Corsica

Olivier Cirendini
Jean-Bernard Carillet
Christophe Corbel
Laurence Billiet
Tony Wheeler

LONELY PLANET PUBLICATIONS
Melbourne • Oakland • London • Paris

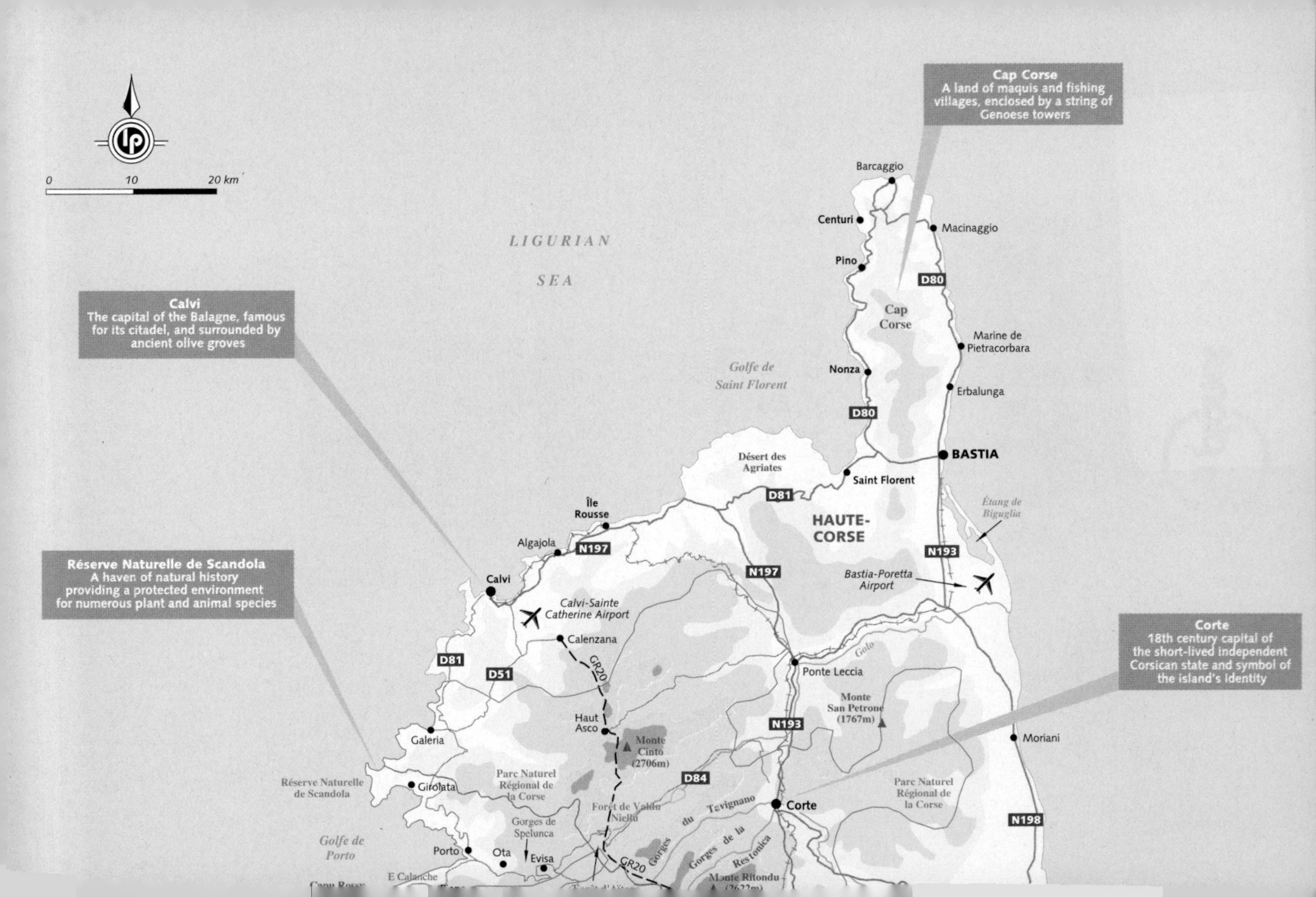

Cap Corse
A land of maquis and fishing villages, enclosed by a string of Genoese towers

Corte
18th century capital of the short-lived independent Corsican state and symbol of the island's identity

Calvi
The capital of the Balagne, famous for its citadel, and surrounded by ancient olive groves

Réserve Naturelle de Scandola
A haven of natural history providing a protected environment for numerous plant and animal species

Barcaggio
Centuri
Pino
Macinaggio
Marine de Pietracorbara
Erbalunga
Nonza
Cap Corse
Saint Florent
BASTIA
Étang de Biguglia
Bastia-Poretta Airport
Morioni

D80
D80
D81
HAUTE-CORSE
N193
N197
N198

Golfe de Saint Florent
Désert des Agriates

Ponte Leccia
Monte San Petrone (1767m)
Parc Naturel Régional de la Corse
Corte
N193
D84

LIGURIAN SEA

Île Rousse
N197
Calvi-Sainte Catherine Airport
Algajola
Calenzana
GR20
Haut Asco
Monte Cinto (2706m)
Forêt de Valdu Niellu
GR20

Calvi
D51
D81
Galeria
Girolata
Gorges de Spelunca
Ota
Porto
Evisa
Golfe de Porto
E Calanche

Réserve Naturelle de Scandola
Parc Naturel Régional de la Corse

0   10   20 km

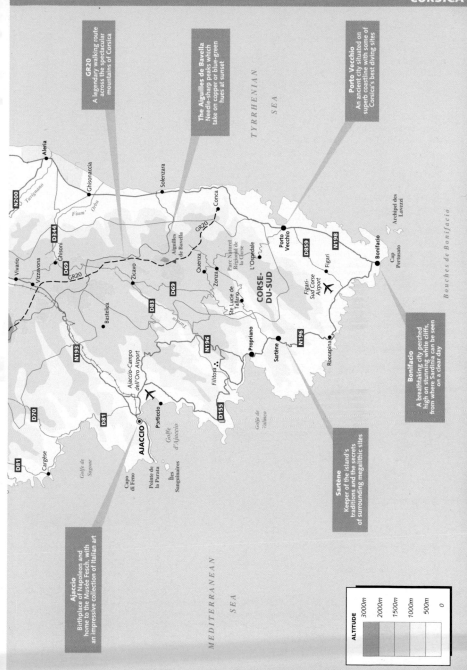

GR20
A legendary walking route across the spectacular mountains of Corsica

The Aiguilles de Bavella
Needle-sharp peaks which take on copper or blue-green hues at sunset

Porto Vecchio
An ancient city situated on superb coastline with some of Corsica's best diving sites

Bonifacio
A breathtaking city perched high on stunning white cliffs, from where Sardinia can be seen on a clear day

Sartène
Keeper of the island's traditions and the secrets of surrounding megalithic sites

Ajaccio
Birthplace of Napoleon and home to the Musée Fesch, with an impressive collection of Italian art

TYRRHENIAN

SEA

Bouches de Bonifacio

MEDITERRANEAN

SEA

Aléria
Ghisonaccia
Solenzara
Conca
Porto Vecchio
Bonifacio
Cap Pertusato
Archipel des Lavezzi
Figari
Figari-Sud Corse Airport
L'Ospedale
Parc Naturel Régional de la Gorse
Zonza
Quenza
Aiguilles de Bavella
Ste Lucie de Tallano
CORSE-DU-SUD
Sartène
Propriano
Roccapina
Filitosa
Zicavo
Bastelica
Vizzavona
Vivario
Ghisoni
Golfe de Valinco
Golfe d'Ajaccio
AJACCIO
Porticcio
Ajaccio-Campo dell'Oro Airport
Pointe de la Parata
Capo di Feno
Îles Sanguinaires
Golfe de Sagone
Cargèse

N200
D344
D69
GR20
D83
D69
N196
N196
D155
N193
D70
D81
D81
N198
D859

Tavignano
Fium' Orbu
Taravo

ALTITUDE
3000m
2000m
1500m
1000m
500m
0

Corsica
1st English edition – August 1999
Translated from Lonely Planet's *Corse* (1st Edition)

Published by
Lonely Planet Publications Pty Ltd A.C.N. 005 607 983
192 Burwood Rd, Hawthorn, Victoria 3122, Australia

Lonely Planet Offices
Australia PO Box 617, Hawthorn, Victoria 3122
USA 150 Linden St, Oakland, CA 94607
UK 10a Spring Place, London NW5 3BH
France 1 rue du Dahomey, 75011 Paris

Photographs
Many of the images in this guide are available for licensing from
Lonely Planet Images.
email: lpi@lonelyplanet.com.au

Front cover photograph
Corsica's most spectacular cliffs are along its southern coast. From here,
the town of Bonifacio looks out to Sardinia. (Christophe Boisvieux)

ISBN 0 86442 792 1

text & maps © Lonely Planet 1999
photos © photographers as indicated 1999

Printed by The Bookmaker Pty Ltd
Printed in China

Contents – Text

2 Contents – Text

DIVING 161

BASTIA & THE FAR NORTH 191

CALVI & THE BALAGNE 217

THE WEST COAST 238

THE SOUTH · 269

THE EASTERN PLAIN · 302

THE CENTRAL MOUNTAINS · 308

LANGUAGE · 321

GLOSSARY · 331

INDEX · 338

MAP LEGEND · back page

METRIC CONVERSION · inside back cover

Contents – Maps

MAP INDEX

Cap Corse & the Nebbio p192

LIGURIAN SEA

Golfe de Saint Florent

The Balagne p218

Île Rousse p229

Calvi p220

Bastia p194

Saint Florent p208

The Eastern Plain p303

From the Golfe de Porto to Ajaccio p239

Porto p242

Golfe de Porto

The Northern GR20 (Calenzana to Vizzavona) p108

Corte p310

Cargèse p251

Golfe de Sagone

The Central Mountains p309

Ajaccio p256

Golfe d'Ajaccio

TYRRHENIAN SEA

The Golfe d'Ajaccio p255

Filitosa p275

The Southern GR20 (Vizzavona to Conca) p109

Around Porto Vecchio p297

Golfe de Valinco

Propriano p272

Sartène p277

Porto Vecchio p291

MEDITERRANEAN SEA

Bonifacio p283

The South p270

0   10   20 km

The Authors

Olivier Cirendini

Although his surname evokes the fragrance of the Corsican maquis, Olivier was born in Paris. After studying English and journalism and spending time in London, he became a journalist, writing on everything from frozen chips to manned space flights. He has travelled widely in his work and has assisted in writing Lonely Planet's English and French-language guides to *Jordan & Syria* and *Mauritius, Réunion & Seychelles* and the French-language guide to *Louisiane*.

Jean-Bernard Carillet

Jean-Bernard trained as a translator before becoming an editor in Lonely Planet's French office. A keen traveller and diving instructor, he will decamp for the sea given the slightest opportunity, but always returns home to his native Lorraine and his daughter Éva, whom he misses greatly while off travelling. Jean-Bernard has also contributed to Lonely Planet's English and French-language guides to *Tahiti & French Polynesia*, and the French-language guides to *Martinique, Dominique et Sainte-Lucie* and *Guadeloupe et ses îles*.

Christophe Corbel

Christophe was born in Paris in 1962, son of a Breton father and Alsatian mother. As a young man, he spent several years in industrial northern France before returning to the capital. A stint in a communications firm enabled him to try his hand at corporate PR and publishing. He then embarked on a promising career as a freelance journalist and became a master at using search engines and other tools of cyberspace. A keen cyclist in Paris, he prefers to travel further afield by train and is no stranger to the railways of China, Eastern Europe and the Baltic countries.

Laurence Billiet

Originally from Lyon, Laurence emigrated to Melbourne to do an MBA. It was there that she came across Lonely Planet in 1993. The following year she returned to Paris and became responsible for marketing and publicity in Lonely Planet's French office. Driven by a constant desire to travel, she has trekked over difficult terrain in Iceland, Réunion, Hawaii and now Corsica. She is fascinated by volcanoes, addicted to vanilla Danette and crazy about football.

Tony Wheeler

Tony was born in England but spent most of his youth overseas. He returned to England to do a university degree in engineering, worked as an automotive engineer, returned to university to complete an MBA then dropped out on the Asian overland trail with his wife, Maureen. They've been travelling, writing and publishing guidebooks ever since, having set up Lonely Planet Publications in the mid-70s.

From the Authors

Olivier Firstly, I would like to thank my ancestors for having sown the seeds of this book in me. I would also like to thank the Rocchini clan (especially Jean-François); Monique and Claude; Marc, Muriel, Raphaëlle and Stan (as well as the entire French football squad); my colleague Jean-Bernard; Linda Peretti; Joëlle Hennemann; Paul-Jo Caitucolli, François Negroni and the Chambres d'Agriculture de Haute-Corse and Corse-du-Sud; the Parc Naturel Régional de Corse; Pierrot, thanks to whom every day is Christmas in Centuri harbour; Stéphanie Le Mao for her valuable insights into history; M de Bernardi; Christophe and Pascale (maybe a spiral staircase is a good thing after all); Leïla de Comarmon and Christine; Monsieur Toison from the Conservatoire du Littoral and Michel Delaugerre from AGENC; Laurence and Bin 266 (where are you, honey?); Didier Buroc for his language expertise; Jean-Paul Giorgetti from Météo-France; Bertrand, who shed more than light on a range of subjects; Isabelle (talking of light); Pascal Cirendini – geologist, uncle and friend (a brotherly embrace to you); Caroline (you know everything) and Nina (what can I say, my little daisy?).

Jean-Bernard Throughout this challenging but exciting experience I have received the support and help of a great many people. I would like to thank Toussaint and Agnès Franceschi, Louise Pirany and her husband, Jean-Paul and Jean-François Quilici, Mme Quilici, Jacques Lusinchi and Michel Folacci, all of whom, in one way or another, made my life up in the mountains more pleasant.

I am eternally grateful to all the instructors and managers in the diving centres, who gave me an unforgettable welcome. Thanks to Sylvie, Pascal, Denis, Walter, Vincent, Michel, Alain, Dominique, Jean-Louis, Yves, Stephen, Yann, Gérard, Johann and all the others for their patience and willingness to cooperate. I am also obliged to Jacques Casanova, whose passion I admire; Patrice Francour, the straight-talking oceanographer; Xavier Baxs; staff at the Ghisonaccia camp site; and Giliane and Robin for their logistic support and encouragement. I will never forget Antoine and

René, the two coral divers, whose situation and work reminded me of the miners where I come from.

A special mention goes to my colleague Olivier Cirendini, who opened the door of his hotel room to me in Calvi, ending 10 nights spent in rather spartan conditions. I take my hat off to Laurence and Arno for their superb work and exceptional involvement in this project. Likewise to Tony, who played the game magnificently. Thanks to them, my work as coordinator was a real pleasure.

Finally, thank you to the entire Lonely Planet team, particularly Zahia, Isabelle, Caroline, Caro, Soph' and Jean-No, who always lend a sympathetic ear.

As regards Chris and my little Éva, I would jump at the chance to savour the delights of this superb island in their company.

Christophe I would like to thank Pascale's mother, who leapt onto the train for Paris to stand in at a moment's notice for relations who were always on the move; Antoine's mother for her active contribution to the Corsican stage; Nina's father for his trust; and Clara's mother for her kind rereading.

Laurence A big thanks to you, Arno, for injecting as much good humour into the difficult two weeks of walking as in our three years of working together in the comfort of our Paris office. Thanks to the entire Lonely Planet team for trusting me and to Jean-Bernard for his encouragement. Love to my parents, who sent me their warmest wishes for the walk, and who gave me a weak knee that has made the owners of a pharmacy in Cozzano a small fortune. I am also grateful to Véronique Muraccioli and her team for their valuable information on the PNRC. Finally, this list would not be complete unless I mentioned the fantastic welcome that we received everywhere on our walk through the Corsican mountains.

This Book

The introductory and regional chapters of this book were written by Olivier Cirendini, apart from The Eastern Plain chapter and the Bastia section, which were written by Christophe Corbel. Jean-Bernard Carillet coordinated the Walking in Corsica and Diving chapters, most of which he also wrote. Laurence Billiet covered the central part of the GR20 walking trail, while Tony Wheeler looked after the first third of the route.

From the Publisher

This English-language edition of Corsica was edited in Lonely Planet's London office by Christine Stroyan, with help from Paul Bloomfield, Rhonda Carrier, David Rathborne and Tim Ryder. It was proofed by David, Rhonda and Paul, and Paul also compiled the index. The text was translated from the original French by Atlas Translations in London.

Tony Battle laid out the book. The maps were drawn in Lonely Planet's French office by Caroline Sahanouk, with help from Philippe Maître, and revised for this edition by Tony, Sara Yorke and David Wenk. Sara also compiled the climate charts.

The cover was designed by Sophie Rivoire, and the illustrations were drawn by Dominique Cordonnier. Many of the photographs were supplied by Lonely Planet Images.

Thanks to Leonie Mugavin for help with the Health section, Quentin Frayne for his linguistic wizardry, Paul Clifton for help with the Gay & Lesbian Travellers section, and to Leonie, Jen Loy, Claire Hornshaw and Simon Calder for checking information for the Getting There & Away chapter.

Thanks also to Zahia Hafs, Caroline Guilleminot, Isabelle Muller, Jean-Noël Doan, Olivier Cirendini, Jean-Bernard Carillet and Christophe Corbel in the French office for their help during the preparation and editing of this book.

Foreword

ABOUT LONELY PLANET GUIDEBOOKS

The story begins with a classic travel adventure: Tony and Maureen Wheeler's 1972 journey across Europe and Asia to Australia. Useful information about the overland trail did not exist at that time, so Tony and Maureen published the first Lonely Planet guidebook to meet a growing need.

From a kitchen table, then from a tiny office in Melbourne (Australia), Lonely Planet has become the largest independent travel publisher in the world, an international company with offices in Melbourne, Oakland (USA), London (UK) and Paris (France).

Today Lonely Planet guidebooks cover the globe. There is an ever-growing list of books and there's information in a variety of forms and media. Some things haven't changed. The main aim is still to help make it possible for adventurous travellers to get out there – to explore and better understand the world.

At Lonely Planet we believe travellers can make a positive contribution to the countries they visit – if they respect their host communities and spend their money wisely. Since 1986 a percentage of the income from each book has been donated to aid projects and human rights campaigns.

Updates Lonely Planet thoroughly updates each guidebook as often as possible. This usually means there are around two years between editions, although for more unusual or more stable destinations the gap can be longer. Check the imprint page (following the colour map at the beginning of the book) for publication dates.

Between editions up-to-date information is available in two free newsletters – the paper *Planet Talk* and email *Comet* (to subscribe, contact any Lonely Planet office) – and on our Web site at www.lonelyplanet.com. The *Upgrades* section of the Web site covers a number of important and volatile destinations and is regularly updated by Lonely Planet authors. *Scoop* covers news and current affairs relevant to travellers. And, lastly, the *Thorn Tree* bulletin board and *Postcards* section of the site carry unverified, but fascinating, reports from travellers.

Correspondence The process of creating new editions begins with the letters, postcards and emails received from travellers. This correspondence often includes suggestions, criticisms and comments about the current editions. Interesting excerpts are immediately passed on via newsletters and the Web site, and everything goes to our authors to be verified when they're researching on the road. We're keen to get more feedback from organisations or individuals who represent communities visited by travellers.

Lonely Planet gathers information for everyone who's curious about the planet – and especially for those who explore it first-hand. Through guidebooks, phrasebooks, activity guides, maps, literature, newsletters, image library, TV series and Web site we act as an information exchange for a worldwide community of travellers.

Research Authors aim to gather sufficient practical information to enable travellers to make informed choices and to make the mechanics of a journey run smoothly. They also research historical and cultural background to help enrich the travel experience and allow travellers to understand and respond appropriately to cultural and environmental issues.

Authors don't stay in every hotel because that would mean spending a couple of months in each medium-sized city and, no, they don't eat at every restaurant because that would mean stretching belts beyond capacity. They do visit hotels and restaurants to check standards and prices, but feedback based on readers' direct experiences can be very helpful.

Many of our authors work undercover, others aren't so secretive. None of them accept freebies in exchange for positive write-ups. And none of our guidebooks contain any advertising.

Production Authors submit their raw manuscripts and maps to offices in Australia, USA, UK or France. Editors and cartographers – all experienced travellers themselves – then begin the process of assembling the pieces. When the book finally hits the shops some things are already out of date, we start getting feedback from readers, and the process begins again ...

WARNING & REQUEST

Things change – prices go up, schedules change, good places go bad and bad places go bankrupt – nothing stays the same. So, if you find things better or worse, recently opened or long since closed, please tell us and help make the next edition even more accurate and useful. We genuinely value all the feedback we receive. Julie Young coordinates a well-travelled team that reads and acknowledges every letter, postcard and email and ensures that every morsel of information finds its way to the appropriate authors, editors and cartographers for verification.

Everyone who writes to us will find their name in the next edition of the appropriate guidebook. They will also receive the latest issue of *Planet Talk*, our quarterly printed newsletter, or *Comet*, our monthly email newsletter. Subscriptions to both newsletters are free. The very best contributions will be rewarded with a free guidebook.

Excerpts from your correspondence may appear in new editions of Lonely Planet guidebooks, the Lonely Planet Web site, *Planet Talk* or *Comet*, so please let us know if you *don't* want your letter published or your name acknowledged.

Send all correspondence to the Lonely Planet office closest to you:

Australia: PO Box 617, Hawthorn, Victoria 3122
UK: 10A Spring Place, London NW5 3BH
USA: 150 Linden St, Oakland CA 94607
France: 1 rue du Dahomey, Paris 75011

Or email us at: talk2us@lonelyplanet.com.au

For news, views and updates see our Web site: www.lonelyplanet.com

HOW TO USE A LONELY PLANET GUIDEBOOK

The best way to use a Lonely Planet guidebook is any way you choose. At Lonely Planet we believe the most memorable travel experiences are often those that are unexpected, and the finest discoveries are those you make yourself. Guidebooks are not intended to be used as if they provide a detailed set of infallible instructions!

Contents All Lonely Planet guidebooks follow roughly the same format. The Facts about the Destination chapter or section gives background information ranging from history to weather. Facts for the Visitor gives practical information on issues like visas and health. Getting There & Away gives a brief starting point for researching travel to and from the destination. Getting Around gives an overview of the transport options when you arrive.

The peculiar demands of each destination determine how subsequent chapters are broken up, but some things remain constant. We always start with background, then proceed to sights, places to stay, places to eat, entertainment, getting there and away, and getting around information – in that order.

Heading Hierarchy Lonely Planet headings are used in a strict hierarchical structure that can be visualised as a set of Russian dolls. Each heading (and its following text) is encompassed by any preceding heading that is higher on the hierarchical ladder.

Entry Points We do not assume guidebooks will be read from beginning to end, but that people will dip into them. The traditional entry points are the list of contents and the index. In addition, however, some books have a complete list of maps and an index map illustrating map coverage.

There may also be a colour map that shows highlights. These highlights may be dealt with in greater detail in the Facts for the Visitor chapter, along with planning questions and suggested itineraries. Each chapter covering a geographical region usually begins with a locator map and another list of highlights. Once you find something of interest in a list of highlights, turn to the index.

Maps Maps play a crucial role in Lonely Planet guidebooks and include a huge amount of information. A legend is printed on the back page. We seek to have complete consistency between maps and text, and to have every important place in the text captured on a map. Map key numbers usually start in the top left corner.

Although inclusion in a guidebook usually implies a recommendation we cannot list every good place. Exclusion does not necessarily imply criticism. In fact there are a number of reasons why we might exclude a place – sometimes it is simply inappropriate to encourage an influx of travellers.

Introduction

Described by Balzac as 'a French island basking in the Italian sun', Corsica is one of the most underrated regions in France and, at the same time, the region most capable of arousing strong passions. The mere mention of its name is enough to evoke images of vendettas, the *maquis* (Corsica's fragrant scrubland), *brocciu* (cheese made from goat's or ewe's milk), chestnuts and, of course, Napoleon Bonaparte. All are undeniably Corsican but, in themselves, they fall short of portraying the complex, elusive and disconcerting nature of this seductive island.

Corsica's countless natural recesses offer everyone the chance to find a corner of paradise. There will always be an inlet, a village or a maquis-covered slope to be explored. For some, Corsica is synonymous with turquoise-blue seas and unnavigable inlets breaking a copper-tinted coastline. For others, its name evokes the smell of the maquis carried by the *libeccio* (south-westerly wind) over the Balagne and Cap Corse, or the stillness of a small village in the Alta Rocca at the end of the day.

Walkers trek to discover its high passes and hidden valleys, the mountain lakes of Melu and Creno and the sharp peaks of Bavella. Divers can explore canyons, rifts and peaks, a mirror image of the island's above-sea terrain, decorated with bunches of gorgonian and red coral and carpeted with flowering anemones. Those seeking a gentler pace of life can relax by the clear waters lapping the shores at Saleccia or

Palombaggia while, beneath plane trees in villages nestling high up in the mountains, gourmets can be found sampling local specialities such as brocciu in brandy, veal with olives, grilled grouper or myrtle liqueur. As for getting to know the Corsican spirit, Corsicans will open up to anyone with time on their hands and a sympathetic ear.

The island has always remained proudly Corsican and kept its distinctive character, despite attempts, first by Rome and then by Pisa and Genoa, to control it. Rooted in its turbulent past and insularity in the same way as its villages cling to the slopes of its mountains, Corsica is both a haven of peace and the *enfant terrible* of the French republic. Unquestionably part of France but Mediterranean by nature, Corsica's preservation of its unique identity makes it a fascinating place to visit.

Facts about Corsica

HISTORY

Corsica's history is a long and turbulent one. The island's strategic position attracted the often unwelcome attentions of the major European and Mediterranean powers. Pisa, Genoa, France, Spain and Britain, not to mention the Moors and the armies of the Roman and Holy Roman Empires, have all fought on Corsican soil. These struggles reflect the Corsicans' own struggle for recognition by their rulers, who were rarely mindful of the islanders' needs.

Origins

While there is little doubt that Corsica was inhabited during the Palaeolithic era, the earliest sign of human existence – the skeleton of Bonifacio Woman, dating from 6570 BC – is from the Neolithic era. The first inhabitants of the island probably came from what is now Tuscany (Italy). They survived by hunting, gathering and fishing, living in rock caves (which can still be seen at Filitosa), equipped with rudimentary tools.

From the discovery of ceramics, arrowheads and agricultural tools the process of settlement can be dated to around 3300 BC. The high point of this early civilisation seems to have been around 4000 BC during the megalithic era, so called because of the megaliths (menhirs and dolmens) that these prehistoric settlers erected on the island, the significance of which is not fully understood. It was shortly after this that the Torréens arrived on the island. Experts believe that the these people were originally Shardanes, a mysterious nautical race which probably retreated into this part of the Mediterranean following a crushing defeat at the hands of Ramses III of Egypt and took up arms against the islanders.

The Torréens destroyed and buried many of the monuments built by the islanders, replacing them with *torri* (towers), imposing round structures with an equally mysterious purpose, which can still be seen on the island today. Some experts, however, believe that the torri were actually built by the original islanders. At any rate, the island's architectural development continued and *castelli* (castles) began to appear, symbols of a settled and organised way of life.

Early Conquerors

Situated at a point where major trading routes intersected, it was not long before Corsica found itself playing host to early explorers. The Phoenicians, a race of explorers and merchants from Asia Minor, are likely to have visited the island, as are the Etruscans and Carthaginians, although no traces of their visits have been discovered. The Greek Phocaeans did settle there, founding Alalia (Aleria) in the 6th century BC. Alalia thrived on trade and Corsica soon rose to fame. Some even claim that the passage in Homer's *Odyssey* where Odysseus fights the cannibalistic Lestrygons was set in the Bouches de Bonifacio.

However, the island eventually became little more than a stop-off point for merchants to replenish their ships until Rome began to take an interest in it, guided by strategic considerations. Rome needed to prevent Corsica, which was so close to the mainland, from falling into the hands of its enemies, the Carthaginians. After 10 expeditions between 260 and 160 BC, the Romans conquered Alalia – which they called Aleria – and soon captured the entire coastline. Life under the Romans was not easy. The Roman way of life was forced upon the islanders, many of whom sought refuge in the mountains away from fierce repression. Rome demanded tributes in kind and sold some of the islanders as slaves and it did little to improve the island. Few roads were built, and the land was not cultivated. The main reason the Romans occupied Corsica was to stop others from doing so, and the island suffered almost 700 years of Roman rule as a consequence. With the benefit of hindsight, however, this period now seems relatively tranquil compared with what was to follow.

Goths, Vandals & Other Invaders

After the collapse of the Western Roman Empire in 476 AD, the distant Byzantine Empire (Eastern Roman Empire) began to take an interest in former Roman territories such as Corsica. The field had been left open for Rome's opponents, such as the Goths, under Totila, and the Vandals, led by Genseric. The latter probably sacked Aleria after laying waste to Gaul. Byzantium's conquest of the island in the first half of the 6th century, which was just as bloody, ended their domination.

Meanwhile, Corsica had also begun to come under attack from the Saracens (Moors, or Muslims, from North Africa). Their forays to the island, during which they raided the villages, became increasingly frequent. Between the 8th and the 18th centuries the island lived in perpetual fear of invasion.

It is known that Christendom retaliated to these attacks, but it is difficult to draw a line between Corsican myth and reality, especially with regard to the crusades. There is no doubt that Pépin le Bref (father of Charlemagne) was involved, while Ugo Colonna, a legendary hero who is believed to have received part of Corsica from Charlemagne, may have freed the island from invaders at one point. Finally, the papacy, taking advantage of dissension within Europe, took over rule of Corsica from the Byzantines.

Lords, Popes & Pisans

The 10th century saw the rise to power of the nobility. Important seigneurial families, which were often of Tuscan or Ligurian origin and sometimes related to Ugo Colonna, created fiefdoms on the island and ruled them with a rod of iron. Some historians believe that the power of Corsican clans dates from this time, when these families owned lands and livestock. Little is known of this period, marked as it was by rivalries

between the families. Yet one thing is certain: it was at the request of Tuscan feudal lords that the Pope renewed his interest in the island. In 1077 he appointed the Bishop of Pisa to manage Corsican affairs.

The powerful Italian city of Pisa, continually battling against its rival, Genoa, had a particular interest in trade; its bishop was more of a merchant in the guise of an ecclesiastic. Corsica benefited from Pisan control and this period was one of peace, prosperity and development, marred only by continuing Saracen forays. Balagne and Cap Corse, in particular, traded with Pisa, and it was around this time that many beautiful churches appeared on the island.

In the meantime, the Genoese had set their sights on Corsica. They were finally rewarded in 1133, when Pope Innocent II divided the island between the two Italian republics. From then on, it was simply a matter of gaining ground.

Genoa undermined its rival's supremacy by fortifying the town of Bonifacio, in the south. Genoese forces then ventured north, where they turned Calvi into a Genoese stronghold. By the 13th century, despite opposition from some of the island's lords, who were loyal to Pisa, Genoa had succeeded in ousting its rival. Pisa's defeat at the Battle of Meloria in 1284 signalled the end of Pisan control of Corsica.

The Genoese Occupation

No name strikes such a dismal chord in Corsican history as that of Genoa. The occupation by the Italian republic lasted for five battle-scarred and brutal centuries. Corsica was important to the Genoese for, unlike Pisa, which had control over a vast area, Genoa had few territories. In addition, its ships had no choice but to sail close to the island. It soon became apparent to Genoa that Corsica was critical to its development and it wasted no time in building a fortress, creating strongholds such as Bonifacio and Calvi and encircling the island with a chain of hundreds of watchtowers.

The Genoese lost no time in taking control of Corsica. More often than not, they simply evicted the Corsicans from strongholds such as Ajaccio and Bonifacio rather than waste time subjugating them. They also used the Corsicans to serve their commercial interests, forcing them to work the land and pay taxes, and punishing severely those who disobeyed. In short, it enforced a colonial system.

The Corsican spirit was not easily crushed, however, and this state of affairs could not last long. The feudal lords were soon dissatisfied with their new masters and Alphonse V, the king of Aragon (who was allied with Venice against Genoa), promised to support the most powerful of the feudal lords, Vincentello d'Istria, in his fight against the Genoese. In 1420 the Aragonese fleet reached Corsica, led by its king. The Genoese stronghold of Calvi was tricked into submission and an attack was launched on the other stronghold, Bonifacio. However, Bonifacio was not so easily

The Terra di Commune

Abuse of the feudal system paved the way for a system of self-government known as the Terra di Commune (literally 'common land'). This system was conceived in the middle of the 14th century by Sambucuccio, the leader of a rebellion against the feudal lords in 1358. The Terra di Commune was divided into *pieve* (parishes) organised according to a community model. Historians have since described this system as 'communism before its time'. The land was equally apportioned so that it could be farmed by local inhabitants and used as grazing for cattle.

Sadly, some of the *caporali* (corporals) who managed the system ended up subjugating the people who had given them power in the first place. The Terra di Commune, which often joined forces with the Genoese in their fight against the feudal lords, was eventually undermined by social divisions on the island.

overcome, and after four months of an unsuccessful siege the disheartened Aragonese fleet departed. Vincentello continued to cause trouble for the Genoese until he was captured and executed in 1434.

In 1453 the Genoese turned to their powerful financial institution, the Office de Saint Georges, to administer their turbulent colony. This was done through repression and strict economic management. The Office de Saint Georges created towns, assumed control of administrative affairs and forced the island's inhabitants to plant olive and chestnut trees and other profitable crops, bringing the island's few plains under cultivation. In this way it hoped to transform Corsica into a rich grain-growing region to supply Genoa with food. At the same time, it raised taxes and used force to curb any local opposition. Over several decades, during which there were thousands of summary executions, it succeeded in 'pacifying' the island, while doing nothing to benefit the Corsicans.

By the mid-16th century the Genoese believed they finally had Corsica under control, defended by their coastal towers. However, the island's strategic importance in Europe would prove them wrong.

Sampiero Corso & the French

In 1552 Henri II, King of France, decided that Italy was a key position on the European political chessboard. Charles V, Holy Roman Emperor and King of Spain, was clearly of the same opinion. Riding roughshod over the Treaty of Crépy (1544), with which France had made peace with the Holy Roman Empire by abandoning its claims in Italy, Henri II launched an attack on Sienna, on the Italian peninsula. Yet again, Corsica found itself caught up in the ensuing chaos due to its location.

In 1553 an expeditionary corps under the command of the Maréchal de Termes and his second in command, the Turkish privateer Dragut, a French ally, reached Bastia. The town was captured, shortly followed by others, and within a few days Corsica was pronounced a French territory.

During this campaign, a Corsican colonel in the French army, Sampiero Corso, became renowned for his courage and came to symbolise the fight against the Genoese (see the boxed text below). Yet his popularity and determination were not enough to safeguard the French victory. The Genoese immediately asked Charles V and Spain for support. Faced with defeat following a series of poorly organised battles, Henri II betrayed the promise that he had given to the Corsicans by signing the Treaty of Cateau-Cambrésis (1559). It was in this treaty he surrendered the island to the Genoese.

After the brief respite under French rule, the Corsicans found themselves again at the mercy of their old enemy and despite a favourable start, Sampiero Corso's attempt to conquer the island in 1564 was short-lived.

Sampiero Corso 'the Fiery'

Born in 1498 near Bastelica, Sampiero Corso became known as 'the most Corsican of Corsicans'. He rose to fame on the Continent as a soldier in the French army. Despite his modest background, his military reputation made it possible for him to marry the noble Vanina d'Ornano, 35 years his junior. Vehemently anti-Genoese, Sampiero fought with great courage alongside the French army in a bid to reconquer his native island. Although this first attempt was unsuccessful, he refused to give up hope. He returned to the island with a band of partisans in 1564, having failed to obtain European backing, and managed to destabilise the Genoese but could not vanquish them. Three years later, Sampiero was assassinated.

One of the most tragic episodes of his life was when his hatred of the Genoese was directed at his wife. Believing that she had betrayed him to his sworn enemies, he killed her with his own hands before burying her with great pomp and ceremony.

Some historians have named the second period of Genoese rule the 'century of fire'. The new Genoese governor had more watchtowers built to protect the island from the increasing number of Saracen raids, while the republic continued where it had left off, governing and suppressing the islanders, favouring the traditional Genoese strongholds and forcing the islanders to cultivate olives, chestnuts and vines. The island's inhabitants remained dissatisfied, especially since they reaped none of the fruits of their labours, and poverty was rife. Excluded from the management of their country's affairs, many Corsican's decided to emigrate.

Uprising & French Intervention

The year 1730 saw the uprising that would mark the start of the Forty Years' War, one of the most important episodes in the island's history. The rebellion began when an elderly man refused to pay tax to a Genoese tax collector. The effects of his action snowballed, with more and more Corsicans refusing to pay their taxes each day. The rebels grew bolder and organised themselves into a group, stealing weapons and gradually weakening Genoese rule. Bastia, Algajola and Saint Florent were taken. With a revolt on their hands, the Genoese successfully appealed to the Emperor of Austria for assistance and Saint Florent and Bastia were subsequently recovered. The Genoese forces were defeated at the Battle of Calenzana (1732), although soon regained control of the situation. It was a transient success, however: the revolt recovered momentum and at a meeting in Corte in 1735, the Corsicans drew up plans for a constitution, establishing Corsica as a sovereign state.

A somewhat comical episode followed. In 1736, an eloquent and rather opportunistic German aristocrat named Théodore de Neuhoff disembarked in Aleria. Seeing him as the leader they had been looking for, the rebels allowed this peculiar man to declare himself King of Corsica (see the boxed text on the next page). He remained

Théodore I, King of Corsica

Born in Cologne in 1694, Théodore de Neuhoff sought a land where he could make a name for himself. Touched by the island's fate after a chance encounter with Corsicans in Livorno, he disembarked in Aleria in 1736. The enthusiasm that greeted his arrival showed how badly in need of a leader the Corsicans actually were. Plausible and charismatic, the German noble won them over. He handed out grand-sounding titles, commanded Corsican leaders, renewed fading rebel hopes and declared himself King of Corsica. Historians are united in the belief that Théodore I had plans for the island, which he could have implemented if only he had received external assistance. In the absence of help he soon gave up and, on the pretext of going in search of reinforcements, fled the island disguised as a priest a few months after his arrival. After trying on more than one occasion to return to Corsica, Théodore de Neuhoff ended his days in London, where he died in 1756, penniless and forgotten.

on the island for a short while, handing out honorary titles and battle orders, then abandoned the throne on the pretext of going in search of reinforcements, which never arrived.

The battle continued in Théodore's absence. The Genoese were so uneasy that they accepted France's offer of help in 1738. Delighted to be involved in the island's affairs again, this time with Genoa's blessing, the French king, Louis XV, sent an expeditionary corps to Corsica under the command of General de Boissieux. The general's mission was one of 'conciliation and arbitration', which only thinly disguised France's real plans. He found himself divided between French cautiousness and the brutal requirements of the Genoese, who were paying for the expedition. The French left Corsica in 1741 in the belief that they had quelled the rebellion but the troubles resurfaced in 1748 and again the Genoese enlisted the French help. The Marquis de Cursay succeeded in regaining administrative control of the island and reconciling Corsican interests with Genoese requirements. He was poorly rewarded for his work: denounced by the Genoese as being too pro-Corsican, he was recalled to Paris and imprisoned. In 1753, Corsica was still under Genoese rule.

Pascal Paoli & the Revolt

In 1755 the troubles on Corsica resurfaced with an insurrection led by Pascal Paoli. An educated man, Paoli came to the assistance of the Corsicans despite the opposition of several important families. In uniting resistance to the Genoese, he succeeded where everyone else before him had failed. In a land subjugated by the Genoese, he created a true state, an independent Corsica (see the boxed text on the next page).

The Moor's Head

Pascal Paoli officially declared the Moor's Head as the emblem of Corsica. Yet no one really knows why the island identifies with this symbol. The word *Maure* or *More* was used to describe Corsica's old enemies, the Saracens. Perhaps this emblem was chosen because it symbolises Corsica's victory over the Saracens. During the crusades, any crusader who had a victory over the 'infidels' could add the Moor's head to their coat of arms. Another theory is that this insignia represents vanquishing one's oppressors and the ability to confront one's destiny. Significantly, the figure shown on the Corsican standard wears his bandeau on his forehead, allowing him to see. The Sardinian arms, on the other hand, depict four Moors' heads with blindfolds.

The Moor's head always faces to the left on the Corsican coat of arms.

However, Paoli's state, based in Corte, did not have enough time to establish itself properly.

In the aftermath of disastrous attempts by the Genoese to regain control of Corsica, France soon established itself as a contender for the island. In 1764 Genoa granted the French permission to occupy the strongholds of Bastia, Ajaccio, Calvi and Saint Florent. The Treaty of Compiègne, which sealed the agreement, was only the beginning: four years later the Treaty of Versailles would formalise the Genoese cession of Corsica to France. From that point on, France began acting as a ruler rather than a mediator. The mobilisation of Paoli's supporters failed to reverse the situation. Their defeat at the Battle of Ponte Novo on 8 May 1769 marked the beginning of French rule of Corsica.

Corsica Under French Rule

Yet again, Corsica had a new ruler. In re-establishing law and order and taking control of the administration, France followed the example of the Genoese, but without their brutality. The French proclaimed a new set of laws, known as the Code Corse, which were specific to the island. There were also some attempts to develop agriculture. The period is characterised by Corsica's integration into the French way of life, one that was about to be totally disrupted by revolution.

The French Revolution received the immediate support of the Corsicans. For the impoverished islanders, it gave new voice to popular dissatisfaction and new hope to the population. In 1789 a decree proclaimed that 'Corsica belongs to the French Empire and its inhabitants shall be governed by the same constitution as the rest of France'. An amnesty was granted to Paoli's supporters, but this did not bring about total reconciliation between Corsica and France. In 1793, Paoli was blamed for the failure of the Sardinian expedition, organised by the Convention (the body that replaced the French National Assembly after the revolution) following a series of disputes with Austria. Furthermore, Paoli opted to side with the moderate wing of the revolutionaries (the

Pascal Paoli – Pioneer

Born in 1725 near Morosaglia, Pascal Paoli is the most celebrated figure in Corsican history, the 'saviour of the homeland'. After being educated in Naples, he began reading the political philosopher Montesquieu, corresponded with the writer and philosopher Jean Jacques Rousseau and made Corsica known in French salons. Like his father Hyacinthe and brother Clément, who had both already won renown in the struggle against the Genoese, he undertook to liberate Corsica. Politician, economist and legislator, Paoli re-established law and order (his strict administration of justice became known as Giustizia Paolina), promulgated a democratic constitution 30 years before the French Revolution, improved agriculture and drained the marshes. Over a period of 15 years, he set up a university, minted coins, made the Moor's head the emblem of the island (see the boxed text on the previous page), founded the coastal town of Île Rousse to compete with the Genoese stronghold of Calvi, ignored Genoese controls over trade and organised military action.

Some historians believe that the Paoli myth has been blown out of all proportion compared with what he actually achieved. However, despite the fact that Paoli really needed more time to implement his original and innovative ideas, he certainly aided Corsica in an unprecedented way. Above all, he proved to the Corsicans that one of their own could take charge of the destiny of their island.

Napoleon Bonaparte

The future Emperor of France was born in Ajaccio in 1769, but in later years his relationship with his native island was somewhat ambiguous.

Sent to France for military training at the age of nine, Napoleon frequently returned to Corsica during his studies (which lasted several years) and while abroad wrote *Lettres sur la Corse*, detailing his attachment to his homeland. At the outbreak of the French Revolution in 1789, Napoleon returned to Ajaccio from Paris and joined the local Jacobin club. However, this attachment to radical revolutionaries did not endear him to the more moderate Pascal Paoli. In 1793 Paoli's men forced Napoleon and his family to leave the island. It was at this point that Napoleon's gaze shifted to greater things and his ardour for Corsica began to cool. He returned to Paris to fight for the Republic, Gallicised his name from the original Napoleone Buonaparte and, after a series of successful military feats and political manoeuvres, was eventually crowned Emperor in 1804. The man whose career took him to the Egyptian pyramids and far-off Russia only ever visited Corsica on one further occasion.

Ultimately, Napoleon did little for the island of his birth. It's ironic that the most famous Corsican in history did the most to Gallicise the island. Fearing internal divisions while he was in power, he even refused to let Corsicans become involved in the island's administration. However, he was always concerned for its future and helped develop his native Ajaccio (see the boxed text 'Napoleon & Ajaccio' in The West Coast chapter).

Despite his distance, it was through the fame of its most famous son that the island gained international recognition and his popularity there never dwindled.

Girondins) rather than the more radical forces (the Montagnards and Jacobins). Refusing to be governed by the Convention, he declared Corsica's secession, and for the first time requested help from England.

On its arrival in Corsica in 1794, the English fleet captured Saint Florent, Bastia and Calvi (it was during a memorable battle for the latter that Admiral Nelson lost an eye). George III, king of England, was proclaimed sovereign of the island. Yet England soon disappointed Paoli, who had believed it to be a model of liberalism. Instead, it adopted a strategic and economic policy that gave little benefit to the Corsicans. Paoli was ousted from power and summoned to London, where he died in 1807.

The Anglo-Corsican kingdom was short-lived; the signing of the Treaty of Paris between France and Sardinia soon undermined English security in the Mediterranean, to the point that England had to abandon Corsica.

Following the English departure in 1796, the island's affairs came under the jurisdiction of Napoleon Bonaparte, a Corsican by birth, who had risen to fame during the French Revolution (see the boxed text on the previous page).

Disagreement & Solidarity

In the 19th century Corsica, as part of France, made sure it received the attention it sought. Rejecting some of the decisions of central government, it showed signs of a continuing clan structure and a worrying propensity towards organised crime. Poverty, development and agriculture remained key issues.

On the other hand, Corsica could not have been more supportive of France in the two world wars. Thousands of Corsicans died on the battlefields between 1914 and 1918. In 1940 the island was occupied by more than 90,000 Fascist and Nazi soldiers. It was here that the term 'Maquis' was coined for the Resistance. Indeed, the island provided several heroes of the Resistance, including Danièle Casanova and Fred Scamaroni. The latter represented the Free French under General de Gaulle and took his own life in prison so that he would not disclose vital information when tortured. In 1942 the submarine *Casabianca*, under Captain L'Herminier, was sent to Corsica with a load of weapons and equipment by Resistance forces based in Algiers. This was the beginning of organised resistance to the Italians by the population of Corsica and led to Corsica being the first French region to be liberated during the war.

However, even these feats of arms did little to improve Corsican-French relations. Many Corsicans decided to emigrate to French colonies after the war but, back home, a certain discontent was beginning to take root.

The Corsican Malaise

It is never easy to describe the recent past, especially where Corsica, which has had a particularly troubled and chaotic history, is concerned.

Although Corsican nationalist and separatist movements emerged in the 1960s, they did not gain a foothold for another 15 years, starting in Aleria. What became known as the 'events in Aleria' were linked to the end of the Algerian war of independence in 1962. At that time, a number of French repatriates from Algeria settled in the lowlands of eastern Corsica, receiving government aid to cultivate vines. The crisis erupted after militants belonging to the Corsican separatist movement led by the Simeoni brothers unearthed a scandal involving fraudulent wine-making practices and the *pieds-noirs* (Algerian-born French) winegrowers, along with the government, were accused of profiteering. A building used to store wine was occupied, and an attempt by the police to resolve the situation ended in two deaths.

The *boues rouges* (red mud) affair, in which an Italian multinational was found to be dumping toxic waste off the coast of Bastia, served as a further catalyst for discontent, which in 1976 manifested itself in the creation of the Front de Libération Nationale de la Corse (FLNC). From then on, Corsican nationalists used force to convey their message. In 1976 there was at least one bombing a day, and the years that followed were marked by a series of nationalist campaigns.

France has consistently adopted a carrot and stick approach to Corsica, alternating between truces (from which it is known that some gained financially) and periods of repression coupled with waves of often random arrests. In 1981 the University of Corte was opened (after the French had closed down Pascal Paoli's university, higher education was only available on the mainland) and in 1982 the Assemblée de Corse was created (the island had previously belonged to the Provence-Alpes-Côte d'Azur region). However, the détente arising from these measures was short-lived. The dissolution of the FLNC by the government in 1983 seriously damaged relations. The nationalist movement continued its campaigns under the name of the 'ex-FLNC'. More than 20 years after the events in Aleria, nationalist groups are still present and active on the island. However, they appear to be suffering a crisis and have split into numerous factions, often in opposition to one another and seemingly outweighed by their armed branches.

The media still depict nationalism in terms of bombings and shows of force (not aimed at tourists) by masked and armed individuals. Yet by the very fact of its existence, the movement is indicative of discontent in Corsican society vis-à-vis a 'motherland' which is often perceived as distant and assimilative. Nationalists have adopted principles, which they will defend by force if necessary, that cover a wide range of fields, from the economy to the environment, including the defence of the Corsican language (see the Language chapter later in this book). It is these principles that see it so firmly opposed to the French government.

The issue of tourism is a striking example of this difference of opinion. For the government departments responsible for land management, tourism is the best means by which Corsica, where industry is virtually non-existent and agriculture unproductive, can become self-sufficient. Yet some separatists see this obsession with tourism as means of forced assimilation which turns the island into a holiday resort for two months of the year while leaving it deserted the rest of the time.

The assassination of the regional prefect, Claude Érignac, on 6 February 1998 was an act of unprecedented violence. Unsolved at the time of writing, the murder triggered a strong reaction in Corsican public opinion and within the French government, which has begun an extensive operation aimed at re-establishing law and order on the island. Similar to Italy's Clean Hands operation, it is particularly aimed at stamping out the system of privileges, and a team of tax inspectors has been sent to the island.

The discontent that has stemmed from this operation has highlighted a mutual lack of understanding between the two sides. For many Corsicans, government policy has contributed to the discrediting of the island. Shocked by the methods employed, many believe that the government – which they claim has been unable to foster economic development on the island and is partly to blame for the current situation – treats all Corsicans like criminals. Others point out that Corsica merely suffers from problems experienced by many regions of France: economic recession, political influence shared between too few people, corruption, extremists, poorly distributed wealth and squandered public money.

For its part, the government thinks that the people of the island, traditionally viewed as thorns in France's side, have gone too far. It refers to the report published in September 1998 by the committee of inquiry into the Corsica question, chaired by Jean Glavany. This lengthy document describes the existence of organised gangs on the island, the emergence of a 'Corsican system' considered to be a proto-Mafia and wide-scale tax evasion. It also denounces the 'wheeler-dealer' tendencies of racketeering nationalist parties.

The report is keen to see shared responsibility between local authorities and the State, and points out the 'inconstancy of government' and 'weakness of local authorities'. It also mentions the scandals involving Crédit Agricole and the Caisse Agricole pour le Développement Économique de la Corse (CADEC; the body responsible for economic development), in which large sums of public money were wasted. Finally, the Glavany report insists that the majority of Corsicans are the victims of, and not responsible for, the current state of affairs on the island.

It would be a mistake to think that modern Corsican society is composed of a mixture of 'partisans of the French State' and nationalists. Most of the island's inhabitants are actually somewhere in between. Generally dissatisfied with the situation on the island, they condemn the violent actions of the nationalist groups, but don't deny the existence of *le malaise Corse*.

GEOGRAPHY

The island of Corsica towers above the sea 150km south of the Italian city of Genoa. At 8722 sq km, the island's surface area is around 20% of that of Switzerland and represents a mere 1.6% of the entire French territory. Lying along a north-south axis, the island is 183km long from tip to tip and spans 85km at its widest part. Cap Corse, the 40km-long peninsula which juts into the Gulf of Genoa at the northern end of the island, gives the island its unusual shape.

Corsica is closer to Italy than to France. Only 90km separate the island from the Italian port of Piombino to the east whereas the nearest continental French town, Nice, is some 170km to the north-west. To the south, 12km separate Bonifacio from the Italian island of Sardinia, which is almost three times as large as Corsica.

The island is extremely mountainous: average height above sea level is 568m. The highest mountain is Monte Cinto (2706m). Other high peaks include Monte Ritondu (2622m), Paglia Orba (2525m), Monte Pedru (2393m), Monte d'Oro (2389m) and Monte Renosu (2354m).

Mountains overhang much of the Corsican coastline. The west coast, exposed to the prevailing winds, is the most jagged, with the deep hollows of the Golfes de Porto, Sagone, Ajaccio and Valinco. On the more monotonous east coast, the long coastal plain of Aleria (or eastern lowlands) can be found.

In addition to its coastal waters, Corsica has many lakes and rivers, though these are often arid-looking. Several rivers rise in the mountains. The Golo, which flows for 80km from the Valdu Niellu forest to south of the Étang de Biguglia, is the fastest flowing. Other rivers include the Tavignano, which flows to Aleria, and, on the other side of the island, the Liamone, Rizzanese and Taravu rivers. Corsica also has 43 glacial lakes.

Corsica's impressive mountainous landscape and clan-based culture, which has existed for centuries, conspire to divide this small island into around 20 'micro-regions'.

These are traditional, not official, and their boundaries can vary from one map to another, depending on whether one is using cultural or economic criteria. Furthermore, the old distinction between the Au-delà-des-Monts (the far side of the mountains) and the En-deçà-des-Monts (this side of the mountains) is still used. Au-delà-des-Monts corresponds to a large region in the south and north-west, from Île Rousse to Solenzara. En-deçà-des-Monts describes the north-eastern part of the island.

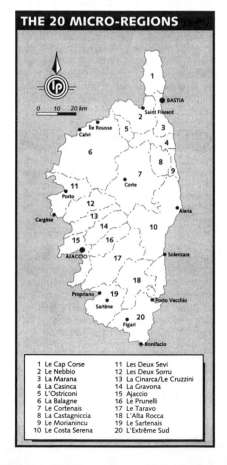

THE 20 MICRO-REGIONS

1 Le Cap Corse	11 Les Deux Sevi
2 Le Nebbio	12 Les Deux Sorru
3 La Marana	13 La Cinarca/Le Cruzzini
4 La Casinca	14 La Gravona
5 L'Ostriconi	15 Ajaccio
6 La Balagne	16 Le Prunelli
7 Le Cortenais	17 Le Taravo
8 La Castagniccia	18 L'Alta Rocca
9 Le Morianincu	19 Le Sartenais
10 Le Costa Serena	20 L'Extrême Sud

GEOLOGY

Geologists are now united in the belief that the massif formed by Corsica and Sardinia, the Corso-Sardinian micro-continent, broke away from Provence around 30 million years ago. The islands ended up in their current position after slowly rotating around an axis somewhere in the middle of the Gulf of Genoa.

The western and southern part of Corsica, from the Balagne to Solenzara, is composed of the original platform that broke away from the continent. This ancient crystalline base consists of magmatic rock (igneous rock formed by magma rising within the earth's crust, which slowly crystallised as it rose), including granite, a hard rock containing feldspar, quartz and mica. This has been eroded to form such dramatic features as the rocky inlets near Piana and the Scandola nature reserve. The same phenomenon created *taffoni* (cavities), which can be seen in various places on the island.

The island's north-eastern fringe, including Cap Corse, bound to its west by Corte and to the south by Solenzara, has a different geological structure. This is composed of complex sedimentary and metamorphic rocks, such as schist. Two stages have been identified in the creation of this alpine, or schistose, scenery. First, a sedimentary platform was formed on the sea floor from deposits produced by the disintegration or alteration of existing rocks, and chemical or biological activity (shell particles, for example). Layer by layer, the platform was built up, eventually rising above sea level. The rocks then metamorphosed, their composition changing as a result of the heat and pressure during the formation of the Alps in the Tertiary era. This is a simplification of the formation of the complex Corsican geology; other factors have also contributed to its development.

A rift zone divided the island in half at Corte, giving the island its herringbone mountain range and numerous east-west valleys. In the Quaternary era, glaciation modified the island's geology, giving it a more alpine relief.

Corsica's mountains are easily classified. The red rocks of the crystalline platform are in evidence around Piana and Scandola. Near Bonifacio white, chalky rocks are found. The island is also home to ophite, a complex magmatic rock created during the major folding periods and which has a distinctive green colour.

Corsica owes the existence of a variety of ornamental rocks and the rare orbicular diorite to geological upheaval. Diorite, an igneous rock, recognisable by its grey honeycomb structure, is found in Sainte Lucie de Tallano in the Alta Rocca.

CLIMATE

The Mediterranean climate, characterised by its summer droughts and sun, gives Corsica an average annual temperature of 12°C. The mountains are cooler, however, and the temperature drops significantly the higher you climb. Snow can be seen above 1600m from October to June, while the sea temperature often rises above 25°C in summer (June to September).

On average, the island has 2700 hours of sunshine each year. Average temperatures often exceed 25°C between June and September; July and August can see temperatures of over 35°C. According to the Ajaccio-based Météo France (the French meteorological office), temperatures climb above 30°C on average 12 days a year in Ajaccio and 32 days in Corte.

Spring and autumn are both fine, with average temperatures of around 15°C and maximum temperatures of 20°C from October to March. Rainfall is highest during the last three months of the year, when there are often severe storms and flooding. Precipitation is minimal in July, but can be considerable in the autumn. The mountains often experience severe winters and some of the island's peaks are snow-capped year-round. Corte has on average 30 days of frost per year, compared with 11 in Ajaccio and three in Bastia. One of the features of Corsica's climate is that it is slightly warmer in the north than in the south.

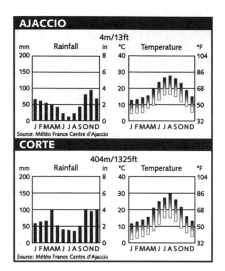

AJACCIO
4m/13ft
Rainfall | Temperature
Source: Météo France Centre d'Ajaccio

CORTE
404m/1325ft
Rainfall | Temperature
Source: Météo France Centre d'Ajaccio

The prevailing winds are the dry, gentle *libeccio*, found especially in Haute-Corse, and the *tramontane*, which comes down from the north in winter. The *sirocco*, warm and moisture-bearing, occasionally blows up from the south-east. Cap Corse and the Bouches de Bonifacio are the windiest points (in 1965 wind speeds hit 288km/h).

ECOLOGY & ENVIRONMENT

Corsica's main attraction is its environment, which is remarkably well-preserved due to a combination of factors. The Corsicans are devoted to their island and react quickly whenever they feel it to be under threat. Action taken by nationalists in the 1980s – sometimes referred to as eco-nationalism – has been a determining factor. Bombings have meant that property developers stay away from the coastline, preventing it from being turned into a kind of Côte d'Azur. Clearly, the island has effective protection mechanisms.

The creation in 1972 of a nature reserve on the island, the Parc Naturel Régional de Corse (PNRC; Corsican Nature Reserve), was a decisive step. As well as being a pro-

tected area of 350,500 hectares, the PNRC actively promotes environmental protection on the island (see the boxed text in the Walking in Corsica chapter).

Unlike the national parks, which cover uninhabited areas, France's regional nature reserves are aimed at 'protecting and encouraging the survival of the natural, cultural and human heritage of the region for the future'. Hence the creation by the PNRC of approximately 2000km of signposted footpaths. This body has also encouraged the preservation of the giant limpet, Hermann's tortoise, the mouflon and the osprey, and was responsible for the reintroduction of the Corsican red deer. The 75 permanent representatives on the board of the PNRC are also involved in the preservation of flora, encouraging the cultivation of fruits no longer grown on the island, breeding livestock and fire prevention.

In addition to the PNRC, there are four nature reserves on Corsica: the Îles Finocchiarola, the Îles Lavezzi, the Îles Cerbicale and the Réserve Naturelle de Scandola (a UNESCO World Heritage Site).

The Conservatoire de l'Espace Littoral et des Rivages Lacustres (Organisation for the Conservation of Coastal Areas and Lakeshores; more commonly known as Conservatoire du Littoral) works to protect the coastline. This public institution, created in 1975, buys land in order to preserve it. Over the years, the Conservatoire has acquired coastal sites all over the island, particularly in Roccapina, the Agriates, the Bouches de Bonifacio, the tip of Cap Corse and the islands of Finocchiarola, Scandola, Cargèse, Piana and the Étang d'Urbino. These sites account for more than 15% of the 1000km of Corsican coastline. The Conservatoire has also gained recognition through its excellent books and brochures on the areas under its protection.

The Agence pour la Gestion des Espaces Naturels de Corse (AGENC; Office for the Management of the Natural Areas of Corsica) provides the Conservatoire du Littoral with technical and scientific guidance (such as studies and ecological surveys, project management and monitoring) on all of its Corsican sites. The organisation also supervises site management and acts as an adviser to local authorities.

One-half of the 28,000 hectares of forest on the island is managed by the Office National des Forêts (ONF; National Office for Forests). The ONF provides seasonal guided visits to the national forests of Bavella, Bonifatu, Marmaro, Chiavari, Valdu Niellu, Aïtone, Pineta, Fangu, San Antone and l'Ospedale.

However, as effective as they are, these organisations cannot fully protect Corsica from ecological damage.

Fire is by far the biggest threat. Stubble-burning, a traditional Corsican custom, produces potash, which is used to improve soil quality. Fires are also the means by which expanses of maquis and forest are replaced by meadows. However, repeated fires are particularly damaging and lead to the desertification of the landscape. The Agriates, which partly owe their current desert-like appearance to this practice, are evidence of this. Many blame shepherds and farmers for starting these fires, often with good reason.

The suckler cow premium, a European Union (EU) system aimed at increasing the island's livestock levels and meeting its grazing requirements, also pushed up the number of fires in the 1980s (see the Economy section later in this chapter). Yet pyromaniacs, careless tourists and the effects of land clearance (since 1976, European subsidies for the uprooting of vines have, in the eyes of some, led to the emergence of a low, fast-burning scrub) have also played a part.

Regardless of how they are started, fires remain the principal threat to the Corsican environment (see the boxed text on this page). No fewer than 22,000 hectares went up in smoke in 1974, while 140,000 hectares were burnt between 1980 and 1990. It is not unusual for 20 fires to be reported on a single summer's day. For information on what action to take if you see a fire starting, refer to the boxed text 'In the Event of Fire ...' in the Dangers & Annoyances section of the Facts for the Visitor chapter.

Forest Fires: Some Facts

- In 1992, 571 forest fires were reported. In 1995, this figure was down to 173, although it rose to 274 in 1998.
- In 1993, 1773 hectares were destroyed by fire. In 1994, this figure reached 12,774 hectares, but had declined to 267 hectares by 1998.
- Of the total of forest fires, 44% have been confirmed as being started deliberately, while 33% were accidental.
- To combat the risk of fire, the Sécurité Civile uses firefighting aircraft, helicopters, observation planes and groups of firefighters stationed at the most critical points on days when the risk is greatest (for instance, in times of high winds, low humidity or intense heat).

The achievements of firefighting aircraft, firefighters and the Sécurité Civile (the civil defence department) are considerable. Controversy erupted on this subject in 1998, when the pilots of Sécurité Civile water bombers refused to be based in certain regions of France, including Corsica, deeming their mission fees too low compared with the cost of living in tourist areas. Fortunately, an agreement was eventually reached.

Tourism also does its share of damage to the environment. An awareness-raising campaign aimed at walkers has attacked the amount of rubbish that appears each year on the footpaths. The sharp increase in the island's population during the summer months also creates a waste problem, particularly in the seaside resorts, and this is aggravated by dumping in the countryside.

On the coast, tourist activity and overgrazing of cattle have contributed towards the destruction of plants that stabilise the Roccapina and Barcaggio dunes. The Conservatoire du Littoral has now remedied this by erecting protective barriers. In addition, some of Corsica's forests suffer damage caused by livestock allowed to roam freely, a traditional farming practice on the island. Pigs in particular contribute to deforestation by disturbing the soil in search of food.

Two environmental issues have surfaced recently in Corsica. The first involves the Canari asbestos mine on Cap Corse. Closed since 1965, it still produces waste and no programme to dispose of the pollution has ever been implemented. The second concerns the Rondinara marine research base between Bonifacio and Porto Vecchio, which should house part of the forthcoming Bouches de Bonifacio marine park. Apparently, this was built in violation of coastal regulations, which prohibit any construction less than 100m from the shore.

These two issues, however, are not yet on the same scale as the *boues rouges* affair, which was triggered in 1973 after it was found that an Italian multinational company was dumping toxic waste off the coast of Bastia.

In spite of all this, Corsica is fortunate enough to have a beautiful and protected natural environment. The nationalist movements, which have taken on the role of environmental protectors in the absence of environmentalist parties on the island, is ensuring the survival of this environment.

FLORA & FAUNA
Flora

The rich Corsican flora is divided into three zones. The Mediterranean zone (up to an altitude of about 1000m) is home to the maquis, holm and cork oaks, and olive and chestnut trees. Pine and beech forests cover a band that extends between 1000 and 1800m. In the alpine zone, above 1800m, vegetation is low and sparse, comprising grasses and small mountain plants. Citron, kiwi and avocado trees grow in the eastern lowlands.

Barbary Fig The Barbary fig was brought back from Central America by Christopher Columbus. A member of the *Cactaceae* family, it resembles a cactus, with prickly,

oval-shaped nopals, 20 to 40cm long, covered in yellow flowers. It produces a sweet fruit with a thick pulp.

Chestnut The chestnut is without doubt the tree that has had the greatest impact on Corsica. Introduced by the Genoese, it soon became widely cultivated in the region to which it gave its name: Castagniccia. The husks open in October, exposing the lovely brown fruit, which is ground down into flour and used in a variety of local dishes. Since WWI, ink disease (caused by a mushroom), lack of plant regeneration and damage caused by domestic pigs has led to a reduction in the number of chestnut trees under cultivation.

Cork Oak Between 15 and 20m in height, the *Quercus suber* is distinguished by its low, twisted branches. Its spongy, fissured bark is removed every eight to 10 years, exposing a reddish-ochre trunk. The bark is then used to manufacture corks. Wood from the cork oak is used for fuel and carpentry. Common in the south, around Porto Vecchio, this tree, which flowers in April or May, is found at the same altitude as the olive tree.

Holm Oak Found below 500m, holm oak, which can grow to around 15m, produces the acorns on which pigs feed. Repeat fires often act as a brake on its growth, however, and it is not unusual to find holm oak in bush form.

Maquis Legend has it that when exiled Corsicans finally returned home, they were able to smell the maquis while still several miles off the coast. The maquis is generally characterised by rather low vegetation (although it can sometimes grow to 5m, fires permitting). Covering around 200,000 hectares, it combines a variety of species, generally sweet-smelling, which usually flower in the spring. The maquis is capable of surviving the intense summer heat. It burns quickly, but soon regrows after a fire. The short list that follows is merely intended as an example of what the maquis might comprise.

The most common species is the **rock rose**. One type of this shrub, the shoots of which secrete a sticky resin, can be recognised by its profusion of white flowers with yellow centres approximately 3cm in diameter. Another type has larger, pinkish-mauve flowers.

Treasured for its blue-black berries, which are used in some excellent liqueurs, **myrtle** flowers in June. Its white flowers give off a peppery aroma. **Tree heather** flowers at the beginning of the year. This often grows to 2m in height and its white flowers exude a honey-like scent. **Strawberry trees** are recognisable by their round, red fruit.

The **mastic tree** also bears red fruit, although these then turn black and exude a resin-like fragrance. **Asphodels**, which can reach up to 1.5m in height, produce groups of small white flowers with narrow petals. Some bear small fruit. Holm oak (see the following section) sometimes appears in the maquis.

Olive Found on the coast below 600m, the olive tree flowers in June and can produce up to a million pollen-rich flowers. The tree is still cultivated for its oil, although it is less prolific now than it was during the Genoese period. The absence of frost in Corsica means that the fruit can be left on the trees until it falls naturally. This explains the long reproductive cycle of Corsica's olive trees, which produce fruit every other year. The olive tree thrives on sunny slopes, particularly in the Balagne.

Pine The main constituent of the forests between 700 and 1500m is the laricio, or Corsican, pine. One of the larger varieties found in the superb Corsican forests, it can grow to around 50m. Some of the trees on the island are 800 years old. As it ages, its foliage spreads horizontally, like a parasol. The laricio pine is more resistant than the maritime pine, also found in Corsica, which does not live as long.

Fauna

Most of the fauna seen on Corsica today are domesticated animals – pigs, cows, goats, sheep and mules. However, the island is home to a number of endemic species.

Trout and eels are found in mountain streams on the island, and the Corsican salamander and Corsican euprocte (related to the triton, but without a backbone or lungs) live on the shores of lakes and on riverbanks.

Walkers will be pleased to hear that there are no vipers on Corsica. The island does, however, have some rare venomous spiders. Small black rats, which used to be common all over Corsica, are now mainly seen on the islands and in Scandola. Corsica has many insects (all harmless), including 40 species of endemic dragonfly, as well as 53 varieties of endemic spider.

Audouin's Gull This sea bird has disappeared from the Continent and is now only found on the shores of small Mediterranean islands such as Corsica, Sardinia and the Balearics. It is smaller and more slender than the herring gull and can be recognised by its dark red and black striped beak, which ends in a small yellow point. It nests among rocks, particularly in the Finocchiarola nature reserve.

Bearded Vulture The wingspan of the bearded vulture, or *altore*, can measure up to 3m. It resembles a falcon during flight. As well as the black 'beard' under its beak, the altore is recognisable by the white or yellowish plumage covering the lower part of its body and by the dark underside of its wings. Solitary, it nests in rocky niches in the mountainous massifs and follows the herds, feeding off carrion. Bone marrow is an important part of its diet; it breaks the bones into pieces by dropping them onto rocks from a great height.

Corsican Nuthatch One of the rare birds endemic to the island, the nuthatch was only discovered at the end of the 19th century. Only the most keen-sighted will spot it: this tiny bird is barely more than 12cm in length. The nuthatch is very light and is an agile climber, enabling it to cling to the most fragile of branches. The Corsican variety is recognisable by the white 'brow' across its head. The nuthatch is sedentary and feeds on pine seeds and insects, which it finds in the conifer forests.

Corsican Red Deer Although it disappeared from the island in the 1960s, the Corsican red deer (*Cervus elaphus corsicanus*) was reintroduced in 1985 from Sardinian specimens. This inhabitant of the maquis lives on brambles, strawberry trees, acorns and chestnuts. The males often grow to over 1m (measured at the withers) and are recognisable by their antlers, which start growing from the age of one. The antlers are shed each spring and grow again in the summer, each time slightly larger. At the instigation of the PNRC around 100 of this species were placed in protected enclosures in Quenza, Casabianda and Ania di Fiumorbu. Some 20 fawns are born each year, and, for the first time, 16 adults were released back into the wild in 1998.

Hermann's Tortoise Formerly very common in France, Spain, Italy, Yugoslavia and Greece, this land tortoise is now one of the rarest reptiles in France. Recognisable by its orange and black stripes, it is relatively common in Corsica. Hermann's tortoise can often be found in the maquis. It is 19cm long on average and lives for 60 to 80 years. It hibernates from mid-November until the end of February under piles of leaves.

Mouflon King of the mountain, the mouflon, a type of short-fleeced sheep, prefers open areas that are free from snow. Seen in south-facing valleys from December to February, this herbivore retreats to higher altitudes in summer. The males are easily recognisable by their huge horns, which become more coiled each year. The white facial markings (or 'face mask'), which spread with age, are also characteristic of the species. Found in their thousands at the

beginning of the century, the number of mouflons is now placed at between 400 and 600, most of which inhabit the Bavella and Asco reserves. The mouflon is a protected species.

Osprey With talons capable of grasping the most slippery of prey and with its sharp eyesight, this enormous predator is a formidable hunter. It is recognisable by its white body and brown wings. The osprey builds large nests on the rocky coasts and headlands of the Réserve Naturelle de Scandola and breeds in early summer. In 1973 there were only three pairs in Corsica, but by 1998 the osprey population had grown to around 20. The osprey species includes many sub-branches found in North America, Africa, Asia and Australia.

Shag This web-footed bird, with its narrow head and black-green plumage, nests in colonies on Corsica's rocky coasts and islands. It is sometimes found on the Finocchiarola islands.

Whales Seen in the triangle of sea between Nice, the Île de Porquerolles and Corsica, the common rorqual is a protected species. It is not unusual for one of these whales, which grow to a length of 24m, to be killed in a collision with a ferry or high-speed vessel, despite being able to travel at 45km/h.

Wild Boar A robust wild cousin of the pig, the wild boar has a dark, silky coat. Dominant in the maquis and forests, this fierce omnivore mainly lives on acorns, chestnuts, roots and fruit. Occasionally, however, it will feed on worms and insects, unearthed by rooting in the soil with its snout, causing extensive damage to the environment. Wild sows and their young live in groups, while males, which are surprisingly fast runners, are solitary creatures. Males also have short but fearsome tusks, which they use to fight other males during the rutting season in November and December. Hunting wild boar is a traditional winter activity in Corsica.

GOVERNMENT & POLITICS

Corsica differs from other French regions, which are governed by a *conseil régional*, or regional council. In 1991, the island was granted special status as the territorial community of Corsica, often referred to as 'Joxe status' after Pierre Joxe, the socialist minister of the interior who was instrumental in the granting of this status. Thus, Corsica has more freedom than other regions without having complete autonomy. For example, as a territorial community, Corsica has more control in areas such as economic and social development, education, culture (particularly aspects linked to Corsican identity) and the environment.

The island is governed by a regional prefect, appointed (like all prefects) by order of the President of the Republic. The most senior State representative on the island, the regional prefect oversees national interests, administration and observance of the law. The current prefect is Bernard Bonnet, who took over after Claude Érignac was assassinated in February 1998.

The territorial community of Corsica has three consultative bodies that work with the prefect. The first is the Assemblée de Corse (Corsican Assembly), whose 51 members, elected for six years by universal suffrage, are consulted on any bills and decrees 'containing provisions specific to Corsica'. The Assemblée has powers of deliberation and can propose statutory changes to the prime minister. It also elects the executive body of the territorial community of Corsica, the Conseil Exécutif (Executive Council). This advises the prefect on the implementation of laws. The Conseil Économique, Social et Culturel (Economic, Social and Cultural Council) advises the Conseil Exécutif on economic, social and cultural matters. The Assemblée de Corse sits in Ajaccio.

The administrative division of Corsica is more traditional. Since 1975 Corsica has been divided into two *départements* (administrative divisions), Corse-du-Sud (prefecture Ajaccio) and Haute-Corse (Bastia). Each comes under the authority of a departmental prefect and has a deliberative assembly, the Conseil Général (General Council), which implements legislation at a local level and manages local amenities. Executive power at departmental level is in the hands of the president of the Conseil Général. The office of regional prefect and departmental prefect of Corse-du-Sud is currently held by the same person.

Finally, Corsica is divided into 360 *communes*, (districts) the basic administrative unit of local government. Each district is presided over by a *maire* (mayor).

On a national scale, each département on the island is represented by two members of parliament (who are elected to the Assemblée Nationale) and two senators (elected to the Sénat, or upper chamber). At the time of writing, these representatives, like the presidents of the general councils, tend to be affiliated to the right.

The question of Corsica's status has not been resolved. The division of the island into two départements is under discussion and there is talk of a return to a single département.

Political Parties

Rather conservative, Corsica has nearly always leaned to the right. The main French parties are represented on the island, including the Rassemblement pour la République (RPR; Rally for the Republic), Parti Socialiste (PS; Socialist Party), Union Démocratique Française (UDF; French Democratic Union) and Parti Communiste Français (PCF; French Communist Party). Environmentalist parties are not represented in Corsica, and neither is the Front National (National Front), which has failed to win support there. According to Corsican political analysts, these absences can be explained by the fact that the island's nationalist parties lobby for the protection of the environment and channel protest votes.

Since the dissolution of the FLNC in 1983, a number of nationalist or separatist movements have been created and dissolved (see the History section earlier in this chapter). At the time of writing, the nationalist movement is represented by A Cuncolta Naziunalista (Nationalist Assembly), Corsica Viva (Living Corsica), Muvimentu per Autodeterminazione (MPA; Movement for Self-Determination), Accolta Naziunalista Corsa (ANC; Corsican Nationalist Assembly) and Unione di u Populu Corsu (UPC; Union of the People of Corsica), the separatist party of the Simeoni brothers (see the History section).

In general, Corsican nationalists campaign for autonomy, recognition of the Corsican people as a distinct nation and protection of the culture and language. In 1994 some branches lobbied for the status of *territoire d'outre-mer* (TOM; French overseas territory). More recently, groups have petitioned for a status similar to that of Nouvelle Calédonie (New Caledonia), a French territory in the Pacific Ocean with considerable autonomy.

The FLNC (in a new incarnation), FLNC Canal Historique and Fronte Ribellu (Revolutionary Front) are the armed branches of the nationalist movement.

The elections to the Assemblée de Corse held in early 1999 produced the following results. Out of a total of 51 seats, the Rassemblement pour la République won 17 seats, Corsica Nazione won eight, Parti Radical de Gauche six, Corse-Social Democrate five, Corse Nouvelle four, Mouvement pour la Corse three, Un Autre Avenir three, Communistes et Démocrates de Progrès three and Parti Socialiste two. This means that the traditional parties of the right now have 21 seats (40% of the total), nationalist parties have eight seats (16%), leftist parties have 16 seats (30% of the total, although these groups do not seem to represent a unified block) and small political groups share the rest. The main difference between the composition of this Assemblée and that of its predecessor is that the nationalists have made gains and the left is more divided. The right has maintained its dominant position and the number of parties represented has increased from five to nine.

ECONOMY

Management of the island's economy is a balancing act. Corsica has very few natural resources and no raw materials. Apart from agriculture, the island's income derives mainly from tourism, the exploitation of which is often controversial. The economy is also affected by Corsica's island status, which has the effect of increasing the price of local produce and complicating logistics. The agro-pastoral way of life seems to belong to the past. Emigration, post-war demographic decline and the existence of customs barriers, combined with the absence of any solid island development programme, have all contributed to the decline of Corsica's economy.

The island has one of the lowest per capita GDPs of all the French regions and the proportion of unemployed is higher than on the mainland. Economic observers insist, however, that Corsica gets considerable support. It receives more per inhabitant in EU subsidy money than any other region in France. It also has special tax status. The classification of the island as a free zone in 1996 reinforced this, along with exemption from social security contributions and corporate income tax. The Glavany report, published in 1998 (see the History section earlier in this chapter), was highly critical of the way in which the island's economic development subsidies had been used.

Corsican agriculture has nearly always been family-oriented. At one time, each family was virtually self-sufficient in food production, growing their own crops, rearing livestock and preparing *charcuterie* (cooked pork meats). However, agricultural production is now on the decline. The amount of farmland (only 14% of the island) also limits the future of Corsican agriculture, although relatively large holdings have appeared in the eastern lowlands, where the best land is. Agriculture represents just 2% of the island's GDP.

The various agricultural subsidies, which do not seem to be able to halt the decline of this sector on the island, include the EU suckler cow premium, a system whereby Corsican farmers were given a premium for each one of their cows that had a calf. Aimed at helping the farming industry, it has become notorious due to abuse of the system (such as fraudulent claims by farmers) and the perverse effects it has had. Since its introduction in the early 1980s, the number of sheep and cattle has increased to such an extent that grazing has become a problem. The system has increased the number of fires started to clear land for grazing, and in some cases herds have been miscounted or divided so that the farmer can receive subsidies.

All this aside, traditional Corsican agriculture is renowned for the quality of its produce. For example, honey is regulated by the Appellation Contrôlée system, traditionally used in France to control the quality of wine. Much of this quality produce is sold to tourists.

At just 5% of the GDP, industry is the Achilles heel of the island's economy. Corsica is the least industrialised region of metropolitan France. The industrial revolution had some impact in the 19th century, when several smelting furnaces were built

on the island. However, the iron and steel industry soon collapsed, as did the new mining industry. Aeronautical engineering, industrial boilermaking, agribusiness and small-scale wood, tobacco and cork industries comprise Corsica's manufacturing sector. Only around 30 companies on the island employ more than 20 people and only one employs more than 100 people. The building industry is worth a mention, however, since it represents 10% of jobs in this sector.

Most of Corsica's electricity is produced in two oil-fuelled thermal power stations in Lucciana and Vazzio. In addition, seven dams supply hydraulic power stations, notably near Calacuccia and on the Prunelli. Any additional electricity requirements are supplied by underwater cable from Italy. The Éole windmills, capable of producing 10% of the island's electricity requirements, should be operational in the year 2000 at 11 sites on the island.

The service sector is the most important in Corsica, accounting for 80% of GDP and almost 70% of jobs. The government and administrative departments are the island's leading employers. In 1994, one-third of Corsican employees worked for the government, local councils and other non-commercial services.

Unsurprisingly, economists see tourism, which currently accounts for 10% of GDP, as the island's best source of income. However, nationalists have denounced this 'obsession' with tourism, preferring to see attempts at promoting traditional activities. Besides this, the tourist season is quite short. Many are in favour of a more exclusive, upmarket type of summer tourism.

POPULATION & PEOPLE

Greatly depleted by losses experienced during WWI and by large-scale emigration, Corsica's population is 262,000, with Ajaccio and Bastia alone accounting for around 100,000. The record high was in 1884, with 276,000 inhabitants, while 1955 saw the lowest recorded figure (170,000).

An INSEE (French National Institute of Economic and Statistical Information) study carried out in 1990 estimated that more than 60% of the population was born on the island. For years, Corsica opened its arms to immigrants. Apart from Italians, many repatriated French settlers from Algeria moved to Corsica at the end of the Algerian war of independence in 1962. This created a number of problems, and was one of the main reasons for the resurgence of the nationalist movement. Since 1975 there have been fewer immigrants, but the number of French settlers from the mainland, known as *pinzuti*, has increased. Non-French immigrants number 22,000, 8% of the total population. Moroccans arrived first (approximately 12,000), followed by Italians and Portuguese (3000 of each), and Tunisians (around 2000).

The island has a low birth rate. Approximately 75 of its towns record more deaths than births. The exodus from the inland villages is also worrying. Between the 1960s and 1990s, the mountain communities lost around 15,000 inhabitants, and some regions have a near-Saharan population density. One-third of the inhabitants of the island's mountain villages is over 60 years old. However, the island does much to keep its mountain culture alive and the PNRC (see Ecology & Environment earlier in this chapter) encourages tourists to explore its mountainous regions.

EDUCATION

Education is compulsory for all between the ages of six and 16. *Lycée* (secondary school) studies are divided into two stages.

Corsica's Emigrants

One of the most salient features of the Corsican nation is that more Corsicans live off the island than on it. For many years, young people have been tempted away from the island, and the richest Corsicans have often made their fortunes in other parts of the world. There are several reasons for this, including the series of foreign occupations endured by the island, poverty and malaria, which was rife along Corsica's shores until the middle of the 20th century. Moreover, for some people life on the island is too limiting.

In the early 19th century, most Corsican emigrants headed for mainland France, where they often joined the army. Others went to Italy, where they studied literature or the sciences. Corsican communities have sprung up in Pisa and Livorno, and the Pope even has a Corsican guard.

Large-scale emigration has taken place from northern Corsica, especially from the Balagne and Cap Corse. Exposed to external influences through the traditions of shipping and trading developed under Genoese rule, many people in northern Corsica have headed for the Americas, particularly Peru, Mexico and Venezuela. On their return to Corsica, some had unusual American-style homes built, which can still be seen today in Cap Corse.

After the Americas, the French colonies became a favourite port of call. Many of Corsica's young yearned to see the French colonies, particularly those in North Africa. In the 1930s the proportion of Corsicans sections of the army and in colonial administration was estimated at almost 20%. After decolonisation these people often returned to France. In the 1960s there were no fewer than 70 Corsican associations in the département of Bouches-du-Rhône alone. Cities such as Paris, Lyon and Marseille still have a large Corsican population.

Overall, it is estimated that 700,000 to 800,000 people have emigrated from Corsica, 500,000 of whom have headed for the French mainland.

The first stage, between the ages of 11 and 15 (generally called *collège*), provides a general curriculum, while at the second stage, which continues until the age of 18, pupils choose between academic and vocational tracks. Students in the academic track can take the *baccalauréat*, the university entrance exam.

Pascal Paoli opened the first university in Corsica in 1765. Unfortunately, it was closed by the French soon after their arrival on the island and for a long time Corsicans intending to go on to higher education had no other choice but to leave the island. This situation was remedied in 1981 with the highly political and symbolic creation of the University of Corsica-Pascal Paoli. Based in Corte, it has 3500 students and offers courses in the arts, languages (including a degree in Corsican), science, technology, law and economics. There are also technical institutes, or IUTs, on the island.

ARTS
Music
Singing, an ancient island tradition, is now undergoing a revival. The *paghjella* is the most famous example of this. These polyphonic chants combine three or four male voices. The men are usually dressed in black and stand with a hand over one ear so that they are not distracted by the voice of the person next to them. This is critical, since each voice sings a different melody: the first provides the tone and basis of the melody, the second provides the bass, while the third, more high-pitched, improvises around a theme. The *voceru*, which is sung during a wake, is more mournful. This monotonous, halting song is sung by sobbing women, who rock to and fro as if in a trance. Vendettas often saw the *voceri* accompanied by cries for vengeance. More gentle, the *lamentu* deplores the absence of a loved one and is also sung by women.

The *chjam'e rispondi* are similar to the call and response style used in blues and spiritual music. This musical form lends itself well to improvisation competitions.

Songs might be accompanied by flutes made out of wood or horn, various percussion instruments and the *cetera*, a 16 chord instrument. Canta U Populu Corsu and other polyphonic groups such as I Muvrini, A Filetta or the Ghjami have now revived these traditional forms of musical expression. Recordings of these groups are available on the island. Older recordings include a set of records entitled *Musique corse de tradition orale*, produced between 1961 and 1963. These provide an opportunity to hear traditional interpretations, some of which were sung by the father of I Muvrini. Also interesting is the *Canzone di i prigiuneri corsi in Alimania 1916-1917*, distributed by La Marge, which were originally recorded on wax rolls by German ethnologists in WWI prisoner-of-war camps.

A religious hymn and a war song, the Corsican *Diu vi Salvi Regina*, is sung a cappella on a variety of occasions.

Literature
Early Corsican storytelling was oral rather than written. Originating in the villages, Corsican narratives were based on poetry, folk tales (*fola*) and stories of daily life, passed on at evening gatherings and related by shepherds on their journeys from summer to winter pasture. Songs, such as bandits' ballads, lovers' serenades and political choruses, were the means by which these stories were told, and they were often modified by the teller. This literary heritage has been adopted by modern Corsican polyphonic groups (see Music).

Literature was slow to become established. As the towns developed, literary circles were formed, such as the Accademia dei Vagabondi, founded in Bastia in 1659. Writers acted as historians (see *La Historia di Corsica* by Anton Pietro Filipoini, 1594) and a type of nationalism flourished. In the 19th century Corsican literature was written in Italian (most famously by Salvatore Viale, 1787-1861), although this was gradually replaced by French.

Two contemporary Corsican writers, widely published on the mainland, have

Theatre Takes to the Maquis in Haute-Corse

In 1998 Robin Renucci formed the first international theatre group in Haute-Corse. A fervent supporter of decentralisation, the actor wanted to revive the culture of the deserted and forgotten villages of central Corsica. Piogiolla, Olmi-Cappella, Mausoleo and Vallica, situated in the mountains near Calvi, offered a variety of locations ideal for staging plays.

After the opening performance, which was a resounding success, several Corsican actors, including the well known Teatrinu, became involved with this artistic and educational project. Mindful of the heritage of Antoine Vitez, a famous actor, director and teacher, Renucci wanted to re-establish links with drama schools. So, for one month in the summer, 70 actors, professional and amateur Corsican and French, young and old, were brought together to work under the guidance of experienced actors such as Mario Gonzales, an expert in commedia dell'arte. Renucci, loyal to the ideal of a public theatre, staged performances free of charge, relying on cooperation between local people and the actors in order to survive. Village squares, disused chapels, maquis and forests provided the settings for a varied repertoire that included Molière, Goldoni, Shakespeare, Ionesco and Culiolo (in Corsican).

immortalised their visions of the island on paper. Bastia-born Angelo Rinaldi meticulously describes post-war Corsican society in *Les Dames de France, La Dernière Fête de l'Empire, Les Jardins du consulat* and *Les Roses de Pline*, in which the author's imagination is fuelled by his childhood memories. Marie Susini, meanwhile, in her work *L'Île sans rivage* (1953), describes the problems relating to Corsican family structure and island confinement. Two contemporary crime writers are also rising to fame. Elisabeth Milleliri, a journalist with *Libération*, has published *Caveau de famille* (1993) and *Comme un chien* (1995), while Archange Morelli has written *La Maison ardente* (1997), a detective story set in Corsica at the beginning of the 16th century.

Architecture

Considered by experts to be one of the richest in Europe, Corsica's Romanesque architecture (from the second half of the 9th century until the end of the Middle Ages) is divided into two distinct periods. During the first, Early Romanesque, period (9th to 11th centuries) hundreds of small churches and rural chapels were built. Only about 10 of these buildings still exist, most of them in ruins. The second period is called Pisan

Romanesque. At the end of the 11th century, Pisa sent architects to Corsica with orders to build small cathedrals. These can mainly be found in the Nebbio, Castagniccia and Balagne. Among the most well known are San Michele de Murato and the Cathédrale de Mariana (south of Bastia), famous for their polychrome walls.

The Baroque style of architecture was introduced to Corsica in the 17th and 18th centuries, during the Genoese period. The Baroque movement was an artistic expression of contemporary religious revival. Many churches in the Balagne and Castagniccia were built in this style, which was very fashionable in northern Italy. Façades with triangular or curvilinear pediments were common, and the sumptuously decorated interiors have been restored to their original magnificence. Some 150 churches were built in this period, of which the best examples (excluding reconstructions) are Saint Jean Baptiste de La Porta (in Castagniccia), the religious buildings in Bastia and the cathedrals of Ajaccio and Cervione.

Other architecture of note includes the island's military buildings – the Genoese towers dotted around the Corsican coastline (67 of these still stand today) and the citadels in coastal towns such as Bastia and

Saint Florent. Built by the Genoese, some were extended by the French, such as the one in Corte, which is Corsica's only example of an inland citadel.

The traditional Corsican house (*casa*) was usually constructed from granite, with the exception of the chalky areas of Bonifacio and Saint Florent and the northern part of the island, where shale was more commonly used. Four or five-storey houses are common. Small apertures in the façades keep the house warm in winter and cool in summer. The roofs are covered in large narrow slates, the colour of which varies, depending upon where the slates come from: grey-blue in Corte, green in Bastia and silver-grey in Castagniccia.

Painting

As with architecture, Corsica has tended to import Pisan and Genoese culture rather than producing its own artistic movements or painters. This is true of the Gothic frescoes produced at the end of the 15th century, which still decorate some 20 churches and chapels. The Musée Fesch in Ajaccio, the biggest museum in Corsica, houses the second-largest collection of Italian paintings in France after the Louvre. Assembled by Napoleon's uncle, Cardinal Fesch, the Italian commissioner for war and later an astute businessman, it contains dozens of early Italian works.

In the 19th century a handful of Corsican artists (such as Charles Fortuné Guasco and Louis Pelligriniles) gained recognition by studying in France. Some even won the Prix de Rome or had exhibitions in Parisian salons.

At the end of the 19th century and beginning of the 20th century, Corsica was visited by several important artists, who came in search of light. Matisse confided that 'it was in Ajaccio that I had my first vision of the South'. Fernand Léger decided to spend several summers on the Corsican coast early in his career. Utrillo and his mother, Suzanne Valadon, also made several visits to the island, as did Signac and the American artist Whistler.

Contemporary island painters such as Lucien Peri, François Corbellini, Pierre Dionisi and Jean-Baptiste Pekle are synonymous with Corsica's artistic reawakening after WWI. Most have taken their inspiration from the island's stunning scenery.

SOCIETY & CONDUCT
Traditional Culture

The traditions and cultural values of the Corsican people remain alive today, especially now that the nationalist movement has made the concept of Corsican identity fashionable.

Many Corsicans proudly lay claim to the legacy of their island's turbulent past. A sense of honour – including keeping one's word – is certainly the most important part of this legacy. Dishonouring a man or woman was considered for years to be the worst possible insult. It is said that merely touching a woman's dress or hair was enough to dishonour her, and injured pride has been the cause of many a bloody vendetta. The island has spawned a number of 'bandits of honour', outlawed and seeking refuge in the maquis, sometimes for years, after having avenged an offence by violent means. Weapons have always been an important part of Corsican culture – and not only for hunting.

The family is also extremely important. Certain rules have served to preserve its unity and continuity. Apart from joint ownership, which prevailed in inheritances, it was a tradition that the first-born would take the name of the paternal grandfather, the second that of the maternal grandmother, the third the paternal grandmother, and so on. This tradition still survives in places today. As is often the case in the Mediterranean, the traditional Corsican family is patriarchal. Males inherited habitable land, but females were bequeathed land near the coast, which was often less useful than that in the hinterland as malaria was rife in those areas at the time. However, many of these women consider themselves fortunate now.

The Vendetta

Of all the Corsican traditions the vendetta is certainly the most fabled. Prevalent between the 16th and 18th centuries, this custom saw families clashing in truly bloody wars that could drag on for years and involve several generations. Yet one would be mistaken in thinking that the vendetta was a substitute for official justice. On the contrary, it tended to be a consequence of the absence of any judicial authority on the island. Whenever the island has been ruled with a strong hand the prevalence of the vendetta has declined.

Far from being an anarchic form of justice, the vendetta has its own code: it was declared as a war and, with the help of mediators, could be ended by the signing of a peace treaty. Vendettas were often caused by deeds or accusations of dishonour, with feuds sparked off by jealous rivalry, disputes over land or even a determination to assert one's power locally.

Jean-Baptiste Marcaggi, in *Bandits corses d'hier et d'aujourd'hui* (1932, republished by La Marge in 1978) defines the vendetta as follows: '… it is not merely a case of one's right to seek revenge, but an obligation to settle the blood feud, or to demand atonement for the dishonouring of a member of the family. In short, those seeking revenge continued in their quest for justice until their ends were achieved'. This obviously leads to a vicious circle: according to the code, which prohibits any material compensation for a murder or offence, one death must lead to another. Many vendettas have only ended once the families have suffered equal losses. This bloody and secular custom, prevalent throughout the Mediterranean and closely associated with the value placed on one's sense of honour, was also ritualistic. Not only did each side keep the bloodstained shirt of the deceased until the death was avenged, but they would refrain from cutting their hair or shaving until they had taken revenge.

Vendettas were more common in southern Corsica. There are no records of vendettas taking place in Cap Corse and they were rarely declared in the Balagne. In the south, however, the tradition took on huge proportions. Some years saw almost 900 murders on the island. Once their revenge was complete, many had no choice but to take to the maquis as outlaws. At this point, it became a question of survival rather than honour, and the fugitives would stop at nothing in order to survive.

The affiliation to a clan automatically provided an extended family, but also included members of a village community in a structure which was protective of its influence and authority. Its members were loyal to the tight-knit group, whose interests they served blindly. Robert Colonna d'Istria describes the clan tradition humorously in *L'Histoire de la Corse* (1995): 'Membership of a clan, the sense of belonging, created ties that stuck to people like Gruyère to pasta'.

Corsica should not be thought of as one big happy family: the island's inhabitants have always demonstrated their lack of unity and the links that exist within families, clans and villages are matched by the antipathy towards other families, clans or villages. At a time when many Corsicans no longer live on the island, to be Corsican can mean fierce loyalty to these values, while the non-Corsican may find a it a society whose village, clan and family structures are not easy to penetrate. This is because Corsicans have come to be wary of anyone from outside their island.

Corsican traditions have to a large extent been protected from the influence of tourism: while Corsica is a mainly mountain culture, with traditional activities taking place in winter – the season of the *figatellu* (a type of sausage), charcuterie, *brocciu* (a local cheese made from ewe's or goat's milk) and hunting – most visitors come to the island in summer.

Visitors who are truly interested in its culture, however, will find the island surprisingly warm and hospitable.

Dos & Don'ts

Your visit to Corsica will be more enjoyable if you stick to a few basic guidelines.

First, some formal conventions are still used in Corsica. For example, you will be expected to say *Merci, monsieur* or *Merci, madame* rather than just *Merci*. As a general rule, rushing around is out of place on the island and there is everything to be gained by being patient. Do not forget to introduce yourself when starting a conversation, since Corsicans like to know whom they are dealing with.

Corsicans sometimes take offence if they invite you to their house and you turn up bearing gifts. The inference is that you brought along what you thought they might not be able to provide. It is also more customary to buy rounds when going for a drink, rather than splitting the bill.

RELIGION

Corsica is predominantly Roman Catholic. Religion manifests itself in various festivals and celebrations, particuarly the lavish Semaine Sainte (Holy Week) processions which take place in towns such as Bonifacio, Sartène and Calvi. Commemorative plaques, often seen at the base of statues, also testify to the extent of religious faith, as do the churches all over the island (some of which are architecturally noteworthy).

Women in Corsican Society

Like many Mediterranean societies typically viewed as male chauvinist, Corsica owes a lot to its women. The traditional portrayal of sombrely dressed women, silent out of deference for their men, is misleading. It was often a mother, for instance, who would declare a vendetta. In his *Guide de la Corse mystérieuse* (1995), Gaston d'Angélis states that if a man was murdered, his wife would often visit the scene of the crime, where she would place her children's fingers in the bullet wound. She would then make the sign of the cross on their foreheads with their father's blood, before making them promise to avenge his death. Legend also has it that when Bonifacio was under siege in 1420, the townswomen gave mothers' milk to its soldiers. This was sometimes used to make cheeses which would then be used to bombard the assailants.

Corsican women demonstrated great courage and determination in 1998. Following the assassination of the prefect Érignac in February, their *Manifeste pour la vie* (Manifesto for Life), a call for an end to violence on the island, hit the headlines. The women agreed to meet on the sixth day of each month outside the gates of the Palais de Justice in Bastia, until the murder was solved. The association known as *51 Femmes pour la Corse de l'An 2000* (51 Women for Corsica in the Year 2000), created shortly afterwards, is more economically oriented.

This is not the first time that Corsican women have unleashed their anger in public. In 1791 Flore Oliva, nicknamed *la colonelle* (the colonel), led the women of Bastia in their revolt against the local bishop, who had pledged support to the French constitution. The bishop was forced to seek refuge from the women in the episcopal palace.

Danielle Casanova, a leading figure in the Corsican resistance who died while being deported in 1943, is also one of the island's *grandes dames*.

Saint Dévote, who was martyred in the 3rd century, is Corsica's main patron. Saint Alexandre Sauli, Saint Appien, Saint Euphrase, Saint Julie, Saint Restitude and Saint Théophile de Corte are also celebrated on the island. However, Catholicism in Corsica exists alongside a variety of mystical and superstitious customs, such as belief in the *spiritu* (the dead who return to visit their homes) and magic spells used to cure illness.

The island also has some Protestant churches (such as those in Ajaccio and Pietranera) and there is a Greek Orthodox church in Cargèse. It is interesting to note that the latter shares a priest with the Catholic church opposite it. Services take place alternately in each.

LANGUAGE

The official language of Corsica is French, but Italian and Corsican (Corsu) are also spoken. Corsican, which was almost exclusively oral until recently, is closer to Italian than French. It constitutes an important component of Corsican identity, and many people (especially at the university in Corte) are working to ensure its survival.

Street signs in most towns are now bilingual or exclusively in Corsican. You'll also see lots of French highway signs 'edited' with spray paint into their *nomi Corsi* (Corsican names). Local usage varies, with both French and Corsican place names used, and this is reflected on maps, where names vary between the French and the Corsican from map to map.

Facts for the Visitor

SUGGESTED ITINERARIES

There are no obvious tourist routes around Corsica. The island's main charm is its scenery, which is fairly evenly spread across its area. Although the best way to get around is by car, you should be able to follow the following itineraries reasonably closely using public transport, although it will take a little longer and you may have to miss out some places – for example, the villages of the Balagne are difficult to get to by bus.

Avoid very rigid and over-detailed schedules. Don't rely too much on road maps, which don't show the relief well: distances can look very short on the map but take hours to travel by road.

Walking itineraries are described in the Walking in Corsica chapter.

One Week

Starting from Bastia, one week would allow you to travel around Cap Corse, and then spend a little time in Saint Florent or in the Agriates before returning to Bastia. Alternatively you could arrive in Calvi and spend two days there before going down towards E Calanche in Piana, the Réserve Naturelle de Scandola and the seaside resort of Porto, before returning to Calvi via the inland villages of the Balagne (if you have a car). In the south, you could do a round trip through Bonifacio, Sartène and Alta Rocca. You could also choose to travel through Corsica's mountains by train (or by car) from Bastia to Ajaccio via Corte, or from Ajaccio to Calvi.

Starting from Ajaccio, it would take a good week to explore the bays on the west coast of the island (Valinco, Ajaccio, Sagone, Porto), Calvi or Bonifacio and the areas around them. If you would prefer a more relaxing holiday, you would be better off in Porto Vecchio or Propriano.

Two Weeks

Starting from Bastia, two very full weeks would allow you to tour Cap Corse, E Calanche and the Réserve Naturelle de Scandola on your way to Calvi. You could then visit Porto before veering east towards Ota, the Gorges de Spelunca, the Forêt d'Aïtone, the Col de Verghio and la Scala di Santa Regina prior to heading back to Bastia.

If you start from Ajaccio, Propriano, Porto Vecchio or Figari, you may prefer a route that links up Sartène and the prehistoric sites of the Sartenais, Bonifacio, Porto Vecchio, L'Ospedale, Bavella and the villages of Alta Rocca: Quenza, Sainte Lucie de Tallano and so on.

Three Weeks

One option would be to add Corte and the Vallée de la Restonica to the first two week itinerary described above. Having said that, many people prefer to finish off their holiday with a week on the beach or a week's walking.

One Month

In a month you can see (almost) everything on Corsica. Some people opt to go all the way round the island, but if you do this don't forget to make a few forays into the spectacular Corsican mountains, to Alta Rocca or even to the heights of Porto.

PLANNING

When to Go

The overwhelming majority of visitors to Corsica go in the middle of summer. This means that the island is at its most overcrowded between the middle of July and the end of August. Therefore, it's during this period that hotel prices are at their highest. Moreover, some of the island's most idyllic sights – Girolata, the Désert des Agriates, Bonifacio, Cap Corse, the GR20 and the numerous coves that litter the coast – do not cope well with the influx of tourists in summer.

Having said that, these months can guarantee good weather conditions. For those who enjoy swimming and diving, the water is warmest in August and September. On the other hand, it can be very hot for walkers in July and August.

May, June and September are the most pleasant months to visit: the temperature is agreeable, tourist levels are acceptable, prices are affordable, the reception is more relaxed and the more seasonal services are available.

Weather Forecasts

The French meteorological office (Météo France) provides seven-day forecasts for each *département*. This service is available on ☎ 08 36 68 08 08. Calls are charged at 2.23FF per minute. The forecasts are updated three times a day.

The Minitel 3615 Météo server provides special bulletins for coastal and mountainous regions for the same price.

Regularly updated forecasts are also available from Météo Consult and Nice-Matin on ☎ 08 36 68 06 50.

A significant number of services on the island (including hotels, camp sites, restaurants, transport and sports facilities) only operate between April and September. During the rest of the year, Corsica can seem dead. Although there can be snow on the peaks into June, some walks – the Mare a Mare Sud and Centre, and the Mare e Monti Sud – are practicable year-round. Spring and autumn are undoubtedly the best seasons for walking.

Maps

Michelin road map No 90, at a scale of 1:200,000 (1cm = 2km), is easy to use and gives a clear overview of the island's road network.

The two IGN 'green series' maps (No 73, Bastia-Corte and No 74, Ajaccio) at a scale of 1:100,000 (1cm = 1km) give a better impression of the relief. These maps are widely available on the island.

For the more detailed maps required for walking see the Walking in Corsica chapter.

What to Bring

The cardinal rule in packing is to bring as little as possible. Start off with too little rather than too much, as virtually anything you could possibly need is available locally.

If you'll be doing any walking with your gear, even just from hotels to trains, a backpack is the only way to go. One of the most flexible ways to carry your belongings is in an internal-frame travel pack whose straps can be zipped inside a flap, turning it into something resembling a nylon suitcase. The most useful kind has an exterior pouch that zips off to become a daypack.

If you plan to stay at hostels and *gîtes d'étape* (mountain lodges), pack or buy your own towel and a plastic soap container when you arrive. Blankets are provided in gîtes d'étape, but it's a good idea to take along your own sleeping bag.

Other items you might need include a torch (flashlight), an adapter plug for electrical appliances (such as a cup or coil immersion heater to make your own tea or coffee), a universal bath/sink plug (a plastic film canister sometimes works), sunglasses and a hat, a few clothes pegs and moist towelettes or a large cotton handkerchief, which you can wet and use to cool off.

TOURIST OFFICES
Local Tourist Offices

There are tourist offices and information centres in the main towns and tourist sites on the island. Some of them are open year-round, others are only open during the main tourist season. The staff are generally competent and often speak English and Italian. These tourist offices provide a range of information on activities, accommodation and transport, together with brochures and maps (although unfortunately these often have mistakes on them).

L'Agence de Tourisme de la Corse (ATC; ☎ 04 95 51 77 77, fax 04 95 51 14 40), 17 blvd du Roi Jerôme, 20000 Ajaccio, can provide a wealth of information that will be useful when planning your holiday. The Minitel service, 3615 Corse, is also a valuable source of information.

Tourist Offices Abroad

French government tourist offices (usually called Maisons de la France) can provide every imaginable sort of tourist information on France, including Corsica, most of it in the form of brochures. They include:

Australia
(☎ 02-9231 5244, fax 9221 8682,
email frencht@ozemail.com.au)
25 Bligh St, 22nd floor, Sydney, NSW 2000
Canada
(☎ 514-288 4264, fax 845 4868,
email mfrance@mtl.net)
1981 McGill College Ave, Suite 490, Montreal, Que H3A 2W9
Germany
Berlin:
(☎ 030-218 2064, fax 214 1238)
Keithstrasse 2-4, 10787 Berlin
Frankfurt-am-Main:
(☎ 069-758 021, fax 745 556,
email maison_de _la_france@t-online.de)
Westendstrasse 47, 60325 Frankfurt-am-Main
Ireland
(☎ 01-703 4046, fax 874 7324)
35 Lower Abbey St, Dublin 1
Italy
(☎ 166 116216, fax 02 5848 622,
email entf@ enter.it)
Via Larga 7, 20122 Milan
Netherlands
(☎ 0900 112 2332, fax 020-620 3339,
email fra_vvv@euronet.nl)
Prinsengracht 670, 1017 KX Amsterdam
UK
(☎ 0891 244 123, fax 020-7493 6594,
email piccadilly@mdlf.demon.co.uk)
178 Piccadilly, London W1V 0AL
USA
Los Angeles:
(☎ 310-271 6665, fax 276 2835,
email fgtola@ juno.com)
9454 Wiltshire Blvd, Suite 715, Beverly Hills, CA 90212-2967
New York:
(☎ 212-838 7800, fax 838 7855,
email info@ francetourism.com)
444 Madison Ave, 16th floor, New York, NY 10022-6903

VISAS & DOCUMENTS
Passport
By law, everyone in France, including tourists, must carry some sort of ID on them at all times. For foreign visitors, this means a passport (if you don't want to carry your passport for security reasons a photocopy should do, although you may be required to verify your identity later) or, for citizens of those European Union (EU) countries that issue them, a national ID card.

Visas
Tourist There are no entry requirements or restrictions on nationals of EU countries, and citizens of Australia, the USA, Canada, New Zealand and Israel do not need visas to visit France as tourists for up to three months. Except for people from a handful of other European countries, everyone else must have a visa.

Visa fees depend on the current exchange rate but a transit visa should cost about UK£7, a visa valid for stays of up to 30 days around UK£18, and a single/multiple entry visa of up to three months about UK£21.50/25.50. You will need your passport (valid for a period of three months beyond the date of your departure from France), a return ticket, proof of sufficient funds to support yourself, proof of pre-arranged accommodation (possibly), two passport-size photos and the visa fee in cash.

If all the forms are in order, your visa will be issued on the spot. You can also apply for a French visa after arriving in Europe – the fee is the same, but you may not have to produce a return ticket. If you enter France overland, your visa may not be checked at the border, but major problems can arise if you don't have one later on (for example, at the airport as you leave the country).

Long-Stay & Student Citizens of EU countries and Switzerland wishing to stay in Corsica for longer than 90 days must apply for a resident's permit from the nearest town hall or from the *service des étrangers* (foreigners' department) of the Corsican prefecture (☎ 04 95 29 00 00, fax 04 95 29 00 36), Palais Lantivy, rue de Sergent Castalonga, 20000 Ajaccio.

Citizens of Australia, Canada and the USA are limited to two stays of 90 days each per year. Those wishing to extend their stay must apply for an extended resident's permit from the French embassy or consulate in their own country.

Non-EU nationals wanting to work or study in France or stay for over three months should apply to their nearest French embassy or consulate for the appropriate *long séjour* (long-stay) visa. Unless you live in the EU, it is extremely difficult to get a visa allowing you to work in France. For any sort of long-stay visa, begin the paperwork in your home country several months before you plan to leave. Applications cannot usually be made in a third country nor can tourist visas be turned into student visas after you arrive in France. People with student visas can apply for permission to work part-time (inquire at your place of study).

Carte de Séjour (Residence Permit)
Non-EU nationals issued with a long-stay visa valid for six or more months will probably have to apply for a *carte de séjour* (residence permit) within eight days of arrival in France. Apply at the foreigner's department of the prefecture in Ajaccio (see the Long-Stay & Student section).

Visa Extensions Tourist visas cannot be extended except in emergencies (for example, medical problems). Again, apply at the foreigners' department of the Corsican prefecture in Ajaccio (see the Long-Stay & Student section).

If you don't need a visa to visit France, you'll almost certainly qualify for another automatic three-month stay if you leave and then re-enter France. The fewer recent French entry stamps you have in your passport the easier this is likely to be. If you needed a visa the first time around, one way to extend your stay is to go to a French consulate in a neighbouring country and apply for another one there.

People entering France by rail, road or even air often don't have their passports checked, much less stamped. Fear not: you're in France legally, whether or not you had to apply for a visa before arriving (though at some point, to show your date of entry, you may be asked to produce the plane, train or ferry ticket you arrived with). If you prefer to have your passport stamped

(for example, if you expect to have to prove when you last entered the country), it may take a bit of running around to find the right border official.

Travel Insurance
You should seriously consider taking out travel insurance. This not only covers you for medical expenses and luggage theft or loss but also for cancellation or delays in your travel arrangements. Cover depends on your insurance and type of ticket, so ask both your insurer and your ticket-issuing agency to explain where you stand. Ticket loss is also covered by travel insurance.

Paying for your airline ticket with a credit card often provides limited travel accident insurance, and you may be able to reclaim the payment if the operator doesn't deliver. In the UK institutions issuing credit cards are required by law to reimburse consumers if a company goes into liquidation and the amount in contention is more than UK£100. Ask your credit card company what it's prepared to cover.

EU citizens are eligible for free emergency medical treatment if they have an E111 certificate. See Predeparture Planning in the Health section later in this chapter for more details.

Driving Licence & Permits
Driving Licence Driving licences issued by member states of the EU allow you to drive in France, as do those from Canada.

International Driving Permit Many non-European drivers' licences are valid in France, but it's still a good idea to bring an International Driving Permit (IDP), which can make life much simpler, especially when hiring cars and motorbikes.

Basically a multilingual translation of the vehicle class and personal details on your local driver's licence, an IDP is not valid unless accompanied by your original licence. An IDP can be obtained for a small fee from your local automobile association – bring along a passport photo and a valid licence.

Hostel Cards

There are two Hostelling International (HI) *auberges de jeunesse* (youth hostels) in Corsica, at Calvi and Poggio Mezzana. A HI card is necessary at these. If you don't pick one up at home, you can buy one at official French hostels for 70/100FF if you're under/over 26 years of age. One night membership (where available) costs between 10FF and 19FF, and a family card is 100FF.

Carte Jeune

A Carte Jeune (120FF for one year) is available to anyone under 26 who has been in France for at least six months. It gets you discounts on things like air tickets, car rental, sports events, concerts and movies. In France, details are available from ☎ 08 03 00 12 26; by Minitel key in 3615 CARTE JEUNES.

Photocopies

The hassles brought on by losing your passport can be considerably reduced if you have a record of its number and issue date or, even better, photocopies of the relevant data pages. A photocopy of your birth certificate can also be useful.

Also copy the serial numbers of your travellers cheques (cross them off as you cash them) and photocopies of your credit cards, airline ticket and other travel documents. Keep all this emergency material separate from your passport, cheques and cash, and leave extra copies with someone you can rely on back home. Add some emergency money, say US$50 in cash, to this separate stash as well. If you do lose your passport, notify the police immediately to get a statement, and contact your nearest consulate.

EMBASSIES & CONSULATES
French Embassies & Consulates

French diplomatic offices overseas include:

Australia
Embassy:
(☎ 02-6216 0100, fax 6273 3193)
6 Perth Ave, Yarralumla, ACT 2600
Consulate:
(☎ 03-9820 0944, 9820 0921, fax 9820 9363)
492 St Kilda Rd, Level 4, Melbourne, Vic 3004
Consulate:
(☎ 02-9262 5779, fax 9283 1210)
St Martin's Tower, 20th floor, 31 Market St, Sydney, NSW 2000

Canada
Embassy:
(☎ 613-789 1795, fax 789 0279)
42 Sussex Drive, Ottawa, Ont K1M 2C9
Consulate:
(☎ 514-878 4385, fax 878 3981)
1 place Ville Marie, 26th floor, Montreal, Que H3B 4S3
Consulate:
(☎ 416-925 8041, fax 925 3076)
130 Bloor St West, Suite 400, Toronto, Ont M5S 1N5

Germany
Embassy:
(☎ 0228-955 6000, fax 955 6055)
An der Marienkapelle 3, 53179 Bonn
Consulate:
(☎ 030-885 90243, fax 885 5295)
Kurfürstendamm 211, 10719 Berlin
Consulate:
(☎ 089-419 4110, fax 419 41141)
Möhlstrasse 5, 81675 Munich

Ireland
Embassy:
(☎ 01-260 1666, fax 283 0178)
36 Ailesbury Rd, Ballsbridge, Dublin 4

Italy
Embassy:
(☎ 06 686 011, fax 06 860 1360)
Piazza Farnese 67, 00186 Rome
Consulate:
(☎ 06 6880 6437, fax 06 6860 1260)
Via Giulia 251, 00186 Rome

Netherlands
Embassy:
(☎ 070-312 5800, fax 312 5854)
Smidsplein 1, 2514 BT The Hague
Consulate:
(☎ 020-624 8346, fax 626 0841)
Vijzelgracht 2, 1000 HA Amsterdam

New Zealand
Embassy:
(☎ 04-384 2555)
34-42 Manners St, Wellington

UK
Embassy:
(☎ 020-7201 1000, fax 7201 1004)
58 Knightsbridge,
London SW1X 7JT

Consulate:
(☎ 020-7838 2000, fax 7838 2001)
21 Cromwell Rd, London SW7 2DQ
The visa section is at 6A Cromwell Place, London SW7 2EW (☎ 020-7838 2051). Dial ☎ 0891 887733 for visa information.

USA
Embassy:
(☎ 202-944 6000, fax 944 6166)
4101 Reservoir Rd NW, Washington, DC 20007
Consulate:
(☎ 212-606 3688, fax 606 3620)
934 Fifth Ave, New York, NY 10021
Consulate:
(☎ 415-397 4330, fax 433 8357)
540 Bush St, San Francisco, CA 94108.
There are other consulates in Atlanta, Boston, Chicago, Houston, Los Angeles, Miami and New Orleans.

Embassies & Consulates in France

All of the following embassies are in Paris, although some countries also have consulates in other major French cities. Only a few countries, including Italy, have diplomatic representation in Corsica.

It's important to realise what your embassy can and can't do to help you if you get into trouble. Generally speaking, it won't be much help in emergencies if the trouble you're in is remotely your own fault. Remember that you are bound by French law. Your embassy will not be sympathetic if you end up in jail after committing a crime locally, even if such actions are legal in your own country. In genuine emergencies you might get some assistance, but only if other channels have been exhausted. For example, if you need to get home urgently, a free ticket home is exceedingly unlikely – the embassy would expect you to have insurance. If you have all your money and documents stolen, it might assist with getting a new passport, but a loan for onward travel is out of the question.

Some embassies used to keep letters for travellers or have a small reading room with home newspapers, but these days the mail holding service has usually been stopped and even newspapers tend to be out of date.

Australia
Embassy:
(☎ 01 40 59 33 00)
4 rue Jean Rey, 15e
The consular section, which handles matters concerning Australian nationals, is open Monday to Friday from 9.15 am to noon and 2 to 4.30 pm.

Canada
Embassy:
(☎ 01 44 43 29 00)
35 ave Montaigne, 8e
Canadian citizens in need of consular services should call the embassy Monday to Friday from 9.30 to 11 am or 2 to 4.30 pm for a weekday appointment.
Consulate:
(☎ 03 88 96 65 02)
rue du Ried, La Wantzenau, 12km north-east of Strasbourg
Consulate:
(☎ 05 61 99 30 16)
30 blvd de Strasbourg, Toulouse

Germany
Embassy:
(☎ 01 53 83 45 00)
13 ave Franklin D Roosevelt, 8e
Consulate:
(☎ 01 42 99 78 00, Minitel 3615 ALLEMAGNE)
34 ave d'Iéna, 16e
Consulate:
(☎ 03 88 15 03 40)
15 rue des Francs Bourgeois, 15th floor, Strasbourg

Ireland
Embassy:
(☎ 01 44 17 67 00 or, after hours in an emergency, 01 44 17 67 67)
4 rue Rude, 16e
Open Monday to Friday from 9.30 am to noon (or by appointment). The phone is answered on weekdays from 9.30 am to 1 pm and 2.30 to 5.30 pm.

Italy
Embassy:
(☎ 01 49 54 03 00)
51 rue de Varenne, 7e
Consulate:
(☎ 01 44 30 47 00)
5 blvd Émile Augier, 16e
Consulate:
(☎ 04 79 33 20 36)
12 blvd Lèmenc, Chambery
Consulate:
(☎ 04 95 31 01 52, fax 04 95 32 56 72)
rue Saint François Prolongée, 20200 Bastia

New Zealand
  Embassy:
  (☎ 01 45 00 24 11 for 24 hour voice mail and
  emergencies)
  7ter rue Léonard de Vinci, 16e
  Open Monday to Friday from 9 am to 1 pm for
  routine matters and from 2 to 5.30 pm for
  emergencies. In July and August it's also open
  on Friday from 8.30 am to 2 pm.
UK
  Consulate:
  (☎ 01 44 51 31 00 or, 24 hours a day in an
  emergency, 01 42 66 29 79)
  16 rue d'Anjou, 8e
  Open weekdays (except public holidays) from
  9.30 am to 12.30 pm and 2.30 to 5 pm.
  Consulate:
  (☎ 04 72 77 81 70, fax 04 72 77 81 70)
  24 rue Childebert, 4th floor, Lyon
  Consulate:
  (☎ 04 91 15 72 10)
  24 ave du Prado, Marseille
  Consulate:
  (☎ 04 93 82 32 04)
  8 rue Alphonse Kerr, Nice
USA
  Embassy:
  (☎ 01 43 12 22 22 or, 24 hours a day in an
  emergency, 01 43 12 49 48, Minitel 3614
  ETATS-UNIS)
  2 rue Saint Florentin, 1er
  Except on French and US holidays, the American Services section is open Monday to Friday
  from 9 am to 3 pm.
  Consulate:
  (☎ 04 91 54 92 00, fax 04 91 55 09 97)
  12 blvd Paul Peytral, Marseille
  Consulate:
  (☎ 04 93 88 89 55)
  31 rue Maréchal Joffre, Nice
  Consulate:
  (☎ 03 88 35 31 04)
  15 ave d'Alsace, Strasbourg

The following countries are represented on
the island by honorary consulates:

Belgium & the Netherlands
  (☎ 04 95 20 89 99, fax 04 95 23 56 44)
  c/o Air Fret Service, aéroport Campo dell'Oro,
  20090 Ajaccio
Germany
  (☎ 04 95 33 03 56) RN 193, zone industrielle
  Furiani, 20600 Bastia
Switzerland
  (☎/fax 04 95 20 80 34)
  2 ave Pascal Paoli, 20000 Ajaccio

CUSTOMS

Check out the duty-free regulations in the
EU before you arrive in Corsica. The following items can be brought into Corsica
duty free from non-EU countries: 200 cigarettes, 50 cigars or 250g of loose tobacco;
1L of strong liquor or 2L of liquor which is
less than 22% alcohol by volume; 2L of
wine; 500g of coffee or 200g of extracts;
50g of perfume and 0.25L of toilet water.

Do not confuse duty-free allowances
with duty-paid items (including alcohol and
tobacco) bought at normal shops and supermarkets in another EU country and brought
into France, where certain goods might be
more expensive. Then the allowances are
more generous: 800 cigarettes, 200 cigars
or 1kg of loose tobacco; and 10L of spirits
(more than 22% alcohol by volume), 20L of
fortified wine or apéritif, 90L of wine or
110L of beer. There are no duty-free shopping facilities in Corsican airports.

Note that your home country may have
strict regulations regarding the import of
meat, dairy products or plants.

Those arriving on the island by boat from
outside the EU must present themselves to
the port authorities when they disembark.
Customs authorities usually board the boat.

MONEY
Currency

The national currency is the French franc,
abbreviated in this book to the letters FF.
One franc is divided into 100 centimes.

French coins come in denominations of
five, 10, 20 and 50 centimes (0.5FF) and
one, two, five, 10 and 20FF; the two highest denominations have silvery centres and
brass edges. It's wise to keep some coins of
various denominations for such things as
parking meters, tolls and laundrettes. Banknotes are issued in denominations of 20, 50,
100, 200, and 500FF. It can often be difficult to get change for a 500FF bill.

See the boxed text 'Introducing the Euro'
on the next page for information on the ad-
vent of the new European currency and its
consequences for the traveller.

Introducing the Euro

On 1 January 1999 a new currency, the euro, was introduced in Europe. It's all part of the harmonisation of the European Union (EU) countries. Along with national border controls, the currencies of various EU members are being phased out. Not all EU members have agreed to adopt the euro, however: Denmark, Greece, Sweden and the UK rejected or postponed participation. The 11 countries that have participated from the beginning of the process are Austria, Belgium, Finland, France, Germany, Ireland, Italy, Luxembourg, the Netherlands, Portugal and Spain.

The timetable for the introduction of the euro runs as follows:

- On 1 January 1999 the exchange rates of the participating countries were irrevocably fixed to the euro. The euro came into force for 'paper' accounting and prices could be displayed in local currency and in euros.
- On 1 January 2002 euro banknotes and coins will be introduced. This ushers in a period of dual use of euros and existing local notes and coins (which will, in effect, simply be temporary denominations of the euro).
- By July 2002 local currencies in the 11 countries will be withdrawn. Only euro notes and coins will remain in circulation and prices will be displayed in euros only.

The €5 note in France (including Corsica) is the same €5 note you will use in all of the other participating countries. There will be seven euro notes. In different colours and sizes they come in denominations of 500, 200, 100, 50, 20, 10 and five euros. There are eight euro coins, in denominations of two and one euros, then 50, 20, 10, five, two and one cents. On the reverse side of the coins each participating state will be able to decorate the coins with their own designs, but all euro coins can be used anywhere that accepts euros.

So, what does all this mean for the traveller? It is somewhat uncertain exactly what practices will be adopted between 1999 and 2002, and travellers will probably find differences in 'euro-readiness' between different countries, between different towns in the same country, or between different establishments in the same town. It is certain, however, that euro cheque accounts and travellers cheques will be available. Credit card companies can bill in euros, and

Exchange Rates

country	unit		franc
Australia	A$1	=	3.85FF
Canada	C$1	=	4.05FF
euro	€1	=	6.56FF
Germany	DM1	=	3.35FF
Italy	L1000	=	3.39FF
Japan	¥100	=	5.13FF
Netherlands	f1	=	2.98FF
New Zealand	NZ$1	=	3.26FF
Spain	100 ptas	=	3.94FF
UK	UK£1	=	9.84FF
USA	US$1	=	6.11FF

At banks and bureaux de change, you can tell how good the rate is by checking the spread between the rates for *achat* (buy rates, that is what they'll give you for foreign cash or travellers cheques) and *vente* (sell rates, that is the rate at which they sell foreign currency) – the greater the difference, the further each is from the interbank rate (printed daily in newspapers, including the *International Herald Tribune*).

Exchanging Money

Post Offices Many post offices change foreign currency at a middling rate. The

Introducing the Euro

shops, hotels and restaurants might list prices in both local currency and euros. Travellers should check bills carefully to make sure that any conversion from local currency to euros has been calculated correctly. The most confusing period will probably be between January 2002 and July 2002 when there will be two sets of notes and coins.

Luckily for travellers, the euro should make everything easier. One of the main benefits will be that prices in the 11 countries will be immediately comparable, avoiding all those tedious calculations.

Also, once euro notes and coins are issued in 2002, you won't need to change money at all when travelling to other single-currency members. Banks may still charge a handling fee (yet to be decided) for travellers cheques but they won't be able to profit by buying the currency from you at one rate and selling it back to you at another, as they do at the moment. However, even EU countries not participating may price goods in euros and accept euros over shop counters.

There are many Web sites dealing with the introduction of the euro but most are devoted to the legal implications and the processes by which businesses may adapt to the single currency and are not particularly interesting or informative for the traveller. The Lonely Planet Web site at www.lonelyplanet.com has a link to a currency converter and up-to-date news on the integration process.

Australia	A$1	=	€0.59
Canada	C$1	=	€0.62
France	10FF	=	€1.52
Germany	DM1	=	€0.51
Italy	L1000	=	€0.52
Japan	¥100	=	€0.78
New Zealand	NZ$1	=	€0.50
Spain	100 ptas	=	€0.60
UK	UK£1	=	€1.50
USA	US$1	=	€0.93

commission for travellers cheques is 1.2% (minimum 16FF).

Post offices accept banknotes in a variety of currencies as well as travellers cheques issued by American Express (denominated in either US dollars or French francs) or Visa (in French francs only).

Commercial Banks Commercial banks usually charge between 22FF and 50FF per foreign currency transaction. The rates vary, so it pays to compare.

Commercial banks are generally open either from Monday to Friday or Tuesday to Saturday. Hours vary but are usually from 8 or 9 am to some time between 11.30 am and 1 pm and from 1.30 or 2 to 4.30 or 5 pm. Exchange services may end half an hour before closing time.

Bureaux de Change Bureaux de change can only be found in the tourist towns along the island's coastline. Some of them demand inflated commissions and it is often worthwhile going to banks instead.

Both banks and bureaux de change often give a better rate for travellers cheques than for cash.

euro currency converter 10FF = €1.52

Cash Generally, cash is not a very good way to carry money. Not only can it be stolen, but in France you don't get an optimal exchange rate. However, it can be a good idea to bring the equivalent of about US$100 in low-denomination notes, so that you can change a small sum when the rate is poor or you need just a few francs (for example, at the end of your stay).

Because of counterfeiting, it may be difficult to change US$100 notes.

Travellers Cheques & Eurocheques In general, banks, bureaux de change and post offices on the island accept travellers cheques. Not all banks accept Eurocheques in francs. Those that do (in particular the many branches of Crédit Agricole) do not charge commission.

Lost or Stolen Travellers Cheques If you lose your American Express (Amex) travellers cheques in France, or they are stolen, call ☎ 0800 90 86 00, a 24 hour toll-free number. If you lose your Thomas Cook cheques, call the company's toll-free customer service bureau on ☎ 0800 90 83 30.

ATMs ATMs (automated telling machines) are known in French as DABs (*distributeurs automatiques de billets*) or *points d'argent*. ATM cards can give you direct access to your cash back home at a superior exchange rate. Cards with the Visa, Master-Card or Cirrus logos are generally accepted.

Some non-US ATMs won't accept PIN codes with more than four digits – ask your bank how to handle this, and while you're at it find out about withdrawal fees and daily limits. If you normally remember your PIN code as a string of letters, translate it back into numbers, as keyboards may not have letters indicated.

ATMs are relatively widespread around the perimeter of the island, with a few notable exceptions (Piana, Cap Corse, the airports). Do not expect to find any in the mountain villages, although it is generally possible to get cash from a post office using a credit card.

Credit Cards Overall, the cheapest way to pay for your time in Corsica is by using a credit or debit card, both to pay for things (in which case the merchant absorbs the commission) and to get cash advances. Visa (Carte Bleue) is the most widely accepted, followed by MasterCard (or Eurocard). Amex cards are not very useful except at upmarket establishments, but they do allow you to get cash at certain ATMs. In general, all three cards can be used to pay for travel by train and in many restaurants.

Exchange rates may change – to your advantage or disadvantage – between the day you use the card and the date of billing.

It may be impossible to get a lost Visa or MasterCard reissued until you get home (Amex and Diners Club International offer on-the-spot replacement cards); hence, two different credit cards are safer than one. Always keep some spare travellers cheques or cash on hand in case of such an emergency.

Cash Advances When you get a cash advance against your Visa card or MasterCard account, your issuer charges a transaction fee and/or finance charge. With some issuers, the fees can be as high as US$10 plus interest per transaction, so check with your card issuer before leaving home and compare rates. Also, French banks generally require you to pay commission for a cash advance on your credit card. You can avoid paying interest (which accrues from the moment you receive the cash, not from the end of the billing period) by depositing lots of money in your credit card account before you leave home, in effect turning it into a bank account and transforming your credit card into a debit card. The biggest problem with cash advances is that there are all sorts of limits on how much cash you can take out per week or month, regardless of your credit limit.

Some unscrupulous bureaux de change advertise that they give cash advances, but instead of giving you French francs, they insist that you take your money in US dollars or some other foreign currency, which they make you buy at their disadvantageous rate. If you need francs, you then have to change your dollars or pounds back again, and take a second loss on the difference between the buy and sell rates.

Lost or Stolen Cards If your Visa card is lost or stolen, call Carte Bleue on ☎ 02 54 42 12 12 (24 hours). To get a replacement card you'll have to deal with the issuer.

Report a lost MasterCard or Eurocard to Eurocard France (☎ 01 45 67 53 53) and, if you can, to your credit card issuer back home (for cards from the USA, call ☎ 314-275 6690).

If your Amex card is lost or stolen, call ☎ 01 47 77 70 00 or 01 47 77 72 00 (24 hours). In an emergency, Amex card holders from the USA can call collect on ☎ 202-783 7474 or 202-677 2442. Amex should now be represented on the island by Corsicatours (☎ 04 95 34 11 12), 1 ave Maréchal Sebastiani, Bastia.

A lost Diners Club card should be reported on ☎ 01 47 62 75 75.

International Transfers In Corsica telegraphic transfers are not very expensive but, despite their name, can be quite slow. Be sure to specify the name of the bank and the address of the branch where you'd like to pick the money up.

It's quicker and easier to have money wired via Amex (US$50 for US$1000). Western Union's Money Transfer system (☎ 01 43 54 46 12) and Thomas Cook's MoneyGram service (☎ 0800 90 83 30) are also popular.

Costs

Because tourism on the island is so seasonal, Corsica is relatively expensive in the summer. In July and August many hotels charge much higher prices than those charged during the rest of the year.

As a general rule, you can expect to pay at least 200FF to 250FF for a decent double room in the peak season (often more in August if you like your creature comforts). You should expect to pay the same minimum rates if you are on your own; there are very few single rooms and you will often have to pay for a double (and generally the least comfortable one).

If you are on a limited budget, you can stay at one of the many camp sites which are scattered across the island. They charge an average of 30FF per person, plus an additional 12FF per tent and a similar amount per vehicle, so that a couple with a car and a tent would pay between 85FF and 90FF per night.

Most restaurants offer tourist menus for about 80FF. However, it is often better to choose a good restaurant and have one good course rather than a mediocre complete meal. The island has quite a large number of good restaurants where you can have an excellent meal for about 120FF. A number of pizzerias are open during the peak season, and although they are not always good – far from it! – they are a relatively economical choice.

Bus travel (which is often seasonal as well) is generally quite expensive if you consider the actual distances travelled (Ajaccio to Bonifacio, 140km, 110FF; Calvi to Bastia, 93km, 80FF). The journey from Ajaccio to Bastia (153km) comes to 121FF if you go by train. Hiring a car will cost you about 1700FF for a week with unlimited mileage and comprehensive insurance. The monthly rate (5000FF) is good because there is little demand for it.

With very few exceptions (such as tours of Porto and Filitosa), cultural sights are free and the museums are cheap.

The best way to reduce your expenditure is to go in June or September – or you can reduce it still further by going in winter. Some three-star hotels offer extremely low prices out of season. The interior of the island is also significantly cheaper than the coast. It has accommodation especially for hikers, where you can get a bed in a dormitory for 60FF. The *refuges* (mountain shelters) along the route of the GR20 charge 50FF per night.

A tax (of 1FF at camp sites and 3FF or 4FF at hotels) is levied on all tourist accommodation in Corsica.

Tipping & Bargaining

French law requires that restaurant, café and hotel bills include the service charge (usually 10 to 15%), so a *pourboire* (tip) is neither necessary nor expected in most cases. However, most people leave a few francs in restaurants, unless the service was bad. They rarely tip in cafés and bars when they've just had a coffee or a drink.

In taxis, the usual tip is 2FF no matter what the fare. Bargaining is rare, except at flea markets.

Taxes & Refunds

France's VAT (TVA) is 20.6% on most goods except food, medicine and books, for which it's 5.5%; it goes as high as 33% for such items as watches, cameras and video cassettes. Prices that include VAT are often marked TTC (*toutes taxes comprises*; all taxes included).

If you are not a resident of the EU, you can get a refund of most of the VAT provided that: you're over 15; you'll be spending less than six months in France; you purchase goods (not more than 10 of the same item) worth at least 1200FF (tax included) at a single shop; and the shop offers *vente en détaxe* (duty-free sales).

Present your passport at the time of purchase and ask for a *bordereau de détaxe* (export sales invoice). Some shops may refund 14% of the purchase price rather than the full 17.1% you are entitled to in order to cover the time and expense involved in the refund procedure.

As you leave France or another EU country, have all three pages (two pink and one green) of the bordereau validated by customs officials at the airport or at the border. Customs officials will take the two pink sheets and the stamped self-addressed envelope provided by the store; the green sheet is your receipt. One of the pink sheets will then be sent to the shop where you made your purchase, which will then send you a *virement* (transfer of funds) in the form you have requested, such as by French franc cheque, or directly into your account. Be prepared for a long wait.

POST & COMMUNICATIONS

There are almost 180 post offices spread around Corsica, including some in tiny hamlets. They are generally efficient and provide services such as fax facilities, parcel delivery and cashing of travellers cheques. They mostly survive either by selling cards or by being located within tobacconists. There are often public telephones either in or near the office.

Postal Rates

Domestic letters up to a weight of 20g cost 3FF. Postcards and letters up to 20g cost 3FF within the EU, 3.80FF to most of the rest of Europe as well as Africa, 4.40FF to the USA, Canada and the Middle East and 5.20FF to Australasia. Aerograms cost 5FF to all destinations.

Worldwide express mail delivery, called Chronopost (☎ 01 46 48 10 00, Minitel 3614 CHRONOPOST for information), costs a fortune.

Sea-mail services have been discontinued and, even if you use *économique* (discount) air mail, sending packages overseas sometimes costs almost as much as the exorbitant overweight fees charged by airlines. Packages weighing over 2kg may not be accepted at branch post offices. Post offices sell boxes in four different sizes for 6.50FF to 12.50FF.

It will cost 35FF (or 20FF economy rate) to send a parcel weighing up to 500g to EU countries or Switzerland, 52FF (25FF economy) to send it to the USA or Canada, and 72FF to send it to Australia or New Zealand.

Sending Mail

All mail to Corsica must include the five digit postcode, which begins with 20, the number of the département.

Mail to France should be addressed as follows:

       John SMITH
       8, rue de la Poste
       20000 Ajaccio
       FRANCE

The surname (family name) should be written in capital letters. As you'll notice, the French put a comma after the street number and don't capitalise 'rue', 'ave', 'blvd' (boulevard) and similar abbreviations. CEDEX after a city or town name simply means that mail sent to that address is collected at the post office rather than delivered to the door.

Receiving Mail

Poste Restante To have mail sent to you via poste restante (general delivery), available at all French post offices, have it addressed as follows:

> SMITH, John
> Poste Restante
> Recette Principale
> 20000 Ajaccio
> FRANCE

Since poste restante mail is held alphabetically by last name, it is vital that you follow the French practice of having your surname or family name (*nom de famille*) written first and in capital letters. In case your friends back home forget, always check under the first letter of your first name (*prénom*) as well. There's a 3FF charge for every piece of poste restante mail you pick up weighing less than 20g; for anything between 20 and 100g, the fee is 4FF. It is usually possible to forward (*faire suivre*) mail from one poste restante address to another. To collect poste restante mail, you'll need your passport or national ID card.

Street Numbers

When a building is put up in a location where they've run out of consecutive street numbers, a new address is formed by fusing the number of an adjacent building with *bis* (twice), *ter* (thrice) or, rarely, *quater* (four times). Thus, the street numbers 17bis and 89ter are the equivalent of 17A or 89B.

Poste restante mail not addressed to a particular branch goes to the town's *recette principale* (main post office) whether or not you include the words Recette Principale in the address. If you want it sent to a specific branch office, include the street address.

The post will generally be kept for about two weeks.

Telephone

Mobile phone reception is poor because of the relief of the island.

International Dialling to Corsica To call Corsica from outside France, dial your country's international access code, then 33 (France's country code), then omit the 0 at the beginning of the 10 digit local number (leaving nine digits, starting with a 4). To call anywhere else in France, dial the international access code, then 33, then again ignore the 0 in the 10 digit local number.

International Dialling from France To call someone outside France, dial the international access code (00), the country code, the area code (without the initial 0 if there is one) and the local number. International Direct Dial (IDD) calls to almost anywhere in the world can be made from public telephones, of which there are a reasonable number on the island. Useful country codes include:

Australia	☎ 61
Canada	☎ 1
Germany	☎ 49
Japan	☎ 81
Ireland	☎ 353
Netherlands	☎ 31
New Zealand	☎ 64
UK	☎ 44
USA	☎ 1

If you don't know the country code (*indicatif pays*) and it doesn't appear on the information sheet posted in most telephone booths, consult a telephone book or dial ☎ 12 for directory inquiries.

To make a reverse-charge (collect) call (*en PCV*, pronounced '**pey-sey-vey**') or a person-to-person call (*avec préavis*, pronounced 'ah-**vek** preh-ah-**vee**'), dial 00, and then 33 plus the country code of the place you're calling (for example, for the USA and Canada, dial 11 instead of 1). There won't be a dial tone after you've dialled 00, so don't wait for one. Don't be surprised if you get a recording and have to wait a while. If you're using a public phone, you must insert a *télécarte* (see Public Phones later in this section) or, in the case of public coin telephones, 1FF to place operator-assisted calls through the international operator.

For directory inquiries concerning subscriber numbers outside France, dial 00 then 3312 and finally the relevant country code (again, 11 instead of 1 for the USA and Canada). You often get put on hold for quite a while. In public phones, you can access this service without a télécarte, but from home phones the charge is 7.30FF per inquiry.

Most of the toll-free 1-800 numbers in the USA and Canada can be called from phones in Corsica but you will be charged for the call at the usual rates.

International Rates From Corsica a call to an EU country costs 1.85FF per minute (1.45FF off-peak). A minute to the USA or Canada costs 2FF (1.60FF off-peak). Off-peak rates apply between 7 pm and 8 am on weekdays and from 7 pm on Friday to 8 am on Monday.

Country Direct Services Country Direct lets you phone your home country by billing the long-distance carrier you use at home. The numbers can be dialled from public phones without inserting a phonecard; with some models, you're meant to dial even if there's no dial tone. The following listed numbers will connect you, free of charge, with an operator in your home country, who will verify your method of payment (for example, by credit card or reverse charge).

Australia (Telstra)	☎	0800 99 00 61
(Optus)	☎	0800 99 20 61
Canada	☎	0800 99 00 16
	☎	0800 99 02 16
Ireland	☎	0800 99 03 53
New Zealand	☎	0800 99 00 64
UK (BT)	☎	0800 99 00 44
	☎	0800 99 02 44
(Mercury)	☎	0800 99 09 44
USA (AT&T)	☎	0800 99 00 11
(MCI)	☎	0800 99 00 19
(Sprint)	☎	0800 99 00 87
(Worldcom)	☎	0800 99 00 13

Domestic Dialling France has five telephone dialling areas. To make calls within any region or between regions, just dial the 10 digit number. The five regional area codes are:

Paris region	☎ 01
north-west	☎ 02
north-east	☎ 03
south-east (including Corsica)	☎ 04
south-west	☎ 05

If you want France Telecom's directory inquiries or assistance service (*service des renseignements*), dial ☎ 12. Don't be surprised if the operator does not speak English. The call is free from public phones but costs 3.71FF from private lines.

It is not possible to make a domestic reverse-charge call. Instead, ask the person you're calling to ring you back (see Receiving Calls at Public Phones later).

Domestic Tariffs Local calls are quite cheap, even at the red tariff (see the following paragraph): one calling unit (0.81FF with a télécarte) lasts for three minutes. For calls of distances up to 100km, one unit lasts somewhere between 72 seconds (25 to 30km) and 32 seconds (52 to 100km) during red tariff periods. Over distances greater than 100km, one unit lasts just 21 seconds in public phones.

Colour codes are used to indicate domestic telephone discounts. The regular rate for calls within France, known as the *tarif rouge* (red tariff), applies from 8 am to 12.30 pm Monday to Saturday and from 1.30 to 6 pm Monday to Friday. You pay 30% less than the tarif rouge with the *tarif blanc* (white tariff), which is in force from 12.30 to 1.30 pm Monday to Saturday and from 6 to 9.30 pm Monday to Friday. The rest of the time, you enjoy 50% off with the *tarif bleu* (blue tariff), except between 10.30 pm and 6 am, when the *tarif bleu nuit* (blue night tariff) gives you a 65% discount.

Note that numbers beginning with 08 36 are always billed at 2.23FF per minute, regardless of the day or the time.

Toll-Free Numbers Two-digit emergency numbers, Country Direct numbers and *numéros verts* (green numbers; toll-free numbers which have 10 digits and begin with 0800) can be dialled from public telephones without inserting a télécarte or coins.

Public Phones Most public telephones in Corsica require a télécarte, which can be purchased at post offices, tobacconists (*tabacs*), supermarket check-out counters and anywhere you see a blue sticker reading *télécarte en vente ici*. Cards worth 50/120 units cost 40.60/97.50FF. Make sure your card's plastic wrapper is intact when you buy it.

In small village post offices, you occasionally find old-style phones for which you pay at the counter after you've made your call.

Using a Télécarte To make a domestic or international phone call with a télécarte, follow the instructions on the LCD display.

When a public telephone's display does not read *hors service* (out of order), the word *décrochez* should appear in the LCD window. If the phone has a button displaying two flags linked with an arrow, push it for the explanations in English. If not, when you see the words *introduire carte ou faire numéro libre* (insert the card or dial a toll-free number), insert the card chip-end first

National Emergency Numbers

These emergency numbers apply in France as well as in Corsica:

Ambulance	☎ 15
Fire	☎ 18
Police	☎ 17

with the rectangle of electrical connectors facing upwards. *Patientez SVP* means 'please wait'.

When the top line of the display tells you your *crédit* or *solde* (how many units you have left), denominated in *unités* (units), the bottom line of the LCD screen will read *numérotez* (dial). As you press the keyboard, the *numéro appelé* (number being called) will appear on the display.

After you dial, you will hear a rapid beeping followed by long beeps (it's ringing) or short beeps (it's busy). When your call is connected, the screen begins counting down your card's value. To redial, push the button inscribed with a telephone receiver icon (not available on all public phones).

If, for any reason, something goes wrong in the dialling process, you'll be asked to *raccrochez SVP* (please hang up). *Crédit épuisé* means that your télécarte has run out of units.

Switching Télécartes Mid-Call It's possible to replace a used-up télécarte with a new one in the middle of a call – an especially useful feature with overseas calls – but only if you follow the instructions exactly. When the screen reads *crédit = 000 unités – changement de carte*, press the green button, wait for the message *retirez votre carte* and then take out the old télécarte. When you see the words *nouvelle télécarte* (not before!), insert a fresh card.

Coin Phones You will occasionally come across phones that take coins (1FF for a local call) rather than télécartes, especially in remote rural areas. Remember that coin phones don't give change.

Most coin phones let you hear the dial tone immediately, but with the very oldest models – the ones with windows down the front and no slot for 2FF pieces – you must deposit your money before you get the tone.

Point Phone Many cafés and restaurants have privately owned, coin-operated telephones – intended primarily for the use of their clients – known as Point Phones. Point Phones require that you deposit 2FF to dial, but you can get half of that back if you make a short call and use two 1FF pieces rather than one 2FF coin. To make another call with your left-over credit (which is shown on the LCD screen), press the *reprise crédit* button.

You cannot get the international operator or receive calls from a Point Phone, but you can dial emergency numbers (no coins needed) and use Country Direct services (insert the 2FF – you'll get it back at the end). To find a Point Phone, look for blue-on-white window stickers bearing the Point Phone emblem.

Receiving Calls at Public Phones All public phones except Point Phones can receive both domestic and international calls. If you want someone to call you back, just give them France's country code, the area code (04 for Corsica) and the number, usually found after the words *Ici le* or *No d'appel* on the tariff sheet or on a little sign inside the phone box. When there's an incoming call, the words *décrochez – appel arrivé* will appear in the LCD window.

Minitel Minitel is a very useful telephone-connected computerised information service, though it can be expensive to use. The most basic Minitels, equipped with a black and white monitor and a clumsy keyboard, are available for no charge to telephone subscribers. Newer models have colour screens, and many people now access the system with a home computer and a modem.

Minitel numbers consist of four digits and a string of letters. Home users pay a per-minute access charge, but consulting the *annuaire* (directory) is free. Most of the Minitels in post offices are also free for directory inquiries (though some require a 1FF or 2FF coin), and many of them let you access pay-as-you-go on-line services.

Fax
Fax services are available in post offices. Details are included under the appropriate towns throughout this book.

Email & Internet Access
So far cybercafés have not sprung up on the island as they have elsewhere in Europe and Internet access is rare. Consequently you will probably have a hard time attempting to find somewhere to collect your email while in Corsica.

Similarly there are very few hotels on the island where the telephone system is sufficiently modern to allow you to connect to the Internet from your room with a modem. The very few places where establishing such a link is possible are described in the text.

INTERNET RESOURCES
The World Wide Web is a rich resource for travellers. You can research your trip, hunt down bargain air fares, book hotels, check on weather conditions or chat with locals and other travellers about the best places to visit (or avoid!).

One of the best places to start your Web explorations is the Lonely Planet Web site (www.lonelyplanet.com). Here you'll find succinct summaries on travelling to most places on earth, postcards from other travellers and the Thorn Tree bulletin board, where you can ask questions before you go or dispense advice when you get back. You can also find travel news and updates to many of our most popular guidebooks, and the subWWWay section links you to the most useful travel resources elsewhere on the Web.

The following list of interesting sites about Corsica is by no means exhaustive:

CorseWeb
www.corsica.net
(features land and villas for sale on the island; in French, English, German and Italian)
Corsica Discovery Pages
www.internetcom.fr/corsica/uk/discov/discov.htm
(illustrated with beautiful photography, allows you to access material either by region or by subject, such as nature, history, language or food)
Diocese d'Ajaccio
www.cef.fr/ajaccio
(official site of the diocese of Ajaccio; French only)
Préfecture de Corse
www.corse.pref.gouv.fr
(official site of the Corsican administration; French only)

BOOKS

Most books are published in different editions by different publishers in different countries. As a result, a book might be a hardcover rarity in one country while it's readily available in paperback in another. Fortunately, bookshops and libraries search by title or author, so your local bookshop or library can best advise you on the availability of the following recommendations.

Lonely Planet

Lonely Planet's *France* is an exhaustive guide to the whole country, and has a chapter devoted to Corsica. *Western Europe* and *Mediterranean Europe* have sections dealing with Corsica. Another useful companion is Lonely Planet's *French phrasebook*.

Travel

James Boswell's *Journal of a Tour to Corsica* (full title: *An Account of Corsica, The Journal of a Tour to That Island, and Memoirs of Pascal Paoli*) was written after his 1765 visit, during which he met numerous memorable people including the Corsican hero Paoli, who made a deep impression upon Boswell. Edward Lear, better known for his body of nonsense poetry, illustrated his *Journal of a Landscape Painter in Corsica* with lavish and romantic illustrations which fired the popular imagination's perceptions of Corsica. Thomasina Campbell, a keen walker and an acquaintance of Lear, wrote an often amusing account of her travels, *Notes on the Island of Corsica*; descriptions of landscape are vivid but the author didn't attempt to understand the island's people.

Dorothy Carrington produced the most insightful recent work in her 1971 volume *Granite Island: a Portrait of Corsica*, which combines accounts of her personal experiences with notes on the history of the island and its people, researched since her first visit in 1948. More recently, Carrington's *The Dream Hunters of Corsica* describes the occult practices of the *mazzeri*, people who can foresee the deaths of others in their dreams. Paul Theroux describes a visit to Corsica during his circuit of the Mediterranean in *The Pillars of Hercules*.

Literature

A number of authors have used Corsica as the setting for novels or stories. During the 19th century, writers from the French mainland began to take an interest in the island, depicting it in Romantic fiction. These works include Guy de Maupassant's *Un Bandit Corse*, *Une Vendetta* and *Histoire Corse*, Honoré de Balzac's *La Vendetta*, Alexandre Dumas' *Les Frères Corse* and Prosper Mérimée's unforgettable *Colomba*, which he wrote following a visit to Corsica. Dumas' novel is available in English as *The Corsican Brothers*; the other stories can be found in various anthologies but are not all currently in print in English.

The Traveller's Literary Companion – France by John Edmondson contains a short section on Corsica featuring extracts from relevant works, including pieces by Maupassant and Mérimée, as well as brief author biographies and pointers for further reading.

For details on Corsican authors, see the Arts section in the Facts about Corsica chapter.

History & Politics

Most English-language books dealing with Corsican history tend to be lengthy and academic. *Feuding, Conflict and Banditry in Nineteenth-Century Corsica* by Stephen Wilson is a comprehensive study of these elements of Corsican life, with insights into other areas of its society.

Various tomes about Napoleon touch on Corsican life and Bonaparte's relationship with the island, although most are currently out of print. *Napoleon and Pozzo di Borgo in Corsica and After, 1764-1821*, by JMP McErlean, describes the feud between Napoleon and his rival, drawing some interesting conclusions about Napoleon's importance in Corsica.

Walking

The Corsican High Level Route – Walking the GR20, by Alan Castle, provides concise details of the famous trail. *Landscapes of Corsica*, by Noel Rochford, lists a number of shorter walking excursions on the island as well as tours suitable for visitors with their own transport.

French-Language

Not surprisingly, the bulk of material relating to Corsica is currently only available in French. *L'Histoire de la Corse*, by Robert Colonna d'Istria, is a recent history book which is easy to read and which seeks to demystify certain episodes in the island's past without descending into polemics. *Plantes et Fleurs Recontrées*, by Marcelle Conrad, details the abundant flora of the island. *Roches et Paysages de la Corse* from the Parc Naturel Régional de Corse (PNRC) is a good reference for those interested in exploring the geology of the island; it's also interspersed with a few routes for geological walks.

Those who are interested in underwater life will want to read the beautiful *La Corse Sous-marine*, with photographs by Georges Antoni. It's richly illustrated with wonderful photos and will make you want to go diving, even if you have never felt the urge before.

NEWSPAPERS & MAGAZINES

The two main daily newspapers are regional editions of newspapers based in mainland France. *Corse Matin* is based on *Nice Matin* and has a circulation of around 40,000. *La Corse* is partially edited by the La Provence group, which is based in Marseilles, and has a circulation of around 16,000. Historically, *Corse Matin* was more right wing and *La Corse* more to the left, but this distinction has now become blurred. The Hachette group, which holds shares in *La Provence*, took a stake in *Nice Matin* in 1998.

There is also a number of publications with limited circulation that are useful if you want to understand modern-day Corsica. *Le Journal de la Corse* styles itself as a 'weekly newspaper that has been defending the interests of the island since 1817' and as 'the doyen of the French press'; it has 10 pages and covers the island's news (5FF). *Arriti* has been supporting Corsican autonomy since 1966; it costs 9FF and deals with Corsican and international news. It also includes poetry and stories in its 12 pages and is available in French and Corsican. The scathing *U Ribombu* (10FF) is the voice of A Concolta Indipendentista, and explains the demands of the main Corsican nationalist movement. *Terre corse* (10FF) is edited by the southern Corsican communist party.

Some English-language newspapers and magazines – for example, the British *Independent* and *Times*, and *Time* – are available on the island in summer.

RADIO & TV

The relief of the island makes it particularly difficult to receive radio signals in large areas of Corsica. This means that many of the stations content themselves with covering the coastal areas, although you can receive Italian radio stations in the interior of the island. As the same stations transmit on different frequencies in different parts of the island, a sophisticated system (with Radio Data System, or RDS, for tracking down changes in frequency) is not considered a luxury on Corsica.

Radio Corse Frequenza Mora (RCFM) is the local station of Radio France and is one of the most popular stations. It has more than 20% of the total audience, and provides news, cultural programmes and music in both French and Corsican. RCFM broadcasts on FM at 101.7 (Bastia), 100.5 (Ajaccio), 102.5 (Corte), 101.8 (Porto Vecchio), 99.2 (Calvi), 88.2 (eastern Cap Corse), 98.2 (Bonifacio), 100.4 (Île Rousse), 100.1 (Sainte Lucie de Tallano) and even on 88.2MHz (eastern plain).

You should be able to receive France Info on 105.4, 105.5 or 105.6MHz FM.

France Inter transmits on 92.4 (Ajaccio and Sartène), 95.9 (Bastia), 92.3 (Bonifacio), 96.8 (Aleria), 96.8 (Porto Vecchio), 89.4 (Vivario), 98.2 and 89.8 (Corte) and 90.8MHz FM (Île Rousse).

Alta Frequenza (news and music) is transmitted on 98.9MHz FM in Bastia; NRJ on 101.2MHz FM in Ajaccio; and Corse Infos (local news) on 95.5MHz FM in the Haute-Corse region.

English-speakers can tune to the BBC World Service, and to the Voice of America, which is broadcast in and around Ajaccio at 96MHz FM.

French terrestrial television channels are also broadcast in Corsica. The island also has another channel, France 3 Corse, which broadcasts regional programmes at certain times of the day. Some hotels also receive international cable channels.

VIDEO SYSTEMS

French TV broadcasts are in SECAM (*système électronique couleur avec mémoire*) and non-SECAM TVs won't work in France. French videotapes can't be played on video recorders and TVs that lack a SECAM capability.

PHOTOGRAPHY & VIDEO
Film & Equipment

Colour film (C41) can be developed for a reasonable price in the larger towns within a few hours. Developing slides (E6) is more expensive and time-consuming because the film is sent off to mainland France.

Standard colour film is easy to come by in Corsica, but it's expensive in the main tourist towns and at the main attractions. Slide film or black and white film is harder to find, as is highly sensitive or specialist film. You will often be charged inflated prices for these types of film if you do find them. Always check the use-by date on the packet and never buy film that has been exposed to heat.

You'll find blank video tapes in supermarkets in the larger towns, but make sure you buy the correct format. It is usually worth buying at least a few cartridges duty-free to start off your trip.

Technical Tips

Corsica is exceptionally photogenic. However, the sun – which wipes out contrast – and the strong light can represent a problem in summer. Use a polarising filter and avoid the light in the middle of the day. It's a waste of time taking film that is too sensitive – 100 ASA will be more than sufficient.

Restrictions

Photography is rarely forbidden, except in museums and art galleries. Of course, taking snapshots of military installations is not appreciated in any country.

Photographing People

When photographing people, it is basic courtesy to ask permission. If you don't know any French, smile while pointing at your camera and they'll get the picture – as you probably will.

Video

Properly used, a video camera can give a fascinating record of your holiday. Video cameras have very sensitive microphones, and you might be surprised how much sound is picked up. This can also be a problem if there is a lot of ambient noise – filming by the side of a busy road might seem OK when you do it, but viewing it back home might simply give you a cacophony of traffic noise. One good rule to follow for beginners is to try to film in long takes, and don't move the camera around too much. If your camera has a stabiliser, you can use it to obtain good footage while travelling on various means of transport, even on bumpy roads.

Make sure you keep the batteries charged and have the necessary charger, plugs and transformer.

Finally, remember to follow the same rules regarding people's sensitivities as for still photography – always ask permission first.

Airport Security

Be prepared to have your camera and film run through x-ray machines at airports and the entrances to sensitive public buildings. The machines are supposedly film-safe up to 1000 ASA, and laptops and computer disks appear to pass through without losing data, but there is always some degree of risk.

The police and gendarmes who run x-ray machines often seem to treat a request that they hand-check something as casting doubt on the power and glory of the French Republic. Arguing almost never works, and being polite is only slightly more effective unless you can do it in French. You're most likely to get an affirmative response if you are deferential and your request is moderate: request that they hand-check your film, not your whole camera (which could, after all, conceal a bomb). They are usually amenable to checking computer disks by hand.

TIME

The time in Corsica is the same as the rest of France. Therefore Corsica is one hour ahead of (that is, later than) GMT/UTC. During daylight-saving (or summer) time, which runs from the last Sunday in March to the last Sunday in October, it is two hours ahead of GMT/UTC. The UK and France are always one hour apart – when it's 6 pm in London, it's 7 pm in Corsica.

New York is generally six hours behind Corsica. This may fluctuate a bit depending on exactly when daylight-saving time begins and ends on both sides of the Atlantic.

The time difference to Melbourne and Sydney is complicated because daylight-saving time in Australia takes effect during the northern hemisphere's winter. The Australian east coast is between eight and 10 hours ahead of France.

Corsica uses the 24 hour clock, with the hours separated from the minutes by a lower-case 'h'. Thus 15h30 is 3.30 pm, 21h50 is 9.50 pm, 00h30 is 12.30 am, and so on.

ELECTRICITY
Voltages & Cycles

The electricity supply in Corsica is 220V at 50Hz AC. You will need an adapter if you are coming from a country where the voltage is different.

While the usual travel transformers allow appliances to run in Corsica, they cannot change the Hz rate, which determines – among other things – the speed of electric motors. As a result, tape recorders not equipped with built-in adapters may function poorly.

There are two types of adapters; mixing them up will destroy either the transformer or your appliance, so be warned. The 'heavy' kind, usually designed to handle 35W or less (see the tag) and often metal-clad, is designed for use with small electric devices such as radios, tape recorders and razors. The other kind, which weighs much less but is rated for up to 1500W, is for use only with appliances that contain heating elements, such as hair dryers and irons.

Plugs & Sockets

Old-type wall sockets, often rated at 600W, take two round pins. The new kinds of sockets take fatter pins and have a protruding earth (ground) pin.

Adapters to make new plugs fit into the old sockets are said to be illegal but are still available at electrical shops.

WEIGHTS & MEASURES
Metric System
Corsica, like the rest of France, uses the metric system. For a conversion chart, see the inside back cover of this book.

Numbers
For numbers with four or more digits, the French use full stops or spaces where writers in English would use commas: one million therefore appears as 1.000.000 or 1 000 000. For decimals, on the other hand, the French use commas, so 1.75 appears as 1,75.

LAUNDRY
Most of the large and medium-sized coastal towns on the island have laundrettes. Allow an average of about 30FF for a machine.

To find a *laverie libre-service* (an unstaffed, self-service laundrette), see the relevant town section in this book or ask at your hotel or hostel.

In general, you deposit coins into a *monnayeur central* (central control box) – not the machine itself – and push a button that corresponds to the number of the machine you wish to operate. These gadgets are sometimes programmed to deactivate the washing machines an hour or so before closing time.

Except with the most modern systems, you're likely to need all sorts of peculiar coin combinations – change machines are often out of order, so come prepared. Coins, especially 2FF pieces, are handy for the *séchoirs* (dryers) and the *lessive* (laundry powder) dispenser.

You can choose between a number of washing cycles:

blanc – whites
couleur – colours
synthétique – synthetics
laine – woollens
prélavage – prewash cycle
lavage – wash cycle
rinçage – rinse cycle
essorage – spin-dry cycle

TOILETS
Public toilets, signposted *toilettes* or *wc*, are rare on the island, but you can use the toilets in any number of restaurants and bars. However, the beaches do not always have toilet facilities. Where there are toilets, they are generally clean.

Except in the most tourist-filled areas, café owners are usually amenable to your using their toilets provided you ask politely (and with just a hint of urgency): *Est-ce que je peux utiliser les toilettes, s'il vout plaît?* Some toilets have washbasins and urinals in a common area through which you pass to get to the closed toilet stalls.

In older cafés and even hotels, the amenities may consist of a Turkish-style toilet (*toilette à la turque*), a squat toilet that people all over Asia prefer to the sit-down type but which some westerners think is primitive and uncomfortable. The high-pressure flushing mechanism will soak your feet if you don't step back before pulling the cord. In some older buildings, the toilets used by ground floor businesses (such as restaurants) are tiny affairs accessed via an interior courtyard.

Many hall toilets are in a little room on their own, with the nearest washbasin nowhere in sight (in hotels, it's more than likely attached to the nearest shower).

It goes without saying that hikers should not leave toilet paper on the paths or in the areas around them. There are a few chemical toilets near the PNRC refuges.

HEALTH
Corsica does not present any particular health risks to the holiday-maker. Most of the following information aims to prepare you for unlikely eventualities, and you should definitely not be alarmed by it.

The sun, walking, diving and the change of climate can give rise to health problems, but anything serious can generally be easily resolved with the assistance of the hospitals and doctors on the island. You can find contact details for hospitals listed in the town sections of this guide.

Predeparture Planning

Health Insurance Make sure that you have adequate health insurance. See Travel Insurance in the Visas & Documents section in this chapter for details.

Citizens of EU countries are covered for emergency medical treatment throughout the EU on production of an E111 certificate, though charges are likely for medication, dental work and secondary examinations, including x-rays and laboratory tests. Ask about the E111 at your local health services department or travel agency at least a few weeks before you travel. In the UK you can get the form from post offices.

Immunisations No particular vaccinations are required for Corsica. However, it is recommended that all travellers are up to date on basic vaccinations (such as polio, tetanus, diphtheria and hepatitis) irrespective of where they are going.

On Minitel, 3615 Visa Santé provides practical advice, health information and useful addresses for more than 150 countries, and 3615 Écran Santé also provides medical information.

Condoms All pharmacies carry condoms (*préservatifs*), and many of them have 24-hour automatic condom dispensers outside the door. Some brasseries, discotheques, metro stations and WCs in petrol stations and cafés are also equipped with condom machines.

Condoms that conform to French government standards are always marked with the letters NF (*norme française*) in black on a white oval inside a red and blue rectangle on the packet.

Other Preparations A trip to the dentist before you leave is a good idea and if you wear glasses take a spare pair and your prescription.

If you require a particular medication take an adequate supply, as it may not be available on the island. Take part of the packaging showing the generic name, rather than the brand, which will make getting replacements easier. It's a good idea to have a legible prescription or letter from your doctor to show that you legally use the medication to avoid any problems.

Medical Treatment in Corsica

Emergency numbers for ambulances, the police and the fire brigade are listed in the Post & Communications section earlier in this chapter.

Major hospitals are indicated on the maps in this book, and their addresses and phone numbers are mentioned in the text. Tourist offices and hotels can recommend a doctor or dentist, and your embassy or consulate will probably know one who speaks your language. You can contact SAMU (☎ 15) to find out where your closest hospital or doctor is.

Public Health System France has an extensive public health care system. Anyone (including foreigners) who is sick, even mildly, can receive treatment in the *service des urgences* (casualty ward or emergency room) of any public hospital. Hospitals try to have people who speak English in the casualty wards, but this is not done systematically. If necessary, the hospital will call in an interpreter. It's an excellent idea to ask for a copy of the diagnosis – in English, if possible – for your doctor back home.

Getting treated for illness or injury in a public hospital costs much less in France than in many other western countries, especially the USA: being seen by a doctor (a *consultation*) costs about 150FF (235FF to 250FF on Sunday and holidays, 275FF to 350FF from 8 pm to 8 am). Seeing a specialist is a bit more expensive. Blood tests and other procedures, each of which has a standard fee, will increase this figure. Full hospitalisation costs from 3000FF a day.

Hospitals usually ask that visitors from abroad settle accounts immediately after receiving treatment (residents of France are sent a bill in the mail).

Dental Care Most major hospitals offer dental services.

Pharmacies French pharmacies are usually marked by a green cross, the neon components are lit when the pharamcy's open. Pharmacists (*pharmaciens*) can often suggest treatments for minor ailments.

If you are prescribed medication, make sure you understand the dosage, and how often and when you should take it. It's a good idea to ask for a copy of the prescription (*ordonnance*) for your records.

Pharmacies co-ordinate their days and hours of closure so that a town or district isn't left without a place to buy medication. For details of the nearest pharmacy that's on night/weekend duty (*pharmacie de garde*), consult the door of any pharmacy, which will have such information posted.

Basic Rules

Water Tap water in Corsica is safe to drink. However the water in most fountains is not drinkable and – like the taps in some public toilets – may have a sign reading *eau non potable* (undrinkable water).

Many people do not hesitate to drink water from streams during their walks. However, this water is not necessarily safe. You may wish to take water purification tablets with you as a precaution.

It's very easy not to drink enough liquids, especially on hot days or at high altitudes – don't rely on feeling thirsty to indicate when you should drink. Not needing to urinate or very dark-yellow urine is a danger sign. There are very few drinking fountains on Corsica, so it's a good idea to carry a water bottle.

Water Purification The simplest way of purifying water is to boil it thoroughly. Note, however, that at high altitude water boils at a lower temperature, so germs are less likely to be killed. You'll need to boil it for longer in these environments.

Simple filtering will not remove all dangerous organisms, so if you can't boil water it should be treated chemically. Chlorine tablets (Puritabs, Steritabs or other brand names) will kill many pathogens, but not some parasites, like amoebic cysts and giar-

Medical Kit Check List

Following is a list of items you should consider including in your medical kit – consult your phamacist for brands available in your country.

- ☐ **Aspirin** or **paracetamol** (acetaminophen in the US) – for pain or fever.
- ☐ **Antihistamine** – for allergies, such as hay fever; to ease the itch from insect bites or stings; and to prevent motion sickness.
- ☐ **Antibiotics** – consider including these if you're travelling well off the beaten track; see your doctor, as they must be prescribed, and carry the prescription with you.
- ☐ **Loperamide** or **diphenoxylate** – 'blockers' for diarrhoea; **prochlorperazine** or **metaclopramide** for nausea and vomiting.
- ☐ **Rehydration mixture** – to prevent dehydration, eg due to severe diarrhoea; particularly important when travelling with children.
- ☐ **Insect repellent, sunscreen, lip balm** and **eye drops**.
- ☐ **Calamine lotion, sting relief spray** or **aloe vera** – to ease irritation from sunburn and insect bites or stings.
- ☐ **Antifungal cream** or **powder** – for fungal skin infections and thrush.
- ☐ **Antiseptic** (such as povidone-iodine) – for cuts and grazes.
- ☐ **Bandages, Band-Aids (plasters)** and other wound dressings.
- ☐ **Water purification tablets** or **iodine**.
- ☐ **Scissors, tweezers** and a **thermometer** (note that mercury thermometers are prohibited by airlines).
- ☐ **Cold** and **flu tablets, throat lozenges** and **nasal decongestant**.
- ☐ **Multivitamins** – consider for long trips, when dietary vitamin intake may be inadequate.

dia. Iodine is more effective in purifying water and is available in tablet form (such as Potable Aqua). Follow the directions carefully and remember that too much iodine can be harmful.

Bites & Stings

Jellyfish stings are generally just rather painful. Antihistamines and analgesics may reduce the reaction and relieve the pain. Bee and wasp stings are also painful rather than dangerous, except in people who are allergic to them. A soothing lotion will give relief and ice packs will reduce the pain and swelling. Scorpion fish and weevers can also sting if you touch them; although the stings are not serious you may need to consult a doctor. There are no adders or poisonous snakes on Corsica.

Environmental Hazards

Fungal Infections Fungal infections occur more commonly in hot weather and are usually found on the scalp, between the toes (athlete's foot) or fingers, in the groin and on the whole body (ringworm). You get ringworm (which is a fungal infection, not a parasite) from contact with infected animals or other people, such as by walking in damp places such as showers.

To prevent fungal infections wear loose, comfortable clothes, avoid artificial fibres, wash frequently and dry yourself carefully. Keep your flip-flops on in showers you don't completely trust. If you do get an infection, wash the infected area at least daily with a disinfectant or medicated soap and water, and rinse and dry well. Apply an antifungal cream or powder. Try to expose the infected area to air or sunlight as much as possible. Change all towels and underwear regularly, wash them in hot water and let them dry in the sun.

Hay Fever Hay fever sufferers should be aware that the pollen count in Corsica is especially high in May and June.

Heat Exhaustion Dehydration and salt deficiency can cause heat exhaustion. Take time to acclimatise to high temperatures, drink sufficient liquids and do not do anything too physically demanding.

Salt deficiency is characterised by fatigue, lethargy, headaches, giddiness and muscle cramps; salt tablets may help, but adding extra salt to your food is better.

Heatstroke This serious, occasionally fatal, condition can occur if the body's heat-regulating mechanism breaks down and the body temperature rises to dangerous levels. Long, continuous periods of exposure to high temperatures and insufficient fluids can leave you vulnerable to heatstroke. Avoid alcohol and exhausting activities when you arrive in a hot country.

The symptoms are feeling unwell, not sweating very much (or at all) and a high body temperature (39 to 41°C or 102 to 106°F). Where sweating has ceased the skin becomes flushed and red. Severe, throbbing headaches and lack of co-ordination will also occur, and the sufferer may be confused or aggressive. Eventually the victim will become delirious or convulse. Hospitalisation is essential, but in the interim get victims out of the sun, remove their clothing, cover them with a wet sheet or towel and then fan continually. Give fluids if they are conscious.

Prickly Heat Prickly heat is an itchy rash caused by excessive perspiration trapped under the skin. It usually strikes people who have just arrived in a hot climate. Keeping cool, bathing often, drying the skin and using a mild talcum or prickly heat powder or resorting to air-conditioning may help.

Sunburn Remember to use a sunscreen and be sure to cover parts of you that would normally be protected – for example, your feet. Although hats provide good protection, do not forget to apply a barrier cream to your nose and lips. Sunglasses often prove indispensable.

Sunstroke Prolonged exposure to the sun can result in sunstroke. The symptoms are nausea, hot skin and headaches. If sunstroke occurs, rest in the dark, apply a compress of cold water and take aspirin.

Health for Divers

Decompression Sickness Corsica is perfect for two activities that it is *not* a good idea to try in the same day: diving and mountain walking. Always avoid climbing at altitude straight after diving; this will allow your body to get rid of the residual nitrogen that it has stored up. Climbing as little as 1500m or even going up in an aeroplane could prove dangerous if you have been diving only a few hours earlier. As a rule of thumb, wait about 12 hours after resurfacing.

The hospital in Ajaccio (☎ 04 95 29 90 90), 27 rue de l'Impératrice Eugénie, has a decompression chamber.

Health for Walkers

Altitude Sickness Lack of oxygen at high altitudes (over 2500m) affects most people to some extent. The effect may be mild or severe and occurs because less oxygen reaches the muscles and the brain at high altitude, requiring the heart and lungs to compensate by working harder. Symptoms include headache, lethargy, dizziness, difficulty sleeping and loss of appetite. These will generally abate after a day or two, but if they persist or become worse the only treatment is to descend – even 500m can help.

Blisters Probably the most common problem for walkers is blisters on the feet. While not serious, a blister on a heel or toe can be a painful ordeal. Prevent blisters by breaking your boots in before embarking on a walking holiday and using thick socks or two pairs of socks to eliminate friction.

As soon as tenderness is felt stop and treat it by applying either moleskin or a cushioned adhesive pad. Once a blister has formed, do not cover it with moleskin. Cut the padded dressing so it surrounds the blister or broken skin. Large blisters can be pricked with a sterile needle and covered with a dressing.

Head Injuries & Fractures A serious fall, resulting in head injuries or fractures, is always a possibility when walking, especially if you are on steep slopes.

If a person suffers a head injury but is conscious, they are probably OK but should be closely monitored for at least 24 hours for any deterioration in their condition. For an unconscious victim, check the airway and breathing immediately and nurse in a recovery position. Bleeding from the nose or ear may indicate a fractured skull. If this occurs, lay the victim so the bleeding ear is downwards and avoid carrying them if at all possible. Seek medical attention urgently.

Indications of a broken bone are pain, swelling, loss of function in a limb or irregularities in the shape of the bones. Fractures in unconscious victims may be detected by gently attempting to bend each bone in turn. If the bone moves it is broken and you should not try to move it any further except to try to straighten out obviously displaced fractures.

Immobilise a non-displaced or straightened fracture by securing one limb to an adjacent one or by applying a splint. Fractures associated with laceration of the skin require more urgent medical treatment, as there is a risk of infection.

Hypothermia Too much cold can be just as dangerous as too much heat, especially if it results in hypothermia. The conditions in the Corsican mountains can be surprising. There can be frost above 2000m on the GR20, even in summer, and at this altitude the temperature and wind and storm conditions are often alpine. The weather can change particularly quickly in Corsica, and cold is the main source of problems for walkers.

Hypothermia occurs when the body loses heat quickly and the core temperature of the body falls. It is surprisingly easy to progress from very cold to dangerously cold due to a combination of wind, wet clothing, fatigue and hunger, even if the air temperature is above freezing. It is best to dress in layers; silk, wool and some of the new artificial fibres are all good insulating materials. A hat is also important, as a lot of heat is lost through the head. A strong, waterproof outer layer is essential. Carry basic supplies, including food containing simple sugars to generate heat quickly and plenty of fluid to drink.

Symptoms of hypothermia are exhaustion, numb skin (particularly toes and fingers), shivering, slurred speech, irrational or violent behaviour, lethargy, stumbling, dizzy spells, muscle cramps and violent bursts of energy. Irrationality may take the form of sufferers claiming they are warm and trying to take off their clothes.

To treat mild hypothermia, first get the person out of the wind and/or rain, remove their clothing if it's wet and replace it with dry, warm clothing. Give them hot liquids – not alcohol – and some high-calorie, easily digestible food. This should be enough to treat the early stages of hypothermia. Do not rub victims, nor place them near a fire, and do not change their clothes when they are exposed to the wind. If possible, make them take a hot bath.

Sprains Ankle and knee sprains can occur when walking, particularly in rugged areas. If you expect such conditions make sure you have all-leather boots with adequate ankle support. Ultra-light, low-cut walking boots are basically glorified tennis shoes and are not suitable.

Mild sprains should be wrapped immediately with a crepe bandage to prevent swelling. Often a day spent resting and elevating the leg will allow you to continue the walk without too much pain. For more serious sprains when the victim is unable to walk, seek medical assistance.

Infectious Diseases

Diarrhoea Simple things like a change of water, food or climate can cause a bout of diarrhoea. Dehydration is the main danger with any diarrhoea, particularly in children. Therefore the first treatment is to drink lots of fluids: ideally you should mix eight teaspoonfuls of sugar and one of salt in 1L of water. Otherwise weak black tea with a little sugar, or soft drinks allowed to go flat and diluted 50% with purified water are recommended. In the case of severe diarrhoea, a rehydrating solution is excellent for replacing lost minerals and salts. When you feel better, continue to eat lightly. Antibiotics can be useful for severe diarrhoea, especially when it is accompanied by nausea, vomiting, stomach cramps or a slight fever. Three days of treatment are generally sufficient, and some improvement is normally seen within 24 hours. However, if the diarrhoea persists for more than 48 hours or if there is blood in the stools, you should consult a doctor.

Viral Gastroenteritis This is caused by a virus rather than by bacteria. Symptoms include stomach cramps, diarrhoea and sometimes vomiting and/or a slight fever. The only treatment is to rest and drink lots of fluids.

Hepatitis Hepatitis is a general term for inflammation of the liver. It is spread through contact with infected blood, blood products or body fluids, for example, through sexual contact, unsterilised needles and blood transfusions or contact with blood via small breaks in the skin. Other risk situations include shaving, tattooing or body piercing with contaminated equipment. In the more discreet forms, the patient has no symptoms. However, the symptoms of the more common forms are fever, lethargy (sometimes intense), stomach pain, nausea, vomiting, dark urine and light-coloured, almost white, faeces. The skin and the whites of the eyes take on a yellow colour (jaundice). Hepatitis can sometimes simply involve a bout of tiredness that can last a few days or a few weeks.

Hepatitis A is the most widespread form of the disease, and there is no medical treatment. You simply have to rest, drink lots of fluids, eat lightly, avoid fatty foods and abstain from alcohol completely for at least six months. There is a vaccine. Hepatitis B is also very widespread, but the vaccination against it is extremely effective. There is currently no vaccine against hepatitis C.

HIV & AIDS Infection with the human immunodeficiency virus (HIV) may lead to acquired immune deficiency syndrome (AIDS), which is a fatal disease. Any exposure to blood, blood products or body fluids may put the individual at risk.

The disease is often transmitted through sexual contact or dirty needles – vaccinations, acupuncture, tattooing and body piercing are potentially as dangerous as intravenous drug use. It is therefore essential to use condoms and to avoid sharing needles in any way.

Sexually Transmitted Diseases There are many different STDs and effective treatments are now available for most of them.

Gonorrhoea, herpes and syphilis are the most common. Sores, blisters or rashes around the genitals and discharges or pain when urinating are common symptoms; these may be less acute or completely non-existent in women. The only way to prevent STDs is always to use condoms during sexual encounters.

Women's Health
Antibiotic use, synthetic underwear, sweating and contraceptive pills can lead to fungal vaginal infections when travelling in hot climates. Fungal infections are characterised by a rash, itch and discharge. The infection can be treated with a vinegar or lemon-juice douche with yoghurt, or ask a pharmacist for nystatin, miconazole or clotrimazole pessaries or a vaginal cream. Good personal hygiene and wearing loose-fitting clothes and cotton underwear may help prevent these infections.

Some women experience an irregular menstrual cycle while travelling because of the upset in routine. Your physician can give you advice about this.

WOMEN TRAVELLERS
Attitudes Towards Women
There are no particular dangers threatening the lone female traveller in Corsica. Although respect for women is traditional on the island, you may encounter a few whistles or remarks during your travels.

Some female travellers have indicated to us that they have occasionally suffered from 'invisibility syndrome' because the islanders sometimes seem to act as if they are not there and exclude them systematically from the conversation.

Safety Precautions
Physical attack is very unlikely but it does happen. As in any country, the best way to avoid being assaulted is to be conscious of your surroundings and aware of situations that could be potentially dangerous: deserted streets, lonely beaches, dark corners of large train stations and so on.

France's national rape-crisis hotline (☎ 0800 05 95 95) can be reached toll-free from any telephone without using a phone card. Staffed by volunteers from 10 am to 6 pm Monday to Friday, it's run by a women's organisation called Viols Femmes Informations. In an emergency, you can always call the police (☎ 17).

GAY & LESBIAN TRAVELLERS
Although there is a gay and lesbian community on the island, there seem to be very few established meeting places. In fact, there are no registered gay or lesbian clubs, discotheques, restaurants or associations in Corsica. However, homosexuality does not seem to represent a problem for this traditional society.

There are rumours that the beach near the Campo dell'Oro airport (Ajaccio), the place de Gaulle and the Jardin Romieux in Bastia, and even the seaside resort of Algajola, near Île Rousse, are favoured by gays.

DISABLED TRAVELLERS
The Ajaccio branch of the Association des Paralysés de France (☎ 04 95 22 25 89, fax 04 95 23 40 43), ave du Maréchal Lyautey, 20090 Ajaccio, publishes details of places in Corsica (hotels, restaurants, cultural sites and so on) that are accessible to disabled.

people. These details can also be obtained from the tourism office in Ajaccio (☎ 04 95 51 53 03, 04 95 51 53 01), 1 place Foch.

Airlines ensure that there are no access problems for disabled travellers on aeroplanes or at the airports. The ferries, the freight/passenger boats *Danièle-Casanova*, *Napoléon-Bonaparte*, *Monte-d'Oro*, *Ile-de-Beauté* and *Paglia-Orba*, and the NGVs (*navires à grande vitesse*) all have some cabins that are accessible to wheelchair users. However, in all cases you must contact the companies in question before travelling. For their details see the Getting There & Away chapter.

The town centres of Bastia, Ajaccio, Bonifacio, Porto Vecchio, Propriano and, to a lesser extent, Sartène are completely accessible, as are most of Corsica's museums.

The following hotels are examples of those that, according to the Association des Paralysés de France, have rooms that are accessible to disabled people:

Ajaccio
  Hôtel Mercure
Bonifacio
  Hôtel Caravelle
  Hôtel-Restaurant du Centre Nautique
Calvi
  Appart'hôtel le Rocher
Erbalunga
  Hôtel Castel Brando
Propriano
  Hôtel Loft
Saint Florent
  Hôtel Tettola
Sartène
  Hôtel Villa Piana
Vallée de la Restonica (Corte)
  Hôtel Dominique Colonna
Vizzavona
  Hôtel du Monte d'Oro

See the sections on the individual places for more details of these hotels.

SENIOR TRAVELLERS
Corsica is an ideal destination for senior citizens. The climate before and after the main season is particularly pleasant. The island also offers a range of good walks accessible to all.

Discounts to which senior travellers in Corsica are entitled are listed in the text as appropriate.

TRAVEL WITH CHILDREN
The family is highly valued in Corsica, and therefore children are always welcome. There are no particular dangers on the island for very young children, even babies, and there is a wide range of sporting activities to occupy them, on the water and on the shore (schools for sailing, windsurfing and so on) and in the mountains.

Many hotels provide additional beds for children and most car hire companies can provide you with child seats, sometimes at no charge. Don't be afraid to haggle.

On the island you can buy nappies, milk for babies up to six months old and between six and 12 months of age, mineral water, a range of medicines and anything else you might need for children.

In summer, make sure that children are protected from the sun: you should use barrier cream and reapply it several times a day, and make sure that they wear a hat. You should try to ensure that they drink lots of water.

DANGERS & ANNOYANCES
The main source of danger in Corsica is driving a car: the roads are very windy, the local drivers are less than patient and livestock can jump out in front of your car at any time. Don't let yourself be distracted by the scenery and don't take your eyes off the road.

There are only very rarely problems with theft on the island. However, avoid leaving anything inside your vehicle where it can be seen (especially if the vehicle isn't registered in Corsica).

When Corsica makes the headlines, it's often because nationalist militants seeking Corsican independence (usually affiliated with one of the quarrelling factions of the

In the Event of Fire ...

All over Corsica, the island's forests bear the scars of the fires which devastate hundreds of hectares of pine forest every year. The civil defence department stations resources at the edge of wooded areas on days when the weather conditions are most favourable to fires starting, but unfortunately even these efforts are not enough to stop the fires.

If you see a fire, telephone ☎ 18 (or ☎ 112 from a mobile phone) and give details of:

- the precise location (road, distance from road etc)
- the type of vegetation (maquis, forest etc)
- the accessibility (track, road etc)

largest separatist organisation, the FLNC) have engaged in some act of violence, such as bombing a public building, robbing a bank, blowing up a vacant holiday villa or murdering the prefect. But the violence, which in 1997 included around 290 bombings and 22 murders (some of them interfactional), is not targeted at tourists, and there is no reason for visitors to fear for their safety.

Some Corsicans are clearly racists, especially against North Africans, who represent a relatively large community on the island.

LEGAL MATTERS
Police

Thanks to the Napoleonic Code (on which the French legal system is based), the police can pretty much search anyone they want to at any time – whether or not there is probable cause.

France has two separate police forces. The Police Nationale, which is under the command of the prefects of the individual départements, includes the Police de l'Air et des Frontières (PAF), the border police. The Gendarmerie Nationale, a paramilitary force which is under the control of the Ministry of Defence, handles airports, borders and so on.

The dreaded Compagnies Républicaines de Sécurité (CRS), riot police heavies, are part of the Police Nationale. You often see hundreds of them, equipped with the latest riot gear, at strikes or demonstrations.

Police with shoulder patches which read Police Municipale are under the control of the local mayor.

If asked a question, the police are likely to be correct and helpful but no more than that (though you may get a salute). If the police stop you for any reason, be polite and remain calm. They have wide powers of search and seizure and, if they take a dislike to you, they may choose to use them. The police can, without any particular reason, decide to examine your passport, visa, residence permit and so on.

French police are very strict about security, especially at airports. Do not leave baggage unattended: they're serious when they warn that suspicious objects will be summarily blown up.

Drinking & Driving

As elsewhere in the EU, the laws are very tough when it comes to drinking and driving, and for many years the slogan has been: *Boire ou conduire, il faut choisir* (To drink or to drive, you have to choose).

The acceptable blood-alcohol limit is 0.05%, and drivers exceeding this amount face fines of up to 30,000FF plus up to two years in jail. Licences can also be immediately suspended.

Litter

The fine for littering is about 1000FF.

Drugs

Importing or exporting drugs can lead to a jail sentence of between 10 and 30 years. The fine for possession of drugs for personal use can be as high as 500,000FF.

Smoking

Many French people do not take seriously laws they consider stupid or intrusive; whether others feel the same is another matter. Laws banning smoking in public places do exist, for example, but no one pays much attention to them. In restaurants, diners will often smoke in the nonsmoking sections of restaurants – and the waiter will happily bring them an ashtray.

BUSINESS HOURS

Many businesses remain open continuously between 8 am and 8 pm – sometimes even later – seven days a week in July and August. On the other hand, others still like to have a siesta and close between noon and 3 or 4 pm. A large number of restaurants are open lunchtimes and evenings every day during this period.

Opening hours are shorter during the rest of the year. As a general rule, opening times are from 8 am to noon and 2 to 6 pm, from Monday to Friday or Saturday. Some places could be mistaken for ghost towns between the end of October and Easter.

The opening times displayed outside shops are not always adhered to.

PUBLIC HOLIDAYS & SPECIAL EVENTS

The following days are public holidays in Corsica:

New Year's Day	1 January
Easter Sunday & Monday	March or April
Labour Day	1 May
VE day	8 May
Ascension	40th day after Easter
Whit Sunday & Monday	8th Monday after Easter
Bastille Day	14 July
Assumption (Napoleon's birthday)	15 August
All Saints' Day	1 November
Armistice Day	11 November
Christmas	25 December

Some of the events below are celebrated outside Corsica as well; others are entirely local.

January
Ile Danse
Festival of dance, held at the Théâtre Kallisté in Ajaccio every year since 1997. Information: ☎ 04 95 22 09 01.

February
A Tumbera
Pig racing festival in Renno on the second weekend in February. Information: ☎ 04 95 26 65 35.
Rencontres de Cinéma Italien de Bastia
Celebrated its 10th anniversary in 1998. Information: ☎ 04 95 31 12 72.

March
Fête de l'Olive
Takes place in mid-March in Sainte Lucie de Tallano. Information: ☎ 04 95 78 80 54.
La Passion
A major event, in the Corsican language, retracing the Passion of Christ, held in Calvi during Holy Week in March or April. Information: ☎ 04 95 65 23 57.
Pâques Orthodoxe (Orthodox Easter)
Celebrated in Cargèse.
Processions de la Semaine Sainte
The most famous processions are those in Bonifacio (Procession of the Five Colleagues) and Sartène. Calvi, Corte, Erbalunga and Bastia also celebrate Holy Week passionately, from late March to early April.
Rencontres de Cinéma Espagnol de Bastia
Information: ☎ 04 95 55 96 37.

April
A Merendella in Castagniccia
Based on local produce, this fair takes place in Piedicroce on the Easter weekend. Information: ☎ 04 95 35 81 26.
Salon de la Bande Dessinée
Cartoons are displayed in Bastia for three days at the beginning of April. Information: ☎ 04 95 32 12 81.

May
A Fera di u Casgia
Cheese fair in Venaco. Information: ☎ 04 95 47 00 15.
Festimare de l'Île Rousse
Festival of the sea, inaugurated in 1998, primarily oriented towards young people. Information: ☎ 04 95 60 08 28.

Foire de Gravana
Information: ☎ 04 95 52 83 37.

June

Allegria de la Saint Jean
Bastia's celebration of Saint Jean with street shows and song. Information: ☎ 04 95 55 96 37.

Calvi Jazz Festival
Mid-June, featuring big names from the international jazz scene. Information: ☎ 04 95 65 00 50.

Fête de Saint Jean de Corse
Day of lectures and concerts staged at the Musée de la Corse and the Citadelle. Information: ☎ 04 95 45 25 45.

Journées Napoléoniennes d'Ajaccio
Exhibitions, son et lumière displays and processions mark three days dedicated to Napoleon. Information: ☎ 04 95 21 85 62.

Rencontres d'Art Contemporain de Calvi
Held at the Citadelle, a collection of works from contemporary painters and sculptors, continuing until September. Information: ☎ 04 95 65 16 67.

Saint Érasme
Blessing of fishing boats, on 2 June in Ajaccio, Bastia and Calvi.

July

Festivoce
Festival of music and song in the Balagne, between Île Rousse and Calvi. Information: ☎ 04 95 61 77 81.

Foire de la Livre Corse de l'Île Rousse
Information: ☎ 04 95 60 27 03.

Foire de l'Olivier
Takes place in mid-July in Montemaggiore, in the Balagne. Information: ☎ 04 95 62 81 72.

Foire de Vin de Luri
The main wine event on the island, at Cap Corse. Information: ☎ 04 95 35 00 15.

Les Estivales d'Ajaccio
Festival of music and dance, from the end of July to the beginning of August. Information: ☎ 04 95 50 40 80.

Les Musicales d'Ajaccio
Classical music lessons and concerts held during the first two weeks of July, begun in 1995. Information: ☎ 04 95 50 40 80.

Nuits de la Guitare de Patrimonio
Big names from the worlds of classical, jazz and flamenco guitar meet in the open-air Patrimonio theatre in the middle of July. Information: ☎ 04 95 37 12 15.

Parcours du Regard d'Oletta
Contemporary art and sculpture in the cellars of the village of Oletta. Information: ☎ 04 95 39 02 50.

Relève des Gouverneurs
On 11 July, this costumed show retraces the arrival of the governors in Bastia. Information: ☎ 04 95 31 09 12.

August

Calvi Allegria
Held in mid-August in Calvi, the Eterna Citadella son et lumière display retraces the history of the Citadelle. Information: ☎ 04 95 65 82 03.

Cavellu in Festa
Horse show in Corte. Information: ☎ 04 95 29 42 31.

Festival de Film de Lama
Festival of European film focusing on rural life; began in 1993. Information: ☎ 04 95 48 21 05.

Festival de Musique d'Erbalunga
Light music, jazz and guitars echo over Cap Corse. Information: ☎ 04 95 33 20 84.

Fêtes Napoléoniennes d'Ajaccio
Includes parades, shows and fireworks, and culminates on 15 August, the anniversary of the birth of Napoleon. Information: ☎ 04 95 50 40 80.

Foire du Pratu
Takes place on the first weekend of the month on the Col de Pratu. Information: ☎ 04 95 39 20 07.

Pèlerinage de Notre Dame des Neiges
Pilgrimage on 5 August, starting from the village of Zonza.

Rencontres Culturelle de Nonza
Opera, concerts and plays are included in this event, inaugurated in 1998. Information: ☎ 04 95 37 89 59.

September

Cinémaffiche de Porto Vecchio
Concentrates on cinema and sculpture. Information: ☎ 04 95 70 35 02.

Fêtes de Notre Dame à Bonifacio
Held on 8 September, this religious festival is also a chance to try stuffed aubergines made the Bonifacio way.

Foire de Niolo
Takes place in early September in Casamaccioli. Information: ☎ 04 95 48 03 01.

Foire de Porto Vecchio
Information: ☎ 04 95 70 67 33.

Rencontres de Chants Polyphoniques de Calvi
Takes place in mid-September in the fantastic setting of the Citadelle. Information: ☎ 04 95 65 23 57.

Rencontres Européennes de Plongée Sous-Marine d'Ajaccio
Exhibition of beautiful underwater images at the end of September. Information: ☎ 04 95 25 12 58.

Settembrini di Tavagna
International music in five villages in this tiny region. Information: ☎ 04 95 36 91 94.

October
Festival de Vent
A celebration of wind in all its forms, in art, sport and science, held in Calvi at the end of October. Information: ☎ 01 42 64 37 69, Web site www.le-festival-du-vent.com.

Musicales de Bastia
Jazz, light music, classical music, song, dance, theatre. Information: ☎ 04 95 32 75 91.

November
Festival du Film des Cultures Méditerranéennes de Bastia
Cinema festival, held since 1982. Information: ☎ 04 95 32 08 32.

Fête du Marron d'Evisa
Information: ☎ 04 95 26 20 09.

Open International d'Échecs de Bastia
Chess tournament, held for the second time in 1998. Information: ☎ 04 95 31 59 15.

December
Foire à la Chataigne
The oldest fair in Corsica, taking place in mid-December in Bocognano. Information: ☎ 04 95 27 43 20.

ACTIVITIES
Corsica is especially attractive to keen walkers and divers, and there are separate chapters in this book dedicated to these activities. However, the sporting activities available on the island don't stop there.

Cycling
Cycling is popular on Corsica and companies in towns all over the island hire out mountain bikes for 80FF to 90FF per day. You can find details of these under the sections on Activities or Getting Around in individual towns, including Ajaccio, Bastia, Calvi, Porticcio, Porto, and Saint Florent. Bear in mind that the combination of the relief and the heat makes cycling a particularly testing experience on the island.

Skiing
Skiing facilities on the island are still limited, although there are resorts in Èse and at the Col de Verghio.

Climbing & Canyoning
The area surrounding the Bocca di Bavella provides opportunities for climbing and canyoning. You can sign up at the tourist information centre in Porto Vecchio (☎ 04 95 70 09 58) or at the Auberge du Col de Bavella (☎ 04 95 57 43 87), which is where you meet the local guides.

The Association Sportive et Culturelle du Niolo (☎ 04 95 48 05 22) can provide you with information on the possibilities for climbing, canyoning and canoeing offered by the region.

Water Sports
In the summer, you can find companies hiring out windsurfers, dinghies and sports catamarans on some of the island's beaches (including Porticcio, around Porto Vecchio and Saint Florent). These operators are detailed in the sections for those towns.

Details of the companies hiring out boats are included in the sections on the relevant harbours.

Horse Riding
You will find a large number of riding centres on Corsica, and some of them are included in this book (for example, see the sections on the Désert des Agriates, Calvi, Île Rousse and Porticcio). The riding centre at Baracci (☎ 04 95 76 08 02, fax 04 95 76 19 48) near Propriano is a good example: it can organise your rides from one centre to the next, meaning that you can cover almost the entire island on horseback.

Organised Tours
Altore (☎ 04 95 37 19 30) has a reputation for its paragliding, adrenaline sports and off-piste skiing. Contact Altore, résidence Sainte Anne, 20217 Saint Florent for their brochure.

Objectif Nature (☎ 04 95 32 54 34, fax 04 95 32 57 58), 3 rue Notre Dame de Lourdes,

Organised Walks

There are a number of companies offering guided walks all over the island, both personalised and in the form of tours, organised by qualified supervisors. They also offer various other leisure activities. Some companies will also carry your luggage from one stage to the next.

A Muntagnola	(☎ 04 95 78 65 19, fax 04 95 32 57 58) Quenza
Alta Strada	(☎/fax 04 95 47 83 01) Moltifao
Altore	(☎/fax 04 95 37 19 30) Saint Florent
Association Sportive et Culturelle du Niolo	(☎ 04 95 48 05 22, fax 04 95 48 08 80) Calacuccia
Compagnie des Guides de Haute Montagne	
Jean-Paul Quilici:	(☎ 04 95 78 64 33)
Pierre Grisgelli:	(☎ 04 95 44 04 50)
Pierre Piétri:	(☎ 04 95 32 62 76)
Didier Micheli:	(☎ 04 95 25 54 24)
Compagnie Régionale des Guides et Accompagnateurs de Corse	(☎ 04 95 48 05 22, fax 04 95 48 08 60) Calacuccia
Cors'Aventure	(☎ 04 95 26 14 49, fax 04 95 23 80 96) Bastellicaccia
Corse Odyssée	(☎ 04 95 78 64 05, fax 04 95 78 61 91) Quenza
Corsica Trek	(☎ 04 95 26 14 49, fax 04 95 26 12 49) Marignana
In Terra Corsa	(☎ 04 95 47 82 69, fax 04 95 47 60 01) Ponte Leccia
Muntagne Corse in Libertà	(☎ 04 95 20 53 14, fax 04 95 20 90 60, Web site www.sitec.fr/mcl) ave de la Grande Armée, Ajaccio
Objectif Nature	(☎ 04 95 32 54 34, fax 04 95 32 57 58) Bastia
Paesolu d'Aïtone	(☎ 04 95 26 20 39, fax 04 95 26 21 83) Evisa

20200 Bastia, arranges guided cycling, walking, horse-riding and fishing trips to the island's interior (for example, along parts of the GR20) as well as sea kayaking, diving and paragliding.

In Ajaccio, contact the Maison d'Informations Randonnées of the Parc Naturel Régional de la Corse (see Information in the Ajaccio section) or Muntagne Corse (☎ 04 95 20 53 14) at 2 ave de la Grande Armée.

WORK

The tourist season generates thousands of seasonal jobs. Getting one is a matter of trying your luck at the various hotels and restaurants on the island.

Permits

To work legally in Corsica you must have a residence permit known as a carte de séjour. Getting one is almost automatic for an EU national and almost impossible for anyone else except full-time students (see under the Visas & Documents section earlier in this chapter).

Non-EU nationals cannot work legally unless they also obtain a work permit (*autorisation de travail*) before arriving in France. Obtaining a work permit is no easy matter, because a prospective employer has to convince the authorities that there is no French – and, increasingly these days, no EU – citizen who can do the job being offered to you.

ACCOMMODATION

The range of accommodation in Corsica is considerably greater between April and October (and even more so from June to September). Many establishments are closed outside this period due to lack of demand. There is a good chance of finding very reasonably priced accommodation before and after the peak season.

Reservations

Advance Reservations Advance reservations are a good way to avoid the hassle of searching for a place to stay each time you pull into a new town; they are especially useful if you won't be arriving in the morning. During periods of heavy domestic or foreign tourism (for example, around Easter, Christmas and the New Year, during the school holiday from February to March and during the period described above), having a reservation can mean the difference between finding a room in your price range and moving on.

Tourist Offices Many tourist offices will help people who don't speak French make local hotel reservations, usually for a small fee. In some cases, you pay a deposit that is later deducted from the first night's bill. The staff may also have information on vacancies, but they will usually refuse to make specific recommendations. You cannot take advantage of reservation services by phone – you have to stop by the office.

By Telephone The relative cheapness of international phone calls makes it eminently feasible to call a hotel in Corsica from anywhere in the world to find out if they have space when you'd like to stay. Double-check to make sure the hotel proprietor understands the date, day of the week and estimated hour of your arrival, and make sure you know what he or she expects in terms of a deposit or written confirmation. It is not fair to the hotelier to make hotel reservations by telephone and then not show up. If you won't be able to arrive as planned, call the hotel and inform them as soon as possible.

Deposits Many hotels, particularly budget ones, accept reservations only if they are accompanied by a deposit (*des arrhes*; pronounced 'dez **ar**') in French francs. Some places, especially those with two or more stars, don't ask for a deposit if you give them your credit card number or send them confirmation of your plans by letter or fax in clear, simple English. But if you send them a fax, don't expect a response by fax.

Quite a few hotel owners frown upon Eurocheques because of the high exchange commission. If you make a deposit by Eurocheque, don't be surprised if the hotel holds it until you arrive and then returns it in exchange for cash. Most hotels will accept personal cheques or banker's drafts (cashiers' cheques) only if they're in French francs.

Postal in Corsica usually takes only a couple of days, so deposits can easily be sent by money order. After you've made your reservations by phone, go to any post office and purchase a *mandat lettre* (money order) for the amount and make it payable to the hotel.

Same-Day Reservations Even during the peak season, most hotels keep a few rooms unreserved, so that at least some of the people who happen by looking for a place can be accommodated. As a result, a hotel that was all booked up when you called three days ago may have space if you ring at 9 or 10 am on the morning of the day you'll be arriving. You can almost always find a place to stay this way, even in the peak month of August.

Most places will hold a room only until a set hour, rarely later than 6 or 7 pm (and sometimes earlier). If you are running late, let them know or they're liable to rent out the room to someone else.

Camping

Corsica has a good network of camp sites, although the quality of service can vary tremendously. Some sites are simply pieces of land equipped with badly maintained toilet blocks, for the simple reason that they are not open more than a few weeks of the year. However, some do offer excellent services, including swimming pools, sports facilities and so on. Most sites fall somewhere between these two extremes.

Most of Corsica's camp sites are open only from June to September. *Camping sauvage* (literally 'wild camping', or camping outside recognised camp sites) is prohibited, in part because of the danger of fires (especially in the maquis). In remote areas walkers can bivouac in *refuge* (mountain shelter) grounds for 20FF a night.

Refuges & Gîtes d'Étape

Refuges offer basic dormitory accommodation. They are exclusively for walkers and can be found in the remote mountain areas of Corsica. The Maison d'Informations Randonnées of the Parc Naturel Régional de la Corse provides lists of mountain refuges and *gîtes d'étape* along the GR20 and other walking trails. Gîtes d'étape are mainly for walkers and provide dormitory accommodation and shared bathroom facilities. They are found in places close to walking routes, and are accessible by road, which means that non-walkers can use them as well, although they normally have to opt for half board.

A night's accommodation in one of the park refuges is 50FF. Nightly rates in a gîte d'étape are from 40FF to 80FF; most offer half board too (145FF to 185FF a night).

B&Bs

The Ajaccio branch of Gîtes de France can provide information on the many B&B rooms available on Corsica. The price is much the same as for a mid-range hotel.

Hotels

Corsica has a good network of two-star hotels. Although the mid-range hotels are not necessarily modern, they are usually adequate. Outside of Bastia, Ajaccio and Corte, most of the hotels close between November and Easter.

There are very few hotels with single rooms. Even if you are travelling alone, you will usually still have to pay for a double room. Prices vary according to the season, degree of luxury (shared or en suite bathroom, shower or bath), view (sea or maquis) and facilities (television, swimming pool and so on). Corsica's budget hotel rooms are more expensive than their mainland counterparts; virtually nothing is available for less than 140FF.

The better hotels are spread around the areas surrounding the more popular seaside resorts. Some of them offer extraordinarily low prices out of season. Although there are very few luxury hotels on the island, there are a few places that used to welcome a more upper-class clientele and have retained a certain old-fashioned charm. They have gradually lowered their prices as the facilities and luxury they offer have been rendered obsolete by time.

Corse-Corsica Hotels-Restaurants, which is published by Logis de France (email info@logis-de-france.fr, Web site www .logis-de-france.fr), lists comfortable hotels in Corsica. Book through the Association des Logis de France office in Bastia (☎ 04 95 54 44 30), BP 210, 20293 Bastia, or in Porto Vecchio (☎ 04 95 70 05 93, fax 04 95 70 47 82), 12 rue Jean Jaurès, 20137 Porto Vecchio.

Rental Accommodation

Many visitors stay in holiday villages, which have to be booked months in advance through a tour operator. Don't expect to be able to stay in one without a reservation. Some private companies rent out villas; for instance, Maison des Îles (☎ 04 95 28 44 00, fax 04 95 28 44 81, 20117 Suarella) offers about 40 different luxury villas – mostly with swimming pools – in the Porto Vecchio area (allow between 10,000FF and 20,000FF per week in July or August).

A more affordable solution is to rent out a self-catering cottage (*gîte rural*) in the country. These can be rented for 1000FF to 2200FF a week; prices double or triple between June and September when most places are booked up months in advance. The cottages are simple but generally fairly comfortable, have their own kitchen and often have the benefit of being out of the way of the main tourist areas. For 50FF, you can buy a brochure detailing all the *gîtes ruraux* in Corsica from the Ajaccio branch of Gîtes de France (☎ 04 95 51 72 82, fax 04 95 51 72 89), 1 rue du Général Fiorella, 20000 Ajaccio.

You will have to book ahead for the summer months.

FOOD

You will find the very best and the very worst food in Corsican restaurants. Many restaurants and pizzerias open in the summer specifically for tourists. The former rustle up 'Corsican specialities' that are often unexciting, and most of them hide their lack of originality behind real rubbish and take great liberties with the traditional island cuisine. So you are likely to find 'Corsican menus' which consist of 'a plate of Corsican cooked meats', followed by a 'Corsican meat dish' and 'Corsican cheeses', with no other explanations.

Right next to these restaurants (which are, admittedly, affordable and sometimes serve acceptable food), you will see restaurants which prepare traditional and quality Corsican cuisine. They are undoubtedly more expensive, but the servings are usually quite generous.

The pizzerias serve up the same pizzas as you can get in Paris, London or anywhere else.

Veal with Olives

Cut the veal into small pieces and brown it in a little olive oil until it is golden. Then sauté some white or red onions in a casserole dish with one clove of chopped garlic. Add a little tomato juice, a glass of white or rosé wine, a pinch of salt, some pepper and a few bay leaves.

Allow to simmer for half an hour, then add some stoned green olives. Continue to cook on a medium heat for half an hour and serve with fresh tagliatelle.

It's better to have one course at a good restaurant rather than a complete but mediocre meal at one of the more tourist-oriented places. However, some delicious specialities are very affordable, especially *omelette au brocciu* and *omelette à la menthe* or *cannelloni au brocciu*.

Corsican cuisine is essentially Mediterranean food embellished with local produce. Some of its more characteristic dishes are best eaten in the winter: game; stews cooked for a long time (*tiani*); soup with green beans, potatoes and ham bones; and casseroles (*stuffati*). You will also find the excellent veal with olives on the menu, as well as the delicate pie made of herbs from the maquis.

brocciu (or *bruccio*) features in a number of different specialities (omelettes with mint, lasagne, sweet and savoury fritters, desserts and so on). This typically Corsican fromage frais is made using a sophisticated recipe based on whey from sheep's and/or goat's milk, which is heated and added to whole milk. This mixture is then reheated and the particles that rise to the surface are skimmed off before being placed in a strainer, one layer at a time. The brocciu (which must come from Corsica to be so-called) can be eaten sweetened (with sugar or jam), salted (or with vinaigrette) or even sprinkled with brandy (aqua vitae). It is typically Corsican, and is not the same as the traditional Provençal or Italian version.

Many producers in the regions of Niolo, Fiumorbu and the area around Vénaco make traditional cheeses from sheep's or goat's milk, with or without rind, with a mild or strong flavour. Generally these cheeses do not have specific names – if they do have one it is the name of the region in which they are produced.

Corsican cooked meats are another renowned product. They derive their flavour from free-range pigs that are allowed to feed on acorns and chestnuts, and the quality of the meats can be attributed to the lengthy drying process. However, not all cooked meats sold on the island come from free-range pigs: in order to cope with the influx of visitors in the summer, a certain proportion is actually imported and then embellished on the island. You can rely on the 'Testa nera' and 'Carte fermière d'identité' labels, which guarantee the quality of the products and that their Corsican origin.

The most widespread cooked meat specialities include *lonzu* (pork fillet preserved whole under a layer of fat) and *coppa* (based on pork spare ribs). You will also find excellent sausages, *prisuttu* (cured ham) and *figatellu*, a long liver sausage prepared in winter and served grilled.

It is not difficult to see that Corsica is no paradise for vegetarians, unless you stick to stuffed aubergines or courgettes (stuffed with brocciu, tomatoes and so on). However, there is some excellent fish (including sea bream and groupers) and seafood. Sea urchins, grilled moray eels, sardines stuffed with brocciu and bouillabaisse are among the seafood available. You can also try freshwater fish (eels or trout).

Another traditional dish, *pulenta* (polenta), which is sometimes used to accompany meat in sauces (such as wild boar casserole), is made using chestnut flour and water. It is served fried and with a sprinkling of sugar (this is one the children will love).

For dessert, try the delicious *fiadone*, a light flan made with brocciu, lemon and eggs, brocciu fritters or *canistrelli*, biscuits made with almonds, walnuts, lemon or

Recipe for Fiadone

Finely grate the zest of one lemon, and mix this in with 500g of brocciu (or ricotta, the closest thing to brocciu), six beaten eggs and 350g of caster sugar in a bowl. Beat until you have a smooth paste. Then turn this mixture into a buttered flan dish and cook at a medium heat until the surface of the fiadone is golden in colour (between 45 minutes and one hour).

aniseed. Corsican jams (made with oranges, figs, chestnuts and so on) are delicious.

Whatever happens, avoid figatellu, brocciu and wild boar in the summer! These are essentially winter dishes and do not cope well with the summer heat. To be available in summer, they must have been preserved in some way, which will have impaired the flavour.

DRINKS
Nonalcoholic Drinks
There are some excellent mineral waters, which come from the springs in Zilia in the Balagne and in Saint Georges (not far from Ajaccio). Orezzo water is a sparkling water from Castagniccia.

Soft drinks and fruit juices are widely available.

Alcoholic Drinks
The island produces two beers. Lovers of pale beer will relish La Pietra, even if it is difficult to taste the chestnuts used in its production. La Serena is a more recent addition, and has less character. It is a pale beer brewed in Furiani.

The Greeks and the Romans introduced vines to Corsica before the Christian era and the Genoese later encouraged the cultivation of this Mediterranean plant. More recently, just after WWI, wine-making on the island suffered as a result of various diseases and subsidies were given to the winegrowers to encourage productivity. Their

Corsican Wines

The wines from the Governor of the Domaine Orenga di Gaffori (Patrimonio), l'Orriu du Domaine de Toraccia (Vin de Corse – Porto Vecchio), the Domaine de Pietri (Coteaux du Cap Corse) and the Domaine Peraldi (Vin de Corse – Ajaccio) are all among the best reds. The white wine with the best reputation is undoubtedly the Clos Nicrosi (Coteaux du Cap Corse).

Other notable wine producing areas are Calvi, Sartène, Figari, the Golo region and the eastern plain.

efforts have since paid off, and Corsican wine production is now distinguished by a few excellent wines, which can be recognised at blind tastings. Although some of the wines are uninteresting, others have real character. It is worth buying wine directly from the producer rather than in the shops or markets.

The island has about 10,000 hectares of vineyards. Most of the wine produced is consumed in the same season; you will not find many vintage wines.

Cap Corse and the vineyards of Patrimonio produce some excellent muscats (sweet white wines) and some aperitifs, which are served chilled and contain various essences from the maquis (including Cap Corse and Rappu) and some liqueurs (including myrtle and citron).

ENTERTAINMENT

Corsica does not have all that many entertainment options, although it is certainly possible to have fun on the island. In general, the more heavily touristed a town is, the more options there will be. Thus, Porticcio, Calvi, Propriano and Porto Vecchio have the most entertainment venues, and the latter is generally regarded as the fun capital of Corsica.

There are cinemas in Ajaccio and Bastia, and some towns on the coast (such as Calvi and Porto) have open-air cinemas in the summer months.

Discotheques can be found in or near Bastia, Saint Florent, Calvi, Ajaccio, Porticcio and Propriano. Again, these are only open in the summer. The most famous disco is Amnésia, between Porto Vecchio and Bonifacio.

Music, dance, cinema, theatre and art feature in the island's many festivals, often held in Calvi and Ajaccio (see the Public Holidays & Special Events section earlier in this chapter). For gamblers, there's the casino in Ajaccio.

In summer, many seaside towns have cafés with terraces which stay open quite late. However, it must be said that away from the coast, entertainment is limited and that during the winter Corsica is definitely not a place for clubbers. Entertainment venues are listed under the relevant towns throughout this book.

SPECTATOR SPORTS

Several large sporting events are held in Corsica over the summer. For tickets phone the numbers listed below:

Corsica Raid Adventure This competition lasts eight days and combines various activities, including mountain running, mountain biking and canyoning. The testing event is held in mid-May, is open to amateurs and celebrated its fifth anniversary in 1998. Information: ☎ 04 95 23 83 00.

Inter-Lac This walking event, which is held in mid-July, links the mountain lakes around Corte. Information: ☎ 04 95 46 12 48.

Mediterranean Trophy This international sailing competition is open to habitable cruisers greater than 8m in length. Information: ☎ 04 95 21 40 43.

Ripcurl This competition counts as the French national funboarding championship and is held in Bonifacio in May. Information: ☎ 04 95 73 11 59.

Tour de Corse Automobile This three day competition is regarded as the rally world championship. The Tour de Corse takes place on the roads (but you should see the roads!) at the beginning of May each year. Information: ☎ 04 95 23 62 60.

Women's International Tennis Open Takes place in Calvi in April. Information: ☎ 04 95 65 21 13.

Also worth mentioning are the Route de Sud (a cycling event held in May, ☎ 04 95 25 08 13); the Corsican triathlon (consisting of swimming, cycling and running, held in May, ☎ 04 95 32 51 64); the Kyrnea Jump (a show-jumping event held in May, ☎ 04 95 20 06 22); and the Six Jours Cyclotouristes de l'Île de Beauté (a six day, 600km cycling event, held in September, ☎ 04 95 21 96 94).

SHOPPING

In the absence of local crafts (many of the items on sale in Calvi's shops come from Asia), you can take home excellent local produce as a souvenir of your stay in Corsica: cooked meats (ham, sausages and so on), chestnut honey, orange wine, myrtle or orange liqueurs, various ratafias, muscat, aperitifs, crystallised citron, table wine, olive oil, chestnut flour, biscuits, cheeses and so on. There are sweet-smelling shops on the island that offer all of this kind of produce, together with cookery books containing recipes that will allow you to make the most of their flavours when you return home. You will also be able to find Corsican produce – sometimes, but not always, cheaper – in the island's markets.

These Corsican specialities are often produced in small quantities using traditional methods, and they are dependent on tourist custom for their survival. They are generally quite expensive but good quality.

Certain shops offer jewellery made of red or pink coral. You can also find cassettes and CDs of traditional polyphonic music in specialist shops. Bookshops also have tempting window displays of books on Corsica (including its flora, fauna and history). The tax on cigars and cigarettes is lower than in mainland France.

Getting There & Away

AIR

Fares quoted in this section are approximate return fares, based on advertised rates at the time of writing. None of them constitutes a recommendation for any airline.

Fares tend to be 40 to 50% lower outside the high season. In Europe and North America the high season is roughly from June to mid-September plus Christmas. The shoulder season is April to May and mid-September to October. In Australia and New Zealand, the high season is roughly December to January.

Airports & Airlines

There are four airports on Corsica (Ajaccio, Bastia, Calvi and Figari). They are all fairly modern and well equipped.

From France, Air France, Air Littoral, Corse Méditerranée, Kyrnair and Air Liberté offer scheduled flights to the island (from December to September only). European airlines with connections to Corsica include Air France, Alitalia, British Airways, KLM-Royal Dutch Airlines, Lufthansa Airlines, Olympic Airways, Sabena and Swissair. From April to October, and particularly during the summer months, the increase in passenger demand is met by charter flights.

Buying Tickets

World aviation has never been so competitive, making air travel better value than ever. But you have to research the options carefully to make sure you get the best deal. The Internet is a useful resource for checking air fares: many travel agencies and airlines have Web sites.

Airlines and travel agencies do not always include airport or departure tax in the price they quote, so, in order to make an accurate comparison, remember to check with the vendor to find out whether or not you have to add these to the price you have been given.

Corsica's Airports

Ajaccio-Campo dell'Oro (☎ 04 95 23 56 56)
Bastia-Poretta (☎ 04 95 54 54 54)
Figari-Sud Corse (☎ 04 95 57 10 10)
Calvi-Sainte Catherine (☎ 04 95 65 88 88)

Some airlines now sell discounted tickets direct to the customer, and it's worth contacting airlines anyway for information on routes and timetables. Sometimes, however, airlines release discounted tickets to selected travel agencies and specialist discount agencies, and these are often the cheapest deals going.

The exception to this rule is the new breed of 'no-frills' airlines, which mostly sell direct. At the time of writing, easyJet and Ryanair are the most useful for getting to Corsica. Unlike the 'full-service' airlines, the no-frills carriers often make one-way tickets available at half the return fare – meaning that it is easy to stitch together an open jaw itinerary where you fly in to one city and out of another. You may also be able to arrange an open jaw ticket through a regular airline, particularly if you are flying in from outside Europe.

Round-the-World (RTW) tickets are another possibility and are comparable in price to an ordinary return long-haul flight. Some airlines also offer student/youth fares – a good travel agency should be able to provide information on such deals. For US and Canadian citizens there is the Europe by Air Pass (formerly the EurAir Pass), with which you can fly between designated cities in Europe with participating airlines for US$90 per flight. Check out their Web site (www.eurair.com) for more details.

You may find that the cheapest flights are being advertised by obscure agencies. Most such firms are honest and solvent, but there are some rogue fly-by-night outfits around. Paying by credit card generally offers protection since most card issuers will provide refunds if you don't get what you've paid for. Similar protection can be obtained by buying a ticket from a bonded agent, such as one covered by the Air Transport Organiser's Licence (ATOL) scheme in the UK. If you feel suspicious about a firm it's best to steer clear, or only pay a deposit before you get your ticket, then ring the airline to confirm that you are actually booked on the flight before you pay the balance. Established outfits such as those mentioned in this book offer more security and are about as competitive as you can get.

Ticketless travel, where your reservation details are contained within an airline computer, is becoming more common. On simple return trips the absence of a ticket can be a benefit, since it is one less thing to worry about. But if you are planning a complicated itinerary that you may wish to amend en route, there is no substitute for the good old paper version.

Travellers with Special Needs

If you have special requirements – you're in a wheelchair, taking the baby, terrified of flying, vegetarian – let the airline know when you book. Restate your needs when you reconfirm, and again when you check in at the airport. With advance warning most international airports can provide escorts from check-in to the plane, although some airlines levy a charge for this service, and most have ramps, lifts and wheelchair-accessible toilets and telephones. Aircraft toilets, on the other hand, present problems for wheelchair users, who should discuss this early on with the airline and/or their doctor.

Guide dogs for the blind will often have to travel in a specially pressurised baggage compartment with other animals, away from their owner, though smaller guide dogs may be admitted to the cabin. They are subject to the same stiff quarantine laws as any other animal entering or returning to rabies-free countries, such as the UK and Australia.

Children under two years old travel for 10% of the standard fare (or free, on some airlines), as long as they don't occupy a seat. They don't get a baggage allowance. Bassinets or 'skycots' – for children weighing up to about 10kg – can usually be provided by the airline if requested in advance. Children between two and 12 years old can usually occupy a seat for between half and two-thirds the full fare, and do get a baggage allowance. Pushchairs can often be taken as hand luggage.

Taxes

Airport tax is quite expensive in Corsica, varying from 120FF to 140FF depending on the destination. Departure tax is 40FF per person. You should check whether these taxes have been included in the ticket price you have been quoted.

The UK

Cheap fares appear in the weekend national papers and, in London, in *Time Out*, the *Evening Standard* and *TNT* (a free magazine which is available from bins outside underground stations).

There are no direct flights to Corsica from the UK, although various airlines offer scheduled flights to the island with just one change en route. Air France (☎ 020-8742 6600, Web site www.airfrance.fr/en) has two flights a day throughout the year to both Ajaccio and Bastia from Heathrow for around UK£230 return, changing in Paris (you have to transfer from Charles de Gaulle airport to Orly by coach). Another Air France option is to fly from London to Nice and then change onto a Corse Méditerranée flight to Calvi, Bastia or Ajaccio (see the following Mainland France section).

Sabena (☎ 020-8780 1444, Web site www.sabena.com) flies to Corsica via Brussels three times a week (Tuesday, Saturday and Sunday). Return tickets are likely to cost around UK£400, but low-season returns to Ajaccio are available for around UK£280 from some travel agencies.

Air Travel Glossary

Baggage Allowance This will be written on your ticket and usually includes one 20kg item to go in the hold, plus one item of hand luggage.

Bucket Shops These are unbonded travel agencies specialising in discounted airline tickets.

Bumped Just because you have a confirmed seat doesn't mean you're going to get on the plane (see Overbooking).

Cancellation Penalties If you have to cancel or change a discounted ticket, there are often heavy penalties involved; insurance can sometimes be taken out against these penalties. Some airlines impose penalties on regular tickets as well, particularly against 'no-show' passengers.

Check-In Airlines ask you to check in a certain time ahead of the flight departure (usually one to two hours on international flights). If you fail to check in on time and the flight is overbooked, the airline can cancel your booking and give your seat to somebody else.

Confirmation Having a ticket written out with the flight and date you want doesn't mean you have a seat until the agent has checked with the airline that your status is 'OK' or confirmed. Meanwhile you could just be 'on request'.

Courier Fares Businesses often need to send urgent documents or freight securely and quickly. Courier companies hire people to accompany the package through customs and, in return, offer a discount ticket which is sometimes a phenomenal bargain. In effect, what the companies do is ship their freight as your luggage on regular commercial flights. This is a legitimate operation, but there are two shortcomings – the short turnaround time of the ticket (usually not longer than a month) and the limitation on your luggage allowance. You may have to surrender all your allowance and take only carry-on luggage.

Full Fares Airlines traditionally offer 1st class (coded F), business class (coded J) and economy class (coded Y) tickets. These days there are so many promotional and discounted fares available that few passengers pay full economy fare.

ITX An ITX, or 'independent inclusive tour excursion', is often available on tickets to popular holiday destinations. Officially it's a package deal combined with hotel accommodation, but many agents will sell you one of these for the flight only and give you phoney hotel vouchers in the unlikely event that you're challenged at the airport.

Lost Tickets If you lose your airline ticket an airline will usually treat it like a travellers cheque and, after inquiries, issue you with another one. Legally, however, an airline is entitled to treat it like cash and if you lose it then it's gone forever. Take good care of your tickets.

MCO An MCO, or 'miscellaneous charge order', is a voucher that looks like an airline ticket but carries no destination or date. It can be exchanged through any International Association of Travel Agents (IATA) airline for a ticket on a specific flight. It's a useful alternative to an onward ticket in those countries that demand one, and is more flexible than an ordinary ticket if you're unsure of your route.

No-Shows No-shows are passengers who fail to show up for their flight. Full-fare passengers who fail to turn up are sometimes entitled to travel on a later flight. The rest are penalised (see Cancellation Penalties).

On Request This is an unconfirmed booking for a flight.

Air Travel Glossary

Onward Tickets An entry requirement for many countries is that you have a ticket out of the country. If you're unsure of your next move, the easiest solution is to buy the cheapest onward ticket to a neighbouring country or a ticket from a reliable airline which can later be refunded if you do not use it. Alternative, you can get an MCO.

Open Jaw Tickets These are return tickets where you fly out to one place but return from another. If available, this can save you backtracking to your arrival point.

Overbooking Airlines hate to fly empty seats and since every flight has some passengers who fail to show up, airlines often book more passengers than they have seats. Usually excess passengers make up for the no-shows, but occasionally somebody gets bumped. Guess who it is most likely to be? The passengers who check in late.

Point-to-Point Tickets These are discount tickets that can be bought on some routes in return for passengers waiving their rights to a stopover.

Promotional Fares These are officially discounted fares, available from travel agencies or direct from the airline.

Reconfirmation At least 72 hours prior to departure time of an onward or return flight, you must contact the airline and 'reconfirm' that you intend to be on the flight. If you don't do this the airline can delete your name from the passenger list and you could lose your seat.

Restrictions Discounted tickets often have various restrictions on them – such as needing to be paid for in advance and incurring a penalty to be altered. Others are restrictions on the minimum and maximum period you must be away, such as a minimum of 14 days or a maximum of one year.

Round-the-World Tickets RTW tickets give you a limited period (usually a year) in which to circumnavigate the globe. You can go anywhere the carrying airlines go, as long as you don't backtrack. The number of stopovers or total number of separate flights is decided before you set off and they usually cost a bit more than a basic return flight.

Stand-by This is a discounted ticket where you only fly if there is a seat free at the last moment. Stand-by fares are usually available only on domestic routes.

Transferred Tickets Airline tickets cannot be transferred from one person to another. Travellers sometimes try to sell the return half of their ticket, but officials can ask you to prove that you are the person named on the ticket. This is less likely to happen on domestic flights, but on an international flight tickets are compared with passports.

Travel Agencies Travel agencies vary widely and you should choose one that suits your needs. Some simply handle tours, while full-services agencies handle everything from tours and tickets to car rental and hotel bookings. If all you want is a ticket at the lowest possible price, then go to an agency specialising in discounted tickets.

Travel Periods Ticket prices vary with the time of year. There is a low (off-peak) season and a high (peak) season, and often a low-shoulder season and a high-shoulder season as well. Usually the fare depends on your outward flight – if you depart in the high season and return in the low season, you pay the high-season fare.

Of the 'no-frills' airlines (see the previous Buying Tickets section), easyJet (☎ 0870 6000 000, Web site www.easyjet.com) flies from both Liverpool and Luton to Nice, from where you can take a connecting flight. Prices start at around UK£90 return and vary according to how far in advance you book and how popular the flight is – Tuesday lunchtime departures are much cheaper than Friday evenings. In summer 1999 Ryanair commenced flights from London Stansted to Genoa for UK£80. From Genoa you can catch a ferry to Corsica (see Italy in the Sea section later in this chapter).

At the time of writing several UK-based no frills airlines were actively considering flights to Corsica.

Charter flights from London to Calvi can be bought from Holiday Options (☎ 01444-881414), 3rd floor, Martlet Heights, 49 The Martlets, Burgess Hill, West Sussex RH15 9NJ. Low-season Sunday flights range from around UK£190 to UK£245. High-season weekly flights (also on Sunday) go to all four airports on Corsica; fares don't vary much between airports. Open-jaw arrangements are available for a charge of around UK£50 per person.

The UK's best-known bargain-ticket agencies are STA Travel (☎ 020-7361 6161, Web site www.statravel.co.uk), Trailfinders (☎ 020-7937 5400), Usit Campus (☎ 020-7730 3402, Web site www.usitcampus.co.uk), Travel CUTS (☎ 020-7637 3161) and Hamilton Europe (☎ 020-7344 3333). All of these firms have branches throughout London and the UK.

Mainland France

The standard fare from Paris to Corsica is usually around 2000FF return, regardless of the season. However, airlines offer various discounts. From April to September flights to Corsica go from many of the larger French cities.

Air France (☎ 08 02 80 28 02, Minitel 3615 Air France) offers daily direct flights from Paris to Bastia, Ajaccio and Calvi. Together with regional airlines Air France also offers flights from Lyon, Marseille, Nice and Montpellier. The Paris-Ajaccio return fare is around 2100FF (1200FF if bought two weeks in advance, student fare 1100FF).

Discount fares can also be found on the airline's Minitel service (in the section *Les coups de pouce*). Fares are posted at midnight on Tuesday and are valid until the following Tuesday.

The large regional airline Air Littoral (☎ 08 03 83 48 34), based in Montpellier, flies to Ajaccio, Bastia and, in the summer, Calvi for around 2100FF, or 1150FF with restrictions. It also has flights from Bordeaux, which stop over in Montpellier, Nantes, Strasbourg or Lille (all ranging from 3700FF to 4000FF). A much cheaper flight is available from Lyon (2450FF).

The British Airways-owned Air Liberté (freephone ☎ 08 03 80 58 05, 04 95 71 10 20, fax 04 95 71 10 43, Minitel 3615 Air Liberté, Web site www.air-liberte.fr) flies only to Figari. Flights depart from Paris (around 2100FF), Marseille and Lyon from early December to March.

Corse Méditerranée (☎ 04 91 24 32 51 for international reservations, or 04 95 29 05 00, fax 04 95 29 05 05) charters planes from Marseille and Nice to Calvi, Ajaccio and Bastia. A return from Marseille to Calvi or from Nice to Ajaccio costs around 1100FF (around 750FF with restrictions).

The small airline Compagnie Kyrnair (☎ 04 95 23 56 85, 04 94 00 83 10) offers flights from Toulon and Clermont-Ferrand to Bastia and Ajaccio. The return flight from Toulon is around 1150FF (around 800FF for students, seniors, families or couples) and from Clermont-Ferrand it's around 1500FF.

Paris travel agencies specialising in bargain flights include Go Voyages (☎ 01 49 23 26 86, Minitel 3615 GO) and Council Travel (☎ 01 44 55 55 44). STA Travel's Paris agent is Voyages Wasteels (☎ 01 43 25 58 35).

Charter Flights The charter flight season is from April to October and during the Christmas holidays.

Nouvelles Frontières (☎ 08 03 33 33 33, Minitel 3615 NF, Web site www.nouvelles-frontieres.fr), with its subsidiary Corsair International, is Corsica's third largest airline. It only operates for six months of the year, chartering from two to five planes a week from Paris to the island's four airports. Fares from Paris range from 900FF to 1400FF, depending on the time of year. Flights from other French cities cost from 850FF to 1300FF in southern France and from 990FF to 1500FF in northern France.

Ollandini Charter (☎ 01 42 33 85 34, 04 95 23 92 93) charters planes between April and September. These fly from Paris (costing around 900/1450FF in the low/high season), Toulouse (700/1250FF), Nantes (900/1350FF), Mulhouse, Strasbourg, Lille, Caen and Chambéry (1000/1300FF) and Brest (1150/1700FF). Flights are usually to Ajaccio, but occasionally go to Bastia, Calvi or Figari.

Continental Europe

Germany Lufthansa Airlines (www.lufthansa.com) has flights from Munich to Bastia, via Nice, for around DM1050 all year.

STA Travel has 27 branches throughout Germany, including at Bockenheimer Landstrasse 133, Frankfurt (☎ 069-703 035) and Goethestrasse 73, Berlin (☎ 030-311 0950). A similar agency in Berlin is SRS Studenten Reise Service (☎ 030-283 3094).

The Netherlands KLM (☎ 0990 750900, Web site www.klm.nl) provides a number of options for getting to places from where it is a short onward trip to Corsica – for example, it flies from Amsterdam to Nice for about f1150. You can also book flights with various regional airlines through KLM – for example, to Marseille (f1050).

In Amsterdam, try the official student travel agency, NBBS Reizen (☎ 020-620 50 71) for up-to-date information.

Other European Cities The Belgian airline Sabena (☎ 02-723 3111) offers direct flights from Brussels to Ajaccio for about Bfr15,000 (Bfr10,500 with restrictions).

Nouvelles Frontières (☎ 02-547 4440), at 2 blvd Lemonnier, 1000 Brussels, offers direct charter flights in the summer from Brussels to Ajaccio. Prices in the low/high season are around Bfr6000/8000.

Air France flies from many European cities via Paris to Corsica. For example, you can fly from Geneva to Corsica with a stopover in Nice or Paris for around Sfr500 return throughout the year (youth/student fare around Sfr470).

The USA & Canada

The *Los Angeles Times*, *New York Times*, *San Francisco Examiner*, *Chicago Tribune*, Toronto *Globe & Mail* and *Vancouver Sun* have big weekly travel sections with lots of ads and information.

There are no direct flights from North America to Corsica. The main gateways are Nice and Paris. From the west coast you would probably pay around US$800/1200 (low/high season) and the fare from the east coast is likely to be around US$650/900.

Two reliable sources of cheap tickets in the USA are STA Travel (toll-free ☎ 800 777 0112, Web site www.statravel.com) and Council Travel (toll-free ☎ 800 226 8624, Web site www.counciltravel.com); both have offices throughout the country.

From Canada, the standard route is to fly with Air Canada, Air France or Canadian Air to Paris and continue from there with Air France. This costs about C$1400 from Vancouver, year-round, or C$850/1100 (low/high season) from Toronto.

Canada's best bargain-ticket agency is Travel CUTS (toll-free ☎ 888 838 2887, Web site www.travelcuts.com), which has some 50 offices.

Travellers over 50 years old might like to check out SAGA Holidays (toll-free ☎ 800 343 0273), which sometimes offers bargain holiday fares.

Australia & New Zealand

Check the travel agencies' ads in the Yellow Pages, and the Saturday travel sections of the *Sydney Morning Herald* and the Melbourne *Age*.

Qantas and Air France have flights from Australia to Ajaccio, via Paris, starting at around A$1800/2150 return (low/high season). AOM French Airlines also flies from Australia to Corsica via Paris for around the same fares.

Airlines from New Zealand also fly to Corsica via Paris. Low-season return fares from Auckland start at around NZ$2350 – for example, Thai International has a flight from Auckland to Paris and onto Ajaccio with Air France. Similar deals are available with a dozen other airlines.

STA Travel and Flight Centres International are major dealers in cheap air fares. STA (www.statravel.com.au) has offices all over Australia and New Zealand including Melbourne (☎ 03-9349 2411), Sydney (☎ 02-9212 1255, Fast Fare Hotline ☎ 1300 360 960, fax 9281 4183) and Auckland (☎ 09-309 9723, Fast Fare Hotline ☎ 09-366 6673, fax 303 9572). Flight Centres (☎ 131 600, Web site www.flightcentre .com.au) has offices all over Australia and New Zealand, including at 19 Bourke St, Melbourne (☎ 03-9650 2899, fax 9650 3751) and 350 Queen St, Auckland (☎ 09-309 6171).

Asia

Although most Asian countries are now offering fairly competitive air fare deals, Bangkok, Singapore and Hong Kong are still the best places to shop around for discount tickets. Travellers from this region will need to travel via Paris to get to any of Corsica's airports.

Khao San Rd in Bangkok is home to many budget travel agencies. Bangkok has a number of excellent travel agencies but there are also some suspect ones; ask the advice of other travellers before handing over your cash. STA Travel (☎ 02-236 0262), 33 Surawong Rd, is a good and reliable place to start.

In Singapore, STA Travel (☎ 737 7188) in the Orchard Parade Hotel, 1 Tanglin Rd, offers competitive discount fares. Like Bangkok, Singapore has hundreds of travel agencies so you can compare prices on

flights; Chinatown Point shopping centre on New Bridge Rd has a good selection.

Hong Kong's travel market can be unpredictable, but some great bargains are available if you are lucky. Hong Kong has a number of excellent, reliable travel agencies and some not so reliable ones. A good way to check on a travel agency is to look it up in the phone book: fly-by-night operators don't usually stay around long enough to get listed. Many travellers use the Hong Kong Student Travel Bureau (☎ 2730 3269), 8th floor, Star House, Tsim Sha Tsui. You could also try Phoenix Services (☎ 2722 7378), 7th floor, Milton Mansion, 96 Nathan Rd, Tsim Sha Tsui.

Africa

There are no direct flights from Africa to Corsica – you will need to go via a European centre. For example, British Airways (www.british-airways.com) has return fares from Nairobi to Paris, via London Gatwick, for around US$850 to US$1000 in the low season and US$1100 in the high. Fares from Johannesburg to Genoa, Marseille or Toulon, all via London, are around R3550 to R3700 in the low season and around R3900 in the high season. Turkish Airways flies from Johannesburg to Nice, via Istanbul, for around R3100/3500 (low/high season).

Middle East

Again there are no direct flights from the Middle East to Corsica. One of the best deals is with Sabena, which flies from Tel Aviv to Corsica, via Brussels, twice a week (about US$600/700 low/high season).

LAND
Bus

Eurolines With the increase in availability of low air fares, buses no longer offer the cheapest public transport around Europe. But if you can't find a cheap flight or prefer to stay on the ground, buses are a good deal. The easiest way to book tickets is through Eurolines, a consortium of coach operators with offices all over Europe.

Eurolines' coaches are fairly comfortable, with reclining seats, on-board toilets and sometimes air-conditioning. They stop frequently for meals, though you'll save a bit by packing your own food.

Discounts depend on the route, but children between four and 12 years old typically get 30 to 40% off, while those aged under 26 and seniors get a 10 to 20% discount on some routes. Fares given here are adult fares. It's a good idea to book at least several days ahead in summer.

Among some 200 Eurolines offices in Europe are the following:

Amsterdam
    Eurolines Nederland
    (☎ 020-560 8787, fax 560 8766,
    Web site www.eurolines.nl)
    Rokin 10, and Amstel Bus Station,
    Julianaplein 5
Frankfurt-am-Main
    Deutsche Touring/Eurolines
    (☎ 069-230 735,
    Web site www.deutsche-touring.com)
    Mannheimerstrasse 4
London
    Eurolines
    (bookings ☎ 0990 143219, information
    ☎ 020-7730 8235, fax 7730 8721,
    Web site www.euro lines.co.uk/euro1.htm)
    52 Grosvenor Gardens, London SW1W 0AU
Madrid
    Eurolines Peninsular
    (☎ 91-528 11 05, fax 468 38 13,
    Web site www .travelcom.es/juliavia)
    Estación Sur de Autobuses
Paris
    Eurolines France
    (☎ 01 49 72 51 51, fax 01 49 72 51 61,
    Web site www.eurolines.fr)
    Gare Routière Internationale de Paris,
    28 ave du Général de Gaulle, Bagnolet
Rome
    Eurolines Italy
    (☎ 06 440 40 09, Web site www.eurolines.it)
    Lato Stazione Tiburtina

In the USA, the Eurolines agent is British Travel International (toll-free ☎ 800 327 6097).

Eurolines Pass For real coach junkies, the Eurolines Pass gives you unlimited travel between 30 major European cities either for 30 days (around UK£230/200 for adults/ youth and seniors in high season) or 60 days (around UK£280/250), although Milan and Rome are currently the closest cities to Corsica covered by the pass.

Busabout This UK-based budget alternative to Eurolines is aimed at younger travellers, but has no upper age limit. It runs coaches along five interlocking European circuits, two of which include Nice, the stop best placed for getting across to Corsica: the Brown Loop, which also includes Paris, Spain and Portugal; and the Green Loop, which also includes Italy. Pick-up points are usually convenient for hostels and camping grounds.

The Busabout Pass costs around UK£249 (UK£199 for youth and student card holders) for 15 days travel on as many of the five circuits as you like. The add-on from London to Paris is around UK£30 return. You can buy Busabout tickets directly from the company (☎ 020-7950 1661, fax 7950 1662, Web site www.busabout.com) or from suppliers such as Usit Campus and STA Travel.

The UK A number of Eurolines services connect London to ports in France and Italy from where it is possible to sail to Corsica.

Sample return fares departing from London's Victoria coach station are: to Nice, high season only, twice weekly, around UK£100/110 (under/over 26); to Genoa, two or three times weekly, low season UK£110/120, high season UK£120/130; to Marseille, two or three times weekly, low season UK£90/100, high season UK£100/ 110; to Toulon, high season only, one departure a week, UK£100/110.

The high season runs from the end of June (sometimes May) to mid-September.

Continental Europe The Eurolines network offers a range of services across the Continent to French and Italian ports. Again the high season runs from May/June to mid-September.

Sample return fares from Amsterdam are: to Nice, high season only, twice weekly, around f330/360 (under/over 26); to Marseille or Toulon, three to five departures weekly, low season f290/320, high season f330/360; to Genoa, high season only, two departures weekly, f295/330. From Germany, there are connections with major cities throughout France and Italy, from where you can travel on to the Mediterranean coast.

Train

Trains are a popular way to get around Europe – comfortable, frequent and generally on time – and they're a good place to meet other travellers. The cost, though, can be higher than flying, unless you have one of the several available rail passes (see the boxed text below).

You're unlikely to have problems buying a long-distance ticket as little as a day or two ahead, even in summer. Amsterdam, Paris, Munich and Vienna are major Western European rail hubs.

If you intend to do a lot of rail travel, consider getting a copy of Thomas Cook's *European Timetable*, updated monthly with a complete listing of train schedules, plus information on reservations and supplements. Single issues cost about UK£10 and are available from Thomas Cook outlets worldwide.

International trains are a favourite hunting ground for thieves, so always carry your valuables with you, keep your bags in sight (or at least chained to the luggage rack) and make sure your compartment is securely locked at night.

From Paris, the main train route to the ports from where you can sail to Corsica is the TGV (*train à grande vitesse*) Sud-Est, which goes through Lyon and Avignon before reaching Marseille, Toulon and Nice.

Rail Passes

If you're planning a wider European trip before or after visiting Corsica, it makes financial sense to get one of the European rail passes. In addition to the following passes, others are available in certain countries only, such as Billets Internationaux de Jeunesse (BIJ) in France. Even with a pass you must still pay for seat and couchette reservations, and supplements on express trains.

Rail Passes for Europeans

Inter-Rail Pass Inter-Rail passes are available to anyone (not just those aged under 26) resident in Europe for six months before starting their travels. The pass divides Europe into zones: for example, zone A is Ireland and the UK; zone E is France, Belgium, the Netherlands and Luxembourg, and so on. A one zone pass is good for 22 specified, consecutive days of travel; the 2nd class price is UK£229 (UK£159 for those aged under 26). Multizone passes are good for one month's travel and are better value. A two zone pass costs UK£279/209, three zones UK£309/229, and all zones UK£349/259.

Euro Domino Pass The Euro Domino Pass (Freedom Pass in the UK) can be used for a number of days travel in a specified country within one calendar month. For those aged under 26, three/five/10 days travel in France cost UK£85/115/185 (UK£105/145/220 for those over 26), and in Italy UK£79/101/140 (UK£99/129/180 for those over 26). Passes are only available in your country of residence (from Rail Europe in the UK, ☎ 0990 848 848), so you have to buy your ticket before you leave home. The pass also brings 30 to 50% discounts on ferries to Corsica.

A new line avoiding Lyon and Avignon will be completed by 2001.

The UK From the UK, the cheapest route by train is from London to Paris by train-boat-train (using the ferry, hovercraft or Seacat to cross the Channel) and then changing trains (and stations) in Paris for the onward journey to the desired port. Tickets for the London-Paris route, as well as for the onward journey, are available from principal train stations in the UK. A 2nd class return ticket from London to Nice via Calais and Paris costs around UK£140 (slightly less for travellers aged under 26). Another way to save on the cost is to buy two or three separate tickets (London-Paris, Paris-Marseille/Nice) from, for example, Rail Europe (see later in this section).

For speed and convenience, the best route is from London Waterloo to Paris via the Channel Tunnel. A 2nd class fare from London to Nice or Marseille costs around UK£120/130 return for travellers aged under/over 26 (the latter must include a Saturday in their trip).

Channel Tunnel services are run by the Eurostar passenger train service (☎ 0990 186 186; London-Paris) or the Eurotunnel vehicle service (☎ 0990 353 535, www.euro tunnel.com; Folkestone-Calais). These operators do not sell tickets to the southern ports. Instead, you should consult Rail Europe (☎ 0990 848 848), which is part of French Railways (SNCF) and arranges rail travel between the UK and many European countries. You can also contact Rail Europe in the USA (☎ 800 4 EURAIL, fax 432 1 FAX) and in Canada (☎ 800 361 RAIL, fax 905-602 4198) or on their Web site (www .raileurope.com). Rail passes (see the boxed text) can be bought from all these offices. See the France section for equivalent SNCF contact numbers.

Rail Passes

Rail Europe Senior Card With this card, travellers aged 60 and over can get discounts of up to 30% on international journeys. It's issued by Rail Europe and costs UK£5. To be eligible you must have a local senior citizens' railcard. In the UK this is called a Senior Railcard; it costs UK£18 and can be bought at train stations. Alternatively, contact any British rail company (for example, Connex ☎ 0870 603 0405) for an application form.

Rail Passes for Non-Europeans

Eurailpass Eurailpass is the Inter-Rail counterpart for non-European residents. A Eurailpass is valid for unlimited rail travel (1st class for those aged over 26, 2nd class for those under 26) in 17 European countries (but not the UK). It includes most supplements for quality trains (such as ICE and most TGV, Eurocity and InterCity trains). The standard Eurailpass costs from US$538 for 15 days up to US$1512 for three months.

Among many variants is the Eurail Flexipass (Eurail Youth Flexipass for those under 26 years), good for any 10 days (US$654/458) or 15 days (US$862/603) of travel in a two month period; a one month continuous pass costs US$890/623.

Eurailpasses are meant to be purchased before you get to Europe, although you can buy them at a few European locations (including Rail Europe) for about 10% more, provided your passport shows you've been in Europe for less than six months.

Europass This provides unlimited 1st class train travel in France, Germany, Italy, Spain and Switzerland, for any five days in a two month period. There's also the option of buying an extra 10 days train travel within the two month period.

For travellers under 26 years, special fares are also available through youth travel specialists such as Usit Campus (see the UK section under Air earlier in this chapter for contact details).

Mainland France SNCF return fares from Paris are around 850FF to Marseille, 900FF to Toulon and 1150FF to Nice. Return fares are 25% cheaper than two singles, so it's more economical to use the same port when travelling to and from Corsica.

In France, SNCF has a nationwide telephone number (☎ 08 36 35 35 35 in French, ☎ 08 36 35 35 39 in English), or you can check them out on Minitel (3615 SNCF) or their Web site (web.sncf.fr).

Car & Motorcycle

Documents In France, drivers must carry the following papers with them at all times:

- a national ID card or passport
- a valid driver's permit or licence (*permis de conduire*); many foreign driving licences can be used in France for up to one year; EU driving licences, as well as those issued in the USA, Canada, Australia and New Zealand, are valid for three months in Corsica
- car ownership papers, known in France as a *carte grise* (grey card)
- proof of insurance, known in France as a *carte verte* (green card)

If you're caught without having all of these documents, you may be subject to a 900FF on-the-spot fine. Photocopies of all of them should be kept in a safe place. Never leave your car ownership or insurance papers in the vehicle.

For information on getting an International Driving Permit, see Visas & Documents in the Facts for the Visitor chapter.

A motor vehicle entering a foreign country must display a sticker identifying its country of registration (for example GB for Great Britain, IRL for Ireland, F for France, and so on).

For more information on motoring on the island, see Road Rules under Car & Motorcycle in the Getting Around chapter.

Equipment A reflective warning triangle, to be used in the event of breakdown, must be carried in the car. Recommended accessories are a first-aid kit, a spare bulb kit and a fire extinguisher. In the UK, the RAC (☎ 0990 275 600) or the AA (☎ 0990 500 600) can provide advice on these items.

A right-hand drive vehicle brought to France from the UK or Ireland must have deflectors affixed to the headlights to avoid dazzling oncoming traffic.

The UK & Mainland France The quickest route from the UK to the south of France is to catch a ferry across the Channel (or the Eurotunnel vehicle service underneath it) to France and drive down.

Eurotunnel (☎ 0990 353 535 in UK or ☎ 03 21 00 50 00 in France) runs a 24 hour service (taking 35 minutes) between Folkestone and Calais. The return fare per car is around UK£280 in the high season (early July to the end of August), or UK£220 if you avoid travelling at the weekend; or UK£220 in the low season (around UK£200 if you travel between 10 pm and 6 am). If you book early enough, you could pay as little as UK£99. The fare includes as many passengers as your vehicle is legally permitted to carry.

Among the ferry companies, P&O Stena Line (☎ 0990 980 980) has the most frequent sailings between Dover and Calais. SeaFrance (☎ 0990 711 711) offers lower fares, and frequencies, on the Dover-Calais route. Fast craft are run by Hoverspeed (☎ 08705-240241) from Dover to Calais and Folkestone to Boulogne.

One option to reduce driving time for those using this route, or when starting in France, is to use Motorail (car transport by rail) for all or part of the trip through France. There is a daily overnight service from Paris to Nice. In the low/high season the return fare for a normal saloon car is UK£280/379, the adult return fare is about UK£75/120 and children aged between four and 11 years travel for around UK£40/60. The cost of a berth is unaffected by the season and is charged per bed per journey. In six berth accommodation you pay UK£12 and in two berth accommodation the cost is UK£52.

For more information, contact Rail Europe (☎ 0990 848 848).

Bicycle

Cycling is a cheap, convenient, healthy, environmentally sound and above all fun way of travelling. One note of caution: before you leave home, go over your bike with a fine-tooth comb and fill your repair kit with every imaginable spare part. As with cars and motorbikes, you won't necessarily be able to buy that crucial spare for your machine when it breaks down somewhere in the back of beyond as the sun sets.

Bicycles can travel by air. You can take them to pieces and put them in a bike bag or box, but it's much easier simply to wheel your bike to the check-in desk, where it should be treated as a piece of baggage. You may have to remove the pedals and turn the handlebars sideways so that it takes up less space in the aircraft's hold; check all this with the airline well in advance, preferably before you pay for your ticket.

SEA

You can sail to one of Corsica's six ports from the Continent. Bastia and Porto Vecchio are on the east coast of the island, and Île Rousse, Calvi, Ajaccio and Propriano on the west. You can sail from either France or Italy.

All the prices quoted in this section are single fares.

Ferry Companies

The sea transport market is divided between five ferry companies. Société Nationale

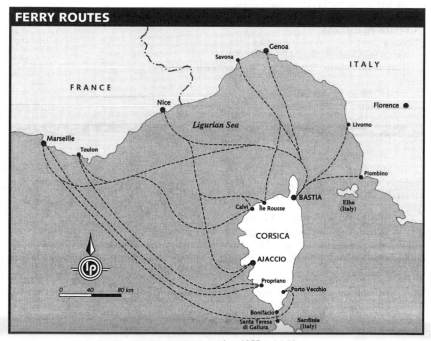

FERRY ROUTES

euro currency converter 10FF = €1.52

Ferries to Corsica

The following are the contact details for the ferry company offices in Corsica, mainland France and Italy:

Compagnie Méridionale de Navigation (CMN)
Corsica
(☎ 04 95 21 20 34, fax 04 95 21 57 60)
Port de Commerce, blvd Sampiero, Ajaccio
(☎ 04 95 31 63 38, fax 04 95 32 37 01)
Port de Commerce, 5bis rue du Chanoine Leschi, Bastia
CMN tickets are also sold in SNCM ticket offices.

Corsica Ferries
Corsica
(☎ 04 95 32 95 95, fax 04 95 32 14 71)
Port de Commerce, 5bis rue du Chanoine Leschi, Bastia
Mainland France
(☎ 04 92 00 42 93) 1 quai Am Infernet, Nice
(☎ 01 47 03 96 30) 25 rue de l'Arbre Sec, Paris
Italy
(☎ 0586 88 13 80) Nuova Stazione Marittima, Calata Carrara, Livorno
(☎ 019 21 60 041) Porto Vado, Savona

Corsica Marittima
Corsica
(☎ 04 95 54 66 95, fax 04 95 32 69 09)
Port de Commerce, 5bis rue du Chanoine Leschi, Bastia
Italy
(☎ 010 58 95 95, fax 010 58 95 93)
GSA/Cemar, Via XX, Settembre 2-10, Genoa

Corse Méditerranéenne (SNCM) Ferryterranée is the largest carrier, sailing from Marseille, Nice and Toulon (in summer only).

SNCM also manages two subsidiaries, the Compagnie Méridionale de Navigation (CMN) and Corsica Marittima, which sails from the Italian ports of Genoa and Livorno.

The French-owned Corsica Ferries sails from Nice and from the Italian ports, and Moby Lines sails from the Italian coast only. See the boxed text on this page for contact details for the five companies.

Over the last few years, sea transport to Corsica has changed considerably. The introduction of NGV services has halved the journey time between the Continent and Corsica. For example, it takes six hours from Bastia to Nice by car ferry, but only 3½ hours by NGV. However, the NGV services, which reach speeds of nearly 70km/h, cannot sail if the waves are over 4m high.

The market is also opening up to competition. Any ship flying the flag of an EU member state can now sail to Corsica from France. Hopefully this will increase competition and bring fares down.

Ferries to Corsica

Moby Lines

Corsica
  (☎ 04 95 34 84 94) Colonna d'Istria & Fils, 4 rue Luce de Casabianca, Bastia
Mainland France
  (☎ 01 55 77 27 00, Minitel 3615 Moby Lines) 45 rue de Paradis, Paris
Italy
  (☎ 010 25 27 55) Port de Commerce, Ponte Assereto, Genoa
  (☎ 0586 82 68 23) Ditta Ghianda-Via Venetto 24, Livorno

Société Nationale Corse Méditerranéenne (SNCM)

Corsica
  (☎ 04 95 29 66 99, fax 04 95 26 66 77, ferry terminal: ☎ 04 95 29 66 63)
  quai L'Herminier, Ajaccio
  (☎ 04 95 54 66 99, fax 04 95 54 66 69, ferry terminal: ☎ 04 95 54 66 60)
  Nouveau Port, Bastia
Mainland France
  (☎ 08 36 67 95 00, fax 04 91 56 35 86, Minitel 3615, Web site www.sncm.fr)
  SNCM Ferryterranée, Marseille
  (☎ 08 36 67 95 00, fax 04 91 56 35 86, ferry terminal: ☎ 04 91 56 38 63)
  61 blvd des Dames, Marseille (head office)
  (☎ 08 36 67 95 00, fax 04 91 56 35 86 12)
  rue Godot de Mauroy, Paris
  (☎ 04 93 13 66 81, fax 04 93 13 66 89, ferry terminal: ☎ 04 93 13 66 66)
  quai du Commerce, Nice
  (☎ 04 94 16 66 66, fax 04 94 16 66 68; ferry terminal: ☎ 04 94 41 50 01)
  49 ave de l'Infanterie de Marine, Toulon

For other SNCM offices in Corsica (such as those in Calvi, Île Rousse, Propriano and Porto Vecchio), see the respective regional chapters of this book.

Fares

Corsica is actually nearer Italy than France, both in terms of distance (Piombino is only 90km from Bastia) and journey time (it's only 2½ hours from Livorno to Bastia by NGV, or *navire à grande vitesse*) – and the fares are often cheaper when travelling from Italy. In general, there is not much variation in price, although the dates for the low and high seasons vary widely between France and Italy. This can make a real difference to the price of a ticket. In summer, for example, departures from Italian ports are sometimes offered at low-season rates.

A passenger ticket from Nice to Bastia can be 240FF (high season), while a Savona-Bastia ticket costs around 170FF (low season). Due to the seasonal nature of tourism in Corsica, it is recommended that you book your ticket several weeks in advance.

The same rules apply for vehicle transport. Choose your departure date carefully and take advantage of the higher number of low-season summer crossings from Italy. If you are travelling by car, it is vital that you book several months ahead.

Fares also vary according to the time of year. Although the price of a passenger ticket is fairly constant (the single fare from Marseille to Bastia goes up by just 15% in the high season), the fare for a car varies considerably, increasing as much as three-fold (from Nice to Bastia, the low and high-season fares are around 220FF and 620FF, respectively).

The fare structure corresponds to four distinct periods: the very low season is from October to mid-April, and the low season from mid-April to the end of June plus the last three weeks in September. Obviously, the two summer months are the most expensive, with Monday to Thursday classed as high season, and Friday to Sunday very high season. There is no difference in price between a ticket purchased in advance and one bought on the day of travel.

The fares published in brochures are exclusive of taxes and harbour duty. The latter varies from around 20FF (Toulon-Calvi) to 50FF (Nice-Ajaccio) per passenger, and from 40FF (Marseille-Calvi) to 70FF (Nice-Ajaccio) per vehicle. In addition, a surcharge of 30FF is added per person per crossing.

The basic fare is based on a passenger ticket with a seat. You can also get a cabin for one, two or four people or a seat in the quiet lounge (for night crossings only). During peak periods, companies sell tickets at a basic fare without a seat but with the option of using seats and benches in the ship's communal areas (such as halls, gangways and bars).

Discounts Children aged between four and 11 can get a 50% discount. Under the age of four, they travel free unless they take up a seat (in which case they pay 50% of the adult fare). Reduced fares are available for those aged between 12 and 25 years (subject to proof of age), families with three children aged under 18 (on presentation of a SNCF family card) and to those aged over 60. Discounts are available irrespective of nationality.

An additional discount is offered to families with four children and to students resident in Corsica.

Corsica Brought Closer to France for 950 Million Francs

The concept of territorial continuity aims to resolve the transport problems that arise as a result of Corsica being an island. The state subsidises transport links between Corsica and mainland France, and in return carriers offer a certain frequency of service and preferential fares for Corsican residents. The first agreements between the state and companies offering services were signed in 1948, but the fares and the inadequate number of crossings, especially in the peak season, were soon criticised. In 1976, the system was remodelled and new agreements signed. In return for increased subsidies, the carriers undertook to run more ships and to stick to fares based on the charge per kilometre used by the French railways. In 1979, the system was extended to airlines. In 1991, negotiations passed into the hands of the Collectivité Territoriale de Corse, which is now responsible for the system. The state now only has a financial role, providing a budget of 950 million francs in 1998.

Mainland France

From France, passengers can sail from Nice, Marseille or Toulon. Nice is the closest port to Corsica, and the only one to have NGV services to Bastia, Ajaccio, Île Rousse and Calvi. These services are chartered by SNCM Ferryterranée and Corsica Ferries. In the summer, at least three or four sail from Nice daily (one or two daily during the rest of the year). There is one car ferry a day from Nice to one of the Corsican ports.

From Marseille, car ferries and general cargo vessels (taking freight and passengers) sail to one of the island's ports at least once a day. The shortest route (Bastia) takes 10½ hours and the longest (Porto Vecchio) 13½ hours. There are sailings from Toulon to Corsica (Propriano, Bastia and Ajaccio) only in the summer.

The basic fare is from around 260FF to 300FF from Toulon and Marseille, and from 210FF to 240FF from Nice. The cheapest accommodation is a seat in the quiet lounge or a cabin for six (costing an additional 40FF, except on general cargo vessels, where it costs an extra 100FF) but you can also opt for a cabin for four (an additional 100FF to 140FF per person) or for two (an additional 180FF to 220FF).

Italy

You can sail to Corsica from four Italian ports: Savona, Genoa, Livorno and Piombino. The shortest route to Corsica is from Piombino to Bastia (90km), although the new NGV services mean that it is now faster to go from Livorno to Bastia (2½ hours), which is an hour quicker than the fastest journey to the island from mainland France (Nice-Bastia).

If you are travelling on the Continent, the Italian ports may prove to be a more convenient option than those in France. For example, from Lyon, Livorno is not much farther than Nice (424km), and from Strasbourg it is quicker to go to Savona (628km) than to Nice (739km).

There are also ferry crossings between Corsica and Sardinia. These are covered under Bonifacio in The South chapter.

The following are sample fares to Bastia: from Livorno, around 100FF to 160FF, depending upon the time of year (plus 30FF to 60FF if going by NGV); from Genoa, 120FF to 170FF (plus 40FF to 70FF for NGV); and from Savona, around 130FF to 180FF (plus 40FF to 70FF).

ORGANISED TOURS
The UK

A number of UK operators offer Corsican packages.

Corsican Places (☎ 01424-460046, Web site www.corsica.co.uk), 16 Grand Parade, St Leonards-on-Sea, East Sussex TN37 6DN, offers package tours to the island year-round. The Corsica Traditional tour costs around UK£450 per person for seven days and UK£900 per person for 14 days. The Corsica Zero tour takes you farther around the island, staying in more basic accommodation; seven days cost around UK£390, 14 days UK£780. Prices don't include flights, although they can be included for an additional cost.

Simply Travel (☎ 020-8987 6103, 598-608), Chiswick High Rd, London W4 5RT, sells flights to all of Corsica's airports, although these are only available from mid-May. Good deals are sometimes available on flights left over from unsold package deals.

VFB Holidays Ltd (☎ 01242-240310, Web site www.vfbhols.co.uk), Normandy House, Lower High St, Cheltenham GL50 3FB, organises tours with set itineraries around the island from May to September. For eight days it costs UK£850 per person, including flights, coach and train travel, and accommodation. VFB also organises self-catering accommodation packages on the island.

Voyages Ilena (☎ 0800 783 9025, Web site www.voyagesilena.co.uk), 1 Old Garden House, The Lanterns, Bridge Lane, London SW11 3AD, organises low and mid-season packages (not from June to September). The participating mid-range hotels are located all over the island and schedules include two or three nights per hotel. Prices include flights, hotels (with breakfast), car hire and insurance (two people for seven days, around UK£560 per person; for 14 days, UK£790 per person).

France

A number of operators sell themed tours to Corsica.

Corse Méditerranée (☎ 04 91 24 32 51) has gastronomic itineraries entitled La Route des Saveurs (The Flavour Trail). These are all-inclusive holidays, usually for three days and two nights, available for Taravu, Alta Rocca or Cap Corse.

Nouvelles Frontières (☎ 08 03 33 33 33, Minitel 3615 NF, Web site www.nouvelles-frontieres .fr) offers chartered flights to a range of destinations in Corsica, but also arranges tours, visits, car hire and sports activities. It has a one week itinerary that combines sampling local cuisine with culture for around 2900FF to 3300FF. Its Liberté tour enables travellers to put together their own itinerary from a list of hotels – the price (from around 2000FF to 2300FF) includes air fare, car hire and hotel accommodation.

Ollandini Voyages (☎ 04 95 23 92 90/93 in Ajaccio; ☎ 04 95 31 11 71 in Bastia) offers a wide range of travel options, including coach tours, excursions, holiday villages, hotels, car hire and boat or plane travel both around and to/from the island.

Union Nationale des Centres Sportifs en Plein Air (UCPA; ☎ 08 03 82 08 30) organises sports holidays to Corsica from mainland France. The activities include horse riding in winter, plus sailing, canoeing and mountain-biking in summer.

The Minitel service 3615 Corse Info provides information on transport, lodging and sports activities. It also offers pre-arranged tours and special rates.

Other Countries

American tour operators specialising in Corsica tend to focus on outdoor activities of one sort or another.

Backroads (☎ 800 GO ACTIVE, Web site www.back roads.com), 801 Cedar St, Berkeley, CA 94710-1800, offers walking, biking and multi-sport holidays on the island. Classico Ciclismo (☎ 800 866 7314 or 781-646 3377, fax 641 1512), 13 Marathon St, Arlington, MA 02474 is a specialist in cycling and walking tours in Italy, but runs some tours to Corsica.

There are no major tour operators in Australia and New Zealand offering tours to Corsica – travellers will need to get to Europe first and take a tour from there.

WARNING

The information in this chapter is particularly vulnerable to change: prices for international travel are volatile, schedules change, routes are introduced and cancelled, special deals come and go, and rules and visa requirements are amended. Airlines and governments seem to take a perverse pleasure in making price structures and regulations as complicated as possible. You should check directly with the airline or a travel agency to make sure you understand how a fare (and ticket you may buy) works. In addition, the travel industry is highly competitive and there are many lurks and perks.

The upshot of this is that you should get opinions, quotes and advice from as many airlines and travel agencies as possible before you part with your hard-earned cash. The details given in this chapter should be regarded as pointers and are not a substitute for your own careful research.

Getting Around

BUS

Numerous bus companies offer services all over Corsica but this does not mean it's easy to get around using this means of transport. On the one hand it is difficult to find your way around; working out which buses stop at any given place can be quite a challenge because many companies only offer a single service. On the other hand many services are infrequent (once or twice a day, often early in the morning) or seasonal.

Services are significantly reduced in the low season and only a handful of intercity buses operate on Sunday and public holidays outside July and August. In the low season some services are combined with school or postal services. In summer (June to September), however, you should be able to catch a bus to most places on the island, except to some of the more remote villages.

Buses serving major routes are generally modern and comfortable. Those heading for the smaller places are smaller and slower.

Fares are relatively high if you consider how short the actual distances are, but this is because the demand is so seasonal. You can buy your ticket from the driver.

There are central bus stations in Ajaccio and Bastia, from where most buses depart. In other places the bus stops for the different companies are detailed in the regional sections of this guide. The main bus routes and companies are as follows:

Ajaccio-Corte-Bastia
Eurocorse (☎ 04 95 31 03 79)
Daily except Sunday and public holidays
Ajaccio-Bastia 110FF; Bastia-Corte 50FF;
Ajaccio-Corte 65FF
Ajaccio-Sainte Marie Sicche-Olmeto-Propriano-Sartène-Roccapina-Bonifacio-Porto Vecchio
Eurocorse (☎ 04 95 31 03 79)
One to four services daily in summer, daily except Sunday and public holidays in the low season
Ajaccio-Bonifacio 110FF (three hours)

Ajaccio-Porto Vecchio through the mountains via Aullène, Quenza, Zonza, Bavella, L'Ospedale
Balési Évasion (☎ 04 95 70 15 55)
Daily except Sunday and public holidays from July to August, Monday and Friday only the rest of the year
Ajaccio-Porto Vecchio 110FF; Porto Vecchio-Zonza 35FF
Ajaccio-Saint Georges-Olmeto-Propriano-Sartène-Sainte Lucie de Tallano-Levie-Zonza (plus Bavella in summer)
Autocars Ricci (☎ 04 95 51 08 19)
One or two services daily
Ajaccio-Sartène 65FF (two hours); Ajaccio-Bavella 90FF (3¼ hours)
Ajaccio-Bastelica
Transports Bernardi (☎ 04 95 28 07 82)
Daily except Sunday and public holidays
50FF
Ajaccio-Pisciatello-Porticcio-Isolella-Mare e Sole
Transports Casanova et Santini (☎ 04 95 25 40 37, 04 95 21 05 17)
Shuttle daily in July and August
Ajaccio-Tiuccia-Sagone-Vico-Renno-Evisa-Marignana
Autocars R Cecaldi (☎ 04 95 21 38 06)
Two or three services daily (except Sunday and public holidays) during school term time
Ajaccio-Porto Pollo-Marinca
Autocars Ricci (☎ 04 95 51 08 19)
Monday, Wednesday and Saturday
Ajaccio-Tiuccia-Sagone-Cargèse-Piana-Porto-Ota
Transports SAIB (☎ 04 95 22 41 99)
One to four departures daily
Ajaccio-Porto 65FF
Ajaccio-Tiuccia-Sagone-Vico-Guagno les Bains-Orto-Soccia
Autocars Arrighi (☎ 04 95 28 31 45)
Bastia-Ponte Leccia-Île Rousse-Algajola-Calvi
Les Beaux Voyages (☎ 04 95 65 15 02)
Twice daily except Sunday and public holidays
Bastia-Calvi 80FF (2¼ hours)
Bastia-Ponte Leccia-Corte
Autocars Cortenais (☎ 04 95 46 02 12)
Monday, Wednesday and Friday from 15 April to 15 September

Bastia-Aleria-Ghisonaccia-Solenzara-Porto Vecchio
 Les Rapides Bleus (☎ 04 95 31 03 79)
 Twice daily
 Bastia-Porto Vecchio 115FF
Bastia-Canari
 Transports Saoletti (☎ 04 95 37 84 05)
 Monday and Wednesday
 40FF
Bastia-Linguizetta
 Transports Poli Xavier (☎ 04 95 38 50 56)
 Monday, Wednesday and Saturday
 80FF
Bastia-Luri
 Transports Luchesi (☎ 04 95 35 10 67)
 Wednesday; plus Tuesday and Thursday from July to September
 45FF
Bastia-Macinaggio
 Transports Saladini (☎ 04 95 35 43 88)
 Monday, Wednesday and Friday
 35FF
Bastia-Moriani
 Autocars Figarella (☎ 04 95 31 07 80)
 Daily
 35FF
Bastia-Saint Florent
 Transports Santini (☎ 04 95 37 04 04)
 Daily except Sunday and public holidays
 30FF
Bastia-Solenzara
 Transports Tibéri (☎ 04 95 57 81 73)
 Daily except Sunday and public holidays
 80FF
Bastia-Vescovato-Venzolasca
 Autobus Casinca (☎ 04 95 36 70 64)
 Daily except Sunday and public holidays
 26FF
Bastia-Erbalunga-Macinaggio-Centuri-Canari-Nonza-Saint Florent-Oletta-Bastia
 Transports Micheli (☎ 04 95 35 64 02)
 Daily except Sunday and public holidays from the beginning of July to the beginning of September
 Complete tour of Cap Corse starting and finishing in Bastia 105FF; Bastia-Centuri 40FF; Centuri-Nonza 28FF
Calvi-Calenzana
 Les Beaux Voyages (☎ 04 95 65 15 02)
 Twice daily except Sunday and public holidays, from July to mid-September
Calvi-Galeria
 Les Beaux Voyages (☎ 04 95 65 15 02)
 Once daily except Sunday and public holidays, from July to mid-September
Calvi-Porto via Bocca a Croce
 Transports SAIB (☎ 04 95 22 41 99)

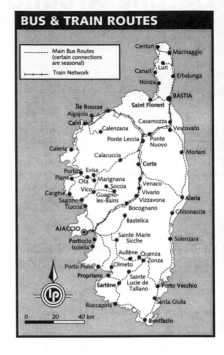

BUS & TRAIN ROUTES

From mid-May to mid-October
 100FF (three hours)
Corte-Aleria
 Autocars Cortenais (☎ 04 95 46 02 12)
 Three times a week in summer
Corte-Calacuccia-Evisa-Porto
 Autocars Mordiconi (☎ 04 95 48 00 04)
 Daily except Sunday and public holidays from July to mid-September
 100FF
Porto Vecchio-Bonifacio
 Eurocorse (☎ 04 95 31 03 79)
 One to four services daily in summer
Porto Vecchio-Santa Giulia
 Eurocorse (☎ 04 95 31 03 79)
 Shuttle service in summer

See Getting There & Away in the sections on individual towns for more information.

TRAIN
The Corsican rail network (Chemins de Fer de la Corse; CFC; ☎ 04 95 32 80 57, 04 95

32 80 61) has four year-round services: Bastia-Ajaccio, Bastia-Corte, Ajaccio-Calvi and Calvi-Bastia. These routes are served by small local trains and offer an excellent opportunity to discover the spectacular scenery in the interior of the island. Prices are very reasonable. Services are slightly reduced in winter.

The main lines are as follows:

Bastia-Ajaccio via Corte
Bastia-Furiani-Biguglia-Casamozza-Ponte Nuovo-Ponte Leccia-Francardo-Corte-Venaco-Vivario-Vizzavona-Bocognano-Mezzana-Ajaccio

   Four trains daily each way from June to September; fewer in winter
   Bastia-Ajaccio 121FF (four hours); fares from Ajaccio include Vizzavona 39FF; Vivario 48FF; Corte 64FF
   The Bastia-Corte service runs once daily except Sunday in each direction
   Bastia-Corte 57FF (1¾ hours); Bastia-Casamozza 17FF (30 minutes)

Ajaccio-Calvi (change at Ponte Leccia)
Ajaccio-Ponte Leccia-Île Rousse-Algajola-Calvi

   Twice daily each way in summer; less frequently in winter
   Ajaccio-Calvi 140FF (4½ hours); Ajaccio-Île Rousse 125FF

Bastia-Calvi
Bastia-Furiani-Biguglia-Casamozza- Ponte Nuovo-Île Rousse-Algajola-Calvi

   Twice daily each way in summer; less frequently in winter
   Bastia-Calvi 92FF (3 hours)

Tramways de Balagne

This local train service provides a link along the coast between Calvi and Île Rousse from April to October. Trains stop in about 20 places, including Lumio, Sant' Ambrogio, Algajola and Davia. They depart every hour between about 8 am and 6.30 pm. A return from Calvi to Île Rousse costs 46FF.

Discounts

There's a discount of 25% on return tickets covering more than 200km (except during July and August). Groups of more than 10 people are eligible for a 20% discount.

Children under 12 years of age are entitled to half-price tickets; those under four years of age travel for free.

Passes

Most rail passes are not valid on the CFC system, though holders of Inter-Rail passes get 50% off the ticket price.

Travellers making a return journey of under 200km within 48 hours are eligible for a *billet touristique* (tourist ticket), which is 25% cheaper than a regular return ticket. These tickets are not available in July, August or the first half of September.

The CFC sells its own rail pass – La Carte Zoom – which is well worth buying if you intend making more than a couple of train journeys within Corsica. The Carte Zoom, which is available from any station year-round, costs 290FF (no reductions for students or seniors) and is valid for seven days unlimited travel on the entire CFC network. It includes a free left luggage service (maximum 20kg).

CAR & MOTORCYCLE

Without a doubt, the best way to get around the island is by car or motorcycle. Some people bring their own cars to Corsica, but it is very easy to hire one when there (see under Car Rental later in this section). There are fewer motorcycle hire companies, but you can hire a motorcycle in most big towns. For information on the documents necessary for driving in France and Corsica see the Car & Motorcycle section in the Getting There & Away chapter.

Be particularly careful when driving in Corsica: most of the roads are spectacular but narrow and harrowing. The hairpin bends on mountain roads are not preceded by any sort of warning, and guard rails – if there are any at all – are usually little more than low stone walls. Shoulders are narrow or nonexistent and bridges are often single-lane. What's more, you run the risk of coming across stray livestock at any time, and some of the local drivers are hurried and impatient. Count on averaging 50km/h.

The most beautiful roads in Corsica include the D84 from Porto to Castel di Verghio via Evisa and the Forêt d'Aïtone, and the D69 from the N193 (near Vivario) via the forests of the PNRC to Ghisoni (where the D344 goes off to the east coast) and Sartène. The fastest road on the island is the N198, which runs along the flat east coast from Bastia to Bonifacio.

A good road map (such as the Michelin 1:200,000 map No 90) is indispensable. Road signs are usually in both French and Corsican.

There are three types of intercity road in Corsica: Routes Nationales (main highways whose names begin with N), Routes Départementales (secondary and tertiary local roads whose names begin with D) and Routes Communales (minor rural roads whose names sometimes begin with C and which are maintained by the smallest unit of government in rural areas, the *commune*).

Road Rules

Motoring in Europe (UK£4.99), published in the UK by the RAC, gives an excellent summary of road regulations in each European country, including the parking rules. Motoring organisations in other countries have similar publications.

Speed Limits Unless otherwise indicated, a speed limit of 50km/h applies in built-up areas; on intercity roads you must slow to 50km/h the moment you pass a white sign with red borders on which a place name is written in black or blue letters. This limit remains in force until you arrive at the other edge of town, where you'll pass an identical sign with a red diagonal bar across the name.

Outside built-up areas, speed limits are 90km/h (80km/h if it's raining) on single carriageway N and D roads and 110km/h (100km/h if it's raining) on dual carriageways. If you observe the speed limit, expect to have lots of cars coming to within a few metres of your rear bumper, flashing their lights and then overtaking you at the first opportunity.

Priorité à Droite For overseas tourists the most confusing – and dangerous – traffic law in France is the notorious *priorité à droite* (give way to the right) rule, under which any car entering an intersection (including a T-junction) from a road on your right has right of way no matter how small the road it's coming from. To put it another way: if you're turning right from a side road onto a main road, you have priority over vehicles approaching from your left. If you're turning left, though, you have to wait for cars coming from your right.

At most larger roundabouts priorité à droite has been suspended so that the cars already in the roundabout have right of way. This is indicated by signs reading either *vous n'avez pas la priorité* (you do not have right of way) or *cédez le passage* (give way) or by yield signs displaying a circle made out of three curved arrows.

Priorité à droite is also suspended on *routes à caractère prioritaire* (priority roads), which are marked by a yellow diamond with a black diamond in the middle. Such signs appear every few kilometres and at intersections. Priorité à droite is reinstated if you see the same sign with a diagonal bar through it.

Alcohol French law is very tough on drunk drivers. The blood-alcohol concentration (BAC) limit is 0.05% (0.50g per litre of blood). Fines for exceeding this limit range from 500FF to 8000FF.

Fines You seldom see the police pulling anyone over for speeding, which may explain why local drivers seem so fearless as they whiz around. If you are stopped, fines for violations deemed serious (such as speeding or driving through a red light) range from 1300FF to 50,000FF. The police can make tourists pay up immediately.

Car Rental

All the international car rental companies are represented at the airports and this is where you will get the widest choice of car. Cars are usually new and rates include

euro currency converter 10FF = €1.52

Road Distances (km)

	Ajaccio	Bastia	Bonifacio	Calvi	Corte	Porto	Porto Vecchio	Sartène
Ajaccio	---							
Bastia	153	---						
Bonifacio	140	170	---					
Calvi	163	94	228	---				
Corte	83	70	150	96	---			
Porto	83	135	207	76	88	---		
Porto Vecchio	130	143	27	213	120	215	---	
Sartène	84	178	54	243	152	167	62	---

comprehensive insurance and, as a rule, unlimited mileage. All insurance is subject to an excess, which is the same as the deposit you pay (between 1500FF and 2000FF). You need to have a credit card to hire a vehicle.

Stiff competition between companies means that if you shop around you may get a better deal – a larger vehicle or an extra day's hire for free, or the tax on car hire many be waived. Expect to pay between 1600FF and 1800FF for a Category A vehicle (three doors, four seats) for a week. The daily rate is about 500FF, while the monthly rate is 4500FF to 5000FF.

At the time of research, Citer and Budget had the most attractive prices. If you have time, contact a number of different companies in advance and ask them to fax you their best price for the period you want. It's likely that many of the rental companies will offer you prices that are lower than their catalogue prices.

The details of the main car rental companies are as follows:

Ada
(☎ 04 95 23 56 57)
Ajaccio-Campo dell'Oro airport
(☎ 04 95 54 55 44) Bastia-Poretta airport
Avis
(☎ 04 95 23 56 90, fax 04 95 10 08 45)
Ajaccio-Campo dell'Oro airport

(☎ 04 95 36 03 56, fax 04 95 36 01 03)
Bastia-Poretta airport
Budget
(☎ 04 95 23 57 21, fax 04 95 23 57 23)
Ajaccio Campo dell'Oro airport
(☎ 04 95 30 05 04) Bastia-Poretta airport
Citer
(☎ 04 95 23 57 15, fax 04 95 23 57 16)
Ajaccio Campo dell'Oro airport
(☎ 04 95 36 07 85) Bastia-Poretta airport
Europcar
(☎ 04 95 23 18 73, fax 04 95 22 07 27)
Ajaccio Campo dell'Oro airport
(☎ 04 95 30 09 50, fax 04 95 30 09 59)
Bastia-Poretta airport
Hertz
(☎ 04 95 23 57 04, 04 95 23 57 05, fax 04 95 23 57 06) Ajaccio Campo dell'Oro airport
(☎ 04 95 30 05 00, fax 04 95 36 14 92)
Bastia-Poretta airport

There arc also car rental companies in the towns (see Getting Around for the individual towns) and at Calvi and Figari airports.

BICYCLE
The summer heat and the relief of the island mean that Corsica is not the easiest place to cycle around. However, cycling is popular and there are companies that hire out mountain bikes (see Activities in the Facts for the Visitor chapter for more details). It costs a flat 73FF to transport your bicycle by train.

HITCHING
Hitching is never entirely safe in any country and we don't recommend it. Travellers who decide to hitch should understand that they are taking a small but potentially serious risk. People who do choose to hitch will be safer if they travel in pairs and let someone know where they are planning to go.

In Corsica, most hitching is done by hikers wishing to reach some of the more remote hamlets that are not well served by public transport. However, while it is fairly easy to hitch along the coast in summer, the low levels of traffic mean that it is considerably more of a lottery on the mountain roads.

BOAT

Unless you bring your own boat or hire one when you arrive, there is little chance of travelling around Corsica by boat. Boats are not used as a means of getting from place to place, although various companies offer boat trips along the coast for tourists and you could try to get a one-way ticket on one of these. In theory, it is possible to travel between Calvi and Girolata, Calvi and Ajaccio, or even Bonifacio and Porto Vecchio by boat. However, prices tend to be high.

Sailors with their own boats can find information about harbour facilities under Getting There & Away in the sections on individual coastal towns.

LOCAL TRANSPORT

Most towns in Corsica are small enough to get around by foot, although Ajaccio and Bastia do have local bus services.

Taxi is often the only other means of transport available (especially when you're heading for some of the airports); this can be expensive if you're on your own. If you do have the money they can be hired for one-day tours (prices are given in the text where this is recommended).

Taxis in Corsica are distinguishable by a 'Taxi' sign on the roof; the cars can be any colour. Details of taxi companies are given under Getting Around in the sections on individual towns.

ORGANISED TOURS

Various companies offer bus tours of different parts of the island, ranging from half a day to two days in duration. Most of the tours take place in the summer months only and depart from Ajaccio, Bastia or Calvi. See under Organised Tours on the sections on individual towns for more details.

As a rule, tours are only run if a minimum number of people have booked, so it's worth booking in advance.

The main Corsican tourist office, Agence du Tourisme de la Corse (ATC; ☎ 04 95 51 77 77, fax 04 95 51 14 40), 17 blvd du Roi Jérôme, 20000 Ajaccio, can give you a complete list of the island's tour operators.

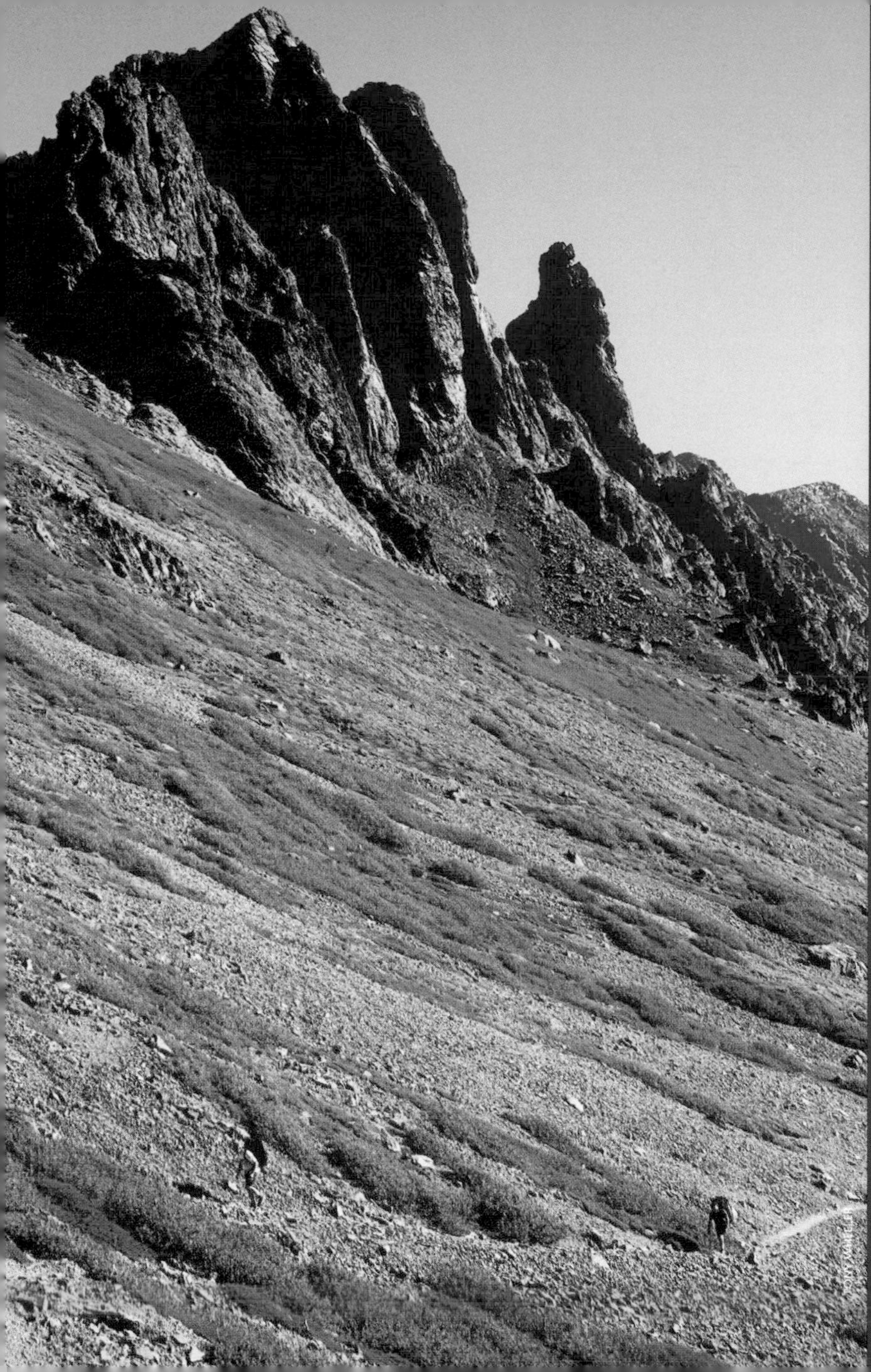

TONY WHEELER

TONY WHEELER

TONY WHEELER

TONY WHEELER

The GR20 walk passes through the interior of the island at an average altitude of 1500m. The scenery along the route includes glacial lakes, pine forests and granite massifs.

Walking in Corsica

The best way to explore Corsica is on foot. The island's mountainous landscape encourages you to leave your car behind and head out onto one of the many paths that crisscross the island from the coast to the most remote spots inland.

This tight network of paths also gives the walker an opportunity to experience the natural and cultural heritage of the inland, more secret Corsica, which is a far cry from the hustle and bustle of the seaside resorts. However, what probably makes Corsica so popular with walkers is the wide range of walks: from the challenging 15 day hike to the gentle coastal stroll, there is something for all tastes and all abilities.

This chapter does not aim to provide an exhaustive list of all the walks available, but rather to provide some technical, practical and cultural information to help you choose the walks best suited to you. All the routes described have been tested. Inevitably, the GR20 is included – its excellent reputation is justified in every respect – as is the Mare a Mare Centre (central sea-to-sea) path, which is for intermediate level walkers. There are also 12 walks lasting from 40 minutes to a few hours, which are easy and suitable for families. Details of accommodation, restaurants and other resources are given for the GR20 and Mare a Mare Centre walks.

Before embarking on any of the walks in this chapter make sure you are healthy and that the walk you have chosen is suitable for your level of physical fitness. For tips on health for walkers and advice on blisters and other walking-related problems see the Health section of the Facts for the Visitor chapter.

The authors and the publisher cannot accept any responsibility for any loss, injury or inconvenience sustained by people using this book. Although they have done their utmost to ensure the accuracy of all information in this guide, they cannot guarantee that the tracks and routes described here have not become impassable for any reason during the interval between research and publication.

The fact that a trip or area is described in this guidebook does not mean that it is safe for you and your walking party. You are ultimately responsible for judging your own capabilities in the light of the conditions you encounter.

A number of companies offer guided walks in various parts of the island. For more information see the boxed text 'Organised Walks' under Activities in the Facts for the Visitor chapter.

The Parc Naturel Régional de la Corse (see the boxed text later in this chapter) is an excellent source of information for walkers. There's also a Minitel service: 3615 Rando.

RESPONSIBLE WALKING

The popularity of walking is placing great pressure on the natural environment. Please consider the following tips when walking and help preserve the ecology and beauty of the Corsican countryside.

Walks for Everyone

- The GR20: a difficult walk for the exceptionally fit. Duration: 15 days (can be divided up into more stages).
- Five intermediate routes: two Mare e Monti (sea and mountains) and three Mare a Mare (sea to sea) routes. Duration: five to 10 days (can be divided up into more stages).
- Seven village walks: easy, circular routes. Duration: three to five hours each.
- Coastal and inland walks. Duration: one to five hours each.

Rubbish

Rubbish is a problem on the GR20 and other walks in Corsica. Follow these guidelines for the proper disposal of rubbish:

- Always carry your rubbish with you and dispose of it in the bins at the refuges at the end of the day. If you can't do this, take it away with you. Don't overlook easily forgotten items such as silver paper, orange peel, cigarette butts and plastic wrappers.

  Empty packaging weighs very little anyway and should be stored in a dedicated rubbish bag. Make an effort to pick up rubbish left by others.
- Never bury your rubbish: digging disturbs soil and ground-cover and encourages erosion. Buried rubbish will more than likely be dug up by animals, who may be injured or poisoned by it. It may also take years to decompose, especially at high altitudes.
- Minimise the waste you must dispose of by taking minimal packaging and taking no more food than you will need. If you can't buy in bulk, unpack small-portion packages and combine their contents in one container before your trip. Take reusable containers or stuff sacks.
- Don't rely on bought water in plastic bottles. Disposal of these bottles is creating a major problem in many countries. Fill up at refuges and springs indicated in the text or use iodine drops or purification tablets in water from other springs.
- Sanitary napkins, tampons and condoms should also be carried to the next bin despite the inconvenience. They burn and decompose poorly.

Erosion

Hillsides and mountain slopes, especially at high altitudes, are prone to erosion.

- Stick to existing tracks and avoid short cuts that bypass a switchback. If you blaze a new trail straight down a slope, it will turn into a watercourse with the next heavy rainfall and eventually cause soil loss and deep scarring.
- If a well used track passes through a mud patch, walk through the mud: walking around the edge will increase the size of the patch.
- Avoid removing the plant life that keeps topsoils in place.

Washing

If you are washing or washing up outside:

- Don't use detergents or toothpaste in or near watercourses, even if they are biodegradable.
- For personal washing, use biodegradable soap and a water container (or even a lightweight, portable basin) at least 50m away from the watercourse. Disperse the waste-water widely to allow the soil to filter it fully before it finally makes it back to the watercourse.
- Wash cooking utensils at least 50m from watercourses using a scourer, sand or snow instead of detergent.

Human Waste Disposal

The lack of adequate sanitation facilities on the mountain trails means that particular care must be taken with human waste.

- Contamination of water sources by human faeces can lead to the transmission of hepatitis, typhoid and intestinal parasites such as giardia, amoebas and roundworms. It can cause severe health risks not only to members of your party but also to local residents and wildlife.
- Where there is a toilet, please use it.
- Where there is none, bury your waste. Dig a small hole 15cm deep and at least 100m from any watercourse. Consider carrying a lightweight trowel for this purpose. Cover the waste with soil and a rock. Use toilet paper sparingly and bury it with the waste. In snow, dig down to the soil; otherwise your waste will be exposed when the snow melts.

Low Impact Cooking

Refuges usually have cooking facilities; camp sites and bergeries usually do not. Lighting fires is strictly forbidden in any part of the PNRC.

Use a lightweight kerosene, alcohol or Shellite (white gas) stove for cooking and avoid those powered by disposable butane gas canisters.

Wildlife Conservation

Do not feed the wildlife, because this can lead to animals becoming dependent on hand-outs, to unbalanced populations and to diseases such as 'lumpy jaw'. Don't leave food scraps behind you. Place gear out of reach and tie packs to rafters or trees.

Do not pick any flowers: most of the species are protected.

The GR20

France has more than 120,000km of marked walking paths, of which the best known set of trails is the *sentiers de grande randonnée* – numbered long-distance footpaths known as GRs. The Corsican route, the GR20, was created in 1972 and has since become an institution. It links Calenzana, in the Balagne, with Conca, north of Porto Vecchio, and attracts some 10,000 brave souls from all over Europe to take on its heights every year.

Roughly speaking, the route is a diagonal from north-west to south-east, following the island's continental divide (hence its Corsican name – Fra Li Monti – which means 'between the mountains'). It's approximately 200km long and is usually split into 15 stages, lasting between five and eight hours each.

The route cuts right through the heart of the Parc Naturel Régional de Corse (PNRC; see the boxed text later in this chapter) and passes through spectacular and primitive scenery in the interior of the island, where the average altitude is between 1000 and 2000m, peaking at 2225m.

The diversity of the landscape makes this an exceptional walk, with forests of beech and laricio pine, granite moonscapes, windswept craters, glacial lakes, torrents, peat bogs, maquis, snow-capped peaks, plains and névés (stretches of ice formed from snow). Nature lovers will be delighted.

Those in search of tranquillity will not be disappointed either – the route only passes through two villages (Vizzavona and Bavella). *Refuges* (mountain shelters) and *bergeries* (shepherd's huts) provide accommodation along most of the route, and there are facilities for camping.

Do not be fooled by the – relatively – low altitudes. The GR20 is a genuine mountain route that requires real physical commitment and should not be taken lightly. The changes in altitude are unrelenting (about 10,000m of positive changes in altitude overall, with up to 800m of climbing in a

What to Bring

- good-quality walking boots
- a 1:50,000 scale map
- a pair of trainers or flip-flops/thongs
- a comfortable, well-fitting rucksack
- a first aid kit, including plasters for blisters and an anti-inflammatory cream
- a windcheater and plastic poncho
- a waterproof/sun hat
- sunglasses
- a pair of shorts
- washing essentials (soap, towel)
- a change of clothes (underwear, T-shirts, socks)
- sun cream
- long trousers (for walking through scrub vegetation)
- a survival blanket
- a fleece jacket
- a torch
- supplies for several days (freeze-dried and high-energy foods)
- a penknife
- a flask and a supply of water (a plastic pouch containing 3L of water, for example)
- a sleeping bag
- a tent to sleep in if accommodation is full
- a mobile phone (optional)
- toilet paper

single stage), the path is rocky and sometimes steep, the weather conditions can be difficult and you have to carry enough equipment to be self-sufficient for a number of days. A good physical condition and advance training are absolutely essential.

Do not overestimate your capabilities, and do consider using the resources available close to the route – villages linked to the GR20 where you can stop off; options to complete half-stages and stock up – which are detailed in the text. Finally, ensure you read the boxed texts in this chapter carefully, particularly 'Making the Most of the GR20'.

THE NORTHERN GR20 (CALENZANA TO VIZZAVONA)

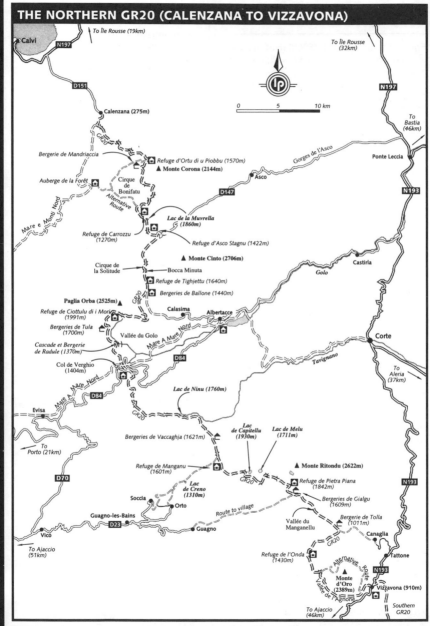

To Île Rousse (19km)

To Calvi

N197

To Île Rousse (32km)

D151

N197

Calenzana (275m)

To Bastia (46km)

Bergerie de Mandriaccia

Refuge d'Ortu di u Piobbu (1570m)
▲ Monte Corona (2144m)

Ponte Leccia

Asco

Gorges de l'Asco

N193

Auberge de la Forêt

Cirque de Bonifatu

Alternative Route

D147

Mare e Monti Nord

Lac de la Muvrella (1860m)

Refuge de Carrozzu (1270m)

Refuge d'Asco Stagnu (1422m)

Castirla

▲ Monte Cinto (2706m)

Cirque de la Solitude

Bocca Minuta

Refuge de Tighjettu (1640m)

Golo

Bergeries de Ballone (1440m)

Paglia Orba (2525m) ▲

Calasima

Corte

Refuge de Ciottulu di i Mori (1991m)

Albertacce

Bergeries de Tula (1700m)

Mare A Mare Nord

Vallée du Golo

Cascade et Bergerie de Radule (1370m)

D84

Tavignano

Col de Verghio (1404m)

Mare A Mare Nord

D84

To Aleria (37km)

Evisa

Lac de Ninu (1760m)

GR20

To Porto (21km)

Bergeries de Vaccaghja (1621m)

Lac de Capitellu (1930m)

Lac de Melu (1711m)

D70

Refuge de Manganu (1601m)

▲ Monte Ritondu (2622m)

N193

Lac de Creno (1310m)

Refuge de Pietra Piana (1842m)

Soccia

Orto

Bergeries de Gialgu (1609m)

Guagno-les-Bains

Route to village

Bergerie de Tolla (1011m)

Vico

D23

Guagno

Vallée du Manganellu

Canaglia

To Ajaccio (51km)

Tattone

Refuge de l'Onda (1430m)

Alternative Route

GR20

N193

▲ Monte d'Oro (2389m)

Vizzavona (910m)

Vallée de l'Agnone

To Ajaccio (46km)

Southern GR20

0   5   10 km

THE SOUTHERN GR20 (VIZZAVONA TO CONCA)

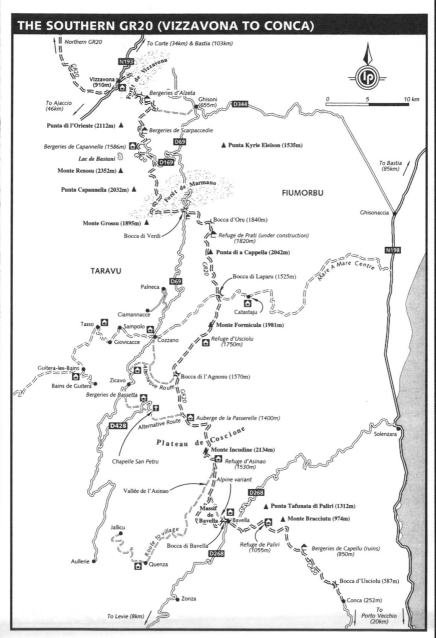

Northern GR20

To Corte (34km) & Bastia (103km)

N193

Forêt de Vizzavona

Vizzavona
(910m)

Bergeries d'Alzeta

Ghisoni
(655m)

D344

To Ajaccio
(46km)

Punta di l'Oriente (2112m) ▲

Bergeries de Scarpaccedie

D69

Bergeries de Capannelle (1586m)

▲ **Punta Kyrie Eleïson (1535m)**

D169

Lac de Bastani

Monte Renosu (2352m) ▲

FIUMORBU

To Bastia
(85km)

Punta Capannella (2032m) ▲

Forêt de Marmano

Ghisonaccia

Monte Grossu (1895m) ▲

Bocca d'Oru (1840m)

N198

Bocca di Verdi

Refuge de Prati (under construction)
(1820m)

▲ **Punta di a Cappella (2042m)**

TARAVU

Mare A Mare Centre

Bocca di Laparu (1525m)

Palneca

D69

Ciamannacce

Catastaju

Tasso

Sampolo

Monte Formicula (1981m) ▲

Giovicacce

Cozzano

Refuge d'Usciolu
(1750m)

Guitera-les-Bains

Alternative Route

Zicavo

Bocca di l'Agnonu (1570m)

Bains de Guitera

Bergeries de Bassetta

D428

Alternative Route

Auberge de la Passerelle (1400m)

Plateau de Coscione

Solenzara

Chapelle San Petru

Monte Incudine (2134m)

Refuge d'Asinao
(1530m)

Alpine variant

Vallée de l'Asinao

D268

▲ **Punta Tafunata di Paliri (1312m)**

Massif
de
Bavella

▲ **Monte Bracciutu (974m)**

Bavella

Jallicu

Route to village

Refuge de Paliri
(1055m)

Bergeries de Capellu (ruins)
(850m)

Bocca di Bavella

D268

Aullerie

Quenza

Bocca d'Usciulu (587m)

Zonza

Conca (252m)

To Levie (8km)

To
Porto Vecchio
(20km)

0   5   10 km

INFORMATION
Times & Distances

The times indicated for each stage in the text represent actual walking time (that is, they do not include resting time) and are valid for walkers of average speed. Adjust them according to the weight of your rucksack (average 15kg), your physical condition, your training, your interests (natural history, photography and so on) and how long you plan to rest for. This means that a stage estimated to take six hours could easily take two to three hours longer. Take this into account when planning your itinerary.

The distances in kilometres are given for information only. In the mountains change in altitude is a more useful reference. Estimates are based on an average walker climbing between 250 and 300m in an hour.

When to Go

The best time of year in which to do the GR20 is between May and October. Some parts of the route are partially covered in snow until June. July and August are the most popular months; the periods before and after the peak season are ideal (June and September).

For details about weather forecasts see the boxed text under Planning in the Facts for the Visitor chapter.

Accommodation & Supplies

The stages of the route are marked with refuges – official bed and breakfast establishments, almost all managed by the PNRC. They are open year-round but are only staffed between June and September.

Beside each refuge is a camp site. In 1998 a night in a refuge cost 50FF per person (20FF for campers) – you pay the warden. Next door to the dormitory (which has wooden partitions, mattresses and duvets) is a communal room with useful equipment (table, benches, gas heaters, cooking utensils and a fire or stove in winter). Campers do not have access to equipment inside the refuge. Outside there's a water point, with toilets (not enough) and showers (not always hot).

Note that there is no reservation system: refuges work on a first-come, first-served basis. Bearing in mind that the capacity is limited (between 20 and 50 places), set out early in the day and take a tent with you, just in case. The comfort and condition of the refuges depends on the wardens. Some are impeccable, others leave a little more to be desired.

It is when it comes to eating that you start to feel the pinch. Do not expect to have a feast in any of these refuges: only some of them offer light refreshments (cooked meats, cheese, eggs and drinks). After complaints from walkers, the PNRC has plans to develop the catering side of its refuges. Fortunately, there are a few private guesthouses and bergeries where you can get a decent meal – a real pleasure after days of freeze-dried food!

Finally, it is worth knowing that the villages in the valleys are only two to four hours walk away on marked routes that lead off the GR20. All the villages have comfortable bed and breakfast facilities and well-stocked shops, so they can be good places at which to stop off and recuperate. Some of them are served by public transport, so they can be good places at which to join or leave the walk.

North-South or South-North?

From what direction should you tackle the GR20? Nearly two-thirds of walkers opt for the north-south route, as does this guide. There are various reasons for this – access to Calenzana is easier, the main guide to the route is in this direction, habit – but logic would dictate going from south to north. The southern section between Conca and Vizzavona is easier, giving your body a chance to get used to the effort. Going in this direction also means that you don't have to walk with the sun in your eyes.

Making the Most of the GR20

Doing the GR20 will give you a sense of pride and achievement, and rightly so. Some GR20 walkers come to escape the stresses of modern life, others are performance freaks. Then there are the organised ones who have prepared their route down to the tiniest detail, calculating rations of freeze-dried food to the nearest gram, and the eccentrics who come along for the adventure, totally unprepared for this legendary route. Figures show that of the 10,000-odd people who take up the challenge every year, more than half do not finish.

But there are those (and their numbers are increasing) who do not see the route as a challenge but as an experience, a voyage of discovery, the rewards of which compensate for the effort. It is from this perspective that this section is written: it aims to highlight the 'GR spirit', which lies largely in pushing oneself to the limit while still indulging the senses. The aim is not to remove the dimension of adventure – after all, it is mainly the GR20's sporting and selective nature that makes it what it is – but to give the walker the keys to making the most of their walk.

Thus, there are details on stop-off points and on getting to the more interesting villages on marked paths off the GR20: it is not a good idea to go down to a village at every opportunity – it would break up the rhythm too much – but you should escape the rigours of the mountains for a day, along with the monotony of freeze-dried food and overcrowded refuges, and simply recharge your batteries. Situated below the GR20, these traditional villages are a veritable oasis of camaraderie. They have comfortable bed and breakfast accommodation where you can feel at home, run by families who will lovingly prepare local delicacies to revive even the weariest of walkers.

Your best bet is probably to go down once between Calenzana and Vizzavona (first week, northern GR20) and a second time between Vizzavona and Conca (southern GR20). When preparing your trip, think about including these detours in your itinerary and make up your own individual GR by using these little side paths. It will also mean that your rucksack is lighter, as you will have no problems stocking up in these villages.

These brief forays into remote valleys will also allow you to get to know these little pockets where the soul of Corsica is still very much alive and well. Don't blindly follow those who go straight to Calenzana from the airport, swallow up the route and then, as soon as they arrive in Conca, take the plane home on the same day. They have only touched the surface.

You can withdraw cash with a credit card (and some form of identification) at post offices, but make sure you have cash or a chequebook to pay for things along the route.

Maps & Signs

The signs consist of two horizontal lines, one red and one white, painted onto tree trunks or rocks. Cairns (small mounds of stones) are also used in certain places where painted signs would not be visible. The path is regularly maintained by the park wardens and navigation should not be a problem. There are some points, however, where the painted marks could do with being a little closer together.

It's a good idea to use a map: the best are the Didier Richard 1:50,000 maps (*Corse du Sud* and *Corse du Nord*) and the 1:25,000 IGN maps (Top 25, blue series).

The paths linking the GR20 to the villages below are marked with yellow painted lines. The markings can be confusing or inadequate on some of the less frequently used paths.

euro currency converter 10FF = €1.52

GR20 Elevation Chart – Stages 1 to 7

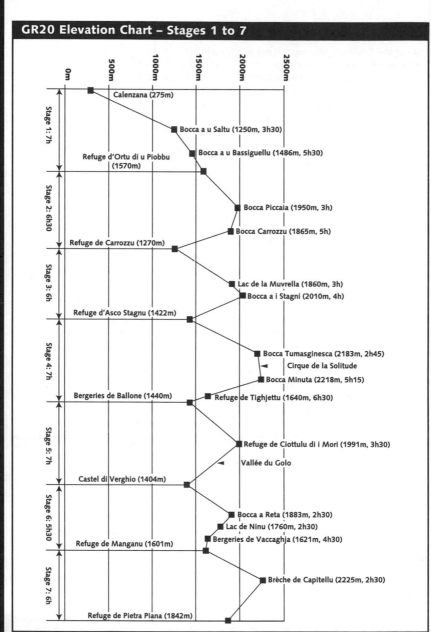

0m | 500m | 1000m | 1500m | 2000m | 2500m

Stage 1: 7h

Calenzana (275m)

Bocca a u Saltu (1250m, 3h30)

Bocca a u Bassiguellu (1486m, 5h30)

Refuge d'Ortu di u Piobbu (1570m)

Stage 2: 6h30

Bocca Piccaia (1950m, 3h)

Bocca Carrozzu (1865m, 5h)

Refuge de Carrozzu (1270m)

Stage 3: 6h

Lac de la Muvrella (1860m, 3h)

Bocca a i Stagni (2010m, 4h)

Refuge d'Asco Stagnu (1422m)

Stage 4: 7h

Bocca Tumasginesca (2183m, 2h45)

Cirque de la Solitude

Bocca Minuta (2218m, 5h15)

Bergeries de Ballone (1440m)

Refuge de Tighjettu (1640m, 6h30)

Stage 5: 7h

Refuge de Ciottulu di i Mori (1991m, 3h30)

Vallée du Golo

Castel di Verghio (1404m)

Stage 6: 5h30

Bocca a Reta (1883m, 2h30)

Lac de Ninu (1760m, 2h30)

Bergeries de Vaccaghja (1621m, 4h30)

Refuge de Manganu (1601m)

Stage 7: 6h

Brèche de Capitellu (2225m, 2h30)

Refuge de Pietra Piana (1842m)

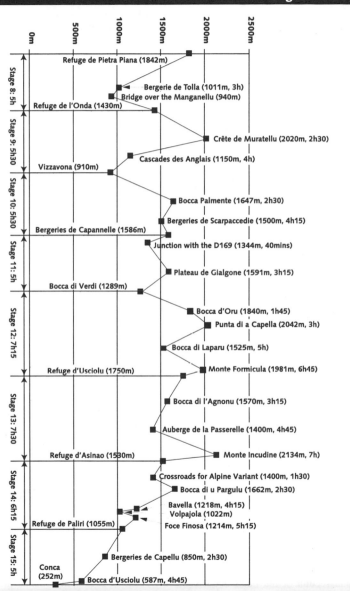

GR20 Elevation Chart – Stages 8 to 15

0m | 500m | 1000m | 1500m | 2000m | 2500m

Stage 8: 5h
Refuge de Pietra Piana (1842m)
Bergerie de Tolla (1011m, 3h)
Bridge over the Manganellu (940m)
Refuge de l'Onda (1430m)

Stage 9: 5h30
Crête de Muratellu (2020m, 2h30)
Cascades des Anglais (1150m, 4h)
Vizzavona (910m)

Stage 10: 5h30
Bocca Palmente (1647m, 2h30)
Bergeries de Scarpaccedie (1500m, 4h15)
Bergeries de Capannelle (1586m)

Stage 11: 5h
Junction with the D169 (1344m, 40mins)
Plateau de Gialgone (1591m, 3h15)
Bocca di Verdi (1289m)

Stage 12: 7h15
Bocca d'Oru (1840m, 1h45)
Punta di a Capella (2042m, 3h)
Bocca di Laparu (1525m, 5h)
Refuge d'Usciolu (1750m)
Monte Formicula (1981m, 6h45)

Stage 13: 7h30
Bocca di l'Agnonu (1570m, 3h15)
Auberge de la Passerelle (1400m, 4h45)
Refuge d'Asinao (1530m)
Monte Incudine (2134m, 7h)

Stage 14: 6h15
Crossroads for Alpine Variant (1400m, 1h30)
Bocca di u Pargulu (1662m, 2h30)
Bavella (1218m, 4h15)
Volpajola (1022m)
Refuge de Paliri (1055m)
Foce Finosa (1214m, 5h15)

Stage 15: 5h
Bergeries de Capellu (850m, 2h30)
Conca (252m)
Bocca d'Usciolu (587m, 4h45)

The GR20 at a Glance

The following information is given here: the start and finish points of each stage with their altitudes, the average duration, alternative routes, opportunities to do a half-stage or stop off in a village, and places to eat.

Stage 1: Calenzana (275m) to Refuge d'Ortu di u Piobbu (1570m); 7 hours.

Stage 2: Refuge d'Ortu di u Piobbu (1570m) to Refuge de Carrozzu (1270m); 6½ hours. Refreshments at Refuge de Carrozzu. Alternative route via the Auberge de la Forêt (food and accommodation) in Bonifatu.

Stage 3: Refuge de Carrozzu (1270m) to Refuge d'Asco Stagnu (Haut-Asco) and Le Chalet Haut Asco (1422m); 6 hours. Food at Le Chalet Haut Asco.

Stage 4: Refuge d'Asco Stagnu (1422m) to Refuge de Tighjettu or Bergeries de Ballone (1440m); 7 hours. Food at Bergeries de Ballone.

Stage 5: Bergeries de Ballone (1440m) to Castel di Verghio (1404m); 7 hours. Possible half-stage as far as Refuge de Ciottulu di i Mori (accommodation only). Optional stop-off in the villages of Calasima and Albertacce at the end of the stage. Food at Castel di Verghio.

Stage 6: Castel di Verghio (1404m) to Refuge de Manganu (1601m); 5½ hours. Optional stop-off in the villages of Soccia and Orto at the end of the stage. Food at Bergeries de Vaccaghja.

Stage 7: Refuge de Manganu (1601m) to Refuge de Pietra Piana (1842m); 6 hours.

Stage 8: Refuge de Pietra Piana (1842m) to Refuge de l'Onda (1430m); 5 hours. Optional stop-off in the villages of Canaglia and Tattone. Food at the Bergeries de Gialgu and at the Refuge de l'Onda.

Stage 9: Refuge de l'Onda (1430m) to Vizzavona (910m); 5½ hours. Alternative route via Monte d'Oro, to the north. Food in Vizzavona.

Stage 10: Vizzavona (910m) to Bergeries de Capannelle (1586m); 5½ hours. Optional stop-off in the village of Ghisoni. Food at the Bergeries de Capannelle.

Stage 11: Bergeries de Capannelle (1586m) to Bocca di Verdi (1289m); 5 hours. Food at Bocca di Verdi.

Stage 12: Bocca di Verdi (1289m) to Refuge d'Usciolu (1750m); 7 hours. Optional stop-off in the village of Cozzano. Refreshments at Refuge d'Usciolu.

Stage 13: Refuge d'Usciolu (1750m) to Refuge d'Asinao (1530m); 7½ hours. Optional stop-off in the village of Zicavo. Possible half-stage as far as Refuge de la Bergeries de Bassetta (accommodation and food). Refreshments at the Refuge d'Asinao.

Stage 14: Refuge d'Asinao (1530m) to Refuge de Paliri, including alpine route (1055m); 6¼ hours. Optional stop-off in the village of Quenza. Possible half-stage as far as Bavella (accommodation and food).

Stage 15: Refuge de Paliri (1055m) to Conca (252m); 5 hours.

Flora & Fauna

A description of the main flora and fauna of Corsica, much of which you will see on the GR20, can be found in the Flora & Fauna section of the Facts about Corsica chapter.

Rules & Regulations

Take note of and observe PNRC rules and regulations; in particular, lighting fires at any point along the route is strictly forbidden, as is camping outside the designated areas near the refuges. There are notices to remind you of this at a few strategic points along the route. See also the Responsible Walking section earlier in this chapter.

Key to Icons

 Walk

 Village

 Places to Stay

 Places to Eat

STAGE 1

Calenzana (275m) to Refuge d'Ortu di u Piobbu (1570m)

Distance: 10km
Standard: Difficult; very little shade
Average Duration: 7 hours
Highest Point: 1570m
Summary: You are confronted with the tough conditions of the GR20 from the very outset. This stage is one long ascent, crossing a series of ridge lines with hardly a downhill break. There's no guaranteed source of water, so bring at least the recommended 2L per person. The other vital necessity is sunscreen: in summer the sun is unrelenting and there are many long stretches with little shade on this and other stages of the GR20.

 The walk starts by winding up to the top of the village, then the path starts to climb steadily through ferns, with good views back to Calenzana and Moncale, another hillside village. Further up, Calvi and the sea come into view as the route climbs into pine forests. At the well-signposted Carrefour de Sentiers (550m), less than an hour from Calenzana, the Mare e Monti Nord route (see the Mare e Monti & Mare a Mare section later in this chapter) splits from the

GR20. Soon after, the trail reaches the rocky Bocca di Ravalente at 616m.

From the pass, the trail skirts a wide terraced valley, staying fairly level and passing a few small streams that usually dry up later in the season, before climbing relatively gently to 820m. After this easy stretch the trail starts to climb steeply, zigzagging uphill to another pass, the **Bocca a u Saltu** (1250m). About 3½ hours from the start, this is a perfect spot for a picnic. The other side of the ridge, on the northeastern face of Capu Ghiovu, the trail starts to climb even more steeply; at times you'll have to clamber over rocks – good practice for the rock climbs you'll encounter in a few days. About halfway up this stretch there's a stream that is sometimes a good source of drinking water, though it tends to dry up later in the season.

The climb becomes less steep before reaching the top (5½ hours into the walk). The wide grassy col at the **Bocca a u Bassiguellu** (1486m) is dotted with shady pine trees and makes another good place for a rest stop. From here the trail crosses a rather rocky and unsheltered stretch but stays fairly level. The refuge comes into view across a valley and at first it looks as if the final half-hour will entail a difficult descent and ascent, but as the refuge gets closer the actual change in height diminishes. A final short climb brings the day to an end. The walk has been almost continuously uphill – reaching each ridge line only starts the climb to the next ridge. For walkers starting the GR20 this first day can be a tough one and the lack of water sources, particularly later in the season, can make it even harder.

 The *Refuge d'Ortu di u Piobbu* (1570m) has 30 beds and plenty of camping space on the slopes below the building and in the trees beyond it. There's just one rather primitive toilet and shower but there is an alternative water source about 200m beyond the refuge along the GR20. Beds in the refuge cost 50FF, camping or bivouacking costs 20FF per person.

Walkers who still feel strong may want to climb nearby **Monte Corona** (2144m). A trail, marked by cairns and flashes of paint, goes up the slope directly behind the **Bocca di Tartagine** (1852m) refuge. From there head south and climb the rocky ridge line until the rounded summit, which is covered in loose stones and marked by a cairn, comes into view. The spectacular view stretches from the refuge below to the north coast. Allow 2½ to three hours to get to the summit and back.

STAGE 2

Refuge d'Ortu di u Piobbu (1570m) to Refuge de Carrozzu (1270m)

Distance: 8km
Standard: Difficult
Average Duration: 6½ hours
Highest Point: 2020m
Note: There are two possible routes: the more traditional route cuts right across a range of mountains, the other avoids the mountains by skirting the range to the west, via Bonifatu.
Summary: A varied day's walk starts with a short ascent and descent followed by a long and arduous climb to an altitude of 2020m. There's then a rocky and often spectacular traverse before a long and seemingly endless descent to the refuge. There is only one relatively certain water source, about two hours into the walk. Supplies may be available at the refuge.

 The day's walk starts with a gentle ascent through pine forest to a ridge line (1630m) with a very disheartening view. In front of you is a sharp drop to the valley bottom and then a long, steep ascent to a much higher ridge line on the other side.

The trail quickly descends to the valley floor, passing the ruined **Bergerie de Man-**

driaccia (1500m) and the Mandriaccia stream, then starts the long climb up the other side. About halfway up the unrelenting ascent there's a good source of drinking water, probably the only one you'll come across all day.

Eventually, about three hours from the start, you'll come to the **Bocca Piccaia** (1950m), a climb of nearly 500m from the valley bottom. There's very little shade on this stretch, making this a tough climb in the heat of the day. At the top there's a dramatic change in scenery; over the other side of the crest the drop is almost precipitous and the scenery rocky and bare, punctuated by thrusting rocky spires. It's a noticeable contrast to what was already a steep and rocky climb on the northern side. It's remarkable how often ridges herald abrupt changes in the topography along the GR20.

The trail does not actually cross the ridge line immediately but stays on the northern side, remaining fairly level until it crosses to the other side and gently descends to the **Bocca d'Avartoli** (1898m). Traversing the southern and western faces of the next ridge line, the trail drops steeply before climbing sharply to cross the next pass to the eastern side of the ridge and then back again to the western side at the **Bocca Carrozzu** (1865m) five hours into the walk.

From here the route commences the long and somewhat tedious descent to the refuge. At first the trail is rather loose and slippery, but at the start of the descent it's worth looking back at the wonderful views enjoyed in the last couple of hours of the walk. Not until well down this descent do trees offer some welcome shade. A short distance before the refuge the trail crosses a stream.

  Refuge de Carrozzu (1270m) is in a magnificent setting, hedged in by sheer rock faces on three sides but with an open terrace looking down the valley to the west. It sleeps 26 and there are plenty of camping spots in the surrounding woods. The standard 50/20FF charges for dormitory/camping apply. In 1998 the young couple who ran the refuge prepared soup, cake and other food. They also sold beer, wine, soft drinks, sausage, cheese and other supplies.

A steep path down from the refuge brings you to a stream with a series of delightful swimming pools.

 There is an alternative low-level route for this stage that skirts the mountain range crossed by the main route. It leads off to the west from the Refuge d'Ortu di u Piobbu, meeting a road after a couple of kilometres, which it follows for about 5km down the valley to **Bonifatu** (540m), with its Auberge de la Forêt (see the section on Bonifatu in the Calvi & the Balagne chapter). From

Bonifatu the route goes back up the road for 1.5km before climbing to rejoin the GR20 just beyond the Refuge de Carrozzu.

STAGE 3

Refuge de Carrozzu (1270m) to Haut Asco (1422m)

Distance: 6km
Standard: Average
Average Duration: 6 hours
Highest Point: 2010m
Summary: This stage is slightly easier than the first two, with a short ascent and descent, the bridge over the Spasimata river and a long and often spectacular rocky ascent to Lac de la Muvrella. From there it's only a short climb to a final ridge before the long descent to the ski resort of Haut Asco. Allow an extra hour to climb the A'Muvrella peak. Once you've left the Spasimata there is little water. At Haut Asco there's a restaurant and bar in the hotel and food supplies are available.

 The day starts with a short, rocky zigzag up through the forest to a ridge line, then a slightly longer drop to the Spasimata river at 1220m, crossed on a rickety suspension bridge that is not for the faint-hearted. At first the trail edges along above the river, crossing long sloping slabs of rock. At some points plastic-coated cables offer reassuring hand holds. These rocky stretches can be dangerously slippery if it rains.

Leaving the river with its tempting rock pools, the trail then starts a long, rocky ascent to **Lac de la Muvrella** (1860m), reached after three to 3½ hours of walking. The lake water is not safe to drink. If you look back during the final stages of the ascent, you'll see Calvi on the north coast. From the lake it's only a short scramble to the knife-edged ridge. After a short drop on the other side,

Clearing the Maquis

Every year a team of about 20 PNRC agents clears the 1500km of paths on the island. This process, which is known as *démaquisage*, generally takes place in the spring, after the rains.

the trail soon starts to climb again, skirting around the side of A'Muvrella to the **Bocca a i Stagni** (2010m). Just before the pass there's a sign indicating that the walk to the Spasimata river, predominantly downhill, takes 2½ hours. Coming the other way, up-hill, has taken around four hours.

A one hour detour from the Bocca a i Stagni takes you to the summit of **A'Muvrella** (2148m) and back. You can also get there from Lac de la Muvrella, rejoining the GR20 at the Bocca a i Stagni, but it's probably easier to leave your rucksack at the ridge and make the ascent from here.

The day is less taxing than the previous two, ending with the 600m descent to Haut Asco, visible far below (the route used to continue from the pass to Refuge d'Altore, until this was destroyed by fire in 1985). Haut Asco looks like any ski resort in the off season – bare, dusty and forlorn – but it's a haven for walkers after the spartan conditions of the last couple of days.

  Refuge d'Asco Stagnu (1422m) has 30 beds in rooms for two, four or six people (50FF). It also has hot showers, a kitchen and dining area and a sun terrace. There's plenty of camping space on the grassy ski slopes (20FF per person). The ski lodge, *Le Chalet Haut Asco* (☎ 04 95 47 81 08), is open from mid-May to the end of September. All 22 rooms all have a shower and toilet. It costs 240FF per night half board between July and September and 200FF in May and June. There's also a *gîte d'étape* (mountain lodge) with beds for 40FF (160FF half board). Showers in the gîte cost an extra 10FF.

Two small *shops*, open from 11 am to 8 pm, sell trekking essentials, including freeze-dried food, sausage, cheese, bread, energy bars, chocolate, cereals and fresh fruit. In the evening the ski lodge's restaurant is quite a scene: large crowds of very hungry walkers shovel down vast quantities of simple food, served with remarkable speed and smiling efficiency by the more than competent staff. It's washed down with equally large volumes of local wine. The three course menu costs 95FF plus drinks, breakfast is 30FF. The hotel has a popular bar and a big outdoor terrace.

The ski lodge and the restaurant accept credit cards. There's a public telephone in the ski lodge bar and a phone box across from the refuge, at the foot of the ski lift.

Haut Asco is also accessible on the D147, which meets the N197 2km north of Ponte Leccia. This means you can leave or join the GR20 at Haut Asco.

STAGE 4

Refuge d'Asco Stagnu (1422m) to Bergeries de Ballone (1440m)

Distance: 8km
Standard: Difficult; technical climbs in the Cirque de la Solitude; little shade
Average Duration: 7 hours
Highest Point: 2218m
Summary: The fact that the altitudes at the beginning and the end of this stage are practically identical could lead you to think this is an easy section – it's not. Generally held to be the most spectacular day on the GR20, it starts with a long climb from Haut Asco ski resort followed by the crossing of the Cirque de la Solitude. After this exhilarating rock climb there's a long descent to the Refuge de Tighjettu and the Bergeries de Ballone. There is water at the Refuge d'Altore, and from there to the bergerie the trail follows a mountain stream. The bergerie has a café, bar and food supplies.

From Haut Asco the trail starts off on the left (south) side of the ski run. It's easy to lose the trail when it runs off the ski slope into the trees. If you do wander off the trail it's not a problem: you can rejoin the route when it climbs above the valley and the ski slopes to cross the glacial moraines. The views over the valley and Haut Asco are stunning.

Allow about two hours to reach the site of the old **Refuge d'Altore** at 2000m. From the small lake at the site a steep 45 minute climb takes you to the **Bocca Tumasginesca**, or Col Perdu (Lost Pass), at 2183m. From the pass the Cirque de la Solitude falls dramatically away beneath your feet. For most walkers this is the highlight of the entire GR20, and one's first reaction is probably sheer amazement that it's possible to descend the steep side of the hanging valley and climb up again on the other side. A close inspection of the equally sheer looking walls on the other side of the valley, however, will reveal the tiny figures of walkers climbing up the other face. In two or three hours you will be there.

The descent and ascent of the **Cirque de la Solitude** is more of a rock climb than a walk. However, there are chains bolted into the rock face to make the climb easier. Since other walkers are often almost vertically below you, it's important to take great care not to dislodge rocks or stones as you climb. Typically it takes about 2½ hours to cross the cirque (a steep-sided basin formed by the erosive action of ice), but much of the route is strictly single file so a single cautious or hesitant walker can slow everybody down.

From the Bocca Tumasginesca it's 200m down to the scree-covered valley floor, where many walkers pause for lunch. On the other side the route crosses rock slabs, often guided by fixed cables, and makes a series of steep, rocky, chain-assisted ascents before emerging into an equally steep gully (or couloir) filled with loose rocks and stones. Towards the top the climb becomes a little gentler, before emerging 240m above the valley floor at the **Bocca Minuta**

(2218m), the second highest point on the GR20.

Past the ridge the scenery is dramatically different, much wider and more open. The trail makes a long and at times steep descent down the **Ravin de Stranciacone**. The path is often loose and slippery to begin with but it soon becomes rockier before reaching the Refuge de Tighjettu about 1¼ hours after leaving the Bocca Minuta.

Refuge de Tighjettu (1640m) charges the standard 50FF for a bed and 20FF for camping or bivouacking. As there is limited camping space around the refuge, many campers prefer to pitch their tents lower down, by the river.

It's only another 30 minutes walk down the valley to the *Bergeries de Ballone* (1440m), open from June to October. The trail descends less steeply as it approaches the old farm, the trees and vegetation become more dense and the pretty little river dances down the valley. There are lots of good spots at which to pitch your tent around the bergerie and camping or bivouacking is free. Beds are also available in a large tent for 10FF.

The bergerie has a popular restaurant and bar, with beers for 12FF and 15FF, wine for 7FF a glass or 60FF a bottle and three-course Corsican meals for 80FF. You can also get breakfast the next morning for 30FF and there is a useful range of food and supplies for sale. After the exhilarating

The Parc Naturel Régional de Corse (PNRC)

The PNRC was created in 1972 and today covers more than one-third of the island, including some of the most beautiful places in Corsica. These include the Golfe de Porto, the Réserve Naturelle de Scandola (a UNESCO World Heritage Site) and the highest peaks on the island, including the Aiguilles de Bavella. The PNRC has a dual mission: protection of the environment and development.

With respect to protection, the PNRC seeks to preserve all the island's endangered animal and plant species, such as the mouflon (a wild sheep native to Corsica) and the Corsican stag. It is also active in protecting sensitive sites, such as the *pozzines* and the high-altitude lakes (see the boxed text later in this section).

Its aim in terms of development is to breathe new life into the interior of Corsica. Walkers will notice how superbly maintained the façades of the bergeries are: in order to boost high-altitude livestock farming, the PNRC undertook to restore the high-altitude bergeries some 20 years ago. Many mills and hundreds of *casgili* (cheese cellars) have also been restored.

The PNRC believes that the best way to develop the central areas of the island is through tourism, and roughly 2000km of walking paths have been created. There are about 100 people responsible for maintaining the paths, clearing the scrub and providing information to the public.

The Maison d'Information Randonnée du PNRC (PNRC Walking Information Office; ☎ 04 95 51 79 10, fax 04 95 21 88 17), 2 rue Sergent Casalonga, Ajaccio, publishes a wealth of information about the park in French, English and Spanish, along with a number of walking guides (mostly in French). It also provides sensible advice on the walking routes available. It is open from 8.30 am to noon and 2 to 6 pm (5 pm on Friday) Monday to Friday.

In summer (June to September) this information is also relayed by five other information offices. Their opening times are subject to change, so ring before you go.

Maison de Calvi
(☎ 04 95 65 16 67) Office de Tourisme, 20260 Calvi

Maison de Corte
(☎ 04 95 46 27 44) La Citadelle, 20250 Corte

Maison d'Evisa
(☎ 04 95 26 23 62) Peasolu d'Aïtone, 20126 Evisa

Maison de Moltifao
(☎ 04 95 47 85 03) Village des Tortues, 20218 Moltifao

Maison de Porto
(☎ 04 95 26 15 14) La Marine, 20150 Porto

crossing of the Cirque de la Solitude, a cold beer on the bergerie's terrace, looking down the pretty forested valley as the sun sinks behind the mountain ridge to the west, makes a fine end to the day.

The only drawback to this pleasant spot is there are no toilet or washing facilities at all. Given the number of walkers who pause for a meal or stop overnight this is a serious oversight. A short walk from the camp site are unpleasant reminders that the lack of toilets could easily be a serious health risk.

STAGE 5

Bergeries de Ballone (1440m) to Castel di Verghio (1404m)

Distance: 13km
Standard: Average; partially shady route
Average Duration: 7 hours
Highest Point: 2000m
Note: Optional half-stage if you stop at the Refuge de Ciottulu di i Mori; access to the villages of Calasima and Albertacce
Summary: A varied walk that ascends through forest before the path becomes steep and rocky as it approaches a pass below Paglia Orba. The walk then circles the southern side of Paglia Orba before dropping down to follow an enticing river that descends into the forested Vallée du Golo and on to the ski resort of Castel di Verghio. There are plentiful supplies of water during the day because much of the walk follows the course of streams. The hotel at Castel di Verghio has a bar, restaurant and food supplies.

 The day begins with a gently undulating ascent through pine forests with streams tumbling down from the hills to the west to join the Viru river at the valley floor. Across the valley to the east you can see the road up from **Albertacce** through **Calasima**, at 1100m the highest village in Corsica. The trail turns west around the eastern slope of Paglia Orba and then emerges from the forest for the steep and rocky slog up to the **Bocca di Foghieghiallu** (Col de Fogghiale; 1962m) after about three hours.

On the other side of the pass a wide valley opens out to the south but the route continues to the west, crossing the slopes of Paglia Orba and climbing slightly to reach the refuge.

 Half-stage *Refuge de Ciottulu di i Mori* (1991m) charges standard rates: 50FF for one of 28 beds or 20FF to camp or bivouac. Along one side of the building there's a terrace looking out over the valley below. Directly behind the refuge is **Paglia Orba** (2525m), the third highest peak in Corsica. Climbers may want to make the three hour round-trip to the summit of the mountain via the Col des Maures, but the final stretch includes some reasonably challenging rock climbing. This is not an ascent for beginners.

 The route continues around to the western side of the Vallée du Golo, descending slightly to 1907m before dropping steeply down to the river at 1700m, just below the ruins of the **Bergeries de Tula**. For the next couple of hours the walk follows the impressively rocky ravine of the **Golo** river, passing a series of rock pools that tempt many walkers to while away an hour or two swimming and sunbathing. The path tracing the lower part of the valley was, for many centuries, a traditional route along which farmers took their livestock when migrating to summer pastures. As the trail descends you'll meet casual walkers who've joined the GR20 from the Fer à Cheval bend on the D84.

The valley narrows before the trail reaches the **Cascade de Radule** (1370m) and the **Bergeries de Radule**, after five to six hours (more if you've indulged in a swim). For the final hour you walk through the beech forests of the Valdu Niellu, passing the signposted turn-off to the Fer à Cheval bend and crossing the Mare a Mare Nord trail before finally emerging on the D84 just 100m west of Castel di Verghio (1404m). The ski slopes are on the other side of the road. Older maps show the GR20 crossing the D84 at the Fer à Cheval bend but the trail has been realigned.

  Hôtel Castel di Verghio (☎ 04 95 48 00 01) gives the impression that it has not been tidied up since the last skiing season. It has 29 rooms, each with a shower and sink (toilets on the landing), that cost 330FF per person for a single room at half-board, 220FF per person for a double room and 170FF per person in the gîte d'étape. Bed-only accommodation in the gîte costs 60FF per person and there's camping for 25FF per person.

The hotel's restaurant offers a 90FF fixed-price menu that attracts hordes of hungry walkers every evening. The hotel bar sells a good range of basic foodstuffs. Credit cards are not accepted and there is only one (unreliable) phone line to the hotel.

A bus service between Corte and Porto runs once daily in each direction via Castel de Verghio.

 Calasima & Albertacce You can get to Calasima (1100m) in 1½ hours via another route from the Bergeries de Ballone. About 2km before the village you pass a memorial to three firefighters killed in an aircraft crash during a forest fire in 1979. The only facility in Calasima is the Bar du Centre but it's only another 5km downhill to Albertacce, which is on the D84. Albertacce has shops, cafés, bars and several places in which to eat, including the Restaurant Paglia Orba, the Auberge U Cintro and the popular little Chez François, all on the main road through town.

STAGE 6

Castel di Verghio (1404m) to Refuge de Manganu (1601m)

Distance: 14km
Standard: Avérage; particularly shady route
Average Duration: 5½ hours
Highest Point: 1760m
Note: Access to the villages of Soccia and Orto at the end of the stage

Summary: This easy day starts with a forest stroll, then entails a steady climb before dropping down to the beautiful Lac de Ninu. From there it's mainly downhill, past a bergerie to the night's stop. Water is available at a spring in a shrine just above Lac de Ninu. After the lake the walk follows a stream most of the way to the night's stop.

 The GR20 runs gently through pine and beech forests, dropping very slightly to 1330m before making a sharp turn to the right (west) and climbing to the small shrine at the **Bocca San Pedru** (Col de Saint Pierre; 1452m), reached after about 1½ hours.

From the pass the route continues to climb, following the carefully laid stones of an ancient mule path. There are great views off to the east of range after range of hills, while to the north the view takes in the hotel and ski runs at Castel di Verghio and the Vallée du Golo up to Paglia Orba. With binoculars it's easy to pick out the Refuge Ciottulu di i Mori. The trail climbs to a ridge, drops off it, climbs back on to it and eventually reaches the **Bocca a Reta** (1883m). It then descends to **Lac de Ninu** (1760m), about 3½ hours from the start. Surrounded by grassy meadows, the lake makes a wonderfully tranquil scene and many walkers stop for a picnic lunch. Basking in the summer sunshine it's hard to imagine the lake is frozen for five to six months of the year.

The trail continues east, following the course of the Tavignano stream draining the lake, across meadows and then through patches of beech forest past the remains of an abandoned refuge to the **Bergeries de Vaccaghja** (1621m), one to 1½ hours from the lake. The bergerie sells wine, cheese and bread. From here you can see the Refuge de Manganu, less than an hour's walk across the valley. The trail drops gently from the bergerie to the **Bocca d'Acqua Ciarnente** (1568m) and finally makes a short, sharp ascent, crossing a bridge over the Manganu stream to the refuge.

 The pleasant *Refuge de Manganu* (1601m) has 25 beds and plenty of grassy camping space around the building, good showers and toilets and a selection of tempting swimming spots in the Manganu stream. The prices are no surprise: 50FF for a bed and 20FF to camp or bivouac.

 Lac de Creno, Soccia & Orto Today's walk has been relatively easy and walkers who have not spent too much time lazing beside Lac de Ninu might consider walking down to Lac de Creno (1310m). Surrounded by pine trees the picturesque lake is a very popular short walk from the mountain village of Soccia (see the Strolls & Country Walks section later in this chapter). The route to the lake off the GR20 turns west just before the Refuge de Manganu; it takes about an hour to walk down the valley to the lake. It's a further hour's walk to a car park then a tedious 30 minutes down the road to Soccia (750m), where there's a church with a 15th century triptych. Resources for the walker are relatively limited. The *Hôtel U Pease* (☎ 04 95 28 31 92, 04 95 28 33 13) offers single/double rooms for 190/275FF. Breakfast costs 34FF. The *Bar-Restaurant Chez Louis* on the main square is the place to meet in the evenings (though despite its name it doesn't serve food). Just below the square, the *Restaurant A Merendella* (☎ 04 95 28 34 91) also proves very popular, probably because it is the only place in the village where you can get a meal. There are no shops where you can stock up, but a supplies van stops in the village almost every day.

Just beyond the lake another trail turns off to the village of Orto (700m), nestling at the foot of a steep-sided valley. Each house looks as if it is almost overhanging the one below. Orto is even more remote than Soccia; the only shop is in the *Bar Chez Titou* at the very bottom of the village.

STAGE 7

Refuge de Manganu (1601m) to Refuge de Pietra Piana (1842m)

Distance: 10km
Standard: Difficult
Average Duration: 6 hours
Highest Point: 2225m
Note: Possible to climb Monte Ritondu (2622m) at the end of the stage
Summary: Almost as spectacular as the Stage 4 crossing of the Cirque de la Solitude, the walk starts with a steep climb to a narrow pass, the highest point along the GR20. From there the walk teeters around a spectacular mountain face high above two glacial lakes before dropping down to the refuge. Water is available from streams during the first ascent and another stream on the final descent to the refuge.

 After crossing the bridge from the refuge, the GR20 immediately begins to climb, emerging onto a small meadow after 30 minutes, climbing again to another brief, horizontal break at around 1970m and then ascending even more steeply up a rocky gully. This finally becomes a scramble to the **Brèche de Capitellu** (2225m), a spectacular small slot through the spiky ridge line of peaks. Around 2½ hours from the refuge, this crossing is the highest point on the GR20 and the view to the east is breathtaking, looking out over **Lac de Capitellu** (1930m) and beyond it **Lac de Melu** (1711m). It's not immediately obvious that the two lakes are at such different levels.

The trail bends round to the south-east and edges around the eastern face of the ridge, high above the lake. Later, looking back towards this ridge, it seems impossible to believe there could be a trail there, the face seems to drop so steeply down to the lake. There's often snow on the path well into the walking season, so take great care;

High-Altitude Lakes & Pozzines

Corsica's 40-odd high-altitude lakes, formed from the glaciers that used to cover the mountains, were unknown to scientists until the 1980s but are now actively monitored by PNRC agents. A number of different analyses have shown that some are endangered by the digging of pigs and the pollution caused by tourist overpopulation in the summer. The PNRC has implemented a protection programme for the most popular lakes – Melu, Ninu and Creno – in the summer. Seasonal workers collect the rubbish left by walkers and ensure that the camping bans are upheld. The GR20 has even been diverted so that it does not contribute to the destruction of the grassy areas around Lac de Ninu. Respect the rules: no fires, no rubbish and no walking at inappropriate times.

The *pozzines* (from the Corsican *pozzi*, meaning pits) are also a fragile environment, threatened by intensive farming. Pozzines are little water holes that are linked together by small streams and are on an impermeable substratum – they're like peat bogs. They feel like a carpet of cool moss to walkers. They are found near Lac de Ninu and on the Plateau de Coscione, between the GR20 and the Refuge de la Bergeries de Bassetta.

it's a long way down. Just before another small pass at 2000m, where the trail crosses to the southern side of the ridge, another trail diverges off to the east and drops down to Lac de Capitellu. It's possible to continue down from there to Lac de Melu and then climb back up to the GR20 at the Bocca a Soglia.

The main route climbs slightly to reach the **Bocca a Soglia** (2052m), about an hour's walk from the Brèche de Capitellu. Far below you can see cars on the D623. Lots of day-trippers drive into the valley from Corte to walk up to the lakes. In the

other direction the village of Guagno is clearly visible to the south-west.

The trail then bends round to the northeast, high above Lac de Melu, climbing to the soft-edged little Bocca Rinosa (2150m) and passing Lac de Rinosa before reaching the Bocca Muzzella, or Col de la Haute Route (2206m), about five hours from the start of this stage. From here it's less than an hour, downhill all the way, to the Refuge de Pietra Piana.

 The small, 24 bed **Refuge de Pietra Piana** (1842m) is nicely situated right on the edge of the ridge, looking south down the Vallée du Manganellu. There's plenty of grassy camping space and good facilities. As usual, the beds cost 50FF, with camping and bivouacs for 20FF per person.

The refuge is used as a helicopter mountain rescue base and there's a landing pad nearby.

 Despite the tough climb at the start of the day and the spectacular walk above the two lakes, this is not a really difficult day and strong walkers may want to consider climbing **Monte Ritondu** (2622m), the second highest mountain in Corsica. This is not a technically difficult climb, although the 800m ascent may be a little tiring at the end of the day. The round-trip from the refuge takes about three hours.

Cairns mark the route to a meadow and dried-up lake just above the refuge. The trail then zigzags uphill before crossing the ridge line at 2260m, south of the peak. Don't descend from the ridge towards the small lakes below – continue north along the eastern side of the ridge, crossing patches of snow until the large **Lavu Bellebone** lake comes into view. The trail drops down to the lake's southern end and edges around the south-eastern side before starting the steep climb up the loose scree slope of the rocky gully that leads to the spiky rock marking the Col du Fer de Lance. From here the trail turns west and climbs to a small metal-roofed shelter, huddled just below the summit. There are superb views in all directions from the summit.

STAGE 8

Refuge de Pietra Piana (1842m) to Refuge de l'Onda (1430m)

Distance: 10km
Standard: Easy; route mostly shady
Average Duration: 5 hours
Highest Point: 1842m
Note: Refreshments available at the Bergeries de Gialgu and Bergerie de Tolla; possible detour to the villages of Canaglia and Tattone
Summary: An easy day's walk that starts with a fairly steep descent past a bergerie, following an ancient shepherds' route into the Vallée du Manganellu. The Bergerie de Tolla is a pleasant place at which to stop and have lunch or just a drink before starting the final ascent to the refuge. The walk follows streams almost all day so water is no problem; you can supplement it with beer and wine at the lunch stop.

 After the dramatic ascents and descents of the previous day, this stage of the walk is gentle and predominantly downhill. As soon as the trail leaves the refuge there's a choice between following the main GR20 through the Vallée du Manganellu or taking an alternative high-altitude route, marked in yellow, which follows ridge lines to the Refuge de l'Onda. The high-altitude route is quicker but less interesting.

The main GR20 starts to drop almost immediately and soon reaches the **Bergeries de Gialgu** (1609m), where bread, cheese and wine can be purchased. The trail continues to drop, following an ancient mule track of neatly laid stones that winds down the hill to the Manganellu stream at 1440m.

It then continues, through often dense forest, to the **Bergerie de Tolla** (1011m), about three hours from the start. This pleasant little haven sells the usual supplies plus other foodstuffs, and also serves snacks and meals. You can break for lunch with a classic Corsican omelette made with brocciu cheese and mint, and a glass of wine or a cold beer. If you're really hungry you can have a complete meal, with wine, for 80FF.

Just below the bergerie a bridge crosses the Manganellu stream (940m). From here you can make a detour off the GR20 to the villages of Canaglia and Tattone (see below).

The GR20 turns upstream from the bridge and almost immediately passes over the Goltaccia, which flows into the Manganellu. Do not cross this bridge but continue upstream and uphill beside the Goltaccia. Eventually the trail crosses the river and climbs away to the north side, soon reaching the busy Bergeries de l'Onda, a hive of activity next to the Refuge de l'Onda's grassy camping site. This is surrounded by fencing to keep out the many pigs poking around the site.

  The *Refuge de l'Onda* itself is higher up the hill, overlooking the bergerie and camp site from 1430m. It charges 50FF for a bed or 20FF to camp or bivouac. The bergerie sells wine, bread, cheese and sausage.

 Canaglia & Tattone It's about an hour's easy walk from the Manganellu bridge on the GR20 to the pretty village of Canaglia. The wide track running alongside the river and the string of little pools make this a popular route with walkers. There's also a road from Canaglia to the Manganellu bridge, but it's open to official vehicles only. At Canaglia's small restaurant, the *Osteria u Capitan Moru*, trout is a speciality. There's a phone in the restaurant.

From Canaglia it's 4km by road to Tattone. For a taxi call Alain (☎ 04 95 47 20 06) in Vivario. Tattone has a large hospital and is on the Bastia-Vizzavona-Ajaccio railway line. It takes just seven minutes and 8FF to get from Tattone to Vizzavona (see Stage 9) by train.

The *Bar du Soleil Camping* (☎ *04 95 47 21 16)* near the train station and charges 22FF per adult, plus 5FF to 10FF for a tent, 10FF for a car and 5FF for a motorcycle. The camp site has a snack bar and supplies and also operates a *navette* (shuttle bus). There's another camp site, *Camping Savaggio*, 2km beyond Tattone.

STAGE 9

Refuge de l'Onda (1430m) to Vizzavona (910m)

Distance: 10km
Standard: Average
Average Duration: 5½ hours
Highest Point: 2159m
Note: Alternative route via Monte d'Oro to the north
Summary: The walk to Vizzavona, traditionally the mid-point of the GR20, starts with a hard and often rocky ascent followed by a descent that starts off equally rocky and bare before reaching the woods around the series of waterfalls and pools known as the Cascades des Anglais. There are plentiful supplies of water during the long descent and Vizzavona, with its train station, hotels, restaurants and cafés is the best-equipped stop along the GR20.

 The route sets off northwards, following the high-level alternative route to the Refuge de Pietra Piana, but soon doubles back to head south up the long climb to the **Crête de Muratellu** (2020m), reached after two to 2½ hours. From this bleak height the rest of the day's walk is a long downhill descent.

An alternative route, marked only by stone cairns, continues up the Crête de

Rubbish & the Environment

Despite all efforts, rubbish is a problem on the GR20. From one end to the other the route is littered with rubbish, empty tins – especially sardine tins – tissues, cigarette ends and, last but not least, toilet paper.

The problem is exacerbated by the lack of sanitation facilities along the route. Camping is restricted to the areas around the refuges and a few of the bergeries. The bergeries do not, as a rule, have any sanitation facilities, and the toilets in the refuges are famously inadequate (about one toilet for every 100 campers), if they work at all.

Muratellu and turns slightly north-east to the **Bocca di u Porcu** (2159m), from where it turns south-east to climb to the summit of **Monte d'Oro** (2389m), the fifth highest mountain in Corsica. There are stretches of difficult rock climbing on this route, which should not be attempted by the inexperienced. It finally rejoins the main GR20 route just before Vizzavona and adds about three hours to the day's walk.

The main GR20 makes a steep and rocky descent from the Muratellu ridge into the upper heights of the Vallée de l'Agnone. The descent becomes less steep and the surroundings greener as the route drops below 1600m and passes the remains of an abandoned refuge at 1500m. The trail passes a high waterfall as it reaches the **Cascades des Anglais** (1150m), roughly four hours from the start. On this stretch you'll see day walkers coming up to the enticing rock pools of the waterfalls. The trail continues through pine forests, sometimes high above the tumbling stream. Monte d'Oro broods over this scene from the north-east.

A snack bar and a **bridge** over the Agnone hint at the proximity of civilisation, and from here into Vizzavona the route makes the transition from walking path to track quite suitable for cars. There are several turns, several bridges and what seems like an interminable trudge before the trail finally emerges on to the road right in the middle of the village of Vizzavona, only a short distance from the train station.

Vizzavona (910m) is a tiny health spa at the foot of the massive Monte d'Oro, and traditionally represents the pivotal point between the northern and southern sections of the GR20. Those who tackle the whole of the GR20 consider it a welcome return to civilisation and generally make the most of the opportunity to restock with provisions and have a decent meal and a good night's sleep in a hotel. Some people finish their walk here while others start it in one direction or the other. Vizzavona is situated at the heart of one of the prettiest forests in Corsica, which is largely made up of laricio pines and beech trees and, together with the surrounding area, provides an excellent setting for a number of well-marked forest walks.

  Hôtel I Laricci (☎/*fax 04 95 47 21 12*) is open from the beginning of April to the end of October. It looks like a big Swiss chalet, and has 12 spacious, renovated rooms that cost 270FF with shower and toilet, 240FF without. Half the rooms have a spectacular view of Monte d'Oro. It's worth booking ahead as the hotel is very much in demand. Fortunately, it has an annexe with three six-bed dormitories costing 145FF per person including an evening meal. There are hot showers and you can do washing for 50FF. The hotel has a big dining room where you will find a simple yet generous fixed-price menu for 85FF. The owners can give good advice on how best to get to know the area on foot. The hotel takes credit cards.

Just opposite the station is the *Resto Refuge de la Gare* (☎ *04 95 47 22 20*), home to a restaurant and two renovated dormitories that are clean and simple and accommodate six people each (60FF per person per night). Meals are optional (there's a fixed-price menu for about 70FF), but there are no self-catering facilities. This

friendly, family-run establishment is open from the beginning of June to the end of September; exact dates depend on how busy it is.

Hôtel Monte d'Oro (☎ 04 95 47 21 06, 04 95 47 23 44, fax 04 95 47 22 05) is an old hotel full of nooks and crannies. It is 3km to the south-west of the village, in the hamlet of Foce, just before the Col de Vizzavona. If you're staying at this hotel, you can leave the GR20 at the Cascades des Anglais and join the N193 at Foce. Alternatively, the hotel will send a shuttle to pick you up if you ring from Vizzavona station. Single/double rooms cost 200/260FF with shared toilet, 250/340FF with shower and toilet and 290/380FF with bathroom. Half board is available. The hotel also has a refuge (60FF per person per night) and a gîte (75FF, or 175FF half board).

Above the N193, at the northern entrance to the town, is **Casa Alta**, which offers bed and breakfast accommodation. This can be a good alternative to Hôtel I Laricci (which is often full) and Hôtel Monte d'Oro (which is some way from the centre).

Campers tend to pitch their tents on a flat piece of land behind the station, which is often full to bursting in summer. It is free to camp here but there are no toilets or washing facilities. An official camp site is being considered.

You can do some serious stocking up at **Épicerie Rosy**, which is in the station itself and run by Madame Zagnoli. It's open from 7.30 am daily, including Sunday and public holidays, and sells everything walkers could want at reasonable prices: Corsican delicacies, freeze-dried foods (38FF), films, bread, cold drinks (between 10FF and 13FF), everyday food supplies, gas refills, batteries and first aid equipment. Credit cards are not accepted.

Just opposite is the **Restaurant-Bar l'Altagna**, which has fixed-price menus for 65FF and 85FF. Local specialities and snacks are also served all day.

There's a telephone box and a post box next to the station, and another phone box next to Hôtel Monte d'Oro.

The train between Ajaccio and Bastia stops at Vizzavona four times a day in each direction. Two of the services continue beyond Bastia to Île Rousse and Calvi.

From Vizzavona, tickets cost 8FF to Tattone, 39FF to Ajaccio, 26FF to Corte, 102FF to Calvi, 82FF to Bastia, 86FF to Île Rousse and 46FF to Ponte Leccia.

STAGE 10

Vizzavona (910m) to Bergeries de Capannelle (1586m)

Distance: 13.5km
Standard: Average
Average Duration: 5½ hours
Highest Point: 1647m
Note: Access to the village of Ghisoni
Summary: This section of the walk is punctuated by magnificent views as you approach Monte Renosu against a background of laricio pine and beech trees.

 From the station in Vizzavona, follow the marked route for the GR20 Sud, which passes in front of Hôtel I Laricci. It crosses the access path to the GR20 Nord on the right and then crosses a little bridge before climbing up to rejoin the N193 and the ONF (Office National des Forêts; National Office for Forests) house. A sign tells you that Bergeries de Capannelle is 4½ hours away, but this is somewhat optimistic. This sign marks the beginning of the dirt track that climbs gently through the woods. Here and there you will come across holly bushes several metres high, lost among the pine trees. The trail goes left at a fork (the right fork leads to a spring after about 450m): you will catch your first glimpse of the **Forêt de Vizzavona** and Monte d'Oro behind you and you'll still be able to hear the faint rumble of the waterfalls.

The route quickly leaves the dirt track behind and makes a twisting ascent up to a high-voltage power cable that marks the start of a long, flat trek through the undergrowth. The pleasant shade from the beech trees is now a thing of the past. The steep little path leads straight ahead until it reaches a junction: here the GR20 goes off to your left, but make a detour 100m down the right fork for a wonderful view of Monte d'Oro and Vizzavona below.

Back on the GR20, the path soon emerges from the undergrowth into a bare, almost lunar landscape from where you can see the **Bocca Palmente** (1647m) ahead. Pay attention to the markings and the junction where the GR20 turns right to get to the pass. If you carry straight on you'll end up at the Palmente spring, about 200m from the GR20. After a 15 minute climb, there's a cairn to indicate that you're almost at the pass. Behind you is the dark silhouette of Monte d'Oro; ahead is the Oculo ridge in the foreground and behind it the Cardo ridge and little **Monte Calvi** (1461m).

The path goes back down towards the **Bergeries d'Alzeta** before continuing on the level. After about 30 minutes a hairpin bend marks the left turn-off that leads to Ghisoni, where you can stop off. This is an ideal spot for a picnic, with a stunning view over the Monte Renosu massif.

 Ghisoni (665m) A wooden sign for Ghisoni on the left marks the spot where the route down to the village diverges from the GR20. The path, which is marked with yellow lines, leads down to the Bergeries de Cardu (where there is a building that can be used as a basic shelter) before crossing a plain. Follow the winding path to the left of the plain (ignore the yellow and blue markings off to the right). It continues through a little forest of maritime pines and over a

canal used to irrigate the gardens of Ghisoni in the 19th century. Before long, you will come to the D69, which, if you turn right, leads to the village. Allow 1½ to two hours to get down to the village and three hours to climb back up again. The change in altitude is 850m.

The peaceful village of Ghisoni makes an ideal stop-off. Nestling at the foot of **Punta Kyrie Eleïson** (1535m), the village awakes from hibernation in the summer when its children return from Bastia or Ajaccio, or even the mainland. As you walk down the streets lined with pretty stone houses, it is easy to see what Ghisoni was like before WWII: there were no less than three dance halls, 12 cafés and an average of 1800 inhabitants year-round (compare to the current figures of 200 in winter and 3000 in summer). At that time Ghisoni's income came primarily from chestnut flour and from exploiting the forest, particularly the laricio pine.

There are shops all along the D344, the main road through the village. Walkers wishing to stay here have two options: *Camping Municipal*, at the intersection of the D69 and the D344, which is simply a sloping piece of land made available to campers and where the only sanitation facility is the communal wash house just below; or *Hôtel Kyrie* (☎ 04 95 57 60 33,

---

Water, Water ...

Water and thirst can be real problems on the GR20. You will be able to find water at every refuge, but between stops there are very few sources of drinking water. These have been detailed in the text. It is a good idea to be cautious and carry water with you (2L per person is the absolute minimum). As far as water from streams is concerned, safety is not guaranteed: do not use it unless strictly necessary and, if possible, purify it using water purification tablets.

fax 04 95 57 63 15), which has 30 slightly old-fashioned but clean rooms with showers and toilets. Double, triple and quadruple rooms range in price from 200FF to 300FF. The hotel is open from the end of April to 10 October and has a restaurant with fixed-price menus for 100FF or 150FF.

For pizza lovers, the *Pizzeria Guy (☎ 04 95 57 60 74)* has recently opened at the bottom of the village, opposite the fire station. It serves good pizzas for 40FF to 50FF and plans to be open year-round. The décor is conventional but the service is friendly. The *Libre-Service Micheli (☎ 04 95 57 60 39)*, with the Super JP/Tabac sign, next to the old church, opens from 9 am to noon and 4.30 to 7 pm daily except Sunday, year-round. It's a grocery selling tinned food, fresh produce, Corsican specialities and supplies for walkers (except freeze-dried foods).

There are no bus services from Ghisoni. You have to hitch to Ghisonaccia (28km south-east) or Vivario (21km north-west) for both national and local buses.

Ghisoni has a post office, open from 8.50 am to noon and 1.50 to 4.30 pm Monday to Friday (8.50 to 11.30 am on Saturday), and two telephone boxes.

 The GR20 continues along the hillside and goes through a forest of laricio pines, some of which are an impressive size. About 1¼ hours later it reaches the three charming **Bergeries de Scarpaccedie** which, surprisingly, have sanitation facilities and electrical equipment.

A short distance on, the route bears to the right. Take a few deep breaths, as the next stretch involves a change in altitude of 150m and a good 20 minutes of solid effort, for which you will be rewarded with a wonderful view of **Monte Renosu** (2352m). The route then follows a metalled road uphill for about 100m before coming to a sign detailing the services available at the **Bergeries de Capannelle** (1586m): straight ahead, the Gîte U Renosu boasts of its hot showers, while the Gîte U Fugone, to the left, coun-

ters with the delights of its draught beer. The two gîtes are 300m apart and your best bet is to go left, as the U Renosu is often shut in the summer.

It's a 20 minute walk to the bergeries, which are at the foot of the ski lifts in the resort of Ghisoni. Although there is only one remaining shepherd, all the bergeries were kept by local families and now serve as cottages for holidaymakers and hunters. They were once lost amid beech forests, but the trees have now been cut down to clear the ski slopes. When the snow melts, the water takes everything in its path with it, which explains why the slopes look so desolate in summer.

 Just before the Gîte U Fugone is the *PNRC refuge*. It is made entirely of stone and is somewhat dubious in terms of comfort. Two planks support 10 mattresses and the décor consists of one gas stove and a few saucepans. One night costs 35FF per person, collected by the warden of the Gîte U Fugone. Whether you stay here or not, it is worth having a look at the PNRC information here about the rest of the GR20.

The *Gîte U Fugone (☎ 04 95 57 01 81)*, run by Paul Maurizi and his wife and open from mid-May to mid-September, is much better value. It's a large building that looks like a high-altitude restaurant and houses dormitories for three to five people. The rooms have recently been renovated and have toilets and hot showers. One night will set you back 55FF (half board 158FF). Those staying at the PNRC refuge can come here for a shower, although it will cost an extra 15FF. There is a little grocery selling basic foodstuffs and a restaurant with fixed-price menus based on Corsican specialities for 60FF and 95FF.

The *Gîte U Renosu*, 300m away, is generally only open in winter. There is a signed walk from the Bergeries de Capannelle to Lac de Bastani, which takes about 2½ hours. It is even possible to climb Monte Renosu from the lake.

STAGE 11

Bergeries de Capannelle (1586m) to Bocca di Verdi (1289m)

Distance: 11.5km
Standard: Average
Average Duration: 5 hours
Highest Point: 1591m
Summary: This stage is relatively short and easy. It skirts the Monte Renosu massif to the east but mostly remains on a plain at an average altitude of 1500m, eventually reaching the Bocca di Verdi. This is the last stop-off point before a series of ridges.

 The route begins at the foot of the ski lift and rapidly retreats into a forest of beech trees that suggest the Bergeries de Capannelle must have been in an idyllic setting before the construction of the ski resort.

It will take you less than 30 minutes to reach the **Bergeries de Traggette** (1520m) and the D169. Fifty metres further on there is a sign to the Bocca di Verdi and the route heads uphill again. There are views over the Fiumorbu region and the Kyrie Eleïson range before the path penetrates a thick forest of pine and beech trees frequented by both wild boar and hunters (if the large numbers of cartridges on the ground are to be believed).

After 45 minutes in the undergrowth, the GR20 rounds a hairpin bend to the right. When the snow is melting you will have to cross a string of streams here, some of which require more acrobatic skills to traverse than others. Another 45 minutes later there's a second hairpin bend, this time in the open.

You are now halfway through the day's walk and right next to **Punta Capannella** (2032m); above you, the Lischetto stream, which flows from the little Lacs de Rina (1882m), cascades down in a profusion of little waterfalls. These little torrents from the eastern face of Monte Renosu converge

a few kilometres downstream to form the Fiumorbu river.

Once you have crossed the **Lischettu**, it will not take more than 30 minutes to get to the **Plateau de Gialgone** (1591m), from where the view over the Bocca di Verdi is invigorating. In front of you is **Monte Grossu** (1895m) and, at the edge of the plain, a wooden sign directs you to the Pozzi, a magnificent grassy plain that may be worth the detour (allow two hours to get there and back).

The GR20 itself carries straight on towards Bocca di Verdi and begins an impressive descent that culminates some 30 minutes later in a little wooden bridge straddling the Marmanu stream, which flows from the Fiumorbu.

A few metres on, a simple wooden sign on the ground indicates a giant fir tree that rises to the amazing height of 53.2m. The path remains flat and enters the undergrowth of beeches before turning to the right and widening out in the middle of a forest of fir trees. After about 20 minutes the trail reaches a large picnic area.

To the right is a path through the forest which goes to the village of Palneca, while a path to the left leads to the **Bocca di Verdi** (Col de Verde) after about 300m.

  Relais San Pedru di Verde (☎ 04 95 24 46 82), better known as the Refuge du Col de Verde, is in a lush green setting on the edge of the D69. It's open from 1 May to the end of September and has capacity for 24 people. It's fairly basic: a wooden cottage equipped with a stove, a table and three wooden planks supporting mattresses. However, there is absolutely nothing wrong with the sanitation facilities and the shower is hot.

A night will set you back 40FF, but camping is free. One of the best things about this refuge is its lovely terrace, where you can treat yourself to generous salads for about 30FF, sandwiches (25FF) and drinks (13FF). In the evening grilled meats and pizzas are on offer.

The Return of the Corsican Stag

The Corsican stag (*Cervus elaphus corsicanus*) first came to the island in ancient times and was widespread – several place names, including Cervioni and Punta di u Cervu, bear witness to this. Relentlessly poached, it finally disappeared from the island in the 1960s.

In 1985 the PNRC went to Sardinia, where the species still lives in the wild, collected two stags and two does and brought them back to a protected enclosure in Quenza. The animals reproduced, and there are now more than 100 stags on Corsican soil, in three enclosures.

The first stags were released into the wild on 3 February 1998, near Quenza. The organisers of the project are optimistic about the species' chances of survival, although poaching remains a threat, as do wild boars, foxes and stray dogs, to the fawns.

STAGE 12

Bocca di Verdi (1289m) to Refuge d'Usciolu (1750m)

Distance: 14km
Standard: Difficult; not much shade; very steep sections and sometimes high winds on the ridges
Average Duration: 7 to 7½ hours
Highest Point: 1981m
Summary: This long stage could be called the 'ridge route'. From the Bocca di Verdi, the trail climbs up to a ridge and continues along it at between 1500m and 2000m almost as far as the Refuge d'Usciolu. At the Bocca di Laparu (1525m) it cuts across the Mare a Mare Centre walk. You almost feel as if you are flying over the region, with spectacular views over Fiumorbu to the east and the Taravu valley to the west.

 After crossing a minor road, the trail climbs gently up into a pine forest. But this doesn't last long: 10 minutes later the GR20 turns off to the left and begins the assault on the mountain. It will take 20 minutes of sustained effort to reach an intermediate plateau, the end of the first section. Looking down to the bottom of the valley you can see the village of Palneca. A stream marks the start of the second steep section (which is at least shaded by beech trees) and after 20 minutes your final goal comes into view.

After another 35 minutes of tough climbing up a steep rocky path exposed to the sun, the trail reaches the **Bocca d'Oru** (1840m), from where there is an excellent view over the eastern plain. If you turn around, you can look back with satisfaction at the distance that you have already travelled on the GR20. You can also make out the chain of Monte Ritondu, Monte d'Oro and Monte Renosu.

A very pleasant walk then leads, after about 15 minutes, to the **Refuge de Prati** (1820m), or at least what is left of it: the refuge was destroyed by lightning in 1997, but there are plans to start rebuilding it in the summer of 1999. It is well worth filling your flask at the refuge's water fountain, as there are no other water sources for the rest of the stage and there's a long way to go yet. The GR20 follows the path to the right (a path to the left marked out in yellow goes down to the village of Isolacciu di Fiumorbu, 1km below to the east) and leads straight on to the ridges.

The stretch of very steep slope only lasts about 20 minutes, but the path remains steep and rocky afterwards. There is a breathtaking bird's-eye view of the villages of Palneca, Ciamannacce and Cozzano, more than 1km below. To the left (east) you can clearly see the village of Prunelli di Fiumorbu, perched up high, and Ghisonaccia down on the plain.

Make the most of the view because you will need all your strength to negotiate the path as it continues its climb through large rocks. This section only lasts 30 minutes, but will prove testing for walkers who suffer from vertigo and could be dangerous in bad weather conditions – so take great care. For the next 1¼ hours the path along the ridge is rock and difficult, coming very close to some frightening precipices at times.

Once past **Punta di a Cappella** (2042m), the trail skirts round the Rocher de la Penta before moving off the ridge and into a little forest that is an ideal spot for a picnic. From here it's less than 30 minutes to the **Bocca di Laparu** (1525m), where the route crosses the Mare a Mare Centre walk (Ghisonaccia to Porticcio). There's a sign to a spring and near this is a very basic refuge (no warden; closed at time of research).

 Cozzano The route from the Bocca di Laparu to Cozzano (about 2½ hours walk) forms part of the Mare a Mare Centre route; see the section on this walk, which also details the tourist resources available in Cozzano, later in this chapter.

 After the pass, the trail continues along the ridge, this time climbing steadily up to **Monte Formicula** (1981m), the highest point of the day and a little less than 500m above Laparu. Allow between 1¾ and two hours for the climb. The setting is magnificent: the vegetation thins out as the altitude increases and the path makes its way through a rocky and chaotic, almost lunar, landscape.

The route initially goes along the eastern side of the ridge before crossing over to the windier western side. Once past Monte Formicula, it is not much further to the Refuge d'Usciolu (roughly 30 to 45 minutes), and rather like a Sunday afternoon walk, it's downhill all the way. The path returns to the eastern side, overlooking a vast grassy plain littered with piles of stones to mark out pastures. It continues along the line of the ridge before tackling the descent itself, first towards this plain, then down to the Refuge d'Usciolu.

  Leaning against the mountain, the *Refuge d'Usciolu* has a bird's-eye view over the whole valley. To the south the valley is dominated by the majestic stature of Monte Incudine (2134m), which almost seems to be within reach. The refuge has 32 beds (50FF) and is clean and well kept. The camp site is just below the refuge (20FF per person). The warden offers light refreshments – sheep's milk cheese (40FF), drinks (13FF), sausage, chocolate and hard-boiled eggs.

STAGE 13

Refuge d'Usciolu (1750m) to Refuge d'Asinao (1530m)

Distance: 14.5km
Standard: Average
Average Duration: 7½ to 8 hours
Highest Point: 2134m
Note: It's possible to do this stage over two days, with a detour to the village of Zicavo or a stop-off at the Bergeries de Bassetta or the Auberge de la Passerelle, climbing Monte Incudine on the second day.
Summary: The stage begins with a walk through the skies, as you stay on the line of the ridge for at least two hours before climbing down to the crossroads at the Bocca di l'Agnonu. From there the trail crosses the undulating Plateau de Coscione before starting the climb up Monte Incudine (2134m), the highest point on the southern section of the GR20. This is followed by a steep descent towards the Refuge d'Asinao.

 A short, steep path from the refuge leads back up to the ridge. There's a sign to Cozzano, where it is possible, but not very practical, to stop off. From here it's a tightrope walk along the **ridge**, which is particularly steep at this stage, for a good two hours. All this time Monte Incudine is ahead of you.

There is little change in altitude, but traversing the slabs of rock can prove very difficult; at times you also have to squeeze through blocks of rock and heaps of knife-like granite. The altitude is an almost constant 1800m, but the trail goes up and down in a continual series of tiny ascents and descents, making the going very hard. This is exacerbated by the lack of shade.

The signs along the route are not always easy to find in the midst of this vast lunar landscape. However, the views over the Taravu valley to the west, the pastures on the plain to the east and, of course, Monte Incudine ahead to the south are sublime.

There's not much in the way of flora on this stretch, which is nothing but smooth, bare rock for more than two hours.

The trail passes a distinctive U-shaped gap, then climbs down towards a wooded area (beeches) on the western side of the ridge. Vegetation appears again. The shrubs and heather are gradually replaced by beech trees.

After about three hours you'll reach a wonderful, huge clearing – an ideal spot for a picnic. It is surrounded by little streams and the trunks of trees struck down in storms, along with majestic beech trees, which provide some very welcome shade. The pastoral setting is in stark contrast to the barren austerity of the route along the top of the ridge. There's also a spring (which is signposted). About 10 minutes from here the trail reaches the crossroads at the **Bocca di l'Agnonu**, about 3¼ hours from the start of this stage.

At the crossroads there's a sign for Asinao, and written underneath in red paint is '*Ravitaillement, gîte, camping à 1 heure*' (Refreshments, accommodation, camping – 1 hour). This refers to the Auberge de la Passerelle, but the time is an underestimate.

Zicavo & the Chapelle San Petru From Bocca di l'Agnonu, you can leave the GR20

and make a detour to the village of Zicavo in the Taravu valley, a walk of less than three hours. Turn off at the sign, following the yellow markings. The route is pleasant, downhill and in the shade most of the way. The path follows a large S shape and is not particularly difficult, but remain vigilant because the signs and the path are not always clear. About two-thirds of the way down (about two hours into the walk) the trail emerges onto a variant route of the Mare a Mare Centre route (orange markings), which it follows as far as Zicavo. The main Mare a Mare Centre route is described later in this chapter.

Zicavo is a pretty village that stretches out along the mountainside at an altitude of 750m. For a long time it relied on agricultural and pastoral activities and served as a base for the shepherds going up to the Plateau de Coscione (see the boxed text 'A Jewel Set in the Mountains'). Those days are gone now and Zicavo relies on tourism.

The history of the village is intimately linked to the Albatucci family, many members of which (including a general) were close to the two Napoleons. The main road through the village is cours Albatucci, and you are sure to be able to find someone who will show you the family home. The village is full of splendid, imposing buildings made of grey granite. The feeling of past greatness and fallen nobility is still tangible today.

Zicavo is an oasis for walkers. The hotels are excellent and the little shops are well stocked. For those wishing to stay here, there are walks to hot springs and nearby villages during which you can discover the Haut Taravu valley in more depth.

At the GR20 end of the village there's a little *gîte d'étape* (☎ 04 95 24 42 13) with six beds. It's clean and functional, well equipped and charges 70FF (inquire at the bar opposite). A short distance away is the *Hôtel-Restaurant du Tourisme* (☎ 04 95 24 40 06), which is very comfortable, is open year-round and has double rooms (with toilet and shower) for around 200FF. At the restaurant there's a choice of fixed-

A Jewel Set in the Mountains

The GR20 crosses a section of the Plateau de Coscione between the Bocca di l'Agnonu and Monte Incudine. This vast expanse of land is actually a mosaic of different environments, which gives the plain a distinct character: beech groves, streams, pozzines, moors, meadows and heaps of fallen rocks all follow one another at an average altitude of 1400m, and the whole plateau is overshadowed by the towering silhouette of Monte Incudine (2134m).

In August, when the monkshood is in bloom, the Plateau de Coscione is strewn with patches of violet. The topography of the plateau, with its gentle oscillations, its terraces and its little valleys, is in stark contrast to the rest of the GR20, where the relief is distinctly less friendly. Walkers tend to think of the walk across the Plateau de Coscione as a welcome respite before the ascent of Monte Incudine.

The Plateau de Coscione is not just a pleasant pastoral scene: it is also important in socio-economic terms as grazing land where pastoral activity has, to a certain extent, survived. You will come across pigs, cattle, sheep and goats. Only a few decades ago, shepherds would come from all over southern Corsica to graze their flocks here in summer. In the early 20th century nearly 600 people lived on the plateau. Those days are long gone, and all that remains is the myth of the Corsican shepherd. The last real Coscione shepherd died in 1997. Today his modern-day counterparts bring their livestock onto the plain in cattle trucks, returning to inspect them every week in their 4WDs. However, some traditions have endured, including the annual shepherds' fair in the village of Zicavo, held in the Chapelle San Petru at the beginning of August. Livestock is blessed during the festival, which would once have attracted more than 1000 people.

In winter the plateau is frequented by cross-country skiers, although there is not always enough snow for skiing.

If you really want to appreciate all the rustic aspects of the Plateau de Coscione, it is worth taking the alternative route via Zicavo and the Chapelle San Petru, or making a detour to the Refuge de la Bergeries de Bassetta, about 1¼ hours to the west of the GR20. This will give you the opportunity to set foot on the pozzines (see the boxed text earlier in this chapter), the water-filled peat bogs that make you feel as if you are walking on a fine English lawn.

---

price menus (home cooking using Corsican products) for 70FF, 100FF and 120FF.

Five minutes away on the D69 towards Cozzano, just after Chapelle Saint Roch, is the *Gîte Le Paradis* (☎ 04 95 24 41 20), run by Louise Pirany, a former teacher who will give you a warm welcome. A night in a room for two, three or four people costs up to 60FF per person. It is also possible to camp in the garden (40FF, with access to the showers). Half board costs 160FF and Madame Pirany prepares Corsican specialities, including a myrtle liqueur and excellent home-made cooked meats. About 100m further on is *Hôtel Le Florida* (☎ 04 95 24 43 11, 04 95 24 40 24), a comfortable hotel that has double rooms with/without bathroom for 160/200FF and fixed-price menus for 90FF and 120FF. Half board is good value at 180FF. Die-hard campers can pitch their tents at the *camp site* (☎ 04 95 24 40 87) run by José Fratini, 1km from the village towards Cozzano. It has hot showers and charges 25FF per person.

If you head south on the D69 you cannot miss the *Pacifique Sud*, a bar-restaurant-pizzeria just beyond the grocery. You can choose between pizzas (from 30FF to 50FF), fixed-price menus for 60FF and 80FF and omelettes for 25FF. On some evenings there's a good atmosphere around the bar.

There's a small, well-stocked *grocery* between Hôtel-Restaurant du Tourisme and Pacifique Sud. It's open from 8 am to 12.15 pm and 3 to 7.30 pm daily from mid-May to mid-September. The owner, Jacques Lusinchi, does everything he can to help walkers. The *bakery* and the post office are both further down in the village.

Autocars Santini provides a service between Ajaccio and Zicavo daily except Sunday (70FF).

To return to the GR20, there is an alternative route south via the Chapelle San Petru and over the most beautiful part of the Plateau de Coscione (the section of the GR20 between Bocca di l'Agnonu and the junction with this route is not as spectacular). From Zicavo, follow the D69 southwards for 1.5km until the path turns off to the left.

Simpler still is to get a lift to the Refuge de la Bergeries de Bassetta (see the Half-stage section below), which is accessible by road (the D69 then the D428). Ask Jacques the grocer, who goes up there almost every day with supplies, or Toussaint Franceschi, the owner of the Refuge de la Bergerie de Bassetta, who often goes backwards and forwards between the refuge and the village. This will save you a 600m change in altitude that is not particularly interesting and entails several hours of walking. From Bassetta, follow the D428 for 1.5km as far as the Chapelle San Petru, where you can make the most of the charming setting and the picnic site.

The trail (which is marked with yellow lines and cairns) is concealed behind the chapel and climbs up to meet a path wide enough for a 4WD in about 20 minutes. It continues to the Refuge de Matalza (very basic: no warden, no water) before reaching the most interesting part of the Coscione, then heads due east to rejoin the GR20, with the massive silhouette of Monte Incudine in the background. Watch carefully for the signs, or you could make any number of wrong turnings. After 1¼ to 1½ hours of easy walking, the route rejoins the GR20 (roughly one hour south of Bocca di l'Agnonu).

 The main route from Bocca di l'Agnonu continues among the beeches for about 20 minutes, leading to an overhang from where there is a wonderful view over the Coscione and, in the background, the imposing spectacle of Monte Incudine. The trail then moves out of the hedges and rapidly leads onto the hilly plain, which is dotted with groves, grassy moors, streams and rocky masses. You have to ford a number of little streams running through the mini depressions carved into the plateau. The route is easy until it reaches the foot of Monte Incudine. Make the most of this because Monte Incudine, which looms ever nearer, is the main item on the day's agenda. After about an hour the trail reaches the junction with the alternative route via Zicavo and the **Refuge de la Bergeries de Bassetta**, 1½ hours walk to the west. There is a sign indicating that the Auberge de la Passerelle is 200m away. Follow the GR20 towards Asinao (signposted); it will take less than 15 minutes to get to the Casamintellu stream and the Auberge de la Passerelle, just next to it.

 Half-stage You have two options if you do not want your day to culminate with the ascent of Monte Incudine.

The first alternative is on the GR20 itself. The private refuge *Auberge de la Passerelle*, essentially a group of wooden shacks on the edge of the Casamintellu stream, is run by Maurice and Jacques, a couple of friendly characters originally from Zicavo. The refuge stands out in comparison with the PNRC refuges: where the others simply sell a few refreshments, this one is a veritable Ali Baba's cave: biscuits, chocolate, soup sachets, cheese, sausage, bread, pâté, hard-boiled eggs, apples and hot and cold drinks – including an aniseed liqueur for 10FF – are all available. And this is not all

Bergeries, or shepherds' huts, provide mountain accommodation.

Suspension bridge.

The view from Monte Ritondu (2622m), Corsica's second highest mountain.

The Refuge de Paliri (1055m).

Approaching Monte Incudine (2134m) on the ridges of the GR20.

The Punta Pinzuta stream between the Refuge de Paliri and Conca on the last stage of the GR20

– they also provide a generous meal of salad, wild boar casserole and pasta for 60FF. There's also a water point. However, the accommodation proves to be basic. The dormitory sleeps 10 (30FF a night) and camping is free. Sanitation facilities are sadly lacking and you will have to make do with a makeshift shower (cold).

The second option is the ***Refuge de la Bergeries de Bassetta*** *(☎ 04 95 25 74 20, 04 95 24 44 50)*, roughly 1½ hours walk off the GR20 (with only a slight change in altitude). This private refuge is an old converted bergerie impeccably run by Toussaint Franceschi and his wife; it is well worth the detour to see its wonderful setting in the most rural part of the Plateau de Coscione. The refuge is 1.5km from the Chapelle San Petru and is also accessible by road from Zicavo, which is about 14km away along the D428 and D69. It costs 60FF (or 150FF half board and 210FF full board). Excellent meals cost 100FF and refreshments are 10FF. The meals are served in a big communal room, with a fireplace decorated with photos of Corsican bandits. There is a dormitory in the main building (18 beds), as well as a smart annexe.

 After the Auberge de la Passerelle, the trail crosses a rickety wooden footbridge over the Casamintellu and the ascent of Monte Incudine begins. As you climb the slope, the beech trees thin out and the landscape becomes more barren. After climbing for about 30 minutes, you reach the ***Aire de Bivouac I Pedinieddi***. This little plateau used to be home to the Refuge de Pedinieddi, until it was destroyed by lightning. It's possible to bivouac here and there is a water supply. After this plateau, the climb continues, often passing through heaps of fallen rocks. Behind you is a magnificent view over the Coscione and the little overlapping valleys.

About one hour's walk from the footbridge, you reach the **Bocca di Luana** (1800m), which is on a ridge. The route turns to the right and begins to climb the

ridge leading to the summit. To the east (left) you can see down the steep-sided valley, with the Tremoli running at the bottom of the barren, rocky scenery. The climb is quite difficult, but there is a 15 minute detour to the west, which brings you to a flat section where you can catch your breath for a little while. After just over two hours of climbing, the cross on the summit of **Monte Incudine**, at 2134m, comes into view. It is not uncommon for there to be névés at this altitude in the month of June.

All that's left now is the descent to the refuge. The first 15 minutes is an easy walk along the ridge. The trail reaches a junction and you can see what lies ahead: the path plummets down to the refuge 500m below. The slope really is impressive, and your joints will certainly feel it.

The path follows the ridge to the east before diving to the south and twisting its way down to the refuge. Allow 1¼ to 1½ hours to climb down from the summit before you can set your rucksack down at the Refuge d'Asinao.

 Refuge d'Asinao (1530m) only has room for 20 people. It costs 50FF (camping 20FF) and sells basic refreshments (cooked meats, honey, cheese, beer and wine). From the refuge you can see the Bergeries d'Asinao below; they are still used and bivouacking is not allowed here.

STAGE 14

Refuge d'Asinao (1530m) to Refuge de Paliri (1055m), via alpine route

Distance: 13km
Standard: Difficult (tricky sections on alpine route); lack of shade when crossing the Bavella massif
Average Duration: 6¼ hours
Highest Point: 1662m

Note: Optional half-stage at the Bocca di Bavella; access to the village of Quenza; alternative route which skirts around the Bavella massif

Summary: One of the most beautiful stages of the southern GR20, the highlight of which is the Aiguilles de Bavella, which can be crossed on the alpine route.

The path continues southwards, overhanging the Vallée de l'Asinao while still shaded by trees, then turns east to the Bavella massif and leads to the path of the same name (1218m). It then continues eastwards and reaches a little depression (1022m) before crossing a mountainous ridge, behind which is the refuge. You will pass from green surroundings to a granite lunar landscape.

 Do not expect to pass the Bergeries d'Asinao, which are below the refuge to the south. The path heads west before gradually changing direction towards the south to reach the valley, where you ford the Asinao after about 30 minutes walk. The descent is gradual and passes through a wooded section dominated by pine trees.

The shape of the Vallée de l'Asinao can be seen clearly; downstream (towards Quenza) the valley widens out, while upstream it becomes very steep. Less than 10 minutes before, you will have passed a sign upstream indicating the path to Quenza, three hours away.

 Quenza The village of Quenza (813m) is actually between three and four hours walk from the GR20 (and a descent of roughly 500m). There's a multitude of reasons to make this detour. The access route (marked in yellow) may be long but it is easy (two-thirds of the path is forest track), the tourist resources are first class and the village itself is a real jewel along the Mare a Mare Sud trail, at the heart of a region with its own inimitable style.

Quenza also has an excellent reputation as a base for leisure pursuits such as walking, pony trekking and canyoning.

To the north of the village is *I Muntagnoli Corsi* (☎ 04 95 78 64 05), which acts as a refuge between the end of May and the end of September. Half board is obligatory and costs 180FF per person; campers pay 20FF per person and 5FF per tent. The refuge has a restaurant service (dinner 100FF, packed lunch 45FF) and serves as a base for leisure activities. There are qualified guides for day-long walks (150FF), canyoning (300FF per person) and canoeing.

If you prefer more luxurious accommodation, head for *Hôtel Sole e Monte* (☎ 04 95 78 62 53, fax 04 95 78 63 88), a two star hotel where the restaurant has a very good reputation. It's at the eastern end of the village, on the main road from Porto Vecchio and Zonza (D420). Single/double rooms with all mod-cons cost between 300FF and 500FF. In the restaurant you can choose between a variety of fixed-price menus (from 150FF) and an extensive à la carte menu with an emphasis on game specialities.

The stables at *Chez Pierrot*, in the isolated hamlet of Jallicu about 5km northwest of Quenza, are an interesting setting. The rooms are functional and clean and sleep four, six or eight people. Half board is obligatory (180FF per person; 20FF extra to hire sheets). An evening meal (traditional local dishes can be prepared on request) will set you back 130FF per person. Pierrot is a horse breeder and you can go pony trekking from here, with a range of options to suit all requirements (one hour, half-day, whole day and so on). The village has two *groceries* where you can stock up, as well as a post office and two telephone boxes. In the tourist season, Autocars Balesi buses stop twice daily in Quenza (Ajaccio to Porto Vecchio line, one each way).

 On the other side of the Asinao river the path climbs gently and then evens out along the side of the mountain at an average altitude of 1300m. You'll see various plants and

Climbing in Bavella

The Bavella massif is popular not only with walkers but also with both novice and expert climbers. Coming along the GR20 from the Refuge d'Asinao, just before you get to the Bocca di Bavella you'll see the training climbs, which are signposted on the slopes themselves. These slopes are ideal for beginners, ranging from 40 to 90m. There are more technical climbs further up in the massif, between Punta di l'Acellu and Punta di u Pargulu (accessible via the alpine route of the GR20). The level of difficulty ranges from 3 to 8a and there are a good number of slopes that are classified as 4 or 5, making them suitable for climbers of medium ability.

If you continue south-east, heading for the Refuge de Paliri along the GR20, you will see other possible climbs, especially on the Punta Tafunata di Paliri, which has a distinctive hole in its summit. The Refuge de Paliri nestles at the foot of this mountain, on the slopes of which is a track made up of some 70m of cables and about 20 bars, suitable for anyone who doesn't suffer from vertigo. You can get to it from the Refuge de Paliri (two hours there and back) or make a day of it from the Bocca di Bavella.

If you would like to know more, consult *Petra di Luna* by Jean-Paul Quilici, the first guide to the high mountains of Corsica. It describes the main climbs in the massif. Alternatively, contact a qualified guide, such as Quilici himself (☎ 04 95 78 64 33), Didier Micheli (☎ 04 95 25 54 24) or Jacques Andreani (☎ 04 95 70 51 93).

---

trees, including alders, pines, arbutuses, violets, bracken and, for the first time on the GR20, silver birches. The route is easy and pleasant, following a ledge above the Asinao for about one hour. There are spectacular views downstream and of the opposite bank, where the rounded valley-side has been etched with deep scars by the ravines running down it. There is also a marked difference in the vegetation on either side; the opposite side is rocky, while this side is much greener. The path is interrupted by a number of little streams. In places you can just about see through the foliage to the towering foothills of the Bavella massif.

After about 1½ hours of walking you reach a crossroads. Straight ahead is the main GR20 route, which skirts the mountainside to the south-west of the massif. To the left, the **alpine route**, which takes you to the heart of the massif, is marked out in yellow. The spectacular alpine version is definitely recommended: it is, without doubt, one of the highlights of the GR20.

However, this route is more taxing than the main route and is considered to be more difficult technically, passing through fallen rocks and stones and requiring you to use your hands across a slab of rock in one section. If you get vertigo or you are not happy with this, it is advisable to take the main route. It is also worth avoiding this option in the wet, as there is a real risk of slipping.

The path for the alpine route turns off at 90° to the normal path and tackles the mountainside directly. The climb is very steep and snakes its way between silver birches and pines, which thin out as the altitude increases and as you go further south-west.

There is a short respite for about 10 minutes, then the path leaves the wooded section and continues to climb towards the **Bocca di u Pargulu** (1662m), reaching it after about one hour. Towards the end, the knife-edge points of the rock faces can feel overwhelming. When you get to the top and see the panoramic views, however, it will all seem unimportant: opposite you is a range of mountains that stretches out in parallel to the one you are on; between the two is a valley, the pass and the village of

The Mule Makes a Comeback

The PNRC regularly uses a helicopter to transport supplies and other materials to the refuges and remove rubbish left by walkers, but this is expensive and noisy, so it is planning to use a method of transport that has been tried and tested over the years: the mule.

This option would allow the PNRC to get to higher altitudes and maintain a constant level of cleanliness in the refuges. Walkers could also profit from the scheme: in some places it is already possible to hire a mule to carry your equipment. This initiative could be of particular interest to those wishing to take children on the walk.

For more information contact the Fédération Nationale Ânes et Randonnées (☎ 04 95 61 80 88, email balagnan@my gale.org).

Bavella; and to the east is the sea. Amid this jagged landscape you can make out peaks that look like huge sharp teeth – these are the Aiguilles de Bavella (Bavella Needles; see The South chapter).

From here the path descends steeply through a stony gully for about 30 minutes until reaching the famous chain across a smooth, steep slab, about 10m in width. After another 30 minutes of tricky progress along rocky slopes you reach a pass, where you have a wonderful view of the peaks and the village of Bavella, close by to the east. The path to Bavella literally plunges through a deep gully of pink granite.

You'll see the rocks used to teach rock climbing (see the boxed text 'Climbing in Bavella' on the previous page) from here. The markings are sometimes less than adequate during this difficult descent. Roughly four hours after you set out, the path rejoins the normal route of the GR20. It is then only a short stroll through a pine forest until you reach the Bocca di Bavella car park.

Go past the Madone des Neiges (a statue of the Virgin Mary) and take the tarmac road (one of the few concessions to civilisation on the GR20) to the left for about 300m. This leads into the village of Bavella.

 Bavella (1218m) It may be worth stopping off in Bavella, as the Refuge de Paliri does not provide refreshments. Some walkers choose to leave the GR20 at this point. This is a shame, as the last part of the walk is particularly picturesque.

Les Aiguilles de Bavella (☎ 04 95 57 46 06), near the Madone des Neiges, is open from 1 April to 15 October and provides food and shelter. It costs 60FF in a room shared between four (half board 170FF) and 180FF for a double room. There is also a kitchenette. The restaurant provides Corsican meals for 65FF, including *raviolis au brocciu* and home-cooked meats. A Corsican soup costs 35FF.

About 300m further towards the village, on a hairpin bend, is the *Auberge du Col de Bavella (☎ 04 95 57 43 87)*, which has an excellent reputation, especially for its food. You can choose between three Corsican fixed-price menus (65FF, 95FF and 120FF) or an extensive à la carte menu featuring mixed salads, home-made specialities (including Corsican ham-bone soup for 49FF), grilled meats, omelettes, pasta and desserts (including a wonderful chestnut tart for 35FF). It costs 70FF in a room for six people (170FF half board). The auberge is open from April to October and accepts credit cards.

Next door is *Le Refuge*, another refuge-restaurant-bar, open from May to September. A room for up to four people will set you back 150FF. The restaurant does pizza for 38FF to 50FF, sandwiches for 25FF and omelettes for 35FF; there are also fixed-price menus for 65FF or 120FF.

There's a *grocery* opposite the Auberge du Col de Bavella, but it's not particularly well stocked.

In the peak season Bavella is served by an Autocars Balesi bus daily except Sunday (line between Ajaccio and Porto Vecchio, one each way).

The Bocca di Bavella marks a real change in the character of the GR20. The green, wooded setting is in distinct contrast to the barren ruins of the Aiguilles de Bavella and the route along the ridge.

If you wish to continue to the Refuge de Paliri, allow another 2¼ hours for this part of the walk, where the only difficult section is around the Bocca di Foce Finosa.

When you reach the auberge on the road into Bavella, take the turning off to the right, which changes into a forest track some 50m further on.

The walk is pleasant and easy, and follows a level route through a forest of pine trees and silver birch for about 15 minutes. The path then narrows before forking to the left and descending to a small stream. About 10 minutes later you come to a forest track – follow it to the right for 50m. Turn left at the fork and cross the **Volpajola** stream on the small concrete bridge.

Opposite you to the east is a long range of mountains, which you will cross via the Bocca di Foce Finosa. Five minutes from the stream, the path forks to the right to begin the ascent. It takes a 45 minute climb to cover the 200m in altitude to the **Bocca di Foce Finosa** (1214m). Once you reach the pass there are views towards the sea in the south-east and the Aiguilles de Bavella the other way.

The last section of the route is the one hour walk to the Refuge de Paliri, down the east face of the range. The descent starts off sharply, before turning towards the north-east and becoming more gentle as it follows the contour line.

A small peak just before you reach the Refuge de Paliri (1055m) marks the end of this long stage, which has lasted more than six hours.

Built on the site of and with the stones of a former bergerie, the little *Refuge de Paliri* (20 beds) is not lacking in style. It is also in a magnificent setting, surrounded by the Punta Tafunata di Paliri, the Anima Dam-

nata, the Punta di Paliri and a strip of green land to the south-east. You can also make out the towering peaks of the mountain range to the south-west. On a clear day you can see as far as Sardinia to the south.

The warden, Madame Quilici, has looked after this refuge almost every summer since 1981. It costs 50FF (20FF for camping, with toilets and use of a kitchenette area with equipment). This refuge does not sell any food, however, and the showers are cold.

STAGE 15

Refuge de Paliri (1055m) to Conca (252m)

Distance: 12km
Standard: Average
Average Duration: 5 hours
Highest Point: 1055m
Summary: This final stage is sometimes left out, but there is no reason to do so. It is a spectacular stage and forms a marked contrast to the previous day's route. Once you have left the south section of the Bavella massif the path joins the maquis with its intoxicating fragrances that you will have forgotten after the rocky surroundings of the previous stages. Towards the end of the stage, the presence of the sea becomes more and more perceptible.

From the refuge the path descends briefly before coming to the heart of a superb forest of maritime pines and silver birch. On the left is the imposing spectre of the **Anima Damnata** (Damned Soul) at 1091m, with its distinctive sugar-loaf shape that becomes all the more obvious when you emerge from the forest. After a short walk along a ledge, you can easily make out the Monte Bracciutu massif to the east and Monte Sordu to the south-east (25 minutes away). The path then follows a ridge that curves north-east around a cirque, in the middle of which are the peaks of the **Massif du Bracciutu**.

To the north-east you can see the hole in the Punta Tafunata di Paliri, which almost looks like a bull's-eye in the line of mountains that extends from the north-east to the south-west with the Refuge de Paliri at its feet. The vegetation is now maquis rather than shrubs. Follow this ledge for about 30 minutes (there's no shade), until you reach the **Foce di u Bracciu** (917m). At this point the trail turns to head due south.

The vegetation here is made up of shrubs, rock rose, lavender and heather. The trail follows the contour line for about 10 minutes before tackling the ascent of the **Bocca di Sordu** (1065m). It takes 30 minutes of difficult climbing to reach the pass, with its distinctive masses of fallen rock. The view from here stretches as far as the sea.

Just after the pass you climb down across a vast granite slab covering about 50m, which is relatively steep (it could easily become a natural slide in the wet). This leads to a sandy path that slices through a pine forest. Five to 10 minutes later it emerges at a little plateau dotted with granite domes and strangely shaped piles of rocks. The background is made up of maquis, a few maritime pines and the trunks of trees destroyed by forest fires. After about 15 minutes in this setting the path starts to descend. The mountainous part of the day's walk fades into the distance as the relief becomes gentler. About 2½ hours after setting out you will reach the (ruined) **Bergeries de Capellu** (850m). A signpost leads you to a spring about 300m to the left of the main path, a good spot for a picnic. About 15 minutes on from here, you come to a little shelf from where you can admire the distinctive sugar-loaf shape of the Punta Balardia to the north-east.

The path climbs steadily down to the **Punta Pinzuta** stream, which you can hear running through the valley although it is still hidden by rows of pine trees that have escaped the flames. Everywhere else the scorched trunks bear witness to the violent forest fires and create a ghostly atmosphere.

The trail fords the stream, then follows the course of the stream for a while before crossing back at a large bend. A good 20 minute climb takes you out of this steep-sided valley and up to a pass. The path continues along the mountainside, almost on the level, describing long curves on a ledge across the maquis for about 45 minutes, until it reaches the **Bocca d'Usciolu** (587m), a narrow U-shaped passage through a wall of granite. From the other side of the pass you can clearly see Conca, the end of the whole GR20, in the valley below. To the south there's a pretty little cove.

The descent into the village (20 to 30 minutes) passes through thick undergrowth, emerging at a tarmac road. Turn left, follow the road to a crossroads and then take the road leading down. You will soon be able to see the main road. For information about the end of the route, see the section on Conca in The South chapter.

The Mare e Monti & Mare a Mare

The Mare e Monti and Mare a Mare routes are five PNRC paths that cover much of the island from the north to the south. Although they are less publicised than the GR20, they have advantages that make them an attractive option. The routes are not as mountainous or as long as the GR20, making them accessible to a greater number of people. They make a good test for those who doubt their ability to cope with the GR20. They also offer more comfort, because walkers can spend the nights in gîtes (with restaurants) or hotels along the way, splitting the walk up however they like. Finally, the routes are less crowded than the GR20.

THE MARE E MONTI & MARE A MARE ROUTES & OTHER WALKS

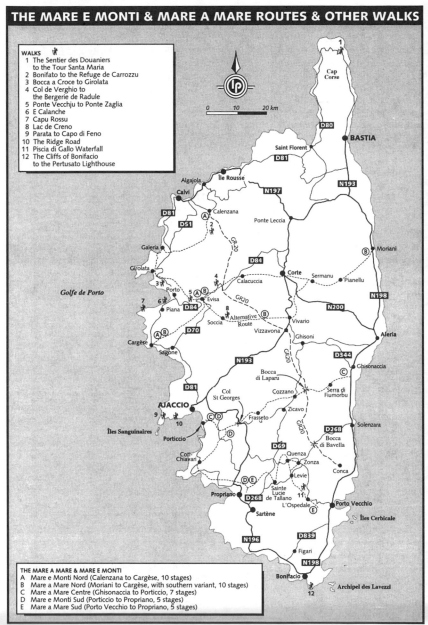

WALKS
1. The Sentier des Douaniers to the Tour Santa Maria
2. Bonifato to the Refuge de Carrozzu
3. Bocca a Croce to Girolata
4. Col de Verghio to the Bergerie de Radule
5. Ponte Vecchju to Ponte Zaglia
6. E Calanche
7. Capu Rossu
8. Lac de Creno
9. Parata to Capo di Feno
10. The Ridge Road
11. Piscia di Gallo Waterfall
12. The Cliffs of Bonifacio to the Pertusato Lighthouse

0   10   20 km

THE MARE A MARE & MARE E MONTI
A Mare e Monti Nord (Calenzana to Cargèse, 10 stages)
B Mare a Mare Nord (Moriani to Cargèse, with southern variant, 10 stages)
C Mare a Mare Centre (Ghisonaccia to Porticcio, 7 stages)
D Mare e Monti Sud (Porticcio to Propriano, 5 stages)
E Mare a Mare Sud (Porto Vecchio to Propriano, 5 stages)

euro currency converter 10FF = €1.52

These walks provide an excellent opportunity to explore the more traditional, inland areas of Corsica. Unlike the GR20, which is largely perched high in the mountains and only passes through two villages, they pass through some of the prettiest villages on the island. The stages are designed to take you from one village to another, which means that you have the opportunity to discover more than just the relief and the natural beauty of the island.

This section gives a general description of each of the walks, with details of the villages through which they pass. More information on some of the villages can be found in the regional chapters, together with a description of places to stay and eat.

Accommodation & Supplies

On both the Mare e Monti and the Mare a Mare there is a gîte at the end of each stage. These are generally well run and more comfortable than the normal refuges. They have small dormitories (four to 10 people), hot showers and blankets (and sometimes sheets). The atmosphere and quality of the services is very much dependent on the wardens, often a local family. Some invest a great deal in upkeep and have earned a good reputation, especially for their food.

You can choose between accommodation only (about 60FF), half board (about 170FF), table d'hôte (traditional meal; about 100FF) and packed lunch, and even camping in some cases. Not all of them have kitchen facilities and half board is obligatory in some cases. Opening times vary from one gîte to another and many are closed out of season (from November to April). It is worth telephoning in advance. In the peak season you will have to make a reservation. You can pay by cash or cheque.

There are hotels in some of the villages. There's also no chance that you will go short of food: in addition to the food at the gîtes there are groceries, self-service shops and even restaurants. Nearly all the villages have a post office (limited opening times) where you can withdraw cash with a credit card (identification required).

Maps & Signs

The routes are marked out in orange (a painted line on tree trunks or rocks). In some places the visibility and frequency of the markings leaves something to be desired. However, you should be suspicious if you have seen no markings for more than 100m. Always retrace your steps and find the last marking.

A detailed map will be extremely useful. Get a Didier Richard map at a scale of 1:50,000 (*Corse du Nord* and *Corse du Sud*) or the IGN maps at 1:25,000 (Top 25, blue series), which are very clear.

The Mare e Monti Routes

As the name suggests, these are paths between the sea and the mountains.

Mare e Monti Nord This is a superb (and not especially difficult) walk which links Calenzana in the Haute-Balagne region to Cargèse, south of the Golfe de Porto. It is divided into 10 stages of four to seven hours each, and its highest point is 1153m. It passes through several exceptional natural sites, such as the Forêt de Bonifatu, the Réserve Naturelle de Scandola and the Gorges de Spelunca. The route stops in a few charming villages, including Galeria, Ota and Evisa. There are gîtes in Calenzana, Bonifatu, Tuarelli, Galeria, Girolata, Curzu, Serriera, Ota, Evisa, Marignana, E Case and Cargèse. Some of these villages also have hotels.

The Mare e Monti Nord is passable year-round, but the periods before and after the main season (May to June and September to October) are preferable to avoid the worst of the heat. The path crosses the Mare a Mare Nord at Evisa and Marignana.

Mare e Monti Sud This path runs between the bays of two well known seaside resorts in the south-west of Corsica – Porticcio and Propriano. It's divided into five stages of five to six hours and ascends to a maximum height of 870m. There are stops in Bisinao, Coti-Chiavari (which towers above the two bays), Porto Pollo and

Olmeto. The walk ends in Burgo (7km north of Propriano).

There are only two gîtes on the route: in Bisinao (☎ 04 95 24 21 66) and Burgo (☎ 04 95 76 15 05). In the other villages you can either stay in a hotel or at a camp site.

The route is characterised by its views over the bays, Genoese towers and beaches (the Baie de Cupabia and Porto Pollo). Like its northern counterpart, this path is passable year-round and is not very difficult. Spring and autumn are the best times. The path meets the Mare a Mare Sud in Burgo.

The Mare a Mare Routes

There are three Mare a Mare (sea to sea) paths, which link the west and east coasts via the mountains in the centre of the island.

Mare a Mare Nord From Moriani on the east coast to Cargèse in the west, this path passes through vastly contrasting areas and is split up into 10 stages, each lasting from four to six hours and reaching altitudes of up to 1600m. For the final section of the walk, between Evisa and Cargèse, the route merges with that of the Mare e Monti Nord.

You will see something of Corte (fourth day), the Bozio (a remote area famous for its chapels and frescos) and the Tavignano before climbing to the Col de Verghio (where the path crosses the GR20). After this the path passes through forests and continues to Evisa and Cargèse. There are gîtes in Pianellu, Sermanu, Castellare di Mercurio, Corte, Calacuccia, Albertacce, Casamaccioli, Evisa, Marignana, E Case and Cargèse.

There's also an alternative route that you can take on the fourth day. From Sermanu, the path goes south to Vivario via Poggio di Venaco, then turns west, passing through Onda, Pastricciola, Guagno, Guagno-les-Bains (the Guagno region is famous for its thermal waters) and Renno before joining the Mare e Monti Nord route at Marignana.

Bearing in mind the altitude of some sections of this walk, it is worth avoiding the period between November and April because parts of the route may still be covered in snow.

Mare a Mare Centre This route is described in detail in the next section.

Mare a Mare Sud This route is passable year-round. It is a famous, easy walk that links Porto Vecchio in the south-east to Propriano in the south-west. The walk is divided into five stages, each of which lasts an average of five hours, and reaches a maximum altitude of 1171m. A stone's throw from the Aiguilles de Bavella and Monte Incudine, it crosses through the magnificent region of Alta Rocca and many of the most beautiful villages on the island. You stop in Cartalavonu, Levie, Serra di Scopamena and Sainte Lucie de Tallano and pass through the wonderful village of Quenza. There is an alternative route via Zonza (allow one extra day).

The Mare a Mare Centre

The Mare a Mare Centre route has been selected for a detailed description. Part of the attraction of this walk is that it is not the best known or most popular of the routes, and it is neither too easy nor too difficult. It also passes through some remote rural areas of Corsica.

The Mare a Mare Centre breaks down into seven stages of three to seven hours each, starting in Ghisonaccia, on the east coast, and finishing in Porticcio, on the west coast. It passes through the little-known districts of Fiumorbu and Taravu, with their charming villages, before crossing the hinterland of Ajaccio. The landscape is spectacular and the walk is an opportunity to see a great deal of Corsican flora.

Many sections of the walk are in the shade. The maximum altitude is 1525m at the Bocca di Laparu; this means that the route is passable mainly between April and November.

STAGE 1

Ghisonaccia to Serra di Fiumorbu (460m)

Markings: Yellow
Standard: Average; a long climb towards the end
Average Duration: 2¾ to 3¼ hours
Highest Point: 460m
Access: Rapides Bleus buses (☎ 04 95 70 10 36) from Bastia and Porto Vecchio, twice a day except Sunday
Summary: This stage takes you away from the sea and into the foothills of the interior. The route is clearly divided into two parts: the first is flat, crossing the farming plain, and the second is simply a climb up to Serra di Fiumorbu.

 The starting point for the Mare a Mare Centre is on the N198, 4.5km south of Ghisonaccia and 1km south of the hamlet of Casamozza, just beyond the bridge over the **Abatescu** and to the right. The start of the walk is marked with a PNRC sign indicating that it is three hours to Serra di Fiumorbu, seven hours to Catastaju (the end of the second stage) and 11 hours to the Bocca di Laparu.

The first part of the walk is flat and follows a little tarmac road that heads due east towards the foothills of the mountains. It passes through fields of farmed chestnut trees, a reminder that the Fiumorbu is a rich and fertile agricultural region. **Asprivu** is the first Corsican village you reach, after less than 30 minutes walk. Watch carefully because the markings are somewhat confusing: when you get to the hamlet you'll see a fork with a pebbly path to the right. Do not take this path, but continue along the tarmac road for another 100m and then take the path off to the right, towards the farm shed (the yellow marking is on the electricity pylon; if you are facing the pylon, take the path to the left). The trail now goes through countryside, featuring alternating

hedges and shrub vegetation. Some 20 minutes later, it reaches the **Fiumorbu** river and follows the course of the water for about 100m along first a narrow ledge then a wider track.

The arable landscape is gradually replaced by trees, including oak, and maquis, which makes the scenery look a little more barren. The next village is **Suartellu**. Go past the little house called Le Palmier, follow the tarmac road for about 800m until you reach a crossroads, cross the road and follow the sign to the left. This tells you that you are one hour from Serra di Fiumorbu (although it is probably more like 1½ hours).

After this things take a turn for the worse when you reach the first climb on this route. About 200m after the first bend, you leave the road for a little path (signposted) that dives into the vegetation. Take a deep breath before starting the long, steep climb. After 45 minutes the path reaches a tarmac road; turn left here and follow the road for about 20m before rejoining the path up the mountainside to the left (although there are orange markings it is not easy to spot). After another 25 minutes of climbing you meet the tarmac road again. This time, follow it to the right towards the village of **Serra di Fiumorbu**, which you can see nestling on the mountainside at an altitude of 460m. As you come into the village you have a wonderful view over the whole of the plain. The gîte is a granite building on the left at the edge of the village.

Some walkers miss out this stage, judging it of limited interest, and start from Serra di Fiumorbu. Others continue to Catastaju for the first night rather than climb up to Serra di Fiumorbu.

 The *gîte d'étape* (☎ 04 95 56 75 48, mobile ☎ 06 81 04 69 49) is run by Madame Guidicelli and sleeps 25 in several dormitories. It costs 50FF per person, or 135FF half board.

At the centre of the village is a *café-grocery*, open seemingly random hours in

July and August. Do not rely on it for your supplies. You'll be better off asking Madame Guidicelli to make you a packed lunch for the following day. There's a telephone box opposite the café.

STAGE 2

Serra di Fiumorbu (460m) to Catastaju (523m)

Markings: Orange
Standard: Easy; no shade on the first part of the route
Average Duration: 4½ to 5 hours
Highest Point: 957m
Summary: This route alternates between ridges, maquis and pine forests and takes you into the heart of the mountains. It starts with a long flat walk along a ridge, followed by several steeper climbs to an altitude of nearly 900m, and finishes with a shady decent towards the hamlet of Catastaju, in a steep-sided valley.

 About 500m out of Serra di Fiumorbu there's a sign for, among other places, Bocca di Juva. Follow this path up to the right. The route goes along a wide south-westerly ridge that mounts regularly and offers magnificent views over a mountain range and the vast depression of Fiumorbu to the west. The villages nestling at the bottom of the valley could easily be in a painting. The vegetation is largely maquis, with rock rose, bellium, purple foxglove and bracken. There is little or no shade in this first section of the route.

The ridge continues to rise, although it barely feels as if you are climbing. The path continues in the open, but there are several tracks where you could go wrong and the markings are less than useful when you need them most. First, you come to a fork with three paths: take the left one. Then you come to another junction: this time take the right-hand option, which follows a steep path up the slope (there are markings on a rock).

After about 1¾ hours the trail reaches a pass, from where there's a stunning view over another valley, then continues along the ridge for about 200m to a crossroads. To the left is a sign for Bovile and Ventiseri and straight ahead is Bocca di Juva, two hours away. The climb gets steeper now and the path leads through thick undergrowth. Then you come to another little valley and the landscape changes, becoming less barren and with more pine trees and bracken.

The climb continues for about 10 minutes until you reach a patch of dense undergrowth, where it is easy to lose track of the markings and the trail itself.

The path curves round to the left and then climbs steeply again for about 10 minutes until it reaches a peak (2¾ hours into the walk). It then begins to descend through spectacular scenery, surrounded by mountains. You go through a pine forest then reach the crossroads at the **Bocca di Juva** (866m), where there's a sign to Ania and Catastaju to the right. From here the descent through the pines is gentle and steep by turns.

Just over one hour after the Bocca di Juva (3¾ hours into the walk) the trail crosses a stream, then climbs for 50m before reaching a crossroads. Don't go straight ahead towards Ania (it is possible to get confused because this route is signposted in orange); turn left and aim for Catastaju.

At the next signpost turn right for Catastaju. You can tell you're almost there when you hear the sound of the Abatescu river; after a good climb downhill you'll see it. The walk has taken 4¾ hours. The gîte is across the footbridge, on the right. A swim in the clear, refreshing waters of the Abatescu is a perfect way to relax at the end of the day.

 The *gîte d'étape* (☎ 04 95 56 70 14, 04 95 56 74 97) is open year-round. It's 3km upstream from the village of San Gavinu di Fiumorbu, overhanging the Abatescu a stone's throw away from where it meets the trail. The building, which used to be a hydroelectric power station, has been comfortably renovated. It sleeps 27 in dormitories. Madame Paoli will give you a warm welcome; her generous meals based on Corsican specialities (allow between 50FF and 100FF) are unrivalled and perk up even the most exhausted of walkers. A night costs 60FF (70FF with sheets), half board is 170FF and a packed lunch will set you back 45FF. Drinks (around 10FF) and light meals are also available.

You can also camp next to the stream for just 10FF.

If you wish to do just a section of the walk, starting or finishing at Catastaju, you can arrange for a car to take you to Ghisonaccia (150FF), Bastia-Poretta airport (300FF) or Cozzano (400FF).

There's a *grocery* in San Gavinu di Fiumorbu, as well as a telephone box.

STAGE 3

 From the gîte, follow the tarmac road uphill for 300 to 400m, then turn right towards Bocca di Laparu. Say goodbye to the tarmac and prepare for a steady but uncompromising ascent to the pass.

The first 30 minutes is uneventful. The climb is slow and regular and follows the course of the Macini stream. Don't let your concentration lapse, because there is a junction that you must not miss: a hairpin bend to the right, at about the same height as the point where the stream goes over the waterfall. Pay attention to the markings on the ground.

After 45 minutes the trail comes to a ledge that towers over the whole Macini valley. This leads, after 30 minutes, to a crossroads: the path to the right goes to San Gavinu di Fiumorbu; continue straight ahead for Bocca di Laparu (signposted). A few minutes later the trail fords a stream, which it then follows uphill along a ridge. A 10 minute climb follows and you cross back over a stream, using large rocks as stepping stones. At this point the markings are barely visible, but there are little cairns and orange markings on the trees on the other side.

From here the path winds through the pine forest, among large rocks and roots. As you progress you'll notice the pines gradually give way to beech trees. After a while the path is blocked by branches on the ground and you have to turn left. The marking, on a little stone, is not visible at first glance.

After about two hours of walking the trail comes to a pass in the form of a little clearing, where you will see the ruins of the **Bergeries de la Scanciatella**. This is a wonderful spot for a picnic, with beautiful views. If you face the valley with the beech forest behind you, the path continues to the right.

A little higher up there is another little bergerie, which has been renovated. About 50m after this the trail enters the beech forest again and follows the contour line. After 15 minutes you cross a little stream.

Catastaju (523m) via Bocca di Laparu (1525m) to Cozzano (727m)

Markings: Orange
Standard: Average; large change in altitude (1000m) over the first section; markings sometimes confusing
Average Duration: 6 to 6½ hours
Highest Point: 1525m
Summary: This long stage is varied and shady; the highlight is the crossing of the Bocca di Laparu, the highest point on the Mare a Mare walks. This pass forms a natural boundary between the regions of Fiumorbu and Taravu. Flora is varied on this part of the trail.

The shape of the route resembles an upturned V: a steady ascent towards the pass followed by a long descent into the Cozzano valley.

Continue walking through the beech forest until you come to a small cairn indicating that you need to turn left. There is an orange line painted on a tree trunk, but the marking is not particularly easy to spot.

The trail arrives at the **Refuge de Laparu** 3¼ hours after you set off. The refuge is a permanent building with no warden; you can sleep here (on a basic mattress) for 20FF. There's a gas stove and a water pipe below if you want to quench your thirst.

To continue, turn left just before the refuge. The trail follows the face of the mountain, then takes a 90° turn uphill. A 15 minute climb leads to a clearing where the signs are a little confusing. Follow the yellow marking on the rock uphill.

The route via the Refuge de Laparu is optional. It involves a slight detour that will add no more than 10 minutes to the day's walk. To avoid the detour, head directly for the Bocca di Laparu at the junction where you can just make out the word Laparu on a stone (the refuge is indicated on a sign that has come away from a tree).

After the clearing you climb for 15 minutes, eventually reaching the **Bocca di Laparu** where the path intersects the southbound GR20 at a right angle. From here there are views over the region of Taravu to the west, for which you are heading. Allow 3½ to 4 hours for the section between Catastaju and Bocca di Laparu.

From the Bocca di Laparu, the trail descends for about 20 minutes before entering a splendid forest of laricio pine and leading to a forest track. Turn left and before long before you'll pass a fast-flowing stream. There's a natural spring next to the path 200m further on. Follow the path, which becomes much wider, until you see a sign for Cozzano pointing towards a little path heading down into the forest.

Half an hour later the trail joins a newly built forest road, which it follows for a short time before turning off to the left on a bend and follows the course of a dry river bed. You now see the first chestnut trees. The path keeps crossing the forest road, so look out for the orange markings carefully.

After about 30 minutes of this crisscrossing, you come first to a wooden gate across the path, then, a few metres on, to a large stream, and finally to a tarmac road. Turn left and the road will take you into the centre of Cozzano. The gîte is on the right-hand side.

  The *Auberge A Filetta* (☎ 04 95 24 45 61, fax 04 95 24 47 05) is on the edge of the village, on the road to Guitera-les-Bains. It has warm, comfortable rooms for 180FF and is open from the end of April to the beginning of October. The place is modern and is often extremely busy in August, so it is worth making a reservation. There's a fixed-price menu for 80FF or specials for 50FF (breakfast 25FF), served in the dining room or on the terrace.

On the other side of the village, towards Palneca (to the north), a large building houses the *Gîte Rural Bella Vista* (☎ 04 95 24 41 59), which has six dormitories for six people each (55FF per person) and three double rooms for 150FF per room. You can also camp in the garden for 25FF and there is a kitchen for walkers to use. If you don't feel like cooking, an evening meal here costs 70FF (breakfast 25FF). As its name suggests, this shelter is set slightly above the village and has a wonderful view over Cozzano.

Cozzano is the only village in the area with a chemist; this is in the main square and is open from 9.15 am to 7.30 pm daily except Sunday. The main square also contains a petrol station and a well-stocked grocery; these are both open from 9 am to 7 pm, Monday to Saturday and on Sunday morning.

The post office is open from 1.45 to 3.45 pm except Sunday. Two bars, the *Central Bar* and the *Snack Bar Terminus*, welcome thirsty walkers, and a baker's van comes to the village daily except Monday at about 8 am.

Autocars Santini buses run between Cozzano and Ajaccio daily except Sunday.

WALKING IN CORSICA

STAGE 4

Cozzano (727m) to Guitera-les-Bains (620m)

Markings: Orange
Standard: Average
Average Duration: 6 hours
Highest Point: 955m
Note: Access to villages along the route
Summary: This rather long stage is probably the least well-marked on the Mare a Mare Centre walk. It is dotted with little villages and is a unique opportunity to discover rural Corsica. It culminates in a long climb down to Guitera-les-Bains past a number of spectacular viewpoints.

 The trail leads off the road to Guitera-les-Bains (D757) 50m before the Auberge A Filetta, by a chestnut tree. After going downhill for about 10 minutes, you come to the **Taravu**, the river that gives its name to the whole region. It is the same Taravu that provides the warm waters for the baths in Guitera-les-Bains, a few kilometres downstream.

Cross the bridge, follow the D28 for about 300m and you'll see a wooden sign pointing to Sampolo on the left. The trail leaves the road and, 100m later, starts up a poorly maintained, steep path that rapidly turns into a narrow gully lined with rocks.

This section of the Mare a Mare Centre is sometimes covered in thick vegetation. If the PNRC has not cleared it you will have to look very carefully for the orange markings until you reach Sampolo. They are often on tree trunks at about eye level. You go through a wooden gate and then navigate your way through a veritable labyrinth of little paths until you reach two pretty houses overhanging the valley.

The path turns to the left and, after a short descent, climbs steeply until it reaches a grave in front of a house. Continuing, it joins the D28, which goes to the little village of Sampolo 200m downstream.

Sampolo used to be frequented by shepherds moving their flocks to summer pastures but now has only about 20 inhabitants in winter. However, this pretty little village is a real godsend for walkers: it has a grocery (the last one before Porticcio), open from 9 am to noon and 4 to 7 pm, and a very nice bar-tobacconist, the Bar des Amis, which is open daily and has been welcoming locals and visitors alike since 1900. One of the walls features a map showing all the former walking paths through the Haut Taravu region.

It will take less than 30 minutes to get to Giovicacce, the next village along the route. The trail goes through Sampolo and arrives at a fork, where it continues along the D28. It passes several little cemeteries, some of which are rather overgrown. The third cemetery is on a bend and here the path leaves the road and heads off to the left. It roughly follows the route of the stone wall before descending into a river bed.

When you get to a crossroads in the open, turn left and you will come to two little wooden bridges in a state of disrepair. Shortly afterwards the path turns right towards **Giovicacce**, where it rejoins the main road (at a telephone box). Follow this road for about 500m until you reach a bridge where a PNRC sign tells you that Tasso is 30 minutes away.

Here the path delves into the undergrowth, following a regular course along a stream. You will notice black plastic pipes – these have long been used instead of traditional open channels to irrigate the terraces around villages. The sophisticated water distribution system in Corsica made it possible for the villages to grow vegetables and fruit trees in the 19th century, but this declined after WWI.

The trail crosses a tarmac road twice. The second time it does so, climb up to **Tasso** on the road rather than try to find the path, which is very badly marked.

  If you do not wish to do the whole stage as far as Guitera-les-Bains, you can stop in Tasso.

The *gîte d'étape* (☎ *04 95 24 52 01)*, run by the aptly named Tassos, is open year-round and can sleep up to 18 people in dormitories for four to six. A whole floor of this large house is reserved for walkers, and there is a common room, a washing machine and a well-equipped kitchen. It costs 60FF a night (half board 175FF).

Auberge de Tasso (☎ *04 95 24 50 54)* is also open year-round and has four smart double rooms for 250FF (including breakfast). There are fixed-price menus for 120FF and 150FF (80FF if you are staying at the auberge). It's a pleasant, modern building with a shady terrace, but the welcome can leave something to be desired.

 It's a 2½ hour walk from Tasso to Guitera-les-Bains. The trail starts along a paved road about 50m from the gîte. It passes several little cemeteries before coming to a group of houses with a spring, which is an excellent source of refreshment. The road then begins to climb up the mountainside before the path branches off it to the left.

It takes nearly an hour to reach a large flat area in the open (955m) where several paths cross. Take the path opposite you, which descends 350m within 30 minutes. Through the gaps there are some sublime views of Zicavo on the opposite side of the valley. In the background you will be able to make out the Bocca di Laparu and the ridges on which the GR20 is perched. When you reach a tarmac road, turn left towards the centre of **Guitera-les-Bains**.

The gîte d'étape is at the bottom of the village, past a spring and a stone wash house. You can walk or hitch from Guitera-les-Bains to the **Bains de Guitera**, a small, natural warm-water swimming pool 5km away.

  The *gîte d'étape* (☎ *04 95 24 44 40)*, an old stone house, is run by Paul-Antoine Lanfranchi. A bed in a dormitory for four costs 65FF. The terrace is a lovely cool haven and the

food is reputedly some of the best in the region. Allow between 80FF and 120FF for dinner. Camping in the garden is tolerated.

STAGE 5

Guitera-les-Bains (620m) to Quasquara (721m)

Markings: Orange
Standard: Easy
Average Duration: 3 to 4 hours
Highest Point: 1048m
Summary: Most of this short, pleasant walk is shady. It passes through the village of Frasseto, where you can stop for a while before tackling the steep climb to Quasquara. This is an excellent way to stretch your legs in preparation for the longer walk tomorrow.

 Climbing back up towards the centre of the village, you pass the Café l'Archia and the village hall (note the period letter box). Carry on until you get to a sign for Frasseto, 3½ hours away. After a 30 minute climb up a rocky track, the trail rounds a hairpin bend, the first in a series. Don't miss the path: it turns off to the left into the forest.

The path comes to a large clearing and turns left, after which there is a fallen tree across the path. You will be able to see holly as the trail continues to wend its way through the undergrowth for another 20 minutes to the **Bocca di Lera** (1048m), the highest point of the day. Once you reach it, ignore the path to Tasso to the right and you will come to a sandy clearing where there's a sign for Frasseto, 1¾ hours away. The following descent is pleasant, regular and shady, and emerges at another large clearing where it heads towards Frasseto to the right.

The descent alongside a chestnut grove reveals a magnificent view of the **Punta di Forca d'Olmu** (1646m) nearly 3km away. Heather and oak trees line the rest of the route, which leads to a tarmac road after less than 45 minutes. Turn right and you will soon be in **Frasseto**, a pretty hamlet with large stone houses that seem to serve as a reminder of a more prestigious past.

  Chez Jean et Pierrette (☎ *04 95 25 79 60*) is a café-restaurant whose charm lies equally in the simplicity of the location and the friendliness of its owners. It's open from May to the end of October and serves as a meeting place for the villagers, who come here for lunch or for a pastis at the bar. For walkers it's an ideal place at which to stop for lunch or a break. The garden is pleasant; you can camp there (with permission).

If you warn her in advance, Pierrette will also prepare you a meal to take with you, because there are no shops in Frasseto.

 It will not take more than 30 minutes to get to the village of **Quasquara**. Walk down Frasseto's main road to the Chiova stream. Don't miss the little turn-off to the right 300m after the bridge. The path, which is poorly maintained, starts to climb. After about 15 minutes it gets to a cemetery and begins to descend just past the first houses in the village.

  The *gîte d'étape* (☎ *04 95 53 61 21*) – ask for Brigitte or Valérie – is a little further on along the main road, just after the old communal oven. It's open year-round and sleeps up to 14 people in dormitories. The setting is spacious and pleasant and there are the added bonuses of a well-equipped kitchen and hot showers. The food, however, is not very inspiring (there's a fixed-price menu for 60FF). Refreshments are available on request and for the modest sum of 200FF the family who runs the gîte can take you to the Col Saint George or Porticcio. They also have apartments for four or eight people further up in the village.

Opposite the town hall is the ***Association Socio-Culturelle de Quasquara***, known as 'le chalet' for reasons that become obvious when you see the building. It serves drinks and has a television, and is currently the only source of entertainment in the village.

STAGE 6

Quasquara (721m) to Col Saint Georges (757m)

Markings: Orange
Standard: Average; little shade along the route
Average Duration: 5 to 6 hours
Highest Point: 1150m
Summary: Early on, this stage scales the heights of the south-westerly ridge of the relief, marked by Punta d'Urghiavari, and it does not really leave the ridge for the rest of the day. At the Col Saint Georges you come back to earth with a bump as you cross the very busy road (N196) leading to Ajaccio.

 Make sure you fill up your flask before setting off because there is no water along the whole of this stage. You start by climbing up through the village – there are even steps for some of the way. Once you reach the last communal oven, follow the sign to Col Saint Georges six hours away. The stage properly begins with a sustained climb of about 1½ hours in duration. If you look back, you will see the village of Bicchisano opposite.

When you reach the open area, you can look with satisfaction at the distance you have covered from Frasseto, which nestles below you. There is a magnificent view across the peaceful valley. The trail continues for another 30 minutes before reaching the highest point of the day, the **Bocca di Foce** (1150m), from where you have a view over both sides of the ridge.

The Water of Saint Georges

Sold across the island, St Georges water comes from a spring about 1km from the Col Saint Georges, on the road to Ajaccio. The water was first bottled in 1980 by two private entrepreneurs, M Livrelli and M Colonna d'Ornano, who were probably the only ones with any faith in the enterprise to begin with. Although the early years were difficult, nearly nine million bottles a year are now sold, both in Corsica and through some outlets in Paris. The factory currently employs 18 people. You can visit the premises if you telephone the Société des Eaux du Col Saint Georges (SECG; ☎ 04 95 25 71 64) in advance. They're based at Col Saint Georges, 20128 Grosseto, Prugna.

The path follows the ridge for about 30 minutes, passing the **Punta d'Urghiavari** (1345m) and descending towards a wooden gate. Here it turns off to the left and, a few hundred metres further on, arrives at the **Bocca di Sant'Antone** (907m). You can clearly make out the sea and the runways at Ajaccio airport for the first time.

It will take nearly 45 minutes to cross the pass, much of which is spent zigzagging through the maquis. You are then faced with a tough climb in the sun, but after only 20 minutes you reach the **Punta Maggiola** (1082m), an ideal place at which to stop for a picnic. The views stretch out to the village of Santa Maria Siché at your feet, Propriano to the south and the highest peaks on the island to the north.

After this the trail begins a long descent though oak trees, leading to a dirt track after about 30 minutes. Turn left and follow the track for about 20m, until the path turns off sharply to the right. There are no markings for another 100m. Go through a metal gate and you'll get to a crossroads in a clearing. Take the left path, which will take you to the **Col Saint Georges** in 30 minutes.

  The *gîte d'étape* in Col Saint Georges is superb – spacious, brand new and more reminiscent of a four star hotel than a traditional walkers' refuge. It has five rooms with four bunk beds, a well-equipped kitchen, a pretty, shady terrace and showers – all for 75FF per person per night. The only drawback is that it is managed by the Auberge du Col Saint Georges, so you will have to put up with the same frosty reception you get there.

The *Auberge du Col Saint Georges* has seven double rooms, which are modern and comfortable and will set you back 250FF (200FF if you have dinner at the auberge). The restaurant is considered to be one of the best in the region and is very popular with the locals. The cheapest thing on the menu is the omelette, which costs 35FF, while the gourmet fixed-price menu costs 160FF. If you wish to eat à la carte (specialities from Corsica and mainland France), allow at least 200FF.

The auberge is on the road between Ajaccio and Bonifacio and is open year-round (closed Monday in the low season).

STAGE 7

Col Saint Georges (757m) to Porticcio

Markings: Orange
Standard: Easy
Average Duration: 5 to 6 hours
Highest Point: 890m
Summary: This dazzling finale takes you from the heights of Col Saint Georges to the beaches of Porticcio, a refreshing haven and an ample reward for the week's hard work. On a clear day there are spectacular views along the descent towards the sea, adding to the beauty of this final stage, which is all too often left out by walkers.

This stage of the route begins a few metres beyond the auberge, on the right, and climbs through green oaks before turning left and starting a climb of no more than 10 minutes in duration.

The vegetation becomes more interesting, and is gradually replaced by superb fields of asphodel.

A sign to Porticcio marks the start of a flat road. A few metres past a solid house, the road splits: take the right-hand fork, even if you cannot see any signs. After 300m there's a small path to the right (keep your eyes open because it's easy to miss) that follows a stone wall through oak trees.

You will come to an electricity pylon after which there's a short steep climb to a signposted turning for Bisinao. Ignore this and continue until you come to a second turning for Bisinao; at this fork the Mare e Monti Sud merges with the Mare a Mare Centre. This marks the beginning of a long descent and for the whole 40 minutes you will have superb views over Ajaccio and the Tour de l'Isolella on the coast.

When you reach the D302, turn right and follow the road for nearly 2.5km as far as the sign for Buselica. Here the trail turns off to the left and joins a second tarmac road for 150m before leaving it again to head for a ruined tower.

The path goes steadily downhill, crossing a maze of junctions on its way, but the route is well marked so you won't get lost. The views of the sea are spectacular but all too fleeting. If you're tired out, you may find it ironic that the municipal cemetery in Porticcio marks the official end of the Mare a Mare Centre walk.

To get to the town centre, turn right onto the road that goes past the Pierre residence and the Terra Bella holiday firm. Go straight ahead at the first crossroads and continue until you come to a roundabout. Head for Porticcio and you will get to the sea in less than 10 minutes.

For details of places to stay and eat in Porticcio, see that section in The West Coast chapter.

Strolls & Country Walks

Walking in Corsica is by no means limited to the GR20 and the Mare a Mare and Mare e Monti walks. There's plenty of choice for those who prefer gentle walks lasting a few hours.

Twelve walks that vary in both interest and location have been chosen and tested. None of them requires sporting prowess. Unless otherwise specified, they are all suitable for families.

There are also a few 'country walks' designed by the PNRC, in various parts of the island. These too are perfectly suited to families and inexperienced walkers. They are all easy round-trip routes lasting between three and seven hours. The walks are based around the inland villages in the lesser-known areas of Alta Rocca, Bozio, Fiumorbu, Niolu, Taravu, Venachese and Giussani. The aim of these walks is to allow the visitor to discover the typical heritage and villages at the heart of the most traditional areas of Corsica and far off the beaten track.

You can get brochures from the Parc Naturel Régional de Corse (see the boxed text earlier in this chapter).

THE SENTIER DES DOUANIERS TO THE TOUR SANTA MARIA

Access & Location: Plage de Tamarone, Macinaggio (Cap Corse)
Markings: Green logo and yellow paint
Standard: Easy; accessible to all; take protection against the sun in summer
Duration: 2 hour circuit
Change in Altitude: Minimal
Summary: A walk along a protected stretch of coastline amid the fragrant maquis of Cap Corse to an exceptional Genoese tower.

To reach the Plage de Tamarone from Macinaggio, head for Camping U Stazzu on the northern edge of town. A poor road continues for about 1km beyond the camp site to the beach. If you follow the beach towards the north you will come to a junction where you can either turn left to reach the inland path to the Chapelle Santa Maria or right for the Sentier des Douaniers (Customs Officers' Route). Take the second option; this will take you onto a path that is well marked out with wooden stakes with a green logo on them and yellow paint markings on the ground.

As the path climbs into the maquis it enters the protected area of Capandala, which belongs to the Conservatoire du Littoral, a coast conservation society (see Ecology & Environment in the Facts about Corsica chapter), and crosses a landscape where the green of the maquis battles with the turquoise of the sea. Continuing, you'll see a sign to the Chapelle Santa Maria, 45 minutes away.

Fifteen minutes later a Genoese tower on a little islet comes into view and the path begins to descend again, towards the area around the Îles Finocchiarola. These three tiny islands were classified as a nature reserve in 1987 and are now an exceptional animal sanctuary covering 3 hectares. Access to the islands is forbidden between 1 March and 31 October.

The path then climbs up to the left, from where you can see Île de la Giraglia to the north and the superb Tour Santa Maria. The path heads down towards the tower, passing the little Chapelle Santa Maria on the way. The Tour Santa Maria is one of the most beautiful towers along the Corsican coastline – it looks as if it is standing on the water.

If you continue past the tower you come to two secluded little coves with sandy beaches, which are ideal for bathing (you can also continue walking from the tower to Barcaggio, on the north coast). You can return to your starting point along the inland route from the Chapelle Santa Maria, a wide path lined with vines.

BONIFATU TO THE REFUGE DE CARROZZU

Access & Location: 20km from Calvi on the N197 and D251 towards Calvi-Sainte Catherine airport, then further along the D251 as far as the Auberge de Bonifatu
Markings: Yellow, then red and white
Standard: Average
Duration: 2 hours there, 1½ hours back
Change in Altitude: 700m
Summary: A flirt with the GR20 against the magnificent backdrop of the Cirque de Bonifatu.

Although this walk is not difficult it can be taxing because it involves a seemingly interminable climb. But it is an opportunity to discover the wonderful barren setting of the Cirque de Bonifatu. It joins the GR20 route and follows it as far as the Refuge de Carrozzu, near which there are vast natural pools where you can swim. You will need good walking shoes. For more information on the cirque see the section on Bonifatu in the Calvi & the Balagne chapter.

When you reach the Auberge de Bonifatu (536m) by road, take the Sentier du Mouflon (Mouflon Route) at the far end of the car park. This is a large forest track accessible to anyone. After 20 minutes you come to a junction, where you go straight ahead for the Refuge de Carrozzu (the path to the left crosses the river before climbing up to the Refuge d'Ortu di u Piobbu). Follow the yellow markings and begin the climb in the shade of the forest. To the left of the path there are views of the barren yet beautiful landscape. After 45 minutes in total the trail crosses over the Figarella river before continuing to climb, with the splendid peaks of the cirque in the background. It crosses another stream, this time with a Nepalese style suspension bridge, and continues as far as a little stone altar and a shelter, where it joins the GR20 with its red and white markings.

At this point, there is a sign pointing right to the Lac de la Muvrella and Asco, and left to the Refuge de Carrozzu, which is 100m away. These 100m offer the most spectacular view over the sharp peaks of the cirque, with their strange red and blue-green hues. In summer you can get a drink at the refuge.

It would be a pity not to go on for another 10 minutes or so. Retrace your steps and take the turning to Asco and the Lac de la Muvrella and you will come to a suspended footbridge, under which the river forms pools where you can swim. For these few hundred metres, the trail crosses slabs of rock with cables to help you avoid slipping. It is an impressive stretch and should not pose any problems if you are sensible.

BOCCA A CROCE TO GIROLATA

> **Access & Location:** At the Bocca a Croce, 22km from Porto on the D81 heading for Galeria; Autocars SAIB (☎ 04 95 26 13 70) buses from Porto to Calvi pass daily except Sunday during the peak season
> **Markings:** Vague traces of white paint; reasonably marked path
> **Standard:** Easy
> **Duration:** 3 hours there and back
> **Change in Altitude:** 250m
> **Summary:** This walk leads to an idyllic hamlet and bay to the north of the Golfe de Porto that are not accessible by road.

The trail sets off on a clear path down a gentle slope through dense maquis. After about 15 minutes you pass a pretty pebbled fountain. Fifteen minutes later you reach a fork; take the left path, which leads down to the Tuara bay. Although the bay should be idyllic, gravel and rubbish carried in by the tide can spoil its charm. Don't spend too much time here; instead walk round to the northern end of the beach. You will be able to see a path to the left that follows the line of the coast and a second, to the right, that heads up the hill. Take the path to the right; there's a 20 minute climb to the junction with the Mare e Monti Nord (orange markings).

Once there, you'll have a stunning view over Girolata and the Golfe de Girolata, havens of tranquility guarded by a small Genoese fort. To the south-west is Capu Seninu and on the other side, to the north-east, is Punta Muchillina (on the edge of the Réserve de Naturelle de Scandola). It takes about 30 minutes to get down to Girolata from this spot.

There are a few good restaurants along the seafront in the village (see Girolata in The West Coast chapter). The only drawbacks are that it can be overcrowded in summer and the beach is disappointing. You might see Guy Ceccaldi, the postman, with his distinctive white beard, who goes from the hamlet to the Bocca a Croce in double-quick time every day to deliver the post.

You can return by a slightly different route. Cross back over the beach in Girolata and follow the path you came on for about 20m. Then, instead of continuing, take the path to the right, which follows a ledge around the coast as far as the Tuara bay.

COL DE VERGHIO TO THE BERGERIES DE RADULE

> **Access & Location:** Col de Verghio, 12km beyond Evisa on the D84
> **Markings:** Yellow
> **Standard:** Easy; some pebbly sections; take good walking shoes
> **Duration:** 40 minutes (one way)
> **Change in Altitude:** 100m
> **Summary:** A lovely path between the forest and the mountains.

The path is marked out in yellow, starting from behind the statue that traditionally marks the border between Haute-Corse and Corse-du-Sud. This is a spectacular walk among mountaintops and forests and is not very difficult. The Bergeries de Radule are on the GR20; when returning take care to follow the yellow markings, not the red and white route of the GR20.

The bergeries are a few little stone shepherd's huts and sheep pens clinging to the side of the mountain and it is very difficult to make them out against their barren background. A shepherd lives here during the summer months. He might show you how to get to a little waterfall a few minutes walk from the bergeries, where the water tumbles into a pool. It could almost be heaven on earth.

PONTE VECCHJU TO PONTE ZAGLIA

> **Access & Location:** Via the D124; between Porto and Evisa, 2km beyond Ota
> **Markings:** Orange
> **Standard:** Very steep section at the end of the walk
> **Duration:** 1 hour there and back; return along the same route
> **Change in Altitude:** Minimal
> **Summary:** A foray into the spectacular Gorges de Spelunca to discover a remarkably well-preserved Genoese bridge.

The path starts at the edge of the double bridge – on the left if you are coming from Ota. It's a former mule track which links the villages of Ota and Evisa, following the line of the Spelunca canyon and running beside Porto stream for part of the way. This is actually a section of the Mare e Monti Nord between Calenzana and Cargèse. The first Genoese bridge, Ponte Vecchju, is about 300m downstream from the start of the path and can be seen from the D124.

The path is rocky and climbs rapidly up the left face of the valley; there is plenty of shade, provided by green oaks. After 30 minutes you come to Ponte Zaglia, a magnificent Genoese bridge in the depths of the vegetation. You can refresh yourself in any number of pools.

It is worth noting that you can start this walk in Ota (just past the Chez Felix restaurant), but it is not as interesting.

E CALANCHE: A WALK TO THE CHÂTEAU FORT

> **Access & Location:** Starts 3.5km from Piana in the direction of Porto
> **Markings:** Blue; blue circles in a white rectangle
> **Standard:** Easy; accessible to all
> **Duration:** 20 to 30 minutes (one way)
> **Change in Altitude:** Negligible
> **Summary:** A short walk with beautiful views over the Golfe de Porto.

This short path leads off from the Tête de Chien (Dog's Head), a distinctively shaped rock signposted on a large bend in the D81, 3.5km from Piana. Its shape is clear if you are coming from Porto. The trail is roughly marked but you are unlikely to get lost because there are always lots of people there in the summer. Avoid wearing sandals because the path, although easy, is rocky.

After 20 to 30 minutes of walking you reach a natural platform, known as the Château Fort (Fortress), from where you have a stunning view (even better at sunset) over the Golfe de Porto and the deep rocky inlets of E Calanche (see The West Coast chapter).

CAPU ROSSU

> **Access & Location:** Take the D81 towards Piana from Porto or Cargèse, then follow the D824 towards Plage d'Arone for about 5km; a notice board behind glass marks the start of the walk
> **Markings:** Obvious path; sections marked with cairns
> **Standard:** Steep path at the end; no shade
> **Duration:** 2½ hours there and back
> **Change in Altitude:** 300m
> **Summary:** One of the most beautiful walks in Corsica, culminating in breathtaking views.

From the road you can clearly make out the silhouette of the Tour de Turghiu out to the west, perched on top of Capu Rossu. The path is pebbly and to begin with is lined with low stone walls. It descends steadily through the maquis. After about 20 minutes, you will see a little bergerie to the left.

A little later, there's a spectacular view to the left over the cove and the white sand of Plage d'Arone. The path skirts around to the south of the rocky base on which the Turghiu tower stands before coming to a second bergerie. Note how the granite here takes on different shades of grey and pink. The path then turns right (northwards) to tackle the climb to the tower. Small cairns are dotted regularly along the route to mark the tight bends as you approach the summit. Allow about 30 minutes, and there's no shade whatsoever. The effort will all seem worthwhile when you reach the Tour de Turghiu, however. From this fabulous viewpoint you can see the Golfe de Porto and the Golfe de Sagone. At your feet is a steep drop down the cliffs to the sea 300m below. Bivouacking is permitted here.

LAC DE CRENO

> **Access & Location:** About 35km northeast of Sagone; take the D70 as far as Vico then the D23 to Soccia
> **Markings:** Yellow (orange on the section from Soccia to Orto)
> **Standard:** Easy
> **Duration:** 2 hours there and back
> **Change in Altitude:** 300m
> **Summary:** The walk takes you to a glacial lake perched at an altitude of 1310m in the heart of the forest.

This tranquil lake in a dense forest of laricio pines is a popular destination. It's best to drive as far as the car park on the other side of the village and pick up the path there; this will spare you an extra 3km walk. There's a small café by the parking area.

The path leaves the car park and climbs the south side of the valley, rising high above the river on the northern slopes of Monte Sant'Eliseo (1511m). Allow about one hour to walk from the car park to the pretty little lake, which covers 2.4 hectares and remains frozen for three or four months of the year. According to legend, the lake was the result of either a hammer blow from the devil or a kick from a horse. The scientific explanation is far more prosaic, tracing the lake's origin back to the last ice age.

You can walk from Soccia to the little village of Orto, close by, before continuing to the lake, but this means walking back along the road between the car park and Soccia, which is somewhat tedious. The route from Soccia to Orto follows the alternative route of the Mare a Mare Nord (orange markings), but it is often overgrown and the markings are difficult to see. There's a great deal of evidence of the pigs that dug out the path. As you approach Orto you have wonderful views of this village nestling in a very narrow, steep-sided valley. Just above Orto is a steep path marked in orange. This climbs up to the ridge through a magnificent chestnut forest, then joins the path from the Soccia car park to Lac de Creno.

PARATA TO CAPO DI FENO

> **Access & Location:** D111 (Route des Sanguinaires) or No 5 bus (Frati stop)
> **Standard:** Average; take water with you
> **Markings:** None
> **Duration:** 1½ hours (one way)
> **Change in Altitude:** Negligible
> **Summary:** This is a fairly easy walk along a shelf overlooking the sea, with wonderful views over the Îles Sanguinaires.

The walk starts from the foot of a small eucalyptus forest opposite the La Parata motel, on the way into Parata.

When you get to a large eucalyptus tree in the middle of the path, the route forks to the left and winds gently up the hill. The eucalyptus gradually give way to pines and then to maquis. The path crosses a tarmac road and passes an upright stone slab before emerging onto a dirt track just above some tennis courts and opposite the Îles Sanguinaires, which were behind you earlier.

Less than an hour later the path reaches two large bays of crystal clear water at the foot of Capo di Feno. The first is the Saint Antoine beach, which has a snack bar, Snack Jérome, open from the end of May to the end of the season.

THE RIDGE ROAD

Access & Location: About 15 minutes walk from the centre of Ajaccio, through the Bois des Anglais; go along the cours Grandval and ave de Général Leclerc as far as the Grotte Napoléon, then skirt round to the right on avenue Nicolas Piétri
Markings: Practically non-existent
Standard: Average; passable year-round, except when there are high winds in the summer (risk of fire); take water with you
Duration: 3 to 4 hours (one way)
Change in Altitude: 300m
Summary: A stone's throw from Ajaccio, this walk allows you to explore the countryside to the north of the Golfe d'Ajaccio.

The walk starts just opposite the Bois des Anglais (English Woods) bus stop. There's a sign reminding you of the basic safety rules and telling you that the path is marked out with blue arrows, although these have long since disappeared.

The dirt track narrows before winding its way through a barren setting dominated by cactus and aloe. As the markings are almost non-existent and there are numerous crossroads, the easiest thing to do is keep on climbing until you reach a wide forest track (this will take between 15 and 40 minutes, depending on the directions you take). This path is known as the Chemin des Crêtes

(Ridge Road), and towers over the town and the Golfe d'Ajaccio; it even affords an interesting perspective on Monte d'Oro, which begins to take shape at the bottom of the Vallée du Gravone to the north-east.

Down below you can see both the old and the new cemeteries. The path runs alongside large, eroded rock forms as it snakes its way through the maquis and eucalyptus bushes. For the entire length of this pretty walk there are wonderful views down over a whole string of beaches and coves. After walking for about two hours you can clearly make out the Îles Sanguinaires.

After this, the path descends for about 30 minutes to the sunny resort of Vignola and the Route des Sanguinaires (D111), which goes along the coast to the west starting from the No 5 bus stop opposite the Hôtel Week-End.

There are some wonderful beaches with snack bars and restaurants to welcome you at the end of this charming walk, then you can return to Ajaccio on the No 5 bus (every hour between 7.30 am and 7.30 pm, daily during the peak season).

PISCIA DI GALLO WATERFALL

Access & Location: Via the D368 between Porto Vecchio and Zonza; about 25km from Porto Vecchio and 1km after the Barrage de l'Ospedale
Markings: Cairns with pictograms
Standard: Very steep section at the end of the walk
Duration: 1½ hours there and back; return along the same route
Change in Altitude: 80m
Summary: The trail leads to a natural curiosity nestled in the heights of Porto Vecchio's hinterland, at the very heart of the wonderful wooded Ospedale massif.

The start of the walk, marked by a signpost, is near a couple of snack bars beside the D368. The first part of the route goes through the middle of a splendid forest of maritime pines down a gently sloping forest track. The path fords two little streams before ascending to a barren little plateau. At this point on the walk you can just see the coast to the west. The trail goes along a ridge that overhangs a steep-sided canyon with a stream rushing through it to the right, the same one that flows over the waterfall further downstream. You then get to a little pass that has wonderful views over the coast and the Golfe de Porto Vecchio. To either side of you there are pink granite massifs stretching down to the sea.

The path then descends across the maquis, dominated by arbutus and heather, and winds between massive lumps of rock. You can clearly hear the sound of the waterfall at this stage. If you want to see the Cascade de Piscia di Gallo ('Chicken Piss' Waterfall), you have to descend through a very steep rocky gully, using your hands and grabbing hold of branches to steady yourself until you reach a little ledge. From this viewpoint you can see the spectacle of the water crashing down onto a rock overhang and splitting into two halves. This last section is not advisable if you have small children with you or if there's wet weather because there's a risk of slipping. Although you cannot bathe under the waterfall, on the way back up you can take a little path down to the left, next to a pine tree. This leads to a stream further down that has inviting pools to swim in.

THE CLIFFS OF BONIFACIO TO THE PERTUSATO LIGHTHOUSE

> **Access & Location:** In Bonifacio, on the road to the upper town; turn left at the bend
> **Markings:** Information point at the start

> **Standard:** Little shade; children must be supervised because the path is close to the cliff edge, especially at the beginning of the walk
> **Duration:** 2½ hours there and back; return along the same route
> **Change in Altitude:** Minimal
> **Summary:** This walk seems a long way from the hustle and bustle of tourism in Bonifacio. It follows the line of the cliffs at the edge of the town and affords excellent views of the spectacular Bouches de Bonifacio (Straits of Bonifacio) between Corsica and Sardinia.

A paved slope climbs to the top of the cliffs from the bend in the road. Follow the path along the cliffs towards the south-east. On your left is low-growing maquis, while on your right there is a sheer drop down to the sea.

After no more than 30 minutes the path joins the D260, which leads to the *sémaphore* (small lighthouse) and the *phare* (lighthouse). Follow this little road as it veers away from the cliff edge for a short distance. The path passes a farm before dipping down into a large depression. It climbs back up and continues past some old military bunkers to the sémaphore, which you'll reach after 45 minutes walk.

After the signal light, the road follows a long hairpin-shaped indentation in the coast. Fifty metres before the lighthouse, a path leads down to a cove edged with golden sand and to Île Saint Antoine.

On the way out you'll be able to appreciate the shape of the chalk cliffs eroded by the sea. On the way back you'll have plenty of time to admire the old town of Bonifacio, balanced precariously on the promontory, and the view of Sardinia to the south. Avoid the hottest parts of the day, as there is no shade and nowhere to get water.

GEORGES ANTONI

GEORGES ANTONI

GEORGES ANTONI

GEORGES ANTONI

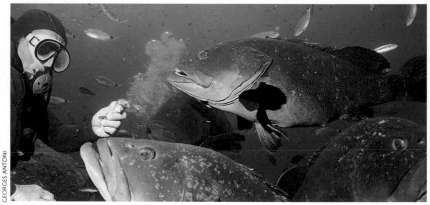

GEORGES ANTONI

The underwater depths around Corsica are rich in marine life. Among other things, you may encounter scorpion fish, moray eels, groupers and highly prized red coral.

Diving

Diving in the waters around Corsica will allow you to experience the Mediterranean at its best. The island has nearly 1000km of coastline with numerous inlets and beaches and, although they're not on a par with tropical seas, Corsica's waters are home to some unique treasures that make the island a favourite destination of experienced and novice divers alike.

Corsica's hilly landscape is echoed in its underwater panorama, which boasts faults, mountains, scree, sharp peaks, canyons and rocky massifs. The scrub on land gives way to gorgonian, yellow flowering anemone and the highly prized red coral, among which grouper, brown meagre and dentex swim. There are a number of easily acces-sible wrecks around the coast. In summer the clarity and temperature of the water, re-markable at this latitude, give this Mediter-ranean world a tropical feel.

Corsica's underwater kingdom is very well preserved, largely due to the near ab-sence of pollution, the lack of intensive fishing and the careful management of two internationally renowned marine nature re-serves, the Réserve Naturelle de Scandola and the Réserve Naturelle des Îles Lavezzi.

Corsica's many diving sites are suitable for all divers, regardless of experience. There are around 30 diving centres with ex-cellent facilities and instructors; staff there can tell you about the various sites.

DIVING SITES
Diving Conditions

In the high season Corsica's waters have much to offer. The water temperature, which is fairly low in winter (around 13 to 14°C), rises to 17°C in May and from 20 to 21°C in June, peaking at around 25°C in August. September is pleasant (23°C) and October very bearable (20°C). These sur-face temperatures are intended as a guide only: for comfort and warmth a suit with a mask is highly recommended in the colder layers below the surface.

In calm seas, particularly in inlets, you will be pleasantly surprised by the visibility. The average visibility in summer is 25m, al-though in August this can rise to 40m when the weather is good. The wind, particularly the *libeccio* (south-westerly wind), can pro-duce a heavy swell at sea and inside the rather exposed gulfs, making diving at some sites impractical. Headlands and rocky overhangs are particularly vulnerable to currents. In unfavourable conditions the diving centres use sheltered zones inside bays.

Few areas of Corsica's coastline have a continental shelf: the island's mountains extend beneath the surface of the water,

---

Corsica's Remarkable Wrecks

Porto Vecchio
The *Pecorella* (5 to 12m) and the *Toro* (20m)

Golfe de Valinco
The yacht on the Sec du Belge (24m) and the *Tasmania* (14 to 19m)

Golfe d'Ajaccio
The *Meulière* (5 to 15m)

Golfe de Sagone
The *Girafe* (18m) and the *Canadair* wreck (30m)

Golfe de Porto
The collier at Punta Muchillina (20 to 30m)

Calvi
The B-17 bomber (27m)

From Calvi to Île Rousse
The *Grand Cerf* (25m)

Saint Florent
L'Aventure (10m) and the *Ça-ira* (18m)

Bastia
The Heinkel-111 (33m), the Thunderbolt (22m) and the *Canonnière* (40 to 45m)

DIVING SITES & CENTRES

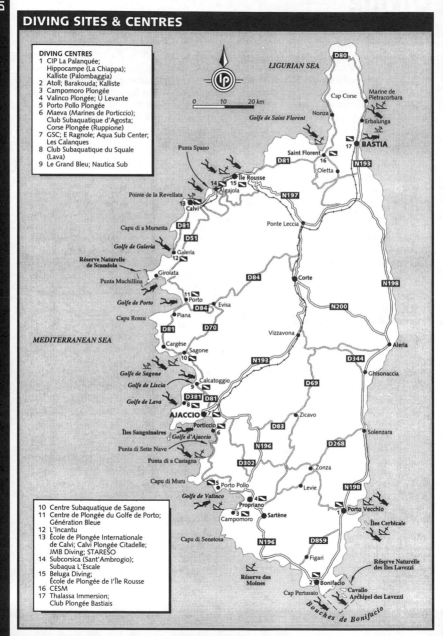

DIVING CENTRES
1 CIP La Palanquée;
   Hippocampe (La Chiappa);
   Kalliste (Palombaggia)
2 Atoll; Barakouda; Kalliste
3 Campomoro Plongée
4 Valinco Plongée; U Levante
5 Porto Pollo Plongée
6 Maeva (Marines de Porticcio);
   Club Subaquatique d'Agosta;
   Corse Plongée (Ruppione)
7 GSC; E Ragnole; Aqua Sub Center;
   Les Calanques
8 Club Subaquatique du Squale
   (Lava)
9 Le Grand Bleu; Nautica Sub

10 Centre Subaquatique de Sagone
11 Centre de Plongée du Golfe de Porto;
    Génération Bleue
12 L'Incantu
13 École de Plongée Internationale
    de Calvi; Calvi Plongée Citadelle;
    JMB Diving; STARESO
14 Subcorsica (Sant'Ambrogio);
    Subaqua L'Escale
15 Beluga Diving;
    École de Plongée de l'Île Rousse
16 CESM
17 Thalassa Immersion;
    Club Plongée Bastiais

LIGURIAN SEA

Cap Corse
Marine de
Pietracorbara
Nonza
Erbalunga
Golfe de Saint Florent
BASTIA

Saint Florent
D81
Oletta
N193

Punta Spano
Île Rousse
Algajola

Pointe de la Revellata
Calvi

N197

Ponte Leccia

Capu di a Mursetta
D81
D51

Golfe de Galeria
Galeria

Réserve Naturelle
de Scandola
Girolata
D84
Corte

Punta Muchillina
Porto
Golfe de Porto
Evisa
N198

Capu Rosso
Piana
D84

N200

D81
D70

MEDITERRANEAN SEA
Cargèse
Sagone
Vizzavona

D344
Aleria

Golfe de Sagone
Calcatoggio
N193

Golfe de Liscia
Ghisonaccia

Golfe de Lava
D381 D81
D69

AJACCIO
Zicavo

Porticcio
D83

Îles Sanguinaires
Golfe d'Ajaccio
Solenzara

Punta di Sette Nave
N196
D268

Punta di a Castagna
Zonza

D302

Capu di Muru
Porto Pollo
Levie
N198

Golfe de Valinco
Propriano
Porto Vecchio

Campomoro
Sartène
Îles Cerbicale

Capu di Senetosa
N196
D859

Figari
Réserve Naturelle
des Îles Lavezzi

Réserve des
Moines
Bonifacio
Cavallo

Cap Pertusato
Archipel des Lavezzi

Bouches de Bonifacio

0   10   20 km

scribed in this guidebook does not mean that it is safe for you and your diving party. You are ultimately responsible for judging your own capabilities in the light of the conditions you encounter.

Around Porto Vecchio

A dozen or so dives can be taken in this area, mainly around the Îles Cerbicale. The small island of **Toro** (The Bull) south-east of this archipelago is ideal for all abilities because it has a number of protected little coves and shallows that descend to a depth of 40m. Its small canyons, which reach a similar depth, are carpeted with encrusted sponges, and there is an abundance of fallen rocks and caves. Comber, rainbow wrasse, bogue and conger eel animate the scene,

forming an impressive landscape of jagged slopes. As a result, on the west coast the water can suddenly get very deep: in places such as the Golfe de Porto it can reach a depth of 800m.

Many *secs*, or shallows, are also found, forming miniature lagoons with a range of depths. On the east coast (around Bastia) this dramatic submarine landscape is replaced by a gently sloping sea bed of sand and silt dotted with massifs.

Beginners should try not to feel intimidated by the shallows and drops, which rarely plunge straight to the bottom, but are often crisscrossed by faults and small plateaus that allow you to control your descent. Most sites can therefore be visited by divers of all abilities.

The descriptions that follow are intended to give an insight into diving in Corsica, based on a selection of popular dives. The names of sites often vary from one centre to another. The most common types of fish to be found are listed, but there is no guarantee that any of them will be seen during a particular dive.

Although the authors and publisher have done their utmost to ensure the accuracy of all information in this guide, they cannot accept any responsibility for any loss, injury or inconvenience sustained by people using this book. The fact that a dive is de-

Environmentally Aware Diving

To minimise the effects of diving on Corsica's fragile marine ecosystem, visitors should try to adhere to the following guidelines.

Don't feed the fish, especially with food that is not part of their normal diet. This could interfere with their metabolism or give rise to unnatural behaviour, particularly in the case of grouper, which lose their natural fear of human beings when fed boiled egg; this turns them into easier targets for predators and makes them more likely to swallow objects such as plastic bags.

Control your buoyancy and stability to avoid accidentally kicking the sea bed. Sessile (non-moving) organisms, particularly sponges and gorgonians, are easily damaged by careless movements.

Don't linger in the caves: bubbles from your regulator will get trapped under the roof, exposing organisms such as encrusted sponges to the air and causing them to decay.

The removal of shells and other fauna from anywhere on the French coastline is strictly forbidden.

and a few dentex, attracted by the current, can also sometimes be seen.

Farther out to sea, the **Danger du Toro** is one of the wildest sites in this area. Three shallows begin several metres below the surface before dropping to 40m. Carved into canyons decorated with gorgonian, they are frequented by grouper, dentex, rainbow wrasse and, near the surface, by damselfish.

La Vacca (The Cow), an islet to the east of the archipelago, has a similar configuration to that of Toro and a depth of approximately 20 to 25m. Farther out to sea lies the **Danger de la Vacca**, where shallows descend in terraces from 3 to 40m. When it's windy or there's a strong current these two sites are exposed and you should keep to the sheltered areas of Toro and La Vacca.

Experienced divers will enjoy **Les Arches**, between Toro and La Vacca, when the sea is calm. This is a huge rocky peak, covered in gorgonian, which extends from 19 to 37m. At 35m a plateau opens up, where divers can pass beneath arches thronged with grouper, moray eel, brown meagre, and predators such as dentex and leerfish.

Two wrecks can be visited in this area. The most famous is the *Pecorella*, which lists on its keel at the northern end of the Golfe de Porto Vecchio. This 45m-long cement carrier, which sank in a storm in 1967, lies on gravel in just 5 to 12m of water in the middle of a Poseidonion bed (see the boxed text 'Small is Beautiful' later in this chapter); this exciting location is often used as a setting for introductory dives, night dives and underwater photography. The wreck is in a remarkable state of preservation and its gangways, chain and cement holds, engine room, davits (crane-like devices for lowering lifeboats) and bridge with its helm can all be explored in safety. Sessile organisms (such as red coral and anemones, which are attached to substrata and are non-moving) adorn part of its metal structure but, apart from a handful of brown meagre and some red scorpion fish, there are few fish.

The *Toro* wreck, near the islet of the same name, is a wooden coaster that shipped tiles and marble slabs; it probably sank between 1910 and 1920. The entire superstructure, which lies at 20m, at the foot of a shallow that rises to 8m, has disintegrated. Some moray eel, red scorpion fish and conger eel can be found there.

Bonifacio

The waters around Bonifacio have been explored more fully than any others in Corsica. The drops here are less frequent than on the west coast and the underwater relief is less pronounced. The Réserve Naturelle des Îles Lavezzi (see the boxed text 'Corsica's Marine Reserves' on page 166), about 20 minutes south-east of the coast, offers a stunning backdrop and exceptional conditions for divers of all abilities. Among chiselled granite rocks, the turquoise-green water of the small inlets, which seem to have been designed for novice divers, is reminiscent of more tropical climes. A bit farther out to sea are several famous sites suitable for more experienced divers.

Corsica's most popular dive site, **Mérouville**, is in the Îles Lavezzi to the east of the archipelago. A rocky mass descends from 17m to a sandy floor at about 30m. The main attraction of the dive is the brown grouper, exclusive to the Mediterranean. Dozens of notoriously friendly specimens, some up to 1.2m long, live here. Accustomed to the presence of divers, they sidle up to you, watching hopefully for titbits, and will allow you to stroke them if you don't make any sudden or uncoordinated movements.

In addition to commercialised Mérouville, which has been a victim of its own success (see the boxed text 'Mérouville'), the Îles Lavezzi are host to a number of other more secluded and wild sites, rich in marine invertebrates. The grouper are more timid here. Near the main island of the Îles Lavezzi, the **Est du Phare** has interesting rocky passages at depths of 3 to 20m but there are few fish. On the south-western side you'll find **Dahbia 1**, **Dahbia 2** and

Mérouville

The success of Mérouville has been a double-edged sword: divers flock here to swim among the friendly grouper and scavenging rainbow wrasse and sargo but the site is overexploited in summer, when it is not unusual to find several dozen boats from Corsica and Sardinia moored here. The sea bed has suffered as a result. Many divers also like to feed the grouper boiled eggs, bread or salami to tame them, but almost all of the diving centres discourage this practice, fearing adverse effects on nature's equilibrium.

The diving centres in Bonifacio are trying to find a compromise between demand and the site's capacity, and a charter is probably going to be drawn up as part of the Bouches de Bonifacio marine park project.

Dahbia 3. The first is a drop spanning 10 to 23m, cloaked in gorgonian and inhabited by moray eel, sea spider, brown meagre and grouper; the second, between 19 and 40m, is a mass of fallen rocks; and the third, between 12 and 30m, is the most beautiful gorgonian-covered drop in the Îles Lavezzi. Grouper, moray eel and red scorpion fish are likely to be spotted here.

West of these sites and farther out to sea, a real treat is in store at the **Écueil des Lavezzi**, a vast rocky plateau marked by a tower that peaks at 5m and gradually descends to 50m. Some have described it as the 'Mediterranean rediscovered'. Out at sea, when conditions are good, you can find wild grouper, brown meagre, dentex, moray eel, rockfish, shoals of sargo and opulent, well-preserved marine invertebrates. The **Tête de Cheval** (Horse's Head), extending from 16 to 50m, is a rock that juts out from the drop, complete with gorgonian, caves and rocky passages.

To the north-west, the **Tête d'Homme** (Man's Head), another rocky ascent staggered between 6 and 40m and accessible to

level 1 divers, is named after the shape of its rocky summit. Gorgonian grows on its side from a depth of 13m and grouper, dentex and brown meagre patrol the waters.

The **Écueil de Sperduto** to the east of the Île Cavallo is a rock visible above the surface of the waves and marked by a tower. This site is suitable for divers of all levels provided the sea is calm. Sargo, moray eel and damselfish can all be found here and you may even come face to face with a barracuda.

Diving in the Îles Lavezzi is not always a picnic, however. Situated right in the middle of the Bouches de Bonifacio, between Sardinia and Corsica, the archipelago is exposed to winds from all directions, particularly westerlies, and to strong currents. The sea can sometimes be capricious and boat trips to the sites can be a little bumpy. Visit the sites in fine weather if you can.

Not all of the diving centres in the area run dives around Bonifacio's chalky cliffs but **Les Grottes**, at the entrance to the harbour, is accessible come rain or shine. A series of caves and passages (only to be explored by the experienced), in less than 10m of water, burrow into the cliff. Cardinalfish, squad lobster, flat lobster and conger eel occasionally appear in this biotope.

To the east of Bonifacio, the Cap Pertusato region contains a number of diving locations, such as **Pertusato**, extending from 3 to 20m, and **Supertusato**, slightly farther east. These two sites teem with small rockfish and are ideal for an introductory dive. For the more experienced diver, a shallow in the form of a vertical drop between 32 and 46m lies just off Cap Pertusato.

Golfe de Valinco

The Golfe de Valinco has an excellent reputation among divers. Its underwater relief is even more dramatic than that of other parts of the west coast (the middle of the gulf reaches a depth of 800m) and it has an abundance of sessile organisms such as gorgonian, parazoa and red coral. The density of the fauna increases and it takes on a

Corsica's Marine Reserves

The preservation of the marine kingdom is not taken lightly in Corsica, which has two nature reserves that include areas of sea.

The **Réserve Naturelle des Îles Lavezzi**, just off Bonifacio at the southern end of the island, was created in 1982. Six of the seven islands in the archipelago are protected areas; the main island, Cavallo, nicknamed 'millionaire's island', is the exception. The 80,000 hectares of sea surrounding the archipelago are also protected. Underwater fishing and the dumping of refuse or waste water are prohibited.

The **Réserve Naturelle de Scandola** on the west coast was created in 1975 and covers 919 hectares on land and 1000 hectares at sea, between Punta Muchillina in the south (at the northern entrance to the Golfe de Porto) and Punta Nera in the north. The Anse d'Elpa Nera, slightly farther north, is also part of the reserve. In terms of subaquatic flora and fauna, Scandola is a true paradise: 450 species of seaweed have been identified here, in addition to 125 species of fish, which find it ideal for breeding.

The restrictions here are more severe than in the Lavezzi reserve: underwater hunting, line fishing (and commercial fishing in the most protected area, classified as the integral reserve), the dumping of rubbish, mooring for more than 24 hours, the removal of marine flora and fauna and scuba diving are all forbidden. The aim is to both protect the area and allow the scientific monitoring of the natural environment. The protective measures help the reserve to act as a natural breeding ground, supplying life to the surrounding areas. Scandola is listed as a UNESCO World Heritage Site.

Several other plans are also in the pipeline. The international marine park project in the

wilder appearance as you near the mouth of the gulf. The most famous dives are over rocky ascents near the shore at the northern and southern entrances to the gulf. For beginners there are sheltered inlets closer to Propriano.

On the southern side of the gulf, halfway between Propriano and Campomoro, **Red Canyon** is a huge rock split open on one side to create a gully rich in red coral (at a depth of about 25m) and other marine organisms. Slightly farther west is the **Sec du Belvédère**, a rocky peak extending from 9 to 30m, famous for its low-level gorgonian and caves adorned with red coral. **Le Tonneau** is remarkable for its varied configuration and is only to be tackled by experienced divers. This huge rock begins at 6m; an arch 23m down, a cave at 47m and, at 41m, a path from which you can re-emerge at 33m are the main features of this renowned dive, during which you will

almost invariably encounter grouper and rock lobster.

At the eastern entrance to the Baie de Campomoro, **Monica** refers to three peaks along the shore. The first extends from 6 to 22m, the second from 7 to 40m and the third from 14 to 40m. A coral cavern is found between 27 and 35m. During the dive you will see large tubes several metres in diameter tangled together at a depth of 12m; these belonged to a ship.

At the entrance to the gulf at the western end of the Baie de Campomoro, the **Sec de Campomoro** is a first-rate dive suitable for divers of all abilities. Several rocky platforms, one of which just breaks the surface of the water, descend to 40m. The site is heavily fissured and gorgonian (at a depth of about 25m), bogue, sargo, rock lobster, dentex, forkbeard and occasionally grouper populate the scene. Behind the Punta Campomoro, the wreck of a yacht lists on the

Corsica's Marine Reserves

Bouches de Bonifacio, which will encompass the current Lavezzi reserve, the Îles Cerbicale and the Maddalena archipelago in Sardinia (an area of 60,000 hectares), will bring new regulations to deal with the problem of overcrowding in the Îles Lavezzi. In summer, it is not unusual to find some 50 yachts and diving boats at one site. There is talk of introducing a quota system, of installing mooring to prevent the use of anchors, of establishing areas classified as integral reserves and of drawing up legislation prohibiting the feeding of grouper.

There are also plans to transform the Scandola reserve into a national marine park, which would be the second-largest in France after Port-Cros. This would extend from the Pointe de la Revellata in the north to Capu Rossu just south of the Golfe de Porto, and would include Galeria and Porto. Three levels of protection with increasingly severe restrictions would be in place: a peripheral zone, a central zone and integral reserves.

Those managing these projects do not have an easy task ahead of them: they must find common ground with diving clubs, ecologists, anglers, yachting enthusiasts and local people, who often have very different agendas. The diving centres welcome the changes despite the restrictions (such as diving quotas, sites reserved for experienced divers and compulsory briefing on protection, the species and all ecological aspects of the reserves) – being situated in a marine park would limit the number of dives that they could run but would allow them to increase prices accordingly.

This change in status will be accompanied by an increase in material and human resources because the parks will be state-run, and Corsica will be able to reap the rewards of a formidable ecological showcase.

Sec du Belge at 24m. This site teems with rock lobster.

Centres in Propriano arrange dives to wild sites outside the gulf, particularly around Capu di Senetosa in the south. These little-visited sites are home to many fish. **Senetosa**, just off Capu di Senetosa, is a shallow extending from 13 to 40m and inhabited by grouper. Nearer the coast, the **Tombant de Conca** falls away sharply from 8 to 47m and is suitable for divers of all abilities.

Valinco Plongée (see under Diving Centres later in the chapter) arranges dives in the Réserve des Moines, out at sea southwest of the Tour d'Olmeto, where it is possible to dive down to the wreck of the *Tasmania*. This 142m-long steamer, which lies at a depth of between 14 and 19m, sank in 1887 on its return to Marseille from the Indies. You can still make out the smokestacks, winches, propeller and stern.

On the northern side, the sites are mainly concentrated around the Punta Porto Pollo at the entrance to the gulf. The most famous is undoubtedly **Les Cathédrales**, a short distance from the small harbour of Porto Pollo. To picture the scene, imagine a scaled-down version of the Aiguilles de Bavella, southwest of Solenzara. Extending from 12 to 40m, its peaks, faults, shelves and arches (at 37m) are home to a variety of creatures that attract marauding predators. Other evocatively named and similarly shaped sites can be found slightly farther west (**La Vallée**, **Les Aiguilles** and **Le Colorado**).

Golfe d'Ajaccio

Dozens of sites can be found in the Golfe d'Ajaccio, between the seldom-visited Îles Sanguinaires in the north and Capu di Muru in the south. **Le Tabernacle**, the main site on this part of the coast, is at the north-western end of the gulf and is ideal for beginners, with a plateau descending from 3 to 22m. Forkbeard, rock lobster, brown meagre, sargo and even grouper are encountered here.

Closer to Ajaccio and 300m from the coast, **Guardiola** suits beginners as well as more experienced divers, falling sharply from the surface to 40m. Gorgonian, rock lobster, grouper and red scorpion fish frequent the site. Local diving clubs visit a handful of other sites between the Îles Sanguinaires and Ajaccio beach.

The most spectacular dives in this area are found mainly in the southern section, between the Tour de l'Isolella (also known as the Punta di Sette Nave) and Capu di Muru. There are several unusual sites around the Pointe de l'Isolella but they get very busy in summer. At the **Punta di Sette Nave** enormous rocks covered in organisms such as gorgonian descend in terraces from 4 to 45m, riddled with small passages and tunnels.

Near the coast, **La Campanina** (suitable for divers of all abilities) is very popular, as is the **Tête de Mort** (Dead Man's Head), also suitable for beginners and experienced divers alike, extending from 0.5m to 40m. A plateau opens out at a depth of 15 to 20m, an ascent tops out at 6m, a chimney and cave can be found at 17m and there is another cave at 10m; it is all brought to life by a wealth of sessile organisms (such as red coral and gorgonian). Brown meagre, sargo, rock lobster, dentex and even leerfish and barracuda can be found.

A short distance from la Campanina is the **Sec d'Antoine**, with similar features.

The Last Maritime Miners

Red coral harvesting is more than just a job, it is part of the history of the Mediterranean. Corsica currently has about 15 coral divers who descend to depths of up to 100m to extract the 'red gold' from the bowels of the sea. Considered a precious stone and prized for its use in jewellery, it is actually an animal species (*Corallium rubrum*) with a hard red skeleton, which lives on the substrata of rocks as far down as 300m.

Coral diving is a high risk profession and divers must be qualified. Their gear consists of a wetsuit (up to three layers), two large cylinders (2x15L or 2x18L), flippers, a dive computer worn on the wrist, a basket for the coral (slung around the neck), a diving torch and a kind of tool, similar to an ice-axe, to detach coral branches.

Deep sea divers face two hazards: failure to decompress when resurfacing and nitrogen narcosis, or 'rapture of the deep', at the bottom. Most divers now use new air/helium mixes in their cylinders to eliminate the risk of nitrogen narcosis, and have recompression chambers on their boats, in which they shut themselves away if they experience the slightest symptom. Before modern techniques were developed, early coral divers used more haphazard methods such as the Saint Andrew's cross (two wooden beams fitted with nets, dragged along the sea bed by boats).

At the end of each season (which extends from May to November) the harvest is sold at Torre del Greco near Naples, the hub of the coral industry. Here a kilo of coral can fetch between 1000FF and 4000FF, depending on the quality, size and thickness of the branches. It is then worked in special cutting shops and sold on to jewellers all over the world in the form of pearls, necklaces, pendants and studs.

The coral divers' days are numbered, however: accessible deposits are becoming rarer in Corsica and the quality of the harvests is low. Corsican coral divers, some of whom have already moved to Tunisia, now have their eyes on Libyan and Albanian shores.

The Punta di Sette Nave and the Tête de Mort are often used for introductory dives. The wild Punta di a Castagna also offers several sites for underwater forays, including the *Meulière*, a minesweeper that sank during WWII and rests at a depth of between 5 and 15m. Two sites are reserved for experienced divers. The first is the **Tombant du Corailleur**, several nautical miles off the gulf; the second, the **Grotte à Corail** (25 to 57m) off Plage d'Agosta, south of Porticcio, is a chimney festooned with gorgonian and coral.

Golfe de Lava

Wild and unvisited, the enchanting Golfe de Lava boasts one of Corsica's most stunning dive sites. The **Banc Provençal**, out at sea to the north, halfway between the Golfe de Lava and the Golfe de Liscia, is only accessible in calm seas. A memorable dive not to be undertaken by the uninitiated, this rocky mass extends from 17 to 80m and consists of a twin summit divided by a fault. One side is formed by a plateau; on the other side rocky shelves form a series of platforms. The rocks, covered by multicoloured sponges, gorgonian and flowering anemones, provide a home for specimens seem to represent all of the Mediterranean's fauna, including brown meagre, forkbeard, rock lobster, moray eel, swallow-tail sea perch, damselfish and a family of grouper living in a cave at 37m.

At the south-western entrance to the Golfe de Lava, the **Sec de Pietra Piombata** shallow is suitable for all divers, ranging in depth from 3 to 60m and embroidered with gorgonian and coral (at 40m). Because it is near the open sea it attracts predators: you may come across dentex, brown meagre or barracuda.

Golfe de Sagone

This huge gulf boasts several exceptional dives. On the southern shore, towards the Golfe de Liscia (part of the Golfe de Sagone), experienced divers can experience a series of drops at **Castellaci**. Nearby, a plateau extends from the coastline in the form of wide steps (15 to 30m, 30 to 50m) honeycombed with caves.

Similar architecture can be found at **Punta Paliagi**, farther east, where small plateaus start at a depth of 3m. At **Punta Palmentoju**, level with the Tour d'Ancone in the Golfe de Liscia, a dozen peaks fall away sharply from 3 to 50m. This spectacular scenery is home to moray eel, gorgonian, rock lobster, brown meagre, dentex and even barracuda. At the nearby **Langue de Feu** (Tongue of Fire), red coral blankets a cavern at around 30m.

If sheer drops are more your thing, you'll enjoy **Punta Capigliolo**, north of the Golfe de Liscia. The rock drops vertically from the surface down to 130m. Farther north, **Punta San Giuseppe** is distinguished by its huge rectangular megaliths, around 20m long and several metres high, found at 20m. From that depth masses of fallen rocks descend to 40m.

The bottom of the Anse de Sagone is the final resting place of two ships, including the *Girafe*, a Napoleonic store ship that transported Corsican pine to be used in shipbuilding. It was scuppered by an English force in the 19th century. Beginners can explore these remains at 18m, where bronze cannons, sections of hull and cannonballs can be seen.

Slightly farther out to sea, at the mouth of the cove, the wreck of a Canadian (firefighting plane) can be visited by seasoned divers. The carcass of the plane, which crashed in 1971 after accidentally veering off course, now lies upside down on a sandy bed at 30m.

Golfe de Porto

Corsica's jewel, the Golfe de Porto is a must, but the dozen sites between Capu Rossu in the south and Punta Muchillina in the north are only used by three diving centres. Granite plunges towards abysses 800m deep in the middle of the gulf, which also borders the Réserve Naturelle de Scandola to the south, home to a complete range of Mediterranean fauna (see the earlier boxed text 'Corsica's Marine Reserves').

Studying Marine Life

The most unusual diving club in Corsica is the oceanographic centre STARESO (STAtion de REcherches Sous-marines et Océanographiques; Submarine and Oceanographic Research Station) at Pointe de la Revellata west of the Baie de Calvi. Founded in 1972 and part of the Université de Liège, it caters for amateur divers, beginners and experienced divers alike, who can rub shoulders with marine experts in a friendly and informal setting. Revenue from tourism helps the centre to continue operating.

STARESO offers an introductory dive for 200FF (departing from the harbour, near the jetty), exploratory dives for between 160FF and 200FF and level 1 instruction for 2500FF. The most frequently used sites are Pointe de la Revellata, Punta Bianca and the Sec du Lion, all less than 15 minutes away. There are occasional trips to the wreck of the B-17 bomber.

STARESO offers a range of bespoke accommodation packages, including full board in summer in a luxury studio or an apartment for two in the research centre (650/550FF respectively per person per night with one or two dives). You can even stay in a room in the lighthouse, for the same price as the studio. Lunch at the centre costs 70FF.

The centre lies 4km west of Calvi at the end of a 4.5km stone track riddled with potholes. To get there, take the D81 from Calvi to Galeria and look out for the lighthouse. Stick to the track, rather than bearing right.

STARESO (☎ 04 95 65 06 18, mobile ☎ 06 12 95 57 51, fax 04 95 65 01 34, email stareso@imaginet.fr) is open daily and arranges two excursions each day.

Diving is prohibited within the reserve but centres in Porto and Galeria arrange dives around its southern boundary, where an abundance of fauna and flora can be found. However, the westerly wind can make boat trips to this area impossible so you may not be able to visit the most stunning diving locations, which are near the northern and southern entrances to the gulf.

As sites for introductory dives and instruction, clubs in Porto have the **Porte d'Aix**, an inlet on the northern shore five minutes from the harbour, **Castagne** in the south, accessible by road or sea, and the **Sec du Château**, also in the south but slightly farther away, consisting of several little shallows near the surface.

Farther west along the southern shore you'll come to **Figajola**, where two headlands descend from 5m to around 35m. They are rich in sessile organisms and often visited by dentex and brown meagre. This site is suitable for both beginners and experienced divers.

Continuing towards Capu Rossu, the delightful **Vardiola** is a sugar-loaf mountain breaking the surface of the waves and encircled by a deep gash at 30 to 10m, which provides an alternative route to the surface. Red coral abounds at the foot of the fault, which rises to a plateau populated by brown meagre, dentex, forkbeard, rock lobster and grouper.

Between Vardiola and Capu Rossu, the **Pitons de Vardiola** are rocky summits that plunge from 8 to 50m. Experienced divers can see the magnificent gorgonian covering the rock face between 30 and 40m.

Facing the open sea, **Capu Rossu** is the outermost point on the southern side of the gulf. Two massive rocks that break the surface of the waves descend in a series of plateaus on the land side and in drops on the side exposed to the open sea. The relief is broken and carved by faults. The proximity of the open sea means you'll probably encounter large fish such as tuna, barracuda and leerfish. This splendid site is suitable for beginners.

The northern side of the gulf is near the Réserve Naturelle de Scandola and culminates in **Punta Muchillina**, with its abundance of marine life. This is a spectacular site suitable for all divers. Near the coast, shallows just 1m or so below the surface descend on the southern side to a depth of 50m. Gorgonian, parazoa, rock lobster, brown meagre, dentex and even barracuda can be seen. On the eastern side the wreck of an old collier lies at 20 to 30m. The machinery room, propeller and boilers can still be made out among the debris, among which fish have a field day.

Five minutes from the harbour, at Monte Rosso, is the gulf's stunning **Voûte à Corail** (coral cavern), 26m below the surface. From a depth of 20m the site, which teems with fish, is used for introductory dives and instruction.

Halfway between Porto and Punta Muchillina is a lovely site called **Punta Scopa**. This drop is suitable for divers of all abilities, who might see predators such as dentex and brown meagre. The next headland, **Seninu**, which is also suitable for all divers, has an excellent reputation. Shallows top out at 1.5m, then tumble down on one side to 50m, furrowed by faults and enlivened by rich sessile organisms, including splendid gorgonian. Grouper, dentex, moray eel, brown meagre, rock lobster and forkbeard may keep you company.

Around Galeria

A wild atmosphere and unique dives characterise the area around Galeria, which has only one diving centre. The sites are scattered between Capu di a Mursetta, to the north, and the northern boundary of the Réserve Naturelle de Scandola.

Heading north from Galeria, the first site you come to is **Ciuttone**, level with the headland of the same name at the eastern end of the Baie de Galeria. This site is accessible to all divers. Red coral is found from a depth of 20m. Farther north, between Ciuttone and Capu di a Mursetta, the **Roche Bleue** (Blue Rock) is for more experienced divers; a sugar-loaf mountain en-

livened with gorgonian, it extends from 30 to 50m.

Farther north, the islet of **Mursetta**, facing the headland of the same name, is spectacular and varied, comprising scree, faults, drops and valleys. The rocks are home to forkbeard, rock lobster and moray eel, and take their colour from sessile organisms such as gorgonian, which becomes denser the deeper you go. Grouper and brown meagre regularly roam the area, which is suitable for divers of all abilities.

Le Tunnel, south of Mursetta, is an L-shaped trench about 50m long that crosses the rock face in places. The entrance is at a depth of 17m and the gully is 2 to 3m in diameter, but you will need a torch (available from the club) to go into it. This dive is suitable for beginners, but going deep into the cliffs can be frightening for those prone to claustrophobia. Inside, the rock is fairly bare and the cowries that crowned the walls have disappeared, but a torch beam almost always surprises forkbeard lurking in crevices. You come out of the gully at 12m. Not far away, **La Faille** gully is slightly deeper, at 16m, but goes back into the rock face for about 30m. At one point you enter an air chamber full of stalactites.

As you get closer to the Réserve Naturelle de Scandola, to the south, the sites become increasingly wild. The islet of **Porri**, a series of rocky ridges parallel to one another at a depth of between 15 and 40m, is of real visual interest and has

Yellow Seaweed

Every year, at the start of summer, a yellow seaweed appears due to the rise in temperature, proliferating and covering the non-moving fauna and rock with a yellowish moss and disfiguring the landscape. This is a perfectly natural phenomenon, and is not caused by pollution as many divers think. Currents gradually cause this rather unsightly moss to disappear.

served as a backdrop for the Championnat Méditerranéen de Photo Sous-Marine (Mediterranean Underwater Photography Championship).

Around Calvi

The area around Calvi is attractive to divers because it is so full of contrasts. The southern part of the bay is nothing to write home about, but once you travel farther west towards the wilderness around the Pointe de la Revellata you'll come across more enticing dives. The Baie de Calvi contains one of the most highly rated sites in Corsica, the wreck of a **B-17 bomber** (see the boxed text 'A Lucky Escape'). Given the depth, the B-17 is for technically experienced divers only, although centres in Calvi are currently taking level 1 divers to where they can see it if the latter are content not to dive down as far as the wreck itself.

La Bibliothèque (the library), so called because of its rocky massifs that resemble

piles of books, is also used for introductory dives. Less than 20m deep, it is home to few fish and mostly sessile (non-moving) organisms are found there. On the other side of the Citadelle, on the way out of Calvi, the **Pointe Saint François** is used for introductory dives and instruction.

To the north-west of Calvi, on the edge of a fishing zone and just south of the lighthouse, **La Revellata** consists of rocky valleys, scree, miniature drops, canyons and faults, at varying depths and exposed to the open sea. In this grandiose setting, with its gorgonian, sponges and flowering anemones, you will probably see grouper, sargo, brown meagre, dentex, leerfish and shellfish; the site, extending from 10 to 40m, is accessible to all divers and combines all of Corsica's underwater delights. Red coral is found below 30m.

Even farther west, experienced divers will enjoy **Mezzu Golfu** (otherwise known as the Sec du Clocher), which plunges down from 27 to 50m. Resembling a flattened ball, it is riddled with faults and caves and covered with gorgonian. You may see grouper and dentex. **Punta Bianca** has rather sharp drops that descend in terraces from 10 to 42m and are covered in gorgonian and red coral. Dentex, conger eel, forkbeard, rock lobster and brown meagre are in more or less permanent residence.

From Calvi to Île Rousse

The area between Punta Spano, west of the Sant'Ambrogio marina, and Algajola, to the east, offers unusual sites suitable for beginners and experienced divers alike. The most famous is the **Danger d'Algajola**, just off Algajola, which is in complete contrast to the type of diving site normally associated with Corsica. The peaks and drops give way to an immense rocky plateau 1.5 nautical miles out to sea, more than 1km long and 400m wide, which descends from 1 to 40m. Due to its size a number of different dives can be made to this site. It is full of nooks and crannies, gorges, small peaks, jagged ridges and miniature valleys, which form an ideal playground for rock-dwelling and

A Lucky Escape

In 1944, as Germans and Americans fought it out relentlessly over the Mediterranean, a B-17 bomber was hit by a Messerschmitt during an air raid on Verona. The pilot attempted to reach Calvi, the nearest base with an airport, but was forced to splash down in front of the Citadelle. Four crew members survived.

Now lying under 27m of seawater 200m from the Citadelle, the B-17 is a major attraction for divers. This imposing metal hulk, about 30m wide, is truncated at the front and rear (the nose and tail were destroyed on landing) but the central part of the fuselage (including the cabin and bomb bay), a section of the landing gear, the wings and four engines with twisted blades are still intact. Don't expect to encounter much fauna: the metal structures are only partially colonised by sponges and fish seem to stay away from the site.

pelagic fish. Divers may find themselves moving through shoals of damselfish and bogue, startling moray or conger eels in their hideaways, encountering marauding grouper, dentex or brown meagre lying in wait and crayfish in their caves, surprising timid octopus or coming face to face with barracuda. The top part of the plateau is devoid of gorgonian but coral can be found farther down.

The Subcorsica club (see under Diving Centres later in this chapter) runs dives at **Pietra Eramer**, an extension of the Punta di Sant'Ambrogio formed by masses of fallen rocks extending from 27 to 43m. Gorgonian provides a beautiful setting for grouper, sargo, dentex, crayfish and lobster.

Another site for experienced divers is **Kalliste**, with its abundance of caves, pinnacles and rocky passages between 23 and 45m. Brown meagre, sargo, forkbeard, moray eel and rock lobster often appear here, and gorgonian and coral are both found below 30m. The remains of the *Grand Cerf*, shipwrecked in the 19th century, are found at 25m; the ribs and derrick are still visible.

Beginners can explore **Cala Stella**, an inlet near the Tour de Spano that was formerly used as a fishing haven; here, in 12m of water, you can swim alongside tiny rock fish between faults and canyons. **Pedra Mule**, an islet near the promontory west of Algajola, is one of the sites used by the Algajola diving centre Subaqua l'Escale. Introductory dives are conducted on the eastern side. On the western side, which is deeper (15m), there is a slight drop inhabited by moray eel and damselfish.

Around Île Rousse

There are few dive sites in the Baie de l'Île Rousse, but the handful found here – rocky ascents rising from a sandy floor and cloaked with magnificent gorgonian, which could be described as the most beautiful in Corsica – will captivate you.

The most famous is **Le Naso**, a huge rock descending from 13 to 32m and accessible to all. It is distinguished by the concentration of conger and moray eel in the crevices around its base; brown meagre and dentex also prowl the area. Nearby, the **Petit Tombant**, between 16 and 42m, has similar features, and shoals of dentex and leerfish swim past its gorgonian-covered surface.

The Petit Tombant becomes the **Grand Tombant**, a plateau at a depth of 20m which, on the side facing the open sea, plunges down to 39m. The vertical rock face is colonised by striking fronds of gorgonian and encrusted sponges, while the plateau is home to sargo and octopus.

Less than 200m from the Grand Tombant towards the open sea, the **Trois Vierges** are three rocks hosting striking fish, particularly brown meagre and dentex, and sometimes tuna or grouper. The depth of the water (between 25 and 42m) means that only experienced divers can visit this site.

Small is Beautiful

Mediterranean fish are less breathtaking and smaller than fish in the tropics, but Corsica is nonetheless an oasis of marine life and will repay those who pay careful attention to its riches. Some divers say they didn't see any fish, while others on the same dive will launch into a description of the many species they encountered. A good instructor familiar with the sites will guide you, but there is nothing like personal curiosity.

To improve your chances, get to know the features of the various biotopes, each of which is home to a particular range of species. Explore each cavern and crevice carefully and acquaint yourself with the behaviour of the most common species. If you get the chance, use a diving torch to accentuate the colours of the sessile organisms (non-moving fauna such as coral, sponges and anemones) and surprise creatures in their hideaways.

The following list is not exhaustive but will help you to familiarise yourself with the underwater kingdom around Corsica.

Fish

Barracuda You will be lucky to see this fish in the wild because it makes only occasional and brief forays into coastal waters.

Bogue One of the few vegetarian fish, this species lives in shoals above Poseidonion beds, the leaves of which it feeds on. It is silver in colour with horizontal golden markings. Born male, specimens grow into females.

Brown meagre A favourite target for hunters, this fairly large predator (40 to 80cm long) is often seen in shoals near the rocky sea floor or Poseidonion beds. It is recognisable by its silvery-grey markings and arched back.

Cardinalfish Also known as 'king of the mullet', the cardinalfish is about 15cm long and lives near the entrances of caves or beneath overhangs. It is recognised by its red colouring and large black eyes.

Comber The most famous variety is the **painted comber**, which owes its name to the patterns on its head. It has vertical black stripes and a blue mark on its underbelly, and tends to live in the Poseidonion beds (see Underwater Flora at the end of this boxed text).

Conger eel Also known as the sea eel, the conger is greyish in colour and can grow to more than 2m in length. By day it hides in holes, between rocks and in wrecks, poking its head out when a diver passes. It leaves its den at night to hunt.

Damselfish These fish form compact, slow-moving shoals relatively near the water's surface and close to shallows. A maximum of 10cm in length, they have grey and black markings and scissor-shaped tails.

Forkbeard This brown fish prefers the shade of caves and overhangs. It is recognised by the two forked barbels under its chin.

Grouper The darling of scuba divers, now thriving after facing extinction (see the boxed text 'The Return of the Grouper'), the grouper can grow to 1.5m. Thickset, it is distinguished by its enormous thick-lipped mouth and whitish flecks on its brownish scales. It spends most of its time in holes but will let divers approach it, particularly if they offer it food (a practice frowned upon by some instructors).

John Dory This fish has superb stripes on its dorsal fin and a black mark on its sides, reputed to be the imprint left by St Peter who, legend has it, was instructed by Christ to catch a John Dory and take a gold coin from its mouth.

Small is Beautiful

Labridae This family's colourful representatives include the inescapable **rainbow wrasse**, the most 'tropical' fish in the Mediterranean, which sometimes approaches divers for food. A maximum of 20cm long, it is found near the surface and has remarkable turquoise and red mottled markings.

Moray eel This fierce predator waits in crevices, from which only its mouth is visible. Growing to 1.5m, it is distinguished by its speed, its sharp teeth and its dark, sometimes yellow-flecked markings.

Red scorpion fish Known locally as capon, the red scorpion fish lies in wait for its prey on the sea floor, using its camouflage skills to blend in with its surroundings. Its body is covered in poisonous spines and outgrowths.

Sargo Extremely common, sargo swim alongside divers who go near the rocky sea floor or beds. The most widespread variety is the silvery **white bream** (around 40cm long), which has two characteristic black marks on its gills and tail. In the same family, the **dentex** is a formidable carnivore that can grow to 1m in length but which makes only fleeting appearances.

Swallow-tail sea perch This small, graceful, orange-red fish is usually found at the entrances to caves or wrecks, away from the light. Born female, specimens change sex when they get older (this is also the case with grouper and rainbow wrasse).

Sessile Organisms & Invertebrates

The most common sessile organisms are **sponges**, which form wide coloured patches on the surfaces of rocks and which filter-feed on phenomenal quantities of water. Cast a glance under the roofs of caves or overhangs to see **yellow anemones** covering the rocks. These colonies of 'flower-animals', which are just a few centimetres long, resemble gold buttons with yellow tentacles.

Red rocks or flowers often turn out to be creatures with rudimentary structures living on the rocky substrata and feeding on suspended particles. Use a diving torch to see them at their best. In the same type of biotope as the sponges, well away from the light but only at depths of between 25 and 30m, is the famous **red coral**. This has hard, ramified branches that are scarlet in colour, often covered in white polyps. A victim of intensive harvesting, red coral is now rare and its branches only grow to 10cm or so. **Red gorgonian** (blue if you're not using a torch) decorates the walls of drops and grows perpendicular to the current. A favourite with photographers, it forms vast fields and blooms in the form of candelabra or as ramified bushes up to 1m wide. It has a supple skeleton, unlike the calcified red coral.

Ascidians resemble soft tubes and grow in a range of colours, usually violet, red or black. They are sometimes transparent, as in the case of **claveline** and the elegant **Neptune's lace**, which forms bushes of pink calcified petals, and the **sea rose**, which is hard and crumbly with pinkish convolutions.

With a bit of luck you'll see a **sabella** (or **spirographe**), part of a worm family. It lives in calcareous tubes 10 to 30cm long attached to rocks or buried in the sand. From there it extends long multicoloured plumes used to filter water.

Mediterranean crustaceans include **crab**, **lobster**, with its enormous pincers, **crayfish**, with its long antenna, and the **hermit crab**, which uses a shell as a squat. The **flat lobster**, a protected species that clings beneath overhangs, and the **squad lobster**, which is reddish with pretty blue stripes, are less well known. Crustaceans live in holes and caves.

Small is Beautiful

The mollusc family includes **cuttlefish**, which propels itself backwards and emits a black fluid at the slightest threat; the **octopus**, with eight sucker-covered tentacles, which usually lives in a hollow but allows itself to be stroked by divers; the **large pearl**, a protected species that can grow to up to 1m and stands upright in the sand near the beds; and **scallop**.

There are also minute creatures such as **dori** and **flabellinidae**, which look like slugs and are less than 5cm long. The dori (of which there are a number of species, including the Dalmatian variety with black markings on a white background) are brightly coloured, while the gracious flabelline is mauve and covered in papulae.

The prickly echinoderms include various types of **sea urchin**, with its characteristic quills, **starfish**, able to turn the stomach inside out to digest particularly large prey, and the **sea-cucumber**, or holothurian, which resembles a large black pudding lying on the sand or among the rocks.

Underwater Flora

There are several varieties of **seaweed** in the Mediterranean; brown, green or red, hard or soft. The calcified varieties can have superb mineral formations. The infamous **caulerpa taxifolia**, which has proliferated along the Côte d'Azur, destroying everything in its path, has so far spared Corsica.

Endemic to the Mediterranean, the Poseidonion (from Poseidon, the god of the sea) is a green plant that forms vast meadows on the sand. Divers generally spurn these grassy beds but they form a choice biotope, home to numerous species of fish seeking shelter or spawning in the foliage.

This is also the case with **Monlouis**, farther out to sea, which descends in terraces from 30 to 47m and is particularly resplendent with gorgonian. To the east, the **Tour de Saleccia**, aligned with its namesake on land, cascades from 25 to 50m. Particularly exposed to the current, these shallows are adorned with gorgonian and sightings of sea bream, rock lobster and skate are possible.

Golfe de Saint Florent

The Golfe de Saint Florent in the north is flanked on its left by the Désert des Agriates. A dozen sites are currently in use on the eastern and western sides of the gulf. To the east, low chalky cliffs extend below the waves. The **Grotte aux Pigeons** is found in such a location. Crevices form gashes in the cliff a few metres below the surface. Farther out to sea, the **Sec des Pigeons** is a rocky plateau extending from 25 to 30m, criss-crossed by small faults where grouper, brown meagre and octopus live.

Leaving the gulf and heading west you'll come to the area around Punta Mortella, near the lighthouse of the same name, which has some unusual dive sites. **Le Gendarme** (The Policeman) is a large boulder that peaks at 17m and descends to 43m; it's home to conger eel, grouper, moray eel and rock lobster. Slightly to the west of Mortella, a rock resembling a **sphinx** juts above the water and drops to 17m.

Near the bottom of the gulf, in the Anse de Fornali, two rows of protruding rocks form a site known as **Les Cormorans**. The modest depth of the water (8m) makes this a good site for introductory dives and instruction.

Two wrecks can be found near the Citadelle in Saint Florent: *L'Aventure*, at 10m, and the *Ça-ira*, which sank north-east

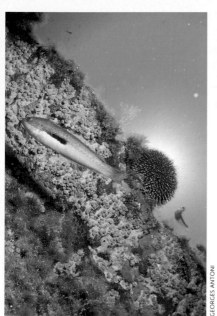

The tropical rainbow wrasse.

GEORGES ANTONI

La Pecorella, off Porto Vecchio (-12m).

GEORGES ANTONI

The wreck of a B17 bomber off Calvi (-27m).

GEORGES ANTONI

Vibrant Gorgonian coral is a common sight in the waters around Corsica.

GEORGES ANTONI

JEAN-BERNARD CARILLET

Setting off for a dive in the Golfe d'Ajaccio from the Plage d'Agosta.

JEAN-BERNARD CARILLET

Final brief before the dive, Îles Lavezzi.

JEAN-BERNARD CARILLET

Snorkelling around the Îles Lavezzi.

JEAN-BERNARD CARILLET

The initial immersion, Îles Lavezzi.

of the Citadelle and now lies at 18m. The latter, a hospital ship dating from the Napoleonic era, has been closely studied by an archaeological group.

The **Sec de la Citadelle**, a small rocky ascent with an abundance of rock masses and hollows in only 6m of water, is perfect for beginners.

Bastia

Unfairly disdained by divers visiting the island, the area around Bastia has a range of fine sites. On this side of the island there are no huge drops, peaks or canyons plunging towards abysses; instead there are gently sloping, sandy, silty floors strewn with rocky outcrops, which are home to a range of creatures.

Gorgonian and red coral are rare, but wreck enthusiasts will be in their element here: there are wrecks just off the coast between Bastia harbour and the Tour de l'Osse on Cap Corse to the north. The names they are known by sometimes differ, depending upon the diving centre. The nearest wreck to the town is that of a Heinkel-111, a German bomber, which lies upturned at a depth of 33m, a short distance from the breakwater of the new harbour. The plane's tail is broken and the engines have come away, but the landing gear is still in place. You can even swim inside the cockpit.

Slightly farther north, the **Roche du 14 Juillet** consists of small cliffs, extending from 17 to 38m, where shoals of sargo, grouper, moray eel and red scorpion fish swim. The **Roche à Mérous** has similar features, at a depth of between 22 and 34m. The **Rocher de Cinquini** consists of overlying rock strata at a depth of between 24 and 36m, partially colonised by a carpet of marine organisms. This honeycombed rock is favoured by shellfish, particularly squad lobster, flat lobster and crayfish, as well as grouper, forkbeard and moray eel. Dentex and sargo can also be seen.

The **Roche des Minelli** comprises three ascents extending between 8 and 22m. Bogue, octopus, red scorpion fish, grouper and moray eel are found among the masses of fallen rocks. Nearby, the **Pain de Sucre**, a sugar-loaf mountain which extends from 28 to 42m, opens out onto a honeycombed plateau at depths of between 36 and 42m, providing an ideal breeding ground for grouper, forkbeard and swallow-tail sea perch.

Farther north, about 20 minutes by boat from Bastia, is the **Ancre Perdue**, a series of sugar-loaf mountains separated by sandbanks; the deepest reaches 42m, the most shallow descends to 24m. The **Roche de Miomio** is a 150m-long sculptured massif ideal for beginners.

Continuing northwards, you will come to two wrecks. A Thunderbolt P-47, a small British fighter plane, still in good condition, lies on seaweed in 22m of water. The *Canonnière* is much farther north, just off Marine de Pietracorbara. This 45m-long wreck sank in 1943. It is at a depth of 40 to 45m so only experienced divers can explore it. You can still see the hull, a section of the deck, the propeller and engine, as well as a cannon. The site teems with grouper, lobster, brown meagre, conger eel and swallow-tail sea perch.

DIVING CENTRES

There are diving centres in nearly all the gulfs as you travel clockwise from Porto Vecchio around to Saint Florent.

They are virtually all affiliated to the Fédération Française d'Études et de Sports

The Return of the Grouper

After decades of unregulated fishing, the grouper, prized for its meat, had virtually disappeared from the western shores of the Mediterranean. On 2 April 1993 it was declared a protected species, and the population is now growing, particularly around Corsica. Its young are seen increasingly often at the dive sites.

Learning to Dive

After the initial introductory dive, the proper theoretical and practical training is essential, indeed compulsory, for safe diving. Several organisations or federations are authorised to provide such training and to issue certificates. These include FFESSM, PADI, CMAS, SSI and NAUI. To the uninitiated, these abbreviations can be confusing. In practice, it does not matter which body you train with, since they all offer similar courses. In any case, diving centres welcome divers regardless of their training background, provided they can produce a certificate. Armed with this qualification, you will be able to dive all over the world.

In France, the main organisation is the Fédération Française d'Études et de Sports Sous-Marins (FFESSM). This offers training in four stages. **Level 1** (CMAS; three to five days, around six dives at sea or in a pool, learning basic techniques and safety rules) allows you to dive accompanied by an instructor down as far as 20m; **level 2** (two weeks) consists of more detailed theoretical and technical training. You can then dive with another diver of the same level as deep as 20m without an instructor, and with an instructor as far as 40m. From **level 3**, you can dive on your own with other divers of the same level. The more professional **level 4** is instructor training.

In England the equivalent of the FFESSM is the British Sub-Aqua Club (BSAC). BSAC-certified divers should be welcome at centres internationally.

The US-based Professional Association of Diving Instructors (PADI) system, widely used in English-speaking countries outside Europe (and increasingly within Europe), works along the same lines. After the 'Discover Scuba' introductory dive, trainees go on to the Open Water Diver, Advanced Open Water Diver, Rescue Diver and Divemaster levels.

Other well known international organisations are Scuba School International (SSI) and the National Association of Underwater Instructors (NAUI). If you want to learn to dive in your own country, ask the diving centre which organisation it's affiliated to.

Sous-Marins (FFESSM; French Federation of Submarine Studies and Sports) and welcome all divers, regardless of their training. Invariably there are one or two instructors who speak English. Most centres have no specific diving itinerary, instead taking into account the weather conditions and divers' experience when deciding which sites to visit on a given day.

Like most leisure activities and tourist facilities in Corsica, diving is highly seasonal. Of some 30 centres on the island, only a handful are open year-round, and some only open on demand or at the weekend. Most open at the end of April and close at the end of October, but in April, May and October they really just tick over. The season proper starts in June and reaches its peak in July and August.

The number of daily excursions is also influenced by seasonal demand. A centre may organise two each day in June (at 8.30 or 9 am and at 2 or 3 pm) and four or five in July and August, especially if it is open seven days a week and employs 15 or so instructors. Go in June, before it gets busy, or in September, when it gets quieter again. At the height of the season the staff are more in demand and the whole experience becomes much less personal.

No matter what time of year it is, it is a good idea to book at least a day in advance. In the high season some centres are fully booked three to four days in advance. The centres are not always staffed when the boats are out, so arrive at least half an hour before the departure time or at the end of the morning or afternoon.

Costs & Facilities

Corsica's diving centres offer a wide range of services, such as introductory dives (for children and adults), night dives, exploratory dives and training for diving qualifications. The price of an introductory dive includes equipment hire, while the cost of an exploratory dive varies according to how much equipment you need to borrow. Expect to pay 80FF to hire all the equipment. If you are planning to make several dives it might be cheaper to bring your own.

Generally clubs have a price for 'equipped divers' (those with a full kit of their own, often including an air cylinder), a 'semi-equipped' price (for those who have some of the equipment) and an 'unequipped price'. The costs given in the centre listings include the cost of hiring all the equipment. All of the centres offer set prices for three, five or 10 dives. Night dives, which are usually more expensive, are arranged either subject to demand or on certain nights.

When it comes to training, only the cost of level 1 instruction is given in our listings because this is the most popular. An indication of the cost of level 1 instruction for the PADI Open Water qualification is given where this is offered. You should make sure the price includes theoretical and practical instruction as well as administrative fees (such as the licence, diving log, diving pass and certificate). Only a handful of centres accept credit cards so bring along cash or travellers cheques.

The boats used to take divers to the sites may be aluminium barges, small semi-rigid 10-seater vessels, large covered 30 or 40-seater launches with all the equipment on board, or even old trawlers or converted tugboats.

Choosing a Centre

Like a hotel or a restaurant, each diving centre has its own personality and style. Some people may feel more comfortable

---

Getting Started

Corsica offers ideal conditions for beginners, with its reassuringly shallow inlets and crystalline, warm water, so if you've always fancied scuba diving but never taken the plunge, now's your chance. Arrange an introductory dive to give you a feel for what it's like to swim underwater; a preliminary session lasts about 20 minutes in a safe location under the watchful eye of an instructor. In some centres, instructors spend half their time taking the uninitiated out on introductory dives, so there's no need to feel embarrassed or nervous.

It's essential that you have confidence in your instructor; call or visit a few clubs, ask questions and listen to your gut instinct. There is no formal procedure but you shouldn't dive if you have a medical condition such as acute ear, nose and throat problems, epilepsy or heart disease (such as infarction), if you have a cold or sinusitis, or if you are pregnant.

Your one-to-one introductory dive will begin on dry land, where the instructor will run through basic safety procedures (such as the use of sign language to indicate that everything is 'OK' or 'not OK', and ear equilibration techniques) and show you the equipment. Special equipment means that children over eight years old can also learn to dive.

You'll practise breathing with the regulator above the surface before going underwater. The instructor will hold your hand and guide your movements for around 20 minutes when you reach the bottom, at a depth of just 3 to 5m. Some centres offer free instruction for apprehensive divers in waist high water in a hotel swimming pool.

If you enjoy your introductory dive you might like to undergo novice training for a certificate that will allow you to dive anywhere in the world (see the boxed text 'Learning to Dive').

with the intimacy and slightly amateurish feel of some of the smaller establishments, others prefer the commercialised professionalism and facilities of a larger American-style centre. Similarly, some customers are reassured by instructors who are strict and methodical, others prefer a more relaxed and flexible approach.

Factors that may influence your decision include the setting (is there a beach nearby so non-divers can go along too?), price, facilities (such as the availability of hot showers or the degree of comfort on the boats), the range of services (such as day trips and special training), the friendliness of the staff, accessibility and whether there are any little extras (are you offered a drink after the dive? Do you have to maintain your own cylinder?). If you are unsure about a centre, go somewhere else, and be wary of word of mouth: each centre has its admirers and critics, especially when there are several centres in one area.

All of the centres listed below are authorised diving centres. They all employ qualified instructors, have modern and well-maintained equipment and observe strict safety regulations.

Rules & Regulations

No special procedures apply for an introductory dive but minors require parental consent. If you are already qualified, you

---

Warning

You should wait at least 12 hours after a dive before climbing or flying. The reduction in pressure that occurs when you gain altitude could interfere with your body's disposal of dissolved nitrogen, with adverse effects ranging from nausea to paralysis of the limbs or even, in the most extreme cases, death. For more on decompression sickness see the Health for Divers section in the Facts for the Visitor chapter.

---

will be asked to produce your certificate and diving card. All divers are welcome, whether they trained with PADI, FFESSM or another body.

If you have not dived for a while, you may be asked to do a refresher dive so that your diving ability and technical skills can be assessed. A medical certificate attesting to your fitness to dive is mandatory for instruction and strongly advised (sometimes compulsory) if you envisage diving regularly with one centre. It can be issued on the spot and costs the same as the medical consultation (115FF).

As for insurance, the situation varies. Some centres require you to take out an FFESSM licence (around 160FF), which includes insurance; others have civil liability insurance for their customers. Make sure your travel insurance covers medical treatment and transport home in case of a diving accident. If it doesn't, you can take out supplementary insurance with the centre.

Accommodation & Transport

Several of the diving centres are part of a hotel, while others can recommend places to stay for a range of budgets, sometimes at a special rate. Some even offer diving packages that include flights, transfers, accommodation and meals.

If you are travelling by public transport, see the Getting There & Away and Getting Around chapters earlier in this book.

Snorkelling in Corsica

The best places for snorkelling in Corsica are the Îles Lavezzi. Several firms in Bonifacio, including two diving centres (Kalliste and Atoll), can take you out to swim in the archipelago's turquoise waters.

Snorkelling is the ideal activity for those reluctant to dive. The best places are inlets or rocky promontories, where small fauna is most abundant, but make sure to consult local diving centres for information on currents, and do not swim alone.

Around Porto Vecchio

CIP La Palanquée
(☎ 04 95 70 16 53, fax 04 95 70 64 48)

This centre, which has been running for more than 20 years, is 400m from the harbour on the road to Bonifacio. It's in a large building on the right, 100m before you get to the Casino supermarket.

Diving prices range from 190FF to 280FF. Expect to pay 1080FF for a six dive package (excluding equipment hire). Introductory dives (usually at the wreck of the *Pecorella*) cost 260FF. Level 1 instruction costs 1990FF.

Alain Desogère, a national FFESSM trainer, has a team of up to 10 instructors, and diver training represents 75% of the centre's activity. The dives take place between the Golfe de Porto Vecchio and the Îles Cerbicale, 20 to 50 minutes away by one of the centre's two boats. A pilot boat has been adapted to seat 30 divers. The divers meet at the club and are taken by van to the departure point in the harbour.

The centre is open year-round (closed Sunday) and runs two excursions daily, at 8.30 am and 2.30 pm. Credit cards are accepted.

Hippocampe
(☎/fax 04 95 70 56 54)

This small centre, which has just three instructors and is owned by a German couple, is on the naturist beach of la Chiappa, south of the Golfe de Porto Vecchio. Follow the main road towards Bonifacio and, as you leave Porto Vecchio, turn left towards Palombaggia. Continue on this road for 7km then bear left towards Chiappa, 2.5km away. Allow at least 20 minutes to get here by car from the centre of Porto Vecchio. Leave your vehicle in the car park and hand over some ID at reception. Divers get in free.

An introductory dive (40 minutes on the beach with the option of a free introductory session in a swimming pool) costs 200FF, an exploratory dive costs between 155FF and 220FF (10 dives for 1400FF to 2000FF) and level 1 instruction costs 1900FF. Instruction for the US SSI Open Water certificate also costs 1900FF.

The sites, between the Golfe de Porto Vecchio and the Îles Cerbicale, are less than 15 minutes away by one of the centre's two semi-rigid vessels. A babysitting service is available at the naturist camp (ask at reception).

The centre is open daily from mid-May to mid-October and runs from two (8.30 am and 2 pm) to five excursions each day, subject to demand.

Kalliste
(☎/fax 04 95 70 44 59, mobile ☎ 06 80 11 71 54)

Approximately 13km from the centre of Porto Vecchio (take the main road towards Bonifacio and, as you leave the town, turn left towards Palombaggia), Kalliste is on the picturesque Palombaggia beach.

Introductory dives (in an inlet in the Îles Cerbicale) cost 330FF, exploratory dives between 195FF and 275FF (six dives for 1115FF to 1570FF), level 1 instruction 2180FF and the PADI Open Water certificate 3200F.

Kalliste has two centres – the second is at Bonifacio harbour. Divers opting for a diving package or those on an instruction course can dive with either establishment.

The 10 instructors employed at the height of the season will take you to the same sites as the other two centres, between the Golfe de Porto Vecchio and the Îles Cerbicale. It takes about 15 minutes by boat (20 seats).

Open daily from April to November, the centre runs from two (8 am and 2 pm) to four excursions each day, subject to demand.

Bonifacio

Atoll
(☎ 04 95 73 02 83, 04 95 73 53 83, fax 04 95 73 17 72)

This centre is perhaps the most famous in Corsica. It is part of the Auberge A Cheda 2km from the marina between Porto Vecchio and Bonifacio but also has an office on the harbour, next to the terminal for ferries to Sardinia.

Despite being one of the largest diving centres on the island, employing 12 instructors at the height of the season, Atoll is very friendly. Its dynamism, professionalism and high level of organisation are reflected in the prices. Introductory dives in the Îles Lavezzi or at Cap Pertusato (Cap Saint Antoine) will set you back 335FF (with the option of a free introductory session in the hotel swimming pool). An exploratory dive costs between 645FF and 295FF. Three dives cost from 645FF to 805FF and six dives will set you back from 1075FF to 1555FF. Level 1 instruction will cost you 2445FF. Atoll is also a PADI-approved centre; expect to pay 3345FF for the Open Water certificate. Photography courses are organised from mid-June to mid-September.

The club's pride and joy is its bespoke 43 seater diving boat, which has all the diving equipment on board. Divers are taken to sites in the Bouches de Bonifacio and the Îles Lavezzi, 20 minutes away. A trip to Mérouville takes place in the morning on Thursday and Sunday. A day trip to Sardinia is organised every Friday (you pay for two dives plus an extra 100FF for lunch on board). Be aware that Atoll's instructors do not condone the feeding of grouper.

Atoll is open year-round and there are daily departures at 8.30 am and 2.30 pm. Credit cards are accepted.

Barakouda
(☎ 04 95 73 13 02, 04 95 73 19 02)
This centre is 1km from the Atoll centre on the road to Bonifacio from Porto Vecchio. It's on the right, 200m after the large roundabout. Established in 1971, it is unconventional in its layout and atmosphere. You will be greeted by the director, Gérard Arend, who is keen to maintain a 'club' atmosphere.

Prices are very reasonable: an introductory dive costs 200FF, an exploratory dive between 130FF and 170FF and a set of five dives from 600FF to 800FF. For the price of level 1 instruction, work out the number of dives you will require then add on the administrative costs.

Boats depart from the beach at Pietranella (there's minibus transfer from the club). The centre has three boats, including a trawler that can carry 40 divers. Arend, who prides himself on having single-handedly domesticated the Mérouville grouper, will only take you to sites in the Îles Lavezzi, which he knows like the back of his hand. In high season Mérouville is on the itinerary every day between noon and 2 pm (two to three times a week at other times of the year). Divers can feed the grouper.

The centre is open daily year-round, subject to demand. There are three excursions each day in the peak season (8.15 am, noon and 2.30 pm). Credit cards are accepted.

Kalliste
(☎ 04 95 73 53 66)
This impeccably maintained centre has a sister centre in Porto Vecchio and charges identical prices (see under Around Porto Vecchio earlier in this section). As you approach Bonifacio from the direction of Porto Vecchio, take the small road on the right just after the Esso petrol station. The centre is situated a few metres back from the harbour, just in front of the Hôtel Résidence.

On board an ultramodern glass-bottomed boat able to carry 40 passengers and store all the equipment, Michel Rossi and his team will take you diving in the Îles Lavezzi, 20 minutes

away, and in the Bouches de Bonifacio. Mérouville is on the itinerary twice a week. Snorkelling enthusiasts (see the earlier boxed text 'Snorkelling in Corsica') can go along for 150FF and non-divers pay 70FF. For 200FF you can be filmed while diving. The programme includes a weekly excursion to the wreck of the *Angelica* in Sardinia. From time to time Rossi takes divers down to wrecks, a speciality of the centre.

Open from April to November, the centre runs two excursions each day (8 am and 2 pm). Credit cards are accepted.

Golfe de Valinco
There are two centres at the foot of the gulf in Propriano and one either side of its entrance in two small seaside resorts.

Valinco Plongée
(☎ 04 95 76 31 01, fax 04 95 76 24 78)
This centre is in a large yellow *algéco* (temporary building). It charges 195FF for an introductory dive at Cala Muretta, an inlet near Portigliolo, or in a cove across from the harbour on the northern shore. An exploratory dive costs from 140FF to 180FF. Five dives cost from 650FF to 850FF and level 1 instruction costs 1400F.

Valinco Plongée uses sites on the southern and northern shores near the mouth of the gulf, such as Le Tonneau, Les Cathédrales and the Sec de Campomoro. Once a week there is a day trip to the Réserve des Moines, with a dive down to the wreck of the *Tasmania* (200FF) and a picnic (additional charge) in an inlet near Capu di Senetosa.

Open from April to October, there are up to six excursions each day between 8 am and 4 pm, subject to demand.

U Levante
(☎ 04 95 76 23 83, fax 04 95 74 03 00)
Just 20m from Valinco Plongée, this centre is also housed in an algéco. Expect to pay from 140FF to 180FF for an exploratory dive, 400FF to 510FF for three dives, 650FF to 850FF for six dives, 1400FF for training or level 1 instruction and 2500FF for the PADI Open Water certificate.

Beginners can go on the usual introductory dive for 195FF (it takes place in an inlet on the southern shore near Portigliolo beach or on the northern shore across from the harbour) or opt for instruction in a hotel swimming pool followed by an introductory dive in the sea, at a cost of 250FF.

Divers are taken to sites in the gulf on one of two aluminium launches. On Sunday you can go to Les Cathédrales. Day trips north or south of the gulf with a picnic lunch in an inlet take place once a week (500FF).

The centre is open daily between April and November and runs two to five excursions a day. Nine instructors work at the height of the season.

Campomoro Plongée

(☎ 04 95 74 23 29, mobile ☎ 06 09 95 44 43)
This small, friendly establishment is in the magnificent Baie de Campomoro at a peaceful seaside resort 15km from Propriano at the southern end of the gulf. The office is on the beach opposite the church. An introductory dive costs 220FF and an exploratory dive costs between 130FF and 200FF. Three dives will set you back from 350FF to 530FF, or pay 550FF to 800FF for five. Expect to pay 220FF per dive and 600FF for theory lessons for level 1 tuition.

Yann Lemoël will take you on a small barge to sites in the southern part of the gulf near the Baie de Campomoro, where there are some real treasures. The centre is ideally placed for dives to the Sec de Campomoro in the west, Le Tonneau or even the Sec du Belvédère in the east. Those diving for the first time will be taken to the western end of the bay, near some small islands just off a Genoese tower, or to the east, near the shore.

Open daily from Easter to the end of October, the centre runs from two to four excursions each day, subject to demand (times vary).

Porto Pollo Plongée

(☎/fax 04 95 74 07 46, mobile ☎ 06 86 03 26 16)
At the northern tip of the gulf, in the village of Porto Pollo, this centre has a relaxed family atmosphere. In an algéco overlooking the small marina, it charges some of the most competitive rates on the island. An introductory dive in an inlet at the mouth of the Baie de Porto Pollo will cost you 150FF, an exploratory dive between 130FF and 160FF, three dives between 360FF and 430FF, six dives between 650FF and 800FF and level 1 instruction an all-inclusive 1600FF.

Porto Pollo Plongée tailors its programme to individual customers. On board an old tugboat, you will explore sites which are less than 15 minutes away in the northern part of the gulf. Other star attractions, such as Les Cathédrales and Les Aiguilles, are barely five minutes from one another.

The centre is open year-round and runs daily excursions at 9 am and 3 pm during the height of the season.

Golfe d'Ajaccio – Southern Shore
Maeva

(☎ 04 95 25 02 40, 04 95 25 10 84)
This centre is located in the Marines de Porticcio, opposite the Elf garage. Expect to pay 220FF for an introductory dive, 160FF to 240FF for an exploratory dive, 858FF to 1320FF for six dives and 1400FF for level 1 instruction. The sites on offer are at Pointe de l'Isolella and Punta di Porticcio, reached in a 30 seater covered vessel or in an inflatable boat. On Sunday morning experienced divers can go to Capu di Muru. A babysitting service is available.

The centre is open daily from April to mid-October. There are departures at 8.30 am and 2 pm.

Club Subaquatique d'Agosta

(☎ 04 95 25 40 26, 04 95 25 58 22, mobile ☎ 06 11 57 77 63)
Located in the Agosta Plage motel (about 3km south of Porticcio) and overlooking a superb white-sand beach, this centre has more than 20 years experience. It tends to cater more for seasoned divers. The morning excursions are for experienced divers only (deep dives are guaranteed) and the afternoon is reserved for instruction.

An exploratory dive costs from 130FF to 210FF, or you can pay between 760FF and 1200FF for six dives. Level 1 instruction will set you back 1950FF. You will dive at sites between Pointe de l'Isolella and Capu di Muru.

The centre is open daily from the beginning of May to mid-October. There are departures at 9 am and 2 pm.

Corse Plongée

(☎ 04 95 25 50 08, mobile ☎ 06 07 55 67 25, fax 04 95 25 46 30)
The clubhouse overlooks the sea in the picturesque village of Ruppione, about 20km south of Ajaccio, just south of the Total garage. An introductory dive costs 220FF, an exploratory dive between 140FF and 220FF, six dives between 800FF and 1280FF, level 1 instruction 2000FF and the PADI Open Water certificate 2200FF.

Corse Plongée operates between Capu di Muru in the south and Punta di Porticcio in the north. The sites are 40 minutes away; divers are taken to them in a covered 40 seater launch that has all the equipment on board, or in a smaller semi-rigid vessel. The itinerary includes all of the famous sites, such as the wreck of the *Meulière*, the Tête de Mort and the Grotte à Corail, but Nicolas Caprili, the director, diver and skipper, prides himself on having several other sites up his sleeve. The centre also offers a certificate in oceanology and diving cruises (see the boxed text 'Diving Cruises'), in addition to day trips that include lunch in a traditional fishing tavern (250FF per dive subject to reservation).

Corse Plongée is open from April to the end of October, with departures daily at 9 am and 3 pm.

Golfe d'Ajaccio – Northern Shore
GSC
(☎ 04 95 21 87 28, mobile ☎ 06 03 58 93 00)
The only club in the centre of Ajaccio, GSC is a small establishment in the Tino Rossi harbour which charges 200FF for an introductory dive (150FF for those under 14 years of age), 130FF to 200FF for an exploratory dive and 750FF to 1100FF for six dives. Introductory

dives take place in an inlet at Pointe de l'Isolella. The programme includes the most popular sites in the gulf, with the exception of the Îles Sanguinaires.

The centre is open daily from the beginning of May to mid-October and runs two excursions each day at 8.30 am and 2.30 pm. An additional excursion may be on the programme in summer.

E Ragnole
(☎ 04 95 21 53 55, fax 04 95 21 53 55)
This relaxed centre is run by a team of young instructors and is part of the Anthinéa fitness club. About 2km from the centre of Ajaccio on the beach side of the Route des Sanguinaires, just after Champion, it charges 190FF for an introductory dive in the sea (100FF on the beach), 150FF to 190FF for an exploratory dive and a mere 900FF for level 1 instruction. The instructors use several sites 400m from the centre, marked by two buoys and a coral reef, but sometimes also take divers in one of the centre's two boats, 14-seater inflatables, to sites in the southern part of the gulf near Pointe de l'Isolella.

Diving Cruises

Combining the joys of sailing with those of diving is an ideal way to discover many of Corsica's delights. Three options are open to those qualified to at least level 2.

Aqua Sub Center in Ajaccio (☎ 04 95 52 01 68, 04 95 10 25 19, fax 04 95 52 08 69) runs a diving weekend exploring the north-western coast of Corsica (Capu Rossu, Porto, Girolata and the fringes of the Réserve Naturelle de Scandola) on a 12m launch. Four dives are listed in the itinerary, including the wreck of the *Jean-Mathieu*, which sank in 1892. Breakfast and lunch are served on board; dinner is taken in a restaurant in the Baie de Girolata. The all-inclusive price is 1500FF per person and with a minimum of four participants and a maximum of eight.

There is an out-of-season cruise (run from November to March) tailor-made by Nicolas Caprili, the director of the Corse Plongée centre in Ruppione (☎ 04 95 25 50 08, mobile ☎ 06 07 55 67 25, fax 04 95 25 46 30), at an all-inclusive price of 550FF per person per day.

The Centre Subaquatique de Sagone at Hôtel Cyrnos in Sagone (☎ 04 95 28 00 01, 04 95 21 09 97, fax 04 95 28 00 77) offers a week exploring the most beautiful locations of the west coast between Girolata and Propriano on board a luxury 18m boat. The trip, which includes 12 dives in the Golfe de Valinco, Golfe d'Ajaccio, Golfe de Sagone, Golfe de Porto and Golfe de Girolata, costs between 2990FF and 3390FF, depending on the time of year (it's run from April to October), including full board and airport transfers. There is a maximum of eight participants. The skipper is an instructor at the centre and has been diving around the island for almost 20 years.

The centre is open daily from May to October (weekends only in low season). Three excursions are run each day in July and August at 9 am, 2.30 pm and 6 pm.

Aqua Sub Center

(☎ 04 95 52 01 68, 04 95 10 25 19, mobile ☎ 06 09 77 34 18, fax 04 95 52 08 69)

In the basement of the Hôtel Stella di Mare, on the route des Sanguinaires approximately 8km from Ajaccio centre, this small establishment offers introductory dives in front of the hotel (200FF), exploratory dives (180FF to 220FF), a six dive package (980FF to 1150FF) and level 1 instruction (1500FF).

Aqua Sub Center usually visits sites on the northern side of the gulf between Ajaccio and the Îles Sanguinaires. It also organises weekend diving cruises (see the boxed text 'Diving Cruises').

The centre is open daily from April to October and runs a minimum of two excursions each day.

Les Calanques

(☎ 04 95 52 09 37, fax 04 95 51 10 88)

Near Aqua Sub Center, this centre is in the Hôtel des Calanques on the right-hand side of the road from Ajaccio. It charges 240FF for an introductory dive, 190FF to 260FF for an exploratory dive, 1000FF to 1600FF for six dives and 1850FF for level 1 instruction.

It is owned by the Nouvelles Frontières group and run by Jean-Pierre Malamas, author of several reference works on diving. The Nouvelles Frontières Group also owns the centre in Le Grand Bleu hotel in the Golfe de Liscia (see under Golfe de Sagone later in this section); the six dives can be used in either centre. The club visits around 10 sites on the northern side of the gulf between Ajaccio and the Îles Sanguinaires.

The centre is open daily from the beginning of May to the end of September (closed Saturday in July and August) and runs four excursions each day between 8 am and 4 pm in high season.

Golfe de Lava

Club Subaquatique du Squale

(☎ 04 95 23 47 23, mobile ☎ 06 07 89 26 30, fax 04 95 20 26 27)

This small centre, in a spruce chalet on Lava beach about 20km north of Ajaccio, is convivial and welcoming. To get here, head towards Mezzavia, then take the D81 towards Cargèse and Porto. After 10km or so bear left

on the D381. Dominique Torre, a staunch proponent of his native Corsica, is happy to adapt to the preferences of his customers. An introductory dive at Pietra Piombata, at the southern entrance to the gulf, costs 220/160FF for adults/children. An exploratory dive costs between 150FF and 200FF, six dives cost 825FF to 1060FF and level 1 instruction costs 1850FF.

A semi-rigid 16 seater vessel takes divers to quiet sites in the Golfe de Lava, such as Pietra Piombata, and in the Golfe de Liscia to the north. It is also ideally placed for the renowned Banc Provençal, about 10 minutes north of the diving centre.

Open from April to the end of November, the centre runs from two (9 am and 2 pm) to three excursions daily in summer.

Golfe de Sagone

Le Grand Bleu

(☎ 04 95 52 24 34, 04 95 52 39 65, fax 04 95 51 10 88)

In the hotel of the same name in the town of Calcatoggio, about 30km north of Ajaccio, this centre is owned by the Nouvelles Frontières Group, like its sister club Les Calanques just outside Ajaccio. From Ajaccio, follow the signs to Mezzavia and Cargèse. At the entrance to the Golfe de Liscia, take the small road on the left that leads to the Tour d'Ancone. Le Grand Bleu is 400m along the beach. Prices and products are identical to those offered by Les Calanques (see Golfe d'Ajaccio – Northern Shore). A free introductory dive in the hotel swimming pool takes place once or twice a week.

Look out for the special course (between the introductory dive and level 1) available to those who are pressed for time; it includes a pool lesson, theory lesson, slide show on fauna and flora and two dives (the first in an inlet) to between 5 and 10m (650FF in season). The sites used are about 10 minutes away on the southern shores of the Golfe de Liscia and the Golfe de Sagone, between Punta Palmentoju and the Banc Provençal (available once a week).

The centre is open from Easter to the end of October (closed on Saturday) and runs from two (8.30 am and 4 pm) to four departures daily.

Nautica Sub

(☎ 04 95 52 27 11)

Nautica Sub, 900m along the beach from Le Grand Bleu, is a small, basic establishment employing a maximum of four instructors. It charges 190/170FF for adults/children for an introductory dive in an inlet or on the beach. An exploratory dive costs from 130FF to 190FF, six dives cost 700FF to 1020FF and level 1 instruction costs 1400FF.

A semi-rigid 12 seater boat takes divers to sites in the Golfe de Sagone and the Golfe de Lava, including the popular Banc Provençal, Pietra Piombata and the *Canadair* wreck.

Open from May to October, the centre runs up to four excursions daily in summer.

Centre Subaquatique de Sagone
(☎ 04 95 28 00 01, 04 95 21 09 97, fax 04 95 28 00 77)
This is a medium-sized centre in the Hôtel Cyrnos in Sagone, next to the main railway line to Cargèse and opposite a superb beach. It charges 200FF for an introductory dive in an inlet at Punta Puntiglione or at the Rocher de Marifaga, or in a sheltered inlet by the harbour if the weather is bad. An exploratory dive costs from 170FF to 200FF, six dives cost 850FF to 1000FF, and level 1 instruction costs 2000FF.

A covered 20 seater launch that used to belong to the customs authorities will take you to sites 15 to 20 minutes away in the Golfe de Sagone, between Punta Paliagi in the south and the Rocher de Marifaga in the north. The *Canadair* and *Girafe* wrecks are out to sea between the two. The Banc Provençal (45 minutes by boat) is normally avoided in summer.

Open daily from May to the beginning of October, there are departures at 9 am and 3 pm. Credit cards are accepted.

Golfe de Porto
Centre de Plongée du Golfe de Porto
(☎/fax 04 95 26 10 29)
Under the management of Sylvie Lannoy, this centre employs 12 instructors at the height of the season. It is just behind Lannoy Sport at the entrance to Porto as you come from Piana, just after the bridge over the Porto river opposite Les Oliviers camp site.

Expect to pay 220/200FF for adults/children for an introductory dive at Castagne, the Sec du Château or Capu Rossu, 150FF to 220FF for an exploratory dive, 810FF to 1180FF for six dives, 1900FF for level 1 instruction and 2400FF for the PADI Open Water certificate.

One of two barges will take you to the key sites in the Golfe de Porto, five to 35 minutes away, between Punta Muchillina in the north and Capu Rossu in the south. In May, June and September a day trip is organised once or twice

a week, involving a dive at Punta Muchillina on the edge of the Réserve Naturelle de Scandola, followed by lunch at Girolata, then a second dive at Capu Seninu or Punta Scopa (you pay for two dives plus 150FF). In July and August, half-day excursions to Punta Muchillina are available once or twice a week (there's an additional charge of 20FF), depending on the weather. Transfers between the centre and the landing stage are by van. There are plans to convert a building right on the harbour for use by the centre. A babysitting service is available if you book in advance.

Open from Easter to October, the centre runs two (9 am and 2.30 pm) to five excursions daily, subject to demand. It's closed on Sunday in May and June. Credit cards are accepted.

Génération Bleue
(☎/fax 04 95 26 24 88)
This centre is run by Pascal Juppet, who is a skiing instructor in winter. It employs up to six instructors at the height of the season and is right on the marina, next to the gangway on the right-hand side. The centre charges 200FF for an introductory dive at Castagne or Capu Rossu, 150FF to 190FF for an exploratory dive, 700FF to 900FF for five dives and 1600FF for level 1 instruction.

The programme is identical to that of the Centre de Plongée du Golfe de Porto. A day trip to Punta Muchillina with lunch at Girolata followed by a second dive at Capu Seninu is organised in the summer (July and August excepted), subject to demand. In summer, Punta Muchillina is a half-day excursion, subject to demand; there's an additional charge of 50FF. Excursions use a covered aluminium barge or semi-rigid vessel.

Open from May to the end of October, from two (10 am and 3 pm) to four excursions are run daily.

Galeria
L'Incantu
(☎ 04 95 62 03 65, fax 04 95 62 03 66)
This centre combines efficiency with a relaxed atmosphere. Part of the hotel of the same name, perched above Galeria in a charming location 300m from the church, it is the largest centre in Corsica but you never feel you're just another in a long line of customers.

The club limits its excursions to two each day even at the height of summer, which is unusual for Corsica, and its diving options are wide-ranging. An introductory dive on a small

Diving Equipment

Above water, diving equipment is heavy and bulky but underwater it allows surprising ease of movement. During an introductory dive your instructor will control and adjust your equipment, the components of which are explained here.

- The **regulator** is connected to tubes on the cylinder and consists of several hoses, one of which leads to a mouthpiece enabling the diver to breathe. Another tube connects to the manometer and a third to the stab-jacket. It provides air at ambient pressure when required.
- Each **cylinder** has a capacity of 12 to 15L and is usually made of steel. Cylinders contain compressed air, allowing the diver to breathe underwater. The autonomy available to the diver varies with the duration and depth of the dive. Special mini-cylinders with capacities of 6 to 8L are available for children.
- **Suits** come in a variety of sizes and thicknesses (from 3 to 7mm). They act as a second skin, keeping divers warm and protecting them from grazing themselves on the coral.
- The **weight belt** compensates for the buoyancy of the suit. Without it, the diver would float to the surface.
- Connected to the cylinder, the inflatable **stabilising jacket**, or stab-jacket, provides comfort and security by allowing divers to stay on the surface, adjust their buoyancy when underwater and resurface effortlessly.
- The **manometer** provides an indication of the pressure in the cylinder, measured in bars, as well as showing how much air is left.
- The **mask** enables divers to see clearly underwater. Short-sighted divers can have specially adjusted masks, and contact lenses may also be worn.
- **Flippers** provide a means of propulsion.
- A **depth gauge**, **dive computer** (worn on the wrist), **knife** and **torch** complete the gear.

beach near the harbour or in an inlet known as Caletta costs 210FF. An exploratory dive costs 180FF to 240FF, or 140FF to 200FF for divers with their own equipment. You can get take dives for 1000FF to 1320FF and level 1 instruction costs 1950FF. It is also possible to train for the PADI Open Water certificate here.

The 15 instructors employed in summer are headed by Daniel Lecouve and Jo Urijens (a former member of the French Foreign Legion). You will be taken by one of two covered 20-seater launches to sites between Capu di a Mursetta, north of the Golfe de Galeria, and the southern edge of the Réserve Naturelle de Scandola. This centre is practically the only one that uses these sites.

Thursday is normally 'Scandola day', with a 1½ hour visit to the reserve, a dive to the famous Punta Muchillina site and a picnic in the Baie de Focolara; this trip costs the price of a dive plus 130FF. Non-divers and children can also go along at a cost of 180/100FF. At lunchtime you can get a diver's meal at the hotel for 70FF, including wine. L'Incantu has

also launched a diving/jazz week in June in conjunction with the Calvi jazz festival, and offers courses in marine biology.

The centre is open year-round and has daily excursions at 9 am and 3 pm. Credit cards are accepted.

Calvi
École de Plongée Internationale de Calvi (Épic)

(☎ 04 95 65 42 22, fax 04 95 65 42 23)
Housed in an algéco at the entrance to the marina, Épic is a family-run centre. Expect to pay 220FF for an introductory dive at Pointe Saint François or Punta Spano, 170FF to 210FF for an exploratory dive, 800FF to 1000FF for five dives and 1700FF for level 1 instruction, all-inclusive. These prices apply in July and August only; reductions are available at other times of the year. A rigid boat or 25 seater covered launch takes divers to the area between the western side of Pointe de la Revellata and the eastern end of the Baie de Calvi, where the B-17 bomber lies near the Citadelle.

The centre is open from April to November. There are departures daily at 9 am and 2.30 pm.

Calvi Plongée Citadelle
(☎/fax 04 95 65 33 67)
A stone's throw from Épic, this high-calibre centre, which employs 10 instructors in summer, does not have an office as such: prospective customers must climb on board one of its two boats moored in the marina. An introductory dive in a rocky inlet at Pointe Saint François, west of the Citadelle, or at Punta Spano, east of the Baie de Calvi, costs 220FF. An exploratory dive costs between 160FF and 220FF, five dives cost between 750FF and 950FF. Level 1 instruction is offered at an all-inclusive price of 1750FF. The centre is also PADI-approved, so you can apply for PADI qualifications such as the Open Water certificate (2250FF).

The sites on offer are scattered between the Sec du Lion, west of Pointe de la Revellata, and Punta Spano, to the east just before you come to Algajola. In the high season there is a day trip to the area around la Revellata once a week on board a covered 20 seater launch; it costs 500FF for two dives, including a cold meal with a drink on board, or 200FF for non-divers.

Open daily from May to September, the centre runs up to four excursions daily. Credit cards are accepted.

JMB Diving
(☎ 04 95 65 12 07, 04 95 65 29 37, fax 04 95 65 39 71)
This family-run centre is temporarily housed in a chalet on the beach in Calvi, at the eastern side of the town (head towards Île Rousse and just past La Camargue nightclub, then turn left down the small road that leads to the beach). Expect to pay 200/210FF for adults/under-12s for an introductory dive at Pointe de la Revellata. An exploratory dive costs from 160FF to 180FF, 10 dives cost 1500FF (equipment supplied) and level 1 instruction is 1500FF.

Divers are taken by a 10 seater aluminium or 12 seater plastic barge to sites 15 to 20 minutes away in the Golfe de Calvi and around Pointe de la Revellata.

Open year-round, the centre runs two to three excursions daily in summer.

From Calvi to Île Rousse
Subcorsica
(☎ 04 95 60 75 38, mobile ☎ 06 81 70 46 25, fax 04 95 60 79 66)
This fairly large centre, established in 1980, is in Sant'Ambrogio marina, about 15km east of Calvi. An introductory dive in an inlet next to the harbour costs 200FF, an exploratory dive costs from 170FF to 220FF, five dives cost 800FF to 1050FF and level 1 instruction is 1600FF, all-inclusive. You might be able to take part in a post-introduction instruction course (four sessions for 800FF).

Subcorsica visits the quiet area between Algajola to the east (including le Danger d'Algajola) and Punta Spano to the west, accessible in 10 to 45 minutes in one of two plastic barges or a restored 15m tartan (a Mediterranean vessel with a lateen sail) dating from 1897. The instructors' favourite sites include the wreck of the *Grand Cerf*, Pietra Eramer and Kalliste. The area around la Revellata, west of the Baie de Calvi, and the B-17 bomber are occasionally included in the itinerary (at an additional charge of 30FF).

The centre is open from May to October and runs excursions daily from June to September, with three to four departures between 9 am and 5 pm, subject to demand.

Subaqua l'Escale
(mobile ☎ 06 08 21 09 51, 06 80 04 65 17)
Subaqua l'Escale is right on the superb beach of Algajola, next to l'Escale restaurant. It charges 210FF for an introductory dive at Pedra Mule, 180FF for an exploratory dive, 850FF for five dives and 1530FF for level 1 instruction. This convivial establishment is run by Ange Benedetti and employs eight instructors at the height of the season. Divers are taken to quiet sites near Algajola, including the popular Danger d'Algajola, accessible in less than 10 minutes on one of two aluminium barges.

The centre is open from Easter to the end of October and runs up to three excursions daily (9 am, 2 pm and 4 pm). It's closed on Sunday.

Île Rousse
Beluga Diving
(☎ 04 95 60 17 36, 04 95 60 52 25, fax 04 95 60 42 75)
In a wing of Hôtel La Pietra, to the side of the ferry terminal near the Genoese tower, this

centre caters mainly to experienced divers. It offers Nitrox dives (with a higher percentage of oxygen through special compressors) on request; prices start at 175FF, excluding equipment hire. An introductory dive in a cove below the hotel costs 230FF, an exploratory dive costs between 145FF and 231FF and level 1 instruction costs 1550FF.

Hans Berz and his eight instructors offer dives in the spectacular underwater landscape west of Île Rousse from a covered 20 seater launch or a semi-rigid vessel. Regularly featured on the programme are Le Naso, the Grand Tombant, the Petit Tombant and the Tour de Saleccia. Day trips are organised once or twice a week to the Baie de Calvi, 1¼ hours away, with dives down to the B-17 bomber and around la Revellata (for an additional charge of 180FF, which includes a meal). From time to time there are day trips to the small island of Centuri, just off the north-west tip of Cap Corse.

The club also offers an introductory course in marine archaeology given by experts, which costs 3000FF per week. The price does not including accommodation.

The centre is open from March to December daily (closed on Sunday), and there are departures at 9 am and 3 pm.

École de Plongée de l'Île Rousse
(☎ 04 95 60 36 85, fax 04 95 60 45 21)
In an algéco near the ferry terminal and run by Jean and Véronique Escales, this centre caters for the general public but specialises in diving for children. An introductory dive in an inlet below Île Rousse lighthouse costs 220FF while an exploratory dive costs from 150FF to 200FF, with a 10% discount available for 10 dives. Level 1 instruction costs 1700FF, all-inclusive.

Sites in the Golfe de Île Rousse, such as Le Naso and the Grand Tombant, are reached in 10 minutes on board a 20 seater covered barge or a smaller 10 seater vessel.

The centre is open year-round and runs from two (9 am and 3 pm) to three excursions daily in summer. Morning dives are for experienced divers only; the afternoon is reserved for beginners and instruction.

Saint Florent
CESM
(☎ 04 95 37 00 61, fax 04 95 37 09 60)
Follow the signs to Oletta to get to CESM, the nautical base of La Roya, from the centre of Saint Florent. As you leave the town, turn right

An ABC of Diving

Thinking of introducing the kids to diving in Corsica? Nothing could be easier: there are small, reassuring inlets with clear, warm water and small rock fauna, and children are guaranteed a warm welcome.

Under French law diving centres can accommodate children from the age of eight, provided they have parental consent. Most clubs take young people from holiday camps or schools during the summer so they're familiar with their needs. Nearly all of the centres have special equipment such as 'bibs', miniature stab-jackets and small mouthpieces and suits.

After the introductory dive kids can go on to obtain special bronze, silver and gold awards.

after the Shell petrol station towards Île Rousse and, when you've crossed the small bridge, turn right immediately into the road to La Roya beach. About 500m later you'll come to CESM, which is part of the sailing school but, like the beach, is not much to look at. The small club has a warm atmosphere, however.

Charges are 185FF for an introductory dive at les Cormorans, near Fornali lighthouse west of the gulf. Exploratory dives cost 185FF, a set of five dives costs from 750FF to 850FF and level 1 instruction costs around 1800FF (10 dives).

Instructors will take you to the Golfe de Saint Florent and Punta Mortella to the west and to Nonza to the north-east on board a 10 seater semi-rigid vessel or a 14 seater aluminium barge.

Open from mid-June to the end of August, the centre runs from two (9 am and 2 pm) to four excursions daily. It's closed on Sunday.

Bastia
Thalassa Immersion
(☎ 04 95 31 78 90, 04 95 31 08 77, mobile ☎ 06 86 37 60 14)
This centre, brilliantly run by three dynamic young instructors, is in a well-equipped, luxurious building about 2km north of Bastia town centre. Follow the signs for Cap Corse

and, after the port of Toga, look out for the Elf petrol station on the left. The centre is opposite the petrol station, down on the beach. An introductory dive at a site rich in marine life near the beach costs 200FF, an exploratory dive costs between 150FF and 180FF, eight dives cost between 1040FF and 1280FF and level 1 instruction is an all-inclusive 1480FF.

The club uses the area between the Heinkel-111 wreck, near the port of Bastia in the south, and the wreck of the the *Canonnière*, just off Pietracorbara in the north, accessible in one hour on board a 15 seater launch. The *Canonnière* is usually offered as a day trip, with lunch at Erbalunga followed by a second dive nearby.

Bookings can be made at the Thalassa diving shop, 2 rue Saint Jean, near the old port. Credit cards are accepted.

The centre is open year-round but closed on Sunday morning. It runs from two (9 am and 2 pm) to four excursions daily.

Club Plongée Bastiais

(☎ 04 95 33 31 28, 04 95 30 56 64, mobile ☎ 06 14 62 56 14)

This centre does not have premises in the strict sense of the word; you have to go straight to its boat, a 20 seater covered launch moored in the old port of Bastia, 20m from the harbour master's office. An introductory dive in the Anse de Ficajola near the harbour costs 180FF (140FF for children aged between eight and 12). An exploratory dive costs between 150FF and 190FF, or buy 10 dives for 1300FF to 1700FF. Level 1 instruction costs 1850FF. On Friday night there's a night dive followed by a light meal, costing 270FF.

The sites visited are the same as those used by Thalassa Immersion, between the Heinkel-111 and the wreck of the *Canonnière*.

The centre is open daily from July to September (except Sunday afternoon) and at weekends during the rest of the year. Departures are at 9 am and 2.30 pm.

Bastia & the Far North

The Cap Corse peninsula, a land of seafarers, is studded with tiny fishing ports nestling between maquis-covered headlands that plunge into the sea. The Nebbio region to the west is a mixture of vineyards, superb expanses of sand and an amazing desert. Bastia, robbed by Ajaccio of its status as Corsica's capital under Napoleon, is still a bustling town.

Bastia

• **pop 38,000**   ✉ **20200**

The largest town on the island, Bastia is Corsica's economic centre. It has the fourth most important port in France. A staging post for those heading south or for Cap Corse from the mainland, Bastia has been trying to tempt visitors to linger for years. The Citadelle quarter (Terra Nova) is currently being renovated for this very reason. Bastia offers a host of attractions, including a lively and busy town centre, long beaches to the south and a rich cultural life.

HISTORY

Although there were settlements on the site in Roman times, Bastia was only officially founded in 1372. The Genoese governor of the time, residing in the poorly defended Château de Biguglia in a malaria-infested area several kilometres away, decided to build a fortress (or *bastiglia* – hence Bastia) on the only rocky headland on this featureless coastline. The site thus became recognised as strategically important. In 1452 the fortress became the provincial capital of Corsica under Genoese rule and the seat of the governors. The Terra Nova quarter grew up around the fortress. Until the 18th century many Corsicans continued to see the Citadelle as the symbol of Genoese domination. On several occasions villagers came down from the mountains and sacked the

Highlights

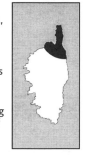

- Savour the cultural attractions of Bastia, Corsica's largest town
- Stroll through the maquis-covered hills of the Cap Corse peninsula
- Explore the stunning barren landscape of the Désert des Agriates

town in protest at Genoese fiscal administration. Yet despite the instability of the period, most of Bastia's architectural heritage dates from around this time (the 17th and 18th centuries).

In 1764 Bastia passed into the hands of the French. In 1791, after two months under siege by Admiral Nelson, it finally surrendered to the English, who remained in control of the town for two years. Under Napoleon, revolts in the town were brutally suppressed and in 1811 Bastia lost its status as capital to Ajaccio. In 1943 it became the only town in Corsica to be bombed by the USA during WWII. In the post-war period the town's port and commerce contributed to its return as the island's economic capital. The Haute-Corse prefecture moved its headquarters to Bastia in 1975.

ORIENTATION

As you come in from the south, from the direction of the airport, the first thing you notice is the imposing Citadelle quarter (Terra Nova). If you are travelling by car, you will probably go through the tunnel hollowed out of the town's rocky crags and

CAP CORSE & THE NEBBIO

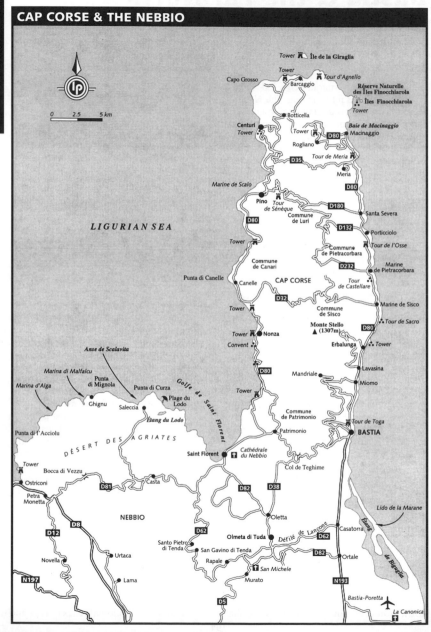

Tower 📷 Île de la Giraglia
Tower
Capo Grosso
Tour d'Agnello
Barcaggio
Réserve Naturelle
des Îles Finocchiarola
Îles Finocchiarola
Botticella
Tower
Centuri
Baie de Macinaggio
Tower
Tower
Macinaggio
D80
Rogliano
D35
Tour de Meria
Meria
D80
Marine de Scalo
Pino
Tour
de Sénèque
D180
D80
Santa Severa
Commune
de Luri
D132
Porticciolo
Tower
Tour de l'Osse
Commune
de Pietracorbara
Marine
de Pietracorbara
Commune
de Canari
D232
CAP CORSE
Punta di Canelle
Canelle
Tour
de Castellare
D32
Marine de Sisco
Commune
de Sisco
Tower
Tour de Sacro
Monte Stello
D80
Tower 📷 Nonza
▲ (1307m)
Convent
Erbalunga
Tower
D80
Mandriale
Lavasina
Miomo
Anse de Scalavita
Marina di Malfalcu
Punta
di Mignola
Golfe de Saint Florent
Tower
Marina d'Alga
Punta di Curza
Plage du
Lodo
Commune
de Patrimonio
Tour de Toga
Ghignu
Saleccia
BASTIA
Étang du Lodo
Patrimonio
Punta di l'Acciolu
DÉSERT DES AGRIATES
Tower
Cathédrale
du Nebbio
Ostriconi
Bocca di Vezzu
Saint Florent
Petra
Monetta
Casta
Col de Teghime
D81
Lido de la Marane
D82
D38
NEBBIO
D12
D8
Oletta
D62
Olmeta di Tuda
Casatorra
Santo Pietro
di Tenda
Défilé de Lancone
D62
Novella
Urtaca
San Gavino di Tenda
D82
Ortale
Rapale
San Michele
N197
Lama
Murato
N193
D5
Bastia-Poretta
La Canonica

LIGURIAN SEA

0   2.5   5 km

pass the old port, before emerging into place Saint Nicolas in the heart of Bastia. Behind the square and parallel to the sea are two busy shopping streets, blvd Paoli and rue César Campinchi. It is a good idea to leave your car in the car park in place Saint Nicolas, to your left as you exit the tunnel.

INFORMATION
Tourist Office
On the northern side of place Saint Nicolas, the small tourist office (☎ 04 95 55 96 96, fax 04 95 55 96 00) is open to the public from 8 am to 8 pm daily in summer. In the low season the office is open from 9 am to noon and 2 to 6 pm, except on Sunday afternoon. A range of brochures is available, including a town plan and brief introduction to Bastia (English version available).

Money
There are several banks on place Saint Nicolas, such as Banque Nationale de Paris and Société Générale, which both have an ATM and bureau de change. You can also exchange money at the post office and in the ferry terminal in summer.

Banque de France, at 2bis cours Henri Pierangeli, is open to the public from 8.45 am to noon and 1.45 to 3.30 pm, Monday to Friday.

Post & Communications
Bastia's main post office is on ave Maréchal Sébastiani. It is open from 8 am to 7 pm Monday to Friday and from 8 am to noon on Saturday.

Bookshop
Maps and walking books are on sale in the Librairie Jean-Patrice Marzocchi (☎ 04 95 34 02 95) at 2 rue du Conventionnel Salicetti. The shop is open daily from 9.30 am to 2 pm and 2.30 to 7 pm (closed on Sunday and Monday morning).

Travel Agency
Ollandini Voyages (☎ 04 95 31 11 71, fax 04 95 32 66 77), at 40 blvd Paoli, sells char-

ter flights to the mainland and tickets for sea crossings and tours in Corsica.

Laundry
The Laverie du Port (☎ 04 95 32 25 51), 25 rue du Commandant Luce de Casabianca, is open from 7 am to 9 pm daily. Expect to pay 34FF for 7kg of laundry (50FF for 15kg).

Medical Services
The hospital (☎ 04 95 59 11 11) is open 24 hours and is several kilometres south-west of Bastia. Bus Nos 1 and 2 go there.

There is a doctor on call during the night, who can be reached on ☎ 04 95 32 23 27, and a 24 hour pharmacist who you can call on ☎ 04 95 31 99 17.

PLACE SAINT NICHOLAS
Almost 300m long, this 19th century square is the focal point of the town. Palm trees and café terraces line its western side. With its Sunday morning flea market and evening rollerbladers, the square attracts people of all ages. It also boasts an imposing **statue of Napoleon**, the powerful torso draped in a Roman emperor's tunic and the head held straight, eyes looking far out to sea. Less than 50km across the water lies the island of Elba. In line with the centre of the square, at 15 blvd du Général de Gaulle, is the **Magasin Mattei** (☎ 04 95 32 44 28), made famous by its Cap Corse apéritif. The shop window contains a display of the spin-off products that have contributed to the brand's success, such as ashtrays, baize, bottle labels and posters. It is open from 9.30 am to noon and 2.30 to 7.30 pm Monday to Saturday.

TERRA VECCHIA
This is the oldest part of the town. It has always been considered a Corsican quarter, unlike the Genoese Terra Nova.

From place Saint Nicolas, follow rue Napoléon past the two baroque chapels, **Chapelle Saint Roch** and **Chapelle de la Conception**. In front of the latter is a square

BASTIA

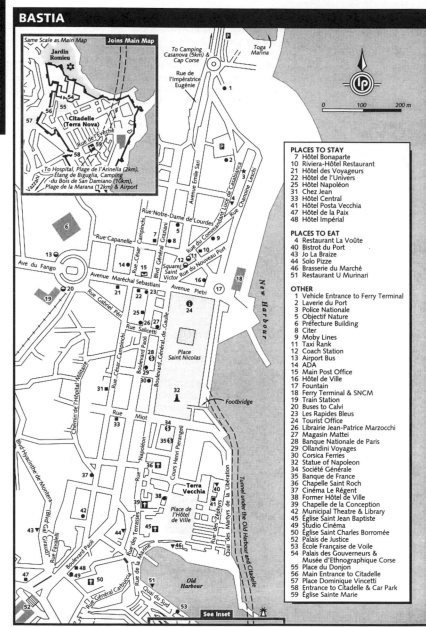

Same Scale as Main Map — Joins Main Map

Jardin Romieu

Citadelle (Terra Nova)

Rue de l'Évéché

To Camping Casanova (5km) & Cap Corse

Toga Marina

Rue de l'Impératrice Eugénie

To Hospital, Plage de l'Arinella (2km), Étang de Biguglia, Camping du Bois de San Damiano (10km), Plage de la Marana (12km) & Airport

0   100   200 m

Rue Notre-Dame de Lourdes

Rue Capanelle

Ave du Fango

Avenue Maréchal Sebastiani

Avenue Pietri

New Harbour

Place Saint Nicolas

Place de l'Hôtel de Ville

Terra Vecchia

Cours Henri Pierangeli

Tunnel under the Old Harbour and Citadelle

Old Harbour

Footbridge

See Inset

PLACES TO STAY
7 Hôtel Bonaparte
10 Riviera-Hôtel Restaurant
21 Hôtel des Voyageurs
22 Hôtel de l'Univers
25 Hôtel Napoléon
31 Chez Jean
33 Hôtel Central
41 Hôtel Posta Vecchia
47 Hôtel de la Paix
48 Hôtel Impérial

PLACES TO EAT
4 Restaurant La Voûte
40 Bistrot du Port
43 Jo La Braize
44 Solo Pizze
46 Brasserie du Marché
51 Restaurant U Murinari

OTHER
1 Vehicle Entrance to Ferry Terminal
2 Laverie du Port
3 Police Nationale
5 Objectif Nature
6 Préfecture Building
8 Citer
9 Moby Lines
11 Taxi Rank
12 Coach Station
13 Airport Bus
14 ADA
15 Main Post Office
16 Hôtel de Ville
17 Fountain
18 Ferry Terminal & SNCM
19 Train Station
20 Buses to Calvi
23 Les Rapides Bleus
24 Tourist Office
26 Librairie Jean-Patrice Marzocchi
27 Magasin Mattei
28 Banque Nationale de Paris
29 Ollandini Voyages
30 Corsica Ferries
32 Statue of Napoleon
34 Société Générale
35 Banque de France
36 Chapelle Saint Roch
37 Cinéma Le Régent
38 Former Hôtel de Ville
39 Chapelle de la Conception
42 Municipal Theatre & Library
45 Église Saint Jean Baptiste
49 Studio Cinéma
50 Église Saint Charles Borromée
52 Palais de Justice
53 École Française de Voile
54 Palais des Gouverneurs & Musée d'Ethnographique Corse
55 Place du Donjon
56 Main Entrance to Citadelle
57 Place Dominique Vincetti
58 Entrance to Citadelle & Car Park
59 Église Sainte Marie

covered in a mosaic of white and green pebbles. Inside, the chapel is carpeted in dark red velvet. The street leads into **place de l'Hôtel de Ville**, also known as place du Marché because there is a market there every morning. The square is lined with some rather dilapidated-looking four-storey buildings. The roofs owe their bluish colour to *lauze*, a stone found only in the area around Bastia. The one restored building in the square is an annexe of the Hôtel de Ville (Town Hall), where weddings are often celebrated. The new Hôtel de Ville building, the most important building in town, is north of place Saint Nicolas.

In the south-western corner of the square is the famous **Église Saint Jean Baptiste**, recognisable by its twin bell-towers. The church was completed in 1666 and redecorated in the Baroque style in the 18th century. Interesting little streets wind their way between tall houses down to the **old harbour** and **Quai des Martyrs de la Libération**. During WWII the buildings nearest the harbour were bombed by the Allies. The quarter behind it is better preserved, particularly as you climb up towards the **Église Saint Charles Borromée**, hidden behind tall narrow buildings, some of which have been restored recently.

CITADELLE & TERRA NOVA

From the south quay of the old harbour, stroll through the **Jardin Romieu** (open from 8 am to 8 pm in summer and 8 am to 5 pm in winter), which will take you to the Citadelle via the steps of the **rampe Saint Charles**.

Unlike in Terra Vecchia, the buildings in Terra Nova have been refurbished, and their ochre, yellow, red and green façades gleam in the sunlight in the narrow streets of the Citadelle. If you are approaching from the Jardin Romieu, you will enter the Citadelle via **place du Donjon**. Immediately on your right is the **Palais des Gouverneurs** (Governors' Palace), which now houses the **Musée d'Ethnographie Corse**. This is closed until 2001 for refurbishment. However, it is still

possible to stroll around the palace courtyard and terraced gardens. There are also plans to rebuild the covered way, part of which has been replaced by post-WWII concrete buildings.

A wander through the narrow streets will bring you to the **Église Sainte Marie**. This former cathedral has an imposing yellow and white façade, set off by a black stripe. A plaque on one of the houses to its right tells you that Victor Hugo lived there as a child from 1803 to 1805, when his father was a general in the town's garrison.

Skirting the former cathedral, you will come to the **Église Sainte Croix**. The walls of the church, which is famous for its **black crucifix**, are covered in thick red velvet. The church is bathed in a warm light reflected off the ochre and red façades of the houses. Look out for the elegant square of green and white pebbles in front of the church.

You can also reach the Citadelle via place Dominique Vincetti, which is used as a car park.

ACTIVITIES

A stone's throw from the bus station at 3 rue Notre Dame de Lourdes is Objectif Nature (☎/fax 04 95 32 54 34, mobile ☎ 06 12 28 52 84). There you'll find a list of organisations offering activities in the region, which could mean anything from exploring the canyons (in la Vacca and Purcaraccia), horse riding (250FF for a half-day or 350FF for a full day), night fishing (350FF for a minimum of eight people), sea kayaking (250FF a day), diving (novice or experienced divers 180FF) or even parapenting and sailing courses. The small shop stocks a selection of ordinary and mountain bikes for hire (100FF a day or 150FF for the weekend).

For further information on diving around Bastia, see the Diving chapter.

The École Française de Voile (☎ 04 95 32 67 33) in the old harbour arranges excursions by catamaran, *optimiste* (coracle) or kayak. The school is open in season from 8.30 am to 12.30 pm and 2 to 6 pm.

COURSES

The association Esse (☎ 04 95 33 03 01, 04 95 34 05 92) arranges classes in the Corsican language. These classes are taught in the CAF community centre, which is near the hospital.

ORGANISED TOURS

In summer the tourist office organises guided tours around the town twice daily at 10 am and 5 pm. Some of these are in English. Tours leave from outside the tourist office and cost 35FF. You can also contact the Association des Guides Professionnels (☎ 04 95 36 26 98) to arrange a private tour in the summer.

Another way to see the town is from a small train (☎ 04 95 31 04 24) that leaves from near the tourist office in place Saint Nicolas.

The train station in Bastia organises day trips to the Forêt de Vizzavona (west of Aleria). The tour includes a visit with a forest guide from the Office National des Forêts (ONF; National Office for Forests). Tours leave from the station at 7 am and return at 6.30 pm. The tour costs 229FF (186FF for children under 16 years of age) and includes a picnic. For information and reservations call ☎ 04 95 32 80 57, fax 04 95 34 01 14.

SPECIAL EVENTS

Each autumn Bastia hosts two major events. One is the Musicales de Bastia, which consists of five days of concerts in the second week of October (information on ☎ 04 95 32 75 91).

The other is the Festival du Film et des Cultures Méditerranéennes during the third week of November (information on ☎ 04 95 32 08 86).

The two events are held in the Théâtre Municipal (☎ 04 95 34 98 00, fax 04 95 34 98 09), rue Favalelli.

For the latest information on cultural events in Bastia, listen to Radio Corse Frequenza Mora on 101.7MHz FM.

PLACES TO STAY

Although few tourists stay in Bastia, it can still be difficult at times to find accommodation. It is vital that you book ahead, especially in summer. At other times of the year, the best places are full by the end of the morning. The accommodation listed in this section tends to be open year-round.

PLACES TO STAY – BUDGET
Camping

Camping Casanova (☎ 04 95 33 91 42) in Miomo (also known as Santa Maria di Lota) is about 5km north of Bastia next to the coastal road. It opens from mid-May to mid-October. Trees provide shade in part of the camp site, which is nothing spectacular. It charges 12/24/12/20/8/4FF per tent/ person/child under seven/car/motorbike/ bike. To get there, catch a bus to Erbalunga from the bus stop opposite the tourist office (Société des Autobus de Bastia, 7.50FF).

Camping du Bois de San Damiano (☎ 04 95 33 68 02, fax 04 95 30 84 10) is on a 12 hectare site by the sea at Lido de la Marana (between the airport and Bastia). A couple with a car and tent will pay 84FF per person. The site also lets chalets for four people by the week (1700FF to 2800FF, depending on the season) and caravans for two (1050FF per week). There is a waterpark with a swimming pool and jacuzzi. A bus goes to Lido de la Marana from Bastia bus station (direction Marana), or you can catch the train, get off at Rocade and walk the rest of the way.

Hotels

Hôtel de l'Univers (☎ 04 95 31 03 38, fax 04 95 31 19 91, 3 ave Maréchal Sébastiani), virtually opposite the post office, has around 30 rooms. The most basic and oldest singles/doubles/triples (shower and toilet upstairs) cost 160/190/230FF. For more comfortable, refurbished rooms including shower, toilet, telephone, cable TV and aircon, expect to pay 260/310/360FF. Breakfast costs 30FF. Guests with motorbikes and bikes can use the hotel car park.

Chez Jean (☎ 04 95 31 50 13, 19 rue César Campinchi) is a small hotel on the first floor of an old building. The 10 or so rooms are basic (washbasin and bidet in some) but most are spacious. Expect to pay 150/180FF for a single/double. The hotel is ideal for those on a shoestring budget but its corridors are noisy, so don't expect to be able to lie in. The rooms don't have double glazing so opt if you can for rooms over-looking the courtyard. The hotel doesn't have a reception: instead go to the 2nd floor and knock on the door to your right.

PLACES TO STAY – MID-RANGE

Riviera-Hôtel Restaurant (☎ 04 95 31 07 16, fax 04 95 34 17 39, 1bis rue du Nouveau Port) is a friendly establishment with 21 rooms on the 1st floor of a building opposite the bus station. Double rooms with outside washroom facilities are 200/230FF in low/high season. A room with a shower, TV and telephone costs 250/300FF. Breakfast costs 21FF, and in the low season the restaurant has a 60FF menu. Two rooms on each floor have a small balcony.

Hôtel Central (☎ 04 95 31 71 12, fax 04 95 31 82 40, 3 rue Miot) is one of the best hotels in town from the point of view of comfort and welcome. The owners have re-furbished the bathrooms, which now have a shower, washbasin and toilet. Some rooms have a small balcony. The manager and his son speak Italian and English. A double room in low/high season costs 200/250FF. The most well-appointed rooms (balcony, fan, TV and telephone) cost 320/380FF. Some rooms have a kitchenette (400FF to 450FF in high season).

Hôtel des Voyageurs (☎ 04 95 34 90 80, fax 04 95 34 00 65, 9 ave Maréchal Sébastiani) is another first-rate hotel. All rooms have TV, air-con, telephone and shower or bath and have recently been redecorated. A single/double room is 250/280FF in low season and 300/350FF in high season. The hotel also caters for families, with a triple room for two adults and a child (350FF) and two family rooms ideal for two adults and

two children (400FF). You are guaranteed a warm welcome.

Hôtel Posta Vecchia (☎ 04 95 32 32 28, fax 04 95 32 14 05, quai des Martyrs de la Libération) is the only hotel offering sea views in Terra Vecchia. The 49 rooms of this two star hotel are excellent. There are two types of double room: smaller rooms cost 240FF (with an additional charge of 20FF in summer) and larger rooms cost 360FF (additional charge of 40FF in summer). The hotel has two small rooms with external bathrooms for 180FF.

Hôtel Impérial (☎ 04 95 31 06 94, fax 04 95 34 13 76, 2 blvd Paoli) has 19 rather dismal rooms that could do with being refurbished. All are well appointed with TV, telephone, hair dryer and double glazing. At the height of the season a single/double/triple costs 300/350/450FF (250/290/350FF in low season). There's a friendly welcome.

Hôtel de la Paix (☎ 04 95 31 06 71, fax 04 95 33 16 95, 1 blvd Giraud) is on the roundabout near the Palais de Justice (law courts). This is a family hotel with 12 small but comfortable rooms. The double rooms have a shower or bath, TV and telephone (250/350FF depending on the season). An extra bed costs 80FF and breakfast is 30FF.

Hôtel Bonaparte (☎ 04 95 34 07 10, fax 04 95 32 35 62, 45 blvd Général Graziani) is in a plain 1960s building. Double rooms cost 300FF from October to March, 350FF from April to June and 400FF from July to September. All the rooms have a shower, TV, double glazing and telephone. They must be vacated before 11 am and breakfast is served between 6 and 11 am (40FF). The rooms are light and some have a balcony but most could do with being completely refurbished. Guests are occasionally treated rather abruptly.

Hôtel Napoléon (☎ 04 95 31 60 30, fax 04 95 31 77 83, 43-45 blvd Paoli) has 13 rooms, each with a bathroom, toilet, TV and mini-bar. Prices for rooms start at 290FF in low season and go up to 590FF in high season (around 15 August, for example). The rooms are rather small and the atmosphere leaves a lot to be desired.

PLACES TO EAT

Brasserie du Marché (☎ *04 95 34 27 11)* is one of a handful of restaurants situated around the old harbour. It is recognisable by its large blackboard on which the menu and daily specials are chalked up. The seafood platter (128FF for the standard size and 266FF for the larger size) prepared in front of the customer is excellent. The daily specials mainly consist of fish. There is an excellent salmon or sea bream with home-made ratatouille for 68FF. Those who are less hungry can pick at warm goat's cheese salad, red pepper salad with anchovy fillets (both 48FF) or flat lobster with mayonnaise (46FF per 100g). The service is discreet and attentive. Wine is served by the glass (25FF for 20cL).

Restaurant U Murinari (☎ *04 95 32 45 99)* is also on the old harbour, opposite Brasserie du Marché. This first-rate restaurant offers three regional menus at 80FF, 100FF and 155FF and a children's menu at 45FF.

Bistrot du Port (☎ *04 95 32 19 83)*, just opposite the entrance to the Hôtel Posta Vecchia (see the preceding Places to Stay section), is a small, excellent restaurant with an intimate atmosphere. It does not offer fixed-price menus but there is a wide range of imaginative à la carte dishes such as sorrel omelette (42FF) and brochette of mussels (55FF). The fish is sold by weight (28FF per 100g, regardless of the type of fish). Try the baked scorpion fish, John Dory with sorrel or gigot of monkfish. Reservations are recommended for this popular place.

Jo la Braise (☎ *04 95 31 36 97, 7 blvd Hyacinthe de Montera)* is a small restaurant two minutes from the Palais de Justice. It is rather plain from the outside but serves delicious and well-prepared food. Jo, the owner, and his wife both work in the kitchen, which leads directly into the dining room. Brochette of mutton, grilled *figatellu* (liver sausage), grilled prawns and tasty pizzas are all cooked in two wooden ovens. The pizzas are small and thick and are cooked in a mould (35FF to 40FF). Finish off your meal with one of the home-made desserts such as banana flambée (35FF). The restaurant is often full and lunch and dinner orders are taken until 2 pm and 9.30 pm respectively.

Solo Pizze (☎ *04 95 31 07 15, 4 place de la Fontaine Neuve)* is a great place for inexpensive food in a shady part of the square, just above rue des Terrasses. The prices of the pizzas and pasta dishes range from 35FF to 50FF. The restaurant is open from Monday to Saturday for lunch and dinner.

La Voûte (☎ *04 95 32 27 82, 6 rue Luce de Casabianca)* is in a quiet street just behind the harbour. It is worth making a detour for its rich and varied menu. For a meal that won't cost the earth, opt for one of the excellent pizzas cooked over a wood fire (45FF to 50FF).

For those who like to get up early, local traders and producers set up their stalls in the market place (place de l'Hôtel de Ville) each morning. You can stock up on local produce such as honey, fruit, *charcuterie* (cooked pork meats) and wine, or simply treat yourself to *feuilleté au bruccio* (brocciu pastry).

Bar Bernard, next to the Église Saint Jean Baptiste, is a good place to rest weary legs. Sit outside on the terrace and enjoy the contrast between the quaint old houses with their blue roofs and the bustle of the busy market.

ENTERTAINMENT
Cinemas

Le Régent (☎ *04 95 31 03 09)*, a multi-screen cinema, is in rue César Campinchi. There is also an art-house cinema, *Studio Cinéma* (☎ *04 95 31 12 94)*, in rue Miséricorde, near the Palais de Justice.

Bars & Discos

Bastia has little nightlife. There are several bars along the waterfront but the two discos in the town are closed during the summer due to competition from those in seaside resorts such as Saint Florent.

Velvet (☎ *04 95 31 01 00*) near the old harbour, just next to the steps leading to the Citadelle, tends to be frequented by people aged under 30. The other is *Urban Jungle*, also closed in summer, which caters for an even younger clientele. The only large disco outside the town open in summer is *L'Apocalypse* (☎ *04 95 33 36 83*) at Lido de la Marana south of Bastia. If you want to go for a drink in a bar that plays techno music, try *Macarana*, next to the new marina (north of the ferry terminal). Alternatively, one of the bars in the village of Petranera puts on rock concerts from time to time.

SHOPPING

You will be spoilt for choice when you go shopping. One of the best places to shop is U Muntagnolu (☎ 04 95 32 78 04, 15 rue César Campinchi), which sells charcuterie, cheese (with special sealed packaging to keep in the smell), wine, liqueurs and honey. It is open year-round from 9 am to 12.30 pm and 3 to 8 pm (closed Sunday). Packages can be mailed for an additional charge.

GETTING THERE & AWAY
Air

Bastia-Poretta airport (☎ 04 95 54 54 54) and its new terminal are 24km south of the town.

Bus

The bus station is virtually opposite the tourist office at the end of rue du Nouveau Port. Bear in mind that some buses leave from the train station, ave Maréchal Sébastiani or ave Pietri.

Ajaccio
Eurocorse (☎ 04 95 21 06 30)
Daily except Sunday and public holidays
Depart from bus station
110FF
Calvi
Les Beaux Voyages (☎ 04 95 65 15 02)
Twice daily
Depart from train station
80FF

Canari
Transports Saoletti (☎ 04 95 37 84 05)
Monday and Wednesday
Depart from bus station
40FF
Corte
Autocars Cortenais (☎ 04 95 46 02 12)
Monday, Wednesday and Friday
Depart from bus station
50FF
Linguizetta
Transports Poli Xavier (☎ 04 95 38 50 56)
Monday, Wednesday and Saturday
Depart from bus station
80FF
Luri
Transport Luchesi (☎ 04 95 35 10 67)
Wednesday (and Tuesday and Thursday from July to September)
Depart from bus station
45FF
Macinaggio
Saladini (☎ 04 95 35 43 88)
Monday, Wednesday and Friday
Depart from bus station
35FF
Moriani
Autocars Figarella (☎ 04 95 31 07 80)
Daily
Depart from bus station
35FF
Porto Vecchio
Les Rapides Bleus (☎ 04 95 31 03 79)
Twice daily
Depart from opposite the post office (ave Maréchal Sébastiani)
115FF
Saint Florent
Transports Santini (☎ 04 95 37 04 04)
Daily except Sunday and public holidays
Depart from bus station
30FF
Solenzara
Transports Tibéri (☎ 04 95 57 81 73)
Daily except Sunday and public holidays
Depart from bus station
80FF
Vescovato & Venzolasca
Autobus Casinca (☎ 04 95 36 70 64)
Daily except Sunday and public holidays
Depart from bus station
26FF

Train

The train station (☎ 04 95 32 80 61) at the western end of ave Maréchal Sébastiani is open from 6.30 am to 8 pm Monday to Saturday and from 7 am to noon and 2 to 7 pm Sunday and public holidays.

In summer there are two trains a day from Bastia to Calvi (3 hours, 92FF), at 8.45 am and 4.35 pm. There are several trains a day to Corte (1½ hours, 57FF), Casamozza (30 minutes, 17FF) and Ajaccio (4 hours, 121FF).

Car
Most of the car rental firms have branches in Bastia and at the airport. At the height of the season it is vital that you book at least a month ahead to be guaranteed a car. ADA (☎ 04 95 31 48 95), at 35 rue César Campinchi, is open from 8 am to noon and 2 to 5 pm Monday to Saturday, as is Citer (☎ 04 95 31 16 15), at 42 rue du Général Graziani.

Boat
The new ferry terminal is at the end of ave Pietri. Inside, tickets are sold for same-day travel; ticket offices open a few hours before the ships arrive. The terminal also has a bureau de change. If you want to buy a ticket to travel on a different day, you will need to go to one of the carriers' offices:

Corsica Ferries
  (☎ 04 95 32 95 95, fax 04 95 32 14 71)
  9 blvd du Général de Gaulle
  Open from 8.30 am to noon and 2 to 6 pm Monday to Friday and 8.30 am to noon Saturday.
Moby Lines
  (☎ 04 95 34 84 94, fax 04 95 32 17 94)
  4 rue Luce de Casabianca
  Open from 8 am to noon and 2 to 6 pm Monday to Friday and 8 am to noon Saturday.
SNCM
  (☎ 04 95 29 66 99, fax 04 95 29 66 77)
  Southern terminal of the commercial port
  Open from 8 to 11.30 am and 2 to 5.45 pm Monday to Friday and 8 to 11.30 am Saturday.

Visiting sailors have a choice between the old harbour in Bastia (☎ 04 95 31 31 10, fax 04 95 31 77 95), right in the centre of town, or the new Toga marina (☎ 04 95 32 79 79, fax 04 95 32 55 61) north of Bastia in the town of Pietrabugno. The former has more

than 250 berths and the latter more than 350. Both have refuelling points, toilets, showers and maintenance workshops.

GETTING AROUND
To/From the Airport
The airport bus (48FF) leaves from in front of the entrance to the Préfecture building, which is on the roundabout in front of the train station. The times are advertised at the bus stop and timetables are available from the tourist office.

A taxi to the airport (☎ 04 95 36 04 65) will cost you 200FF (up to 250FF at night, on Sunday and on public holidays).

Bus
Bus No 1 goes to the airport (7.50FF) from the Toga marina via blvd Paoli and the Citadelle (place Dominique Vincetti).

Taxi
Taxis Radio Bastiais (☎ 04 95 34 07 00, place Saint Victor) operates 24 hours. You can also call Taxis Bleus (☎ 04 95 32 70 70).

Bicycle
Objectif Nature hires out bikes by the day – see under Activities earlier in this section.

AROUND BASTIA
Étang de Biguglia
Measuring 11km by 2.5km and with a surface area of 1450 hectares, this is the largest lake in Corsica. Declared a nature reserve in 1994, it is an important staging post for birds migrating between Europe and Africa. There are more than 100 rare species of bird here.

The northern part of the lake is linked to the sea by a canal but the rest is freshwater. Eel and mullet are farmed here and there are many footpaths where you might spot some of the reserve's inhabitants. There is an information kiosk (open during the summer) on the eastern shore. Sailing and bathing are prohibited.

Lido de la Marana is a narrow stretch of coastline more than 10km long, wedged between the Étang de Biguglia and the sea. Much of the area is devoted to tourism, with shops and businesses, residential areas, camp sites (see Places to Stay earlier in this section), discos and even a riding centre. The beach is nothing special but at least you will have room to stretch out on a towel. As you approach from Bastia you come to a long car park that fringes the beach. After this the road heads inland slightly and parking is more limited.

A cycle track borders the lake on its eastern side and is frequently used by rollerbladers, cyclists and pedestrians.

Getting There & Away There are several buses a day from the coach station in Bastia (direction Marana) to the Lido and the lake. You can also catch the Casamozza train as far as Rocade. The Étang de Biguglia is 200m away on foot.

Mariana & the Cathédrale de la Canonica

At the southern end of the Étang de Biguglia, a short distance from Bastia-Poretta airport, is the small archaeological site of Mariana and the Cathédrale de la Canonica, recognisable by its polychrome walls. The cathedral is right on the D107 and the surrounding area is rather unattractive, but it is worth visiting. The Église de San Parteo (which is closed to the public) towards the runway is in a rather more bucolic setting.

Cap Corse

No one knows whether it is in silent reproach or in search of its homeland that Cap Corse (Capi Corsu in Corsican) reaches towards Italy and the Golfo di Genova. Often described as an 'island within an island', this maquis-covered peninsula 40km long and around 10km wide gives Corsica its characteristic outline and has a history that sets it apart from the rest of the island.

Genoese Towers

Around 60 of the 85 Genoese towers built in Corsica by the Office de Saint Georges in the 16th century remain. Mostly round but occasionally square, these fortified structures are about 15m high and are particularly common in Cap Corse.

The towers were intended to protect the island from the countless Saracen raids but you can't help thinking that in building them Genoa also sought to protect its strategic and commercial interests in Corsica. Placed around the coastline so that each was visible from the next, the towers formed a vast surveillance network. A system of signals enabled a message to circle the island in one hour.

Marine de Scalo, Pino, Erbalunga and the Sentier des Douaniers (which takes you to the lovely Santa Maria tower) all have Genoese towers. Many towers still stand at other points on the island, including Porto, Campomoro and Calvi.

The peninsula was ruled for a long time by important families of lords from Liguria, such as the Da Mare, Avogari and Gentile families. They had close links with the republic of Genoa and thrived on trade in wine and oil. Genoa became accustomed to considering Cap Corse as an ally, and history rarely proved it wrong. This part of Corsica also has a long maritime tradition. Apart from Bonifacio, it is the only region of Corsica where the inhabitants have made a living from fishing.

The only merchants and sailors on an island of mountain dwellers closed to an outside world that was often considered hostile, the inhabitants of Cap Corse soon felt the need to broaden their horizons. After having made the region one of the most prosperous on the island, many turned to distant shores, thus contributing to the island's depopulation over the years. The apéritif bearing the region's name became a mascot for the émigrés and a symbol of their nostalgia for their homeland. Many of them won renown in the French colonies in North Africa and the Americas. Once they had made their fortune, many returned to Corsica, where some of them had unusual colonial-style houses built. Some of these 'American homes' can still be seen in the region today, particularly in Sisco and Canelle.

Encircled by an large number of towers built under the Genoese to protect the vulnerable peninsula from Saracen raids, the cape is dotted with fishing villages and small communities perched precariously on its hills. Much of the region consists of gentle highlands covered in maquis. The east and west coasts are very different in appearance, with the wilder west coast undoubtedly the more spectacular.

Cap Corse tourist office (☎ 04 95 32 01 00, fax 04 95 31 77 79) is in the Maison du Cap Corse on the outskirts of the town of Retrabugno, a few kilometres north of Bastia. It is open from 9 am to noon and 2.30 to 6 pm Monday to Saturday. The times vary in winter. Brochures and programmes for the region's cultural events are available here.

The following description of the region starts in Bastia and follows the coastline around to Saint Florent. Don't be surprised to find that some villages have more than one name. The main hamlet of each district in the region is often also known by the same name as the district itself. Morsiglia is thus also known as Baragona, Botticella is Ersa, and so on.

ERBALUNGA

Erbalunga is around 10km north of Bastia. Little of the town can be seen as you pass along the main road through it. However, it would be a shame to allow its peaceful narrow streets to go unexplored. The streets form a close network around a tiny fishing harbour, where a few colourful boats are moored. A Genoese tower adds the finishing touch to the scene. The town is famous for its processions during Holy Week.

You will find several grocery stores and a post office in Erbalunga but no bank or ATM.

Places to Stay

Castel Brando (☎ 04 95 30 10 30, fax 04 95 33 98 18) is the only hotel in Erbalunga. This three star hotel is in a charming restored house. The comfortable, light and spacious rooms all have air-con, TV and telephone. Double rooms are available for 380FF in April, May, September and October, 430FF in June and from 480FF in July and August. The hotel has a lovely swimming pool and you are assured of a warm welcome.

Hôtel Les Roches (☎ 04 95 33 26 57) is in Lavasina, a few kilometres away in the direction of Bastia. This hotel is a rather cheaper alternative to Castel Brando. Its rustic double rooms cost 200FF without a bathroom, 250FF with bathroom and 300FF with bathroom and sea view. The hotel is open year-round. Only rooms with a sea view are available in winter, when they cost 250FF.

Places to Eat

A Piazetta (☎ 04 95 33 28 69) is the cheapest place to eat in Erbalunga, with pizzas for 45FF and main courses from 55FF. The restaurant, in the main square, is open daily in summer. It is closed on Tuesday in winter and for the whole of January and February.

Le Pirate (☎ 04 95 33 24 20) is a lovely restaurant in the small harbour: you can eat lunch or dinner with the waves virtually lapping at your feet. The à la carte menu includes fish soup (60FF), pasta with basil and garlic (70FF) and meat dishes (from 90FF to 120FF). It's open from April to October but closed Monday, except in July and August.

L'Esquinade (☎ 04 95 33 22 73), also down in the harbour, has a 120FF menu (which includes local ham and mullet à la Provençale), pasta from 60FF to 80FF and meat dishes from 90FF. It is open for lunch and dinner year-round but is closed on Wednesday except in summer.

ROGLIANO (RUGLIANU)

• pop 480

A few kilometres inland from Macinaggio, Rogliano (also called Bettolacce) had its heyday when the village was home to the powerful Da Mare family.

Its hour of glory came in 1869, when the ship bringing Empress Eugénie home from Egypt was forced to take shelter in the port of Macinaggio. The empress and her retinue climbed up to the village and legend has it that she went to gather her thoughts at the Église Sant'Agnello. Behind its beautiful façade, the 16th century church has a high altar made from Carrara marble.

Several wine-growers are located nearby, including the Gioielli and Pietri estates. Le Clos Nicrosi (☎ 04 95 35 41 17), one of the most famous vineyards on the island, is signposted from the village. In the pretty building with its column pediment you can buy and taste wine from 9.30 to 11.30 am and 2.30 to 7 pm, Monday to Friday. An annual wine festival is held in Luri at the beginning of July.

Places to Stay & Eat

The pretty *U Sant'Agnellu* inn (☎/fax 04 95 35 40 59) is open from April to October. This has light, pleasant double rooms costing from 280FF to 340FF depending upon the season. The first-rate 80FF menu includes Corsican charcuterie, grilled steak with herbs or cannelloni with brocciu, and cheese or dessert. An Olympian calm and a superb panorama also feature among its attractions.

A shuttle between Macinaggio and the village operates free of charge in summer.

MACINAGGIO (MACINAGHJU)

The harbour is reputed to have had the best mooring in Cap Corse since time immemorial. Macinaggio was a naval base at the time of Pascal Paoli and will appeal particularly to sailing enthusiasts.

The large marina, frequented by Italian navigators, is not the prettiest in the area but offers a range of facilities such as refuelling points, water, ship dealers, bars, restaurants and a bureau de change. Showers and weather forecasts are available from the harbour master's office (☎ 04 95 35 42 57).

Macinaggio also prides itself on its lovely **Plage de Tamarone**, undoubtedly the most stunning beach in the region. To get there, follow signs to Camping U Stazzu, then to Santa Maria, on the road from Macinaggio towards Centuri. Follow the winding camp site road for about 800m. The road is about 1km away from the beach. In summer you will find a refreshment stall with a reasonably priced menu but there are no toilets.

The **Sentier des Douaniers** (Customs Officers' Route) leads away from the beach, climbing through fragrant maquis before dropping down to the protected shore that runs alongside the Îles Finocchiarola and Capandola reserve, where the wonderful Genoese Santa Maria tower rises out of the shimmering water. See the Walking in Corsica chapter for more on this path.

Places to Stay & Eat

There are a handful of hotels and restaurants in the area but camp sites are few and far between in this region.

Camping U Stazzu (☎ 04 95 35 43 73) is signposted 800m on the right as you leave the town heading towards Centuri. It charges 27/16FF per person/pitch. The site is near the beach and village and has decent washrooms and shady pitches. It's open from April until 1 October.

BARCAGGIO (BARCAGHJU)

From Botticella (more commonly referred to as Ersa, the name of the district), the lovely but rather narrow D253 winds its way through the maquis for 10km before reaching the northernmost village in Cap Corse. In its far-flung location, Barcaggio seems eternally lost in silent contemplation of the remote Île de la Giraglia and its *sémaphore* (a small lighthouse), which took 10 years to build. There is no bus service to this village.

From the beach at Barcaggio you can join the Sentier des Douaniers (see the Macinaggio section above and the Walking in Corsica chapter), which is poorly signposted at this point. The trail begins behind the wooden fencing around the beach and continues as far as the Tour d'Agnello, before going on to Santa Maria and Macinaggio. The fencing was erected at the instigation of the Conservatoire du Littoral (coast conservation organisation) to combat the disappearance of plants stabilising the sand dunes, such as dune grass and lesser bindweed, which are now rarer as a result of tourism and overgrazing. The beach car park costs 10FF a day in summer.

Capo Grosso, west of Barcaggio and the village of Tollare, offers a breathtaking view over the cape. From the D153, a pitted and bumpy road reaches the viewing point after 2.5km: it is not signposted but is the only tarmac road heading west before you get to Tollare.

Places to Stay & Eat

Hôtel La Giraglia (☎ 04 95 35 60 54, fax 04 95 35 65 92) takes advantage of its monopoly, charging rather inflated rates. The single/double/triple rooms are comfortable but basic and cost 390/440/550FF. Credit cards are not accepted. The restaurant is open from April to September.

U Pescatore (☎ 04 95 35 64 90) is the only restaurant in Barcaggio. It is open daily for lunch and dinner, June to September. In simple surroundings you can order fish soup, omelette made with local herbs from the maquis or even grilled steak with herbs (140FF).

Tents and caravans are prohibited in this area, except in the few designated parking areas.

CENTURI
• pop 200

Nestling below Col de la Serra, the tiny port of Centuri keeps the local tradition of rock-lobster fishing going. Established by the Romans as Centurium, the village was once a busy trading centre. It was also used as a military base, as testified by the old cannons converted into mooring posts in the harbour. In the 18th century Pascal Paoli based part of his rapid-response fleet here.

Tourism is important to the town: work is currently underway to extend the sea wall and the restaurant illuminations that light up the town in summer. The pretty little harbour is sometimes too quiet at the height of the tourist season. Nevertheless, it is charming and soulful and remains one of the most attractive spots in the region. One of the town's most famous inhabitants is a friendly fisherman who looks like Santa Claus and has appeared in various advertisements.

Above the village, the Moulin Mattei flaunts the merits of 'Mattei Cap Corse, an exquisite citrus liqueur' from Col de la Serra. Liqueur aside, this point offers a superb panorama over Île de la Giraglia and the mainland mountains that weave their way towards the sea.

Information

The nearest post office is in Orche, 4km from the harbour. It is open from 9 am to noon and 1.30 to 4 pm Monday to Friday and from 9 am to noon Saturday. You should be able to cash travellers cheques into francs (2% commission) and get cash using Visa, MasterCard or Eurocard (minimum commission 20FF).

Places to Stay

Camping L'Isulottu (☎ 04 95 35 62 81) is 1.5km from Centuri harbour. This is a pleasant place with decent washroom facilities, a mini-market and a snack bar. There is access to a small shingle beach 10 minutes away. Expect to pay 28FF per person, 15FF to 18FF per tent, and 10/30FF per car/camper van. Credit cards are accepted for amounts over 300FF. The site is closed from 20 December to 20 January.

Don't miss the *Hôtel-Restaurant du Pêcheur* (☎ 04 95 35 60 14). This pretty green building on the harbour offers clean and freshly decorated double rooms with an unrestricted view over the harbour for

The Best Views on Cap Corse

A number of sites offer fine viewing points over Cap Corse. In addition to **Capo Grosso** and the **Moulin Mattei** (see the sections on Barcaggio and Centuri), there is the **Tour de Sénèque**, which dominates the hills above Pino on the western coast of the peninsula and offers views of the eastern and western coasts.

Half a kilometre from Pino (where Église Santa Maria Assunta houses a 15th century triptych attributed to the Florentine painter Fra Bartolomeo and classified as a historic monument), follow the D180 for around 6km. Once you reach the Col de Santa Lucia look out for the small road on the right next to the chapel. After 1km this brings you to a cluster of abandoned buildings where you can leave your car. There is a steep 15 minute climb to the tower along a path signposted in red. To get to the well-preserved tower, turn left onto the stone slabs once you reach the undergrowth.

200FF (300FF in August). Open from April to October, this is a good choice for those on a tight budget.

Hôtel U Marinaru (☎ 04 95 35 62 95) is around 200m from the harbour. This is less well situated than Hôtel-Restaurant du Pêcheur but slightly more comfortable. Its large double rooms, each with a terrace and bathroom, cost 200FF. The hotel is open year-round. Half board is compulsory in August.

Hôtel-Restaurant Le Vieux Moulin (☎ 04 95 35 60 15, fax 04 95 35 60 24) is the most comfortable hotel in Centuri. Its prices are reasonable: you can expect to pay 280FF for a lovely double room with a shower, TV and telephone. Larger chalets for two to three people with a terrace are available for 330FF. Le Vieux Moulin is an excellent place to stay and is open year-round (except during its annual holiday). There is a disco under the hotel terrace in a vaulted room that was used as a warehouse when Centuri thrived on trade. Established in 1960, this small friendly disco is the oldest in Corsica.

Places to Eat

Le Snack Cavalu di Mare is near Hôtel-Restaurant Le Vieux Moulin. Its prices are reasonable: sandwiches cost from 17FF to 22FF, hamburgers cost 20FF and omelettes and salads cost from 30FF to 40FF. There are fixed-price menus at 55FF and 60FF. It is only open in July and August.

Hôtel-Restaurant Le Vieux Moulin (see Places to Stay) has a 190FF menu (herb tart, grilled lobster and dessert) but is rather expensive. There are generous fixed-price menus for 115FF or 145FF, with a good fish soup, meat or baked fish (despite the proximity of the sea, fish costs an extra 30FF), cheese and fruit. Snacks are more reasonably priced but the à la carte menu is pricey.

Many of the hotels in the harbour also have restaurants.

Mini-Market Agostini is open daily in summer and is near Hôtel-Restaurant Le Vieux Moulin. It is well stocked and sells newspapers.

Getting There & Away

There is no harbour master's office in the tiny harbour and sailors can berth there free of charge. Mooring is limited, however, both at the quayside and out of the water. There are no showers or toilets in the harbour. This could all change after completion of the extension work on the jetty and the dredging in progress at the time of writing, which should enable around 15 sailing boats to be accommodated.

NONZA

Records of Nonza date back to the Middle Ages. The village is partly built over a spectacular rocky crag on the summit of which stands a Genoese tower, more than 150m above the shingle beach.

Nonza is also famous for its 16th century **Église Sainte Julie**, next to the road. In addition to its ochre façade and painted and sculpted walls and ceiling, the lovely church, which is a listed historic monument, has a Baroque altar in polychrome marble made in Florence in 1693, and a painting of Saint Julie on the cross. Across the road, peaceful but steep narrow streets lead down to the village behind the square 16th century **tower**.

Nonza rose to fame in 1768. Besieged by the French, to whom the Genoese had just ceded Corsica in the Treaty of Versailles, the village was fiercely defended by one of its inhabitants, Jacques Casella. Single-handedly operating a large number of fire-arms, he managed to convince his attackers that Nonza was being defended by a dozen people. He eventually surrendered, to the stupefaction of his adversaries. The viewing point offers a superb panorama over the village, gulf and beach below.

Around 50m from Église Sainte Julie in the direction of Cap Corse, a path descends to the supposedly miraculous **Fontaine Sainte Julie**. There is a memorial plaque dedicated to Corsica's patron saint on the pediment of the white chapel, recalling that in the year 303:

Saint Julie was martyred and crucified for her Christian beliefs. After her death, her breasts were cut off and hurled against the rock, from where the miraculous waters sprang.

Beneath the fountain the path drops sharply down to a shingle **beach**. Swelteringly hot in summer, the beach offers no shade and the climb back up is difficult, but it is pos-sible to get there and back by car: continue towards Cap Corse for around 2km until you get to a narrow tarmac road, which will take you down to the shore in a couple of minutes.

Nonza has a small grocery shop and post office, open from 9 am to noon and 2 to 4 pm Monday to Friday and from 9 to 11.30 am on Saturday. You can exchange travellers cheques into francs here (with a 1.2% commission charge) and get cash using Visa, Eurocard or MasterCard. There is no ATM.

Places to Stay & Eat

L'Auberge Patrizi (☎ 04 95 37 82 16) in the main square has comfortable rooms in vari-ous stone buildings in the village. The pleasant single/double rooms, each with bathroom, cost 250/300FF in low season (including breakfast) and 300/400FF in summer. The inn also has a 120FF menu (charcuterie, cannelloni with brocciu or sauté of veal, cheese and dessert) and daily specials (60FF) served under a pleasant bower.

At *Le Café de la Tour*, near L'Auberge Patrizi, you can have a drink in the shade of the trees. A small shop opposite the café sells pizza slices and sandwiches for 18FF to 40FF.

L'Auberge du Chat Qui Pêche (☎ 04 95 37 81 52) is around 10km north of Nonza on the D80. This pretty stone house with its oleander groves has small but pleasant attic rooms with bathroom for 200FF. The inn offers a 95FF menu and daily specials for 50FF, which mainly consist of grilled dishes and fresh produce cooked on a wood fire. This charming inn is open year-round ex-cept January and February. The view from the terrace is breathtaking at certain times of the day.

Getting There & Away

The firm Micheli (pronounced 'Migueli'; ☎ 04 95 35 64 02) organises coach tours of the region from July to the beginning of September. The itinerary starts and finishes in Bastia and takes in Erbalunga, Macinag-gio, Centuri, Canari, Nonza, Saint Florent and Oletta. The complete tour costs 105FF, Bastia to Centuri costs 40FF and Centuri to Nonza costs 28FF. Coaches leave the bus station in Bastia at 9 am Monday to Satur-day (except 14 July and 15 August) and re-turn to Bastia at around 5 pm.

Other companies provide a service to Cap Corse from Bastia the rest of the year. Transports Saoletti (☎ 04 95 37 84 05) runs buses to Canari (40FF) on Monday and Wednesday. Saladini (☎ 04 95 35 43 88) runs buses to Macinaggio (35FF) on Mon-day, Wednesday and Friday. Transport

Luchesi (☎ 04 95 35 10 67) operates a bus service to Luri (45FF) on Wednesday, and on Tuesday and Thursday between July and September.

The Nebbio

With the vineyards of Patrimonio, the seaside town of Saint Florent and the Désert des Agriates, the Nebbio (Nebbiu in Corsican) is a region of contrasts. Behind the stark exterior of the desert lies one of the most beautiful beaches in Corsica, while art connoisseurs will delight in the number of Pisan churches in the area.

SAINT FLORENT (SAN FIURENZU)
• pop 1450   ✉ 20217
Away from the maquis of Cap Corse, the landscape becomes more undulating, varied and cultivated. Saint Florent is the principal town in the Nebbio region. This pleasant seaside town 23km from Bastia is a good place in which to spend a few days, and its bay, marina and beach are popular with tourists.

History
More would be known about the town's past if the base of the Cathédrale du Nebbio were excavated. This fine example of religious architecture was built on the site of the Roman city, which was located here because at the time of its construction malaria was rife along the coast. The explanation of the origin of the town's name changes depending on whom you talk to: some believe Saint Florent was an African bishop exiled to Corsica by the Vandals in the 15th century, others tell of a Roman soldier who converted to Christianity and was subsequently martyred.

The town rose to fame under the Pisans. It became a pawn in the fight against the Genoese due to its strategic position (it provides a safe harbour across the water from the military port of Toulon). Subsequently neglected, little was heard of the town until the new harbour and the development of tourism made it popular once more.

Orientation
The main road from Patrimonio skirts the north-eastern side of the town and takes you to place des Portes, Saint Florent's focal point. The narrow streets of the old town stretch westwards.

Crossing the Poggio river, the road continues south towards Plage de la Roya, accessible from the beach road on the right just after the metal bridge over the Aliso river.

Information
Tourist Office The friendly staff in the tourist office (☎ 04 95 37 06 04) are professional and experienced. The office is in the Centre Administratif (Civic Centre) opposite Hôtel Madame Mère on the main road, which also houses the post office and town hall. Useful information on the town, the Nebbio region and the Désert des Agriates is available from the office, which is open from 9 am to noon and 2 to 5 pm daily in July and August (Monday to Friday and Saturday morning the rest of the year).

Money Société Générale, on the main road, exchanges currency and travellers cheques. An ATM outside the bank accepts Eurocard, MasterCard and Cirrus. It is open from 9 am to noon and 2 to 4.45 pm Monday to Friday.

Across the road, Crédit Agricole also has an ATM and exchanges currency and travellers cheques. Expect to pay a commission of 35FF (Eurocheques in francs are exchanged free of charge). It is open from 8.10 to 11.55 am and 1.35 to 4.50 pm, Monday to Friday.

The post office (see Post below) exchanges some travellers cheques for a commission of 1.2%.

Post The post office is in the Centre Administratif and is open from 9 am to noon and 2 to 5 pm Monday to Friday and from 9 am to noon Saturday.

SAINT FLORENT

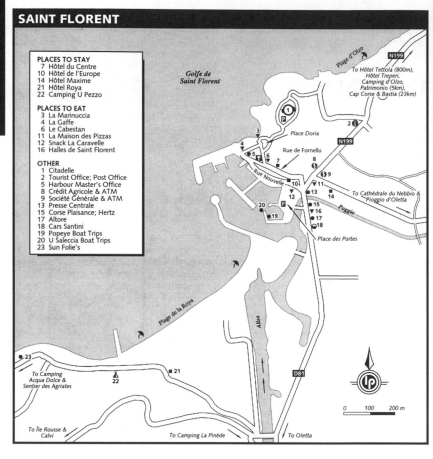

PLACES TO STAY
7 Hôtel du Centre
10 Hôtel de l'Europe
14 Hôtel Maxime
21 Hôtel Roya
22 Camping U Pezzo

PLACES TO EAT
3 La Marinuccia
4 La Gaffe
6 Le Cabestan
11 La Maison des Pizzas
12 Snack La Caravelle
16 Halles de Saint Florent

OTHER
1 Citadelle
2 Tourist Office; Post Office
5 Harbour Master's Office
8 Crédit Agricole & ATM
9 Société Générale & ATM
13 Presse Centrale
15 Corse Plaisance; Hertz
17 Altore
18 Cars Santini
19 Popeye Boat Trips
20 U Saleccia Boat Trips
23 Sun Folie's

Bookshop Presse Centrale (☎ 04 95 37 13 79), in the place des Portes, sells French and foreign newspapers (in summer) as well as a selection of books and film.

It is open daily (closed Sunday afternoon) from 7.30 am to 8.30 pm in summer and from 8 am to 12.30 pm and 2 to 7 pm in the low season.

Medical Services The nearest hospital is 23km away in Bastia. A doctor is available 24 hours year-round on ☎ 04 95 37 00 04.

Citadelle

Perched above the harbour, the sandy-coloured Citadelle built under the Genoese looks remarkably like a Moroccan casbah. Its ramparts were destroyed in Genoese times. At the time of writing it was undergoing renovation.

Cathédrale du Nebbio (Église Santa Maria Assunta)

Built in the 12th century by the Pisans, this fine example of religious architecture is a

The multihued maquis lent its name to the French Resistance.

Saxifrage.

Purple foxglove.

Between Bocca di Verdi and the Refuge de Prati on the GR20.

Asphodels.

Montpelier rock rose and fern.

Arbutus.

Broom in bloom.

JEAN-BERNARD CARILLET

Between the mountains and the sea: a church rises from the maquis in Cap Corse.

OLIVIER CIRENDINI

Cap Corse is studded with tiny hamlets.

OLIVIER CIRENDINI

Centuri's fishing industry is very much alive.

OLIVIER CIRENDINI

About 60 Genoese towers survive on the coast.

reminder that in the fourth century Saint Florent became the home of the Bishop of Nebbio. The cathedral is around 800m east of the town centre, built on the site of the Roman city. The Roman façade incorporates amazing sculptures of snakes and wild beasts. In his *Guide de la Corse mystérieuse*, Gaston d'Angélis relates that the bishops of Nebbio were entitled by their office 'carry a sword and to officiate with two pistols on the altar'.

The cathedral is permanently staffed in summer. Ask at the tourist office for the key if you want to visit in the low season. Entrance is free.

Plage de la Roya

This long ribbon of sand around 2km southwest of the town centre gives you a lovely view over the town and the Nebbio hills. From June to September Sun Folie's Location (☎ 06 09 54 19 39) hires out sailboards (50FF to 90FF per hour), sailing dinghies (110FF per hour), racing catamarans, kayaks and jet skis. Two comfortable deck chairs and a parasol will set you back 60FF per half-day.

The Patrimonio Vineyards

Several wine-growers have shops in the town centre where you can taste and buy local wines. Better still, you can go straight to the *domaines* (estates), around 6km from Saint Florent. Domaine Gentile (☎ 04 95 37 01 54) on the northern outskirts of the town is closest. Other domaines are discussed under Patrimonio later in this chapter.

Boat Trips to the Agriates

Two companies organise summer boat trips to the superb Plage du Lodo near the Désert des Agriates. The *Popeye* (☎ 04 95 37 19 07), an old fishing boat recognisable from the Rolling Stones mouth painted on its prow, leaves the quay three times a day in summer. The journey to Plage du Lodo takes around 30 minutes and costs 55FF return (30FF for children). You can hire diving masks (30FF) and parasols (20FF) on board. The launch *U Saleccia* (☎ 04 95

36 90 78) makes two return trips a day in summer; it charges the same as the *Popeye*.

A debate broke out at the beginning of the 1998 season when the district authority responsible for managing this stretch of coastline asked companies running boat trips to pay for the right to use the landing stage at Plage du Lodo. The matter was eventually resolved but it might be a good idea to ask whether the landing stage is still there before you buy your ticket (otherwise you will disembark onto an inflatable pontoon, which can sometimes be a bit tricky).

Activities

Altore (☎/fax 04 95 37 19 30) next to Halles de Saint Florent offers courses in canyoning, parapenting and climbing, but you can also do winter sports such as skiing and hiking in snow shoes. The shop is open from April to October but can be contacted by telephone in winter.

See the Diving chapter for information on diving in the area.

Places to Stay – Budget

Camping d'Olzo (☎ 04 95 37 03 34) on the northern outskirts of the town is open from 1 April to 30 September. This three star camp site with quiet, shady pitches is without doubt one of the best in Saint Florent. You will pay 29/16/16/10FF per person/pitch/car/motorbike.

Camping La Pinède (☎ 04 95 37 07 26) lies south of the town towards Plage de la Roya. Turn off the main road just after the metal bridge: the camp site is on the banks of the Aliso. Shady and pleasant with a swimming pool, it's open from 1 May to the end of September.

More basic camp sites can be found on Plage de la Roya. *Camping U Pezzo* (☎ 04 95 37 01 65) opposite the sailing school has decent pitches and facilities but is often packed in summer. Expect to pay 20/12/11/8FF per adult/tent/car/motorbike. It's open from April to October.

Camping Acqua Dolce (☎ 04 95 37 08 63), slightly farther away from town, is similar. Its bar will appeal to football lovers.

Hôtel du Centre (☎ 04 95 37 00 68, *rue de Fornellu*) is a lovely and inexpensive family hotel. Situated in the old town, a stone's throw from the harbour, it has 10 impeccable rooms with TV, bathroom and telephone. The double rooms range from 200FF to 300FF depending on the time of year. The hotel is open year-round.

Hotel de l'Europe (☎ 04 95 37 00 03, *place des Portes*) has single/double/triple rooms at 150/200/250FF in the low season. Expect to pay an additional 100FF in July and 200FF in August. The hotel is open from April to September.

Hôtel Maxime (☎ 04 95 37 05 30, *fax 04 95 37 13 07*) is a white-fronted building above the Poggio river at the beginning of the road leading to the cathedral. It has lovely light and comfortable double rooms with telephone, TV and mini-bar for 340/380/280/250FF (July/August/September/October to June). It's open year-round. Parking is available.

Places to Stay – Mid-Range & Top End

Hôtel Tettola (☎ 04 95 37 08 53, *fax 04 95 37 09 19*) on the northern outskirts of town combines the advantages of a lovely swimming pool and a beach. The comfortable double rooms overlooking the sea are the most popular and the most expensive (up to 620FF in July and August) but the more noisy rooms overlooking the road only cost between 260FF and 480FF. All rooms cost 260FF in the low season. The hotel, which has a warm and friendly atmosphere, is closed in November, January and February.

Hôtel Treperi (☎ 04 95 37 40 20, *fax 04 95 37 04 61*), hidden among the vineyards north of the town, will also give you a warm welcome. It is easiest to get to it by car: it's signposted just after the Elf garage on the right as you come from Saint Florent. Its charms include a swimming pool, tennis courts and a menu featuring Corsican produce. It has 18 rooms, each with a terrace and a view over the gulf and vineyards. The owners have produced a leaflet with a dozen or so ideas for walks around Saint Florent. Expect to pay anything from 220FF to 400FF for a double room, depending on the time of year.

Hôtel Roya (☎ 04 95 37 00 40, *fax 04 95 37 11 29*), on Plage de la Roya, is also worth a mention. It belongs to the British chain Mark Warner and is a favourite haunt of Anglo-Saxons: English is spoken more than French here. The pleasant hotel has an ochre façade and private access to a pretty corner of the beach. The comfortable rooms are usually booked up but you can always try your luck. Expect to pay from 200FF to 270FF per person, including breakfast.

Places to Eat

Budget *Snack La Caravelle* in place des Portes serves inexpensive dishes such as *bruschetta* (toasted bread rubbed with garlic with various toppings, such as tomato, cheese and olives) for 35FF to 42FF, salads for 30FF to 35FF and omelette and chips for 20FF to 25FF. The snack bar is open daily from April to October.

La Maison des Pizzas (☎ 04 95 37 08 52) on the main roundabout sells pizzas cooked over a wood fire for 40FF to 75FF year-round. It is open until 11 pm or midnight daily in July and August.

Those who want to shop for their food can head for the *Halles de Saint Florent* supermarket just south of the river. It is open from 8 am to 8 pm daily in summer.

Mid-Range & Top End *Le Cabestan* (☎ 04 95 37 05 70, *rue de Fornellu*), in the heart of the old town, is certainly one of the best-value restaurants in Saint Florent. The excellent 85FF menu has a wide range of dishes: start with fish soup or *gambas flambées* (flambéed Mediterranean prawns) and as a main course try the excellent sea bream with fennel, grilled mullet with maquis herbs or *tripettes* (tripe) with beans. Finish off with cheese or a dessert. Le Cabestan opens two weeks before Easter and closes in mid-November. It is open daily for lunch and dinner. Credit cards are accepted.

La Gaffe (☎ 04 95 37 00 12) in the harbour is a good seafood restaurant that also caters for those on a budget (seafood tagliatelle for 51FF). The monkfish stew with tagliatelle is wonderful (95FF). The 99FF menu has fish soup, grilled swordfish and cheese or dessert and the à la carte desserts and Patrimonio wines are reasonably priced. The restaurant is open daily (except Tuesday in the low season), and is closed from mid-November to mid-December.

La Marinuccia (☎ 04 95 37 04 36, place Doria) is on a terrace over the water and is an ideal place to eat dinner while watching the sun go down. The simple 95FF menu includes fish soup or local ham in port, followed by lamb chops with herbs and cheese or dessert. The 110FF menu includes foie gras, sardines stuffed with brocciu and cheese or home-made dessert. La Marinuccia is open until 10.30 or 11 pm daily from April to October. The only drawback is that the Patrimonio wines are expensive considering they are produced just down the road. Don't be confused by the restaurant's neon sign in the square: its concealed entrance is on the left of the square a few metres in front of a low parapet.

Entertainment
La Conca d'Oro (☎ 04 95 39 00 46) disco is 5km from the town on the way to Oletta. It's open in summer.

There are open-air screenings of films in July and August – ask at the tourist office.

Getting There & Away
Bus Transports Santini (☎ 04 95 37 02 98, 04 95 37 04 04), just after the bridge over the Poggio on the main road, operates a bus service from Saint Florent to Bastia. Buses usually leave twice daily except on Sunday and public holidays.

Car The small Hertz agency (☎ 04 95 37 16 19) is open from 1 June to 30 September. It is in a corner of the Corse Plaisance chandlery just south of the Poggio.

Boat The harbour master's office (☎ 04 95 37 00 79, fax 04 95 37 11 37) is next to Église Sainte Anne. Showers (15FF), chand-

lery supplies, water, fuel and weather reports are available in the harbour. This large, attractive marina reserves around 120 berths for visitors. Expect to pay from 85FF to 142FF to moor a 9m boat, depending on the time of year.

Getting Around
You can get around the town on foot but transport is useful if you want to go to the beach. Corse Plaisance (☎ 04 95 37 00 58) is open from 9 am to noon and 3 to 5 pm Monday to Friday year-round (Saturdays and Sunday morning in summer). It has scooters and motorbikes for hire from 270FF a day.

PATRIMONIO
As you head towards Cap Corse you will come to the peaceful village of Patrimonio, 6km from Saint Florent and surrounded by vines. The tall 16th century Église Saint Martin, with its half-moon pediment and stone scrolls, overlooks the town.

Most visitors come to the area in search of wine. The predominant variety of grape in the region is muscat. The area, which was the first in Corsica to be granted an *appellation d'origine contrôlée* (AOC) label, produces red, rosé and white table wine with varying degrees of success. Around 600 hectares are divided between some 35 wine-growers, who are happy to let you taste their wines. A tour of the vineyards is a must if you have a car.

As you leave Saint Florent and head for Cap Corse you will come to the locally renowned **Domaine Gentile** on your left (☎ 04 95 37 01 54). A few kilometres farther along on the right is the white building of **Domaine Orenga de Gaffori** (☎ 04 95 37 45 00), about 200m before you get to the roundabout at the lower end of Patrimonio. The estate's Cuvée du Gouverneur (around 50FF) is one of the best red wines produced on the island. You can taste and buy it in season.

Once you get to the village (signposted to the right at the roundabout), stop off at

Clos Marfisi (☎ 04 95 37 01 16), where tastings are held between 9 am and noon and 2 and 7 pm daily from March to October (by appointment only the rest of the year). The table wine costs between 37FF and 40FF and muscat costs 54FF.

Clos de Bernardi (☎ 04 95 37 01 09), above the road to the church, offers tasting tours for small groups in a lovely stone house. The friendly M de Bernardi produces a good red wine and is also proud of his rosé (table wine costs 35FF, muscat 50FF).

As you leave the village, pause to visit **Domaine Lazzarini** (☎ 04 95 37 13 17). This vineyard receives a number of coach parties in summer. As well as an excellent muscat (45FF), it produces orange, peach and table wines that can be sampled and bought.

With one or two exceptions, wines produced in these cellars are not for laying down but for immediate consumption.

COL DE TEGHIME
High up on the ridge, Col de Teghime (536m) halfway between Bastia and Saint Florent offers a breathtaking view over the entire region. To the east you can see as far as Bastia, the Étang du Biguglia and, on the horizon, the island of Elba (in clear weather). To the west lie the Patrimonio vineyards, the Golfe de Saint Florent and the Désert des Agriates.

The pass is around 10km from Bastia (from the town centre follow the diversion signs towards Calvi then head for Saint Florent). Just before you get to the pass, you'll see a large open-air rubbish tip that attracts birds of prey and seagulls.

At the pass, you can get to the summit of the **Sierra di Pigno** (961m) on a narrow tarmac road (bear right as you come from Bastia). The 4.5km climb, very pleasant on foot, will afford you a magnificent view over the two sides of the pass and over Cap Corse.

The windy summit is more difficult to get to. Look out for the unsightly radio masts and a small military area.

DÉFILÉ DE LANCONE
The Défilé de Lancone in the Massif du Monte Pinzali was sculpted by the U Bevincu river, which is torrential at this point and goes on to flow into the Étang de Biguglia. From the Bocca di Santu Stefanu roundabout two roads overhang the narrow gorges: the D82 joins the N193 at Ortale, while the more spectacular D62 goes to Casatorra. The D62 is quite narrow, however, and becomes difficult if traffic is heavy.

OLETTA & POGGIO D'OLETTA
• pop 900 & 150
Oletta and Poggio d'Oletta cling to the hillside between Saint Florent and Bastia. The hills here slope gently down to the Vallée du Guadello and the vineyards of Patrimonio. The two small villages stretch out over several kilometres and are linked by a road offering a superb view over the Golfe de Saint Florent.

A stroll through the narrow streets of Oletta will take you to the workshops and cellars of around 10 local **artisans**. Their workshops are usually open to the public from 11 am to 12.30 pm and 6 to 8 pm in summer.

In Poggio d'Oletta two small churches in a superb location below the town hall face Saint Florent. The Église de San Cervone is the better restored and is open to the public (ask at the town hall for the key). The choir dates from 1145 but its current form is 18th century. The clock tower was added in the 19th century.

Places to Stay & Eat
Restaurant A Maggina (☎ 04 95 39 01 01) on the northern outskirts of Oletta serves the best food in either village. It's family-run and has a small dining room with a view. It offers a choice of two menus, one at 110FF (terrine of *figatellu*, duck with olives, cheese or dessert), the other at 140FF. À la carte dishes include a platter of Corsican cheeses (35FF), fish (30FF per 100g) or meat (from 80FF). The restaurant

has three rooms to let in a very pretty stone house that overlooks the road. Expect to pay 200FF for a room with a bathroom and small garden. In July and August half board is encouraged. The restaurant has a car park (essential in summer) and is open from April until the end of October.

Pension Casette (☎ 04 95 39 02 71, fax 04 95 32 73 16) is in Casette on the southern outskirts of Oletta. This simple family home has four rooms. Double rooms are 250FF (450FF for four) with external washroom facilities. It is open from April until the beginning of September.

Bar-Restaurant U Lampione (☎ 04 95 39 02 97) is near the church in the centre of Oletta. It is run by a Frenchman with a Corsican accent. You can order thick-cut sandwiches made using fresh bread (30FF with a drink) and relax in the shade of the trees. From 15 August (when the wild boar season opens) hunters come here on Sunday for an apéritif and to compare their trophies.

There is a small **grocery shop** near the Église d'Oletta and a **mini-market** at the southern end of the village as you head towards Olmeta di Tuda.

MURATO

A few hundred metres south of the Église de San Michele, Murato is a large village with pretty houses. During independence, the mint where the coins of the new state were struck was located in the village. This is also the birthplace of Giuseppe Fieschi and of the father of Raúl Leoni, who symbolise the rich and eventful history of Corsican emigration (see the boxed text 'The President & the Terrorist').

You can eat lunch, have dinner or dance in one of the restaurants – **Le Monastère** (☎ 04 95 37 64 18) is the most pleasant – or discos.

Église de San Michele de Murato

The green and white Romanesque Église de San Michele de Murato is in a meadow surrounded by rocky crags above the tranquil

---

The President & the Terrorist

At the age of 58 Raúl Leoni was voted president of Venezuela in the December 1963 elections. His Murato-born father Clément Leoni had left Bastia for Caracas at the age of 22 to try his luck in the new South American republic 68 years earlier. He had four children, including Raúl, who made his first and only visit to Corsica in 1970. Father and son are now heralded as symbols of successful Corsican migration.

Born in Murato in 1790, Giuseppe Fieschi led a more turbulent life. A petty criminal, he left Corsica for Paris, where he worked for some time with the secret police. He infiltrated the republican movements and in 1835 organised an attempt on the life of Louis-Philippe and the royal family during the anniversary of the July 1830 revolution. The daring assassination attempt failed but 19 people were killed. Fieschi and his accomplices were condemned to death and executed a year later. Today Fieschi's memory lives on in the town, overshadowing that of Raúl Leoni.

Vallée de Saint Florent and the Désert des Agriates. The white chalk came from Saint Florent and the green serpentine was taken from the bed of the nearby U Bevincu river. The colours are laid out in monochrome horizontal bands and then in an irregular patchwork. Local legend has it that the church was built in a hurry in just one night. What is certain is that it dates from around 1140. It was restored in the Baroque style and visited by the French author Prosper Mérimée, who wrote about and sketched it. To see the wall frescoes inside, get the key from Murato town hall.

Around Murato

U Mulinu (☎ 04 95 39 06 16) restaurant near an old mill on the U Bevincu river is only open in summer. You can order pizza or one of the dishes from the Corsican menu, and children can go for a dip in the cold shallow water. To get there, turn right 200m after the Église de San Michele de Murato. The restaurant is at the end of a track, on your left before you get to the bridge over the river.

After visiting the Église de San Michele, head down to Saint Florent via the villages of Rapale, San Gavino di Tenda and Santo Pietro di Tenda. **Rapale** is a charming village with several cafés. You can also walk from here to the ruins of a church that resembles the Église de San Michele de Murato. The path is signposted from behind the church in the village.

DÉSERT DES AGRIATES

Between Saint Florent and the mouth of the Ostriconi lie 30km of arid landscape known as the Désert des Agriates, where the maquis is scorched by the sun and from which rise low chalky mountains. Even the plants seem rock-like. It's hard to believe that the area was once used to grow food for Genoa. Until the beginning of the 20th century, life in the area was governed alternately by transhumance and sowing. In October shepherds from the Nebbio and the Vallée de l'Asco would bring their goats and ewes here for the winter. In June farmers from Cap Corse would follow them, arriving in flat boats. The region was even famous for its olive groves. *Ecobuage* (cultivation on burnt stubble) and fires fanned by the prevailing winds are mainly to blame for transforming the fertile soil into a stony desert.

The Agriate coast has had the same radiant appearance since time immemorial. Its trump card is undoubtedly the outstanding **Plage de Saleccia**, which stretches for nearly 1km and is up there with the best of what any tropical island has to offer. The smaller but equally stunning **Plage du Lodo** and **Plage de l'Ostriconi**, at the western end of the Agriates, are also superb. Some say the latter has the finest sand in Europe.

Almost 5000 hectares bought by the Conservatoire du Littoral, together with the ad-

Posidonia Oceanica

The long brownish leaves that often carpet Corsica's sandy beaches (and upset some swimmers) are one of the most important elements of the Mediterranean marine ecosystem. Often mistaken for seaweed, they are part of the aquatic plant *Posidonia oceanica*, found to a depth of 35m. Its leaves form underwater meadows, producing oxygen and providing a breeding ground and a source of food for small marine fauna. The plant beds also cushion the effect of the waves, thus contributing to the protection of the sandy beaches. *Posidonia oceanica* is a protected species in Corsica.

joining common land, make up the protected natural site of the Agriates, managed by the Syndicat Mixte Agriate (Joint Agriate Association; ☎ 04 95 37 09 86). As well as protecting this area of outstanding interest and beauty, its work is aimed at safeguarding the species of bird, butterfly and plant that populate this ecosystem.

Off-road motor vehicles, fires, camping and bivouacking, and the dumping of rubbish are prohibited in the Agriates.

Exploring the Agriates

Boat The easiest way of getting to the Agriates is by boat. Two companies organise boat trips to Plage du Lodo (30 minutes on foot from Plage de Saleccia) from Saint Florent.

See the section on Boat Trips to the Agriates in the Saint Florent section.

Car Two roads descend into the Agriates from the D81. Both are around 12km long. The first starts in the village of Casta, the second from Bocca di Vezzu, 10km from Casta in the direction of Île Rousse.

Neither road is accessible unless you are in a 4WD vehicle because both are rough and stony (don't be deceived by the short strip of tarmac at Bocca di Vezzu), especially if rain has created ruts in the ground that have then been baked hard by the sun.

Walking There is a coastal path to the area from Saint Florent (Plage de la Roya). You can walk to Plage de l'Ostriconi at the other end of the Agriates in three days. The walk is divided into three stages: Saint Florent to Saleccia (around 5½ hours); Saleccia to Ghignu (around 2¾ hours); and Ghignu to Ostriconi (around 6½ hours). The route, passable year-round, is not particularly hard-going but make sure you have plenty of water with you.

Accommodation is available at Plage de Saleccia and Ghignu. See the following section on Places to Stay & Eat.

Don't make the difficult journey from Casta to Saleccia on foot in summer.

Cycling This is a favourite with the more sports-oriented visitor. Although the sandy coastal path (see Walking above) is not suitable for mountain bikes, you can get from the village of Casta to Plage de Saleccia. Rather than following the coast, the 12km-long rough track gives you the chance to explore the interior of the Désert des Agriates. Bear in mind that the hard, stony ground makes the descent particularly challenging, especially for novices – the expression 'blazing sun' takes on new meaning here in summer.

Make sure you have plenty of water, a hat, sun cream and time. It is better to attempt the descent early in the morning so that you avoid the hottest part of the day and can spend the rest of the day on the beach. The dusty track takes you through breathtaking scenery and descends amid fragrant maquis overshadowed by pale mountains. The view from here makes the whole effort seem worthwhile. Allow 1½ to 2 hours for the difficult climb back up to Casta (expect to do much of it on foot pushing the bike).

You can hire brand new mountain bikes from Relais de Saleccia (☎ 04 95 37 14 60) in Casta, about 100m off the track. Expect

to pay 90FF per day: the price includes the loan of an instant puncture sealant. It's open from April to October.

It's also possible to hire mountain bikes in Île Rousse. See Activities in the Île Rousse section of the Calvi & the Balagne chapter.

Horse Riding Horse riding is available between Ostriconi and Île Rousse. Arbo Valley (☎ 04 95 60 49 49) organises rides around the Agriates: a half-day excursion will cost you 300FF, including a meal. The centre, which is approved by the Association Nationale du Tourisme Équestre (National Association of Equestrian Tourism), can also organise excursions with a bivouac to other parts of the island lasting several days. It is signposted on a bend 4km from Île Rousse on the D81: follow the rough track to the pretty valley in which it is located for 800m.

Les Agriates à Cheval (☎ 04 95 60 10 05, in the Village de l'Ostriconi complex) organises rides to the Agriates (180FF for three hours, 300FF for six).

Places to Stay & Eat
Relais de Saleccia (☎ 04 95 37 14 60) in Casta has six lovely double rooms (there will soon be 10) which cost 250FF (300FF in August) including breakfast. Half the rooms have a terrace and an unrestricted view over the Agriates. The hotel has a good-value Corsican menu at 80FF, which includes Corsican soup, cannelloni with brocciu, and cheese or dessert (including an excellent *fiadone*). It's open from April to October.

Camping U Paradiso (☎ 04 95 37 82 51) is at the end of the track from Casta to Plage de Saleccia, 12km from the D81. This is a good camp site that charges 15/15/10/5FF per person/tent/car/motorbike. It has a small grocery store, public telephones, a bar, a billiard table and a children's play area. The washroom facilities are reasonable. The site, around 100m from Plage de Saleccia, also has a few pretty stone chalets for 250FF per person (half board). These are often booked up well in advance. There is a pleasant dining room open from June to September. The 90FF dinner menu is changed daily. At lunchtime you can order salad (from 35FF to 50FF), steak and chips (65FF) or the daily special.

Les Paillers de Ghignu are old *bergeries* (shepherd's huts) near Plage de Ghignu. Used by walkers along the coastal path, they offer basic accommodation. Bring a sleeping bag with you because you will be sleeping on a stone surface (a foam sleeping mat is also a good idea). There is an outside washing block with hot water and drinking water. Meals are not provided. The bergeries charge 50FF a night and are open between April and October. You should make a reservation by contacting the Syndicat Mixte Agriate (☎ 04 95 37 09 86) in Casta, on the left as you come from Saint Florent, around 5km from Relais de Saleccia. The office is open from 9 am to 4 pm Monday to Friday (it keeps longer hours in summer).

Village de l'Ostriconi (☎ 04 95 60 10 05, fax 04 95 60 01 47) is pleasant but in need of modernisation. On the D81 across from Plage de l'Ostriconi, it has camping facilities (32.50/13.50/13.50FF per person/tent/car), a swimming pool, a grocery store and tennis courts. Double rooms are available for 170FF and 260FF, in addition to functional chalets with kitchenette for four to five people (from 295FF to 490FF depending on the time of year). It's open from Easter to October.

Ferme-Auberge de Pietra Monetta (☎ 04 95 60 24 88) is on the D81 from Saint Florent towards Île Rousse, not far from the Ostriconi river. This lovely stone building has four rustic double rooms with bathroom (but shared toilet) for 200FF, including breakfast (150FF for a single person). The 110FF menu includes grilled lamb or pork stew. The charcuterie, vegetables and oil used in the meals are produced on the farm. The inn is closed on Wednesday and from March to October.

Calvi & the Balagne

The Balagne is a secluded territory in the north-west of the island, bordered by the Désert de Agriates to the north, the Vallée du Fango to the south and the foothills of Monte Cinto to the east. There is a sharp divide between the fertile north (two-thirds of the region) and the southern desert.

The Balagne is one of the largest regions in Corsica and its landscape has a gentleness that stands out from the barrenness of some of the other regions on the island. Known as the 'orchard of Corsica', it owes its success to fertile land, strategically positioned ports and its proximity to mainland France. The region has long been prosperous due to its flourishing olive groves and citrus fruit plantations. It became one of the first regions on the island to open up to tourism when Calvi became a fashionable holiday destination in the period between the two world wars.

Today the Balagne, with its beautiful villages perched high up in the mountains and the delightful resort town of Calvi, continues to attract a large number of visitors in the summer months thanks, in part, to its good transport links through the ports of Calvi and Île Rousse and Calvi-Sainte Catherine airport.

The Coast

CALVI
• **pop 4900**   ✉ **20260**

Calvi, the capital of the Balagne, is a thriving little town stretched out along its bay under the watchful eye of two giants: the Citadelle and Monte Cinto (2706m). The closest town to France, Calvi was once a Genoese stronghold and the Genoese influence is still discernible today.

The attractions of its beach, the Citadelle and the cultural festivals it stages every year make Calvi one of the most popular resorts on the west coast.

Highlights

• Ride the Tramways de Balagne train along the beautiful coastline between Calvi and Île Rousse

• Breathe the pure air of the Bonifatu forest as you watch the sun set over the cirque

• Feast your eyes on endless groves of olive trees, typical Balagne scenery

History

Although the Golfe de Calvi has been a port of call for sailors since ancient times, the foundations of the town were laid by the Romans in the 1st century AD. Later destroyed by Saracen raiders, Calvi recovered a little under the Pisans (from the 11th to the 13th century) but rivalries between local lords, especially those from Cap Corse, led the population to turn to Genoa for protection in 1278. The powerful Italian republic was handed the opportunity to exert its power on the island and took no time in turning the inhabitants of Calvi into good Genoese citizens. From this point on the history of the town became so inextricably linked with its loyalty to this republic that many other parts of the island considered it the oppressor (the finger is still sometimes pointed at Calvi, even today).

The town grew in strength under the influence of the Genoese and the Citadelle was built. At the same time Genoa used the Office de Saint Georges (a financial institution that administered the island) to transform Calvi into a thriving town, so that by

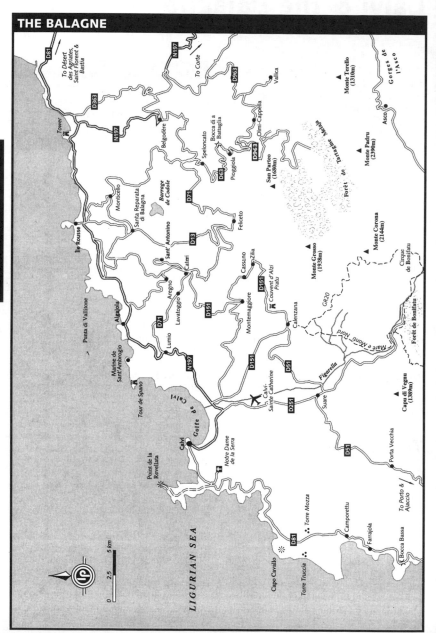

THE BALAGNE

LIGURIAN SEA

0   2.5   5 km

the 15th century it was thoroughly Genoese, along with Bonifacio. It remained so until the 18th century, although in the meantime it was attacked by two powerful forces.

The first attack occurred in the middle of the 16th century, when the rivalry between Henri II of Navarre (France) and Charles V of Spain turned Corsica into an important strategic target. In 1553 France dispatched a squadron made up of French troops, supporters of Sampiero Corso (see the boxed text in the History section of the Facts about Corsica chapter) and Turkish forces under the command of the Turkish privateer Dragut. This fleet captured Bastia, Saint Florent and Bonifacio but failed to take Calvi. It was on this occasion that Genoa gave the town its motto in recognition: *Civitas Calvi Semper Fidelis* (Ever-faithful City of Calvi).

The second episode was less successful for Calvi. In 1794 the town, which had been ceded to France by the Genoese in 1764, came under attack from the British army and separatist forces led by Pascal Paoli. It was heavily bombarded and largely destroyed during the fighting (which cost Nelson his right eye), and eventually capitulated. The Anglo-Corsican kingdom was short-lived, however, and Calvi returned to French control in 1796.

Orientation

The Citadelle – also known as the Haute Ville (Upper Town) – is built on a promontory to the north-east of the Basse Ville (Lower Town).

Most activity is centred around quai Landry (along the marina), ave de la République, blvd Wilson and, to a lesser extent, ave Christophe Colomb. A section of the lower town to the east of blvd Wilson is pedestrianised. There's a long beach stretching out to the south-east of the *port de plaisance* (marina).

Information

Tourist Office The tourist office (☎ 04 95 65 16 67, fax 04 95 65 14 09) is in the marina, above the harbour master's office

---

A Calvian Called Columbus

Place Christophe Colomb, ave Christophe Colomb, a plaque commemorating the anniversary of Columbus' discovery of America ... Nearly every town on the island has its own hero: in Ajaccio it is Napoleon, in Île Rousse it is Pascal Paoli, in Bastelica it is Sampiero Corso and in Calvi it is the discoverer of the New World.

But why does the ghost of the famous navigator haunt the alleyways of the Citadelle? The answer is simple: some people maintain that Christopher Columbus was born in Calvi, in a section of the Citadelle that is now in ruins. So what if most sources say Columbus was Genoese – wasn't Calvi Genoese when he was born in around 1450?

So little is known about the early life of the explorer that it is difficult to prove or disprove the story. Even if it can be proved that Columbus was the son of a Genoese weaver, there is no way of proving whether his distant ancestors were Corsican, Galician, Catalan or Genoese. Whatever the truth is, the bold adventurer quickly set his sights on America and left Corsica as nothing but his alleged birthplace.

(*capitainerie*). It can provide you with a variety of brochures and information about the town. The office is open daily from 9 am to 1.30 pm and 2.30 to 7 pm between June and October, and from 9 am to noon and 2 to 5.30 pm in winter (closed Saturday afternoon and Sunday). The staff speak English and Italian as well as French.

Money There's a branch of Société Générale on blvd Wilson; it's open from 8.10 to 11.55 am and 2 to 4.55 pm Monday to Friday. The bureau de change is open from 8.30 to 11.30 am and 2 to 4.30 pm; there's a commission charge of 25FF on cash transactions, plus 1% of the transaction for travellers cheques in a foreign currency. Eurocheques are not accepted.

CALVI & THE BALAGNE

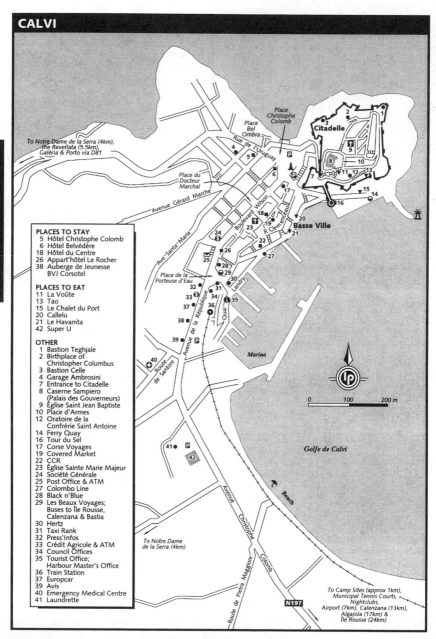

CALVI

Place Christophe Colomb

Place Bel Ombra

Citadelle

Basse Ville

Rue de l'Uruguay

Place du Docteur Marchal

Avenue Gérard Marche

Boulevard Wilson

Ave-Santa-Maria

Rue Clemenceau

Place de la Porteuse d'Eau

Avenue de la République

Quai Landry

Marina

To Notre Dame de la Serra (4km), the Revellata (5.5km), Galéria & Porto via D81

Route de Santore

Golfe de Calvi

Beach

To Notre Dame de la Serra (4km)

Route Christophe Colomb

Route de Pietra Maggiore

N197

To Camp Sites (approx 1km), Municipal Tennis Courts, Nightclubs, Airport (7km), Calenzana (13km), Algajola (17km) & Île Rousse (24km)

0   100   200 m

PLACES TO STAY
5 Hôtel Christophe Colomb
6 Hôtel Belvédère
18 Hôtel du Centre
26 Appart'hôtel Le Rocher
38 Auberge de Jeunesse BVJ Corsotel

PLACES TO EAT
11 La Voûte
13 Tao
15 Le Chalet du Port
20 Callelu
21 Le Havanita
42 Super U

OTHER
1 Bastion Teghjale
2 Birthplace of Christopher Columbus
3 Bastion Celle
4 Garage Ambrosini
7 Entrance to Citadelle
8 Caserne Sampiero (Palais des Gouverneurs)
9 Église Saint Jean Baptiste
10 Place d'Armes
12 Oratoire de la Confrérie Saint Antoine
14 Ferry Quay
16 Tour du Sel
17 Corse Voyages
19 Covered Market
22 CCR
23 Église Sainte Marie Majeur
24 Société Générale
25 Post Office & ATM
27 Colombo Line
28 Black n'Blue
29 Les Beaux Voyages; Buses to Île Rousse, Calenzana & Bastia
30 Hertz
31 Taxi Rank
32 Press'Infos
33 Crédit Agricole & ATM
34 Council Offices
35 Tourist Office; Harbour Master's Office
36 Train Station
37 Europcar
39 Avis
40 Emergency Medical Centre
41 Laundrette

Crédit Agricole at 8 ave de la République, opposite the council offices, has an ATM. You can also change money there (35FF commission on travellers cheques). The bank is open from 8.15 to 11.50 am and 2 to 5 pm Monday to Friday (4.50 pm on Thursday and Friday).

There's also an ATM at the post office.

Post The post office on blvd Wilson is open from 8.30 am to 5.30 pm (6.30 pm in July and August) Monday to Friday and on Saturday morning.

Poste restante mail should be addressed to Bureau de poste de Calvi, blvd Wilson, 20260 Calvi, Corsica.

Bookshops Press'Infos (☎ 04 95 65 17 43) on ave de la République has a large range of French and foreign newspapers and magazines. It's open daily from 7 am to 10 pm (sometimes even later) in the peak season. The rest of the year, opening hours are 7.30 am to 12.30 pm and 2 to 7.30 pm.

Originally just a record shop, Black n'Blue (☎ 04 95 65 25 82) at 20 blvd Wilson now also sells a choice of foreign-language books (none in English) that are an improvement on the normal level of holiday reading. It's open year-round from 9 am to noon and 2.30 to 5 pm Monday to Saturday (and Sunday morning in summer).

Laundry There is a laundrette in the car park of the Super U supermarket on ave Christophe Colomb. It's open daily from 8 am to 9 pm and a load costs 34FF (plus 25FF for 30 minutes of drying).

Medical Services Although there is no hospital in Calvi, there is an emergency medical centre (☎ 04 95 65 11 22, fax 04 95 65 10 15) in route du Stade, a few minutes walk south of the town centre. It's attached to the hospital in Bastia and is open 24 hours year-round.

The centre only handles emergencies, but the nursing staff will be able to put you in touch with the town's GPs and specialist doctors if necessary.

Citadelle

Built at the end of the 15th century by the Genoese, Calvi's Citadelle towers over the town from its rocky promontory. Unlike the citadel in Bonifacio it is not an integral part of the town and usually stands empty, although a few cafés and restaurants set out their tables in the shadow of its ochre walls. The majority of the buildings within are closed to the public, but the Citadelle is definitely worth a detour for its peculiar atmosphere, its various religious buildings and the spectacular view over the Golfe de Calvi and surrounding area.

Crossing place Christophe Colomb, you reach the Citadelle through a porch over which the town motto is inscribed. A succession of little alleyways lead to the place d'Armes, to the left of which is the **Palais des Gouverneurs Génois** (Genoese Governors' Palace). This imposing building, which has been renamed Caserne Sampiero, was built by the Genoese in the 13th century and extended by the Office de Saint Georges. It now houses a division of the French Foreign Legion and is closed to the public.

The **Église Saint Jean Baptiste** is up the street from the palace, halfway up a little alley. This 13th century church is built in the shape of a Greek cross and very nearly did not make it to the present day: in 1567 the explosion of a powder store nearby was very nearly fatal. However, the church was rebuilt three years later and consecrated as a cathedral in 1576. As well as a splendid dome, the interior boasts a high altar of polychrome marble dating from the 17th century, to the right of which is the *Christ des Miracles*. This ebony statue has been venerated since the town was besieged in 1553. According to legend, the ships of the besieging forces sailed out to sea after the population of Calvi carried the statue in a procession through the streets of the city.

Also in the church, the large statue of the *Vierge du Rosaire* (Virgin of the Rosary) has three different robes: a black one for Good Friday, a purple one for the Wednesday after Palm Sunday and a rich brocade

CALVI & THE BALAGNE

robe for processions. Only women are allowed to dress her. According to some sources, she was donated to the city by a Calvian who brought her back from Peru. Others maintain that she is Spanish in origin. There are also some screened loges which were formerly used by the women of the local elite.

If you retrace your steps and take a little street on the other side of the place d'Armes you will come to the **Oratoire de la Confrérie Saint Antoine** (Oratory of the Saint Antoine Brotherhood), a charity that has been active in Corsica since the 16th century. Behind the ornate façade of the building, which features a slate lintel depicting the abbot Saint Antoine, are walls covered in frescoes from the 15th and 16th centuries (some in very bad condition) and an ivory Christ attributed to the Florentine sculptor Jacopo d'Antonio Tati, known as 'le Sansevino'.

Farther along the street on this side of the Citadelle is the **Palais des Évêques de Sagone**, the former palace of the bishops of Sagone, which now houses the Tao restaurant and piano bar (see Places to Eat and Entertainment later in this section).

The Citadelle has five **bastions**, erected after the 15th century, which provide wonderful views. To the north-west is the Bastion Celle, flanked by a stone sentry box placed above the ramparts to survey the area. Nearby is the plaque marking the alleged birthplace of Christopher Columbus (see the earlier boxed text 'A Calvian Called Columbus'). It's also worth seeing the **Tour du Sel** (Salt Tower), a pretty round tower on quai Landry (outside the ramparts) once used to store the town's salt.

The tourist office organises two-hour guided tours of the Citadelle which cost 45FF (15FF per person for groups). Book in advance.

Église Sainte Marie Majeure
Behind the pink exterior of the Baroque church of St Mary the Elder (Santa Maria Maggiore in Corsican) at the heart of the lower town is an impressive dome.

Built between 1765 and 1838, the church houses 16th and 18th century canvasses and a statue of the Assumption that is carried through the town every year during the Assumption Day procession which takes place at the end of August.

Beach
The beach in Calvi stretches 4km from the marina along the bay to the east. To get to it by foot from the centre of town, follow ave Christophe Colomb south until you reach Chemin de la Plage (the beach path), which turns off to the left after the Casino supermarket.

Boat Trips
Between April and October Colombo Line (☎ 04 95 65 32 10) offers various trips on modern glass-bottomed boats that allow you to see into the depths. The first option is a full-day trip costing 270FF per person. It leaves at 9.15 am, coasts around the coves of the Réserve Naturelle de Scandola for about an hour, then heads for Girolata, where passengers are given two hours for lunch, returning to Calvi by 3 or 4 pm. A similar, half-day trip costing 220FF leaves at 2 pm and returns at about 5 pm.

During the high season there is a third outing twice a week for 320FF. Leaving Calvi at 8.30 am, it tours the Réserve Naturelle de Scandola and the deep rocky inlets of Piana (E Calanche), then goes on to Ajaccio, where the boat stops for four hours before returning to Calvi at about 5.30 pm. All these trips are dependent on the weather so it is wise to check in advance.

The Colombo Line office is in the harbour. Children between four and ten years of age pay half price (children under four go free).

Activities
Tennis The municipal tennis courts (☎ 04 95 65 21 13) are along the beach, towards Camping La Pinède. There are six courts, four of which are floodlit. They all cost 40FF an hour between noon and 4 pm and 70FF an hour at other times. Add an extra

10FF an hour for the lights if you like to play at the end of the day. The club is open daily year-round and has a pleasant clubhouse. Every April these courts host the Women's International Tennis Open.

Cycling Garage Ambrosini (☎ 04 95 65 02 13), not far from rue de l'Uruguay, hires out mountain bikes for 100FF a day (250FF for three days). It's open daily in summer from 8 am to noon and 2 to 6 pm (closed weekends in winter). You will be required to leave a deposit of 1500FF.

Horse Riding Two kilometres from the centre of town, towards the airport, is A Cavallu riding centre (☎ 04 95 65 22 22), which gives pony trekking and riding lessons year-round for 100FF an hour. Confident riders can even go swimming with the horses.

Paragliding & Extreme Sports Altore (☎ 04 95 61 80 09), east of Calvi on the D151 between Montemaggiore and Cateri, organises paragliding flights between April and December (350FF each). In winter this club, which specialises in extreme sports, organises off-piste skiing and snowshoe trekking.

Diving See the Diving chapter for details.

Organised Tours

Les Beaux Voyages (☎ 04 95 65 11 35) offers six different coach trips that allow you to discover a little of the island: the Forêt de Bonifatu (half-day, 55FF), Cap Corse (full day, 150FF), villages of the Balagne (half-day, 75FF), the maquis (circular route via Île Rousse, Scala di Santa Regina, Col de Verghio, Piana and Porto; full day, 150FF), Ajaccio via Corte and Col de Vizzavona (full day, 180FF) and a two day tour of the island as far as Bonifacio (500FF). The tours only take place if a minimum number of people turn up.

The agency's offices are on place de la Porteuse d'Eau and open from 9 am to noon and 2 to 7 pm, Monday to Saturday between May and October and Monday to Friday the rest of the year.

Corse Voyages (☎ 04 95 65 00 47), in conjunction with Autocars Mariani, organises excursions with similar routes and prices. Its offices on blvd Wilson are open from 9 am to noon and 2 to 7 pm Monday to Saturday year-round.

Special Events

Calvi hosts a range of festivals between Easter and October:

La Passion
Holy Week is celebrated with a major show in the Corsican language retracing Christ's Passion. Information: ☎ 04 95 65 23 57.

Rencontres d'Art Contemporain
A collection of works by contemporary painters and sculptors, held in the Citadelle between June and September. Information: ☎ 04 95 65 16 67.

Calvi Jazz Festival
Towards the middle of June big names from the international jazz scene come to Calvi for open-air or indoor concerts and jam sessions. Information: ☎ 04 95 65 00 50.

Calvi Allegria
In mid-August the Eterna Citadella son et lumière display retraces the history of the Citadelle. Information: ☎ 04 95 65 82 03.

Rencontres de Chants Polyphoniques
A gathering of polyphonic expression that takes place around mid-September in Église Saint Jean Baptiste, at the Poudrière and in place d'Armes in the Citadelle. Information: ☎ 04 95 65 23 57.

Festival du Vent
An opportunity to discover more about the way the wind works, both in artistic terms and in relation to sport and science. The Festival of the Wind is held at the end of October. Information: ☎ 01 42 64 37 69 or Web site www.le-festival-du-vent.com.

Places to Stay – Budget

Camping La Pinède (☎ 04 95 65 17 80, fax 04 95 65 19 60), close to the beach about 1.5km from the town centre, is a good choice. Sheltered by pine trees, the pitches are quiet, and the camp site has a restaurant, bar, laundrette and supermarket. There's also a swimming pool, table tennis tables, crazy golf, children's play areas and two tennis courts (30FF per hour). Prices are 36/12/12FF per person/tent/car. The camp site is open from 1 April to 15 October. Almost opposite this camp site, along ave Christophe Colomb, is *Camping Paduella* (☎ 04 95 65 06 16), which is less pleasant but cheaper, at 29/12/12FF per person/tent/car. It's open between May and October.

You will receive a warm welcome at the *Auberge de Jeunesse BVJ Corsotel* (☎ 04 95 65 14 15, fax 04 95 65 33 72, ave de la République), one of the few such establishments on the island. It is practically opposite the station and has the words Youth Hostel emblazoned across its wide yellow front. It's open from the beginning of March to the end of November and has 133 beds in simple but clean rooms (with bathroom) for two to eight people. A night costs 120FF, including a generous breakfast. Evening meals are available, costing 60FF. There is no maximum age and you don't have to belong to an affiliated youth hostel network.

If you are travelling as a couple outside the peak season, you may be able to find a more comfortable double room at a competitive price in a hotel. However, you will find no better price if you are travelling on your own in the high season.

Hôtel du Centre (☎ 04 95 65 02 01, 14 rue Alsace Lorraine) is the most economical place after the youth hostel. It has decent double rooms with basin for 160FF (230FF in August). Rooms with showers cost between 180FF and 250FF, depending on the season. Small studio apartments for two people are available for between 200FF and 290FF. The Hôtel du Centre is open from the beginning of June to the end of September. It does not accept credit cards.

Places to Stay – Mid-Range & Top End

Hôtel Belvédère (☎ 04 95 65 01 25, fax 04 95 65 33 20, place Christophe Colomb), open year-round, has pleasant, comfortable double rooms with bathroom and TV for 200FF in the low season, 250FF in July and September and 350FF in August. There are

also rooms sleeping three people (250/300/400FF) or four people (300/350/450FF). Single travellers may get a discount.

Hôtel Christophe-Colomb (☎ 04 95 65 06 04, fax 04 95 65 29 65, rue de l'Uruguay), near Hôtel Belvédère, is open from April to the end of September. It has good double rooms with telephone, TV and bathroom for between 200FF and 250FF in the low season, 300FF in July and 400FF in August.

Although its prices are a little higher, you can save money on restaurant bills at the *Apart'hôtel le Rocher* (☎ 04 95 65 20 04, fax 04 95 65 36 71, blvd Wilson), which lets impeccable apartments for two, three or four people with bathroom, kitchenette, air-conditioning and telephone. The hotel is open from the end of May to the beginning of September; it's often fully booked for weeks on end in July and August but may be worth a try. In June and September a studio for two/three/four costs 355/470/550FF. These rates increase to 500/650/700FF in the most popular weeks in July and 740/890/980FF in August. A studio apartment for three people for a week costs between 2550FF and 5300FF, depending on the season.

Places to Eat

You will find any number of stalls selling sandwiches, *panini* (filled bread rolls) and other snacks in the harbour and the pedestrianised streets around it. There are many pizzerias and restaurants offering traditional Corsican menus, although their authenticity is often somewhat dubious.

Budget Away from the restaurants near the harbour, which can sometimes err on the side of tackiness, beyond the Tour du Sel on the ferry quay, is *Le Chalet du Port* (☎ 04 95 65 46 30), a pleasant little bar where the décor combines the colours of the Mediterranean with old adverts for *Nice-Matin* or Ricard. You will be given a warm welcome and the food is simple, good and affordable: grilled pizzas (35FF) and kebabs (30FF), chips (15FF) or a plate of cold cooked meats (48FF). All this, together with good retro music and long opening hours (6 am to 2 am in high season).

If you're not that hungry, *Le Havanita* on the harbour offers tapas for between 20FF and 25FF, including peppers stuffed with *brocciu* (a Corsican cheese), pickles, tortillas and Corsican ham. It has a little terrace and is open daily from 5 pm to 2 am between the beginning of May and the end of September.

Another cheap option is the large *Super U* supermarket on ave Christophe Colomb. During the summer it's open from 8 am to 8 pm Monday to Saturday and 8 am to 1 pm on Sunday. Winter opening hours are 8.30 am to 12.30 pm and 3 to 7 pm Monday to Saturday.

La Gelateria Solea opposite the Église Sainte Marie Majeure serves generous portions of excellent ice cream, with flavours to tempt even the most difficult customers, starting at 8FF. It's open from 10.30 am to midnight in summer.

Mid-Range & Top End *La Voûte* (☎ 04 95 65 12 83) is in a little room with subdued lighting under the old courtrooms in the Citadelle; it would have been where criminals condemned to death spent their last moments. The welcome is now warmer and the two fixed-price menus for 100FF are good value. The Corsican Menu starts off with a plate of cooked meats, followed by, for example, an excellent Calenzana veal. The Corsican Fisherman's Menu consists of fish soup followed by deep sea Mediterranean prawns. Both are rounded off with good desserts (the brocciu charlotte is divine), and the restaurant normally offers the traditional Corsican myrtle liqueur. La Voûte is open every evening from June to September.

The family-run *Calellu* (☎ 04 95 65 22 18), on the harbour, has a reputation for friendly service and good fish. The fixed-price menu costs 100FF and consists of fish soup or tomatoes with fromage frais and olive oil, then grilled sea bass with maquis herbs or roast quail, followed by a selection of Corsican cheeses or a home-made dessert. It's open lunchtimes and evenings between 1 March to 30 October, evenings only in July and August.

Tao (☎ 04 95 65 00 73) has become a real institution over the years. It was set up by Tao Kanbey de Kerekoff, who left his native Caucasus to accompany Prince Lousoupov (who took part in the assassination of Rasputin) into exile. He arrived in Calvi in the early 1920s after a long journey and fell in love with the Citadelle, so he acquired what was once the palace of the bishops of Sagone and, in 1935, opened the first cabaret in Corsica. It was passed on to his children, and although it is still most famous as a piano bar it now doubles as a restaurant offering excellent food and a wonderful view over the bay.

Main courses (such as grilled fish, monkfish kebabs with fruit or duck breast) cost from 95FF to 140FF, with desserts for between 35FF and 45FF. Tao is open from 7 pm to midnight between the end of May and the end of September. To get there, take the little road off to the right when you get to place d'Armes.

Entertainment

The vaulted rooms decorated in pastel shades at *Tao* (see Places to Eat) are the old cellars of the palace. Decorated by Toni Casalonga, an artist from Pigna, they are open to revellers every evening during the high season from 11 pm to 5 am. Tao-By, one of the founder's sons, begins the evening by playing the piano before passing over to Alain, a DJ who is allergic to dance and techno music, preferring the sounds of the 60s and 70s. Cocktails cost between 50FF and 80FF, beer is 45FF.

La Camargue disco (☎ 04 95 65 08 70), 1.5km out of Calvi in the direction of Île Rousse, has a swimming pool, a piano bar, a restaurant and an open-air dance floor. There's a free shuttle service from the harbour. Admission costs between 60FF and 80FF; La Camargue is open from April to October. High season hours are 8 pm to 5 am.

CALVI & THE BALAGNE

There's another disco, *L'Acapulco* (☎ *04 95 65 08 05)*, 5.5km from the town centre towards Calenzana.

An open-air cinema, *Airpop Cyrnos* (☎ *04 95 65 01 24)*, shows films at 9.45 pm in summer. The films change every evening and cost 39FF. Head for the corner of Casino supermarket on ave Christophe Colomb.

Getting There & Away

Air There's a brand new terminal at Calvi-Sainte Catherine airport (☎ 04 95 65 88 88), which is very large considering the volume of traffic that actually passes through it. The airport is 7km south-west of the town centre. The runways are so close to the mountains that flights are often redirected to Bastia when there are high winds. There is no ATM or bureau de change at the airport and no way of getting into town apart from by taxi. However, there are car rental companies at the airport (see under Car).

The Getting There & Away chapter has details of flights to Calvi.

Bus Les Beaux Voyages (☎ 04 95 65 15 02) runs buses to Bastia (80FF, 2¼ hours) via Algajola, Île Rousse and Ponte Leccia Monday to Saturday year-round (except on public holidays). The buses leave at 6.45 am from opposite the agency's offices in place de la Porteuse d'Eau. In July and August the company also has a service to Galeria (35FF, one hour) and Calenzana (25FF, 30 minutes). In winter the school bus will take you to Calenzana every weekday except Wednesday.

Between mid-May and mid-October SAIB (☎ 04 95 22 41 99) provides a service to Porto via Bocca a Croce which goes through some spectacular scenery. The bus leaves from the marina at 3.30 pm (100FF, three hours).

Train Calvi's train station (☎ 04 95 65 00 61), on ave de la République, was extended in summer 1998. There are two departures a day to Ajaccio (140FF), Bastia (92FF), Corte (77FF) and Vizzavona (102FF).

Between April and October there are local train services, operated by Tramways de la Balagne, along the coast between Calvi and Île Rousse. They stop in about 20 places along the way, including Lumio, Sant'Ambrogio, Algajola and Davia. There are departures roughly every hour between 8 am and 6.30 pm. A return from Calvi to Île Rousse costs 46FF.

Car There's a Hertz car rental agency (☎ 04 95 65 06 64) hidden in one corner of place de la Porteuse d'Eau. Avis (☎ 04 95 65 06 74) and Europcar (☎ 04 95 65 10 35) are in ave de la République, on either side of Auberge de Jeunesse BVJ Corsotel.

There's also a wide choice at the airport. The following companies have offices in the terminal:

Avis (☎ 04 95 65 88 38)
Budget (☎ 04 95 65 36 67)
Europcar (☎ 04 95 65 10 19)
Hertz (☎ 04 95 65 02 96)

If there is no one at the counter, try the companies' parking lots on the other side of the road from the terminal.

Boat SNCM operates a high-speed boat (2½ hours) to and from Nice daily or every other day between April and mid-October. The same company, together with CMN, takes freight and passengers between Calvi and Marseille (one to four times a week in winter, less in summer). Finally, Corsica Ferries operates a departure for Nice (2½ hours) daily between mid-May and mid-September.

The agent for CMN and SNCM in Calvi is CCR (Corse Consignation et Representation; ☎ 04 95 65 01 38), in the harbour opposite the Colombo Line office. It's open Monday to Friday from 9 am to noon and 2 to 6 pm during the high season and from 8.30 am to noon and 2 to 5.30 pm in the low season (to noon on Saturday).

Corsica Ferries is represented in Calvi by Les Beaux Voyages (see under Organised Tours earlier in this section). For more

The Road from Calvi to Porto

The D81 between Calvi and Porto (known as the D81B as far as Galeria) traverses some spectacular coastal scenery before plunging into the Parc Naturel Régional de Corse (PNRC), but if you're driving you will hardly have the chance to appreciate it because you'll be concentrating too hard on the road.

Maps cannot reflect the poor condition of the D81, particularly after Galeria, where the parapet has been partially destroyed by falling rocks and the tarmac has been patched up again and again. On this stretch the road rarely goes in a straight line for more than 200m and the white line sometimes leaves no more than 1.5m of overtaking space, which makes passing other vehicles a very tricky business involving a lot of gesticulation.

You have to take this road to get to Bocca a Croce, which comes after Bocca a Palmarella – where you pass into Corse-du-Sud – and is the point at which the mule track leading down to Girolata starts (see the Bocca a Croce to Girolata walk in the Walking in Corsica chapter). Some improvements were carried out on the section around Galeria in the summer of 1998 and the D81 does get better after Partinello, before passing through a wonderful landscape of red rocks with one of the most beautiful views of the town of Porto. You'll have to wait for this, though – it is not unusual for it to take nearly 1½ hours to cover the 45km between Galeria and Porto.

information on boat links to the mainland, see under Sea in the Getting There & Away chapter.

Within Corsica it is, at least in theory, possible to get from Calvi to Porto by boat between May and October, but this is expensive. Take the Colombo Line launch to Girolata (170FF) then the Nave Va boat as far as Porto (80FF).

About 180 berths in the beautiful marina in Calvi are reserved for visiting sailors. There are chandlers, mechanics and sail repairers in the harbour and, of course, fuel and water facilities. Charges are between 69FF and 155FF depending on the season for a 9 to 10m boat and from 90FF to 225FF for an 11 to 12m boat. Hot showers are available for 15FF.

The harbour master's office (☎ 04 95 65 10 60) is below the tourist office and opens from 7.30 am to 1 pm and 2 to 7.30 pm.

Getting Around
You will easily be able to get around Calvi on foot.

To/From the Airport There are no public transport services to the airport; use a taxi (see below).

Taxi There's a taxi rank (☎ 04 95 65 03 10) opposite the local council offices on place de la Porteuse d'Eau.

It costs about 70FF to get to the airport (90FF at weekends), about 190FF to the Forêt de Bonifatu, 270FF to Galeria and 130FF to Calenzana.

AROUND CALVI
Pointe de la Revellata
Its jagged edges sprayed with fine white foam, this cape offers views of the beautiful, wild coastline of the Golfe de Calvi. La Revellata, 6km west of Calvi's Citadelle, has a sandy beach lapped by gorgeous turquoise waters nestling in a little cove on its eastern side. Many maps still point out the seal grotto (Grotte des Veaux Marins) on the western side of the cape although the numbers of seals have been decimated and the creatures no longer visit this part of the coast.

You can get here on foot or by mountain bike. Take the D81 from place Christophe Colomb towards Galeria and Porto until you reach the footpath down to the cape. After 1km there's a turning off to the right, towards the beach.

Notre Dame de la Serra

Notre Dame de la Serra owes its reputation not only to its chapel and its statue, which was erected facing out to sea in 1950, but also to the exceptional view over the Golfe de Calvi from this wild and windswept point. The view is particularly breathtaking at the end of the day, when Calvi is lit up. During the day the shade given by the pine trees makes it an ideal spot for a picnic.

You can get to it from a turning opposite the road to Pointe de la Revellata on the D81, where there is a sign pointing to Notre Dame de la Serra 1.5km to the left. You can also reach it on foot along a circular route from Calvi; ask at the tourist office for information.

Algajola

This old town on the coast between Calvi and Île Rousse, once strongly Genoese, is somewhat eclipsed by Île Rousse but is given a new lease of life each tourist season. A quiet seaside resort, it has a train station that links it to Île Rousse and Calvi in the summer (see Getting There & Away in the Calvi section), a post office, a few restaurants and shops and, above all, a beautiful long sandy beach.

There is evidence that the town was occupied by the Romans at one time. The Genoese citadel, which was ravaged by Saracen attacks in the middle of the 17th century, was the seat of government of the Balagne for several years. It is now under private ownership.

Algajola was once famous for its porphyritic granite (a magma rock rich in coloured crystals) quarry, which is no longer mined.

Places to Stay Close to the little train station, *Hôtel Saint Joseph* (☎ 04 95 60 72 12) has very clean, pleasant double rooms for between 200FF and 340FF, depending on the season. The price includes breakfast. This is the best reasonably priced place to stay in Algajola and is open between the end of April/beginning of May and mid-October.

Hôtel Beau Rivage (☎ 04 95 60 73 99, fax 04 95 60 79 51) is farther into the village, next to the beach. It's fairly luxurious and the prices reflect this: rooms with a balcony and sea view cost 185/255FF per person in the low/middle season and 395FF (half board obligatory) in July and August. The hotel also has 10 less comfortable, more affordable rooms in an annexe a few hundred metres away in the village. It is open from April or May to September.

ÎLE ROUSSE (ISULA ROSSA)
• pop 2350   ✉ 20220

Its cobbled streets and the plane trees in place Paoli give Île Rousse a certain charm. The town remains peaceful, despite the influx of tourists attracted by its fine sandy beach, which is reached by a miniature railway. The beach stretches out along the lovely promenade A Marinella. The town's name comes from the red colour of the granite of the former Île de la Pietra, where ferries dock (now linked to the town by a jetty).

History

Some sources suggest that the ancient city of Agilla mentioned by Ptolemy once stood on the site where the port of Île Rousse now stands. The Romans set up a trading post here, but this was abandoned, probably as a result of Saracen invasions.

The town came back to life in 1758 when the visionary patriot Pascal Paoli chose what was then a modest fishing village as a port city to rival the Genoese capital, Calvi. Île Rousse remained a thriving commercial centre until WWI, after which it began to decline before being given a new lease of life by tourism.

Orientation

Coming from the direction of Bastia, you enter Île Rousse along ave Paul Doumer, which takes you via ave Piccioni to place Paoli in the centre of town. North of the square are four little alleys (rue Notre Dame, rue Paoli, rue de Nuit and rue

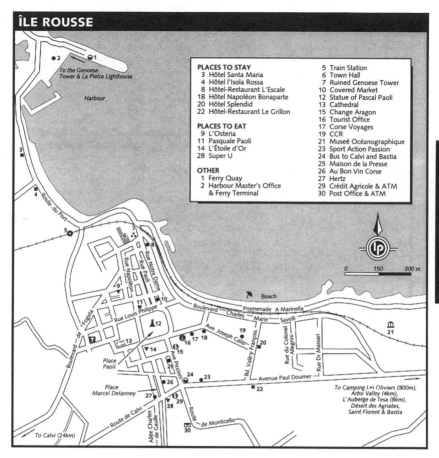

ÎLE ROUSSE

PLACES TO STAY
3 Hôtel Santa Maria
4 Hôtel l'Isola Rossa
8 Hôtel-Restaurant L'Escale
18 Hôtel Napoléon Bonaparte
20 Hôtel Splendid
22 Hôtel-Restaurant Le Grillon

PLACES TO EAT
9 L'Osteria
11 Pasquale Paoli
14 L'Étoile d'Or
28 Super U

OTHER
1 Ferry Quay
2 Harbour Master's Office
   & Ferry Terminal
5 Train Station
6 Town Hall
7 Ruined Genoese Tower
10 Covered Market
12 Statue of Pascal Paoli
13 Cathedral
15 Change Aragon
16 Tourist Office
17 Corse Voyages
19 CCR
21 Museé Océanographique
23 Sport Action Passion
24 Bus to Calvi and Bastia
25 Maison de la Presse
26 Au Bon Vin Corse
27 Hertz
29 Crédit Agricole & ATM
30 Post Office & ATM

CALVI & THE BALAGNE

Napoléon) on either side of the covered market, where most of the town's restaurants and shops are.

The ferry quay is on the Pietra peninsula, to the north of the town about 750m from the train station. The beach is east of place Paoli.

Information
Tourist Office The tourist office (☎ 04 95 60 04 35) is on place Paoli, right in the town centre. In the high season it's open from 9.30 am to 12.30 pm and 2.30 to 7 pm Monday to Saturday, and from 10 am to noon and 4 to 7 pm Sunday and public holidays. In winter it's open from 9 am to noon and 2 to 6 pm Monday to Friday.

Money Change Aragon, on ave Piccioni about 50m from place Paoli, is open from mid-March to mid-October. There is no commission charge for foreign-currency travellers cheque and cash transactions (5% for French franc travellers cheques). It is open from 8.30 am to midnight in July and August (8 pm the rest of the year, when it also closes for lunch). You should also be able to get cash on a credit card for an average commission of 5%. In the same road is Société Générale, which has an ATM and a bureau de change.

There's an ATM at Crédit Agricole, next to the Super U supermarket near place Marcel Delanney. It charges a commission of 35FF for changing money or cashing travellers cheques (no commission for Eurocheques). There's also an ATM in front of the post office.

Post The post office is on route de Monticello, which is an extension of ave Piccioni a few minutes walk from place Paoli. It is open from 8.30 am to 5 pm Monday to Friday and on Saturday morning.

Bookshop Maison de la Presse (☎ 04 95 60 30 41) on ave Piccioni has a good range of books, guides, magazines and foreign-language publications. It's open daily from 6 am to midnight in the high season and from 6 am to 12.30 pm and 3 to 7 pm the rest of the year.

Things to See & Do
In addition to the pleasures of the **beach**, Île Rousse is a great place to just stroll around: wander under the plane trees in place Paoli (don't miss the statue of the man himself), along **promenade A Marinella** beside the beach and through the cobbled streets of the **old town** behind the **covered market**. This market is worth a visit, not only for the stall-holders, who come every morning in summer (and who are not averse to giving out free samples), but also for the architecture. The 19th century building, with its 21 columns, is classed as a historical monument.

You can also walk (or take the little tourist train) to the Île de la Pietra, where there is a **Genoese tower** and a lighthouse.

Finally, it would be a shame to miss the **Musée Océanographique** (☎ 04 95 60 27 81) – an aquarium with a difference. M

Perno, who set it up in the 1980s, aims to interest his audience in the often rather spiny and plain-looking fish of the Mediterranean by providing a humorous yet educational commentary along with various demonstrations, including one on the way to tell the difference between male and female sea spiders. Tours last 1½ hours and take place between April and October. There are tours in English at noon and 2 pm and in French at 11 am, 3 pm and 4.30 pm. They cost 44FF (34FF for children). The museum (with a shark sign outside) is along the beach, past the little railway.

Activities
Cycling Sport Action Passion (☎ 04 95 60 15 76), on ave Paul Doumer, hires out mountain bikes for about 100FF a day. The shop is open daily from 7 am to 7.30 pm in summer and from 9 am to noon and 2.30 to 7 pm Monday to Saturday in winter.

Horse Riding Arbo Valley riding centre (☎ 04 95 60 49 49) is about 4km out of Île Rousse on the road to Bastia. Turn off at the porch and the centre is down about 800m of track. It's approved by the Association Nationale du Tourisme Équestre (National Equestrian Tourism Association) and its services range from one-hour rides (100FF) to treks lasting from two to six days.

Diving See the Diving chapter for details.

Places to Stay – Budget
About 800m on the road out of town towards Bastia is *Camping les Oliviers* (☎ 04 95 60 19 92, fax 04 95 60 30 91), a pleasant (and flowery) site. It charges 29/16/10FF per person/tent/car (with a 10% reduction if you stay longer than seven days). Open between April and October, it has a clean toilet and shower block and a washing machine.

Hôtel-Restaurant Le Grillon (☎ 04 95 60 00 49, fax 04 95 60 43 69, ave Paul Doumer) is the cheapest in Île Rousse. It has clean rooms for two/three/four people for 180/200/240FF in the low season and

200/250/280FF in July. Half board is compulsory in August and will set you back 540FF per person. Le Grillon is closed from mid-November to the beginning of March. The reception is at the bar.

Places to Stay – Mid-Range

Hôtel-Restaurant L'Escale (☎ 04 95 60 10 53, rue Notre Dame) in the old town has four light, clean rooms with bathroom and offers the best value in town. Two of the bedrooms have a wonderful view over the sea (250FF), the other two (200FF) overlook the road and are noisier (the noise does die down in the early evening). Add 50FF to these prices in July and 100FF in August. The friendly, family-run hotel is open year-round and also lets a few comfortable studio apartments in a building near the harbour; they cost 2600FF a week in July.

The beautiful *Hôtel Splendid* (☎ 04 95 60 00 24, fax 04 95 60 04 57) on ave Joseph Calizi has good rooms with bathroom; they are a little expensive at 290/360FF for a double in the low/high season but the hotel does have a swimming pool. It's open from the end of May to the end of October.

Towards the harbour, *Hôtel l'Isola Rossa* (☎ 04 95 60 01 32, fax 04 95 60 33 02) has 20 comfortable rooms with TV, telephone and bathroom. Doubles cost 200FF between October and February, 250FF between March and May, 300FF in June and 400FF in July and August. Rooms with balconies are a little more expensive.

Places to Stay – Top End

Hôtel Napoléon Bonaparte (☎ 04 95 60 06 09, fax 04 95 60 11 51), with an imposing ochre façade flanked by two crenellated towers in one corner of place Paoli, is a monument in itself. This former palace was built in 1870 and between 1953 and 1954 was home to the exiled Mohammed V of Morocco and his son, the future Hassan II. Although it has seen better days (the rooms cannot really be described as luxurious any more), it has a certain quaint charm. Prices for a double range from 430FF to 820FF,

depending on the season and the view (sea or garden). The hotel also has a swimming pool.

The town's most luxurious hotel is the *Santa Maria* (☎ 04 95 60 13 49, fax 04 95 60 32 48) on the road towards the harbour. Prices for a double room in this three star hotel range from 280FF to 400FF in the low season, 360FF to 550FF in the mid season and 560FF to 720FF between mid-July and the end of August. The hotel has 58 comfortable though slightly cramped rooms with air-conditioning, TV and telephone, and a lovely pool.

Places to Eat

Budget There are pizzerias and cafés serving sandwiches along the streets of the old town, in place Paoli and along the beach.

Hôtel-Restaurant L'Escale (see Places to Stay above) has generous daily specials that are good value for money, especially the excellent *omelette au brocciu* (45FF). The dining room has a wonderful view over the bay and there is a billiard room (tournaments are organised on Tuesday evenings in the low season).

Super U supermarket on ave Paul Doumer, at the top of ave Piccioni, is open from 8.45 am to 8 pm Monday to Saturday and on Sunday morning in summer; low season hours are 8.45 am to 12.30 pm and 3.30 to 7.30 pm Monday to Saturday.

Mid-Range & Top End *Pasquale Paoli* (☎ 04 95 60 39 11, 2 place Paoli) has fixed-price menus for 70FF and 85FF. The latter consists of a starter, lamb sautéed in Corsican wine and cheese or dessert. There's a pleasant little terrace in the square and the restaurant is open daily between April and October.

L'Osteria (☎ 04 95 60 08 39, rue d'Agilla), off rue Napoléon, welcomes diners in a lovely, rustic room. There's a fixed-price menu for 115FF, consisting of Corsican soup or herb tart, sautéed veal with olives or tripe, followed by cheese or *fiadone* (tart made with brocciu and lemon), all prepared without the aid of a freezer or a microwave,

CALVI & THE BALAGNE

according to the menu. The restaurant provides carafes of house wine at reasonable prices. It's open every evening in July and August and lunchtimes and evenings in the low season (closed Wednesday and in January).

L'Étoile d'Or (☎ 04 95 60 45 58, place Paoli) will appeal to a wide range of budgets with its fixed-price menus, which range from 70FF (Mediterranean prawns with herbs and spices, grilled beef or sole meunière, and dessert) to 178FF (mountain charcuterie or terrine de figatellu, herb tart or sautéed veal, dessert of the day). The restaurant is open daily.

For a culinary treat, head for Auberge de Tesa (☎ 04 95 60 09 55), 8km from Île Rousse. It claims to be an inn rather than a restaurant, which means you are treated as a guest rather than a customer, and it is not unknown for all the guests to end up at the same table. But it's worth it – the fixed-price menu for 180FF is incredibly generous (everything is included; you won't even get charged for an extra coffee). The meal might begin with cold starters – brocciu, liver mousse, dried tomatoes, onion preserve – followed by hot starters, including some wonderful courgette fritters. Next up is veal with olives or the delicious lamb with thyme, followed by cheese and desserts (including a divine fiadone or a marbled chocolate and chestnut pudding). Most products come from local producers and the auberge bakes its own bread.

It also has a few impeccable rooms with bathroom for 300FF. Half board for two people costs 550FF – a bargain. It is next to a little stream and is wonderfully quiet: the only sounds are a donkey braying or a peacock squawking. You'll need a car to get here: follow the main road for 6km towards Bastia then turn right at the sign for the auberge and follow the road for 2km.

Shopping

There are a number of craft shops along the little streets of the old town. The covered market, open every morning, sells various Corsican foodstuffs.

You could also try Au Bon Vin Corse (☎ 04 95 60 15 14) on place Marcel Delanney. This shop/wine bar, decorated with barrels, is a good place to stop for a glass of wine or to buy honey, liqueurs, olive oil and so on. It's open until about 9 pm year-round, daily except Sunday afternoon.

Getting There & Away

Île Rousse is 25km from Calvi-Sainte Catherine airport.

Bus Les Beaux Voyages (☎ 04 95 65 15 02), based in Calvi, provides a bus service linking Île Rousse to Calvi, Ponte Leccia (connecting service to Ajaccio) and Bastia from Monday to Saturday. It stops outside the Le Sémiramis bar, on the corner of ave Paul Doumer and ave Piccioni.

Train There are two departures daily from Île Rousse train station (☎ 04 95 60 00 50) to Bastia (76FF), Corte (61FF), Vizzavona (86FF), Ajaccio (125FF) and various villages along the way.

Tramways de la Balagne also link Île Rousse and Calvi (30FF) via Lumio and Davia roughly every hour from 8 am to 6.30 pm between April and October.

There's a left-luggage facility at the station (15FF per item for 24 hours).

Car Hertz (☎ 04 95 60 12 63) is on the corner of place Marcel Delanney and route de Calvi.

Boat There's a high-speed boat link between Île Rousse and Nice (operated by SNCM), a service to Marseille (SNCM and CMN) and a service to Savona in Italy (Corsica Ferries).

CCR (☎ 04 95 60 09 56), formerly called Tramar, on ave Joseph Calizi, is the representative for these companies. It's open from 9 am to noon and 1.45 to 5.30 pm Monday to Friday and from 8.45 am to noon on Saturday.

Corse Voyages (☎ 04 95 60 11 19), in place Paoli, also sells ferry tickets.

The Interior

GETTING AROUND

There are no bus services to Belgodère, Speloncato and the forests of Tartagine Melaja and Bonifatu.

Les Beaux Voyages (☎ 04 95 65 15 02) operates a seasonal service between Calvi and Calenzana (25FF, 30 minutes) from 1 July to 15 September. The buses leave from place de la Porteuse d'Eau in Calvi at 2 and 7 pm, with the return services leaving Calenzana 30 minutes later at 2.30 and 7 pm. There is no service on Sunday and public holidays. In the low season you can use the school buses. Contact Les Beaux Voyages for more information.

You can also take a taxi from Calvi to Calenzana or the Forêt and Cirque de Bonifatu; the price is reasonable for four people.

If you want to get straight to Calenzana from the airport, it's best to take a taxi rather than going into Calvi to catch the bus. The taxi fare is 120FF to 130FF during the week, 160FF to 170FF on Sunday.

BELGODÈRE (BELGUDÈ)

• pop 340

This tiny village high above the olive groves in the Vallée du Prato 10km from Île Rousse has a richer history than might at first appear to be the case: not only was a prior put to death in the 17th century by villagers who could not bear his authority, but a curate was also driven out in 1847. By way of revenge the latter wrote a 48 verse poem about everything that was wrong with the village and its people. The visit of the painter Maurice Utrillo with his mother, artist Suzanne Valadon, between 1912 and 1913, was more peaceful: he painted a portrait of Valadon in the village square, a copy of which is kept in the village hall.

For a long time Belgodère belonged to a rich family of Tuscan origin, the Malaspinas, who lived in the big white building on the way out of the village towards Speloncato.

The church in Belgodère is worth a visit for its Baroque altarpiece. It's often shut but if you ask at the cafés next door someone will tell you who has the key. The other interesting feature of the village is the fort, some of which is in ruins, from which there is a wonderful view over the surrounding valleys with their numerous olive trees. To get to it, go through an archway between the two cafés behind the war memorial in the square, then follow the little alleyways.

Places to Stay & Eat

Hôtel-Restaurant Niobel (☎ 04 95 61 34 00, fax 04 95 61 35 85), a few hundred metres from the square on the road to Ponte Leccia, has a good reputation for its food. This family-run establishment is open between Easter and All Saints' Day (1 November) and offers fixed-price menus for 75FF to 120FF. The 100FF menu consists of lamb's liver mousse followed by sautéed lamb with polenta, Corsican cheeses and home-made desserts. The hotel has 12 pleasant rooms with bathroom and telephone. Some rooms have a balcony and a superb view over the valley. A single/double/triple costs 200/230/ 310FF in the low season and 240/300/ 380FF in July and August. The owner's father is an unbeatable authority on the history of Belgodère.

The village has a post office and cafés, which are open year-round.

SPELONCATO (SPILUNCATU)

• pop 200

Eleven kilometres south-west of Belgodère along a road that snakes up the mountainside, Speloncato is without doubt one of the most beautiful villages in the Balagne. Perched at an altitude of 500m not far from an ancient Roman site, it owes its name to the nearby grottoes (*e spelunche* in Corsican) and its charm to its little streets with their densely packed stone houses.

Église Saint Michel combines Romanesque style with a Baroque chancel built in 1755, and is worth a visit not only for its paintings and sculptures but also for its

CALVI & THE BALAGNE

magnificent Tuscan organ (1810) and 17th century wooden reliquary. The bell-tower was added in 1913.

Places to Stay & Eat

Hôtel A Spelunca (☎ *04 95 61 50 38, fax 04 95 61 53 14*) is the only hotel in the village and is open from May to September. It's a beautiful building that was built in 1850 by Cardinal Savelli, the director general of the police in Rome under Pope Pius IX and a native son of Speloncato. It has 18 comfortable rooms around a central staircase. A double will set you back 250FF or 300FF (depending on the view) in the low season and 270FF or 330FF in the high season. The cheapest rooms are the pleasant attic rooms. Single rooms cost 220FF or 250FF.

The bars and restaurants in the village square are open for lunch and dinner.

FORÊT DE TARTAGINE MELAJA

This makes a pleasant day trip but you'll need some sort of vehicle to get here. From Speloncato take the D63 then the D963 to get to the Tartagine Melaja forest. This mountainous route begins by climbing to Bocca di a Battaglia (1099m), the pass that marks the boundary of the PNRC. The contrast between the scenery on each side of the pass is spectacular: on the coastal side the maquis-covered mountain slopes seem to slide gently down towards the waves, while on the other side, from where you can look back to the artificial lake behind the Codole dam, there are trees.

The pass is 3km from the village of Pioggiola. The road winds through another 16km of stunning landscapes before reaching the forest. The scenery is barren while the narrow road, along which you are more likely to pass cattle than other vehicles, follows a ledge along the mountainside, but the scattered pines become more dense as you approach the forest. The road reaches the forestry lodge about 3.5km after the sign indicating the start of the forest. A few hundred metres on you can swim in the river, have a picnic or go for a walk along one of the marked paths (including a fire-wall path) that stretch out along the streams in the shade of the pines.

This forest of laricio and maritime pines and oaks is state-owned and covers more than 2700 hectares.

Places to Stay & Eat

Auberge Aghjola (☎ *04 95 61 90 48, fax 04 95 61 92 99*) in Pioggiola is open to guests between March and October. This pretty, ivy-covered house has a little swimming pool and 10 pleasant double rooms with bathroom for 300FF or 375FF. Half board (375FF per person) is obligatory in July and August. The restaurant has a good reputation and serves local specialities. You can even try the shepherd's menu, *spuntina*, for 75FF: it consists of a plate of cold cooked meats, a selection of cheeses and caramelised apple sorbet.

One kilometre farther on towards the forest, at the junction of the D63 and the D963, is *Hôtel A Tramala* (☎ *04 95 61 93 54*), a big stone house with spacious double rooms with shower. The price of a double room ranges from 250FF to 330FF depending on the season.

Next door is *Auberge La Tornadia* (☎ *04 95 61 90 93, fax 04 95 61 92 15*), a restaurant that has been open for more than 30 years and has a good reputation locally. It's open for lunch and dinner and guests are served either in a warm room or on a terrace shaded by chestnut trees. The auberge has fixed-price menus costing from 100FF to 140FF. For 110FF you can have courgette fritters, locally produced meat in sauce with a gratin of potatoes or green mountain beans, followed by cheese and a dessert. The extensive wine list starts at 70FF per bottle. The auberge is closed from mid-November to mid-March.

CALENZANA
• pop 1500

Thirteen kilometres from Calvi, Calenzana was once a pocket of opposition to the Genoese occupation. In 1732, during the

The Olive Tree

Since ancient times the olive tree has been considered a symbol of peace, although according to Greek legend it was created from turmoil: it is supposed to have sprung up in the Acropolis after Athena, the goddess of war and wisdom, threw a spear during a battle with Poseidon. Far from ancient Greece, this supposedly eternal tree spread across Corsica in Roman and Genoese times. The Genoese authorities forced every family to plant olive trees in large numbers, along with chestnut trees, cereals and vines.

Olive trees flower in June and can bear up to one million flowers each – they produce so much pollen that locals describe the fine golden powder that spreads across the Balagne as a 'yellow wind' – but only 1 to 5% of the flowers actually produce olives.

There is no frost in Corsica, so the fruit can simply be harvested by waiting until it drops onto large coloured nets. The olives stay on the tree until they are completely ripe, soaking up all the flavours in the environment. This gives the oil produced on the island its superior flavour and explains the reproduction cycle of the olive trees, which only bear fruit every two years. Oil produced in this way is a pure juice, obtained simply by cold pressing the ripe olives (the black olives; green olives are collected before they ripen and are for eating).

After a period of decline following WWII, caused by competition from other oils and later by fires (one in 1971 only spared 500 trees out of the 35,000 in the Balagne), the future of olive growing is now looking more rosy. Indeed, it has been flourishing since the early 1990s thanks to the professionalism of the producers and the fact that olive oil is becoming more fashionable. The Balagne is the main area of production in Corsica. In the mid-19th century olive growing accounted for more than 90% of resources in the Calvi area. Although current production levels are lower than in the past, the quality is still as good as it has ever been.

Olive trees like sunny hillsides up to a maximum altitude of 600m, and contribute to the beauty of the scenery in the Balagne. In a letter to his brother Theo, Vincent Van Gogh described the olive as 'silver, sometimes blue, sometimes greenish, bronzed and paling on land which is yellow, pink, purplish or orangey, and ranges all the way through to red ochre'.

There are two annual olive festivals in Corsica: on the third weekend in July in the hills above Calvi and in Sainte Lucie de Tallano in the Alta Rocca (southern Corsica) in March.

Corsican uprising, it was the scene of a battle between Genoese soldiers, backed up by Austrian troops they had called to their aid, and the Corsican partisans.

The village is the northern starting point for the GR20 and is also on the route of the Mare e Monti Nord, making it very popular with walkers.

Work on the **Église Saint Blaise** in the village square began in 1691 and took 16 years. The cornices, decorated with acanthus leaves, were added in 1722 and the high altar in polychrome marble (based on drawings by Florentine architect Pierre Cortesi) in 1750.

The splendid Baroque bell tower was built between 1862 and 1875. Word has it that the church was built on the tombs of 500 German mercenaries recruited by the Genoese and killed in battle in 1732.

Places to Stay

The *gîte d'étape municipal* (☎ 04 95 62 77 13) is a few hundred metres along the road to Calvi, on the right-hand side past the ervice station. It has clean, comfortable dormitories for eight people and costs 50FF a night. You can also pitch a tent nearby (15FF, plus 25FF per person). There's a café which serves simple meals, including

The Balagne Craft Road

Anxious to show that the Balagne has preserved its traditional crafts, the association A Strada di l'Artigiani (☎ 04 95 32 83 00) and the Chambre des Métiers de Haute-Corse (Haute-Corse Chamber of Trade) have marked out the Route des Artisans de Balagne (Balagne Craft Road), which snakes through the hills between Calvi and Île Rousse, passing through towns and villages where there are cutlers, beekeepers, cabinet-makers, stringed-instrument makers, bookbinders, wine-makers and potters. Their workshops are open to the public in, among other places, Feliceto, Lumio, Calenzana, Olmi-Cappella, Pigna, Belgodère and Cateri.

If you would like more information, pick up the Strada di l'Artigiani leaflet from the tourist office in Calvi.

breakfast for 30FF. The shelter is open year-round and the showers are hot.

Hôtel Bel Horizon (☎ 04 95 62 71 72, 04 95 62 70 08) opposite the church offers clean rooms with en suite shower (shared toilet). It's open from April to September and is popular with weary walkers. Single/double/triple rooms cost 180/200/300FF in the low season and 200/240/350FF between July and September. The rooms at the front have a lovely view over the church, with vistas of the mountains as the spectacular background.

Hôtel Monte Grosso (☎ 04 95 62 70 15), on the edge of the village towards Calvi, has single rooms for 220FF and doubles at 250FF and 290FF.

Places to Eat

A popular spot is *La Calenzana* (☎ 04 95 62 70 25) on the main road behind the church. It serves grilled pizzas (36FF to 45FF) and has a fixed-price Corsican menu for 90FF, which includes wild boar with spaghetti during the hunting season. The restaurant is open from April to October.

U Stazzone (☎/fax 04 95 62 80 44) is open year-round and serves more sophisticated meals. The restaurant is in an old forge and the fixed-price menu for 90FF combines local delicacies with garden vegetables. The owners can organise guided walks and pony treks in the area. The manager is English. U Stazzone is closed on Sunday in winter.

Of the other alternatives, *Pizzéria Prince Pierre* (☎ 04 95 62 81 97), in front of the church, is worth a mention. It serves pasta and pizza for between 35FF and 50FF.

Spar, at the edge of the village on the road towards Calvi, is a well-stocked little supermarket open from 8.30 am to 12.30 pm and 3 to 7 pm (3.30 to 7.30 pm in summer) Monday to Saturday, and 8.30 am to 12.30 pm on Sunday.

AROUND CALENZANA

About 1.5km to the east of the town is the Romanesque Chapelle de Santa Restituta, who was martyred on the same spot in 303 AD. The saint's grave dates back to the same century but was renovated in 1951. Ask for the key to the chapel at the tobacconists by the bar next to the church, where there is also an information board about the chapel.

The village of Montemaggiore (altitude 400m) a few kilometres to the north of Calenzana is well worth a detour for the wonderful view from the foot of the Baroque church of Saint Augustin (17th century). You can stop off en route to taste wine at the cellars of Domaine d'Alzipratu (☎ 04 95 62 75 47), near the former convent of the same name 2.5 km from Calenzana on the D151. The cellars are open daily from 8 am to noon and 2 to 7.30 pm and are not far from the Zilia mineral water spring.

FORÊT & CIRQUE DE BONIFATU

The word Bonifatu means 'place of good life' and in the early years of the 20th century the area around the cirque was frequented by convalescents because of its pure air. The forest has managed to preserve some of this purity and is still populated by mouflons (wild sheep native to Corsica), foxes, bearded vultures, Corsican nuthatches and wild boars.

Between altitudes of 300 and 1950m the forest consists of maritime and laricio pines, green oaks and other broad-leaved trees. These different species cover a total area of about 3000 hectares, mostly in the cirque. More than just a basin, the cirque looks like a series of tangled ridges and crests. At the end of the day the sun lends it amazing reddish, copper and blue-green hues.

At one time the forest and the cirque were traversed by nomads taking their flocks between winter and summer grazing grounds. Now they are mainly frequented by walkers tackling the GR20.

You will need a car to get there. From Calvi take the road towards the airport (D251) and continue along it for about 20 minutes. There's a sign for the Forêt de Bonifatu 7km after the turn-off for Calenzana. Two kilometres farther on you come to Bocca Rezza (510m), which overlooks a barren landscape sometimes called the Chaos de Bocca Rezza. The pass is a little before the forestry lodge, an inn and the car park.

A little footpath known as the Sentier du Mouflon (Mouflon Path) starts from the car park. It's a small forest track (see Bonifatu to the Refuge de Carrozzu under Strolls & Country Walks the Walking in Corsica

chapter) that is closed to traffic and is an easy walk along the Figarella river, where you can swim in summer before drying out on the rocks. After about 20 minutes this track leads to the paths that take you to the Refuge de Carrozzu (two hours) or the Refuge d'Ortu di u Piobbu (about three hours) on the GR20 route.

These fairly quick walks are a good way of exploring the cirque, because you can only get a vague impression from below.

Places to Stay & Eat

Auberge de la Forêt (☎ *04 95 65 09 98*) next to the car park is open from April to the end of September. It has five comfortable rooms with en suite bathroom (shared toilet) costing 280FF for a double and 390FF for a triple (half board is 238FF per person, 280FF if you are on your own). The auberge also has two impeccable dormitories with 16 bunk beds and a bathroom for 70FF (178FF half board). It is also possible to camp for 38FF (the price includes a hot shower).

Auberge de la Forêt is popular with walkers and serves a generous fixed-price menu for 98FF on a pretty terrace. The menu starts off with cooked meats or Corsican soup, followed by a choice of *cannelloni au brocciu* or wild boar casserole and a selection of cheeses and pastries. Sandwiches (25FF) are also available.

Another option would be to walk to the Refuge de Carrozzu (see the Walking in Corsica chapter).

The West Coast

The Golfe de Porto, the Golfe de Sagone and the Golfe d'Ajaccio are home to natural treasures, beach-fringed seaside resorts and historical towns. Traditional villages cling to the mountainside a few kilometres out of Porto or in the Liamone region, while Ajaccio, Corsica's capital, has some real cultural gems.

Golfe de Porto

RÉSERVE NATURELLE DE SCANDOLA

Created in 1975, Scandola nature reserve at the northern end of the Golfe de Porto occupies 920 hectares of land and approximately 1000 hectares of sea. Owing its exceptional ecological richness to a varied geology as well as a particularly favourable climate and regular sunshine, it is home to a variety of plant and animal species, including osprey, cormorant, puffin, coral and seaweed. Scientists come in droves to study this flora and fauna.

Although the reserve itself was estab-·lished too late to save the last colonies of monk seal and Corsican deer (now reintroduced around Quenza in the Alta Rocca),

Highlights

- Observe the multitude of fascinating plant and bird species in the Réserve Naturelle de Scandola

- Explore the countryside around the towering, coppercoloured E Calanche rock formations

- Sample Corsican culture and sun in the museums and beaches of Ajaccio

Scandola is a unique breeding ground for grouper and osprey (see the boxed text 'The King of Scandola Reserve' on page 240). A type of calcareous seaweed that is so hard it forms pavements on the water's surface is another of its curiosities.

Bound in the north by Punta Palazzu and in the south by Punta Muchillina, the reserve is under the management of the Parc Naturel Régional de Corse (PNRC), which was awarded a special certificate recognising its work by the Council of Europe in 1985. A portion of the coastline belongs to the Conservatoire du Littoral, and Scandola is also on the UNESCO world heritage list. The Isola di Gargali and tower, as well as the Isola di Garganellu, are in the western part of the reserve, renowned for its wildlife and its volcanic caves and faults. Birdwatchers are usually in luck until the end of June.

Getting There & Away

The only way to get to the reserve is by boat: there are no footpaths to the Scandola peninsula. Several companies organise boat

THE WEST COAST

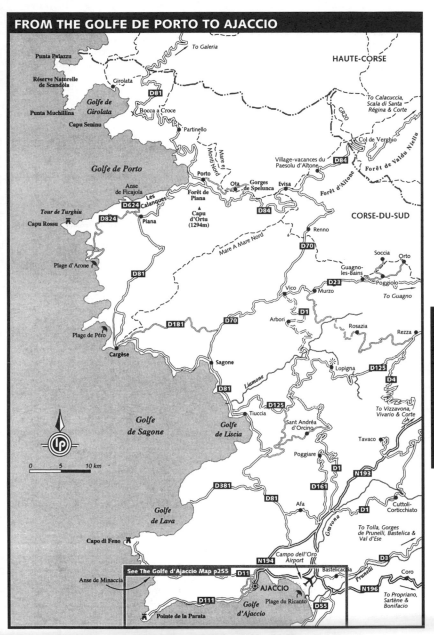

FROM THE GOLFE DE PORTO TO AJACCIO

HAUTE-CORSE

Punta Palazzu

Réserve Naturelle
de Scandola

Girolata

To Galeria

D81

Golfe de
Girolata

Bocca a Croce

Punta Muchillina

Capu Seninu

Partinello

To Calacuccia,
Scala di Santa
Régina & Corte

GR20

Col de Verghio

Village-vacances du
Paesolu d'Altone

D84

Forêt de Valdu Niellu

Golfe de Porto

Porto

Mare e Monti Nord

Ota

Gorges
de Spelunca

Evisa

Anse
de Ficajola

Forêt de
Piana

Forêt d'Aïtone

Les Calanques

D624

Tour de Turghiu

D824

Piana

Capu
d'Ortu
(1294m)

D84

CORSE-DU-SUD

Capu Rossu

Renno

Mare A Mare Nord

D70

Plage d'Arone

Soccia

Orto

Guagno-
les-Bains

D23

Poggiolo

Vico

Murzo

To Guagno

D81

D181

D70

D1

Arbori

Rosazia

Rezza

Plage de Péro

Cargèse

Sagone

Lopigna

D125

D4

To Vizzavona,
Vivario & Corte

D81

Liamone

Golfe
de Sagone

Golfe
de Liscia

Tiuccia

D125

Sant Andréa
d'Orcino

Tavaco

0   5   10 km

Poggiare

D1

N193

D381

D161

Golfe
de Lava

D81

Afa

D1

Cuttoli-
Corticchiato

Capo di Feno

To Tolla, Gorges
de Prunelli, Bastelica &
Val d'Ese

Gravona

D3

Coro

Campo dell'Oro
Airport

N194

Bastelicaccia

Prunelli

See The Golfe d'Ajaccio Map p255

D11

N196

To Propriano,
Sartène &
Bonifacio

Anse de Minaccia

AJACCIO

D111

Golfe
d'Ajaccio

Plage du Ricanto

D55

Pointe de la Parata

THE WEST COAST

The King of Scandola Reserve

The Scandola peninsula was home to just three osprey pairs in 1973; today there are about 20 pairs. A large bird of prey with a white body and brown wings, the osprey is a magnificent sight, especially when it's hunting. It soars in wide circles until it spots a fish moving just below the water's surface, then dives towards the waves. At the very last minute it draws its feet forward to seize its prey.

trips to the reserve from Porto, Cargèse, Sagone or Ajaccio: see under Things to See & Do in the sections on these towns later in this chapter. Trips from Calvi are detailed in the Calvi & the Balagne chapter.

GIROLATA

Although not officially part of the Réserve de Scandola, Girolata and the surrounding area are outstanding. The town's main feature is its Genoese fortress. Capu Seninu attracts sailing enthusiasts and those seeking secluded and deserted beaches. You can get to Girolata either by boat or on foot: it's a 1½ hour walk from Bocca a Croce. This walk is described in the Walking in Corsica chapter.

Despite its remoteness, this superb natural harbour gets very busy in July and August and some people complain that the beach gets rather dirty. However, Girolata is the jewel of the Corsican coast and is well worth a visit.

Places to Stay

Girolata lies on the Mare e Monti path and has two gîtes d'étape. *Le Cormoran Voyageur* (☎ 04 95 20 15 55), a red stone house lovingly tended by Joseph Teillet, a fisherman well known to the locals, is near the village on the edge of the beach and has 20 beds divided among three reasonably comfortable rooms. Half board costs 170FF (there are no self-catering facilities). The

menu includes fish soup and a fish dish such as pandora, sea bream or sargo, or local pork. Le Cormoran Voyageur is open from 1 April to the end of October. Credit cards are not accepted.

La Cabane du Berger (☎ 04 95 20 16 98) on the beach is primarily a bar and restaurant but is also used as a gîte d'étape. You can choose between wooden chalets with bunk beds (50FF per person per night or 160FF for half board), a camp site (40FF) or a double chalet (160FF for two). Showers and toilets are communal. It's open from April to mid-October.

Places to Eat

There are several restaurants particularly well situated above the beach and beneath the Genoese fortress; they all have excellent fish-based menus and are open daily in the high season for lunch and dinner.

Le Bel Ombra (☎ 04 95 20 15 67) just above Le Cormoran Voyageur gîte has an unrestricted view over the cove and offers fixed price menus which cost between 80FF and 165FF; dishes include fish soup, local cheese and homemade lemon tart. There are also à la carte dishes (including salads and fish dishes) costing from 50FF to 170FF. It is open from May to October. *Le Bon Espoir* (☎ 04 95 10 04 55) next door has a Corsican menu (fish soup, swordfish, tuna or sauté of veal) at 118FF, daily specials from 70FF to 80FF and a chef's special which costs 125FF. *La Cabane du Berger* (see under Places to Stay) offers similar menus and dishes. Expect to pay between 80FF and 155FF. All three restaurants take credit cards.

There's a small grocery shop, as well as a public telephone, on the beach.

PORTO

✉ 20150

The main attraction of Porto, for years just the port for the mountain village Ota, is its location at the foot of a lovely square tower erected by the Genoese in the 16th century to protect the superb Golfe de Porto from

The charming seaside resort of Calvi.

The hero of Corsica is celebrated in Île Rousse.

The village of Speloncato, high in the Balagne.

Tiny Belgodère, perched above olive groves.

Take the scenic route from Calvi to Île Rousse.

The pastel-shaded town of Ajaccio, birthplace of Napoleon Bonaparte.

Relaxing at the end of a long day.

Been fishin' ... in the Golfe d'Ajaccio.

Saracen forays. This small seaside resort seems to have mushroomed suddenly but retains a certain charm. Packed in summer but deserted in winter, it makes a good base for exploring the remote inland scenery and exceptional wild coast of the Réserve Naturelle de Scandola. Porto and Ota have a combined population of 460.

Orientation

Porto's pharmacy is one of the few buildings visible from the D81, the main road through this part of the coast, and is a useful landmark because it is at an intersection with the road that leads to the area of La Marine 1.5km away. Between the pharmacy and La Marine lies the quarter known as Vaïta, or Porto-le-Haut. La Marine is cut in two by the Porto river, over which there is a footbridge. Those travelling by car to the southern side of La Marine should take the road signposted 'Porto rive gauche' on the D81 towards Piana.

Information

Tourist Office The friendly and efficient tourist office (☎ 04 95 26 10 55) in La Marine's car park is open from 9 am to 7 pm daily in July and August and from 9 am to noon and 2 to 6.30 pm Monday to Friday the rest of the year. Most of the staff speak English; they can provide you with information on activities and walks in the area. The PNRC information office (☎ 04 95 26 15 14) is also in La Marine.

Money The only ATM is on the D84 in Vaïta. It takes all major credit cards. The town also has three bureaux de change. The first, next to the post office, exchanges travellers cheques and currency for a commission of 20FF per transaction. It is open from 7 am to 8 pm daily from April to October. The second and most efficient is next to the pharmacy. You can get cash using Visa or MasterCard (5% commission) and exchange travellers cheques and Eurocheques for 20FF commission per transaction. It's open daily in July and August, weekdays only the rest of the year. From June to August it's open right the way through from 7 am to 8 pm. The third bureau de change is next to Timy supermarket.

Post & Communications The small post office on the D84 in Vaïta is open from 9 am to 12.30 pm and 2 to 4 pm Monday to Friday and from 8.30 to 11 am on Saturday.

There are public card-operated telephones opposite the post office. There's a fax transmission service at the tourist office; it costs 5FF per page for destinations in France and 10FF per page for overseas destinations.

THE WEST COAST

Bookshop L'Aiglon in La Marine sells French and foreign newspapers, beach accessories and camera film. It is open from 8.45 am to 8 pm April to October and until midnight in the peak season.

Laundry There is a laundrette on the D84 in Väita; expect to pay 35FF for washing and 25FF for drying.

Genoese Tower
Standing guard over the entrance to the fishing harbour, the Genoese tower is an ideal place from which to watch the sun set over the gulf. The lovely square tower, built in 1549 at the same time as the other 85 towers around the Corsican coast, is on the UNESCO world heritage list.

It was restored in 1993 and is open from 9 am to 8.45 pm daily in summer only. Admission costs 10FF. You reach the tower via a series of steps starting next to La Tour Génoise restaurant. In fine weather you can see the Tour de Piana on the southern side of the gulf from the top of the tower.

Boat Trips
Two companies arrange boat trips from Porto from April to October.

Nave Va (information from Hôtel Le Cyrnée, ☎ 04 95 26 15 16) runs three-hour trips to the Réserve de Scandola, with lunch at Girolata. There are two excursions each day in summer at 9.30 am and 2.30 pm and tickets cost 180FF (children aged between 6 and 12 travel half-price).

Porto Linea (tickets and information from Hôtel Monte Rosso; see Places to Stay later in this section) organises a similar excursion (2¾ hours, 150FF). It also runs a shorter trip that lasts from 6 to 7.30 pm and costs 100FF (no food included). Porto Linea occasionally uses a yellow boat with about 12 seats called Mare Nostrum; because of its size this can explore inlets more easily than bigger boats. It is always a good idea to listen to weather reports before going on boat trips.

Those wishing to explore the Golfe de Porto on their own can hire inflatable motor dinghies from 400FF for a half-day – ask at the crazy golf course in La Marine.

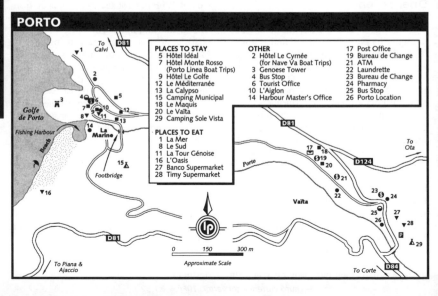

PORTO

PLACES TO STAY
5　Hôtel Idéal
7　Hôtel Monte Rosso (Porto Linea Boat Trips)
9　Hôtel Le Golfe
12　Le Méditerranée
13　La Calypso
15　Camping Municipal
18　Le Maquis
20　Le Vaïta
29　Camping Sole Vista

PLACES TO EAT
1　La Mer
8　Le Sud
11　La Tour Génoise
16　L'Oasis
27　Banco Supermarket
28　Timy Supermarket

OTHER
2　Hôtel Le Cyrnée (for Nave Va Boat Trips)
3　Genoese Tower
4　Bus Stop
6　Tourist Office
10　L'Aiglon
14　Harbour Master's Office
17　Post Office
19　Bureau de Change
21　ATM
22　Laundrette
23　Bureau de Change
24　Pharmacy
25　Bus Stop
26　Porto Location

Other Things to See & Do

It is not the most stunning beach in Corsica but the Plage de Porto should content those keen on sunbathing and swimming.

There is an open-air cinema, Cinesia, which screens films in the eucalyptus forest in La Marine in summer.

For information on diving around Porto, see the Diving chapter.

Places to Stay – Budget

Camping Sole Vista (☎ *04 95 26 15 71, fax 04 95 26 10 79*) on the outskirts of Porto on the D81 is friendly with shady, secluded sites and clean washroom facilities. It costs 29/10/10/20FF per person/tent/car/camper van.

Camping Municipal (☎ *04 95 26 17 76*) in the marina at the other end of town has basic facilities and is open from June to September. Expect to pay 28/10/22FF per person/site/camper van. To get there by car, take the road signposted 'Porto rive gauche' on the D81 heading towards Piana.

There are lots of hotels in Porto but the town virtually shuts down at the end of summer. *Le Maquis* (☎ *04 95 26 12 19, fax 04 95 26 12 77*) is about 2km from the sea at the intersection of the D81 and the road to Ota, and is renowned for its food. This pleasant hotel is open year-round (except a few weeks in November/December and January/February) and offers five very basic double rooms, among the cheapest in Porto. Those with outside toilets cost 120FF or 150FF depending on the season, those with a shower and toilet cost 180FF and those with bathroom and toilet cost 200FF. Half board is compulsory in August and costs 200FF or 250FF per person, depending on the room.

Hôtel Le Golfe (☎ *04 95 26 13 33*) in the marina has 10 decent rooms with toilet and shower costing from 160FF (180FF in July and August).

Places to Stay – Mid-Range

Hôtel Idéal (☎ *04 95 26 10 07, fax 04 95 26 11 57*) at the bottom of the slope that leads to La Marine is clean and pleasant but rather impersonal. Its double rooms with bathroom cost 180FF in spring and 220/230FF in July and August. Rooms overlooking the sea have terraces; those on the other side are larger and can accommodate an extra bed for a surcharge of 70FF. The hotel is open between Easter and the end of October.

Le Vaïta (☎ *04 95 26 10 37, fax 04 95 26 12 81*) on the D81 in Vaïta is open from April to November. The new owners are gradually refurbishing the 26 rooms; at the time of writing, the best rooms (with TV) were on the 2nd floor, while rooms at the front have a terrace. A double room costs between 300FF and 360FF in July, 350FF to 420FF in August and 170FF to 200FF the rest of the year. There is a pleasant lounge and restaurant.

Hôtel Monte Rosso (☎ *04 95 26 11 50, fax 04 95 26 12 30*) has a prime location in La Marine. The rooms are decent and have bathrooms; they cost 240FF (300FF in July and August). It's open between April and mid-October.

Le Méditerranée (☎ *04 95 26 10 27*) in La Marine has double rooms for 250FF (300FF in July and August). Its swimming pool has a view of the tower but contrary to the sign outside it no longer has tennis courts.

La Calypso (☎ *04 95 26 11 54, fax 04 95 26 12 17*) opposite the small harbour has pleasant studios with air-conditioning, TV, telephone and a small kitchenette for 300FF to 340FF for two people, depending on the time of year (330FF to 370FF for three people). There is a minimum stay of two nights, or a week in August (3600FF for two people). It is open from April to September; you're advised to phone ahead for reservations.

Places to Eat

Lots of restaurants and hotels along the seafront have inexpensive menus and serve pizza. *La Tour Génoise* (☎ *04 95 26 17 11*) has pizza from 38FF to 55FF, pasta from 48FF to 60FF and a Corsican menu for 85FF.

THE WEST COAST

Le Maquis (☎ 04 95 26 12 19) at the intersection of the D81 and D124 to Ota has a mouthwatering menu for 90FF: try the fish soup or fillet of poached forkbeard, followed by cheese or apple tart. This pleasant family restaurant also has a Corsican menu (140FF) that includes a selection of local *charcuterie* (cooked pork meats) and a *ballotin* of sea bass in Sartenais wine.

L'Oasis (☎ 04 95 26 10 53) at the end of the beach at the other end of Porto is renowned for its fish platter (80FF), a stew with three types of fish accompanied by vegetable fritters (the recipe for which is jealously guarded by the chef) and a glass of wine. The menu also includes dishes costing from 45FF (fresh tagliatelle with basil and garlic) to 110FF (*blanquette* of monkfish), or there is a 140FF fixed menu. This friendly establishment is open daily for lunch and dinner between April and October.

Le Sud (☎ 04 95 26 14 11), with its superb terrace beneath the Genoese tower, has a 110FF menu consisting of fish soup or terrine of forkbeard with sesame followed by grilled mullet or roulade of scorpion fish with leek fondue, rounded off with cheese or dessert. It also has good, reasonably priced local wine, carefully prepared accompaniments and a refined atmosphere. It is open until 11 pm daily in summer.

La Mer (☎ 04 95 26 11 27) in La Marine serves good fish on its terrace overlooking the gulf and the Genoese tower, which is illuminated at night. The wine is expensive but there are reasonably priced menus at 99F and 138FF.

Banco supermarket on the D81, near the pharmacy, is open from 8 am to 12.30 pm and 3 to 7.30 pm Monday to Saturday and Sunday morning from 1 April to the end of October. *Timy* supermarket is right next door and there is a small grocery shop in La Marine.

Getting There & Away

Porto is on the SAIB (☎ 04 95 22 41 99) Ajaccio-Ota bus route. Between one and four buses a day (depending on the time of year and the day of the week) link the seaside resort with Ota, Piana, Cargèse, Sagone, Tiuccia and Ajaccio. A single fare to Ajaccio costs 65FF.

SAIB (☎ 04 95 22 41 99) operates a bus service from Porto to Bocca a Croce from 15 May to 10 October. Buses leave at 8 am and take one hour. It also runs a bus from Calvi, leaving at 3.30 pm and taking one hour 40 minutes. The service operates from Monday to Saturday (daily in August).

Mordiconi (☎ 04 95 48 00 04) runs buses from Porto to Calacuccia and Corte daily (except Sunday) from July to mid-September. The Porto-Corte journey costs about 100FF.

Buses stop at the pharmacy and La Marine; ask at the tourist office for further information.

Sailing enthusiasts should note that space for mooring in Porto harbour is limited due to its size and shallowness. Expect to pay 85FF for a boat 4.5 to 8m in length and 120FF for a boat between 8 and 10m long. The washroom facilities at Camping Municipal, 10 minutes walk away, can be used. The harbour master's office (☎ 04 95 26 14 90) is on the quayside.

Getting Around

Porto Location (☎/fax 04 95 26 10 13) opposite Banco supermarket on the D81 hires out cars (420FF per day), scooters (300FF per day) and mountain bikes (90FF per day; summer only). It is open in the tourist season only, from 8.30 am to 9 pm.

FROM PORTO TO COL DE VERGHIO

This route takes you to Ota, with its Genoese bridges, then on to the superb Gorges de Spelunca in Evisa, the Forêt d'Aïtone and Col de Verghio (Bocca di Verghju), above which lies the Niolo (Niolu) region. From here you can go on to the Forêt de Valdu Niellu, Calacuccia, the Scala di Santa Regina and Corte (see the Central Mountains chapter).

Ota
✉ 20150

Perched at an altitude of 310m above its cemetery, the pretty village of Ota clings to the mountain 5km east of Porto. It is renowned for its peaceful atmosphere, its stone houses, its war memorial and its inexpensive gîtes near the Mare e Monti path.

Two exceptional **Genoese bridges** about 2km farther along the D124 are worth a look. The graceful Pont de Pianella to the south of the road forms a perfect arch. You can walk down to the bridge and river and go for a swim. The second bridge, a few hundred metres away, crosses the Aïtone and Tavulella rivers, one after the other. A path then leads off to the right; you can walk along the river to Ota in about 40 minutes.

There is a lovely walk from the Genoese bridges into the Gorges de Spelunca nearby. An old mule track follows the Défilé de la Spelunca as far as the Ponte Vecchju before climbing up to the overgrown Pont de Zaglia and ending up in Evisa. This route is described in more detail in the Walking in Corsica chapter.

Places to Stay & Eat *Chez Félix* (☎ 04 95 26 12 92, 04 95 26 14 60, place de la Fontaine) is divided into dormitories, each with six bunk beds and a bathroom (60FF per person per night), and has a large communal kitchen. It also rents out rooms and studios, and runs the only taxi service in Porto or Ota. Half board will set you back 160FF. The gîte is renowned for its family cooking: the generous 100FF Corsican menu includes soup, meat with sauce, cheese and dessert.

Chez Marie, Le Bar des Chasseurs (☎ 04 95 26 11 37) has impeccable rooms costing the same as those at Chez Félix. There is also a double room that costs 120FF for two, available to couples on a first-come first-served basis. The 100FF menu includes Corsican soup, omelette with *brocciu*, wild boar in winter and dessert.

Chez Félix and Chez Marie are both friendly places with terraces that open out over magnificent mountain scenery.

The grocery shop near the church is open from 8 am to noon and 3 to 5 pm Monday to Saturday. From June to August it stays open until 8 pm and is also open on Sunday.

Getting There & Away SAIB (☎ 04 95 22 41 99) operates a bus service from Ota to Porto, Piana, Cargèse, Sagone, Tiuccia and Ajaccio year-round. There are usually two buses a day except on Sunday and public holidays, but from 1 July to 15 September SAIB buses and minibuses run daily. Buses leave from place de la Fontaine, not far from Chez Félix.

Evisa
• pop 265   ✉ 20126

The peaceful village of Evisa is at an altitude of 830m between the Gorges de Spelunca and the Forêt d'Aïtone. It is popular with walkers in summer because it is where the Mare a Mare and Mare e Monti paths meet. Evisa is famous for its chestnuts (there is even a special 'chestnuts from Evisa' label) and a chestnut fair is held there every November.

There is a post office in the village.

Places to Stay & Eat The *Gîte d'Étape d'Evisa* (☎ 04 95 26 21 88) near the post office at the end of a narrow street is prized among walkers for its warm reception. It is open from April to October and charges 60FF per night in a dormitory, 160FF for generous half board.

La Châtaigneraie (☎ 04 95 26 24 47) at the entrance to the village as you come from Porto or Sagone is probably the best place to stay here. Its lovely double rooms with bathroom start at 180FF in low season and cost 200FF from 15 May to 15 July and 250FF from mid-July to mid-September. Its restaurant has an excellent reputation: in summer the 80FF lunch menu includes *crudités* and Corsican cheese, melon and Corsican ham, and dessert. The 95FF menu includes a selection of charcuterie, lamb

THE WEST COAST

chops with herbs or sauté of veal with cep mushrooms, a cheese board, and custard tart with apples or sponge cake with pine kernels. The wines are reasonably priced and credit cards are accepted. La Châtaigneraie is open from March to October.

U Pozzu (☎ *04 95 21 11 45*) on the outskirts of Evisa as you head for the Forêt d'Aïtone is open from May to the end of September and has nice studios for four to five people for 1500/2000FF a week, depending on the time of year. The hotel's restaurant, *U Mulinu*, serves crêpes and Corsican specialities such as omelette with brocciu and mint.

L'Aïtone (☎ *04 95 26 20 04, fax 04 95 26 24 18)*, opposite U Pozzu, has pleasant double rooms with a terrace, although these are expensive (from 420FF to 600FF), and cheaper rooms for just 180FF to 200FF, according to the time of year. Open from May to September, it has a panoramic view and a swimming pool. Its fixed-price menus cost from 95FF to 120FF.

A number of cafés in the village serve snacks and there are several grocery shops.

Getting There & Away Ceccaldi (☎ 04 95 20 29 76) operates a bus service between Evisa and Ajaccio via Vico year-round. Buses leave daily except Sunday and public holidays and tickets cost 60FF.

Forêt d'Aïtone

The Forêt d'Aïtone – 1670 hectares at a height of between 800 and 2000m – begins a few kilometres outside Evisa. In the 17th century the Genoese built a path through these trees to Sagone, from where timber from the forest was sent to shipyards in Genoa. Corsican pine is the dominant species, covering around 800 hectares. Beech covers around 200 hectares and you'll also come across maritime pine, fir and larch. The forest has been famous for its plant extracts for years.

Look out for the signs to the tiny waterfall and natural basin which forms a miniature swimming pool on the left-hand side of the road as you come from Evisa. About 10 minutes walk from the road, the site is idyllic, cool and peaceful.

Two kilometres above the waterfall is Village-vacances de Paesolu d'Aïtone, a holiday village that contains the PNRC information centre (☎ 04 95 26 23 62). The latter has an interesting exhibition on the fauna and flora of the forest but is usually closed; you may be able to get the key from the holiday village. There is a branch of the tour operator UCPA in the holiday centre; it organises cross-country skiing courses here in winter.

A few hundred metres away, the short Sentier de la Sittelle (Nuthatch Path) signposted by the ONF, offers the chance to explore the forest (signposts feature the nuthatch, a bird endemic to the island). The path bears off to the left from the road along the Piste des Condamnés, (track of the condemned), named in memory of the prisoners who worked in the forest in the 19th century.

Places to Stay *Village-vacances du Paesolu d'Aïtone* (☎ *04 95 26 20 39, fax 04 95 26 21 83)* was designed for those who want to stay in the heart of the forest and has 60 fairly simple chalets, each with a kitchenette. Built in 1975, they are let by the week (costing from 1940FF to 2600FF) and can accommodate between four and six people. The holiday village is particularly popular with cross-country skiers in winter. Wild boar forage in the area year-round.

Getting There & Away There's no public transport service to the forest but you can take a taxi to Ota. The waterfall is about 4km from Evisa along a pleasant trail.

Col de Verghio

About 6km above the Village-vacances de Paesolu d'Aïtone, Col de Verghio (1467m) marks the boundary between Haute-Corse and Corse-du-Sud. As you cross this boundary you'll pass a statue by the sculptor Bonardi; it is said to represent Jesus dressed in a long cloak with one hand reaching forward palm upwards.

There are a number of walking paths from Col de Verghio, which has unrestricted views over the Forêt d'Aïtone on one side and the Forêt de Valdu Niellu on the other. The friendly stallholders selling Corsican produce and drinks in the car park in summer can recommend walks in the area. The walk to the bergerie on the GR20 is described in the earlier Walking in Corsica chapter.

The Niolo region and the Forêt de Valdu Niellu stretch eastwards from Col de Verghio. A few parcels of forestry land are used to study the longevity of the Corsican pine. Some of its trees are 300 years old and have grown to a height of 30m.

In addition to Castel di Verghio hotel and restaurant (see the Walking in Corsica chapter), which caters mainly for walkers, accommodation is available in Calacuccia, about 20km from Col de Verghio (see The Central Mountains chapter).

PIANA

- pop 500   ⊠ 20115

Located 68km from Ajaccio and 12km south-west of Porto, Piana overlooks the Golfe de Porto from a small plateau at an altitude of 438m. E Calanche, its famous rocky inlets, cast a golden shadow over the village, through which many visitors pass but in which few stop. It is a pleasant village in which to spend some time, however.

In the 15th century the village was ruled by the seigneurs de Leca, who governed a vast area on the west coast of the island. Rebelling against Genoa, they were massacred alongside the defenders of the parish. The Genoese then banned anyone from living in Piana, which only came to life again in 1690, after the decline of the Genoese republic. The Église Sainte Marie, which contains several exceptional statues, was built out of public funds between 1765 and 1772.

Apart from E Calanche (see later in this chapter) and the village itself, there is little to see in Piana. Its church and narrow streets are worth a look however, and it is a

good base for walks into the surrounding countryside.

Orientation

Arriving from Porto, the first thing you'll come to is the Hôtel des Roches Rouges. The path to the gîte is on a bend just before you get to Mare e Monte hotel. The tourist office is a few hundred metres farther along on the left, before you get to the post office, the village square with its church and restaurants, and the Hôtel Continental on the outskirts of Piana towards Cargèse.

Information

Tourist Office Staff at the tourist office (☎ 04 95 27 84 42) on the main road can supply you with brochures and information on walks and hikes in the area. From 15 June to 15 September it's open from 9 am to noon and 2 to 7 pm daily; in spring it's open from 9 am to noon and 2 to 7 pm daily except Sunday; and in winter it's open from 9 am to noon weekdays only. Ask at Le Glacier restaurant if it is closed.

Money There are no banks, bureaux de change or ATMs in Piana but you should be able to get cash using a credit card or exchange your travellers cheques (1.2% commission) at the post office.

Post The post office in the building next to the town hall is open from Monday to Friday and on Saturday morning (9 am to 3 pm in summer; 9 am to 12.30 pm and 2 to 4 pm during the rest of the year).

Places to Stay

Camping de la Plage d'Arone (☎ 04 95 20 64 54) is 600m from the Plage d'Arone. Open from 1 June to 30 September, it costs 30/13/12FF per person/tent/car. It's a lovely camp site with decent washroom facilities but offers little shade. About 11km from the village, it is the only camp site near Piana.

The *Gîte d'Étape Giargalo*, owned by Le Glacier restaurant, was basic at the time of writing but was due to be replaced by a more modern structure with a restaurant, ice-cream parlour and patisserie in time for the 1999 season. Rooms with between two and four beds cost 50FF per person per night (half board costs 160FF) and there is a communal kitchen. To get to the gîte, turn off the main road once you get to the bend at Mare e Monti hotel. Continue along this road for several hundred metres until you get to a grey stone building; reception is in Le Glacier restaurant.

Hôtel Continental (☎ 04 95 27 83 12) on the southern outskirts of Piana is good value. Simple but pleasant singles/doubles with rustic wooden floorboards and shared bathroom cost 160/190FF. The hotel, which is open from April to September, also has an annexe with more modern and comfortable double rooms with bathrooms and balconies (270FF), but some guests think these have less charm.

Mare e Monti hotel *(☎ 04 95 27 82 14, fax 04 95 27 84 16)* is a good place in which to stay at the other end of the village. Its rooms are rather quaint in style but are immaculate and comfortable, with bathroom, telephone and balcony. They cost 200FF in the high season and 180FF in the low season. The hotel also has two triple apartments (with the third beds in separate rooms) for 250FF.

Hôtel des Roches Rouges (☎ 04 95 27 81 81, fax 04 95 27 81 76) is below the road in the north-eastern outskirts of Piana. Established in 1912, it is in a large building that has seen better days but retains an outmoded charm. In addition to a terrace with a lovely view over the Golfe de Porto, it has 30 excellent, traditionally furnished double rooms with parquet flooring for 340FF. Rooms with a sea view are the most popular. This charming hotel is open from 1 April until 15 November.

Places to Eat

Le Casanova (☎ 04 95 27 84 20) opened in 1998 in a lovely stone house with a pleasant little terrace in place de la Coletta, the main square. Open during the high season, it serves large pizzas cooked on a wood fire (38FF to 55FF) and pasta.

Le Glacier (☎ 04 95 27 82 05) offers simple and inexpensive daily specials: pasta dishes cost around 40FF and there is also a selection of pizza, Corsican specialities, pastries and excellent home-made ice cream costing from 40FF to 50FF. A stone's throw from the main square, it is open for lunch and dinner daily from April to the end of September.

The restaurant at the *Hôtel des Roches Rouges* (see Places to Stay earlier in this section) combines culinary refinement with superb décor. Comfortably installed in a cane armchair, you can sample the excellent cuisine in a dining room decorated with frescoes and columns opening onto a view over the Golfe de Porto. The fixed-price menus start at 120FF and the 150FF menu includes salad with scallops and myrtle brandy, *croustillant* of mullet with basil sauce, and dessert. Credit cards are accepted. The restaurant is open during the same months as the hotel.

Getting There & Away

SAIB's (☎ 04 95 22 41 99) Ajaccio-Porto bus service stops in Piana. The buses run twice a day Monday to Saturday (apart from public holidays) year-round, daily from 1 July to 15 September.

E CALANCHE

Piana's Calanche (rocky inlets) tower almost 400m above the Golfe de Porto. In French they are known as Les Calanques (from the Corsican word; singular *calanca*). UNESCO, deeming them of international interest, has designated these strange geological formations a World Heritage Site, and they attract crowds of visitors. Guy de Maupassant, who visited Corsica in 1880, likened them to 'the fantastic characters from fairy tales, preserved by some supernatural force'. This amazing stone garden, part of the PNRC, was formed by wind and sea erosion. At the end of the day the setting sun gives it coppery tones that contrast with the matt colour of the few clumps of vegetation that have become established there.

The D81 begins to wind its way through the Calanche, which start 1.5km from Piana, on its way to Porto; the route twists and turns for several kilometres through the ochre-red rocks.

Walks

You can explore the site and surrounding area on one of the numerous walks that are possible year-round. The first three routes described below start at the Pont de Mezzanu, approximately 1.5km from Piana in the direction of Porto (halfway between the Chalet des Roches Bleues souvenir shop and Piana). A brochure and a map detailing the paths are available from the tourist office in Piana.

Many visitors pull over in their cars along the road through E Calanche to explore the scenery on foot and obstruct the areas cut into the rock face to allow two cars to pass. Park in the designated parking areas near the Tête du Chien if you can.

The Sentier Muletier Walk This route takes about an hour and follows the mule track that linked Piana and Ota before the D81 was built in 1850. It is signposted in blue.

The Forêt de Piana Walk This comprises two alternative routes, taking 2½ and three hours respectively, passing through the pine forests and chestnut groves above E Calanche.

The Capu d'Ortu Walk This starts like the Forêt de Piana walk before ascending to a rocky spur. The walk takes six hours and takes you to the Capu d'Ortu plateau (1294m).

The Château Fort Walk Leading to a rocky promontory over the Golfe de Porto and E Calanche, this walk takes about 40 minutes, there and back. The path is signposted from the Tête du Chien (Dog's Head), a rock on the D81 3.5km from Piana towards Porto. This route is described in the Walking in Corsica chapter.

Getting There & Away

It is easy to get to E Calanche on foot from Piana. SAIB buses between Ajaccio and Porto can also drop you off here or at the souvenir shop.

AROUND PIANA

You may find it useful to have a car to explore the area.

Anse de Ficajola

The Anse de Ficajola is an inlet in which lobster-fishing boats used to take shelter. From the church in Piana, follow the D824 towards the Plage d'Arone for 1km then turn right onto the D624, which winds its way down through superb rocky red mountains for about 4km. You can pause to admire the wonderful views over E Calanche. Leave your vehicle and walk for about 10 minutes down a path to reach the marina, where a refreshment room is open during the summer.

Plage d'Arone

This lovely beach is reached by following the D824 from the church in Piana for 12km. You'll drive along a ridge that offers wonderful views over the Golfe de Porto before cutting through superb wild mountain scenery and maquis to end up south of Capu Rossu.

The long fine sand beach has a special place in Corsican history: it was here that the first weapons for the Corsican resistance arrived on the submarine *Casabianca* in 1942, under the command of Captain L'Herminier (after whom several quays in Corsican harbours are named). A number of bars and restaurants open along the beach in summer.

Capu Rossu

Between the Golfe de Porto and the Golfe de Sagone this scrub-covered headland with pink-grey rock plunges into the sea 300m below and is crowned by the Tour de Turghiu. There is an excellent walk along the headland and the view over the Golfe de

THE WEST COAST

Porto and the Plage d'Arone is breathtaking. To get to the headland, follow signs to the Plage d'Arone from Piana (D824). The beach is about 7km from Capu Rossu, along a road that cuts through a superb wild landscape. The walk to Capu Rossu from the D824 is described in the Walking in Corsica chapter.

Golfe de Sagone

CARGÈSE (CARGHJESE)
• pop 900   ⊠ 20130

Make sure you allow time on your trip to visit this sleepy town, which was built on a promontory over the sea. Created in 1774 to house a Greek community exiled in Corsica under the Genoese (see the boxed text 'From the Peloponnese to Cargèse' below), it owes its unique atmosphere to its history, although its charm lies in its quiet streets and white façades rather than any Greek atmosphere.

Among its population, it is difficult to differentiate between the immigrants' descendants and the founding Corsicans. Its Greek heritage lives on in its lovely Greek church and in the celebration of Greek Orthodox religious festivals.

Orientation

Most of the hotels and restaurants in Cargèse lie along the main road (D81) while the old town and the churches are to the right as you come from Piana. Several streets lead off the main road down to a small fishing harbour, which is of little interest to visitors today.

The Plage du Péro (Peru) is 1.5km north of Cargèse.

Information

Tourist Office The tourist office (☎ 04 95 26 41 31) is off the main road, in the old town. It is open from 9.30 am to 12.30 pm and 4.30 to 8.30 pm daily in summer and from 10 am to noon and 3 to 5 pm on weekdays in winter.

Money Banque Populairc Provençale et Corse in rue Colonel Fieschi is open from 8.15 am to noon and 2 to 5 pm Monday to Friday. You can exchange currency and travellers cheques in French francs for a commission of 20FF. There is a 30FF commission charge for transactions involving travellers cheques in other currencies and 35FF for cash advances on credit cards. Eurocheques are not accepted. Crédit Agricole, in the same street as the Banque

From the Peloponnese to Cargèse

In 1663, 800 Greeks from the southern Peloponnese fled the Ottoman occupation and entered into talks with the Genoese authorities to find a new land. Twelve years later the Genoese granted them the territory of Paomia, about 50km from Ajaccio. In March 1676 the surviving immigrants (120 of them had perished on board *Le Saveur* en route to Genoa) set foot on Corsican soil for the first time. The original colony prospered until the Corsicans rebelled against the Genoese in 1729. The Greeks sided with the Genoese, prompting the Corsicans to sack Paomia. The Greek community moved to Ajaccio, where it lived unobtrusively for about 40 years.

Relations between Greeks and Corsicans began to improve from 1768 and six years later the Greeks built 120 houses in Cargèse. The country was still in turmoil, and during the French Revolution this new territory was repeatedly attacked by inhabitants of the neighbouring village of Vico. After four years of exile in Ajaccio, most of the Greeks returned to Cargèse. Hostilities with the Vicolais continued until 1830, since when Corsicans and Greeks have lived in perfect harmony.

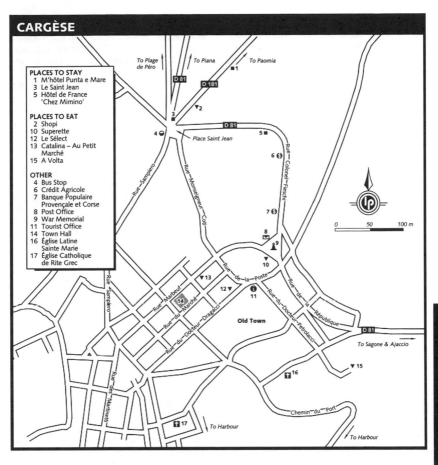

CARGÈSE

PLACES TO STAY
1 M'hôtel Punta e Mare
3 Le Saint Jean
5 Hôtel de France
   'Chez Mimino'

PLACES TO EAT
2 Shopi
10 Superette
12 Le Sélect
13 Catalina – Au Petit
    Marché
15 A Volta

OTHER
4 Bus Stop
6 Crédit Agricole
7 Banque Populaire
   Provençale et Corse
8 Post Office
9 War Memorial
11 Tourist Office
14 Town Hall
16 Église Latine
    Sainte Marie
17 Église Catholique
    de Rite Grec

To Plage de Péro
To Piana
To Paomia
Place Saint Jean
Old Town
To Sagone & Ajaccio
To Harbour
To Harbour

0   50   100 m

THE WEST COAST

Populaire, exchanges currency and travellers cheques for 35FF per transaction (no commission for exchanging Eurocheques). A similar commission is charged for withdrawals made using a credit card. It is open from 8.45 am to 12.15 pm and 1.45 to 5 pm Monday to Friday (to 4.30 pm Thursday and Friday).

You should also be able to exchange travellers cheques and draw money on your credit card in the post office (see under Post) for a commission of 1.2%.

The nearest ATM is in Sagone 14km to the south-east on the D81, outside Crédit Agricole, which has the same opening hours as the Cargèse branch. It takes Visa, MasterCard and Cirrus.

Post The post office at the intersection of the main road and the old town is open from 9 am to 4.45 pm on weekdays from June to August and from 9 to 11.45 am and 2.30 to 4.45 pm the rest of the year. It is also open on Saturday morning from 9 to 11.45 am.

euro currency converter 10FF = €1.52

Église Catholique de Rite Grec

This white-fronted church stands opposite the Église Latine. The icons, several of which were brought back from Greece in 1676, the illuminations and the internal staircase are worth a look. The church was built in 1852 to replace the original building on the same site, which had become too cramped. It took 20 years to build and the congregation was frequently enlisted to help. Like all Greek churches, it is distinguished by the richness of its ornamentation and iconostasis (a traditional painted wooden partition separating the sanctuary from the nave).

Église Latine Sainte Marie

Built in the neoclassical style with a stone façade, this church dates back to 1817, when the town's non-Greek families started a fund to build a Latin church. Work began eight years later and continued until 1828. Its roof was blown off in 1835 and it didn't have any interior fittings until 1845. The square tower was added in 1847. The absence of rivalry between the Orthodox and Catholic faiths is illustrated by the fact that the two churches share the same priest; Catholic and Orthodox services are held alternately in the appropriate church.

Boat Trips

Renaldo (☎ 04 95 26 41 31) organises boat trips to Capu Rossu, E Calanche and the Réserve de Scandola from May to September. Boats leave the harbour at 9 am and return at 4 pm. Tickets cost 200FF (100FF for children under 10 years of age, free for children under five) and are on sale in the tourist office. The trip includes a two hour stop at Girolata and a half-hour swim in an inlet.

Places to Stay

Hôtel de France 'Chez Mimino' (☎ 04 95 26 41 07), rue Colonel Fieschi, is open from April to the end of October. This family business has 12 good rooms with bathrooms. Doubles/triples are a reasonable 160/180FF (200/220FF in August).

Le Saint Jean (☎ 04 95 26 46 68, fax 04 95 26 43 93) has utilitarian but comfortable rooms with air-con, TV, terrace and telephone. A double room with a sea view costs from 250FF to 420FF, depending on the time of year. Rooms which overlook the maquis cost 200FF to 380FF (plus 80FF for an extra bed). The hotel is in place Saint Jean (on the D81) and is open year-round.

At *M'hôtel Punta e Mare* (☎ 04 95 26 44 33, fax 04 95 26 49 54), a few hundred metres from place Saint Jean on the way to Paomia (D181), impeccable, quiet double rooms cost from 200FF to 300FF, depending on the time of year. Small apartments (with kitchenette) for four people are available by the week for 1500FF to 2000FF. Credit cards are not accepted.

Places to Eat

There are lots of traditional restaurants along the main road. In the old town *Le Sélect* (☎ 04 95 26 43 41) is a pleasant little café that serves pizza (35FF to 42FF) and pasta (42FF to 60FF) and has fixed price menus for 75FF to 125FF. At *A Volta* (☎ 04 95 26 41 96), in a cul-de-sac at the end of rue du Docteur Petrolacci in the old town, you can eat lunch or dinner at tables with a splendid view of the sea. The 98FF menu includes fish soup or terrine, fillet of forkbeard or omelette with brocciu, followed by cheese or dessert.

There are two pizzerias by the harbour and plenty of supermarkets in the town. *Catalina – Au Petit Marché*, a small grocery shop in the old town, is open daily until 8 pm in summer. The *Superette* opposite the post office is open from 7 am to 12.30 pm and 4 to 7.30 pm daily (closed Sunday afternoon). There's a *Shopi* store 100m from place Saint Jean in the direction of Paomia.

Getting There & Away

SAIB (☎ 04 95 22 41 99) buses on their way to Ajaccio and Porto stop in either place Saint Jean or at the post office in the evening. Ask at the tourist office for more information.

SAGONE & TIUCCIA

These seaside resorts to the south of Cargèse are renowned for their beaches. Sagone, an old Roman city, had a bishop's palace from the 6th to the 16th century but no trace of it remains today.

Information

Crédit Agricole in Sagone has one of the few ATMs along this stretch of the coastline. It accepts Visa, MasterCard and Cirrus.

Boat Trips

Renaldo (☎ 04 95 26 41 31) in Cargèse organises boat trips to Capu Rossu, E Calanche and the Réserve de Scandola from Sagone from May to September. Boats leave at 8.30 am and return at around 4 pm. Tickets cost 200FF (100FF for children aged under 10, free for children under five); the trip includes a two hour stop at Girolata and a half-hour swim. Tickets are sold in L'Ancura restaurant in Sagone (☎ 04 95 28 04 93) or Chez Manette bookshop (☎ 04 95 52 21 22) in Tiuccia.

Places to Stay & Eat

There are plenty of bars, hotels and restaurants near the two resorts.

Getting There & Away

Arrighi (☎ 04 95 28 31 45, 04 95 22 20 62) operates a daily return bus service between Ajaccio and Soccia via Tiuccia and Sagone.

LE LIAMONE

Between Sagone and Col de Verghio, this mountainous, green and wild micro-region, also known as les Deux-Sorru, takes its name from the river that flows into the Golfe de Sagone. Its largest villages are Renno (Rennu) and Vico (Vicu), which has an imposing convent. The villages detailed below lie along the northern Mare a Mare path.

Guagno-les-Bains

The road that winds its way up behind Vico leads to a picturesque cluster of villages perched on the mountainside. Guagno-les-Bains, the first village you come to, became a popular thermal spa in the 18th century because of its hot springs, and villagers are now trying to entice people here to experience the curative powers of Corsica's mineral waters once again – with minimal success.

Places to Stay & Eat *Hôtel des Thermes* (☎ 04 95 28 30 68, fax 04 95 28 34 02), open from 1 May to 24 October, is grand and luxurious but rather forlorn. Singles/doubles cost 370/480FF (including breakfast) in August and 310/410FF the rest of the year. Half board is 500/740FF in August and 440/670FF the rest of the year. Its restaurant is usually deserted but the food is excellent.

Soccia & Orto

Perched at an altitude of 750m, the pretty village of Soccia is set on terraces on the side of the mountain 6.5km above Guagno-les-Bains. A great place to escape from the GR20, it is the starting point for the pleasant Lac de Creno walk (see the Walking in Corsica chapter). The village church dates from 1875 and contains a 15th century triptych. It is supposed to be open from 10 am to noon and 4 to 7 pm but times vary. The war memorial in the picturesque village square is a testimony to the importance of local involvement in WWI – it lists almost 50 names. Accommodation options and restaurants are detailed in the section on the GR20 (Stage 6) in the Walking in Corsica chapter.

Orto, a few kilometres from Soccia, is even more remote, at the bottom of a narrow, steep valley where each house seems to overhang the one below.

Guagno

From Guagno-les-Bains follow the winding road up the valley for 8.5km until you reach Guagno (altitude 750m), only three hours walk from the GR20. There are several paths from Guagno to this walking route, which you can join either at Bocca a Soglia or just to the south of the Pietra Piana refuge. The village hosts a gîte d'étape, a small grocery shop and a public telephone.

Getting There & Away
Based in Soccia, Arrighi (☎ 04 95 28 31 45, 40 95 22 20 62) operates a bus service daily (except Sunday) between Ajaccio and Soccia. Buses go via Tiuccia, Sagone, Vico, Guagno-les-Bains, Poggiolo and Orto. Buses leave Soccia at 6.55 am and depart from the Ajaccio shipping and freight terminal at 3.35 pm. The journey between Ajaccio and Soccia costs 75FF.

Golfe d'Ajaccio

AJACCIO (AJACCIU)
• **pop 59,000**   ✉ **20000**
The site of the Assemblée Territoriale de la Corse and the provincial capital of Corse-du-Sud, the port of Ajaccio is the largest town on the island. Famous as the birthplace of Napoleon Bonaparte, it's a pleasant enough place, despite having noisy and rather unattractive parts, which rub shoulders with the narrow streets of the old town. The largest vessel to dock in the harbour is the *Napoléon-Bonaparte*, a ferry that sails to the continent. The pedestrian shopping street, rue du Cardinal Fesch, is a good place for a stroll and the town's museums, particularly Musée Fesch, should content even the most demanding culture vulture.

The Citadelle is a military area closed to the public. Most of Ajaccio's museums and monuments are given over to the memory of Napoleon I.

History
Some sources attribute the town's origins to the mythical Greek hero Ajax, while others claim that its name derives from that of a Roman camp, but Ajaccio was most probably created in 1492, when the Genoese moved families here from elsewhere on the island. Corsicans were banned from living in Ajaccio until 1553, when Sampiero Corso and French troops, assisted by the Turkish privateer Dragut, took the town.

Napoleon & Ajaccio

Ajaccio rose to fame under Napoleon, its most illustrious son. In 1811 an imperial decree made Corsica a single *département*, and Ajaccio was made capital. There was an outcry in Bastia, which lost its status as the island's principal town, but Napoleon justified his decision by asserting that Ajaccio 'should be the capital ... since it is a natural harbour that lies across the water from Toulon and is thus the closest to France after Saint Florent'. In accordance with the emperor's wishes, Ajaccio went on to spearhead the campaign to Gallicise the island.

Shortly afterwards a citadel was built on the site of the Genoese castle. Recaptured in 1559 by the army of the Republic of Genoa, the town was not truly open to Corsicans until 1592.

The birth of Napoleon on 15 August 1769 was a turning point in the town's history. In accordance with a decree of the emperor, Ajaccio replaced Bastia as the island's capital in 1811 (see the boxed text 'Napoleon & Ajaccio'). This new status initiated the rise of Ajaccio, which is now a busy and thriving town.

Orientation
The main road through the town, cours Napoléon, links place de Gaulle (place du Diamant) with the train station. The old town is bordered by place de Gaulle, place Foch and the Citadelle. The Route des Sanguinaires (D111), which leads to Pointe de la Parata, borders the town to the west.

Information
Tourist Office The tourist office (☎ 04 95 51 53 03, fax 04 95 51 53 01) at 1 place Foch has a range of brochures and information on the town. In July and August it is open from 8 am to 8 pm Monday to Saturday and from 9 am to 1 pm on Sunday; the

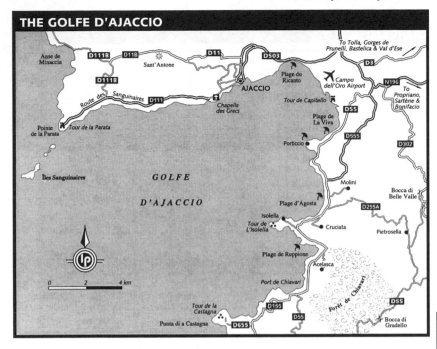

THE GOLFE D'AJACCIO

rest of the year it's open from 8.30 am to 6 pm Monday to Friday and from 9 am to 5 pm on Saturday. Staff speak English, Italian and German.

Maison d'Informations Randonnées du PNRC This office (☎ 04 95 51 79 10, fax 04 95 21 88 17) at 2 rue Sergent Casalonga can provide you with all sorts of useful information on walking in Corsica. It's open from 8.30 am to noon and 2 to 6 pm Monday to Friday from June to October.

Money Banque de France, at 8 rue Sergent Casalonga, is open from 8.45 am to noon and 1.45 to 3.30 pm Monday to Friday. You will only be charged commission (1%) for transactions involving travellers cheques in francs; currency and travellers cheques in foreign currency are exchanged free of charge. Crédit Lyonnais, at 59 cours Napoléon, exchanges travellers cheques and cur-

rency for 30FF (for amounts less than 300FF) or 50FF commission. Eurocheques are exchanged free of charge. It's open from 9 am to 12.15 pm and 2 to 4.15 pm Monday to Friday.

You should be able to exchange American Express, Visa and Thomas Cook travellers cheques at the main post office (see the following Post & Communications section for details) without being charged commission.

There are lots of ATMs in the town, including one at Banque Populaire Provençale et Corse in place Foch at 6 ave Antoine Serafini. The one outside BNP, at 33 cours Napoléon, accepts Visa and MasterCard.

Post & Communications The main post office, at 13 cours Napoléon, is open from 8 am to 6.30 pm Monday to Friday and Saturday morning. Letters and parcels can be sent to: poste restante, poste principale

euro currency converter 10FF = €1.52

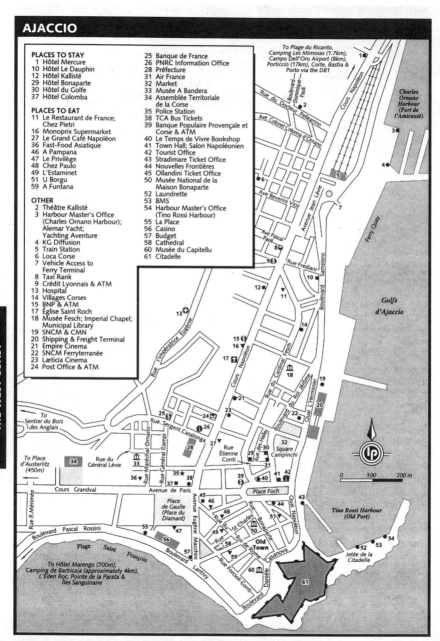

AJACCIO

PLACES TO STAY
1 Hôtel Mercure
10 Hôtel Le Dauphin
12 Hôtel Kallisté
29 Hôtel Bonaparte
30 Hôtel du Golfe
37 Hôtel Colomba

PLACES TO EAT
11 Le Restaurant de France;
   Chez Pietri
16 Monoprix Supermarket
27 Le Grand Café Napoléon
36 Fast-Food Asiatique
46 A Pampana
47 Le Privilège
48 Chez Paulo
49 L'Estaminet
51 U Borgu
59 A Funtana

OTHER
2 Théâtre Kallisté
3 Harbour Master's Office
   (Charles Ornano Harbour);
   Alemar Yacht;
   Yachting Aventure
4 KG Diffusion
5 Train Station
6 Loca Corse
7 Vehicle Access to
   Ferry Terminal
8 Taxi Rank
9 Crédit Lyonnais & ATM
13 Hospital
14 Villages Corses
15 BNP & ATM
17 Église Saint Roch
18 Musée Fesch; Imperial Chapel;
   Municipal Library
19 SNCM & CMN
20 Shipping & Freight Terminal
21 Empire Cinema
22 SNCM Ferryterranée
23 Læticia Cinema
24 Post Office & ATM

25 Banque de France
26 PNRC Information Office
28 Préfecture
31 Air France
32 Market
33 Musée A Bandera
34 Assemblée Territoriale
   de la Corse
35 Police Station
38 TCA Bus Tickets
39 Banque Populaire Provençale et
   Corse & ATM
40 Le Temps de Vivre Bookshop
41 Town Hall; Salon Napoléonien
42 Tourist Office
43 Stradimare Ticket Office
44 Nouvelles Frontières
45 Ollandini Ticket Office
50 Musée National de la
   Maison Bonaparte
52 Laundrette
53 BMS
54 Harbour Master's Office
   (Tino Rossi Harbour)
55 La Place
56 Casino
57 Budget
58 Cathedral
60 Musée du Capitellu
61 Citadelle

THE WEST COAST

d'Ajaccio, cours Napoléon, 20000 Ajaccio. Mail is kept for two weeks. The post office also has a fax service: it costs 15FF for the first page and 12FF per page thereafter to send a fax within France.

Bookshops The stall opposite the main post office on cours Napoléon is open daily from sunrise to 7 pm (morning only on Sunday) and sells foreign, national and local newspapers. There is another stall open from 6 am to 8 pm daily year-round in place Foch.

The large bookshop and stationery shop Le Temps de Vivre, at 2 place Foch, has a wide selection of books, including a small section of English and German publications. It is open from 8.30 am to noon and 2.30 to 7 pm daily except Sunday and on Sunday morning in summer.

Medical Services The hospital (☎ 04 95 29 90 90) at 27 rue de l'Impératrice Eugénie has a 24 hour emergency department.

Laundry The laundrette in the old port is open from 7 am to 9 pm. Expect to pay 40FF to wash 7kg of laundry.

Musée Fesch

Built at the instigation of Cardinal Fesch (see the boxed text on this page) to house a collection that he donated to the town in 1839, Musée Fesch (☎ 04 95 21 48 17), 50 rue du Cardinal Fesch, has some outstanding 14th and 19th century Italian paintings by Titian, Fra Bartolomeo, Veronese, Botticelli and Bellini. On level 1 look out for *La Vierge à l'enfant soutenu par un ange sous une guirlande* (*Mother & Child Supported by an Angel under a Garland*), one of Botticelli's masterpieces. *Portrait de l'homme en gant* (*Portrait of the Gloved Man*) by Titian matches a piece hanging in the Louvre.

Level 2 displays 17th and 18th century Italian works. In the basement there is a rather disappointing Napoleonic collection. The emperor is depicted standing, sitting, on a camel, on horseback, in alabaster, bronze, ivory, sculpted, painted, engraved, on razors, knives, paper knives, plates, and represented in any other way you might care to imagine.

Admission costs 25FF (15FF for groups of more than 10, students and seniors). Entrance to the **Imperial Chapel** next door, where the tombs of several members of the imperial family are found (Napoleon is buried in Les Invalides in Paris) costs 10FF. The chapel was closed for renovation at the time of writing.

From 15 June to 15 September Musée Fesch is open from 10 am to 5.30 pm daily except Tuesday. In July and August it is sometimes open from 9.30 pm to midnight. From 16 September to 14 June it is open from 9 am to 12.15 pm and 2.15 to 5.15 pm (closed Sunday and Monday).

Municipal Library

Situated next to Musée Fesch, on rue du Cardinal Fesch, Ajaccio's municipal library (☎ 04 95 51 13 00) is a rare treat. The entrance is decorated with two lions donated by Cardinal Fesch, modelled on the

Cardinal Fesch

The maternal uncle of Napoleon, Joseph Fesch (1763-1839) was the Archdeacon of Ajaccio and the Archbishop of Lyon. He was made cardinal despite his having turned his back on the Church for several years to act as war commissioner for Italian troops.

According to the history books it was through his uncle that Napoleon succeeded in convincing Pius VII to crown him emperor. But Fesch went unrewarded for his efforts: his opposition to Napoleon's views on how France should deal with the papacy led to his eventual disgrace and withdrawal to Rome, where he died at the age of 76.

An art lover, Fesch bequeathed an impressive collection of books and paintings to Ajaccio, his native town.

beasts guarding the tomb of Pope Clement XIII at St Peter's in Rome. Inside you can admire the walnut panelling – classed as a historic monument – the 18m-long central table, the shelves weighed down by old books and the wooden ladders of this impressive rectangular room. The library was built in 1868, to plans by the architect Caseneuve.

Napoleon's brother Lucien Bonaparte commissioned the library in 1801 to house the thousands of works stacked under the museum gables. He donated 12,310 volumes confiscated from émigrés and members of the religious congregation in Paris during the French Revolution. The library continued to receive gifts and works from Cardinal Fesch's private collection and now displays over 25,000 volumes, as well as keeping around 20,000 items in storage. The oldest dates from 1475. This shrine to Corsican history, which also houses many recent works and contains a wealth of information on Corsica, is open from 1.30 to 6 pm Monday to Friday. Admission is free of charge.

Musée A Bandera

Tucked away in rue du Général Lévie, the interesting Musée A Bandera (☎ 04 95 51 07 34), or flag museum, provides an overview of Corsican history from its origins until WWII, through documents, artefacts and dioramas. One of the highlights is the grapnel of *La Sémillante*, which sank in 1855 off the Îles de Lavezzi, taking with it 700 soldiers and sailors. You can also see a collection of fine metal artefacts from the Saracen period and study copies of the *Petit Journal* and *L'Illustré* from the end of the 19th century, which recount the arrest of famous Corsican bandits.

The museum, which has a rather martial flavour, is non-profit-making and aims to familiarise people with Corsica's history and inhabitants. It is open from 9 am to noon and 3 to 7 pm Monday to Saturday in summer, and in winter from 9 am to noon and 2 to 6 pm. Admission costs 20FF (concessions 10FF).

Musée National de la Maison Bonaparte

This museum (☎ 04 95 21 43 89, rue St Charles) gets busy in summer but is difficult to find. The simplest way to get to it is along rue du Roi de Rome, off which you will find rue St Charles, indicated by a sign saying Maison Bonaparte on one side and Strada Malerba on the other. Its attractions include several bejewelled items of furniture, an ivory and ebony crib brought back from Syria and the room in which the emperor was born. The Bonaparte family tree completes the visit, which some people find disappointing.

Admission costs 22FF (15FF concessions, free to those under 18 years). Visitors are asked to dress in a respectful manner. The museum is open from 9 am to noon and 2 to 6 pm in summer and from 10 to noon and 2 to 5 pm in winter (closed on Sunday afternoon and Saturday morning).

Salon Napoléonien

On the first floor of the town hall, the Salon Napoléonien (☎ 04 95 51 52 62) is worth a brief visit. Entrance costs 10FF; children under 16 years of age get in free. Information sheets in French, English, Italian and German describe the features of the two rooms, such as the sculptures and paintings of the imperial family, furniture from the 'return from Egypt' period, a Bohemian crystal light and numerous medals. The salon is open from 9 to 11.45 am and 2 to 5.45 pm daily from 15 June to 15 August (closed Sunday and public holidays). Between 16 September and 14 June it closes at 4.45 pm (closed on Saturday, Sunday and public holidays).

Musée du Capitellu

This small private museum (☎ 04 95 21 50 57) at 18 blvd Danièle Casanova (a famous member of the Corsican resistance) provides a fascinating glimpse of the town's history. It is open daily (except Sunday afternoon) from 10 am to noon and 2 to 6 pm from 15 March to 15 October. Admission is 25FF (10FF for children aged under 10).

Cathedral

The Venetian-style cathedral was built in the second half of the 16th century; you can see the font used for Napoleon's baptism and the *Vierge au Sacré-Coeur* by Delacroix. The cathedral, which has an ochre façade and is in the shape of a Greek cross, stands in the old town at the corner of rue Forcioli Conti and rue St Charles.

Place d'Austerlitz

About 1km from place de Gaulle, this square contains an immense statue of Napoleon, with a cave behind it. Both were undergoing restoration at the time of writing.

Boat Trips

Stradimare (☎ 04 95 51 31 31) in the old port organises boat trips to the Îles Sanguinaires (100FF), the Réserve de Scandola via the E Calanche, Piana and Girolata (220FF) and Bonifacio (240FF) from April to the end of September, usually daily at the height of the season. It is a good idea to confirm the times and book ahead: the office is open from 9.30 am to 12.30 pm and 4 to 7.30 pm. Children go for half-price.

Beaches

Those who like to laze around on golden sand will be in their element here. The large Plage du Ricanto lies at the tip of the gulf between south-east Ajaccio and the air terminal, about 6km from the town on the No 1 bus. Smaller expanses of sand can be found in Ajaccio itself and around Pointe de la Parata, which you can reach on the No 5 bus. The seaside resort of Porticcio on the other side of the Golfe d'Ajaccio (see Porticcio later in this chapter) prides itself on its long sandy beach.

Activities

KG Diffusion (☎ 04 95 20 51 05, fax 04 95 20 70 12) and Alemar Yacht (☎ 04 95 20 92 55, fax 04 95 20 90 08) above the harbour master's office in Charles Ornano harbour both hire out sailing dinghies. The friendly team at Yachting Aventure (☎ 04 95 10 26 25), also above the harbour master's office,

hire out three-seater jet skis (from 1000FF to 1500FF per day depending on the time of year) and motor boats.

For information on diving around Ajaccio, see the Diving chapter.

The Ridge Road walk is described in the Walking chapter.

Organised Tours

Ollandini (☎ 04 95 23 92 40) runs six coach trips from Ajaccio to the maquis and the area around Bastelica (half-day, Monday, 90FF); Bonifacio, with a return via Sartène (Tuesday, 170FF); Vizzavona and Corte (train and bus, Wednesday, 190FF); Girolata, Piana, E Calanche and Porto (bus and boat, Thursday, 300FF); Bavella (Friday, 165FF); and the Forêt de Vizzavona and Cascade des Anglais (Saturday, 150FF). Its office at 3 place de Gaulle (on the corner of rue du Roi de Rome) is open from 8.30 am to 12.30 pm and 1.30 to 6.30 pm Monday to Friday and from 9 to 11.45 am on Saturday.

Ceccaldi (☎ 04 95 21 38 06) at 1 route d'Alata, not far from Camping Les Mimosas, organises similar tours.

Festivals

Ajaccio's calendar of events includes a dance festival (held in the Théâtre Kallisté) and Spanish cinema festival in January. Les Journées Napoléoniennes in June includes parades, torchlight processions and firework displays. Les Musicales d'Ajaccio takes place in July, and the town celebrates Napoleon's birthday on 15 August.

Places to Stay – Budget

It is difficult to find cheap accommodation in Ajaccio, although there are reasonably priced two-star hotels in town. Many two and four-star hotels are found along the Route des Sanguinaires but a lot of these are expensive for what they offer. It is a good idea to book your room in advance if planning to stay in the summer.

Camping de Barbicája (☎ 04 95 52 01 17) next to a beach on the Route des Sanguinaires about 4.5km from the town centre is open from April to the end of September.

THE WEST COAST

Its washroom facilities are adequate. Expect to pay 40/12/14FF per person/tent/vehicle. It is often packed in high season. To get there catch the No 5 bus from blvd Lantivy.

Camping les Mimosas (☎ 04 95 20 99 85), 3km from the town centre along route d'Alata, is small and rather unattractive but is relatively shady and has decent washroom facilities and a small grocery shop. It is open from 1 April to 15 October. Expect to pay 28/11/11FF per adult/tent/car. The No 4 bus will drop you off 900m from the site.

Hôtel Colomba (☎ 04 95 21 12 66, 8 ave de Paris) is the cheapest hotel in Ajaccio. Its decent, clean double rooms will set you back a mere 150/180FF, depending on the time of year. On the 3rd floor of a rather dark building, it is open year-round.

Places to Stay – Mid-Range

Hôtel Bonaparte (☎ 04 95 21 44 19, 1 rue Étienne Conti) is a friendly family hotel in a good location. The 16 rooms have TV, telephone, bathroom and harbour view and cost 250/280/320FF (single/double/triple). Rooms with numbers ending in 4 can accommodate two to three people; those with numbers ending in 2 or 3 are smaller and do not have a toilet. This two star hotel is open from April to October.

Hôtel Kallisté (☎ 04 95 51 34 45, fax 04 95 21 79 00, 51 cours Napoléon) is a favourite haunt of independent travellers. It offers a wide range of facilities, including a bureau de change, car, motorbike and mountain bike hire and a car park. Rooms are clean and have bathroom, satellite TV and telephone; many are nonsmoking. Some were recently redecorated to expose the original stone walls, others have a more old-fashioned décor. The Kallisté probably offers the best value for money in Ajaccio for a single traveller. A single room costs 200/220/300FF (October to June/July to September/August). Expect to pay 250/275/340FF for a double room and 325/365/450FF for a triple over the same periods. There is an extra charge of 50FF for rooms

with air-conditioning or a kitchenette. The owner speaks English.

Hôtel Marengo (☎ 04 95 21 43 66, fax 04 95 21 51 26, 2 rue Marengo) just outside the town centre will appeal to those in search of sun, sand and relaxation. Its 16 lovely rooms have balcony, TV, telephone and air-conditioning, and there are a few parking spaces outside. Doubles with a shower room (shared toilet) cost from 230FF to 280FF depending on the time of year. Expect to pay 260FF to 330FF for a double room with bathroom. Single rooms cost the same as doubles. Le Marengo is closed from 15 December to 15 March.

Hôtel le Dauphin (☎ 04 95 21 12 94, fax 04 95 21 88 69, 11 blvd Sampiero) offers single rooms costing between 202FF and 250FF, double rooms from 238FF to 290FF and triple rooms from 292FF to 390FF (including breakfast) depending on the time of year. With shower, TV, toilet and telephone, the rooms are pleasant, though some are rather old-fashioned in appearance. The hotel is opposite the ferry terminal; reception is in the bar.

Places to Stay – Top End

Hôtel Mercure (☎ 04 95 20 43 09, fax 04 95 22 72 44, 115 cours Napoléon) near the station has 49 identical and comfortable rooms, often used by business travellers. They have air-conditioning, bathroom with bath, TV, telephone with modem connection and free garage parking. Expect to pay 330FF to 410FF for a single room and 380FF to 480FF for a double, depending on the time of year.

Hôtel du Golfe (☎ 04 95 21 47 64, fax 04 95 21 71 05, 5 blvd Roi Jérôme) is a pretty three star hotel which overlooks the Golfe d'Ajaccio. Single/double/triples cost 310/350/450FF. Singles/doubles with a sea view are more expensive at 390/420FF but have pleasant balconies. Prices go up by 15% between 1 and 25 August. Although not truly luxurious, rooms have soundproofing, air-conditioning, mini-bar, telephone and TV.

L'Éden Roc (☎ 04 95 51 56 00, fax 04 95 52 05 03) is a four star hotel 10km from the town centre in the direction of Pointe de la Parata. A double room will cost between 280FF and 1210FF depending on the level of comfort and time of year. The hotel has a fitness room, swimming pool and pleasant lounge area.

Places to Eat

Budget *Fast-food asiatique (☎ 04 95 21 23 31, 1 rue Maréchal Ornano)* offers unbeatable prices: fried noodles cost 22FF, chicken curry 30FF and the daily special 30FF. There are a few tables if you want to eat in. It's open daily from 11 am to 3 pm and 5.30 to 11 pm.

Several restaurants and pizzerias along rue des Anciens Fossés, a narrow street in the old town, cater for tourists. The setting is pleasant and the food cheap. *U Borgu (☎ 04 95 21 17 47, rue des Anciens Fossés)* has pasta from 37FF, good pizzas from 44FF to 55FF, salads for around 40FF and fixed price menus from 65FF. It is open daily year-round; orders are taken from 11.30 am to 2.30 pm and 6.30 to 11 pm and credit cards are accepted. *Chez Paulo (☎ 04 95 51 16 47, rue du Roi de Rome)* pizzeria is open daily for lunch and dinner until 5 am.

There are plenty of supermarkets. The well-stocked *Monoprix* in cours Napoléon is open from 8.30 am to 7.15 pm Monday to Saturday (to 8 pm in summer).

Mid-Range *Le Restaurant de France, Chez Pietri (☎ 04 95 21 11 00, 59 rue du Cardinal Fesch)* is charming but rather old-fashioned. The 95FF menu includes warm leek tart with beurre blanc or feuilleté of chicken livers, followed by fillet of forkbeard with basil or ray poached in butter, and apple pie. The à la carte menu includes a succulent duck cutlet with onion compote (80FF), Corsican specialities (125FF) and excellent cannelloni with brocciu. Expect to pay between 90FF and 145FF for a bottle of Corsican wine. The restaurant is open for lunch and dinner and serves until 10.30 pm daily except Sunday. Credit cards are accepted.

L'Estaminet (☎ 04 95 50 10 42, 6 rue du Roi de Rome) has a pretty dining room and terrace in the heart of the old town. The menu shuns Corsican specialities in favour of dishes such as aubergines with compote of onion (50FF), carpaccio of fresh salmon (70FF), duck cutlet with green pepper (80FF), smoked salmon (75FF), veal chop grilled with *sel de Guérande* (95FF) and courgette fritters (75FF). The restaurant is friendly and the food good. It is open from 12 to 2 pm and 7.30 to 10.30 pm (closed on Sunday and at Monday lunchtime). Credit cards are not accepted.

Top End *Le Grand Café Napoléon (☎ 04 95 21 42 54, 10 cours Napoléon)* has a lovely candlelit dining room with a grand piano, plants and white tablecloths. Start off with velvet crab and turtledove soup (60FF), then try the medallion of monkfish with ginger (110FF) or the excellent duck cutlet with citrus fruit (90FF). There is also a 130FF menu. The setting is refined and the food carefully prepared. The restaurant is open daily except Sunday from noon to 2 pm and 7 to 10.30 pm.

A Pampana (☎ 04 95 21 19 66, 14 rue du Roi de Rome) has a menu devised each morning according to what the market has to offer. The owner and her daughter prepare refined Mediterranean cuisine using mainly fresh produce. Various types of fish are served, including mullet and the occasional sumptuous fricassee of monkfish with spider crab sauce. Expect to pay about 220FF (excluding drinks) for an excellent meal. This captivating restaurant is open from Tuesday to Saturday; it is a good idea to book in advance.

A Funtana (☎ 04 95 21 78 04, 9 rue Notre Dame) is another good restaurant. Try the two types of foie gras poached in yellow peaches (140FF), the salad of local fish fried in olive oil (90FF), the roast weever (100FF) or the salmi of pigeon with sherry vinegar. Expect to pay 80FF for a lunch menu and 150FF for dinner, not including drinks. The restaurant serves until 11 pm (closed Sunday and Monday).

THE WEST COAST

Entertainment

There is more to do in Porticcio than in Ajaccio, which is often deserted at night.

The *Empire* (☎ *04 95 21 21 00)*, *Laeticia* (☎ *04 95 21 07 24)* and *Bonaparte* (☎ *04 95 51 26 46)* cinemas on cours Napoléon all screen new releases. Tickets cost around 45FF. Screenings are usually at around 7 and 9.30 pm, with additional shows at around 2 and 4 pm on Wednesday, Saturday and Sunday.

There are a number of bars around rue du Roi de Rome. You can also try *Le Privilège* (☎ *04 95 50 11 80, place de Gaulle)*, a piano bar that regularly hosts variety acts.

La Place (☎ *04 95 51 09 10, blvd Lantivy)* next to the casino is the only disco in Ajaccio. It is open from 11 pm onwards on Wednesday, Thursday, Friday and Saturday nights.

The *casino* (☎ *04 95 50 40 60, blvd Lantivy)* is rather plush but has a good reputation. Its slot machines, bureau de change, restaurant and bar are open to anyone over the age of 18, but there is a dress code. The gaming room, which has roulette and blackjack, opens at 9.30 pm. The casino is open from 3 pm to 3 am year-round.

Shopping

There is a market in square Campinchi every morning. At the weekend clothes and craft sellers join the stalls selling fruit, vegetables and Corsican produce.

Villages Corses (☎ 04 95 51 08 05), at 44 rue du Cardinal Fesch, is packed with charcuterie, cheese, liqueurs, wine, chestnut flour, honey, candied mandarin and other delicious Corsican produce. The shop is open daily from 8 am to 12.30 pm and 2.30 to 7.30 pm.

Getting There & Away

Further information is contained in the Getting There & Away chapter at the start of this book.

Air The glass and metal terminal building at Campo dell'Oro airport (☎ 04 95 23 56 56) was still under construction at the time of writing, which might explain the lack of a bureau de change and ATM. The airport does have a bar, souvenir and craft shops and a bookshop. It is 8km south-east of the town and is well served by public transport.

Air France (reservations and general information: ☎ 0802 802 802, fax 04 95 20 59 00) at 3 blvd du Roi Jérôme is open from 8.30 am to noon and 2 to 6 pm Monday to Friday. Other airline offices can be found in the airport itself. Nouvelles Frontières (☎ 04 95 21 55 55), 12 place Foch, is open from 9 am to noon and 2 to 6 pm Monday to Friday (to noon on Saturday).

Bus A number of bus companies have offices in the modern shipping and freight terminal (☎ 04 95 51 55 45) on quai L'Herminier and there are bus services to most parts of the island from Ajaccio. There are at least four buses a day in summer to Bonifacio (two on Sunday and public holidays). They leave at 8 and 8.30 am and 3 and 4 pm. Allow three to four hours to get to your destination, depending on the number of stops. Tickets cost 110FF. There are four buses a day in summer to Sartène (two hours, 65FF) and two a day to Zonza and Bavella (3¼ hours, 90FF). There is at least one bus a day to Porto (two hours, 65FF) and around six buses a day between Ajaccio and Porticcio (20 minutes, 20FF). There is also a service to Vizzavona, Vivario and Corte.

Train Four trains a day leave Ajaccio station (☎ 04 95 23 11 03) for Vizzavona (39FF), Vivario (48FF) and Corte (64FF). There are four trains each day to Bastia (121FF) and two to Île Rousse (125FF) and Calvi (140FF). The left-luggage facility in the station costs 10FF for the first day and 15FF per day thereafter.

Boat Ajaccio has two yachting harbours: the Charles Ornano is bigger but the Tino Rossi is a favourite with crews. The harbour master's office in the first (☎ 04 95 22 31 98, fax 04 95 20 98 08, VHF channel 9) is open from 7 am to 9 pm in summer and from 8.30 am to noon and 2 to 6 pm during the rest of the year. The Charles Ornano harbour has 850 berths, 40 reserved for visitors, and was known as the Port de l'Amirauté until it was renamed after a former mayor: most of the town's inhabitants use the old name.

Water, fuel, showers, toilets, weather reports, a careening area and a chandlery can all be found in the harbour. The daily rate for a 12m boat from November to March is 69FF; it costs 151FF in April, May and October and 326FF from June to September. Multihull vessels are charged an additional 50%.

The harbour master's office in Tino Rossi harbour (☎ 04 95 51 22 72, fax 04 95 21 93 28), the old port, is open from 8 am to noon and 2 to 6 pm. Washroom facilities, showers, shops, a laundrette, a ship's chandler, weather reports, restaurants, mechanics and a sail repair shop are just some of the services. Smaller than Charles Ornano harbour, it reserves more berths for visitors. Expect to pay 93/133FF in the low/high season for a 8m boat, 124/178FF for a 10m boat and 180/249FF for a 12m vessel. The high season runs from 1 June to 30 September.

Ferries leave from the shipping and freight terminal (☎ 04 95 51 55 45) on quai L'Herminier. This large building, which also serves as a coach station, is open from 6.30 am to 8 pm (when the last ship sails).

SNCM Ferryterranée (☎ 04 95 29 66 99, 04 08 36 67 95 00) has two offices in the harbour. The office next to the CMN sells tickets for same-day travel; the other, opposite the shipping and freight terminal, handles reservations. Both are open from 8 to 11.45 am and 2 to 6 pm Monday to Friday and on Saturday morning. CMN (☎ 04 95 21 20 34, 08 01 20 13 20) also runs crossings and its offices on quai L'Herminier are open from 8 am to noon and 2 to 6 pm.

Getting Around

To/From the Airport TCA buses run between the airport and the town centre 8km away. Buses leave from the car park

signposted 'departures' at the end of the air terminal. The journey to the shipping and freight terminal usually takes around 20 minutes, though it can last longer if traffic is heavy. Tickets cost 20FF. The service runs every hour from 6.30 am to 10 pm; buses leave the airport at set times and the shipping and freight terminal on the half-hour.

A taxi from the airport to the town centre costs around 100FF except between 7 pm and 7 am and on Sunday and public holidays, when you'll pay 130FF. Add 12FF for airport tax. Taxis can take up to four people but there's a 6FF supplement if there are more than three people.

Bus Ajaccio is well served by TCA buses. Tickets cost 7.5FF each or 58FF for a carnet of 10. You can get timetables and a network map from the TCA shop in ave de Paris (☎ 04 95 51 43 23).

The main lines are as follows:

No 1: Airport-town centre-les Crêtes
No 2: Mezzavia-town centre-les Crêtes
No 3: Town centre-Pietralba
No 4: Budiccione-town centre-Hôpital de la
    Miséricorde
No 5: Town centre-Pointe de la Parata (Route
    des Sanguinaires)
No 6: Station-Castelluccio
No 7: Loretto-town centre-Empereur

Car There are a number of car hire firms with representatives in the car park opposite Campo dell'Oro airport. They are theoretically open from 9 am to about 11 pm in summer and from 9.30 am to 9 pm during the rest of the year. The first two companies listed below seem to be the cheapest for weekly car hire but you should take the opportunity to get quotes from different firms.

Ada
    (☎ 04 95 23 56 57)
Avis
    (☎ 04 95 23 56 90, fax 04 95 10 08 45)
Budget
    (☎ 04 95 23 57 21, fax 04 95 23 57 23)

THE WEST COAST

Castellani Sixt
(☎ 04 95 23 57 00, fax 04 95 23 56 99)
Citer
(☎ 04 95 23 57 15, fax 04 95 23 57 16)
Europcar
(☎ 04 95 23 18 73, fax 04 95 22 07 27)
Hertz
(☎ 04 95 23 57 04, 04 95 23 57 05,
fax 04 95 23 57 06)

In town, Budget (☎ 04 95 21 17 18, fax 04
95 21 00 07), at résidence Diamant, 1 blvd
Lantivy, has cars for hire for 530FF per day
(including 100km), 1570FF per week (including 1750km) or 4000FF per month (unlimited mileage). These prices, which are
subject to change, include comprehensive
insurance cover.

Motorcycle & Bicycle Loca Corse (☎ 04
95 20 71 20), at 10 ave Beverini Vico, hires
out 125cc motorbikes (350FF a day or
1850FF a week), scooters (from 250/300FF
a day to 1330/1670FF a week in low/high
season) and mountain bikes (80FF a day or
440FF a week). It is open from 9 am to
noon and 2.30 to 6.30 pm daily except Sunday. BMS (☎/fax 04 95 21 33 75, mobile 06
09 24 56 55), Jetée de la Citadelle, has
mountain bikes for 80FF a day, scooters for
290FF a day or 1700FF a week and motorbikes. There is a 10 to 15% discount out of
season.

Taxi There is a taxi rank on the corner of
cours Napoléon and ave Pascal Paoli. You
can order a taxi on ☎ 04 95 23 25 70.

AROUND AJACCIO
Îles Sanguinaires
These four small islands with their jagged
coastlines take their name (Bloody Islands)
from their distinctive red rock. They lie just
off Pointe de la Parata at the mouth of the
Golfe d'Ajaccio and are a good place for a
walk.

Stradimare (☎ 04 95 51 31 31) organises
boat trips to the islands from Tino Rossi
harbour in Ajaccio for 100FF. The No 5 bus
will take you as far as Pointe de la Parata.

PORTICCIO
The nearest seaside resort to Ajaccio, Porticcio looks over at Napoleon's birthplace
from the southern side of the Golfe d'Ajaccio. Some people find this new town devoid
of charm; others like it for its long fine-sand
beach and its liveliness in summer.

Orientation
The town stretches along the length of
its beach. A series of modern complexes
known as La Viva, Les Marines and Les
Marines 2 on either side of the D55 form its
focal point.

Coming from Ajaccio, the first thing
you'll see is the 666 disco on your left. A bit
farther along on the right-hand side is La
Viva, with its bars and restaurants. There is
a turning on the left towards the equestrian
centre, a few hundred metres away from
Camping Les Marines de Porticcio. You
eventually come to Les Marines, which has
a tourist office, bookshop, cinema, the Blue
Moon disco and a landing stage. Across the
road, Les Marines 2 has a petrol station, a
taxi rank, banks, a post office and a Champion supermarket.

The Plage d'Agosta, Plage de Ruppione
and Plage de Mare e Sole are in the southern part of the gulf.

Information
Tourist Office This small white kiosk
(☎ 04 95 25 01 01) in Les Marines is open
year-round. It is open from 8.30 am to 1 pm
and 2.30 to 8 pm daily in summer and from
9.30 am to 12.15 pm and 2.30 to 6.45 pm
Monday to Saturday in winter. Its staff are
very helpful.

Money Société Générale next to the post
office has an ATM that accepts Visa, Eurocard, MasterCard and Cirrus. The bank is
open from 8.15 am to noon and 1.45 to
4.45 pm Monday to Friday and has a bureau
de change. Next door, Crédit Agricole
charges 35FF to exchange currency and
travellers cheques in foreign currency.
There is no commission on transactions involving Eurocheques in francs. It is open

from 8.30 to 11.45 am and 2.15 to 5 pm Monday to Friday (to 4.30 pm Thursday and Friday). There is an ATM outside.

Post The post office behind the Elf petrol station in Les Marines 2 is open from 8.30 am to 6 pm Monday to Friday and also on Saturday morning during the summer. The opening hours are shorter outside the high season.

Bookshop The newsagent in Les Marines sells French and foreign newspapers and a small selection of books. It is open daily except Sunday afternoon.

Things to See & Do

Porticcio's main attraction is its **beaches**. The beautiful Plage de La Viva that fringes the town is the most popular; it boasts bars and restaurants as well as stalls that hire out sailboards and deckchairs. The Plage d'Agosta, Plage de Ruppione and Plage de Mare e Sole farther south are less popular and hence often more pleasant.

A kiosk (☎ 04 95 25 94 14) near the tourist office in Les Marines organises **boat trips** on a 20m launch from April to October. The boat sails for Scandola at 8.30 am and returns at 6.30 pm; the trip includes a 2½ hour stop at Girolata and costs 240FF. There are also excursions to Bonifacio and the Îles Sanguinaires. Boats for Bonifacio leave at 9 am and return at 6.30 pm, making a three hour stop in Bonifacio. Tickets cost 250FF. Boats for the Îles Sanguinaires leave at 3 pm and return at 6.30 pm. There is an hour's stop at the islands and tickets cost 110FF.

Activities

Water Sports Rive Sud Nautique (☎ 06 09 98 87 56) on Plage de La Viva hires out jet skis from June to September. Prices are 200FF for 15 minutes or 550FF to 660FF per hour for two-seaters. The firm organises half-day jet ski excursions for 1200FF for two people. Loconautique (☎ 04 95 21 70 23) next door hires out inflatable dinghies from 600FF a day.

For information on diving in the area, see the Diving chapter.

Other Activities Hôtel-Motel de Porticcio has hard tennis courts available by the hour (60FF per hour, 50FF for hotel guests); ask at reception.

The Centre Équestre de Porticcio (☎ 04 95 25 11 05) offers horse riding (100FF per hour) or exercises at the centre itself. Turn off the main road at the 666 disco and continue for 1km. The centre is signposted.

You can hire mountain bikes from Rive Sud Sport et Chasse-Pêche (☎ 04 95 25 01 97) in the La Viva complex. Expect to pay 80FF per day, 200FF for three days and 400FF per week. The shop is open from 9.30 am to 12.30 pm and 3.30 to 8 pm daily in summer and from 9 am to noon and 2.30 to 7.30 pm Monday to Saturday in winter. The local diving centre hires out mountain bikes at the same rates.

Places to Stay – Budget

Porticcio has little accommodation for the independent traveller. *Camping Les Marines de Porticcio* (☎ 04 95 25 09 35, fax 04 95 25 95 11) a shady camp site near the beach and the town centre, is fairly quiet. Expect to pay 30FF per adult (35FF in July and August) and 10FF per car (13FF in July and August). The camp site is on a small hill and you pitch your tent on one of its terraced sites. Small prefabricated chalets are available by the week in July and August for 1600FF to 2600FF for three to four people, depending on the exact date. The camp site has a children's play area and is open from June to September.

Camping de l'Europe (☎ 04 95 25 42 94, fax 04 95 25 59 66), open from May to October, is 5.5km from Porticcio near the Plage d'Agosta, 600m from the D55. It is rather remote and has old-fashioned washroom facilities. It also has a bar and laundry. It costs 28/11/11FF per person/tent/car.

Places to Stay – Mid-Range

Hôtel-Motel de Porticcio (☎ 04 95 25 05 77, fax 04 95 25 11 11) is on a bend in

THE WEST COAST

the road near Les Marines. It has good single/double rooms with bathroom which cost 190/220FF in the low season and 290/370FF in August. A friendly place, it has 30 rooms and 17 fully equipped studios, plus five pleasant double rooms with bathroom but no toilet; these are offered at a cheaper rate. Studios for four people with kitchenette and loggia cost between 350FF and 550FF per night depending on the time of year.

Hôtel Kallisté (☎ *04 95 25 54 19, fax 04 95 25 59 25*) is 5km from Porticcio in the hills above Plage d'Agosta. It is a good hotel but you need a car to get here. Its lovely, light rooms have air-conditioning, TV and telephone and are away from the rather overrated hustle and bustle of Porticcio. A double room overlooking the garden/sea costs 260/320FF in spring and autumn. These rates go up to 320/380FF in July and September and to 480/540FF in August. Rooms overlooking the sea have a balcony, and the hotel, which belongs to the owner of the Hôtel Kallisté in Ajaccio, also has apartments with a view over the Golfe d'Ajaccio. Signposted 700m above the main road, it is open from April to October.

Places to Eat

Porticcio is not a mecca for gourmets; what it does offer is a lot of snack bars and restaurants serving fairly standard food, particularly in Les Marines and on the beach. Nearly all of these places have wide terraces overlooking the sea and tables on the beach.

A Marana (☎ *04 95 25 10 56*) in La Viva serves simple hearty fare such as pizza cooked on a wood fire (36FF to 48FF), grilled meat, kebabs and pasta (45FF to 68FF). It is open daily until late year-round.

Next door, *A Merendella* (☎ *04 95 25 08 27*) serves good crêpes; the kitchen is open from noon to midnight during the summer and 11 pm during the rest of the year. It is open daily year-round.

For self-caterers, there is a *Champion* supermarket behind Les Marines 2; to reach it, go past the side of Hôtel-Motel de Porticcio.

Entertainment

Les Trois Stars (☎ *04 95 25 91 82*) cinema in Les Marines has two screens showing up to six different films each day, year-round. Tickets cost 40FF.

The *666* (☎ *04 95 25 12 35*), a disco on the main road just before the turning for the equestrian centre, has two dance floors, neon lights and a smoke machine and plays techno and dance music. Entrance costs 60FF (including a drink); women get in free on Wednesday night before 1 am. The club is open from 10.30 pm to 5 am.

Many people prefer *Blue Moon* (☎ *04 95 25 07 70*), above Les Marines. Its entry charge and opening times are the same as the 666 but the atmosphere is more relaxed. There is a large terrace and dance floor. The club is open daily between July and mid-September, and at the weekend during the winter.

Le Pub Saint-James (☎ *04 95 25 97 92*) above La Viva is open until 3 am every night year-round and puts on good live blues and rock acts. A different band plays here every two weeks. You can sit outside on the terrace and quench your thirst with one of 40 different beers (20 to 50FF). Spirits and cocktails cost between 28 and 55FF.

Getting There & Away

Bus There is a bus service (☎ *04 95 25 40 37*) between Ajaccio and Plage de Mare e Sole from 1 July to 15 September. Buses leave approximately every 20 minutes from 8.30 am until 6.55 pm from Ajaccio and from 7.30 am until 6 pm from Mare e Sole. They stop at Porticcio, Agosta and Isolella. The fare from Ajaccio to Porticcio is 15FF. There is a morning and evening shuttle in winter.

Boat Launches go to and from Porticcio and Tino Rossi harbour in Ajaccio in summer. There are five return journeys a day, starting at 8.30 am. The journey takes around 20 minutes and costs 30FF one way,

50FF return. Call ahead (☎ 04 95 25 94 14) to make sure the service is available.

Getting Around

You can get around the area on foot, by mountain bike, by bus or by taxi. There is a taxi rank in the Elf garage car park in Les Marines 2.

THE GORGES DU PRUNELLI, BASTELICA & VAL D'ESE

After leaving Ajaccio the D3 winds its way up into the mountains for about 25km until it reaches the village of Tolla and a lake. It then continues along the Gorges du Prunelli, which can be seen from below at bends in the road, until it gets to Bastelica (population 400).

This rustic mountain village is famous for its charcuterie, made from local store pigs, and for being the native village of Sampiero Corso (see the boxed text 'Sampiero Corso the Fiery' in the History section of the Facts about Corsica chapter), whose statue graces the entrance to the village. A rough road leads from the village to the Val d'Ese ski resort 16km away, passing through superb mountain scenery offering fine views of interesting and varied Corsican geology. It also passes a rubbish dump and a bergerie. The ski resort (altitude 1700m) has little impact on the environment: there are only two buildings and no hotel or restaurant. You can hire ski equipment in Bastelica.

Places to Stay & Eat

Hôtel-Restaurant le Sampiero (☎ 04 95 28 71 99) is next to the town hall and opposite the statue of Sampiero Corso. It has rather old-fashioned but clean and comfortable rooms with TV and telephone. Single rooms cost 260FF. Doubles with shower cost 260FF, those with bath cost 290FF.

Auberge Castagnetu (☎ 04 95 28 70 71, fax 04 95 28 74 02) is 1.5km from the Église de Bastelica. The auberge's pleasant, neat rooms cost 290FF for two people out of season and 330FF in July and August. The food has been acclaimed by various gastronomic associations; the 150FF menu includes local charcuterie, *gambas flambées au whisky* or *feuilleté* of scrambled eggs

Store Pigs

There are no longer any wild pigs (except wild boar) in Corsica: pigs seen at the sides of mountain roads are domestic animals known as *cochons coureurs*, or store pigs. It is estimated that there are 15,000 store pigs in Haute-Corse and 30,000 in Corse-du-Sud.

Corsican pork derives its flavour from the store pigs' diet of acorns and chestnuts (supplemented with other food at certain times of the year). The charcuterie produced in Corsica is excellent but expensive and some of the specialities sold on the island are actually made from imported pork meat.

with brocciu, followed by *effeuillé* of duck with chestnuts or *deux tiani*, a sauté of veal and ragoût of beans with cep mushrooms. The meal ends with cheese or dessert. There are daily fixed-price menus in summer for around 100FF, served in the hotel's lovely rustic dining room.

Getting There & Away

Bernardi (☎ 04 95 28 07 82) operates a daily bus service between Ajaccio and Bastelica. Tickets cost 50FF. Buses leave from the Claridge Bar in Ajaccio (☎ 04 95 23 22 87), 67 cours Napoléon. There is no service on Sunday or public holidays.

The South

Southern Corsica reveals a variety of vistas from Propriano to Porto Vecchio. The Sartenais, the area around the noble Sartène, is home to some of the most famous prehistoric sites on the island. A countryside of cork oaks, the extreme south boasts a wonderful coastline and Bonifacio, a breathtaking city suspended between sky and sea. Finally, the relief of Alta Rocca conceals little villages and numerous footpaths. Although the south of the island has been somewhat slower to capitalise on tourism than other parts, it is certainly catching up now.

Highlights

- Marvel at the prehistoric sites of Filitosa and the Sartenais with their carved menhirs
- Explore the spectacular coastal town of Bonifacio, perched on chalk cliffs
- Drift through the tranquil hills and villages of Alta Rocca

Propriano & Filitosa

PROPRIANO (PRUPIÀ)
- pop 3200

Founded by the Genoese as early as 1640, for a long time Propriano remained a modest hamlet in the shadow of the village of Fozzano.

The town is at the eastern end of the Golfe de Valinco, from where Sampiero Corso coordinated an attempt to liberate the island in 1594. Its late spurt of growth was largely a result of the construction of its harbour early in the 20th century, which has made Propriano the centre of maritime activity in the Sartenais region.

The arrival of tourists to the Golfe de Valinco's shores did the rest; Propriano is now a popular seaside resort. Although the area around the harbour is still pretty, the town is losing its charm, especially in the little streets by the sea; however, it is still a good base for discovering the Sartenais and Filitosa.

Orientation

Avenue Napoléon, which runs alongside the harbour, and rue du Général de Gaulle, which veers off to the south-east, are the main streets of the town centre and the focus of most activities. If you arrive from the north, you'll come into Propriano along the rue de 9 Septembre (the wide coastal road), which comes out at the junction of the above two roads.

Information

Tourist Office The tourist office (☎ 04 95 76 01 49) can be found at the marina. In summer it is open from 8 am to 1 pm and 3 to 8 pm, Monday to Saturday, and Sunday morning. The rest of the year it's open from 8.30 am to noon and 1.30 to 6 pm, Monday to Friday. The office changes money free of commission (but using rounded-up figures) outside normal banking hours.

Money There is an ATM outside Société Générale, at 1 rue du Général de Gaulle, which changes foreign currency travellers cheques and cash for an average commission of 25FF plus 1% of the amount, or commission-free for travellers cheques made out in French francs. The bank is open from 8.15 am to noon and 1.45 to 5 pm, Monday to Friday. There is another ATM

THE SOUTH

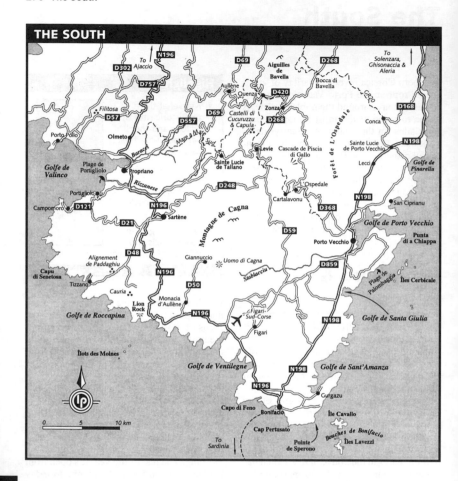

outside Crédit Agricole, on rue du Général de Gaulle.

U Scambiu, on rue Capitaine Pietri, a bureau de change within the Loft Hôtel, charges 20FF to change foreign currency and travellers cheques. It is open in the summer from 10 am to 1 pm and 4 to 8.30 pm, daily except Sunday.

Post The post office is on route de la Paratella, a little way out of the town centre and a few minutes walk south of the har-bour. In summer it is open from 8.30 am to 6.30 pm, Monday to Friday, and Saturday morning. The rest of the year it is open from 9 am to noon and 2.30 to 5.30 pm, Monday to Friday, and Saturday morning.

Bookshop La Maison de la Presse (☎ 04 95 76 06 77), on the corner of ave Napoléon and rue du Général de Gaulle, stocks a large range of paperbacks and books about Corsica, as well as French and foreign newspapers. It's open from 7 am to 11.30 pm daily in the high season and from 7.30 am to 12.30 pm and 2.30 to 7.30 pm, Monday to Saturday and Sunday morning, in the low season.

Laundry There is a laundrette on rue du Général de Gaulle, open from 7.30 am to 7 pm (it closes at noon on Sunday and public holidays). Washing costs 25FF per load.

Boat Trips
I Paesi di u Valincu (☎ 04 95 76 16 78), at the harbour next to the tourist office, organises trips in an aluminium boat that has been specially adapted for underwater viewing.

The trips available include a visit to the Réserve Naturelle de Scandola via the Golfe de Valinco, the Îles Sanguinaires and Capu Rossu (departing at 8 am, returning at 7 pm, 280FF); discovering the protected coastline of the Sartenais (departing at 9.30 am, returning at 5.30 pm after a stop for a swim, 200FF); a two hour tour of the Golfe de Valinco (90FF); and night trips to see the lights of Corsica (from 9.30 to 11 pm, 70FF). The boat can take up to 100 passengers and operates between Easter and All Saints' Day (1 November). Children aged between six and 12 pay half-price.

Boat trips in a cruise catamaran are also available – inquire at the tourist office.

Beaches
There are a few little beaches in the town, the best of which are Plage du Lido, west of the lighthouse, and Plage du Corsaire.

There are better places to swim in the Golfe de Valinco, especially Plage de Portigliolo, 7km south of the town.

Activities
Mountain Biking Ventura Location (☎ 04 95 76 11 84) is on ave Napoléon, near the ferry quay. It hires out good mountain bikes at bargain prices (60FF per day) and 125cc trail bikes for 350FF per day. It's open from 9 am to noon and 3 to 7 pm daily during the high season, (closed on Sunday in the low season). The shop organises motorcycle trips in the winter.

Horse Riding The Ferme Équestre de Baracci (Baracci Riding Centre; ☎ 04 95 76 08 02, fax 04 95 76 19 48) is on route de Baracci, about 2km north of Propriano. It stables 15 Corsican horses, which you can take out riding or trekking with a guide or qualified supervisor. A two hour ride (suitable for all abilities, but not for children) in the maquis and along the coast will set you back 200FF. There is also a one day route that takes you along a mule track to the village of Fozzano (the scene of the 1833 vendetta that inspired Prosper Mérimée to write *Colomba*) before a stop for a swim in a natural pool. The whole day costs 490FF, including a picnic. Advanced riders can even sign up for a long trek of at least a week without a guide, spending the nights bivouacking or in *bergeries* (shepherd's huts).

The centre has a reputation for high-quality service. It's open from April to May and from September to October. A long trek normally takes place in December or January.

Diving See the Diving chapter for details of diving in the region.

Places to Stay – Budget
Camping Tikiti (☎ 04 95 76 08 32) overlooks the main road towards Ajaccio about 1.5km north of Propriano. The site is huge, and covered with flowers and greenery; it's not built up like many of the other camp sites in the area. It has its own pizzeria, playgrounds washing machines, spotless washing facilities, and, above all, plenty of space. The site is open year-round; allow 32/12/12FF per person/tent/car.

Ferme Équestre de Baracci (☎ 04 95 76 08 02, fax 04 95 76 19 48) is a few hundred metres farther along the same road, on the right-hand side of route de Baracci. As well as riding lessons, it offers accommodation year-round, costing 85FF per person (including breakfast) in a room sleeping four people with shared bathroom, or 125FF per person in a twin room with bathroom. There is also one double room with bathroom

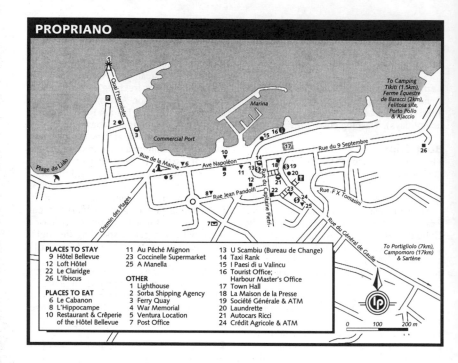

PROPRIANO

To Camping
Tikiti (1.5km),
Ferme Équestre
de Baracci (2km),
Felitosa site,
Porto Pollo
& Ajaccio

Marina

Commercial Port

Quai l'Herminier

Plage du Lido

Rue de la Marine

Ave Napoléon

Chemin des Plages

Rue Jean Pandolfi

Rue du Capitaine Pietri

Rue du 9 Septembre

Rue F. X Tomasini

Rue du Général de Gaulle

To Portigliolo (7km),
Campomoro (17km)
& Sartène

0   100   200 m

PLACES TO STAY	11 Au Péché Mignon	13 U Scambiu (Bureau de Change)
9 Hôtel Bellevue	23 Coccinelle Supermarket	14 Taxi Rank
12 Loft Hôtel	25 A Manella	15 I Paesi di u Valincu
22 Le Claridge		16 Tourist Office;
26 L'Ibiscus	**OTHER**	Harbour Master's Office
	1 Lighthouse	17 Town Hall
PLACES TO EAT	2 Sorba Shipping Agency	18 La Maison de la Presse
6 Le Cabanon	3 Ferry Quay	19 Société Générale & ATM
8 L'Hippocampe	4 War Memorial	20 Laundrette
10 Restaurant & Crêperie	5 Ventura Location	21 Autocars Ricci
of the Hôtel Bellevue	7 Post Office	24 Crédit Agricole & ATM

(230FF). The rooms are simple and clean, although a little small.

Places to Stay – Mid-Range

Hôtel Bellevue (☎ 04 95 76 01 86, fax 04 95 76 27 77), on ave Napoléon near the harbour, can be recognised by its distinctive pink façade and blue shutters. All of its bedrooms have en suite bathrooms and some have a view over the harbour. The rooms are pleasant, if a little noisy. A double room will set you back between 200FF and 240FF (350FF between the middle of July and the end of August), a triple room between 260FF and 300FF (440FF in the high season). The hotel also has a few single rooms without bathroom, which cost from 200FF to 250FF depending on the season. The reception is in the bar.

Le Claridge (☎ 04 95 76 05 54) is owned by the same people. It is an ochre-coloured building a few streets back from the harbour and offers spacious and comfortable rooms with bathroom, TV, air-conditioning and telephone. The setting is not as pleasant but it's distinctly quieter than the Hôtel Bellevue. The hotel also has a car park. Doubles cost 230FF or 280FF, depending on the room, rising to 330FF or 370FF in the high season.

Loft Hôtel (☎ 04 95 76 17 48, fax 04 95 76 22 04), on rue Jean Pandolfi parallel to ave Napoléon, is open between March and September. Most of its rooms, which are all spacious and absolutely spotless, have a double bed and two bunk beds. The attic rooms on the 1st floor definitely have a little less charm. Those on the right-hand side of the ground floor have a more limited view and no TV, but cost 20FF less than standard rooms. Doubles cost 280FF between April and June and in September,

Looking over Bonifacio harbour from the old town high on the cliffs.

The cliffs of old Bonifacio.

The Îles Lavezzi, a protected paradise in the far south.

The walk from Bonifacio to Cap Pertusato affords splendid views of the headland and the cliffs.

The seaside resort of Campomoro, on the Golfe de Valinco, has a 16th century Genoese tower.

Sainte Lucie de Tallano – one of the prettiest and most prosperous villages in Corsica.

from 300FF to 320FF in July and 350FF in August. Add 80/100FF for an extra child/adult bed. There is a car park, and the owner is happy to point out good walks and things to see in the area.

L'Ibiscus (☎ 04 95 76 01 56, fax 04 95 76 23 88) is a modern, rather characterless building on the way out of town towards Ajaccio. It has good, functional rooms with TV and balcony. It's open year-round; singles/doubles cost 260/300FF in the low season, 340/440FF in the high season.

Places to Eat

There are lots of cafés and restaurants along the marina.

Budget The *Coccinelle supermarket*, rue du Général de Gaulle, is open from 7.30 am to 12.30 pm and 3 to 7.30 pm, Monday and Saturday and Sunday lunchtime (it doesn't close for lunch in August).

Au Péché Mignon (☎ 04 95 76 01 71) is a patisserie by the harbour. It has a few little tables and is ideal for a breakfast of hot drinks and pastries. It's open from 8 am daily in summer, and from Tuesday to Sunday in winter.

The *Restaurant & Crêperie of the Hôtel Bellevue* (see under Places to Stay) serves sweet and savoury crêpes for between 20FF and 30FF (with fixed crêpe menus at 40FF and 55FF) on a pretty little terrace with rattan chairs and a lovely view of the harbour.

Mid-Range *L'Hippocampe* (☎ 04 95 76 11 01), on rue Jean Pandolfi, is not far from the market and a little way from the restaurants by the harbour. It specialises in fish, and has a fixed menu costing 98FF consisting of fish soup or raw fish marinated in lime, followed by a wing of skate or a fillet of fish grilled with herbs, and a dessert. L'Hippocampe is open daily for lunch and dinner between 1 April and 30 September.

A Manella (☎ 04 95 76 14 85, 18 rue du Général de Gaulle) is open lunchtimes and evenings (until 11.30 pm) daily between June and the end of September, and from

Thursday to Saturday between November and February. The chef has conjured up a fixed menu based on local produce and costing 95FF: fish soup or Cap Corse melon, sautéed veal or shredded skate from the bay braised in pesto, followed by a dessert. The restaurant also serves pizza and a more sophisticated fixed menu for 140FF. You have to go down a few steps to get to this friendly restaurant with its little terrace, where a bottle of Alzipratu costs 75FF.

Le Cabanon (☎ 04 95 76 07 76), on ave Napoléon, has a good reputation for its fish, its quiet terrace and its 85FF fixed menu: country ham or fish soup, leg of lamb with thyme or fisherman's selection, followed by cheese or a dessert. The restaurant also serves shellfish and a seafood platter for 120FF. It is open lunchtimes and evenings until 10.30 pm daily between Easter and All Saints' Day (1 November). It is worth booking in advance if you want to eat on the terrace. Service can be a little slow when the restaurant is busy.

Entertainment

There are two discos, the *Midnight* and the *Kallisté*, opposite one another on the steps in rue Grosseli, right in the centre of town.

Getting There & Away

Bus Autocars Ricci (☎ 04 95 76 25 59), on ave du Général de Gaulle, provides a regular service between Ajaccio and Propriano (60FF, one hour 40 minutes). Departures from Propriano are at 7.15 am (daily except Sunday, year-round) and 9.15 am (daily in summer). The return buses leave Ajaccio at 4 pm (daily except Sunday, year-round) and 3 pm (daily in summer). The buses leave from in front of Autocars Ricci's offices.

Car Ventura Location (see under Mountain Biking) represents Citer car hire. A small car costs 390/1750FF per day/week.

Boat Ferries between Propriano and mainland France are operated by SNCM (Marseille and Toulon) and CMN (Marseille).

THE SOUTH

The Sorba shipping agency (☎ 04 95 76 04 36, fax 04 95 76 00 98, quai L'Herminier) represents these two companies. It's open for ticket sales from 8 to 11.30 am and 2 to 4.30 pm Monday to Friday.

The harbour master's office (☎ 04 95 76 10 40) shares the premises of the tourist office. Depending on the season, it costs between 100FF and 165FF to moor a 9 to 10m boat in the marina, which has fuel, electricity, chandlers, mechanics and hot showers (10FF). Multihulled vessels pay a 50% supplement.

Getting Around

There is a taxi rank on rue du Capitaine Pietri, which is often called 'rue des taxis'. Some drivers organise excursions in the summer. Ask at the tourist office for details.

GOLFE DE VALINCO

This bay is all the more surprising if you approach it from the sea. Two little seaside resorts sit on opposite sides of the mouth of the bay, both with excellent diving (see the Diving chapter for details): Campomoro, to the south, and Porto Pollo to the north. Seven kilometres south of Propriano, the beautiful **Plage de Portigliolo** stretches out on either side of a little aerodrome that seems in keeping with the scenery of this protected coastline. The beach is 4km long and cut in two by the Rizzanese river.

The road leading south-west from Portigliolo (D121) climbs a little before reaching Belvédère, just before the seaside resort of **Campomoro**, where you will find the **Tour de Campomoro** (Campomoro Tower). There is a little footpath leading to the tower, with several information boards along the route telling you about the tower and its surroundings. Built in the 16th century by the Genoese, it is one of the largest on the island, and is also the only one to have been fortified with a star-shaped surrounding wall. Lovingly restored in 1986, it is now in the care of the Conservatoire du Littoral (coast conservation organisation). It is about 17km from Propriano.

To the north of the bay, Plage de Baracci is just one of the beaches you come across before you reach **Porto Pollo**. There are hotels, restaurants and bars here, the closest village to the megalithic site at Filitosa.

Places to Stay & Eat

Camping Lecci et Murta (☎ 04 95 76 02 67), near Plage de Portigliolo, has isolated, shady pitches, a children's play area and a pizzeria with a pleasant terrace. There are also tarmac tennis courts (50FF per hour, 40FF for campers) at the site, which is open from June to September. Allow 30/10/10FF per person/tent/car (34/14/14FF in July and August). You will need a car to get there from Propriano: head for Sartène for about 3km, then follow the D121 for 5km until you come to a sign for the site, which is 300m to the left.

There are also places to stay in Porto Pollo, on the other side of the bay. *Camping U Caseddu* (☎ 04 95 74 01 80) covers a large area, but has little shade. It is on the edge of Porto Pollo and tends to get full in the summer. It is open between the end of May and the beginning of October and has clean washing facilities, washing machines and a restaurant. Allow 29/10/8FF per person/tent/car.

Hôtel du Golfe (☎ 04 95 74 01 66) is the cheapest in Porto Pollo. It is right on the edge of the village, near the little harbour. Its basic but clean double rooms cost 200FF and have bathrooms with a décor that is straight out of the 1960s. Reception is generally at the pizzeria of the same name, by the harbour.

Hôtel Kallisté (☎ 04 95 74 02 38, fax 04 95 74 06 26) has comfortable, spotless rooms with telephone and bathroom and is definitely the best option in Porto Pollo. Allow 280/310FF for a double room in the low season (maquis/sea view), 300/350FF in July. Half-board is available in July (350FF per person) and obligatory in August (400FF). The Kallisté has fixed-price menus for 125FF and 140FF. The Corsican-style kid sometimes on the menu is excellent and the desserts are also very good.

The hotel is open between 1 April and 15 October.

Getting There & Away

Casabianca (☎ 04 95 74 05 58) offers a daily bus service between Propriano and Porto Pollo during the summer (18FF, 45 minutes). The first bus (there are six shuttles a day) leaves Porto Pollo at 7.35 am and Propriano at 8.20 am.

Autocars Ricci (☎ 04 95 51 08 19) goes to Porto Pollo from Ajaccio on Monday, Wednesday and Saturday.

FILITOSA

Even though it is the most famous prehistoric site in Corsica, there are still many mysteries about Filitosa that remain to be solved. The site was discovered in 1946 by the owner of the land, Charles-Antoine Césari (whose family still runs the site reception), and owes a great deal to the archaeologist Roger Grosjean, who was responsible for the excavations. What is special about Filitosa is that the remains on the one site stretch back over an extremely long period of history, from ancient Neolithic (around 6000 to 5000 BC) to Roman occupation. Of these times, the megalithic period is most interesting because of its statuary, which reached its peak around 1800 BC.

The oldest remains reveal that the human population lived in rock shelters, although only a specialist could detect signs of human habitation now. Remnants of pottery, arrow heads and farming tools show that settlement began around 3300 BC.

The *menhir* (standing stone) statues of the megalithic period are more impressive. The fact that they were even erected marks a major step forward. However, the meaning of these granite monoliths, which are 2 to 3m high and carved to represent human faces or weapons, is still unclear: it's unknown whether they are phallic symbols to symbolically fertilise the land, representations of local horsemen (the Paladini) or monuments to ward off the threat of the

Torréen invaders (see the boxed text 'Mysterious People of the Sea' on the next page).

However, there seems to be complete agreement that the Torréens arrived at the peak of the megalithic period. They were better armed and more advanced than the communities on the island, and seem to have expelled the creators of the statues from Filitosa in around 1500 BC. They destroyed a large number of the statues, or buried them face down, and replaced them with circular structures, known as the *torri*, whose role is just as mysterious. The central and western monuments in Filitosa are examples of these.

Filitosa is worth a one hour visit. Once you have got your ticket (22FF, children free), you have to go through the little museum (it is better to visit it on the way out) to get to the menhir statue known as Filitosa V. This has a distinctive rectangular head,

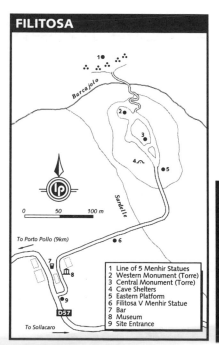

FILITOSA

To Porto Pollo (9km)

To Sollacaro

0   50   100 m

Barcajolo

Sardelle

1 Line of 5 Menhir Statues
2 Western Monument (Torre)
3 Central Monument (Torre)
4 Cave Shelters
5 Eastern Platform
6 Filitosa V Menhir Statue
7 Bar
8 Museum
9 Site Entrance

D57

THE SOUTH

and is the largest and best-armed statue in Corsica. Look out for the clearly visible sword and dagger decorating the statue.

If you continue along the path you come to some rock shelters and the foundations of some huts (there are signs showing you where to find these simple blocks of rock) before you get to the central torre with its six little statues, including the one known as Filitosa IX, the face of which is considered a masterpiece of megalithic art.

The western monument, where a pile of stones forms the cavity of a torre, is a few metres farther on, before the path goes down towards the highlight of the visit: five menhir statues lined up in an arc around the foot of an ancient olive tree. Behind them is a little granite quarry, from where the ancient sculptors probably got their materials.

To be honest, you would have to be a specialist to appreciate the real archaeological value of the site, and the meagre information provided is not enough to excite the novice. However, there is a peaceful atmosphere, especially at the end of the day, and the geometry of the last five statues is interesting when viewed from the western monument.

It is worth spending a few minutes in the museum before you leave. It houses three more menhir statues, some pottery, some human remains, a few stone tools and information about the Torréens-Shardanes. There is also a bar and a souvenir shop at the site.

Filitosa (☎ 04 95 74 00 91) is open from 8 am to sunset daily, between April and June.

Places to Stay & Eat

The nearest camp sites and hotels are in Porto Pollo (see under Golfe de Valinco earlier in this section). To get there by car from

Mysterious People of the Sea

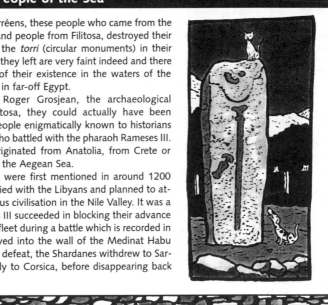

Who were the Torréens, these people who came from the sea, drove the island people from Filitosa, destroyed their statues and built the *torri* (circular monuments) in their place? The traces they left are very faint indeed and there is only evidence of their existence in the waters of the Cyrenaic Sea and in far-off Egypt.

According to Roger Grosjean, the archaeological authority on Filitosa, they could actually have been Shardanes, the people enigmatically known to historians as 'sea people', who battled with the pharaoh Rameses III. They probably originated from Anatolia, from Crete or from the coast of the Aegean Sea.

The Shardanes were first mentioned in around 1200 BC. They were allied with the Libyans and planned to attack the prosperous civilisation in the Nile Valley. It was a mistake: Rameses III succeeded in blocking their advance and sinking their fleet during a battle which is recorded in hieroglyphics carved into the wall of the Medinat Habu temple. After this defeat, the Shardanes withdrew to Sardinia and probably to Corsica, before disappearing back into obscurity.

Filitosa, take the D57 towards Propriano for 4.5km, then turn right onto the D157 for the same distance.

Getting There & Away

There are no real bus services to Filitosa. The only possibility is the line between Ajaccio and Porto Pollo operated by Autocars Ricci (☎ 04 95 51 08 19), which passes 2km from the site.

The Sartenais

In more than one way, the Sartenais is a reminder of what Corsica used to be like; the region fervently perpetuates traditions going back to the Middle Ages, while to the south of the town there are prehistoric remains that provide information about the lifestyle of the first inhabitants of the island.

SARTÈNE (SARTÈ)
• pop 3650   ✉ 20100

'The whole place breathes war and vengeance', Paul Valéry said about Sartène. In fact, this shadowy town seems to watch over the Rizzaneze valley with an austere eye from its high granite walls, and can look somewhat severe. It was a bastion for large families of noblemen who didn't want anyone meddling in their business, and even today Sartène doesn't give much away about its past. However, it was the subject of numerous raids by the Saracens in the 15th and 16th centuries and pirates from Algiers took 400 of its inhabitants into slavery in 1583.

Danger for Sartène didn't always come from the outside – far from it. The town takes pride of place in the history of one of the most famous Corsican traditions: the vendetta. As well as the consequences of the Colomba Carabelli vendetta (it is said that a curate, a protagonist in the affair, remained shut away in his home in Borgo for nine years for fear of reprisals), there was a famous rivalry between two Sartène families in the first half of the 19th century. One

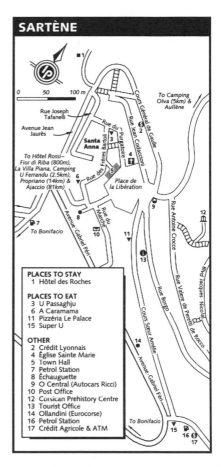

SARTÈNE

0   50   100 m

To Camping Olva (5km) & Aullène

Rue Joseph Tafanelli
Avenue Jean Jaurès
Santa Anna
To Hôtel Rossi–Fior di Riba (800m), La Villa Piana, Camping U Ferrandu (2.5km), Propriano (14km) & Ajaccio (81km)
Place de la Libération
To Bonifacio
To Bonifacio

PLACES TO STAY
1 Hôtel des Roches

PLACES TO EAT
3 U Passaghju
6 A Caramama
11 Pizzéria Le Palace
15 Super U

OTHER
2 Crédit Lyonnais
4 Église Sainte Marie
5 Town Hall
7 Petrol Station
8 Échauguette
9 O Central (Autocars Ricci)
10 Post Office
12 Corsican Prehistory Centre
13 Tourist Office
14 Ollandini (Eurocorse)
16 Petrol Station
17 Crédit Agricole & ATM

of the families came from the Borgo quarter, the other from Santa Anna, and the whole thing turned the town's streets into the set for a miniature civil war. Calm only returned to the town after a peace treaty was signed in the Église Sainte Marie. Some sources suggest that a quarrel about a dog was the cause of the bloody confrontations between the two families.

Perhaps it was this deep attachment to the island's values that provoked Mérimée's comment that Sartène was the 'most Corsican of all Corsican towns'.

THE SOUTH

The Procession du Catenacciu

On the eve of Good Friday, Sartène is the setting for one of the oldest religious traditions on the island: the Procession du Catenacciu. In a colourful re-enactment of the Passion, the Catenacciu (literally, 'the chained one'), an anonymous, barefoot penitent covered from head to foot in a red robe and cowl, carries a huge cross through the town while dragging a heavy chain shackled to the ankle. The Catenacciu is followed by a procession of other penitents (eight dressed in black, one in white), members of the clergy and local notables. As the chain clatters by on the cobblestones, local people look on in great (if rather humourless) excitement. Needless to say, everyone is curious to find out the identity of the penitent, selected by the parish priest from among applicants seeking to expiate a grave sin.

The chains and cross of the Catenacciu can be seen in the Église Sainte Marie.

For a long time isolated and introverted, the town is now effectively the guardian of the island's traditions. The Catenacciu procession has been followed religiously since the Middle Ages (see the boxed text above).

Orientation

Sartène is built around place de la Libération, from which cours Sœur Amélie and cours Général de Gaulle, the town's main streets, lead off.

The old quarter of Santa Anna stretches out to the north of place de la Libération. Many of its little streets have more than one name, and just as many signs.

Information

Tourist Office The tourist office (☎ 04 95 77 15 40), 6 rue Borgo, is near to place de la Libération and is open from 9 am to noon and 4 to 7 pm, Monday to Saturday, from May to September.

Money Crédit Lyonnais, on cours Général de Gaulle, doesn't charge commission on travellers cheques in French francs; however, you will have to pay 30FF per transaction to change cash or foreign currency travellers cheques into francs. It's open from 8.15 am to 12.15 pm and 1.40 to 4.40 pm, Monday to Friday.

The only ATM in Sartène is outside Crédit Agricole, at the bottom of cours Sœur Amélie near the petrol station.

Post The post office is on rue du Marché, not far from place de la Libération. It's open from 8.30 am to 12.30 pm and 2 to 5.30 pm, Monday to Friday, and Saturday morning.

Old Town

The old town is a stone labyrinth, a maze of steps and little streets, some of which are so narrow that a man can hardly pass through them. One of the benefits of these alleyways, particularly appreciated in summer, is that they provide the pedestrian with some welcome shade during the day, while the warmth that has accumulated in the granite is retained for several hours after sunset.

Église Sainte Marie can be found above place de la Libération, which is still sometimes called place Porta. It was built in 1766 on the site of an older building that collapsed not long after it was built. It boasts a superb altarpiece, made of polychrome marble, which came from the Couvent Saint François in Sainte Lucie de Tallano, and canvasses depicting the stations of the Cross, painted by an artist who was passing through in 1843. You will also be able to see the chains and cross used during the Procession du Catenacciu.

Next to Église Sainte Marie is the building that now houses the **town hall** but which, in the 16th century, was the palace of the Genoese lieutenants. It is now classed as a historic monument and is home to some anonymous Italian canvasses that have, unfortunately, been poorly restored. It's open from 8.30 am to noon and 2 to 6 pm Monday to Friday; admission is free. If you go through the gateway below this former palace you come to the real jewel of the old town, the **Santa Anna quarter** and its narrow streets.

South-west of place de la Libération is an **échauguette** (watchtower), which indicates just how important the people of Sartène used to consider it was to keep a lookout around the city. The échauguette is not open to visitors.

Corsican Prehistory Centre

Perhaps it is to reinforce Sartène's austere atmosphere that the town museum (☎ 04 95 77 01 09) is in a former prison – to which the bars on the windows, the thick walls and the sinister hinges still bear witness. It consists of one room and five cells, and houses a collection of items of diverse origins and various ages, ranging back to the Neolithic era. The most interesting thing about this little museum is its pottery (especially some beautiful painted pieces from the Middle Ages) and stone objects: arrow heads, tools, jewellery and so on.

To get there, follow the steps off rue Antoine Crocce, to the right behind place de la Libération. It's open from 10 am to noon and 2 to 6 pm, daily except Sunday, from 15 June to 15 September. Admission costs 15FF (children and group members 10FF).

Places to Stay

Camping U Farrandu (☎ 04 95 73 41 69) is the closest camp site to the town, 2.5km north of Sartène on the right-hand side of the Propriano road, just after a bend. Toilet and washing facilities are clean, the service is friendly and the pitches are private and shady. Allow 33FF (total) for the first night and 30FF for subsequent nights. This little camp site is open from April to October, and also has a tennis court and mini-golf.

Camping Olva (☎ 04 95 77 11 58) is to the north of town, 5km out on the D69 towards Aullène. It is quiet, shaded by eucalyptus trees and has a lovely tennis court, a swimming pool and a little supermarket. It costs 33/16/13FF per person/tent/car. There is a free shuttle service between the site and

the town in summer. You can get information from Ollandini (☎ 04 95 77 18 41) on ave Gabriel Péri.

Hôtel des Roches (☎ 04 95 77 07 61, fax 04 95 77 19 93), at the bottom of ave Jean Jaurès, is the only hotel in the centre of Sartène. Its rooms have en suite bathroom, TV and telephone, are slightly on the old-fashioned side but are clean and have good bedding. The best rooms, which are slightly more expensive, have a beautiful view over the valley. A night in a single room will cost you 240/250FF (town/valley view), a double 260/280FF and a triple 350FF. A generous breakfast costs 35FF. The hotel is open year-round and also has a restaurant (the fixed menu costs 110FF).

Hôtel Rossi – Fior di Riba (☎ 04 95 77 01 80, 04 95 77 09 58) is a good choice. With a warm, family atmosphere, it offers spotless and comfortable double rooms costing from 230FF (low season) to 340FF (high season). Located 800m from town on the Propriano road, it welcomes visitors from mid-March to mid-October, and has a small swimming pool.

La Villa Piana (☎ 04 95 77 07 04, fax 04 95 73 45 65) is just next to the Hôtel Rossi – Fior di Riba, and also has good, comfortable double rooms ranging from 250FF to 370FF and 330FF to 440FF in the low and high seasons respectively. It's open from the beginning of April to the end of September. Guests can also use the pleasant pool and the tennis court.

Places to Eat

If you are self-catering, head for the *Super U*, at the bottom end of cours Sœur Amélie near the petrol station. It is open from 8.30 am to 7.45 pm, Monday to Saturday.

U Passaghju (☎ 04 95 77 21 84), at the northern end of rue des Frères Bartoli, is open lunchtimes and evenings daily between April or May and September. The restaurant is in the pleasant setting of the alleyways of the old town, and has fixed-price menus for 75FF and 95FF, plus a lunch menu for 60FF (stuffed mussels, fish kebab, dessert).

THE SOUTH

A Caramama (☎ *04 95 77 07 84)* is in the old town; turn left after you go through the gateway by the town hall from place de la Libération. It serves good pizzas costing between 38FF and 52FF, to eat in or take away. The restaurant has tables in the street and serves a wide range of fixed menus until late in the evening; it's open from the end of May to mid-October.

Pizzéria Le Palace (☎ *04 95 77 02 97, 4 cours Sœur Amélie)* also serves pizzas (costing from 35FF to 55FF) and grilled meat and fish (starting at 75FF). The balcony is perched above the street, and its few tightly packed tables provide a wonderful opportunity to eat in the fresh air on a summer evening.

Getting There & Away

Autocars Ricci (☎ 04 95 51 08 19, 04 95 76 25 59) buses leave Sartène for Ajaccio at 7 and 9 am daily, year-round. The service goes via Propriano, Olmeto and Saint Georges. There are also departures at 4.35 and 5.35 pm for Sainte Lucie de Tallano, Levie and Zonza. There is a shuttle service to the Bocca di Bavella in summer. The base for Autocars Ricci in Sartène is the O Central bar, on place de la Libération.

Ollandini (☎ 04 95 77 18 41), ave Gabriel Péri, is the representative for Eurocorse, whose buses leave for Ajaccio at 6 and 8 am and 4 pm year-round (different timetable on Sunday and public holidays). There are also two buses a day to Bonifacio and Porto Vecchio and one to Zonza (except Sunday and public holidays). Ollandini is open from 7.30 am to noon and 2.30 to 6.30 pm, Monday to Friday, and Saturday morning.

PREHISTORIC SITES OF THE SARTENAIS

Very little is known about Corsica's dolmens and menhirs. Although historians seem to agree that the dolmens mark burial sites, the menhirs remain unexplained. It has been suggested that they were representations of divinities, the deceased or enemies, sculpted with a view to warding off their

power, but there is no way of finding out for certain.

The heterogeneity of these structures complicates the task still further: some of them are simple, crude standing stones, whereas others represent human faces or weapons. Others, like those in Filitosa, have phallic connotations, which have led some to conclude that they were fertility symbols for the land.

In the absence of an irrefutable scientific explanation, it is probably best to consider these sites as good places for walks. Although the laborious sculpture by our very distant cousins can be fascinating for prehistorians and archaeologists, it can be somewhat disappointing for the demanding aesthetes that we have become in the intervening few thousand years. Having said that, there is a certain charm, almost a mystique, about the prehistoric sites of the Sartenais and the sight of these statues fashioned by *Homo sapiens* an eternity ago is certainly food for thought. This is especially so if you make the most of the calming light at the end of the day to visit these prehistoric relics.

To the south of Sartène are the sites of Cauria and Paddaghiu – these are absolutely free from tourists and among the most famous sites on the island. You will need a vehicle to get there.

Cauria

About 15km from Sartène is the beautiful, deserted plain of Cauria, which is home to three megalithic curiosities: the *alignements* (lines) of menhirs of Stantari and Rinaghiu, and the Funtanaccia Dolmen. You don't have to pay to see any of these sites, which are right out in the maquis; however, don't expect to find a snack bar, shade or any sort of explanatory information.

To get to the sites, you will have to go across rudimentary grids designed to keep animals within certain areas. This makes the walk difficult for people with reduced mobility. Allow about one hour.

From Sartène, follow the road to Bonifacio for 2km before turning off on the D48, a winding road down to the right. The megalithic site at Cauria is signposted off to the left after a few kilometres and is another 4.5km along a poorly maintained road which leads to a sign riddled with bullet holes. The sign points to the menhirs and the dolmens, along a driveable track to the right; you can also park your car in the shade here and go on foot.

Follow the road down for 900m and you will come to the **Alignement de Stantari**. There are nine menhirs in total: the fourth from the left represents a sword, the one to the right of it is a stone face with its mouth open in a muted cry. The **Alignement de Rinaghiu**, which is more anarchic, is 300m away and has spent thousands of years at the foot of a little wood that some say is sacred.

If you retrace your steps to the Alignement de Stantari, you go across a wooden grid made from the two main branches of a cork oak to get to the **Funtanaccia Dolmen**. From here it's another 350m to the megalithic monument, which is the largest of its type and more worth the detour than the lines of menhirs.

The path to the dolmen crosses another path after a few hundred metres. Follow this path to the right and it will bring you back to the path you were on originally.

Alignement de Paddaghiu

With nearly 260 menhirs, either standing or lying, the Alignement de Paddaghiu is the largest collection of megalithic statues in the Mediterranean. There are four lines of between four and eight standing menhirs, some of which are sculpted, and these are the main attraction at the site, which is in an enclosure between maquis and vines.

To get there by car from Cauria, drive the 4km back to the D48 and turn left towards Tizzano. The site is next to a wine-tasting building for the wine-producing *domaine* (estate) of Mosconi (the domaine is 1km before, on the left-hand side). Leave your car in the car park, and follow the arrows for about 1km along the path, which is not accessible by car. Access is free.

PROTECTED COASTLINE
Marine de Tizzano

About 5km south-west of the Alignement de Paddaghiu is this little cove, which was once watched over by a fort, now in ruins. Here you'll find a beach and a few little creeks.

At *Hôtel-Restaurant du Golfe* (☎ 04 95 77 22 34, fax 04 95 77 14 76), double rooms cost between 350FF and 520FF, depending on the season. The rooms, which are light and pleasant, have TV, telephone and bathroom; those on the top floor cost 20FF more but have a wonderful view and a bath. The restaurant serves sophisticated food at reasonable prices. The hotel is open between the end of March and October.

Chez Antoine (☎ 04 95 77 07 25) is well known for its grilled fish and its stone bower on the edge of the harbour.

Roccapina

The Roccapina site, which is protected, is 20km from Sartène and 30km from Bonifacio. It is famous for a geological curiosity, a naturally eroded sculpture in the shape of a lion. The big cat can be found opposite Auberge la Corralli, in the direction of the sea from the N196. Although it is not as perfect as the Sphinx in Egypt, it is nonetheless easy to make out the animal: two enormous blocks of rock on top of a ridge crowned by a Genoese tower make out the shape of a stretching lion, with a few standing rocks as his mane. The lion is not the only curiosity at the site. Next to a snack bar there is also a rocky block whose shape is reminiscent of a gorilla's head looking out to sea. The site is 2km after Auberge la Corralli in the direction of Bonifacio. If you have a good imagination, you may also be able to make out the shape of an elephant in the rocks (recognisable by its trunk).

To get to the beach at Roccapina, take the track leading off the main road next to Auberge la Corralli and follow it downhill for 2km. The dunes of juniper, damaged by campers in the years prior to 1985, are now protected by the Conservatoire du Littoral, which also seeks to protect limpets. These

THE SOUTH

large shellfish move at night to eat seaweed, and change sex to become female when they get larger than 4cm across. The larger females were often eaten by lovers of molluscs, and the species was in danger of extinction before it became protected.

There is a path from the beach up to the lion rock.

Places to Stay & Eat

There are a few places that you can stay in the area. However, you run the risk of feeling a little cut off.

Camping Municipal Arepos (☎ 04 95 77 19 30) is at the bottom of the path. It's open between May and September, and charges 65FF for two people (with a tent and car) for the first night and 60FF for subsequent nights. It has few attractions, but is very close to the beach.

Auberge la Corralli (☎ 04 95 77 05 94) is on the main road and has four good rooms with bathroom, balcony and TV. Doubles start at 250FF, and half-board (530FF for two people) is obligatory in July and August. Fixed menus are offered for 80FF and 120FF.

Getting There & Away

Eurocorse buses (☎ 04 95 21 06 30, 04 95 70 13 83) stop at Roccapina on the route between Ajaccio and Bonifacio.

The Far South

There is a narrow plain separating the coast from the rocky foothills of the island, which gives the very south of the island its own particular look. Popular with tourists for its exceptional coastline, this landscape of cork oaks is dominated by Bonifacio.

BONIFACIO (BUNIFAZIU)
• pop 2700   ✉ 20169

Standing atop chalky cliffs, watched over by its citadel, Bonifacio is a wonderful place that is worth the trip to Corsica on its own. The town owes a great deal of its beauty to its extraordinary coastal location: imagine a fjord about 100m wide plunging 1.5km into cliffs of white rock sculpted by the sea and the wind. Then imagine a citadel perched on top of these cliffs, dominating the turquoise depths of the Bouches de Bonifacio from a height of almost 70m.

At the far south of the island, the 'Corsican Gibraltar', separated from Sardinia by only 12km of water, is a pleasant, rewarding and, above all, popular destination.

History

The discovery of Bonifacio Woman, the remains of a young woman who lived near the present town about 8500 years ago, proves that the area was inhabited in the Neolithic period. There is no doubt that the site was active a few thousand years later. There are even some people who suggest that the episode of the Odyssey in which Odysseus meets the Lestrygons, a race of giant cannibals, at the foot of 'sheer cliffs on either side' could have taken place at the entrance to the Goulet de Bonifacio (Bonifacio Narrows), and not facing the Italian coast.

The town was probably founded by the Marquis de Toscane Boniface, who gave the town its name in 828.

When all of the town's inhabitants were gathered for a wedding in 1187, the powerful Genoese republic seized its chance and took over the town. It sent in its settlers, and the many financial benefits convinced them to stay. True to form, the Genoese drove the native islanders out of town.

The Genoese colony of Bonifacio had to defend itself on two occasions. The first was in 1420, when Alphonse V of Aragon laid siege to the town for five months on the grounds that Pope Boniface VIII had given Corsica to Spain. According to legend, the Escalier du Roi d'Aragon (King of Aragon's Stairway) was carved at this point, and he was forced to retreat after a Genoese squadron was dispatched to assist the colony.

The second siege took place in 1553. The alliance between French troops, supporters of Sampiero Corso and the Turkish pirate

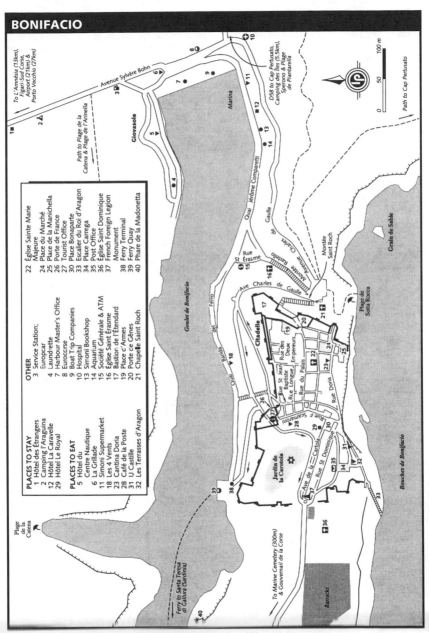

BONIFACIO

PLACES TO STAY
1 Hôtel des Étrangers
2 Camping l'Araguina
12 Hôtel La Caravelle
29 Hôtel Le Royal

PLACES TO EAT
5 Hôtel du
   Centre Nautique
6 La Grillade
11 Simoni Supermarket
18 Les 4 Vents
23 Cantina Doria
28 Café de la Poste
31 U Castille
32 Les Terrasses d'Aragon

OTHER
3 Service Station;
   Europcar
4 Laundrette
7 Harbour Master's Office
8 Eurocrse
9 Boat Trip Companies
10 Hospital
13 Simoni Bookshop
14 Aquarium
15 Société Générale & ATM
16 Église Saint Érasme
17 Bastion de l'Étendard
19 Place c'Armes
20 Porte ce Gênes
21 Chapelle Saint Roch
22 Église Sainte Marie
   Majeure
24 Place du Marché
25 Place de la Manichella
26 Porte de France
27 Tourist Office
30 Place Bonaparte
33 Escalier du Roi d'Aragon
34 Place Carrega
35 Post Office
36 Église Saint Dominique
37 French Foreign Legion
   Monument
38 Ferry Terminal
39 Ferry Quay
40 Phare de la Madonetta

THE SOUTH

Dragut aimed to liberate the island from its Genoese occupation. The town surrendered, after resisting the siege bitterly for 18 days, following the treachery of one of its inhabitants. Together with the rest of the island, it was returned to the Genoese in 1559 by the treaty of Cateau-Cambrésis.

Orientation

Bonifacio can be separated into two main sections: the marina at the end of the Goulet de Bonifacio, and the Citadelle – also known as the Vieille Ville (Old Town) or Ville Haute (Upper Town) – perched on the cliff-top between the goulet and the sea. There are two ways into the Citadelle: the beautiful Porte de Gênes (Genoa Gate; pedestrian access only) at the top of montée Saint Roch, and the Porte de France (France Gate; vehicle access), which overlooks the ferry terminal.

Information

Tourist Office The tourist office (☎ 04 95 73 11 88), 2 rue F Scamaroni, is very close to the Porte de France. It is open from 9 am to 8 pm daily in summer, and from 9 am to noon and 2 to 6 pm, Monday to Friday, during the rest of the year.

Money Société Générale, at 7 rue Saint Érasme on the southern side of the harbour, is the only bank in Bonifacio; it also has the town's only ATM. It's open from 8.15 to 11.30 am and 2 to 4.30 pm. Changing money will set you back 25FF per transaction (plus 1% of the total for travellers cheques). Eurocheques are not accepted.

There's a bureau de change inside the ferry terminal that charges 30FF commission for exchanging foreign currency. Changing travellers cheques made out in French francs and Eurocheques (only accepted in francs) costs a minimum of 50FF, or 5% of the total for transactions over 1000FF. Changing foreign currency travellers cheques costs 30FF, or 1% of the total for transactions over 3000FF. The bureau de change is open in the high season between 8 am and 8pm.

Post The post office is hidden in place Carrega in the Citadelle, and is open between 8.30 am and 6 pm Monday to Friday and on Saturday morning until noon in the summer. During the rest of the year it's open from 9 am to noon and 2 to 5 pm Monday to Friday and Saturday morning.

Photography Film prices can reach record levels in Bonifacio because of the number of tourists. It is not unusual for a 100 ASA film to cost 68FF in the summer. If you are unlucky enough to need film, try Photo & Cie (☎ 04 95 73 55 05), 7-9 montée Rastello, where the prices are reasonable.

Bookshop Simoni (☎ 04 95 73 02 63), on the harbour near the aquarium, is a bookshop and stationers stocking a very wide range of French and foreign daily newspapers, periodicals and books in the summer. It is open from 8 am to midnight daily during July and August (closed between 1 and 4 pm on Sunday) and from 8 am to noon and 3.45 to 7 pm, Monday to Saturday and Sunday lunchtime, in the winter.

Laundry There is a laundrette on the northern side of the marina. Allow 35FF per wash.

Medical Services The hospital in Bonifacio (☎ 04 95 73 95 73) is just east of the marina and has an emergency unit open 24 hours daily. The emergency number for an ambulance is ☎ 04 95 73 95 95.

Citadelle & Ville Haute

There are two sets of steps from the harbour to the Citadelle, which was built by the Genoese. **Montée Saint Roch**, which starts as montée Rastello, links rue Saint Érasme to the Porte de Gênes. The second ascends to the Porte de France from quai Banda del Ferro, not far from the ferry quay. The montée Saint Roch and Porte de Gênes route is undoubtedly the best way to enter the Citadelle.

The **Porte de Gênes**, which was fitted with a drawbridge in the last few years of the 16th century, was the only way of getting into the Citadelle until the Porte de France was built in 1854. To the north is the **Bastion de l'Étendard**, a remnant of the fortifications built as a result of the siege in 1553. It is home to the **Mémorial du Passé Bonifacien** (Memorial to Bonifacio's Past; admission 10FF) where various episodes in the town's history have been recreated. To the south of the bastion are **place du Marché** and **place de la Manichella**, from where there are some wonderful views over the Bouches de Bonifacio.

The main road in the Citadelle during the Genoese occupation was the **rue des Deux Empereurs**, which owes its name to Charles V and Napoleon I, who both stayed in the town, the former on his way to Algiers in 1541, the latter in 1793. There are only commemorative plaques to mark the visits of these two emperors (at Nos 4 and 7); the houses in question are not open to visitors.

Église Sainte Marie Majeure was built by the Pisans and completed in the 14th century. Although it has been modified on numerous occasions and has gradually lost its original style, it retains its main feature: the **loggia**, under the arches of which the notables of the town used to gather. Opposite it is the old **communal tank**, which was once used by the town to collect rainwater gathered by the many aqueducts running above the streets of the old town. Many of the stone features in the Citadelle were built in an attempt to resolve the knotty problem of supplying water to the town. For a long time the water was supplied by means of mule-powered scoop wheels.

In its own way, the **Escalier du Roi d'Aragon** is a result of the same problem. Legend has it that the 187 steps down from the south-western corner of the Citadelle to the sea 60m below were carved in a single night by the King of Aragon's troops during the 1420 siege. It is more likely that this impressive scar down the side of the cliff was carved to allow access to a spring discovered by monks.

To the west of the Citadelle is **Église Saint Dominique**, one of the few Gothic religious buildings in Corsica. It houses an altarpiece made of polychrome marble that dates back to the mid-18th century, as well as the reliquaries carried in processions through the town during a number of religious festivals.

The **marine cemetery**, with its immaculate lines of tombs, stretches out to the sea a few hundred metres farther to the west. Although the surroundings are far from brilliant, there is a spectacular view over the Sardinian coast, about 12km away. An **underground passage** dug by hand during WWII leads to the **Gouvernail de la Corse** (Helm of Corsica), a rock in the water a few dozen metres out with a shape reminiscent of the helm of a ship. The passage is open to the public in the summer (10FF), but closes at around 6 pm.

Marina

Église Saint Érasme was built in the 13th century and is dedicated to the patron saint of fishermen. It is at the foot of montée Rastello.

The **Aquarium** (☎ 04 95 73 03 69) is in a natural cave in quai Jérôme Comparetti and features the marine flora and fauna of the Bouches de Bonifacio; admission costs 22FF (students 16FF, children 11FF).

Beaches

A very steep path leads down from the bottom of the montée Saint Roch to Plage de Sotta Rocca, which you can see below you, nestled at the foot of the cliffs, opposite the Grain de Sable and the amazingly clear turquoise waters.

The little Plage de la Catena and Plages de l'Arinella stretch out at the back of the coves of the same name, on the northern side of the goulet. There is a path leading to them from the corner of the U Veni snack bar on ave Sylvère Bohn. However, both of these beaches unfortunately tend to collect the rubbish from the goulet.

Boat Trips

The beauty of the seascapes on view around Bonifacio means that there are inevitably numerous companies offering boat trips, jostling for position along the quays of the marina.

There are two main routes. The first includes the goulet, the *calanche* (deep rocky inlets; *calanques* in French) and the Grotte du Sdragonato (Little Dragon Cave); tours cost from about 50FF to 65FF, depending on the duration, which is generally between 30 and 50 minutes. The second route heads for the Îles Lavezzi and costs about 100FF. The launches for this second trip are about 10m long and offer a shuttle service, so you can spend as long as you like on the islands; it is worth taking some water and food with you, as there are no facilities there. On the way back, the boats pass close to Île Cavallo, the Pointe de Sperono, the calanche and the cliffs.

It would be a shame to miss out on this excellent opportunity to discover the area around the Goulet de Bonifacio. The Citadelle, perched on its limestone promontory, is even more beautiful when seen from the sea and there are a number of curiosities along the coast that are best admired from a boat: the Escalier du Roi d'Aragon, the Gouvernail de la Corse, the Grain de Sable (Grain of Sand, a section of the cliff a few dozen metres from the coast that seems to have escaped erosion) and the Grotte du Sdragonato (famous for a hole the shape of the island in its roof, through which sunlight illuminates the seaweed carpeting the seabed).

The boat trips are available from 9.30 am to 7 pm between April and October. All of the companies provide similar services. There is friendly but nonetheless real competition between the boat trip operators, and generous reductions can be obtained. When making your choice, consider the appearance of the boat and the discounts offered.

Activities

Walking There is a sign describing the footpaths along the coast at the foot of montée Saint Roch. Don't miss the one that goes to the Cap Pertusato (see the Walking in Corsica chapter).

Diving See the Diving chapter for information on diving in the Bonifacio area.

Places to Stay

The majority of the hotels in Bonifacio have three stars; however, there are also some more reasonable accommodation options.

Camping *Camping l'Araguina* (☎ 04 95 73 02 96), on ave Sylvère Bohn north of the marina, is open from April to October. Although the pitches are tightly packed, the main advantage of this site is that it is only a few hundred metres from the harbour. It is quite shady, with clean toilet and washing facilities and a laundrette (30FF per wash). It also rents out eight pretty and comfortable bungalows costing from 2300FF to 4400FF per week for four to five people. Allow 32FF per person, 11FF per tent and car and 7FF per motorbike. Guests also get a reduction on Cristina boat trips.

Camping des Îles (☎ 04 95 73 11 89) is 5.5km from the town, on the road to Cap Pertusato (signposted route). It's in a wonderful setting, with plenty of flowers and facilities worthy of some hotels, including mini-golf, a very nice pool, a little supermarket, a laundrette and a play area. It's opposite the Sperono golf course and about 1km from Plage de Piantarella. The only negative aspect is that it lacks any shade. The site is open between 1 April and 31 October and charges between 27FF and 43FF per person, depending on the season, between 10FF and 16FF per tent and between 10FF and 14FF per car.

Hotels *Hôtel des Étrangers* (☎ 04 95 73 01 09, fax 04 95 73 16 99, ave Sylvère Bohn) can be found a few hundred metres north of the marina, on the western side of the road. It is a good choice for its friendly service and the fact that it is undoubtedly one of the few establishments in Bonifacio whose prices are appropriate for independent travellers. Its rooms all have bathrooms and are simple with comfortable beds. Prices vary according to the season, the rooms' size and position: on the road side (warm and noisy) or at the back (cool and quiet). Some of the rooms have air-conditioning and TV. Doubles overlooking the road with no air-conditioning or TV cost 200FF (236FF in July and August); better rooms at the back, with air-conditioning, cost 200FF (386FF in July and August). Prices include a good breakfast. The hotel is open between April and October and has a car park.

Hôtel Le Royal (☎ *04 95 73 00 51, fax 04 95 73 04 68)* is in the heart of the Citadelle. Whether you are on your own or with three other people, one of its huge rooms will cost 450FF in July, 600FF in August and between 280FF and 350FF in the low season. All 14 rooms have air-conditioning, TV and bathroom. An extra bed costs 50FF.

Hôtel La Caravelle (☎ *04 95 73 00 03, fax 04 95 73 00 41, 35 quai Jérôme Comparetti)* at the marina is open from the end of March to 15 October. It is a three star hotel and offers comfortable rooms with air-conditioning, TV and telephone. The most expensive rooms also have a view over the harbour. Allow between 450FF and 550FF, depending on the season, for a double room overlooking the courtyard, and between 600FF and 1000FF for one with a view over the harbour. Suites are available and cost between 1000FF and 1500FF.

Places to Eat
Budget There are many shops and cafés by the harbour where you can get sandwiches, pizzas and *panini* (bread rolls).

The *Simoni supermarket* is on the southern side of the marina and is open from 7 am to 8 pm daily in the summer and from 8 am to 12.30 pm and 3.30 to 7.30 pm, from Monday to Saturday and Sunday morning, in the winter.

La Grillade (☎ *04 95 73 55 50)*, on the north side of the marina, serves good value, unpretentious food under an arbour of Virginia creeper. Dishes include salads (30FF), sandwiches, omelettes, plates of *charcuterie* (cooked pork meats; 40FF) and barbecued meat in the evening (from 70FF). It's open lunchtimes and evenings daily in the high season, evenings only in low season.

Les Terrasses d'Aragon (☎ *04 95 73 51 07, place Carrega)* is one of the many pizzerias in Bonifacio. It is in the Citadelle, opposite the post office, and has a terrace with a wonderful view. Open daily (closed in January), it serves pizzas (from 40FF to 65FF) and has fixed-price menus.

Mid-Range & Top End *Café de la Poste* (☎ *04 95 73 13 31, 5 rue F Scamaroni)* can cater to all tastes, thanks to its extensive choice: snacks, fixed lunch menus for 58FF (daily special, dessert and a 0.25L carafe of wine), pasta dishes from 48FF, pizzas, grilled meat and fish (grilled swordfish costs 84FF) and fixed menus of Bonifacio specialities for 85FF or 115FF. Meals are served at lunchtime and in the evening year-round. The café's large terrace is near the post office in the Citadelle, very close to the tourist office.

Cantina Doria (☎ *04 95 73 50 49, 27 rue Doria)* is a pleasant little restaurant that has chosen to bring traditional Corsican mountain cuisine down into the Citadelle in Bonifacio. The fixed evening menu (70FF) – Corsican soup with vegetables, beans and ham bone, followed by cheese or a dessert and a 0.25L bottle of wine – is deservedly successful, as is the country atmosphere of the room, where you sit on long wooden benches. The menu also includes a reasonable house wine for 40FF, daily specials for 55FF and an *omelette au brocciu* for 35FF. This 'canteen' is open year-round (except January), daily in the summer, but closed on Sunday and Tuesday evening in the winter.

Les 4 Vents (☎ *04 95 73 07 50, quai Banda del Ferro)*, near the ferry quay, is popular for its fish in the summer and its Alsace specialities in the winter. It serves fixed menus starting at 90FF and is open daily at lunchtime and in the evening in the high season (closed on Tuesday in the low season).

U Castille (☎ *04 95 73 04 99, rue Simon Varsi)* is in a lovely stone room in the heart of the Citadelle. The menu includes fish and meat (from 90FF to 120FF). There is a fixed

THE SOUTH

menu for 120FF (squid *à la romaine*, fillet of bass with saffron, grilled steak with herbs). The restaurant also offers a fixed menu for 80FF, and various pizzas.

The restaurant in the *Hôtel du Centre Nautique* (☎ *04 95 73 02 11)* is on the northern side of the harbour, on the opposite side to most of the restaurants and on the side with the best view of the Citadelle when it is lit up in the evening. This restaurant is only a few metres away from the pontoons and has a very maritime feel, with teak tables and chairs, lighting from storm lamps and so on. It is frequented by a classy clientele from Sperono, some of whom are a little snobbish, but it serves excellent pasta dishes: tagliatelle with artichokes (75FF) or Saint Jacques scallops (95FF), farfalle with aubergines (70FF), macaroni with four cheeses (80FF), linguini with Mediterranean prawns (140FF), and more. A bottle of wine costs between 55FF and 120FF. The restaurant is open at lunchtime and in the evening year-round (food served till about 11 pm) and is a pleasant place to spend the evening, although the bill can easily come to 150FF.

Entertainment

Concerts are sometimes staged on the terraces of the marina's bars and restaurants in the summer.

L'Amnésia (☎ *04 95 72 12 22)* is on the N198, halfway between Bonifacio and Porto Vecchio, and is famous for hosting Eddy Barclay's 'white night'. It is considered to be *the* club in Corsica, and opens at 11 pm. There is a free shuttle service from Bonifacio harbour (it leaves from close to the Eurocorse offices).

Getting There & Away

Air Figari-Sud Corse airport (☎ *04 95 71 10 10)* is in the middle of the maquis, 21km north of Bonifacio, near the village of Figari. This is a good location, as it means the airport can serve both Bonifacio and Porto Vecchio. There are daily flights to Marseille, Nice and Paris, plus charter flights in summer.

Like most airports in Corsica it has no ATMs or bureaux de change, despite being renovated in 1996.

Boat Ferries operated by Moby Lines sail between Santa Teresa di Gallura (Sardinia) and Bonifacio. Moby Lines is an Italian company, represented in Bonifacio by Les Voyages Gazano (☎ 04 95 73 00 29), which is open at the ferry terminal from 7 am to 8 pm and 9.30 to 10 pm, Monday to Friday and Saturday morning, in the summer. There are 10 return services daily to the Sardinian port (crossings take about one hour) between the beginning of April and the end of September.

Also at the terminal is Saremar (☎ 04 95 73 00 96), which operates crossings to Santa Teresa di Gallura daily year-round (four daily in summer, two during the rest of the year). The offices are open from 9 am to 9 pm in summer, and from 9 to 11 am and 2.30 to 4.30 pm during the rest of the year (although the offices are only open at departure times on Sunday in the winter).

The companies charge similar prices: between 48FF and 60FF per person and from 140FF to 240FF per vehicle, one way, depending on the size of vehicle and the season.

The harbour master's office (☎ 04 95 73 10 07, fax 04 95 73 18 73) in Bonifacio is by the marina and is open between 7 am and 10 pm in July and August, from 7.30 am to noon and 3 to 7 pm in June and from 8 am to noon and 2 to 6 pm during the rest of the year. Chandlers, fuel, water and showers (12FF) are available at the harbour. Depending on the season, it costs between 90FF and 127FF to moor a 9 to 10m boat.

Bus Eurocorse (☎ 04 95 21 06 30, 04 95 70 13 83), whose offices by the harbour are open all day, operates services between Bonifacio and Porto Vecchio, Roccapina, Sartène, Propriano, Olmeto, Sainte Marie Sicche and Ajaccio. There are up to four departures daily during the high season (6.30 and 8.30 am and 12.30 and 2.15 pm) and two departures daily in the low season (at 6.30 am and 2 pm, except on Sunday and public holidays). There are two services on Sunday and public holidays in the summer (8.30 am and 2.15 pm). The journey to Ajaccio takes 3½ hours and costs 110FF.

Car There is a Europcar agency (☎ 04 95 73 10 99) on the northern route into town, near the petrol station. It is open daily from 8 am to 1 pm and 3 to 8 pm (daily in July and August), between 1 April and 30 October.

Les Voyages Gazano (☎ 04 95 73 00 29), in the ferry terminal, represents Avis.

As in other towns, the airport has the widest choice of car rental companies. Many companies open specifically for the arrival and departure times of the flights. The main ones are:

Avis	☎ 04 95 71 00 01
Budget	☎ 04 95 71 04 18
Citer	☎ 04 95 71 02 00
Europcar	☎ 04 95 71 01 41
Hertz	☎ 04 95 71 04 16

Getting Around

Bonifacio is a dead end and a trap for vehicles. It has been known for the traffic jam in the town centre to stretch back as far as the roundabout on the main road in summer. There are few car parks in the town centre, and all of them are expensive in the high season. Your best bet is to choose a hotel with a car park and get around on foot.

To/From the Airport Transports Rossi (☎ 04 95 71 00 11) provides a shuttle service between the airport and Bonifacio from the end of June to the beginning of September. The departure times correspond to the arrivals and departures of the flights. The journey to Bonifacio costs 50FF and takes about half an hour. The departures for the airport leave from the harbour car park.

The trip from the airport to the centre of Bonifacio comes to about 185FF in a taxi. Add 50% on Sunday or public holidays, or at night.

BOUCHES DE BONIFACIO

This narrow stretch of sea separates the far south of Corsica from Sardinia and is home to some of the island's natural treasures.

Archipel des Lavezzi

The Archipel des Lavezzi (Lavezzi Archipelago) is a group of about 10 main islands, a protected paradise between sky and sea. The islands' beauty owes a great deal to their colours, ranging from the turquoise and ultramarine of the water to the clear tones of the granite. The rocks have been sculpted by the erosion of sand and sea, and some of them are reminiscent of the scales of a strange sea monster. Others are polished, rounded, and more sensual in form.

Île Lavezzi, which gives its name to the whole archipelago, is the most accessible and the southernmost point of Corsica. The lighthouse keepers are the only inhabitants of this 65 hectare island, which stands out

---

The Sad End of the *Sémillante*

The line of graves in the Achiarino cemetery on the Île Lavezzi is a reminder of the tragic events of the night of 15 February 1855. The *Sémillante* had left Toulon the night before with more than 350 crew and 400 soldiers on board. She was bound for Sebastopol with reinforcements for the Crimean War (1854-56). Heading out at night into the Bonifacio Straits, which were very poorly marked out, the three mast frigate was surprised by a sudden gust of wind and was shipwrecked off the Île Lavezzi with her 773 passengers still on board. Only the captain could be identified and given a named grave; the other victims of the tragedy were buried anonymously in the peaceful little cemetery on the island. In his *Lettres de mon moulin* (published in English as *Letters from my Windmill*), Alphonse Daudet describes the shipwreck, which is still the worst shipping disaster ever in the Mediterranean.

THE SOUTH

because of the purity of its waters and the beauty of its scenery. In the high season there are a number of shuttle services between the island and Bonifacio; take some food and water with you, as there are no facilities on the island. See Boat Trips under Bonifacio for more details of boat trips.

In addition to superb little pools that are perfect for swimming, the island also hosts the cemetery for the victims who perished on board the *Sémillante* (see the boxed text on the previous page).

Although not part of the Réserve Naturelle des Îles Lavezzi, **Île Cavallo**, north of the Îles Lavezzi, is a protected paradise for billionaires. It is almost twice as large as Île Lavezzi and closed to people whose bank balances don't run to the requisite number of digits. It's home to the luxurious villas of the jet set.

Cap Pertusato

Recognisable by its resemblance to a sinking ship, Cap Pertusato (also called Pointe Saint Antoine) is a good place to walk to from Bonifacio. The route along the chalky cliffs from the top of montée Saint Roch is described in the Walking in Corsica chapter. You can also cover the 4km separating it from the town by car if you join the D58 near the hospital. It would be a real challenge to attempt to describe the view from the cape, over the cliffs, the open water, the Îles Lavezzi and the Citadelle. Suffice it to say that the cape is the best spot for a fantastic view of the town from across the open sea that you can get without stepping aboard a boat.

Pointe de Sperono

As a favourite place for international celebrities, Pointe de Sperono is under close surveillance. The golf course overlooking it was created by importing the fertile soil needed to grow the grass for perfect greens and is now one of the most famous in Europe. To the north is the little Plage de Piantarella, which is open to the public. On the beach, Piantarella Nautic (☎ 04 95 73 51 64) hires out inflatable dinghies for 400FF

a day. There is also a snack bar and windsurfing equipment can be hired during the summer.

PORTO VECCHIO (PORTIVECCHJU)
• pop 9400   ✉ 20137

Porto Vecchio owes its appeal not so much to the remains of its Citadelle but more to the superb coastline stretching out on both sides of this odd 'salt city'. The town is also an excellent base if you want to discover Alta Rocca, the Forêt de l'Ospedale, the Bocca di Bavella and Aiguilles de Bavella, and the surrounding villages.

History

In a bid to establish itself on the eastern coast of the island, the Genoese republic set its sights on Porto Vecchio in the 15th century. This site, which was definitely inhabited in ancient times, is set at the back of a deep bay, and provided the best shelter between the fortified towns of Bonifacio and Bastia. The Genoese settled at the top of the bay, where they created the Ville Haute (Upper Town), which they soon fortified with thick ramparts.

This attempt to distance themselves from the dangers of the coastline did not prove successful, however: malaria was prevalent along the coast and decimated the first settlers. A few years later a second attempt to populate the town, this time with forcibly recruited Corsicans, was no more successful. Porto Vecchio was essentially abandoned before re-emerging in 1564, when it was chosen by Sampiero Corso as a new base for his attempts to liberate the island. The town was besieged and forced to capitulate a few months later.

The town did not really begin to thrive until the malaria-infested swamps around it were transformed into salt marshes. Fortified by its new-found healthiness, the town started again from scratch. The beauty of the beaches stretching away on either side of the bay helped to make it the active and popular tourist town that it is today.

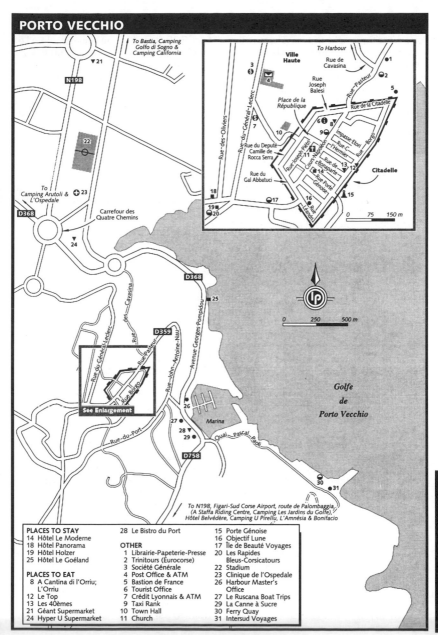

PORTO VECCHIO

To Bastia, Camping
Golfo di Sogno &
Camping California

To
Camping Arutoli &
L'Ospedale

Carrefour des
Quatre Chemins

Ville
Haute

To Harbour

Rue de
Cavasina

Rue
Joseph
Balesi

Place de la
République

Rue du Député
Camille de
Rocca Serra

Rue du
Gal Abbatuci

Citadelle

0   75   150 m

D368

D359

See Enlargement

Marina

Quai   Pascal   Paoli

D758

Golfe
de
Porto Vecchio

0   250   500 m

To N198, Figari-Sud Corse Airport, route de Palombaggia,
(A Staffa Riding Centre, Camping Les Jardins du Golfe),
Hôtel Belvédère, Camping U Pirellu, L'Amnésia & Bonifacio

PLACES TO STAY	28 Le Bistro du Port	15 Porte Génoise
14 Hôtel Le Moderne		16 Objectif Lune
18 Hôtel Panorama	OTHER	17 Île de Beauté Voyages
19 Hôtel Holzer	1 Librairie-Papeterie-Presse	20 Les Rapides
25 Hôtel Le Goéland	2 Trinitours (Eurocorse)	Bleus-Corsicatours
	3 Société Générale	22 Stadium
	4 Post Office & ATM	23 Clinique de l'Ospedale
PLACES TO EAT	5 Bastion de France	26 Harbour Master's
8 A Cantina di l'Orriu;	6 Tourist Office	Office
L'Orriu	7 Crédit Lyonnais & ATM	27 Le Ruscana Boat Trips
12 Le Top	9 Taxi Rank	29 La Canne à Sucre
13 Les 40èmes	10 Town Hall	30 Ferry Quay
21 Géant Supermarket	11 Church	31 Intersud Voyages
24 Hyper U Supermarket		

THE SOUTH

euro currency converter 10FF = €1.52

Orientation

Porto Vecchio is split in two. There is the Ville Haute with its little streets and the ruins of the Citadelle, and below this the more modern harbour, which stretches along ave Georges Pompidou. Rue de Cavasina, which leads off the first roundabout to the north of the marina, links the two parts. The carrefour des Quatre Chemins, to the north, is the focus for much of the activity in the town.

Information

Tourist Office The tourist office (☎ 04 95 70 09 58) is open from 9 am to 8 pm, Monday to Saturday and on Sunday until 1 pm in the summer, and from 9 am to noon and 2 to 6 pm, Monday to Friday and on Saturday morning during the rest of the year. Its on rue du Deputé Camille de Rocca Serra. The staff are efficient and speak English.

Money Crédit Lyonnais, on the corner of rue du Général Leclerc and rue Scamaroni, is not far from the post office. It charges 30FF and 50FF for changing foreign currency and travellers cheques respectively. Eurocheques in French francs are not accepted but there is an ATM outside the bank.

Société Générale on rue du Général Leclerc also has a foreign currency exchange facility. It's open from 8.15 to 11.45 am and 2 to 4.30 pm.

During the summer, the bureau de change in the harbour master's office building, will change foreign currency and travellers cheques for a commission of 20FF. There is an ATM at the post office, which also changes travellers cheques for an average commission of 1.2%.

Post The post office on rue du Général Leclerc is open year-round from 8.30 am to 6 pm, Monday to Friday, and on Saturday morning.

Bookshop Librairie-Papeterie-Presse (☎ 04 95 70 07 71), 12 rue Pasteur, stocks a range of French and foreign newspapers, a small selection of books and stationery. It's open from 7.30 am to 8 pm in summer (closed on Sunday afternoon) and from 8 am to noon and 2 to 7 pm, Monday to Saturday and Sunday morning in the low season.

Laundry There's a laundrette in the same building as the harbour master's office on ave Georges Pompidou (20FF per wash).

Medical Services The Clinique de l'Ospedale, between the Hyper U supermarket and the stadium, close to the carrefour des Quatre Chemins, has an emergency unit (☎ 04 95 72 09 76). The nearest hospital is in Bonifacio.

Ville Haute

There are a few traces of the old Genoese Citadelle here, especially the Porte Génoise and the Bastion de France (closed to the public). The beautiful rue Borgo gives an impression of what the city was once like.

Beaches

Although there is no beach in the town, some of the most famous beaches on the island stretch out on either side of Porto Vecchio. In particular, Plage de Palombaggia and Plage de Santa Giulia are extremely popular in summer. See under Around Porto Vecchio later in this section for more details.

Boat Trips

Le Ruscana is an old fishing boat aboard which you can explore the coast as far as Bonifacio. Its offices (☎ 04 95 71 41 50) are opposite the harbour master's office building at the marina. Commentaries are provided by the friendly crew and the trips last a day, passing the Réserve Naturelle des Îles Cerbicale and the beaches to the south of Porto Vecchio before reaching the Îles Lavezzi, Île Cavallo, the Pointe de Sperono and Bonifacio (weather permitting).

The price of 300FF (children 150FF) includes a picnic and a stop for a swim in a lovely little cove. The ticket office is open from 10 am to 12.30 pm and 5 to 9.30 pm during the summer.

If you would prefer to explore the coast yourself, Locorsa (☎ 04 95 70 12 13), in the harbour master's office building, hires out inflatable dinghies (no permit required); prices start at 600FF per day. Locorsa is open from 9 am to noon and 3 to 8 pm daily in summer, and can also be reached by phone in the low season.

Activities
Riding The A Staffa riding centre (☎ 04 95 70 47 51) is open year-round. To get there, take the N198 south, turn off onto route de Palombaggia, and the centre is on your right after about 300m.

Diving See the Diving chapter for information on diving in the Porto Vecchio area.

Places to Stay – Budget
Camping Arutoli (☎ 04 95 70 12 73) is 1km from the carrefour des Quatre Chemins on the road towards L'Ospedale and Zonza, making it the closest to the town. There are signposts to the site from the D368. The pitches are quiet and shaded by pine trees, the toilet and washing facilities are good and it has a laundrette and a lovely pool. Allow between 29FF and 34FF per adult, depending on the season, and 13FF per tent or car. The site also rents out bungalows sleeping four people for between 1500FF and 2000FF per week, depending on the season.

There are many other camp sites all around the town but you will need a car to get to them. See under Around Porto Vecchio for details.

Although *Hôtel Panorama* (☎ 04 95 70 07 96, 12 rue Jean Nicoli) doesn't have the panoramic view that its name suggests, it is one of the cheapest places in the town, costing 240FF for a double with shared shower and toilet in the summer, or 330FF for a room with en suite shower (a prefabricated cubicle) and toilet. It's a little basic, and prices fall to 220/310FF in June and September. It also has some triples (between 310FF and 360FF) and quads (between 350FF and 390FF). There's a car park.

Places to Stay – Mid-Range
Hôtel Le Goéland (☎ 04 95 70 14 15, ave Georges-Pompidou) owes a great deal of its charm to its waterside location, between the harbour and the roundabout before the carrefour des Quatre Chemins. It's a family-run hotel and a good choice: it's quiet, and has a garden, which is a lovely place to sit for a drink. The atmosphere is pleasant and relaxed. Single or double rooms with shared toilet cost from 250FF to 280FF or 280FF to 330FF, depending on the season, while a double room with a bathroom and toilet costs from 330FF to 440FF. It's open between Easter and November. English and Spanish are both spoken.

Hôtel Holzer (☎ 04 95 70 05 93, 12 rue Jean Jaurès) is not far from the centre of the Ville Haute (it also has a door on rue Jean Nicoli) and offers comfortable, spotless rooms with satellite TV, telephone and air-conditioning; it's open year-round and is a little like a maze. Doubles cost 280/ 380/420FF in winter/July/August. Triples costs 320/420/480FF, while singles cost 260FF year-round, except during August (320FF). The Holzer is a good choice.

Hôtel Le Moderne (☎ 04 95 70 06 36, 10 cours Napoléon) is a white building with blue shutters opposite the church. Its double rooms, with shared toilet, are light and pleasant; these cost 300/350FF in July/ August. Rooms with en suite bathroom cost 350/400FF in July/August. Although the location of the hotel is a little noisy, rooms 20 and 21 look out over a large terrace towering over the town and harbour, and are quieter. The hotel is open between May and October.

Places to Eat
Budget The *Hyper U supermarket* (on the carrefour des Quatre Chemins) and the *Géant supermarket* (on the next roundabout to the north) should be a boon to self-caterers. Both are in large shopping complexes with lots of shops.

Les 40èmes is a crêperie on rue Borgo in the Ville Haute. It serves savoury crêpes costing between 20FF and 54FF. The house

THE SOUTH

specialities are crêpes with mozzarella, such as the *vent d'est* (tomatoes, mozzarella, mint and lemon). It's open from 3 pm to midnight, June to September.

Mid-Range & Top End *A Cantina di l'Orriu* (☎ 04 95 72 14 25, *cours Napoléon*) is a wine bar that serves the same products sold in the shop L'Orriu next door. You can try some excellent Bastelica ham or charcuterie from Evisa (between 60FF and 90FF), Corsican cheese (50FF) or even liver pâté from ducks fed on chestnuts (95FF). For dessert, try the brocciu with sugar and brandy (25FF). This sophisticated little 'canteen' also serves little tasters (15FF) to go with a glass of wine (15FF to 30FF). It is a charming place right in the heart of the Ville Haute and is open from 11 am to 2 pm and 6 to 11 pm, daily except Sunday lunchtime, between May and the end of September.

Le Bistro du Port (☎ 04 95 70 22 96, *ave Georges Pompidou*) has a good reputation for its fish and its 98FF fixed menu: rock fish soup or hot goat's cheese salad, selection of bay fish with sea urchin roe or *bavette* (a cut of beef) with shallots, followed by cheese or dessert. The setting is pleasant and the atmosphere maritime.

In the Ville Haute, rue Borgo is home to a number of restaurants that back on to the ramparts and have lovely terraces facing out over the sea; *Le Top* is one of these. The fixed menu (75FF) consists of marinaded peppers grilled with pesto or lentil salad with brocciu, sardines in lime and chervil sauce or old-fashioned Corsican sautéed veal, followed by a dessert. There is also a wide range of fish dishes on the menu.

Entertainment

Objectif Lune (☎ 04 95 70 47 37, *rue Léandri*) is an active outfit that organises jazz, blues and soul concerts in a venue whose décor owes a great deal to the adventures of Tintin. It is open from 9 pm to 1 am. Draught beer costs between 15FF and 20FF, and cocktails cost between 25FF and 35FF (10FF extra on concert nights).

On the harbour is *La Canne à Sucre* (☎ 04 95 70 35 25), which allows you to while away the evening (until 2 am during the high season) over an ice cream or a cocktail. It's open from June to October.

You'll find the monumental white entrance to *L'Amnésia* (☎ 04 95 72 12 22), supposedly the best night club in Corsica, on the N198, halfway between Porto Vecchio and Bonifacio.

Shopping

L'Orriu (☎ 04 95 70 26 21), on cours Napoléon, is fragrant with the hams hanging from the ceiling, the cheese sitting on the shelves between the bottles of wine and spirits, and the jams and pâtés. It's open from 9 am to 1 pm and 3 pm to midnight daily in the high season (closed in November and March).

Getting There & Away

Air Figari-Sud Corse airport is only about 20km away from Porto Vecchio. See Bonifacio Getting There & Away for more details of flights.

Bus Les Rapides Bleus-Corsicatours (☎ 04 95 70 10 36), 7 rue Jean Jaurès, operates a twice-daily service (daily in winter except Sunday and public holidays) to Bastia via Sainte Lucie de Porto Vecchio, Solenzara and Ghisonaccia (115FF, departures at 8 am and 1.30 pm). They also operate a shuttle service to Santa Giulia in the summer, via Camping Arutoli (15FF, four shuttles daily). The office is open from 8.30 am to noon and 2 to 6.30 pm, Monday to Friday, and Saturday morning.

Île de Beauté Voyages (☎ 04 95 70 12 31), 13 rue du Général de Gaulle, represents Balési Évasion, whose buses go to Ajaccio via the mountains (Zonza, Bavella, Aullène and so on). Buses depart daily except Sunday and public holidays in July and August, and on Monday and Friday only in winter (110FF to Ajaccio, 35FF to Zonza).

Eurocorse is represented by Trinitours (☎ 04 95 70 13 83), on rue Pasteur, which can be found at the Cavasina junction on the way into the Citadelle. Eurocorse operates a service to Ajaccio along the coast (via Bonifacio, Sartène and Propriano). In summer there are four services daily between Monday and Saturday and two on Sunday and public holidays; inquire in advance for the winter timetable. During the high season, the same company operates a shuttle service to Bonifacio (36FF, 30 minutes) and a 'beach service' to Palombaggia (20FF, 30 minutes). Trinitours is open from 8.30 am to noon and 2 to 6.30 pm, Monday to Friday, and on Saturday morning.

Buses depart from in front of the offices.

Car There are car hire facilities in the building housing the harbour master's office on ave Georges Pompidou. Budget, Europcar (☎ 04 95 70 24 49) and Citer (☎ 04 95 70 16 96) are all represented and open in the summer.

The following car hire companies are represented at Figari-Sud Corse airport:

Avis	☎ 04 95 71 00 01
Budget	☎ 04 95 71 04 18
Citer	☎ 04 95 71 02 00
Europcar	☎ 04 95 71 01 41
Hertz	☎ 04 95 71 04 16

Boat The *Monte d'Oro* can take more than 500 passengers. It links Porto Vecchio with Marseille (SNCM) on mainland France and with Livorno in Italy (Corsica Marittima).

SNCM and Corsica Marittima are both represented by Intersud Voyages (☎ 04 95 70 06 03), whose offices can be found in the tinted-glass building topped with a red metal column opposite the ferry quay.

There are about 100 moorings in the marina in Porto Vecchio that are reserved for visitors. The harbour master's office (☎ 04 95 70 17 93) is housed in a building on ave Georges Pompidou that is home to a number of different shops and services, including car hire and a laundrette. Showers, fuel, water and chandlers are to be found at the marina. During the high season, the harbour master's office is open between 8 am and 9 pm, and in the low season it is open

during normal office hours. Allow between 64FF and 121FF, depending on the season, to moor a 9 to 10m boat.

Getting Around
To/From the Airport A shuttle service is operated by Transports Rossi (☎ 04 95 71 00 11) between Figari-Sud Corse airport and Porto Vecchio from the end of June to the beginning of September. The times of the buses correspond to flight arrival and departure times. The journey takes 30 minutes and costs 50FF. The buses depart from the Bar de la Marine by the harbour.

Allow about 230FF for a taxi (320FF on Sunday, on public holidays and at night).

Taxi There is a taxi rank (☎ 04 95 70 08 49) on cours Napoléon.

AROUND PORTO VECCHIO
Although it is difficult to believe when you see the coastline around Porto Vecchio, this stretch of the coast was once a health hazard due to malaria. Between the Golfe de Pinarellu and the Golfe de Sant'Amanza the serrated coastline is softened by stretches of beautiful white sand lapped by clear waters. Sadly, these heavenly beaches are no secret and often get extremely overcrowded at the peak of the tourist season.

South of Porto Vecchio
For some people, the best example of the beauty of the Corsican coastline is **Palombaggia**. This long ribbon of sand edged by pine trees opposite the Réserve Naturelle des Îles Cerbicale is without doubt the most famous beach in the south of the island, and is definitely the most popular in the summer. **Santa Giulia**, at the back of its own bay a few kilometres farther south, is almost as beautiful.

The road to Palombaggia is well marked. It turns off the N198 to the south of Porto Vecchio; it's 14km from here to the beach.

Places to Stay & Eat There's a string of camp sites along the road to Palombaggia, and during the high season bars and

THE SOUTH

restaurants open along the edge of the beach. Santa Giulia is more oriented towards visitors staying in holiday villages and offers few opportunities for the independent traveller.

Camping Les Jardins du Golfe (☎ 04 95 70 46 92, route de Palombaggia) is 4km from Porto Vecchio and 10km from the Plage de Palombaggia. It's open year-round and has a pizzeria, a supermarket, children's play areas and table-tennis tables. A spot in the shade of the site's palm trees costs 14/32/14FF per person/tent/car in the high season.

Camping U Pirellu (☎ 04 95 70 63 13) is about 4km from the Plage de Palombaggia. It's open from Easter to the end of September and has a lovely pool, a supermarket, good shower and toilet blocks, a bar, a pizzeria, half-size tennis courts (50FF per hour), mini golf (25FF) and a sauna. It costs from 12/28/12FF to 15/38/15FF per person/tent/car, depending on the season.

Hôtel Belvédère (☎ 04 95 70 54 13, fax 04 95 70 42 63) is 6km from town on the edge of the Golfe de Porto Vecchio. It is an intimate three star hotel with 16 rooms (with balconies) and three suites, all with air-conditioning, TV, telephone and minibar. The Belvédère has a large swimming pool and lovely gardens. Prices for a double range from 270FF to 990FF, depending on the season. The hotel restaurant serves some tempting dishes.

North of Porto Vecchio

The N198 goes north from Porto Vecchio to Trinité de Porto Vecchio where the D468 turns off to the east and heads towards the popular beaches at **Cala Rossa** and the **Baie de San Ciprianu**. Farther to the north is the stunning peninsular of **Pinarellu** (Pinaraddu) with its Genoese tower and beautiful stretches of sand all around.

If you get fed up with white sand, turquoise sea, shady pine trees and the warmth of the sun, head for the village of **Lecci**, just before Sainte Lucie de Porto Vecchio on the main road. As you come into the village you will see a sign for the **Domaine de Torraccia** (☎ 04 95 71 43 50), another 1.5km towards the sea. The owners of this 43 hectare estate produce sweet wines, marc brandy, olives and oil, but the estate is best known for its red, rosé and white wines, costing between 30FF and 35FF per bottle.

The Domaine de Toraccia red is excellent and l'Orriu (52FF), a 'prestige' vintage from grapes of outstanding years, is certainly one of the best Corsican red wines. Torraccia is also one of the few wine-producers which allows its red wine to mature and you can buy vintage bottles there. In summer the estate is open from 8 am to noon and 2 to 8 pm, Monday to Saturday (to 6 pm in the low season).

Places to Stay & Eat *Camping Golfo di Sogno (☎ 04 95 70 08 98)* is about 6km

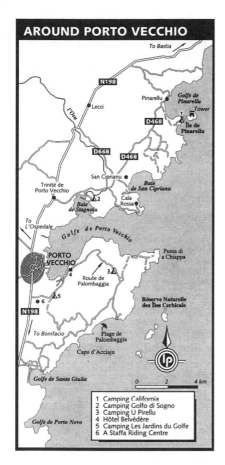

AROUND PORTO VECCHIO

To Bastia

N198

Pinarellu

Golfe de Pinarellu

Lecci

D468

Île de Pinarellu

Tower

D668   D468

San Ciprianu

Trinité de Porto Vecchio

Baie de San Ciprianu

Cala Rossa

Baie de Stagnolu

Golfe de Porto Vecchio

To L'Ospedale

PORTO VECCHIO

Punta di a Chiappa

Route de Palombaggia

N198

To Bonifacio

Réserve Naturelle des Îles Cerbicale

Plage de Palombaggia

Capu d'Acciaju

Golfe de Santa Giulia

0   2   4 km

Golfe de Porto Novo

1 Camping California
2 Camping Golfo di Sogno
3 Camping U Pirellu
4 Hôtel Belvédère
5 Camping Les Jardins du Golfe
6 A Staffa Riding Centre

north-east of Porto Vecchio on the N198 and D468, in the Baie de Stagnolu. It's open from 1 May to mid-November and is essentially a luxury camp site. It has large green pitches, a bar, a restaurant, direct access to the beach, two tarmac tennis courts (70FF per hour) and facilities for hiring mountain bikes or windsurfing equipment. A pitch costs 60FF for a tent and a car, plus 34FF per person. The camp site also has basic bungalows.

Camping California (☎ *04 95 71 49 24*) is about 10km farther along the D468,

on the Pinarellu peninsula. There are two beaches (nudist sunbathing is allowed on one of them) stretching out on either side of this site, which has good shower and toilet facilities and a tennis court (60FF per hour). It's open from June to September and costs 15/33/9FF per person/pitch/car.

Places to eat open along the beach during the high season.

Alta Rocca

Alta Rocca is a region crisscrossed by footpaths, nestling in the foothills of the mountain range which forms the spine of the island and looking out towards the Golfe de Porto Vecchio to the east. The tranquillity of L'Ospedale, the prehistoric remains in Levie and the area around it, the beauty of the villages clinging to the rocks and the stunning Bavella massif all combine to make Alta Rocca a region worth visiting.

The tourist office (☎ 04 95 78 41 95, fax 04 95 78 46 74) for the Alta Rocca region is in Levie.

GETTING THERE & AWAY

Autocars Ricci (☎ 04 95 51 08 19) operates a daily year-round service between Ajaccio and Zonza via Propriano, Sartène, Sainte Lucie de Tallano and Levie. The fare from Ajaccio to Zonza is about 90FF. Buses depart from Ajaccio at 4 pm, Propriano at 5.45 pm, Sartène at 6 pm and Sainte Lucie de Tallano at 6.30 pm, arriving in Zonza at about 6.50 pm. Coming from the other direction, buses leave Zonza at 6 am and arrive in Ajaccio at 8.50 am. The service goes on to the Bocca di Bavella in summer.

Balési Évasion (☎ 04 95 70 15 55) has services linking Zonza (and Bavella in summer) to L'Ospedale, Porto Vecchio, Quenza and Ajaccio. In summer buses run daily except Sunday. During the rest of the year, services run on Monday and Friday only; they terminate in Zonza, but if you ask in advance they will take you on to Bavella, if the pass is open.

THE SOUTH

Buses from Porto Vecchio leave from the offices of Île de Beauté Voyages. The fare from Porto Vecchio to Zonza is 35FF.

L'OSPEDALE

L'Ospedale holds a special place in the hearts of the inhabitants of Porto Vecchio. The area takes its names from a former 'hospital', or health spa, and has long been synonymous with peace and coolness away from the heat of the coast. About 1km up from the village of L'Ospedale, the **Forêt de l'Ospedale** starts. It covers vast plains above Porto Vecchio, and still bears the scars of recent fires in 1990 and 1994.

A short way into the forest on the D368 from L'Ospedale, a road branches off to the left for the hamlet of Cartalavonu. After about 2km on this you can turn off onto the **Sentiers des Rochers** (Rock Path), also known as the Sentiers des Taffoni, an ideal way to explore this tranquil forest of laricio pines on foot.

The path has been well marked out by the ONF and is a good place for an easy, mainly flat walk among the trees and the *taffoni*, cavities formed in the rocks by erosion (see Geology in the Facts about Corsica chapter). After about 30 minutes you come to a little grassy plain littered with rocks, which is crossed by the Mare a Mare Sud walk. The view from here is wonderful.

If you're feeling brave you can continue along the path (which is now not as well-marked) to the left towards Punta di a Vacca Morta (1314m), from where you can look down over the Golfe de Porto Vecchio and the Lac de l'Ospedale. You can also start the walk at the Refuge de Cartalavonu or the Bocca a Melu on the Mare a Mare Sud.

The forestry lodge at Marghese (☎ 04 95 70 01 49), a short distance along the road to Cartalavonu from the D368, organises walks in the forest accompanied by ONF guides, leaving at 9 am on Friday morning during July and August.

If you continue on the D368 towards Zonza, you will come to the lake formed by the Barrage de l'Ospedale, from where you

can walk to the **Cascade de Piscia di Gallo** (see Strolls & Country Walks in the Walking in Corsica chapter).

Places to Stay & Eat

Le Refuge (☎ 04 95 70 00 39) in Cartalavonu is popular with walkers tackling the Mare a Mare Sud. The shelter is open year-round and has good dormitories (with bathroom) sleeping six people, and with a large common room, for 60FF per night (160FF half board). There are also three lovely double rooms costing 260FF. The restaurant serves good home-cooked food: mountain soup, *figatellu* (liver sausage) in winter, blood sausage or braised lamb and chestnut polenta with brocciu. The refuge is in a pretty stone building, right at the end of the village.

ZONZA

• pop 2600

This mountain village was briefly home to the exiled Mohammed V of Morocco in 1953 before he moved on to Île Rousse, and is now frequented by walkers and those heading for the famous peaks of Bavella by car. Its excellent location goes some way towards explaining the village's amazing hotel resources.

Places to Stay & Eat

Camping Municipal de Zonza (☎ 04 95 78 62 74) is a haven of tranquillity in the depths of the forest, on the D368 3km east of the village. It's open between mid-May and the end of September and charges 20/14/14FF per person/tent/car or motorcycle. There are very few camper vans on the site and the facilities are clean.

Hôtel-Restaurant de la Terrasse (☎ 04 95 78 67 69) is the least expensive hotel in Zonza, with double rooms costing between 220FF and 270FF. The cheapest room is a little on the dark side but the others are acceptable and all have en suite bathroom. You can try home-made charcuterie in the restaurant. The hotel is open from 1 April to 31 October.

Hôtel-Restaurant l'Incudine (☎ *04 95 78 67 71)* has good double rooms with bathroom, with prices starting at 260FF. Half board is obligatory in July and August, costing from 260FF to 290FF per person, depending on the room. The restaurant has a fixed menu for 100FF consisting of wild boar pâté, Corsican veal chop or sirloin grilled over a wood fire and home-made desserts.

Hôtel-Restaurant Le Tourisme (☎ *04 95 78 67 72)* has 13 bedrooms with TV, telephone and balcony. It's a good hotel, open from 1 May to the end of October. Doubles cost from 250FF to 320FF in the low season and 280FF to 360FF in the high season.

L'Aiglon (☎ *04 95 78 67 79)* is a restaurant with a good reputation for local cuisine. The fixed menu costing 115FF promises a leg of pork with creamy fig sauce followed by a sophisticated home-made dessert. The A Muntanera selection (90FF) includes brocciu, grilled figatellu, chestnut polenta and a spinach gratin. The restaurant is part of a family-run hotel with small but pretty, well-kept rooms, available on a half-board basis only.

QUENZA

This little village is a gem set high up in the mountains a few kilometres to the west of Zonza along the D420, which then continues to Aullène. The village has a number of sporting facilities and is dealt with in more detail in the Walking in Corsica chapter (see Stage 14 of the GR20).

CONCA

Backing onto the mountains but still close to the coast (6km as the crow flies), Conca is a little town nestling at the foot of Punta d'Ortu (695m), best known to walkers as the end (or start) of the GR20.

The *gîte d'étape* (mountain lodge) *La Tonnelle* (☎ *04 95 71 46 55)* is clean, functional and open year-round. It's on the road into the village, just opposite the cemetery, and is run by Michael Follacci, a cook,

walker and traveller who can speak some English. A night in a room sleeping two/three/four people costs 100/80/70FF per person. Each room has an en suite bathroom and there's a large common room and a kitchenette. It's also possible to camp for about 30FF per person. Breakfast costs 30FF and lunch or dinner is 70FF. Foreign currency can be changed here and staff at the gîte can arrange a shuttle service on request to Sainte Lucie de Porto Vecchio (15FF) to connect with the bus for Porto Vecchio.

Hôtel San Pasquale (☎ *04 95 71 56 13, fax 04 95 71 42 10)* charges between 200FF and 350FF, depending on the time of year, for a double room with bathroom. The setting of the hotel is pleasant and the rooms are functional.

There's a choice of snack bars and restaurants in the centre of the village. Conca also has a post office and a well-stocked grocery, open daily in summer.

There are no public transport services to Conca. Ask at La Tonnelle for more information on transport options.

AIGUILLES DE BAVELLA

Bocca di Bavella (Bavella Pass; 1218m), 9km above Zonza, is overlooked by the imposing silhouette of one of the most beautiful landscape features in the south of Corsica: the Aiguilles de Bavella. These peaks, which rise to a height of more than 1600m and which are also known as the Cornes d'Asinao (Asinao Horns), are jagged points, the colour of which changes depending on the position of the sun in the sky, ranging from ochre to golden. Behind these stone 'needles' looms the profile of Monte Incudine (2134m), which the GR20 links to the Bocca di Bavella. From the pass you can see the statue of Notre Dame (or Madone) des Neiges. If you look farther, you may be able to see the horns of mouflons (mountain sheep) which frequent the area.

The Bavella massif is a wonderful place for climbing, canyoning and walking. There

THE SOUTH

is also an alpine version of the GR20 which splits off beyond Notre Dame des Neiges and allows you to approach the peaks. Some of the guides in the area meet at the *Auberge du Col de Bavella (☎ 04 95 57 43 87)*; look out in particular for Jean-Paul Quilici and Didier Micheli. The alternative alpine route on the GR20 is described, along with the rest of the walk, in the Walking in Corsica chapter.

ARCHAEOLOGICAL SITES OF PIANA DE LEVIE

The *piana* (Corsican for the French *commune*, a small administrative area) of Levie is home to two remarkable archaeological sites: the *castelli* (castles) of Cucuruzzu and Capula. The Cucuruzzu site was discovered in 1963 and is an interesting example of Bronze Age monumental architecture. Set in a chaotic granite landscape, the remains indicate that this was the site of a genuine, organised community whose activities were originally based on farming and agriculture, but diversified during the recent Bronze Age (1200 to 900 BC) to include milling, pottery and weaving. The Castellu de Capula is more recent, although it is likely that it coincided with the Cucuruzzu village at some point; it was probably inhabited into the Middle Ages.

Besides a wonderful view over the Aiguilles de Bavella, these castelli are worth a detour for their presentation as much as anything. Personal stereos are provided at the entrance to the site, with a recorded commentary backed by traditional polyphonic chants (see Arts in the Facts about Corsica chapter) which brings what is essentially ineloquent material to life with explanations of such things as the taffoni, the chestnut trees and even the use of granite in Corsican architecture over thousands of years. The commentaries are available in French, English, Italian and German.

The archaeological sites (☎ 04 95 78 48 21) are signposted to the right off the D268, 3.5km after the village of Levie in the direction of Sainte Lucie de Tallano, and are

about 4km after the turn-off. Allow about 1½ hours for the visit, which follows a circular route. Opening hours are 9 am to 6 pm (8 pm in July and August) daily from April to October. The admission price of 25FF (13FF for children) includes the loan of the personal stereo, but you do have to leave a form of identification as a deposit.

LEVIE (LIVIA)

The peaceful village of Levie was a bastion of Corsican resistance during WWII and is now frequented by walkers on the Mare a Mare Sud route. One of the main attractions of the hamlet is its **archaeological museum** (Musée de l'Alta Rocca; ☎ 04 95 78 47 98), which is not to be missed. It is currently housed in the stables of a former residence of the Spanish ambassador, just behind the village hall, but there are plans to move it into a larger building.

The museum includes a presentation of the geology, climate, flora and fauna of the island, but more importantly this is where the Dame de Bonifacio (Bonifacio Woman), the oldest human remains found in Corsica, is displayed. The 'young' lady is thought to have lived on the island about 8500 years ago and it is amazing how much scientists have been able to conclude about the state of her health at her death, which was probably a result of a lesion to the first right molar.

The museum also displays cutting tools made of obsidian, flint and rhyolite, arrow heads, Neolithic vases and some wonderful Bronze Age pottery.

The Iron Age is represented here by a woman's skeleton which was found at the Capula site, textiles and jewellery (bracelets, brooches, chains, rings and belt buckles) with some remarkable workmanship. There's also a Genoese coin.

Places to Stay

The *Gîte d'Étape de Levie (☎ 04 95 78 46 41)* is in a stone building above the police station. It's open from April to October and charges 65FF per night (160FF for half board).

SAINTE LUCIE DE TALLANO (SANTA LUCIA DI TALLA)
• pop 430

Sainte Lucie de Tallano would definitely be among the contenders if anyone decided to award a prize for the prettiest village in Corsica. Although time has robbed the hamlet of many of its inhabitants, it has taken away none of the charm of its little houses with their reddish-orange tiled roofs, nestled tightly together against the deep green backdrop of the surrounding forest and maquis.

The village has restaurants and cafés, a post office, and an information centre (☎ 04 95 78 80 13) in the village hall. Open from June to mid-September, the centre is a veritable mine of information; you can hire a personal stereo with a commentary (10FF) for a tour of the village.

Throughout the summer there are twice-daily visits to the **moulin à huile** (oil mill), which illustrates the importance of olive trees in the history of the village. Sainte Lucie de Tallano is also famous for its deposits of **orbicular diorite**, which are no longer mined. This is a rare igneous rock with distinctive grey cavities that has been used to decorate the pedestal of the war memorial in the village square. The **Église Sainte Lucie** is also worth a visit, as is the Renaissance-style **Couvent Saint François**. This is an imposing building which sometimes stages theatrical events. It's on the edge of the village on road to Levie. Ask for the key at the bars and restaurants in the village square if it's closed.

Craft fairs are held in Sainte Lucie de Tallano in early March (Fête de l'Olive) and around 20 July.

Places to Stay & Eat

The *Gîte d'Étape U Fragnonu* (☎ 04 95 78 82 56) is about 300m away from the main square, in the direction of Zonza. It has nine spacious dormitories, each with four beds and a spotless en suite bathroom. The building is modern and offers an exceptional level of comfort for a gîte, including a large, pleasant common room. Open year-round, it charges 70FF a night. Non-walkers are strongly encouraged to go for half board at 170FF. You are unlikely to regret it: the lasagne with brocciu and spinach, pork with cep, corn polenta and veal casserole are certainly worth it. There are also restaurants under the plane trees on the main square.

MONTAGNE DE CAGNA

This isolated massif overlooks Figari, and is famous for the **Uomo di Cagna**, a huge rock balanced on a block of granite at the summit, the shape of which resembles a human profile. The Cagna mountain has wonderful views and is a popular place for a walk. The climb starts from Giannuccio, a village at the end of the D50 north of Monacia d'Aullène. The path, which goes through impressive granite landscapes, is roughly marked out with cairns and starts above the highest house in the village. Make sure you take some water with you if you plan to go as far as the hamlet of Uomo di Cagna, which is a three hour walk away.

The Eastern Plain

LA CASINCA

A few kilometres south-west of Bastia-Poretta airport is the small region of La Casinca, stretching along the eastern side of Monte Sant'Angelu (1218m) between the Golo and the Fium'Alto rivers. From Torra (on the N198 north-east of Vescovato) the D237 wends its way through La Casinca's traditional villages for about 20km. It takes a few hours to follow this route; more if you stop for a meal in Vescovato.

Vescovato to Castellare di Casinca

Formerly a fortified town, hilltop **Vescovato** (population 2350) got its name from the word *vescovo* (bishop); it was the site of the bishops' palace in the 15th century, before this was transferred to Bastia.

It is best to leave your car at the edge of the village and explore the little alleyways and stairways between the tall houses on foot. At the top of the village is a wide square lined with plane trees and several little cafés. This leads on to the Baroque **Église San Martino**, built on a small terrace that overlooks the roofs of the surrounding houses. If you want to look inside, ask the neighbours for the keys.

If you carry on past Vescovato cemetery to the south-east you'll come to **Venzolasca** (population 1500). To the north of this village is the *Ferme-Auberge U Frangnu* (☎ 04 95 36 62 33), one of the prettiest restaurants in the area. It is run by a hearty young grandfather who serves a fixed-price menu (150FF at lunchtime, 180FF in the evening) around an olive press inside or on an outside terrace overlooking the fields. Children's meals are half-price or 50FF, depending on the age of the child. The restaurant is open every evening in summer, and on Thursday, Friday and Saturday evenings and Sunday lunchtime during the rest of the year (closed in October). Bookings are essential.

The road continues to **Loreto di Casinca** (D7), **Penta di Casinca** (D206) and **Castellare di Casinca** before returning to the N198, passing **Chapelle San Pancraziu** on the way.

LA CASTAGNICCIA

Bordered by the Golo river to the north, the Tavignano river to the south and the central mountains to the west, La Castagniccia owes its name to the Genoese, who planted its first chestnut trees in the 16th century (see the boxed text 'Corsican Manna' on page 305). It is scattered with streams, hills and mountains and covered with a dense blanket of vegetation, from which emerge villages linked by small, sinuous roads.

The region was one of the main bastions of nationalism in the 18th century. During the 19th century it had more than 50,000 inhabitants and was the most prosperous region on the island, but it suffered severe depopulation after WWI and today its villages are almost deserted. Tourist accommodation in the area is extremely limited.

La Porta & Around

La Porta, the former capital of La Castagniccia, can be reached via a little road (the D506) that winds through chestnut trees. The **Église Saint Jean Baptiste** is at the entrance to the town. Built between 1648 and 1680, and recently renovated, it is now among the most beautiful Baroque buildings on the island. Its traditional organ, which dates back to 1780, was originally destined for the Couvent Saint Antoine de Casabianca but was offered to the church at the time of the French Revolution by Commissioner Salicetti. An annual concert of classical organ music is made into a CD (it's available at the little grocery shop on the main street or can be ordered by email from coriolan@wanadoo.fr).

The ruins of **Couvent Saint Antoine de Casabianca** (destroyed by Commissioner Salicetti) are at the Bocca de Saint Antoine about 8km north of La Porta on the D515. This community was founded in 1420 and it was here that Pascal Paoli was proclaimed general of the nation.

Morosaglia, north-west along the D71 (via Quercitello, about 15km from La Porta), is the birthplace of Pascal Paoli and boasts a **museum** in his honour. The museum is open daily (except Tuesday) from 9 am to noon and 2.30 to 7.30 pm in summer, 9 am to noon and 1 to 5 pm during the rest of the year. Admission costs 10FF.

From the Bocca di u Pratu (along the D71 from Morosaglia) a footpath leads to **Monte San Petrone** (1767m), the highest point in La Castagniccia. Allow four to six hours for the return climb.

Walking La Porta is the starting point for a number of paths crisscrossing the heights of La Castagniccia. Suitable for walkers of all abilities, the paths are an easy way to reach the passes (such as **Bocca di u Pratu**, 70 minutes), or other villages such as **Quercitello** (20 minutes), **Croce** (40 minutes) or **Ficaja**. Even in midsummer the paths are cool in the shade of the forest, which gets more dense after La Porta. There are also a number of walks starting at Croce.

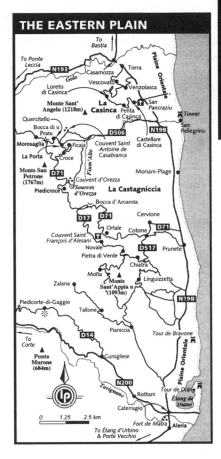

Horse Riding Soliva riding centre (☎ 04 95 39 22 92) in Croce (at an altitude of 800m) organises horse riding for riders of all abilities; it costs 400FF per person per day, including a meal, in groups of 10 to 12 people. The centre has a restaurant (see under Places to Stay & Eat).

Places to Stay & Eat The only way to find accommodation in La Porta itself (there are no hotels) is to contact *Felix Taddei* (☎ 04 95 39 20 51), who rents out two rooms in a building next to the post

The Waters of Orezza

The Sources d'Orezza were classified as producing among the 'iron-bearing, sparkling waters of France' at the beginning of the 19th century; some people even said they had 'the most powerful iron-bearing water in France, if not the world'. In 1866 the water began to be bottled and distributed across the island and exported to mainland France, and in 1896 a thermal spa centre with massage rooms, showers and baths was built. Pascal Paoli came here every year to recuperate, as did the polite society of Bastia and Ajaccio. The English discovered Orezza in the early 20th century.

Despite the competition from mainland spas Orezza developed rapidly, but the buildings had to be abandoned in 1934 after a violent storm destroyed the pipes. During WWII the occupying Germans set up a small bottling plant; after the war the property changed hands numerous times but the little bottles with the green caps continued to be sold. When no buyer could be found in 1995 production had to stop, but the springs were finally bought by the Conseil Générale de Haute-Corse, which plans to restore the buildings. Until that time you can refresh yourself with sparkling water direct from the springs.

office. The usual cost is about 200FF per room.

Chez Élisabeth (☎ 04 95 39 22 00), on the main road, is the only decent restaurant in the village. Its large dining room has bay windows overlooking the gardens of surrounding houses. There are fixed-price Corsican menus (100FF and 150FF) and generous pizzas (35FF to 45FF, evenings only). The restaurant is open daily between mid-March and mid-November, closed on Monday during the rest of the year. Booking is recommended. It is worth arriving before or after the tourist coaches.

Soliva riding centre (see under Horse Riding) has four bedrooms, each with a bathroom and four bunk beds. Accommodation costs 130FF per person with breakfast, 200FF for half board.

La Porta to Cervione

From La Porta the D515 goes through Ficaja and Croce before rejoining the D71 towards the **Vallée d'Orezza**, where you can visit the **Couvent d'Orezza**, now in ruins, and the **Sources d'Orezza** (see the boxed text above). On the way out of **Piedicroce** take the D146 towards **Bocca d'Arcarota**, then the D17 towards the old **Couvent Saint François d'Alesani**.

To get back down to Cervione via Cotone from Bocca d'Arcarota, take the D71, or the D17 to **Novale** and **Chiatra**, turning north on the D517 to Cotone when you come to the **Barrage de Alesani**.

Places to Stay & Eat *Hôtel Le Refuge* (☎ 04 95 35 82 05, 04 95 35 81 08) is in a characterless, modern, one storey building in Piedicroce. The best rooms have a spectacular view over the valley; doubles overlooking the valley cost 280FF, while those on the road side cost 250FF (with shower and toilet). The hotel also has a restaurant. It is closed between 15 November and Easter.

Auberge des Deux Vallées (☎/fax 04 95 35 91 20) at Bocca d'Arcarata is open between May and September. A pleasant chalet-style building with a terrace facing Monte San Petrone, this walkers' refuge contains 10 beds. A night in the six bed dormitory costs 60FF; a double room with bunk beds costs 120FF or 150FF, depending on the season. The shelter serves a fixed menu costing 80FF, which includes cold cooked meats, *figatellu* (liver sausage), fromage frais fritters, and trout stuffed with fromage frais. A bed and a meal costs 160FF for walkers.

The austere stone walls of Sartène have seen some bloody vendettas.

OLIVIER CIRENDINI

The Funtanaccia dolmen, one of the megalithic sites on the Cauna plateau not far from Sartène.

OLIVIER CIRENDINI

JEAN-BERNARD CARILLET

The spectacular jagged peaks of the Aiguilles de Bavella (Bavella needles) shouldn't be missed.

OLIVIER CIRENDINI

Dam at the gorge of Scala di Santa Regina.

JEAN-BERNARD CARILLET

The gentle landscape of the Coscione plateau.

Corsican Manna

There were chestnut trees in Corsica before the arrival of the Genoese but the latter encouraged chestnut growing in the late Middle Ages. Before long, chestnut trees had colonised La Castagniccia (from *castagnu*, meaning chestnut).

The nuts were turned into flour, which rapidly became one of the staple ingredients of the islanders' diet – it is used to make polenta. Chestnuts became the focal point of the local economy and were even used as a currency. Many were exported to mainland France.

The chestnut industry began to decline after WWI: depopulation, ink and hemp disease, the failure to replant, and damage by wild pigs, which tear up the roots and furrow the soil, dealt a fatal blow to an industry and methods which had not changed for centuries. Just 2000 tonnes of chestnuts were harvested in 1992, compared with 150,000 tonnes in the 1880s.

Cervione

This village is home to the **Musée Ethnographique** (☎ 04 95 38 12 83), open from 10 am to noon and 2.30 to 6 pm, Monday to Saturday. Its rich and varied collection covers a wide range of island traditions and skills. It's in the community centre in the heart of town.

PLAINE ORIENTALE

Stretching from Bastia in the north to Aleria in the south (nearly 70km), this alluvial plain – a flat landscape surrounded by a narrow sandy strip – is the only real plain in Corsica. It was uninhabited until WWII because of the prevalence of malaria; the first people to exploit the land were Algerian repatriates, who were given government sponsorship to plant vines and use modern farming techniques in the 1960s (see the boxed text 'Simeoni's Stand' on the next page). The government encouraged the creation of wine cooperatives and built dams to improve irrigation. Today, production also includes citrus fruits, including clementines and citrons, and kiwi fruit.

The region's narrow beach stretches over over tens of kilometres; it is fairly uninspiring but a number of tourist complexes have sprung up along the coast for avid sunworshippers, especially just to the south of Bastia (see Around Bastia in the Bastia & the Far North chapter) and around Aleria.

ALERIA
• pop 2050

Formerly the capital of Corsica, known as Alalia, Aleria is a charmless little town on the N198 between Bastia and Porto Vecchio. It has few attractions but its Roman ruins and archaeological museum are worth a visit. The Étang de Diane and Étang d'Urbino to the north and south, respectively, are excellent places for walking, as are the banks of the Tavignano river.

Information
Tourist Office The tourist office (☎ 04 95 57 01 51), on the main road, is open from 9 am to 12.30 pm and 3.30 to 8 pm in summer, from 9 am to noon and 3 to 7 pm during the rest of the year. It runs free trips to the Roman ruins and the Étang de Diane. Staff speak English.

Money There are a number of banks with ATMs along the main road. You can change money at Crédit Agricole, open from 8.15 to 11.55 am and 1.30 to 4.45 pm, next to Super U supermarket, and at Marina d'Aleria camp site.

Musée Archéologique Jérôme Carcopino & Roman Ruins
Jérôme Carcopino Archaeological Museum (named after the historian of ancient Rome) is in the magnificent **Fort de Matra**. Built by the Genoese in 1484, it towers over the Vallée du Tavignano and the Étang de Diane. The objects on display were unearthed at the former site of Alalia and bear witness to the town's Etruscan, Phocaean and Roman

past. The exhibition rooms are open from 8 am to noon and 2 to 7 pm in summer, to 5 pm during the rest of the year. Combined admission to the museum and the Roman ruins costs 10FF.

The ruins are a 300m walk south-west of the fort. Excavations started in 1921 but were first organised in a methodical way in 1958. The site now boasts the remains of a forum, a citadel, some temples and part of the centre of the Roman town, but most of the city is still to be excavated.

Activities

Marina d'Aleria camp site (see under Places to Stay) hires out bicycles by the hour (20FF) or day (80FF), as well as windsurfing equipment (50FF per hour), kayaks (30FF per hour), one-person boats (60FF per hour) and two-person canoes (45FF per hour).

Domaine de Bravone naturist club (see under Places to Stay) has a diving centre. A 2½ hour dive costs 1700FF (children 1000FF).

Organised Tours

ONF (☎ 04 95 32 81 90 in Bastia) organises trips to the Forêt de Marmanu (Tuesday at

Simeoni's Stand

On 21 August 1975 Edmond Simeoni, the leader of the pro-independence movement, barricaded himself in a wine cellar in Aleria to protest against the French government's financial support of repatriates from Algeria who were living in this fertile region in the 1960s, and who Simeoni considered to be 'dispossessing' the native Corsicans. The police attacked, with fatal consequences: two policemen lost their lives. This was the first event which drew attention to the growing conflict between the nationalists and the 'invaders' – the French state and the repatriated French from Algeria.

2.30 pm; two hours) and the Forêt de San Antoine (Friday at 10 am; 2½ hours), southwest of Aleria. Tickets cost 30FF (children aged under 12 free) and are available at the tourist office.

Places to Stay

Marina d'Aleria (☎ 04 95 57 01 42, fax 04 95 57 04 29), a four star camp site at the eastern end of the N200, is shady and stretches for 500m along the edge of the long sandy beach. The price for a tent and two adults is 64/96FF in low/high season. It is almost essential to book in July and August. The camp site also has bungalows with a double bed and two small bunk beds suitable for children. They cost 630FF per day in August and 250FF out of season.

Three naturist clubs near Aleria provide accommodation right next to the beach. Of these, the closest is *Riva Bella* (☎ 04 95 38 81 10, fax 04 95 38 91 29), which has camping facilities. The best-equipped is *Domaine de Bravone* (☎ 04 95 38 80 30, fax 04 95 38 83 47), 10km north of Aleria; a chalet sleeping two people costs 174/357FF in the low/high season. It has tennis courts, a diving centre and mountain bikes (100FF per day), windsurfing equipment and catamarans for hire. There are also facilities for horse riding (100FF per hour).

Hôtel Les Orangers (☎ 04 95 57 00 13, fax 04 95 57 05 55), the only one star hotel in town, is 50m from the crossroads where the N200 and the N19 meet in the direction of the beach. Large double rooms with sink cost 180FF. The hotel is clean and well-kept but can be a little noisy.

Hôtel L'Empereur (☎ 04 95 57 02 13) is on the N198 but has rooms at the back away from the traffic noise. These rooms all have a bathroom and cost 220/300FF during the low/high season (rooms facing the road cost 200/260FF).

Next door, the *Atrachjata* has similar facilities and charges the same prices.

Places to Eat

There are lots of bars and restaurants along the N198 and on the seafront.

Oyster Farming

The Étang de Diane north-east of Aleria is a natural port famous for its oyster farming; its large surface area (600 hectares) and its depth (up to 11m) make it ideal for this.

In ancient times the oysters were exported, primarily to Rome. The flesh was extracted from the shells and preserved in either salt or olive oil and vinegar in amphorae. Production levels were so great that you can still see a little island formed from the shells discarded in the lake, where oysters and fish are still farmed today.

Le Bounty (☎ *04 95 57 00 50)* is on Plage de Padulone; you can eat pizzas (upwards of 40FF) and fish (roasted sea bream with rice, 80FF) on its terrace facing the open sea. The décor is a little tacky.

Aux Coquillages de Diana (☎ *04 95 57 04 55)* is on the N198 on the banks of the Étang de Diane; it's open between June and September and has fixed menus costing 90FF and 150FF. The nearby *Le Chalet* (☎ *04 95 57 04 46)* is open when Aux Coquillages de Diana is closed, from October to the end of May (closed in January and every Wednesday). It has the same menu at the same prices.

Getting There & Away

Aleria is on the bus line operated by Les Rapides Bleus (☎ 04 95 31 03 79) between Bastia and Porto Vecchio. Autocars Cortenais (☎ 04 95 46 02 12) operates a service to Corte (50FF, one hour).

Buses arrive at and depart from the post office on the N198.

The Central Mountains

Corte, the capital of Paoli's state, remains a symbol of Corsican identity. South of the town, despite large-scale depopulation, the inhabitants of picturesque villages try to preserve a way of life that has been undermined by modern civilisation.

The towns and villages in this part of Corsica are linked by the Chemins de Fer de la Corse (CFC), Corsica's metre-gauge single-track railway, which winds through forests and mountains. As many walkers will testify, the central part of Corsica boasts some spectacular scenery, including the Vallée de la Restonica and Scala di Santa Regina.

Highlights

- Relax in the fascinating historic town of Corte, home of Corsica's university

- Bathe in the beautiful pools of the Vallée de la Restonica

- Hike through the awesome Scala di Santa Regina

Corte

- **pop 6000** ✉ **20250**

At the mouth of the Restonica and Tavignano valleys, surrounded by mountains, Corte (Corti in Corsican) seems rooted to its rocky headland. Its Citadelle dominates both the Ville Haute (Upper Town) and the Ville Basse (Lower Town). Lashed by strong winds in winter and basking in sweltering heat in summer, Corte is frequently visited by walkers, who find it a peaceful place in which to take a break. Home to Corsica's only university (with 3500 students) and the Musée de la Corse (or Musée Régional d'Anthropologie), the town is trying to become an emblem of Corsican culture once again.

HISTORY

Corte was founded in 1419 by the Corsican viceroy Vincentello d'Istria, who built a small fort that became known as the Nid d'Aigle (Eagle's Nest) on the rocky headland. The only fortified town in central Corsica, Corte – halfway between Bastia and Ajaccio – witnessed all of the battles against Genoese rule. Between 1755 and

1769 Pascal Paoli founded the first independent Corsican government in the town and got one of the first democratic constitutions in the world voted in, in the Couvent d'Orezza. In 1765 the university was established, but four years later Paoli was defeated by the French. From then on Corte was a garrison town, and was even used as a base by the French Foreign Legion when it left North Africa in 1962.

ORIENTATION

The main street, cours Paoli, divides the small town in two. To the west, steps lead to the Ville Haute and the Citadelle. To the east, you descend into the Ville Basse and the new quarter, which stretches down the valley. Ave Jean Nicoli, on which the Università di Corsica Pasquale Paoli is situated, leads onto cours Paoli. The train station is about 800m from the town centre.

INFORMATION
Tourist Office

The tourist office (☎ 04 95 46 26 70, email cortetourisme@wanadoo.fr), at 15 quartier

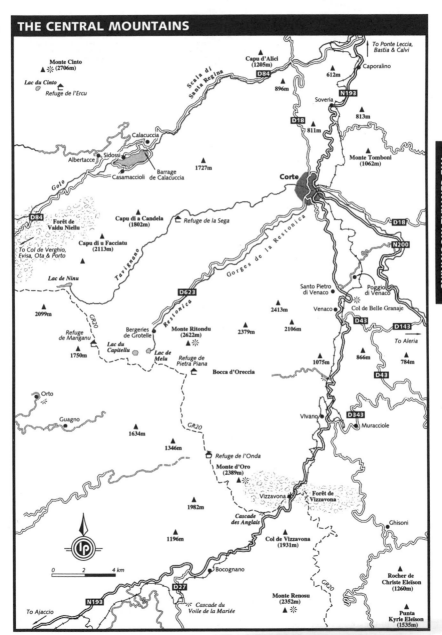

THE CENTRAL MOUNTAINS

To Ponte Leccia, Bastia & Calvi

Monte Cinto (2706m)

Lac du Cinto

Refuge de l'Ercu

Capu d'Alici (1205m)

D84

896m

612m

Caporalino

N193

Soveria

813m

D18

811m

Calacuccia

Sidossi

Albertacce

Casamaccioli

Barrage de Calacuccia

1727m

Monte Tomboni (1062m)

Corte

Golo

D84

Forêt de Valdu Niellu

Capu di a Candela (1802m)

Refuge de la Sega

D18

To Col de Verghio, Evisa, Ota & Porto

Capu di u Facciatu (2113m)

Tavignano

Gorges de la Restonica

N200

D623

Santo Pietro di Venaco

Poggio di Venaco

Lac de Ninu

2099m

Restonica

2413m

Venaco

Col de Belle Granaje

D43

D143

GR20

Refuge de Manganu

1750m

Bergeries de Grotelle

Lac du Capitellu

Lac de Melu

Monte Ritondu (2622m)

Refuge de Pietra Piana

2379m

2106m

To Aleria

1075m

866m

784m

D43

Orto

Bocca d'Oreccia

Guagno

1634m

1346m

GR20

Vivano

Muracciole

D343

Refuge de l'Onda

Monte d'Oro (2389m)

Vizzavona

Forêt de Vizzavona

Ghisoni

1982m

1196m

Cascade des Anglais

Col de Vizzavona (1931m)

Rocher de Christe Eleison (1260m)

Bocognano

D27

N193

To Ajaccio

Cascade du Voile de la Mariée

Monte Renosu (2352m)

GR20

Punta Kyrie Eleison (1535m)

0   2   4 km

THE CENTRAL MOUNTAINS

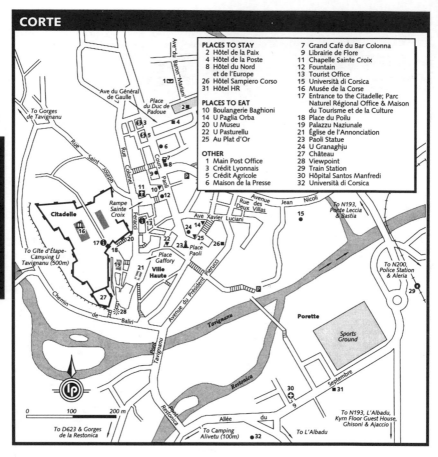

CORTE

PLACES TO STAY
2 Hôtel de la Paix
4 Hôtel de la Poste
8 Hôtel du Nord
   et de l'Europe
26 Hôtel Sampiero Corso
31 Hôtel HR

PLACES TO EAT
10 Boulangerie Baghioni
14 U Paglia Orba
20 U Museu
22 U Pasturellu
25 Au Plat d'Or

OTHER
1 Main Post Office
3 Crédit Lyonnais
5 Crédit Agricole
6 Maison de la Presse
7 Grand Café du Bar Colonna
9 Librairie de Flore
11 Chapelle Sainte Croix
12 Fountain
13 Tourist Office
15 Università di Corsica
16 Musée de la Corse
17 Entrance to the Citadelle; Parc
   Naturel Régional Office & Maison
   du Tourisme et de la Culture
18 Place du Poilu
19 Palazzu Naziunale
21 Église de l'Annonciation
23 Paoli Statue
24 U Granaghju
27 Château
28 Viewpoint
29 Train Station
30 Hôpital Santos Manfredi
32 Università di Corsica

des Quatre Fontaines, is open in summer it's open from 9 am to 6 pm Monday to Saturday; the rest of the year it's open weekdays from 9 am to noon and 2 to 3 pm. At the time of writing the office was moving to premises above the Parc Naturel Régional de Corse office in the Citadelle (entrance on place du Poilu) and renaming itself the Maison du Tourisme et de la Culture. Staff distribute a small map of the town and the surrounding area as well as a list of places to stay, but they don't take bookings.

A pamphlet entitled *Parcours patrimonial*, published by the Société Historique de Corte, lists the main points of interest in the town. It's available from the tourist office.

Parc Naturel Régional de Corse Office

The PNRC office (☎ 04 95 46 27 44), on the right as you enter the Citadelle, is open daily in summer and autumn. You can obtain walking brochures and advice on itineraries here.

Money

You will find several banks to the north of cours Paoli, including Crédit Lyonnais and Crédit Agricole, which both have ATMs. It is possible to change money on weekdays from 8.15 to 11.55 am and 1.45 to 4.50 pm. Expect to pay a commission of 35FF for cash transactions and when cashing travellers cheques.

Post

The main post office on ave du Baron Mariani is open from 8 am to noon and 2 to 5 pm Monday to Friday and from 8 am to noon on Saturday.

Bookshops

The Librairie de Flore at 5 cours Paoli is open daily in summer from 9 am to 8 pm, except on Sunday afternoon. It sells maps, guidebooks on Corsica and a small selection of English-language books. French newspapers can be bought from the Maison de la Presse, also on cours Paoli. Foreign newspapers are also on sale there during the summer.

Library

The library in the Centre de Recherches Corses in the Palazzu Naziunale is open weekdays from 9 am to noon and 2 to 6 pm and has everything that has ever been written on Corsica and the area around Corte, on subjects as diverse as flora and fauna and history. You can also leaf through the nationalist press, including the famous *Il Ribombu*, the official publication of the A Cuncolta Naziunalista (Nationalist Assembly) party.

Medical Services

Open 24 hours a day, Hôpital Santos Manfredi (☎ 04 95 45 05 00) is on allée du 9 Septembre, in the Porette quarter near the train station.

Emergency

The police station is on the outskirts of Corte on the N200, heading south-east towards Aleria.

CITADELLE

Triangular in shape and some 100m above the town, the Citadelle dominates Corte. To its south, at the top of steps cut into the Restonica marble, is the old **château**. Prettily restored, this building, which resembles a small fort, was built in 1419 and extended by the French in the 18th and 19th centuries. Vauban, the famous French military engineer, constructed huge ramparts here. The view of the covered way is excellent.

After entering the Citadelle you reach two large buildings facing one another, the **Casernes Serrurier and Padoue** (Serrurier and Padoue Barracks). Built under Louis-Philippe, they were used for a variety of purposes, including as a prison and later as a barracks for the French Foreign Legion from 1962 to 1983. Today the Caserne Serrurier houses the Musée de la Corse. Since 1981 the Caserne Padoue has been used for teaching by the university. It should soon accommodate the Maison du Tourisme et de la Culture.

The FRAC (Fonds Régional d'Art Contemporain) is also in this building. It organises four exhibitions a year, one of which is usually dedicated to a Corsican artist. For further information call ☎ 04 95 46 22 18.

MUSÉE DE LA CORSE (MUSÉE RÉGIONAL D'ANTHROPOLOGIE)

Inaugurated in December 1997 by the minister of culture, Catherine Trautman, this building was restored by the Italian architect Andrea Bruno, who kept the long façade and enlarged the windows to allow more light to enter the rooms.

On the 1st floor the **Galerie Doozan**, named after a priest who between 1951 and 1978 collected almost 3000 traditional Corsican objects, exhibits items which display artistry and skill.

The 2nd floor, or '**musée en train de se faire**' (museum under construction), covers more contemporary subjects, such as industry, tourism and music. The ground floor is reserved for temporary exhibitions.

THE CENTRAL MOUNTAINS

euro currency converter 10FF = €1.52

In July and August the museum is open daily from 10 am to 8 pm. In spring and autumn it closes at 6 pm and is shut on Monday and public holidays. From November to the end of March it closes at 5 pm and on Sunday. The entry fee is 20FF for adults (35FF during temporary exhibitions) and 15FF for children over 10 years old. Cassette tours can be rented in English or French for 10FF. Free 1½ hour guided tours are available by booking ahead only.

A special edition of *Beaux Arts Magazine* which features the museum is on sale in the entrance hall (55FF).

PALAZZU NAZIUNALE (NATIONAL PALACE)

On your left before you go into the Citadelle you will see a large rectangular building. This used to be the palace of the Genoese lieutenant, and it housed the first and only independent Corsican government under Paoli. Paoli lived in the palace, which was also the site of the university – it still houses some of the university departments and a library. The ground floor is used as an exhibition room for local artists.

Below the palace on place Gaffory is the **Église de l'Annonciation**, built in the middle of the 15th century. It was transformed and enlarged in the 17th century.

UNIVERSITÀ DI CORSICA PASQUALE PAOLI

One of the demands of the nationalists in the 1960s was that Corsica should have its own university. The state finally conceded to this in 1975, and in October 1981 students pushed open its doors, almost two centuries after the first university was established during Corsican independence. Each year it takes in around 3500 students of such subjects as the social sciences, biology, languages and economics. The main building is on ave Jean Nicoli near the entrance to the Ville Basse.

Student life in Corsica poses certain problems due to the town's size. Accommodation is in short supply (students often have to take rooms in hotels) and the public transport infrastructure is inadequate.

ACTIVITIES

L'Albadu equestrian centre (see Places to Stay – Budget below) offers a number of horse-riding packages. A full day costs 450FF (including a meal) and a half-day 200FF. An hour's riding costs 90FF. You can also get information from the Association Régionale du Tourisme Équestre en Corse (☎ 04 95 46 31 74) at 7 rue du Colonel Ferracci.

ORGANISED TOURS

You can take a small train around Corte (mobile ☎ 06 09 95 70 36) from the Tuffeli car park at the lower end of cours Paoli. The tour lasts 30 minutes (or one hour, with stops) and costs 25FF. Tours are in French.

Autocars Cortenais (☎ 04 95 46 02 12) organises a range of excursions in the Vallée de la Restonica, including the Bergeries de Grotelle (70FF return) and the Pont de Tragone (60FF return).

PLACES TO STAY – BUDGET

Camping Alivetu (☎ 04 95 46 11 09), open from mid-April to the beginning of October, is on allée du 9 Septembre, south of the Pont Restonica and approximately 900m from the train station. It charges 30/15/15FF per adult/tent/car.

Gîte d'Étape-Camping U Tavignanu (☎ 04 95 46 16 85) is open from Easter to October. It charges 22/10FF per adult/tent. To get there, head west along chemin de Baliri on the west side of the Citadelle and look out for signs to the camp site, which is at the end of a narrow road 500m after the bridge. U Tavignanu also has dormitory beds (80FF including breakfast). It is open year-round and is near the Mare a Mare Nord walking trail.

L'Albadu (☎ 04 95 46 24 55), an equestrian centre on the old Ajaccio road in the heart of the countryside, has a number of small, clean rooms with shower and outside toilet for 200FF. You can also pitch your tent on terraced plots. Expect to pay 50FF a day for two people with a tent (plus 10/5FF for a car/motorbike). The easiest way to get there is to take the main road to Ajaccio, then turn right after 1km (it is signposted). If you are on foot, they will pick you up if you telephone.

Hôtel de la Poste (☎ 04 95 46 01 37, 2 *place du Duc de Padoue*) is in a charming old building. It has not been awarded any stars but has 12 basic rooms. Double rooms cost 170FF to 190FF depending on their size. At the height of the season prices go up by 10FF. Rooms 5 and 6 have balconies and rooms 9 and 10 wide terraces. The hotel is open year-round and a warm welcome is guaranteed.

Hôtel HR (☎ 04 95 45 11 11, fax 04 95 61 02 85, 6 allée du 9 Septembre) is the largest hotel in Corte (135 rooms) and also one of the cheapest. It is around 150m from the train station in a building devoid of charm but the rooms are pleasant; doubles start at 145FF (199FF with shower and toilet). The hotel, open year-round, has a sauna and fitness room as well as private parking for two-wheeled vehicles. Make sure you book ahead, even out of season.

PLACES TO STAY – MID-RANGE

Hôtel de la Paix (☎ 04 95 46 06 72, fax 04 95 46 23 84, ave du Général de Gaulle) is in a 1960s building at the end of a quiet street perpendicular to cours Paoli. The rooms, which have toilet, shower and telephone, start at 250FF, regardless of season. A family room costs 300FF. Breakfast is 35FF. The 60 rooms could do with being given a new lease of life. The hotel does not accept bank cards. It is open year-round except New Year.

Hôtel du Nord et de l'Europe (☎ 04 95 46 00 68, 22 cours Paoli) is first-rate. The 13 rooms all have showers and some are studio size. Doubles cost 200FF (240FF with toilet), rooms with two large double

beds cost 260FF (300F with toilet). The hotel charges 320FF for four people. The rooms all have double glazing, which is vital because some of the rooms overlook the street. The east-facing rooms are the quietest. The hotel also runs Le Grand Café du Bar Colonna on cours Colonna (left as you come out of the hotel), where you can eat breakfast (30FF). Walkers are welcome and can leave their rucksacks in a locked room in the café. The hotel has details of English-speaking guides and is open year-round.

Hôtel Sampiero Corso (☎ 04 95 46 09 76, ave du Président Pierucci) is a modern building with double rooms for 270FF and triple rooms for 400FF. Cots cost 100FF. Each room has a bathroom, toilet and telephone. The hotel is in a noisy street but all the windows have double glazing.

Le Kyrn Floor (☎ 04 95 37 01 83) on your left if you are coming from Corte, about 3km along the Ajaccio road, is an attractive large stone guesthouse above the N193. As well as distilling essential oils such as rosemary and myrtle, the owners have been taking in guests for more than 10 years. The five rooms, each with shower, toilet and washbasin, cost 300FF (including a generous breakfast). You can opt for one of the studios (350FF) on the same level as the garden, where you can have a barbecue or eat breakfast alfresco. A studio for four (with mezzanine bedroom) costs 550FF with breakfast. The rooms are perfect and you are assured of a hearty welcome. Sadly, however, one is aware of the proximity of the main road, particularly in the studios.

PLACES TO EAT
Snacks

Baghioni (☎ 04 95 46 02 67, 7 cours Paoli) is a poky little bakery that sells delicious, freshly baked sweet and savoury pastries. Try the *gâteau aux châtaignes* (chestnut cake) in season. *U Pasturellu*, in the small street leading to place Paoli in the Ville Haute, sells L'Empereur pâté sandwiches on bland white bread for 25FF, but it would

THE CENTRAL MOUNTAINS

be cheaper to go to the small supermarket on place Paoli, where you can buy the bread and pâté to make your own and sample the delicious *fougasses* (bread with olives, sometimes with onion and bacon).

In the evening two vans – one in place du Duc de Padoue and the other at the corner of ave Xavier Luciani and cours Paoli – sell substantial but uninspiring pizzas cooked on wood fires for between 30FF and 45FF.

Restaurants

U Museu (☎ 04 95 61 08 36, rampe Ribanelle) is a first-rate restaurant in the Ville Haute, to your right before you enter the Citadelle. The atmosphere and service are excellent and the prices reasonable. It even has a shaded terrace. The fixed-price menus are good value – there is one at 89FF that includes fish soup, trout in *peveronatta* sauce (pepper, wine and tomato), cheese and dessert. The 75FF menu includes a starter or dessert and main course. The children's menu costs 35FF. Make sure you try the excellent wild boar stew with wild myrtle (65FF), *tripettes à la bordelaise* (tripe with red wine sauce and shallots; 49FF) or omelette with brocciu and mint. The restaurant is open daily in summer but closed on Sunday and during the school holidays out of season. There is a menu in English.

Au Plat d'Or (☎ 04 95 46 27 16, 1 place Paoli) is a small restaurant where tourists rub shoulders with locals. You can eat in one of two quiet dining rooms or on the shrub-screened terrace. For a starter, you can choose from a selection of imaginative salads such as *la marocaine* (semolina flavoured with cumin and white grapes), chicken liver and nut salad (49FF) or quenelles of chicken liver mousse (45FF). The refreshing terrine of brocciu with sweet peppers on a *coulis de tomates* (similar to tomato purée) is also excellent (60FF), as are the *millefeuille* of omelette with ground pepper (60FF) and the brochettes of beef with fresh mushrooms flavoured with cumin (100FF). There are delicious home-made desserts and service is quick and attentive.

U Paglia Orba (☎ 04 95 61 07 89, ave Xavier Luciani), above a busy street, offers three menus at 65FF, 80FF and 95FF. The first includes a plate of *Prisuttu* (Corsican raw ham), meat cannelloni and a crème caramel. You might like to try specialities such as escalope of veal rolled and stuffed with mint (75FF) or steak with hazelnuts (72FF). There are a few pizzas on the menu, starting at 45FF. The restaurant is open from Monday to Saturday.

L'Albadu equestrian centre (see under Places to Stay – Budget) has an extensive, traditional 80FF menu with soup, cannelloni with brocciu, fruit tart, coffee and wine. You must book in advance. The meal can be combined with a ride on one of the horses (see the earlier Activities section).

ENTERTAINMENT

Although there are a few bars on cours Paoli and in place Paoli (such as *Le Grand Café du Bar Colonna* on cours Colonna and *Bip's* farther south on cours Paoli), nightlife in Corte is rather limited. At the time of research, the only disco in the town centre was about to relocate to allée du 9 Septembre to be closer to the university.

SHOPPING

In the Ville Haute (between the Citadelle and place Paoli) several craft shops sell handmade items such as pottery, wooden toys and paintings.

At U Granaghju (☎ 04 95 46 20 28, fax 04 95 46 19 78), 2 cours Paoli, you can stock up on traditional local produce.

GETTING THERE & AWAY
Bus

Corte is on the Bastia-Ajaccio bus route operated by Eurocorse (☎ 04 95 21 06 30). Buses leave from Le Grand Café du Bar Colonna daily. A single to Bastia costs 50FF and a single to Ajaccio 65FF.

From 15 April to 15 September Autocars Cortenais (☎ 04 95 46 02 12) runs buses between Corte and Bastia via Ponte Leccia three times a week (Monday, Wednesday and Friday). The journey takes 1¼ hours and costs 50FF. The bus leaves from the Corte Voyages agency at 19 cours Paoli.

Autocars Cortenais also provides a bus service to Aleria three times a week (Tuesday, Thursday and Saturday). The bus leaves from the train station and tickets cost 50FF.

Autocars Mordiconi has buses going to Porto via Calacuccia and Evisa (100FF) daily except Sunday and public holidays. They leave from place Paoli.

Train
There are four trains daily to Ajaccio (☎ 04 95 46 00 97). The journey takes two hours and tickets cost 64FF. There are also trains to Bastia (1½ hours, 57FF), Calvi (77FF), Île Rousse (60FF) and Vizzavona (26FF). There is an additional charge of 73FF for bikes. Left luggage costs 15FF per day.

Around Corte

SCALA DI SANTA REGINA
North-west of Corte, this awesome mountain pass was for years the only way of getting to Calacuccia and the villages in the tiny Niolu region. The deep granite gorges that plunge down to the bed of the Golo river make this one of the island's most dramatic mountain landscapes, all the more so because of the colour of the rock.

The narrow road, sometimes little more than a ledge with reinforced verges supported by arches, winds its way through the pass for around 20km until it gets to the outskirts of Calacuccia. The only blot on the landscape is the chain of rusty electricity pylons that follow the line of the river.

A dam and hydroelectric power station, which can dramatically alter the water levels, make any descent into the gorges perilous. You can go down a narrow walkway 4km from Calacuccia but the view from the road is just as stunning.

You need a car to get to Scala di Santa Regina. From Corte, head north on the N193 as far as Francardo, then turn west on the D84.

CALACUCCIA
• pop 320
Resplendent above its lake, Calacuccia is a popular haunt of hikers following the Mare a Mare Nord route. There is not much to do in the town, especially now that the lake, managed by the electricity company EDF, is off-limits to swimmers. Signs posted around the lake prohibit sailing, bathing and fishing, although there is the occasional canoeing competition. Locals tend to swim in the mountain streams between Casamaccioli and Albertacce.

The town lies in the shadow of Monte Cinto (2706m). A series of five jagged peaks known as Les Cinq Moines (The Five Monks) resembles the dorsal spine of some giant prehistoric creature.

There is a memorial plaque in the town to Gracieux Lamperti, the French and European boxing champion in 1959, who came from Calacuccia.

Calacuccia has bars, restaurants, a petrol station, two grocery shops and a post office (behind the town hall).

Information
The tourist office and the Association Sportive et Culturelle du Niolu (☎ 04 95 48 05 22) are 1km out of the village towards Scala di Santa Regina. These two organisations, which promote tourism in the Niolu area, can give you information on climbing, exploring the canyons and canoeing. The offices are open from July to September, from 9 am to noon and 2 to 5 pm Friday to Sunday and from 9 am to 12.30 pm and 2 to 6 pm Monday to Thursday.

Places to Stay
Gîte d'Étape du Couvent (☎ 04 95 48 00 11) is just above the road 1km south of Calacuccia. It is a favourite port of call among walkers. Dorm beds cost 60FF and

THE CENTRAL MOUNTAINS

the six double rooms cost 200FF. The gîte is open year-round.

Gîte d'Étape d'Albertacce (☎ *04 95 48 05 60)* is 2.5km south of Calacuccia. This fine stone house on the outskirts of the quiet village of Albertacce has dormitories for four, a communal area, a kitchen and clean bathrooms. Expect to pay 60FF per night, 25FF for breakfast and 165FF for half board.

Hôtel des Touristes (☎ *04 95 48 00 04)* is a large grey building not entirely without charm that offers comfortable and traditionally furnished single/double rooms for 200/250FF (with bidet), 270/300FF (with shower) and 300/370FF (with bath).

Hôtel Acqua Viva (☎ *04 95 48 06 90)*, the second largest hotel in Calacuccia, is in the building above the petrol station. Double rooms cost from 280FF to 380FF, depending on the time of year.

Places to Eat

Auberge Casa Balduina (☎ *04 95 48 08 57)* opposite the convent offers good home cooking. The 85FF menu includes locally produced *charcuterie* (cooked pork meats), meat with sauce, cheese and fruit. The 60FF menu includes a salad and dessert.

Le Restaurant du Lac (☎ *04 95 48 02 73)* at Sidossi, around 2km from Calacuccia on the edge of the lake, is reputed to be the town's best restaurant, and its fresh produce does it credit. The restaurant has two menus, one at 75FF, which includes a salad, sautéed pork with peppers and olives, and cheese or fruit. A more mouthwatering one costs 128FF; it includes carpaccio of *manzu* (free-range veal), bean salad with smoked duck cutlet, or crumbled cod with green salad and balsamic vinegar, then escalope of lamb or grilled manzu, followed by cheese and dessert.

Getting There & Away

Bus Mordiconi (ask at Hôtel des Touristes; see Places to Stay above) runs buses to Corte, Evisa and Porto from July to mid-September. They leave at 9 am for Porto and 5.30 pm for Corte.

VALLÉE DE LA RESTONICA

Despite being extremely popular in summer, Vallée de la Restonica is one of the highlights of the Corte area. The river, rising in the grey-green mountains, has hollowed out pretty little basins in the rock that provide a sheltered setting for bathing or sunbathing. The D623 winds its way through the gorges from Corte until it gets to the Bergeries de Grotelle, which have made a number of concessions to modern civilisation and tourism.

You can bathe in nearly all the gorges. The most suitable areas are between the Auberge de la Restonica and the information point (near a small chapel with lovely natural swimming pools), and along the last 3km of the road before you get to the bergeries.

A number of walks are also signposted along this road; they can take from 30 minutes to several hours. Most visitors come to the gorges to see the **Lac de Melu** at 1711m, an hour's climb, and the **Lac du Capitellu** at 1930m, around 1¾ hours away on foot. The path to the lakes is signposted in yellow from the Bergeries de Grotelle car park (1370m). Be sure to wear good walking shoes if you plan to go on foot, and avoid times of day when the sun is strongest. Bear in mind that the mountains are often still snow-capped in May.

The path to the Lac de Melu follows the right bank of the Restonica for most of the way, before branching into two tracks. The track that continues along the bank is harder going than the one that crosses the river but you are less likely to come across snow in winter and spring.

The huge number of tourists in the Vallée de la Restonica in summer has led to the introduction of bylaws enforced by local officials. You must not park in spots along the gorges that are not special parking zones (such as the spaces for cars to pass each other). Caravans and camper vans are not allowed beyond Tuani, 7km from Corte. The car park at the bergeries costs 20FF in summer. Fires, bivouacs, camping on unauthorised sites and the dumping of waste in or near the river, which supplies Corte with drinking water, are forbidden.

Information
The information point (☎ 04 95 46 33 92) in Vallée de la Restonica is 6km from Corte. It is open from 8 am to 8 pm daily mid-June to mid-September, although times may vary within those dates.

Places to Stay & Eat
The following places are listed in the order in which you will find them as you come from Corte. The last is therefore closest to the Bergeries de Grotelle and the start of the lake walk.

Auberge de la Restonica (☎ 04 95 45 25 25, fax 04 95 61 15 79) is less than 2km from Corte. This lovely stone house, just metres from a pretty waterfall and natural pool, has six rooms and one small split-level apartment costing 250FF to 350FF for two people out of season. Half board is compulsory in summer (from 670FF to 770FF for two). There is also a superb swimming pool. This lovely hotel is open year-round, although the restaurant is closed in winter.

Hôtel Dominique Colonna (☎ 04 95 45 25 65, fax 04 95 61 03 91), opposite the Auberge de la Restonica (and owned by the same family), is named after the current owner's father, a former professional football player. Its three-star double rooms, each boasting a bath, balcony, TV and telephone, cost from 300FF to 580FF depending on their size, the view they offer and the time of year. The hotel, which uses the same swimming pool as the Auberge de la Restonica, is closed between mid-November and mid-March.

Hôtel-Restaurant Le Refuge (☎ 04 95 46 09 13, fax 04 95 46 22 38), around 800m from Auberge de la Restonica, has comfortable rooms with bathrooms. It offers the best value for money in the valley, with double rooms costing from 280FF to 300FF, depending on the time of year. Half board (540FF to 600FF for two) is compulsory from mid-July to the end of September. The

hotel is open from April to September and you can swim in the nearby gorges. It is a good idea to book in advance, since the accommodation and food of this lovely hotel make it a popular destination.

Le Relais des Lacs, Chez César, is open from noon to 5 pm June to September. It is renowned for its meat dishes cooked on a wood fire (44FF to 61FF) and for its trout (54FF). Fixed-price menus cost from 69FF.

Camping Turni (☎ 04 95 46 11 65), opposite the Vallée de la Restonica information point, is a vast, shaded camp site with fairly basic facilities; it costs 30/14/12FF per person/tent/car. The ground is very hard, as is often the case in Corsica, but the site is pleasant and you can swim here. It also has a bar and pizzeria. It is 11km from Corte and 5km from the Bergeries de Grotelle, where you can buy cold drinks and snacks. It's open from April to September.

Getting There & Away
In summer Rinieri Minibuses (☎ 04 95 46 22 89, 04 95 46 02 12) takes passengers from Corte to the Bergeries de Grotelle. Tickets cost 70FF and there's a minimum of 10 passengers. A taxi from Corte (☎ 04 95 46 04 88) will take up to four passengers to the Bergeries and back for 200FF.

VENACO
• pop 620
At an altitude of 600m, Venaco looks down into the Vallée du Tavignano. Famous for the trout from its streams and its ewe's milk cheese, this once-bustling village is now rather subdued, like many of Corsica's mountain villages. Yet it still has a post office (at the bottom of the village in a building shared with the town hall, school and fire service), cafés and a grocery shop. The train station is at the foot of the village 600m from the main road.

Just south of Venaco the D43 drops down into the valley. This leads to the D143 and the Pont de Noceta, on the route of the Mare a Mare Nord. The bridge crosses the

THE CENTRAL MOUNTAINS

Vecchio river, which dominates a superb mountainous landscape. You can swim in the river here. There is also a lovely view over the village from the road.

Places to Stay & Eat

Hôtel U Frascone (☎ *04 95 47 00 85)* on the south side of the village is the only hotel here. Open year-round, it has double rooms costing from 200FF to 250FF. The restaurant has fixed-price menus at 75FF (charcuterie, cannelloni with brocciu or grilled trout, and dessert) and 130FF (herb turnover, roast lamb with local herbs).

Camping-Auberge de la Ferme de Peridundellu (☎ *04 95 47 09 89)*, next to the D143 3.5km from Venaco, is a small and friendly family-run camp site on a headland facing the valley. Open between Easter and October, it charges 28/16/14FF per adult/tent/car. The farm serves delicious meals: look out for its basic 90FF menu of local farm produce.

Other accommodation is available in Santo Pietro di Venaco north of Venaco. *Gîte d'Étape de Saint Pierre de Vénaco*

(☎ *04 95 47 07 29)* is a favourite stopover for people walking the Mare a Mare Nord. This lovely stone house, built in the traditional Corsican style, has large dormitories for four people (160FF half board) and single/double rooms at 200/250FF. The owner, a mountain guide, can organise walks and help you explore the area. To get to the gîte, go up to the top of the village, passing behind the church, then turn right when you get to the Office National des Forêts (ONF; National Office for Forests) sign. The gîte is renowned for its friendly atmosphere and good food, and is often full in summer.

Hôtel Le Torrent (☎ *04 95 47 00 18)*, open from July to September, is a rather quaint but pleasant traditional French inn with double rooms with bathrooms costing from 220FF. The menu is good value at 70FF. The hotel is signposted from the N193.

Getting There & Away

Eurocorse (☎ 04 95 21 06 30) runs buses twice daily (except Sunday and public holidays) that stop in Ajaccio, Vizzavona, Vivario, Venaco, Corte, Ponte Leccia and Bastia. They leave both Ajaccio and Bastia at 8.30 am and 3 pm to travel in opposite directions. Expect to pay 55FF for a ticket from Ajaccio to Venaco; the trip takes about one hour and 20 minutes.

CFC also goes to Venaco: four trains daily link the village with Ajaccio, Corte and Bastia via Vizzavona and Vivario. Departures are usually at 7 and 9 am and 2.30 and 4.35 pm from Ajaccio, and at 7.20 and 9.05 am and 2.30 and 3.50 pm from Bastia.

VIVARIO
● pop 500

Nestling among mountains and clustered around a church, this pretty village, with its tiled roofs standing out against the green of the surrounding forests, is worth a visit. On an alternative route of the Mare a Mare Nord, it dates back to Roman times. One of its curiosities is the bridge that crosses the Vecchio 3km to the north. The small stone road lies under the tall supports of a metal-covered railway viaduct inspired by the work of Gustave Eiffel. A rather unsightly concrete bridge is currently under construction alongside it, apparently to avoid a bend in the road.

Vivario has a bar, pizzeria and small grocery shop. The train station is around 500m north of the village.

Places to Stay
Le Macchje Monti (☎ *04 95 47 22 00)* near the church is the only hotel in Vivario; double rooms cost 200FF from March to October. The welcome can be lukewarm.

Getting There & Away
Eurocorse (☎ 04 95 21 06 30) runs buses to Vivario from Ajaccio, Vizzavona, Venaco, Corte and Bastia twice daily except Sunday and public holidays. The ride from Ajaccio costs 50FF and takes 70 minutes.

There are four trains daily from Vivario to destinations such as Ajaccio, Bastia, Corte, Venaco and Vizzavona. The trip from Ajaccio to Vivario costs 48FF and takes between 1½ and 1¾ hours.

GHISONI
Before WWII Ghisoni boasted three dance halls, 12 cafés and 1800 inhabitants. Its population has since dwindled to about 180. The village lies peacefully at the foot of Punta Kyrie Eleïson, a mountain south-east of Vivario. Robert Colonna d'Istria, in his *L'Histoire de la Corse*, explains where its unusual name came from: in the 14th century members of the Giovannali sect, who were of Franciscan origin but resented Church authorities, were burnt alive on the mountain. Legend has it that as the flames rose and the priest sang the prayer of the Kyrie Eleïson, a white dove began to wheel above the burning woodpiles.

Ghisoni has a camp site, hotel, pizzeria, grocery shop and post office. Further information can be found in the Walking in Corsica chapter.

Getting There & Away
There are no buses to Ghisoni. The train to Vivario or the bus to Ghisonaccia are the closest you can get by public transport.

VIZZAVONA
Beneath the towering 2389m of Monte d'Oro, the fifth-highest peak on the island, Vizzavona is familiar to the many walkers who start or end their GR20 trek there. The small village, with its few dozen inhabitants, consists of a cluster of houses and hotels around a train station 700m from the main road. Places to stay and eat are detailed in the earlier Walking in Corsica chapter.

The Forêt de Vizzavona, where bandits held travellers to ransom in the 19th century, is now a haven of peace. You are spoilt for choice by the numerous footpaths that run through it. It covers 1633 hectares and consists mainly of beech and Corsican pine trees, some more than 800 years old. Despite the humid climate there have been five major fires in the forest since 1866.

Cascades des Anglais
Two and a half kilometres from the spot where the road from Ajaccio branches off towards the train station, the short path to these waterfalls is signposted on the right. This gentle forest trail, marked out in green by the ONF, drops down into the superb pine and beech forest. After 15 minutes you come to the GR20, where there is a refreshment stall in summer. To your left are the waterfalls. You can get to Vizzavona station in 30 minutes by taking the GR20 to your right.

In summer the waterfalls are not so much white-water rapids as a series of clear pools ideal for swimming in. You can sunbathe on the smooth rocks. The pools extend up the mountain for another 15 minutes. Easily accessible, they owe their name to the British holiday-makers who used to flock to Vizzavona, undeterred by the cold water. In these pools its easy to imagine you've found a corner of paradise.

THE CENTRAL MOUNTAINS

Cascade du Voile de la Mariée

Continue south-west along the main road for a few kilometres until you get to the village of Bocognano. The road to the Cascade du Voile de la Mariée is on the left as you leave the village, at the Bar-Restaurant Le Copacabana. The narrow road passes a railway bridge, then comes to a second bridge, recognisable by its iron guardrails, 3.5km from the main road. A small wooden ladder on the left allows you to get over the fence. Continue along the path that climbs through the undergrowth, roughly marked out with lengths of rope tied between the trees. After around 10 minutes of rather difficult terrain you come to a tall, broad waterfall. Fast-flowing in winter, it is rather disappointing in summer but allows you to freshen up. The rocks on the edge of the waterfall are slippery, so be careful.

Getting There & Away

Vizzavona and Bocognano are both on the Eurocorse (☎ 04 95 21 06 30) Ajaccio-Bastia route. There are two departures daily except Sunday and public holidays. Allow one hour to get to Vizzavona from Ajaccio or Corte. Tickets from Ajaccio are 45FF. Departures are at 8.30 am and 3 pm from the coach station in Ajaccio and at 9.45 am and 4.15 pm from Corte.

There are four trains daily from Vizzavona to destinations including Ajaccio, Bastia, Vivario, Venaco and Corte. The trip from Ajaccio to Vizzavona costs 39FF and takes around 80 minutes. Departures are at 7 and 9 am and 2.30 and 4.35 pm from Ajaccio, at 7.20 and 9.05 am and 2.30 and 3.50 pm from Bastia, and at 8.59 and 11.10 am and 4.13 and 5.44 pm from Corte, although times are subject to change.

Language

CORSICAN

The vitality of the Corsican language is immediately apparent to anyone setting foot on the island. Far from being folkloric and obsolete, Corsican is spoken daily by many of the island's inhabitants. You'll also encounter it in newspapers, songs and poetry. Yet all Corsicans also understand and speak French and usually Italian.

Corsican has its roots in Italian. In his book *Corse* Fernand Ettori remarks that 'its closest relatives can be found in Tuscany'. However, this linguistic foundation has been moulded by the various societies which have presided over the island through the centuries.

The Corsican language thus contains elements of Iberian, Ligurian and Genoese. French was then grafted onto this, particularly after it became compulsory to learn French on Corsica at the end of the 19th century. For years it was an offence to speak Corsican, just as the inhabitants of Brittany were forbidden to speak Breton.

Language has pride of place in the Corsican sense of identity. The islanders are stout defenders of their dialect and anything else that symbolises the specificity of their island in relation to France. Although most road signs in Corsica are bilingual (Corsican/French), it is not unusual to see the French translation crossed out, erased, or even bullet-riddled.

With the rise of the separatist movement in the 1970s, several associations – such as *Scola Corsa* – began to offer courses in Corsican. The language was finally recognised in 1974 when it was included in the framework of the French *loi Deixonne*, a law on regional languages.

To this day, the debate over the Corsican language is problematic from a constitutional point of view. Recognising Corsican is to admit that it is spoken by a select group of people, thus distinguishing between the Corsicans and the French. This sensitive issue has not yet been fully resolved.

There are no English-language guides or phrasebooks to Corsican. The following are of use to French-speakers. Assimil has published a manual entitled *Le Corse sans peine* but this work doesn't contain a vocabulary listing. The *Dictionnaire français-corse* by DCL Éditions is comprehensive but bulky, and therefore not easy to carry around. Fernand Ettori has compiled the *Anthologie des expressions corses Rivages*.

It is possible to study Corsican at the Università di Corsica Pasqual Paoli in Corte. The association Esse in Bastia (☎ 04 95 33 03 01) also runs courses in Corsican.

Pronunciation & Grammar

The letters **k**, **w**, **x** and **y** do not exist in Corsican but the alphabet uses the groups of letters **chj** 'tyi' and **ghj** 'diè'. As a general rule, **ch** is pronounced 'g', **u** is pronounced 'ou', **c** is often pronounced 'tch' and **g** is often pronounced 'dg'. The last vowel of a word often has a 'sh' sound, and sometimes it is not pronounced at all. Porto Vecchio, Portivecchju in Corsican, is thus pronounced 'pourti vechj'.

Corsican pronunciation also varies between north and south (or even from one village to the next). The letter **v** in southern Corsica is pronounced 'b' in the north. Double **l** in the north becomes a double 'd' in the south (Pinarellu, for example, is pronounced and written Pinareddu). The inhabitants of Bonifacio (Bunifaziu) have preserved their own language, which is closely related to Genoese.

Emphasis is often on the penultimate syllable (if the word has no accent), but can also be on the last syllable, particularly with the infinitive form of the verb, in which case it has an accent grave (eg à). Occasionally, emphasis is on the third from last syllable. The plural is formed with *i*, so *u trenu* (train), *i treni* (trains).

Greetings

Hello/Good day.	*Bunghjornu.*
Goodbye.	*A venicci.*
Thank you.	*Grazie.*
Cheers!/ Good health!	*A salute!*
Best wishes!	*Pace i salute!*

Basics

I	*eiu*
you/you (plural)	*tù/voi*
he	*ellu*
we	*noi*
they	*ellu*
the	*u*
Yes.	*Iè.*
No.	*Innò.*
How many/much?	*Quantu?*
Where?	*Duve?*
When?	*Quandu?*
Who?	*Quale?*

Numbers

1	*unu*
2	*dui*
3	*trè*
4	*quattru*
5	*cinque*
6	*sei*
7	*sette*
8	*ottu*
9	*nove*
10	*dece*
20	*vinti*
30	*trenta*
40	*quaranta*
50	*cinquanta*
60	*sessanta*
70	*settanta*
80	*ottanta*
90	*novanta*
100	*centu*
1000	*mille*

Some Useful Words

Variations can be found between the northern and southern parts of the island.

boy	*maschju*
girl	*figliola*
man	*omu*
woman	*donna*
daughter	*figlia*
son	*figliolu*
mother	*mamma*
grandmother	*mammone*
grandfather	*babbone*
married man/ woman	*sposu; casatu*
unmarried man/ woman	*figliu; scàpulu*
child	*zitellu; bambinu*
summer	*estate*
autumn	*autunnu*
winter	*invernu*
spring	*veranu*
to arrive	*arrivà*
to be	*esse*
to drink	*bèi; bià*
to drive	*cunduce*
to eat	*manghjà*
to greet	*salutà*
to have	*ave*
to leave	*parte*
to like/love	*amà; tene caru*
to pay	*pagà*
to sleep	*dorme*
to walk	*marchjà; caminà*
true	*veru*
false	*falsu*
open	*apertu*
closed	*serratu*
large	*grande*
small	*chiùca; picculu*
ill	*malatu*
doctor	*duttore*
pain	*dulore*
attack	*attaccu*
politeness	*crianza*
tiredness	*fatica*
vengeance	*vindetta*
thirst	*sete*
mouth	*bocca*
kiss	*basgià*
bed	*lettu*
bedroom	*càmera*
dormitory	*dormitoriu*
shower	*duscia*

maquis	*machja*
mountain	*muntagna/* *monte* (summit)
myrtle	*morta; murta*
sea	*mare*

Transport

bicycle	*velò*
bus	*vitturonu*
path/road	*caminu; strada*
plane	*avione*
road	*strada*
street	*carrughju*
train	*trenu*

Food

acqua	water
acquavita	eau-de-vie (brandy)
agnellu	lamb
brocciu/bruccio	Corsican goat's or ewe's milk cheese
caffè	café
caldu	hot
carne	meat
carne vaccina	beef
cena	dinner
cignale; cignali	wild boar
dulciumi	dessert
fame	hunger
fiadone	flan made with brocciu, lemon and eggs
figatellu	liver sausage
freddu	cold
fruttu; frutta	fruit
furmagliu; casgiu	cheese
merenda	lunch
ortiglia	vegetable
pane	bread
pastadolce	cake
pesciu	fish
prisuttu	cured ham
pulenta	polenta
salame	charcuterie (cold cooked pork meats)
sdiunu	breakfast
suppa; minestra	soup
té	tea
vinu	wine
vitella; manzu	veal

FRENCH
Pronunciation & Grammar

This guide gives only a basic overview of French. For a more comprehensive guide to the language get hold of Lonely Planet's *French phrasebook*.

Most letters in French are pronounced more or less the same as their English equivalents. Here are a few which may cause confusion:

j	as the 's' in 'leisure', eg *jour* (day)
c	before **e** and **i**, as the 's' in 'sit'; before **a**, **o** and **u** it's pronounced as English 'k'. When undescored with a 'cedilla' (ç) it's always pronounced as the 's' in 'sit'.

French has a number of sounds that are difficult for Anglophones to produce. These include:

- The distinction between the 'u' sound (as in *tu*) and 'oo' sound (as in *tout*). For both sounds, the lips are rounded and projected forward, but for the 'u' the tongue is towards the front of the mouth, its tip against the lower front teeth, whereas for the 'oo' the tongue is towards the back of the mouth, its tip behind the gums of the lower front teeth.

- The nasal vowels. With nasal vowels the breath escapes partly through the nose and partly through the mouth. There are no nasal vowels in English; in French there are three, as in *bon vin blanc* (good white wine). These sounds occur where a syllable ends in a single **n** or **m**; the **n** or **m** is silent but indicates the nasalisation of the preceding vowel.

- The **r**. The standard **r** of Parisian French is produced by moving the bulk of the tongue backwards to constrict the air flow in the pharynx while the tip of the tongue rests behind the lower front teeth. It's similar to the noise made by some people before spitting, but with much less friction.

An important distinction is made in French between *tu* and *vous*, which both mean 'you'. Tu is only used when addressing people you know well, children or animals.

If you're addressing an adult who isn't a personal friend, *vous* should be used unless the person invites you to use *tu*. In general, younger people insist less on this distinction, and you will find that, in many cases, they use *tu* straight away on meeting someone.

All nouns in French are either masculine or feminine and adjectives reflect the gender of the noun they modify. The feminine form of many nouns and adjectives is indicated by a silent *e* added to the masculine form, as in *étudiant* and *étudiante*, the masculine and feminine for 'student'.

In the following phrases both masculine and feminine forms have been indicated where necessary. The masculine form comes first, separated from the feminine by a slash. The gender of a noun is often indicated by a preceding article: 'the/a/some', *le/un/du* (m), *la/une/de la* (f); or a possessive adjective, 'my/your/his/her', *mon/ton/son* (m), *ma/ta/sa* (f). With French, unlike English, the possessive adjective agrees in number and gender with the thing possessed: 'his/her mother', *sa mère*.

Basics
Yes.	*Oui.*
No.	*Non.*
Maybe.	*Peut-être.*
Please.	*S'il vous plaît.*
Thank you.	*Merci.*
You're welcome.	*Je vous en prie.*
Excuse me.	*Excusez-moi.*
Sorry/Forgive me.	*Pardon.*

Greetings
Hello/Good morning.	*Bonjour.*
Good evening.	*Bonsoir.*
Good night.	*Bonne nuit.*
Goodbye.	*Au revoir.*

Small Talk
How are you?	*Comment allez-vous?* (polite)
	Comment vas-tu?/ Comment ça va? (informal)
Fine, thanks.	*Bien, merci.*
What's your name?	*Comment vous appelez-vous?*
My name is ...	*Je m'appelle ...*
I'm pleased to meet you.	*Enchanté* (m)/ *Enchantée* (f).
How old are you?	*Quel âge avez-vous?*
I'm ... years old.	*J'ai ... ans.*
Where are you from?	*De quel pays êtes-vous?*
I'm from ...	*Je viens ...*
Australia	*d'Australie*
Belgium	*de Belgique*
Canada	*du Canada*
England	*d'Angleterre*
Germany	*d'Allemagne*
Ireland	*d'Irlande*
the Netherlands	*des Pays-Bas*
New Zealand	*de Nouvelle Zélande*
Scotland	*d'Écosse*
the USA	*des États-Unis*
Wales	*du Pays de Galle*

Language Difficulties
I understand.	*Je comprends.*
I don't understand.	*Je ne comprends pas.*
Do you speak English?	*Parlez-vous anglais?*
Could you please write it down?	*Est-ce que vous pouvez l'écrire?*

Getting Around
I want to go to ...	*Je voudrais aller à ...*
I'd like to book a seat to ...	*Je voudrais réserver une place pour ...*
How long does the trip take?	*Combien de temps dure le trajet?*
What time does the ... leave/arrive?	*À quelle heure part/arrive ...?*
aeroplane	*l'avion*
bus (city)	*l'autobus*
bus (intercity)	*l'autocar*
ferry	*le ferry(-boat)*
train	*le train*
Where is (the) ...?	*Où est ...?*
bus stop	*l'arrêt d'autobus*
train station	*la gare*
ticket office	*le guichet*

I'd like a ... ticket.	*Je voudrais un billet ...*
one-way	*aller-simple*
return	*aller-retour*
1st class	*première classe*
2nd class	*deuxième classe*
left-luggage locker	*consigne automatique*
platform	*quai*
timetable	*horaire*
I'd like to hire ...	*Je voudrais louer ...*
a bicycle	*un vélo*
a car	*une voiture*
a guide	*un guide*

Signs

ENTRÉE	ENTRANCE
SORTIE	EXIT
COMPLET	NO VACANCIES
RENSEIGNEMENTS	INFORMATION
OUVERT/FERMÉ	OPEN/CLOSED
INTERDIT	PROHIBITED
(COMMISSARIAT	POLICE STATION
DE) POLICE	
CHAMBRES	ROOMS
LIBRES	AVAILABLE
TOILETTES, WC	TOILETS
HOMMES	MEN
FEMMES	WOMEN

Around Town

I'm looking for ...	*Je cherche ...*
a bank/	*une banque/*
exchange office	*un bureau de change*
the ... embassy	*l'ambassade de ...*
the hospital	*l'hôpital*
the market	*le marché*
the police	*la police*
the post office	*le bureau de poste/ la poste*
a public phone	*une cabine*
a public toilet	*les toilettes téléphonique*
the tourist office	*l'office de tourisme*
Where is (the) ...?	*Où est ...?*
beach	*la plage*
bridge	*le pont*
church	*l'église*
lake	*le lac*
old city (town)	*la vieille ville*
the palace	*le palais*
quay/bank	*le quai/la rive*
ruins	*les ruines*
sea	*la mer*
square	*la place*
tower	*la tour*
What time does it open/close?	*Quelle est l'heure d'ouverture/ de fermeture?*
I'd like to make a telephone call.	*Je voudrais téléphoner.*

I'd like to change ...	*Je voudrais changer ...*
some money	*de l'argent*
travellers cheques	*chèques de voyage*

Directions

How do I get to ...?	*Comment dois-je faire pour arriver à ...?*
Is it near/far?	*Est-ce près/loin?*
Can you show me on the map/ city map?	*Est-ce que vous pouvez me le montrer sur la carte/le plan?*
Go straight ahead.	*Continuez tout droit.*
Turn left.	*Tournez à gauche.*
Turn right.	*Tournez à droite.*
at the next corner	*au prochain coin*
behind	*derrière*
in front of	*devant*
opposite	*en face de*
north	*nord*
south	*sud*
east	*est*
west	*ouest*

Accommodation

I'm looking for ...	*Je cherche ...*
the youth hostel	*l'auberge de jeunesse*
the camp site	*le camping*
a hotel	*un hôtel*
Where can I find a cheap hotel?	*Où est-ce que je peux trouver un hôtel bon marché?*

LANGUAGE

What's the address? *Quelle est l'adresse?*
Could you write *Est-ce vous pourriez*
it down, please? *l'écrire, s'il*
vous plaît?
Do you have any *Est-ce que vous avez*
rooms available? *des chambres*
libres?

I'd like to book ... *Je voudrais réserver ...*
a bed *un lit*
a single room *une chambre pour*
une personne
a double room *une chambre*
double
a room with a *une chambre avec*
shower and toilet *douche et WC*

I'd like to stay *Je voudrais coucher*
in a dormitory. *dans un dortoir.*

How much is it ...? *Quel est le prix ...?*
per night *par nuit*
per person *par personne*

Is breakfast *Est-ce que le petit dé-*
included? *jeuner est compris?*
Can I see the room? *Est-ce que je peux voir*
la chambre?
Where is the toilet? *Où sont les toilettes?*

I'm going to stay ... *Je resterai ...*
one day *un jour*
a week *une semaine*

Shopping
How much is it? *C'est combien?*
It's too expensive *C'est trop cher*
for me. *pour moi.*
Can I look at it? *Est-ce que je peux*
le/la voir? (m/f)
Do you accept *Est-ce que je peux*
credit cards? *payer avec ma*
carte de crédit?
Do you accept *Est-ce que je peux*
travellers *payer avec des*
cheques? *chèques de voyage?*

more/less *plus/moins*
cheap *bon marché*
cheaper *moins cher*
bookshop *la librairie*
chemist/pharmacy *la pharmacie*

Emergencies

Help! *Au secours!*
Call a doctor! *Appelez un*
médecin!
Call the police! *Appelez la police!*
Leave me alone! *Fichez-moi la paix!*
I've been robbed. *On m'a volé.*
I've been raped. *On m'a violée.*
I'm lost. *Je me suis égaré/*
égarée. (m/f)

laundry/laundrette *la laverie*
market *le marché*
newsagency *l'agence de presse*
stationers *la papeterie*
supermarket *le supermarché*

Time, Dates & Numbers
What time is it? *Quelle heure est-il?*
It's (two) o'clock. *Il est (deux) heures.*
When? *Quand?*
today *aujourd'hui*
tonight *ce soir*
tomorrow *demain*
yesterday *hier*
in the morning *du matin*
in the afternoon *de l'après-midi*
in the evening *du soir*

Monday *lundi*
Tuesday *mardi*
Wednesday *mercredi*
Thursday *jeudi*
Friday *vendredi*
Saturday *samedi*
Sunday *dimanche*

January *janvier*
February *février*
March *mars*
April *avril*
May *mai*
June *juin*
July *juillet*
August *août*
September *septembre*
October *octobre*
November *novembre*
December *décembre*

1	*un*
2	*deux*
3	*trois*
4	*quatre*
5	*cinq*
6	*six*
7	*sept*
8	*huit*
9	*neuf*
10	*dix*
11	*onze*
12	*douze*
13	*treize*
14	*quatorze*
15	*quinze*
16	*seize*
20	*vingt*
100	*cent*
1000	*mille*

one million	*un million*

Health

I'm sick.	*Je suis malade.*
I need a doctor.	*Il me faut un médecin.*
Where is the hospital?	*Où est l'hôpital?*
I have diarrhoea.	*J'ai la diarrhée.*
I'm pregnant.	*Je suis enceinte.*

I'm ...	*Je suis ...*
diabetic	*diabétique*
epileptic	*épileptique*
asthmatic	*asthmatique*
anaemic	*anémique*

I'm allergic ...	*Je suis allergique ...*
to antibiotics	*aux antibiotiques*
to penicillin	*à la pénicilline*

antiseptic	*antiseptique*
aspirin	*aspirine*
condoms	*préservatifs*
contraceptive	*contraceptif*
medicine	*médicament*
nausea	*nausée*
sunblock cream	*crème solaire haute protection*
tampons	*tampons hygiéniques*

Food

breakfast	*le petit déjeuner*
lunch	*le déjeuner*
dinner	*le dîner*
grocery store	*l'épicerie*

I'd like the set menu.	*Je prends le menu.*
I'm a vegetarian.	*Je suis végétarien/ végétarienne.*
I don't eat meat.	*Je ne mange pas de viande.*

Starters & Soup

bouillabaisse
  Mediterranean-style fish soup, originally from Marseille, made with several kinds of fish, including *rascasse* (spiny scorpion fish); often eaten as a main course
croûtons
  fried or roasted bread cubes, often added to soups
entrée
  starter
potage
  thick soup made with puréed vegetables
soupe de poisson
  fish soup
soupe du jour
  soup of the day

Meat, Chicken & Poultry

agneau	lamb
bifteck	steak
bœuf	beef
bœuf haché	minced beef
boudin noir	blood sausage (black pudding)
canard	duck
cervelle	brains
charcuterie	cooked or prepared meats (usually pork)
cheval	horse meat
chèvre	goat
côte	chop of pork, lamb or mutton
côtelette	cutlet
dinde	turkey
escargot	snail
foie	liver

foie gras de canard duck liver pâté
jambon ham
lapin rabbit
lard bacon
mouton mutton
oie goose
pieds de porc pigs' trotters
porc pork
poulet chicken
rognons kidneys
sanglier wild boar
saucisson large sausage
saucisson fumé smoked sausage
steak steak
tripes tripe
viande meat
volaille poultry

Common Meat & Poultry Dishes
blanquette de veau or *d'agneau*
    veal or lamb stew with white sauce
bœuf bourguignon
    beef and vegetable stew cooked in red
    wine (usually burgundy)
cassoulet
    Languedoc stew made with goose, duck,
    pork or lamb fillets and haricot beans
chou farci
    stuffed cabbage
choucroute
    sauerkraut with sausage and other pre-
    pared meats
confit de canard or *d'oie*
    duck or goose preserved and cooked in
    its own fat
coq au vin
    chicken cooked in wine
civet
    game stew
fricassée
    stew with meat that has first been fried
grillade
    grilled meats
marcassin
    young wild boar
quenelles
    dumplings made of a finely sieved
    mixture of cooked fish or (rarely) meat
steak tartare
    raw ground meat mixed with onion, raw
    egg yolk and herbs

Fish & Seafood
anchois anchovy
calmar squid
chaudrée fish stew
coquille Saint- scallop
    Jacques
crabe crab
crevette grise shrimp
crevette rose prawn
fruits de mer seafood
gambas king prawns
homard lobster
huître oyster
langouste crayfish
langoustine very small saltwater
    'lobster'
moules mussels
palourde clam
poisson fish
sardine sardine
saumon salmon
thon tuna
truite trout

Vegetables, Herbs & Spices
ail garlic
aïoli or *ailloli* garlic mayonnaise
anis aniseed
artichaut artichoke
asperge asparagus
aubergine aubergine (eggplant)
avocat avocado
betterave beetroot
carotte carrot
céleri celery
cèpe cep (boletus
    mushroom)
champignon mushroom
champignon de button mushroom
    Paris
chou cabbage
concombre cucumber
courgette courgette (zucchini)
crudités small pieces of
    raw vegetables
épice spice
épinards spinach
haricots beans
haricots blancs white beans
haricots rouge kidney beans

haricots verts	French (string) beans
herbe	herb
laitue	lettuce
légume	vegetable
lentilles	lentils
maïs	sweet corn
oignon	onion
olive	olive
panais	parsnip
persil	parsley
petit pois	pea
poireau	leek
poivron	green pepper
pomme de terre	potato
ratatouille	casserole of aubergines, tomatoes, peppers and garlic
riz	rice
salade	salad or lettuce
tomate	tomato
truffe	truffle

Cooking Methods

à la broche	spit-roasted
à la vapeur	steamed
au feu de bois	cooked over a wood-burning stove
au four	baked
en croûte	in pastry
farci	stuffed
fumé	smoked
gratiné	browned on top with cheese
grillé	grilled
pané	coated in breadcrumbs
rôti	roasted
sauté	sautéed (shallow fried)

Sauces & Accompaniments

béchamel
  basic white sauce
huile d'olive
  olive oil
mornay
  cheese sauce
moutarde
  mustard
pistou
  pesto (pounded mix of basil, hard cheese, olive oil and garlic)

provençale
  tomato, garlic, herb and olive oil dressing or sauce
tartare
  mayonnaise with herbs
vinaigrette
  salad dressing made with oil, vinegar, mustard and garlic

Fruit & Nuts

abricot	apricot
amande	almond
ananas	pineapple
arachide	peanut
banane	banana
cacahuète	peanut
cassis	blackcurrant
cerise	cherry
citron	lemon
datte	date
figue	fig
fraise	strawberry
framboise	raspberry
mangue	mango
marron	chestnut
melon	melon
noisette	hazelnut
orange	orange
pamplemousse	grapefruit
pastèque	watermelon
pêche	peach
poire	pear
pomme	apple
prune	plum
pruneau	prune
raisin	grape

Desserts & Sweets

crêpe
  thin pancake
crêpes suzettes
  orange-flavoured crêpes flambéed in liqueur
flan
  egg-custard dessert
frangipane
  pastry filled with cream flavoured with almonds or a cake mixture containing ground almonds

galette
    wholemeal or buckwheat pancake; also a
    type of biscuit
gâteau
    cake
gaufre
    waffle
gelée
    jelly
glace
    ice cream
tarte
    tart (pie)
tarte aux pommes
    apple tart
yaourt
    yoghurt

Snacks

croque-monsieur
    a grilled ham and cheese sandwich
croque-madame
    a croque-monsieur with a fried egg
frites
    chips (French fries)
quiche
    quiche; savoury egg, bacon and cream tart

Basics

beurre	butter
chocolat	chocolate
confiture	jam
crème fraîche	cream
farine	flour
huile	oil
lait	milk
miel	honey
œufs	eggs
poivre	pepper
sel	salt
sucre	sugar
vinaigre	vinegar

Utensils

bouteille	bottle
carafe	carafe
pichet	jug
verre	glass
couteau	knife
cuillère	spoon
fourchette	fork
serviette	serviette (napkin)

Drinks
Nonalcoholic

café	coffee
café au lait	coffe with milk
café crème	coffee with cream
chocolat chaud	hot chocolate
eau minérale/ eau de source	mineral water
eau de robinet	tap water
express	espresso coffee
jus d'orange	orange juice
lait	milk
(petit) noir	black coffee
thé	tea
thé au citron	tea with lemon
thé au lait	white tea
tisane	herbal tea

Alcoholic

bière	beer
champagne	champagne
cidre	cider
cognac	brandy
gin	gin
pastis	aniseed liqueur served with water
vin	wine
vin blanc	white wine
vin mousseux	sparkling wine
vin rouge	red wine
vodka	vodka
whisky	whisky

Glossary

AGENC – Agence pour la Gestion des Espaces Naturels de Corse; Office for the Management of the Natural Areas of Corsica
aiguille – rock mass or mountain peak shaped like a needle
algéco – temporary building
appellation d'origine contrôlée – mark of quality for wines and cheeses
ATM – automated teller machine; cashpoint
auberge – inn
auberge de jeunesse – youth hostel

baie – bay
bain – bath
barrage – dam
bastiglia – fortress
bergerie – shepherd's hut, often used as accommodation for walkers
bocca – mountain pass
bouches – straits
brèche – breach, gap
brocciu/bruccio – Corsican goat's or ewe's milk cheese
bruschetta – toasted bread rubbed with garlic served with various toppings

calanche (Cor)/calanque (Fr) – rocky inlets
capu (Cor)/cap (Fr) – cape
cascade – waterfall
casgili – cheese cellar
castellu, castelli (pl) – castle
chapelle – chapel
chapon – red scorpion fish
charcuterie – cold cooked pork meats
cignale (Cor) – wild boar
cirque – a semicircular or crescent-shaped basin with steep sides and a gently sloping floor, formed by the erosive action of ice
clos – vineyard
col – mountain pass
commune – smallest unit of local government in rural areas
Conseil Général – General Council; implements legislation at local level

Conservatoire du Littoral – Conservatoire de l'Espace Littoral et des Rivages Lacustres; Organisation for the Conservation of Coastal Areas and Lakeshores
Corsu – Corsican language
couloir – deep gully on a mountain side
couvent – convent
crête – ridge

défilé – gorge, narrow pass
démaquisage – scrub clearance
département – unit of French regional administration
désert – desert
dolmen – megalithic tomb
domaine – estate, especially one which produces wine

ecobuage – cultivation on burnt stubble
église – church
étang – lake

fiadone – flan made with *brocciu*, lemon and eggs
figatellu – type of liver sausage
fola – folk tale
forêt – forest
FLNC – Front de Libération Nationale de la Corse; Corsican National Liberation Front

gîte d'étape – mountain lodge, more comfortable than the basic *refuges*
golfe – bay, gulf
goulet – narrows; bottleneck at entrance to a harbour

île – isle/island

lac – lake
laricio – type of pine native to Corsica
lauze – type of stone found only in the area around Bastia
libeccio – south-westerly wind

maison – office, house
maquis – scrub

menhir – single standing stone, often carved, dating from the megalithic era
mouflon – wild sheep native to Corsica

névé – mass of porous ice; also known as a firn

ONF – Office National des Forêts; National Office for Forests
optimiste – coracle

panini – filled bread rolls
phare – lighthouse
pieds noirs – repatriated French from Algeria
pieve – small region; parish
pinzuti – settlers from the French mainland
place – square
plage – beach
plongée – diving
PNRC – Parc Naturel Régional de Corse; Corsican Nature Reserve
port de plaisance – marina
pozzi – pits
pozzines – interlinked water holes
préfecture – unit of regional administration in France
priorité à droite – give way to the right
prisuttu – Corsican raw ham

punta (Cor)/pointe (Fr) – point; headland

randonnée – walk (noun)
refuge – mountain accommodation ranging from basic huts to simple hostels

sanglier (Fr) – wild boar
Saracen – Moor; Moorish
sec (Cor) – shallow (diving; noun)
sec (Fr) – dry
Sécurité Civile – civil defence department
sémaphore – small lighthouse
Shardanes – 'sea people'; ancient nautical race
son et lumière – night-time presentation at a historic site using lighting and sound effects and narration
source – spring

taffoni – cavities (geology)
torre, torri (pl) – tower
Torréens – invaders who conquered Corsica at some point after 4000BC; probably *Shardanes*
tour – tower

vallée – valley
vendetta – blood feud

LONELY PLANET

Phrasebooks

Lonely Planet phrasebooks are packed with essential words and phrases to help travellers communicate with the locals. With colour tabs for quick reference, an extensive vocabulary and use of script, these handy pocket-sized language guides cover day-to-day travel situations.

- handy pocket-sized books
- easy to understand Pronunciation chapter
- clear & comprehensive Grammar chapter
- romanisation alongside script to allow ease of pronunciation
- script throughout so users can point to phrases for every situation
- full of cultural information and tips for the traveller

'...vital for a real DIY spirit and attitude in language learning'
– *Backpacker*

'the phrasebooks have good cultural backgrounders and offer solid advice for challenging situations in remote locations'
– *San Francisco Examiner*

Arabic (Egyptian) • Arabic (Moroccan) • Australian *(Australian English, Aboriginal and Torres Strait languages)* • Baltic States *(Estonian, Latvian, Lithuanian)* • Bengali • Brazilian • Burmese • Cantonese • Central Asia • Central Europe *(Czech, French, German, Hungarian, Italian, Slovak)* • Eastern Europe *(Bulgarian, Czech, Hungarian, Polish, Romanian, Slovak)* • Ethiopian (Amharic) • Fijian • French • German • Greek • Hill Tribes • Hindi/Urdu • Indonesian • Italian • Japanese • Korean • Lao • Latin American Spanish • Malay • Mandarin • Mediterranean Europe *(Albanian, Croatian, Greek, Italian, Macedonian, Maltese, Serbian, Slovene)* • Mongolian • Nepali • Papua New Guinea • Pilipino (Tagalog) • Quechua • Russian • Scandinavian Europe *(Danish, Finnish, Icelandic, Norwegian, Swedish)* • South-East Asia *(Burmese, Indonesian, Khmer, Lao, Malay, Tagalog Pilipino, Thai, Vietnamese)* • Spanish (Castilian) *(also includes Catalan, Galician and Basque)* • Sri Lanka • Swahili • Thai • Tibetan • Turkish • Ukrainian • USA *(US English, Vernacular Talk, Native American languages, Hawaiian)* • Vietnamese • Western Europe *(Basque, Catalan, Dutch, French, German, Greek, Irish)*

LONELY PLANET

Guides by Region

Lonely Planet is known worldwide for publishing practical, reliable and no-nonsense travel information in our guides and on our Web site. The Lonely Planet list covers just about every accessible part of the world. Currently there are nine series: travel guides, shoe-string guides, walking guides, city guides, phrasebooks, audio packs, travel atlases, diving and snorkeling guides and travel literature.

AFRICA Africa – the South • Africa on a shoestring • Arabic (Egyptian) phrasebook • Arabic (Moroc-can) phrasebook • Cairo • Cape Town • Central Africa • East Africa • Egypt • Egypt travel atlas • Ethiopian (Amharic) phrasebook • The Gambia & Senegal • Kenya • Kenya travel atlas • Malawi, Mozambique & Zambia • Morocco • North Africa • South Africa, Lesotho & Swaziland • South Africa, Lesotho & Swaziland travel atlas • Swahili phrasebook • Trekking in East Africa • Tunisia • West Africa • Zimbabwe, Botswana & Namibia • Zimbabwe, Botswana & Namibia travel atlas
Travel Literature: The Rainbird: A Central African Journey • Songs to an African Sunset: A Zimbabwean Story • Mali Blues: Traveling to an African Beat

AUSTRALIA & THE PACIFIC Australia • Australian phrasebook • Bushwalking in Australia • Bush-walking in Papua New Guinea • Fiji • Fijian phrasebook • Islands of Australia's Great Barrier Reef • Melbourne • Micronesia • New Caledonia • New South Wales & the ACT • New Zealand • Northern Territory • Outback Australia • Papua New Guinea • Papua New Guinea (Pidgin) phrasebook • Queensland • Rarotonga & the Cook Islands • Samoa • Solomon Islands • South Australia • Sydney • Tahiti & French Polynesia • Tasmania • Tonga • Tramping in New Zealand • Vanuatu • Victoria • Western Australia
Travel Literature: Islands in the Clouds • Sean & David's Long Drive

CENTRAL AMERICA & THE CARIBBEAN Bahamas and Turks & Caicos • Bermuda • Central America on a shoestring • Costa Rica • Cuba • Eastern Caribbean • Guatemala, Belize & Yucatán: La Ruta Maya • Jamaica • Mexico • Mexico City • Panama
Travel Literature: Green Dreams: Travels in Central America

EUROPE Amsterdam • Andalucia • Austria • Baltic States phrasebook • Berlin • Britain • Central Europe • Central Europe phrasebook • Czech & Slovak Republics • Denmark • Dublin • Eastern Europe • Eastern Europe phrasebook • Estonia, Latvia & Lithuania • Finland • France • French phrase-book • Germany • German phrasebook • Greece • Greek phrasebook • Hungary • Iceland, Greenland & the Faroe Islands • Ireland • Italian phrasebook • Italy • Lisbon • London • Mediterranean Europe • Mediterranean Europe phrasebook • Paris • Poland • Portugal • Portugal travel atlas • Prague • Romania & Moldova • Russia, Ukraine & Belarus • Russian phrasebook • Scandinavian & Baltic Europe • Scandinavian Europe phrasebook • Slovenia • Spain • Spanish phrasebook • St Petersburg • Switzer-land • Trekking in Spain • Ukrainian phrasebook • Vienna • Walking in Britain • Walking in Italy • Walking in Switzerland • Western Europe • Western Europe phrasebook
Travel Literature: The Olive Grove: Travels in Greece

INDIAN SUBCONTINENT Bangladesh • Bengali phrasebook • Bhutan • Delhi • Goa • Hindi/Urdu phrasebook • India • India & Bangladesh travel atlas • Indian Himalaya • Karakoram Highway • Nepal • Nepali phrasebook • Pakistan • Rajasthan • South India • Sri Lanka • Sri Lanka phrasebook • Trekking in the Indian Himalaya • Trekking in the Karakoram & Hindukush • Trekking in the Nepal Himalaya
Travel Literature: In Rajasthan • Shopping for Buddhas

LONELY PLANET

Mail Order

Lonely Planet products are distributed worldwide.They are also available by mail order from Lonely Planet, so if you have difficulty finding a title please write to us. North and South American residents should write to 150 Linden St, Oakland, CA 94607, USA; European and African residents should write to 10a Spring Place, London NW5 3BH, UK; and residents of other countries to PO Box 617, Hawthorn, Victoria 3122, Australia.

ISLANDS OF THE INDIAN OCEAN Madagascar & Comoros • Maldives • Mauritius, Réunion & Seychelles

MIDDLE EAST & CENTRAL ASIA Arab Gulf States • Central Asia • Central Asia phrasebook • Iran • Israel & the Palestinian Territories • Israel & the Palestinian Territories travel atlas • Istanbul • Jerusalem • Jordan & Syria • Jordan, Syria & Lebanon travel atlas • Lebanon • Middle East on a shoestring • Turkey • Turkish phrasebook • Turkey travel atlas • Yemen
Travel Literature: The Gates of Damascus • Kingdom of the Film Stars: Journey into Jordan

NORTH AMERICA Alaska • Backpacking in Alaska • Baja California • California & Nevada • Canada • Florida • Hawaii • Honolulu • Los Angeles • Miami • New England USA • New Orleans • New York City • New York, New Jersey & Pennsylvania • Pacific Northwest USA • Rocky Mountain States • San Francisco • Seattle • Southwest USA • USA phrasebook • Washington, DC & the Capital Region
Travel Literature: Drive Thru America

NORTH-EAST ASIA Beijing • Cantonese phrasebook • China • Hong Kong • Hong Kong, Macau & Guangzhou • Japan • Japanese phrasebook • Japanese audio pack • Korea • Korean phrasebook • Kyoto • Mandarin phrasebook • Mongolia • Mongolian phrasebook • North-East Asia on a shoestring • Seoul • South-West China • Taiwan • Tibet • Tibetan phrasebook • Tokyo
Travel Literature: Lost Japan

SOUTH AMERICA Argentina, Uruguay & Paraguay • Bolivia • Brazil • Brazilian phrasebook • Buenos Aires • Chile & Easter Island • Chile & Easter Island travel atlas • Colombia • Ecuador & the Galapagos Islands • Latin American Spanish phrasebook • Peru • Quechua phrasebook • Rio de Janeiro • South America on a shoestring • Trekking in the Patagonian Andes • Venezuela
Travel Literature: Full Circle: A South American Journey

SOUTH-EAST ASIA Bali & Lombok • Bangkok • Burmese phrasebook • Cambodia • Hill Tribes phrasebook • Ho Chi Minh City • Indonesia • Indonesian phrasebook • Indonesian audio pack • Jakarta • Java • Laos • Lao phrasebook • Laos travel atlas • Malay phrasebook • Malaysia, Singapore & Brunei • Myanmar (Burma) • Philippines • Pilipino (Tagalog) phrasebook • Singapore • South-East Asia on a shoestring • South-East Asia phrasebook • Thailand • Thailand's Islands & Beaches • Thailand travel atlas • Thai phrasebook • Thai audio pack • Vietnam • Vietnamese phrasebook • Vietnam travel atlas

ALSO AVAILABLE: Antarctica • Brief Encounters: Stories of Love, Sex & Travel • Chasing Rickshaws • Not the Only Planet: Travel Stories from Science Fiction • Travel with Children • Traveller's Tales

LONELY PLANET

Lonely Planet Online
www.lonelyplanet.com *or* **AOL keyword: lp**

W hether you've just begun planning your next trip, or you're chasing down specific info on currency regulations or visa requirements, check out Lonely Planet Online for up-to-the minute travel information.

As well as mini guides to more than 250 destinations, you'll find maps, photos, travel news, health and visa updates, travel advisories, and discussion of the ecological and political issues you need to be aware of as you travel. You'll also find timely upgrades to popular guidebooks which you can print out and stick in the back of your book.

There's also an online travellers' forum where you can share your experience of life on the road, meet travel companions and ask other travellers for their recommendations and advice.

And of course we have a complete and up-to-date list of all Lonely Planet travel products including travel guides, diving and snorkelling guides, phrasebooks, atlases, travel literature and videos, and a simple online ordering facility if you can't find the book you want elsewhere.

Lonely Planet Diving & Snorkelling Guides

K nown for indispensible guidebooks to destinations all over the world, Lonely Planet's Pisces Books are the most popular series of diving and snorkelling titles available.

There are three series: **Diving & Snorkelling Guides**, **Shipwreck Diving** series, and **Dive Into History**. Full colour throughout, the **Diving & Snorkelling Guides** combine quality photographs with detailed descriptions of the best dive sites for each location, giving divers a glimpse of what they can expect both on land and in water. The **Dive Into History** series is perfect for the adventure diver or armchair traveller. The **Shipwreck Diving** series provides all the details for exploring the most interesting wrecks in the Atlantic and Pacific oceans. The list also includes underwater nature and technical guides.

LONELY PLANET

FREE Lonely Planet Newsletters

We love hearing from you and think you'd like to hear from us.

Planet Talk

Our FREE quarterly printed newsletter is full of tips from travellers and anecdotes from Lonely Planet guidebook authors. Every issue is packed with up-to-date travel news and advice, and includes:

- a postcard from Lonely Planet co-founder Tony Wheeler
- a swag of mail from travellers
- a look at life on the road through the eyes of a Lonely Planet author
- topical health advice
- prizes for the best travel yarn
- news about forthcoming Lonely Planet events
- a complete list of Lonely Planet books and other titles

To join our mailing list, residents of the UK, Europe and Africa can email us at go@lonelyplanet.co.uk; residents of North and South America can email us at info@lonelyplanet.com; the rest of the world can email us at talk2us@lonelyplanet.com.au, or contact any Lonely Planet office.

Comet

Our FREE monthly email newsletter brings you all the latest travel news, features, interviews, competitions, destination ideas, travellers' tips & tales, Q&As, raging debates and related links. Find out what's new on the Lonely Planet Web site and which books are about to hit the shelves.

Subscribe from your desktop: www.lonelyplanet.com/comet

Index

Text

Bold indicates maps.
Italics indicates boxed text.

Boxed Text

MAP LEGEND

BOUNDARIES

▬▪▬▪▬▪▬ ....International
▬▪▬▪▬▪▬ ....State
▬ ▬ ▬ ▬ ....Disputed

HYDROGRAPHY

............Coastline
............River, Creek
............Lake
............Intermittent Lake
............Salt Lake
............Canal
→→ ....Rapids
→╫←═ ....Waterfalls
............Swamp

ROUTES & TRANSPORT

............Freeway
............Highway
............Major Road
............Minor Road
══════ ....Unsealed Road
............City Freeway
............City Highway
............City Road
............City Street, Lane

⇒⌇═══⌇............Tunnel
├──•──┤ ....Train Route & Station
──Ⓜ── ....Metro & Station
............Tramway
╫─╫─╫─............Cable Car or Chairlift
─ ─ ─ ─ ....Walking Track
• • • • • ....Walking Tour
─ ─ ─ ─ ....Ferry Route
............Pedestrian Mall

AREA FEATURES

............Building
✿ ....Park, Gardens
+ + × × ....Cemetery
............Market
............Beach, Desert
............Urban Area

MAP SYMBOLS

✪ **CAPITAL** ....National Capital
◉ **CAPITAL** ....State Capital
● **CITY** ....City
● **Town** ....Town
● **Village** ....Village
○ ....Point of Interest

■ ....Place to Stay
Ⓐ ....Camping Ground
⛺ ....Shelter
🏠 ....Trekking Hut

▼ ....Place to Eat
🍺 ....Pub or Bar

🛩 ....Airplane Wreck
✈ ....Airport
............Ancient or City Wall
∴ ....Archaeological Site
🏖 ....Beach
🏯 ....Castle or Fort
⌒ ....Cave
🏛 ....Church
............Cliff or Escarpment
◤ ◥ ... Dive Centre, Dive Site
☯ ....Embassy
✚ ....Hospital
❋ ....Lookout
⚱ ....Monument

▲ ....Mountain or Hill
⌒⌒ ....Mountain Range
🏛 ....Museum
← ....One Way Street
Ⓟ ....Parking
)(............Pass
★ ....Police Station
✉ ....Post Office
⚓ ....Shipwreck
◎ ....Spring
☎ ....Telephone
❶ ....Tourist Information
🚶 ....Trail Head
⊖ ....Transport

Note: not all symbols displayed above appear in this book

LONELY PLANET OFFICES

Australia
PO Box 617, Hawthorn, Victoria 3122
☎ (03) 9819 1877 fax (03) 9819 6459
email: talk2us@lonelyplanet.com.au

USA
150 Linden St, Oakland, CA 94607
☎ (510) 893 8555 TOLL FREE: 800 275 5555
fax (510) 893 8572
email: info@lonelyplanet.com

UK
10a Spring Place, London NW5 3BH
☎ (020) 7428 4800 fax (020) 7428 4828
email: go@lonelyplanet.co.uk

France
1 rue du Dahomey, 75011 Paris
☎ 01 55 25 33 00 fax 01 55 25 33 01
email: bip@lonelyplanet.fr
minitel: 3615 lonelyplanet *(1,29 F TTC/min)*

World Wide Web: www.lonelyplanet.com *or* AOL keyword: lp
Lonely Planet Images: lpi@lonelyplanet.com.au